	DATE		

*Insect Pests of Tropical
Food Legumes*

Insect Pests of Tropical Food Legumes

Edited by

S. R. Singh

JOHN WILEY & SONS

Chichester · New York · Brisbane · Toronto · Singapore

Other Wiley Editorial Offices

John Wiley & Sons, Inc., 605 Third Avenue,
New York, NY 10158-0012, USA

Jacaranda Wiley Ltd, G.P.O. Box 859, Brisbane,
Queensland 4001, Australia

John Wiley & Sons (Canada) Ltd, 22 Worcester Road,
Rexdale, Ontario M9W 1L1, Canada

John Wiley & Sons (SEA) Pte Ltd, 37 Jalan Pemimpin #05-04,
Block B, Union Industrial Building, Singapore 2057

Library of Congress Cataloging-in-Publication Data:
Insect pests of tropical food legumes / edited by S. R. Singh.
      p.   cm.
   Includes bibliographical references.
   ISBN 0-471-92390-7
   1. Legumes—Diseases and pests—Tropics.   2. Insect pests—Tropics.
   3. Legumes as food—Tropics.   4. Tropical crops—Diseases and pests—Tropics.
   I. Singh, S. R.
   SB608.L4154   1989
   635'.65'0913—dc20   90–34517
                                                                            CIP

British Library Cataloguing in Publication Data:
The insect pests of tropical food legumes.
   1. Tropical regions. Crops. Pests: Insects. Control
   I. Singh, S. R.
   632.70913

   ISBN 0-471-92390-7

Printed and bound in Great Britain by Biddles Ltd., Guildford, Surrey

Reginald H. Painter
1901–68

This book is dedicated to Dr. Reginald H. Painter, world authority and pioneer in research on host-plant resistance, under whom I had the distinct privilege of doing my doctoral research.

Contents

List of Contributors

Dr C. B. Adalla   *Asst Professor, Dept of Entomology, University of the Philippines at Los Banos, College of Agriculture, College Laguna 4031, Philippines*

Dr C. Cardona   *Entomologist, Bean Program, Centro International de Agricultura Tropical (CIAT), Apartado Aereo 6713, Cali, Colombia*

Dr K. M. Dick   *Legume Improvement Program, International Crops Research Institute for the Semi-Arid Tropics, ICRISAT Patancheru PO 502324, Andhra Pradesh, India*

Dr J. H. Ribeiro dos Santos   *Entomologist, CCA/UFC, Fortaleza CE, Brazil*

Dr J. A. Duke   *Germplasm Services Laboratory, Building 001 Room 133, United States Dept. of Agriculture, BARC/West, Beltsville, Maryland 20705, USA*

Dr S. K. Green   *Asian Vegetable Research & Development Center (AVRDC), Shanhua, Tainan, Taiwan*

Dr C. G. Gold   *Legume Improvement Program, International Crops Research Institute for the Semi-Arid Tropics, ICRISAT Patancheru PO 502324, Andhra Pradesh, India*

Dr L. E. N. Jackai   *Entomologist, Grain Legume Improvement Program, International Institute of Tropical Agriculture, PMB 5320, Ibadan, Nigeria*

Dr A. K. Karel   *Professor of Entomology, Department of Zoology, MOI University, PO Box 3900, Eldoret, Kenya*

Dr G. G. Kundu   *Division of Entomology, Indian Agricultural Research Institute, New Delhi, India*

Dr S. S. Lateef   *Entomologist, Legume Improvement Program, International Crops Research Institute for the Semi-Arid Tropics, ICRISAT Patancheru PO 502324, Andhra Pradesh, India*

Dr K. M. Makkouk   *International Center for Agricultural Research in the Dry Areas (ICARDA), Aleppo, Syria*

Dr F. J. Morales   *Centro Internacional de Agricultura Tropical (CIAT), Cali, Colombia*

Dr A. R. Panizzi   *Centro Nacional de Pesquisa de Soja (CNPSo), Empresa Brasileira de Pesquisa Agropecuaria (EMBRAPA), Londrina, Parana, Brazil*

Dr G. V. Ranga Rao   *Legume Improvement Program, International Crops Research Institute for the Semi-Arid Tropics, ICRISAT Patancheru PO 502324, Andhra Pradesh, India*

Dr D. V. R. Reddy   *Legume Improvement Program, International Crops Research Institute for the Semi-Arid Tropics, ICRISAT Patancheru PO 502324, Andhra Pradesh, India*

Dr W. Reed   *Legume Improvement Program, International Crops Research Institute for the Semi-Arid Tropics, ICRISAT Patancheru PO 502324, Andhra Pradesh, India*

Dr H. W. Rossel   *Virologist, International Institute of Tropical Agriculture, PMB 5320, Ibadan, Nigeria*

Dr T. G. Shanower   *Legume Improvement Program, International Crops Research Institute for the Semi-Arid Tropics, ICRISAT Patancheru PO 502324, Andhra Pradesh, India*

Dr S. R. Singh   *Director, Grain Legume Improvement Program, International Institute of Tropical Agriculture, PMB 5320, Ibadan, Nigeria*

Dr K. P. Srivastava   *Division of Entomology, Indian Agricultural Research Institute, New Delhi, India*

Dr G. Thottapilly   *Virologist, International Institute of Tropical Agriculture, PMB 5320, Ibadan, Nigeria*

Dr J. S. Wightman   *Principal Entomologist, Legume Improvement Program, International Crops Research Institute for the Semi-Arid Tropics, ICRISAT Patancheru PO 502324, Andhra Pradesh, India*

Foreword

I am delighted to write the foreword for a book that exemplifies collaboration between centres within the Consultative Group on International Agricultural Research (CGIAR) system. The book synthesizes what is known about insect pest management for a group of crops that hold much promise for feeding people in developing countries and for putting into place sustainable systems of food production.

I congratulate Dr S. R. Singh and the other scientists from five of the international agricultural research centres who have worked so hard to bring this book to fruition; because of their strategic locations throughout the world, they were able to draw on colleagues from the national research programs in Africa, Asia and Latin America. Through such efforts, one can look forward to a time when food legumes have fulfilled their promise.

Food legumes contain comparatively high concentrations of protein and, as a complement to cereals such as maize, can supply nutrients for people who cannot afford higher-priced sources of protein. Also, because of food legumes' capacity to increase nitrogen in the soil, they make ideal companion crops to maize and other cereals that require heavy inputs of nitrogen.

I have no doubt that this book will serve as a valuable reference for food legume researchers all over the tropics, especially for those seeking to design integrated pest management systems. Insect pests cause major damage to the food legumes feeding poor populations in the Third World — cowpeas, soybeans, beans, pigeon pea and groundnut. Control of these pests has been difficult; insecticides and sprayers are beyond the reach of most of the farmers in the developing world, and where they can be purchased, their use has prompted concerns about environmental degradation, health hazards to humans and animals, and the emergence of insects resistant to their effects. All are real concerns, as has been clearly demonstrated in parts of Latin America.

This book focuses on the development of crops that are resistant to infestation by insects, and it details other methods to minimize chemical control. Crop production may never be totally free from insect attack, but judicious use of cultural, biological and chemical control along with insect-resistant crop varieties will limit damage from insects and stabilize yields where moisture is not a limiting factor for production. The information in this book is collated by crop so that individuals who concentrate efforts on a single commodity can easily find the insects that constrain production and the stages of growth when they attack and damage the plants.

I am pleased to note that the book has been dedicated to an outstanding entomologist, Dr Reginald H. Painter, who was a pioneer in the field and a father of research on host-plant resistance.

L. D. Stifel
Director general
International Institute of Tropical Agriculture

Preface

In the tropics, insect pests are often the major constraint for crop production, particularly in food legumes. In most regions, food legumes are grown as secondary crops on marginal soils, and under subsistence conditions, particularly in Africa, farmers consider food legume production risky.

Compared with cereal crops, feed legumes have received limited attention from crop-improvement specialists, and their yields have remained relatively low. Recently, they have gained some impetus from the drive to promote sustainable systems, as part of their demand for nitrogen can be met by biological nitrogen fixation, the rhizobia in the soil colonizing their roots and capturing nitrogen from the air.

In this book, an effort has been made to collate the information on advances made in the control of insect pests of tropical food legumes, namely cowpeas, soybeans, beans, pigeon peas and groundnuts (or peanuts). Entomologists from the International Institute of Tropical Agriculture (IITA), Centro Internacional de Agricultura Tropical (CIAT) and the International Crops Research Institute for the Semi-Arid Tropics (ICRISAT), along with researchers in national programmes in Africa, Latin America and Asia have contributed. 'The introduction, which deals with the general morphology, ecosystems, regions, distribution and uses of the crops, comes from a well known scientist at the United States Department of Agriculture. A chapter on virus vectors and transmission of viruses has been included, representing efforts from virologists working at IITA, CIAT, ICRISAT, the International Center for Agricultural Research in the Dry Areas (ICARDA) and Asian Vegetable Research and Development Center (AVRDC).

I am delighted that we have been able to muster such a collaborative effort in the production of this book, and I gratefully acknowledge the work that went into preparing the chapters for this volume. The quality of the work is clear in the comments by reviewers, who are eminent scientists in their own right.

I would like to take this opportunity to thank Prof. Thomas R. Odhiambo director of the International Centre of Insect Physiology and Ecology

(ICIPE), Nairobi, Kenya, for encouraging me to undertake the task of editing and compiling the book. He was instrumental in my decision.

Finally, I want to thank Dr L. D. Stifel, director general, and Dr K. S. Fischer, deputy director general (research), both of IITA, for their continued belief in academic research as a means of improving food production in the tropics and their support for the publication of this book.

I want to thank the late Amy Chouinard for editorial assistance and J. Ojurongbe and E. Nwulu, IITA, for designing the cover.

S. R. Singh
Director
Grain Legume Improvement Program
International Institute of Tropical Agriculture

Reviews

The book is a very well designed presentation of the pests of each of the five important food legumes. The five chapters which comprise the heart of the book are likely to remain the principal references of food legume entomology in the tropics for the 1990s and beyond.

Equally informative is the closing chapter—a review of virus and mycoplasma diseases which is often bypassed by entomologists.

The authors are to be congratulated on a first-class job.

Thomas R. Odhiambo
Director, The International Centre
of Insect Physiology
and Ecology

I should like to congratulate you on the excellent work of bringing together, analyzing and presenting the body of knowledge on what I would refer to as 'integrated pest and disease management in food legumes'.

The book is an excellent background and analysis which clearly demonstrates the interdependence of disciplines in the evolution of environment-conscious and sustainable strategies for integrated pest and disease management.

The work emphasizes the fundamental need for an improved understanding of the complex interactions of food legume crops and their production systems, insects and disease organisms, and the tropical environment. It is a significant contribution to our knowledge and a vital guidepost to future collaborative and interdisciplinary research.

T. Ajibola Taylor
Senior Research Officer,
International Service for
National Agricultural
Research

I extend to you and your co-authors heartiest congratulations and commendation for an outstanding job which is badly needed and fills a void. It is well planned and well written and with the inclusion of plates and references will be an excellent book.

M. D. Pathak
Director-General,
U.P. Council of
Agricultural Research

This book provides extremely valuable, carefully edited, and extensively referenced summaries of the pests involved, the damage they cause and the control measures that can be applied. A particularly important feature is the emphasis placed on the opportunities for integrated pest management. The major contributions that can be made to this approach from cultural control, and particularly from legume varieties resistant to insect attack, are highlighted, and the key role of natural enemies in biological control is covered.

This major book provides by far the most comprehensive and valuable overview of its field and is an indispensible reference for all workers on tropical legumes.

D. F. Waterhouse
Commonwealth Scientific
and Industrial Research
Organization, Australia

I think that this book will serve as an excellent reference text to those workers in the field. It is authoritative and its comprehensive treatment of the subject and its breadth of coverage of crops and insect pests should make it useful to a very wide audience.

John J. McKelvey, Jr
Former Director,
Rockefeller Foundation,
New York, USA

Insect Pests of Food Legumes
Edited by S. R. Singh
©1990 John Wiley & Sons Ltd.

Introduction to Food Legumes

JAMES A. DUKE[a]
[a]*Germplasm Services Laboratory, ARS, BARC-West, Beltsville, Maryland, USA*

As noted by H. K. Jain in the introduction to *Pulse Crops* (Balder *et al.*, 1988), pulses are second only to cereal crops, nicely complementing them, in feeding the developing world. Interestingly, Balder and colleagues (1988) contrast the picking of legumes (from *legere*: to gather) with the threshing of cereals. This book on tropical legumes complements the pulse book, with overlap only on the pigeon pea (*Cajanus cajan*).

We treat, in addition, South America's major leguminous contributions — beans and peanuts — Africa's major leguminous contribution — cowpea — and China's major contribution — soybean — all covered cursorily in my *Handbook of Legumes of World Economic Importance* (Duke, 1981).

Martin (1984) voiced optimism for legumes in the tropics, 'As a class, the legumes are probably potentially the most important plants of the tropics and possibly for the temperate zone as well... Tropical legumes that produce dry, edible seeds (pulses) are numerous.'

In a survey of the world's 30 major crops, Noel Vietmeyer (1986) ranked soybean ninth in production (Table 1) at 60 million t (2.5 per cent of total production), peanut 23rd at 20 million t (0.8 per cent of total production), and beans 27th at 10 million t (0.4 per cent of total production).

More than a decade has passed since I first drafted my *Handbook of Legumes*. Since then, the handbook has been translated to Japanese, and the translator acuminately helped me improve the text. It's hard to keep up with all the literature on a single crop, much less 140.

A lot of literature accumulates in a decade, and I've only skimmed it since Dr S. R. Singh invited me to write this introduction. His welcome invitation gave me the opportunity to update the summaries on five most important legumes for the tropics, the bean, cowpea, peanut, pigeon pea, and soybean. Together, these legumes provide protein eaten by most people in the tropics and nitrogen to the soils. Also, they provide much-needed vitamins, minerals, and fibre to carnivorous humans, some of whom are fibre deficient.

For example, in 1985, the world had 432,000 ha producing 2.94 million t

Table 1. Top 30 crops in world production of food (Vietmeyer, 1986)

Crop	Production (million t)	% of total food production
Wheat	360	15.3
Rice	320	13.6
Corn	300	12.7
Potato	300	12.7
Barley	170	7.2
Sweet potato	130	5.5
Cassava	100	4.2
Grapes	60	2.5
Soybean	60	2.5
Oats	50	2.1
Sorghum	50	2.1
Sugar cane	50	2.1
Millets	45	1.9
Banana	35	1.5
Tomato	35	1.5
Sugarbeet	30	1.3
Rye	30	1.3
Orange	30	1.3
Coconut	30	1.3
Cottonseed oil	25	1.0
Apple	20	0.8
Yam	20	0.8
Peanut	20	0.8
Watermelon	20	0.8
Cabbage	15	0.6
Onion	15	0.6
Beans	10	0.4
Peas	10	0.4
Sunflower	10	0.4
Mango	10	0.4

haricots (6783 kg/ha), 25.28 million ha producing 14.62 million t dry beans (578 kg/ha), 52.37 million ha producing 100.83 million t soybeans (1925 kg/ha), and 18.96 million ha producing 21.26 million t groundnuts (1122 kg/ha) (FAO, 1986, which did not give statistics for cowpea and pigeon pea). Soybean contributed more than $11 billion to the American economy in 1988, peanuts and beans closer to $1 billion each (Duke, 1989). Neither Vietmeyer nor FAO gives comparable recent data for all five legumes treated in this book so the most up-to-date data are from the 1970s (Table 2).We and Gaia might be better off if wealthy people substituted legumes for some of the meat and dairy products eaten.

Table 2. Legume production data (ca 1970) (Martin *et al.*, 1976)

	Area (million ha)		Production (million t)		Yield (t/ha)	
	World	US	World	US	World	US
Soybeans	35.4	16.9	45.5	31.0	1.32	1.83
Peanuts[a]	18.7	0.6	17.6	1.3	0.94	2.17
Dry beans	22.8	0.6	11.4	0.8	0.50	1.38
Cowpeas	3.1	0.3	1.1	0.2	0.40	0.61
Pigeon peas	2.9	—	2.0	—	0.68	—

[a]The shells constitute about 27 per cent of weight.

Albeit, some people are allergic to legumes (e.g., four people in the U.S. died in a 2-year period because of allergy to peanuts; Lockey and Bukantz, 1989); even more people are ethnically allergic, if not fatally so, to the faba bean, *Vicia faba*. Still more lactase-deficient people may be allergic to milk and other dairy products.

It takes about 10 kg fodder to make 1 kg of meat. And ruminant animals, via eructations, are contributing significantly to the methane half of the greenhouse acceleration. Two cosmopolitan changes, strictly hypothetical because undesirable to many, could lower the methane content of the atmosphere markedly:

- switching from omnivory to vegetarianism with legumes (coupled with non-replacement of the expendable ruminants); and
- replacing paddy rice with rainfed or irrigated terrestrial legumes.

Some speculate that adding epazote (*Chenopodium ambrosioides*) to beans would reduce the flatus among consumers and further suggest that the addition of epazote or qing hao (*Artemisia annua*) to fodder would lower the methane in ruminant eructations.

First-world countries with high rates of atherosclerosis, cancer, diabetes, hypertension, and obesity are being advised, sometimes officially, to eat more vegetables, including legumes, and less meat, especially fatty meat. In the U.S., the advice is to bring the percentage of fat in the diet down from 35 per cent to at most 30 per cent.

Popular writer Jean Carper (1988) listed several of the 'health food aspects' of beans (under which she includes many of those discussed in this book). She noted that a cup of cooked, dried beans every day should lower the low-density lipid (LDL) cholesterol, regulate blood sugar and insulin, lower blood pressure, and regulate the bowels, preventing gastrointestinal troubles, even hemorrhoids and possibly cancer of the gut. She cited studies showing that bean diets improved the ratio of high- to low-density lipids (HDL:LDL) by 17 per cent. Even a 7.5-oz. (213 g) can of pork and beans a day can lower cholesterol by an average 12 per cent. Individuals with type I diabetes can cut their insulin requirements by 38 per cent if they increase their bean intake a cup (about 184 g) a day. The protease inhibitors in beans (responsible for indigestion when one eats too many beans) block the development of breast and colon cancer, turning off the oncogenes. Replacing half the protein from meat with soybean protein reduced atherosclerosis by 50 per cent in experimental animals. Among Japanese, a bowl of soybean soup a day reduced the risk of stomach cancer by 30 per cent.

The family of the yam (Dioscoreaceae) triggered North America's second revolution, the Sexual Revolution, by serving as the source for the steroid contraceptive. Today it is the yambean family (Fabaceae) that continues what *Dioscorea* sp. began. 'The days are over regarding production of steroids from Mexican barbasco... all commercially available steroids start with soya sterols' (E. W. McCloskey, President, Berlichem, personal communication, 31 March 1989). The soybean is now the prime source of steroidal drugs, including contraceptives and steroidal anti-inflammatory drugs. Other genera of legumes are also sources for drugs: anthraquinones from *Cassia* and *Senna*; balsams from *Myroxylum*; bufotenine from *Mucuna*; castanospermine from *Castanospermum*, choline from most, if not all, legumes; chrysarobin from *Andira*, coumarins from *Dipteryx*, *Melilotus*, etc.; desmethyldiazepam (at only 3−15 ppt) in *Glycine* and *Lens*; diazepam (Valium) from *Glycine* (Unseld and Klotz, 1989); levadopa from *Mucuna*, *Vicia*, etc.; epicatechins from many woody legumes; fenugreekine from *Trigonella*; glycyrrhizin from *Glycyrrhiza*; gum tragacanth from *Acacia*; indigo from several legumes; lecithin from most, if not all, legumes; lectins from several legume seeds (including *Abrus*, *Arachis*, *Bauhinia*, *Canavaha*, *Caragana*, *Cicer*, *Cytisus*, *Dolichos*, *Erythrina*, *Glycine*, *Laburnum*, *Lathyrus*, *Lens*, *Phaseolus*, *Pisum*, *Psophocarpus*, *Robinia*, *Sophora*, *Tetragonolobus*, *Ulex*, *Vicia*, *Vigna*, *Wisteria*); mimosine from *Leucaena*; monocrotaline from *Crotalaria*; physostigmine from *Physostigma*; psoralen from *Psoralea*; resins from *Copaifera*; rotenone from *Derris*, *Mundulea*, *Tephrosia*; rutin from *Sophora*; swainsonine from *Astragalus* and *Swainsonia*; tragacanth from *Astragalus*; trigonelline from dozens, if not most, legumes; in addition to many bioactive alkaloids from *Cytisus*, *Erythrina*, *Erythrophleum*, and *Sophora*.

Legumes are the meat substitute for the poor in the Third World and the medicine for the over-carnivorous in the First and Second World. Strange that legumes are now being advocated as a cure for those who have measured the rise in their standard of living by their increase in meat consumption.

Even stranger how a gene from the Third World Brazil-nut (*Bertholettia excelsa*) may improve legumes' ability to serve as a complete food for the hungry poor and for the wealthy vegetarian. A story from *Science News* (13 May 1989) is a reminder that legumes do not provide all the amino acids needed by humans and other monogastric animals to build and repair their tissues. Working with tobacco, Samuel Sun (University of Hawaii, Honolulu) inserted a Brazil-nut gene, coding for high methionine, and got a tobacco plant with 30 per cent more methionine, predicting a methionine-rich transgenic soybean to consumers within 2–3 years. Also interesting that this would couple genes from a tree species (the Brazil-nut) that is dependent on the rain forest and is the best known source of organic selenium, with a Chinese herb, the soybean.

This development may fan the flames of initiative at the Food and Agriculture Organization of the United Nations (FAO), getting legumes into the limelight of agropolitics. As the original source of the soybean and still the best potential reservoir of soybean genes for tolerance to diseases and insect predation, China may view with disdain the economic figures showing the value of soybeans to the American and Brazilian economies. Soybean politicians are doing battle with those promoting other tropical oils, and they had reason to celebrate when soybean oil proved to be a source of the fatty acids (omega 3s and 6s) found to reduce the levels of cholesterol in human blood and, hence, potentially to support higher prices and health food claims.

The oil-palm politicos have come back with their own challenges, and the peanut promoters have a cultivar high in monounsaturated fatty acids (MUFA) in response to the success of MUFA in olive oil. Farmers feed their pigs MUFA peanuts to produce pork with healthier ratios of saturated to monounsaturated and polyunsaturated fatty acids (SFA : MUFA : PUFA).

Advocates of Extractive Reserves in the Amazonian rain forest claim that, after 10 years, the standing forest has yielded, and continues to yield, greater economic returns than forests felled for the production of cattle or soybeans. At the same time, Brazilian soybean advocates may hint that American soybean interests are secretly supporting Extractive Reserves to eliminate the competition. Talk about a hot non-potato! If Honolulu scientists develop a high-methionine soybean by combining Chinese soybean genes with Brazil-nut genes, one hopes it will feed more starving Brazilians and Chinese than the biotechnologists who introduced these unrelated genes and arranged the strange marriage.

Might the new, improved soybean, by becoming more valuable than ever relative to the Brazil-nut, contribute to the demise of the forest that nurtured and conserved the Brazil-nut? Thanks to Gaia, the Brazil-nut survived deforestation long enough to make this important contribution to world nutrition.

As Hulse reminded everyone in 1979:

> It is well established that the proteins of food legumes and cereal grains are nutritionally complementary, the essential amino acids that are deficient in the one being provided in the other. Consequently, when eaten together, both cereal and legumes are used more efficiently than if either is eaten alone.

Legumes and cereals also complement each other in intercrops, with most tropical legumes annually fixing about 100 kg N/ha. However, the output is not free. Under conventional farming, the price for nitrogen contributed by legumes is clear from biomass yields of, say, C-4 grasses, C-3 grasses, and legumes. Though relatively higher in nitrogen and protein, the legumes yield only half as much total biomass as the C-3 grasses, which in turn yield only half as much total biomass as the C-4 grasses, a simple ratio of 1:2:4. These are the biological costs of nitrogen fixation and excessive photorespiration. The ratio holds true in the so-called super-yield targets of the U.S.: 100 bushels of soybeans per acre and 400 bushels of corn (Duke, 1983).

Appropriate combinations of legumes and grasses give the best yields of forage and hay and probably also biomass where water is not limiting. The C-4 grass gives the highest yields for awhile but cannot sustain the yields without added N, be it from legumes, crop residues, manure (green or brown), sewage sludge, or energetically expensive chemical nitrogen. For high-quality leaf protein, the legume seems indispensable for animal food, human food, and chemurgic utilization (Duke, 1983). In developing countries, where chemical nitrogen is out of reach for most producers, the contribution by legumes (Table 3) assumes particular importance.

A brief look at the contributions, composition and distribution of each of the five legumes highlighted in this book is worthwhile.

Table 3. Productivity, including nitrogen fixation, by five food legumes (Duke, 1983, 1985)

	N fixation (kg/ha)	Net primary productivity (t/ha)
Arachis hypogaea	41–222	2–7
Cajanus cajan	98–280	2–12
Glycine max	1–168	2–20
Phaseolus vulgaris	10–65	3–7
Vigna unguiculata	73–354	3–6

Arachis hypogaea L. Fabaceae

When crushed, groundnut or peanut seeds yield a non-drying, edible oil used in cooking, in margarines, in pharmaceuticals, in cosmetics, in emulsions for insect control, and in fuel for diesel engines. The oil cake is a high-protein livestock feed and may be used for human consumption. Other products include dyes, ice cream, massage oil, paints, and a milk. Seeds are eaten raw, whole roasted and salted, or chopped in confectioneries, or ground into peanut butter. Young pods may be consumed as a vegetable. Young leaves and tips are suitable as a cooked green vegetable (Martin and Ruberte, 1975). The Javanese use the tips for lablab and the germinating seeds to make toge (Oschse, 1931). Scorched seeds serve as a coffee substitute. The hulls can be used for furfural, fuel, as a filler for fertilizers and for livestock feed or sweeping compounds. The foliage provides silage and forage. Peanuts bred for high-MUFA, may improve the fatty-acid profile in pork as hogs glean the fields following the harvester. Most of the peanuts grown in the U.S. enter the market ground (as peanut butter, 50 per cent); salted, whole (21 per cent), or mixed in confectioneries (16.5 per cent). Elsewhere, peanuts are processed mainly for oil (Duke, 1981).

My colleague and I (Duke and Wain, 1981) cited folk usage of peanut as an aphrodisiac, as a decoagulant and as treatment for cholecystosis, inflammation, and nephritis. Peanuts play a small role in folk pharmacopoeia. In China the nut is considered demulcent, pectoral, and peptic; the oil aperient and emollient, taken internally in milk for gonorrhea, applied externally for rheumatism (Duke and Ayensu, 1985). In Zimbabwe the peanut is used in remedies for plantar warts. Hemostasis and vaso-constriction have been reported as effects of peanut, and the alcoholic extract is said to affect isolated smooth muscles and frog hearts like acetylcholine.

The alcoholic lipoid fraction of the seed is said to prevent hemophilia and to be useful in treatment of some blood disorders (e.g., arthritic hemorrhages) in hemophilia. Heinerman (1988) encourages hemophiliacs to eat more raw peanuts and peanut butter. Further he suggests peanut butter as an adhesive for cloves applied to aching dental caries and as a vehicle for more unpleasant herbal drugs like cayenne. Shelled, uncooked seeds are reported to average, per 100 g, more than 500 kcal (2092 kJ), 4–13 g moisture, 21.0–36.4 g protein, 35.8–54.2 g fat, 6.0–24.9 g total carbohydrate, 1.2–4.3 g fibre, 1.8–3.1 g ash, 49 mg Ca, 409 mg P, 3.8 mg Fe, 15 µg beta-carotene equivalent, 0.79 mg thiamine, 0.14 mg riboflavin, 15.5 mg niacin, and 1 mg ascorbic acid (Table 4). Roasted seeds contain, broadly per 100 g: 595 kcal (2490 kJ), 1.8 g moisture, 23.2 g protein, 50.9 g fat, 21.7 g total carbohydrate, 3.2 g fibre, 2.4 g ash, 42 mg Ca, 354 mg P, 0.45 mg thiamine, 0.11 mg riboflavin, and 15.3 mg niacin.

Table 4. Composition of 100 g of the edible portion of raw peanuts (*Arachis hypogaea*) (USDA 1986)[a]

Nutrient (unit)	Amount in 100 g, edible portion		
	Mean	Standard error	Number of samples
Proximate			
Water (g)	6.50	0.093	31
Food energy (kJ)	2374		
Protein (N x 5.46) (g)	25.80	0.242	78
Total lipid (fat) (g)	49.24	0.297	98
Carbohydrate, total (g)	16.14		
Crude fibre[b] (g)	4.85	0.043	12
Ash (g)	2.33	0.064	26
Minerals			
Calcium (mg)	92		45
Iron (mg)	4.58		49
Magnesium (mg)	168		45
Phosphorus (mg)	376		45
Potassium (mg)	705		47
Sodium (mg)	18		35
Zinc (mg)	3.27		45
Copper (mg)	1.144		45
Manganese (mg)	1.934	0.057	44
Vitamins[c]			
Ascorbic acid (mg)	0.0		
Thiamine (mg)	0.640	0.034	24
Riboflavin (mg)	0.135	0.005	20
Niacin (mg)	12.066	0.305	24
Pantothenic acid (mg)	1.767	0.100	8
Vitamin B_6 (mg)	0.348	0.020	8
Folacin (μg)	239.8	15.874	8
Vitamin B_{12} (μg)	0.0		
Vitamin A (IU)	0.0		
Lipids			
Fatty acids[d]			
Saturated, total (g)	6.834		
14:0 (g)	0.025		
16:0 (g)	5.154		
18:0 (g)	1.100		
Monounsaturated, total (g)	24.429		
16:1 (g)	0.009		

Nutrient (unit)	Amount in 100 g, edible portion		
	Mean	Standard error	Number of samples
18:1 (g)	23.756		
20:1 (g)	0.661		
Polyunsaturated, total (g)	15.559		
18:2 (g)	15.555		
18:3 (g)	0.003		
Cholesterol (mg)	0.0		
Phytosterols (mg)	220		
Amino acids			
Tryptophan (g)	0.250		128
Threonine (g)	0.883		144
Isoleucine (g)	0.907		140
Leucine (g)	1.672		140
Lysine (g)	0.926		147
Methionine (g)	0.317		22
Cystine (g)	0.331		29
Phenylalanine (g)	1.337		141
Tyrosine (g)	1.049		137
Valine (g)	1.082		141
Arginine (g)	3.085		140
Histidine (g)	0.652		140
Alanine (g)	1.025		135
Aspartic acid (g)	3.146		135
Glutamic acid (g)	5.390		133
Glycine (g)	1.554		134
Proline (g)	1.138		130
Serine (g)	1.271		134

[a] Common measures in cooking are 1 oz = 28 g (about one-fourth the values cited) and 1 cup = 146 g (about 1½ times the values); shells constitute about 27 per cent of total weight.
[b] Insoluble dietary fibre as determined by the neutral detergent fibre method: 5.9 g/100 g.
[c] Alpha-tocopherol is present: 8.33 mg/100 g.
[d] Because of rounding or incomplete recording of fatty acids, columns do not always add up.

Boiled seeds contain, per 100 g: 235 kcal (984 kJ), 44.6 g moisture, 16.8 g protein, 8.3 g fat, 26.3 g total carbohydrate, 6.1 g fibre, 4.0 g ash, 45 mg Ca, 260 mg P, 5.1 mg Fe, 0.44 mg thiamine, 0.16 mg riboflavin, and 1.4 mg niacin. Raw leaves contain, per 100 g: 69 kcal (289 kJ), 78.5 g moisture, 4.4 g protein, 0.6 g fat, 14.9 g total carbohydrate, 4.6 g fibre, 1.6 g ash, 262 mg Ca, 82 mg P, 4.2 mg Fe, 7735 µg beta-carotene equivalent, 0.23 mg thiamine, 0.58 mg riboflavin, 1.6 mg niacin, and 98 mg ascorbic acid.

The oilseed cake is said to be a good source of arginine and glutamic acid, used in treating mental deficiencies (Perry, 1980). Hager's handbook states that seeds contain 20–30 per cent nitrogenous matter, 2–5 per cent cellulose, 8–21 per cent starch, alpha-cephalin, xanthine, glutathione, delta- and gamma-tocopherol, arginine, guanosine, choline, lecithin, saccharose, conglutin, conarachin, L-(-)-cystine, sarkosine, biotin, thiamine, vitamin P, conenzyme A, alpha-ketoglutaric- and gamma-methylent-alpha-ketoglutaric acid, traces of 4-methyleneproline, allantoinase, phospholipase D, isocitratylase, and fumarase.

Yoshida and Hasegawa (1977) reported 2.14 nmol/g stizolamine (1-methyl-3-guanidino-6-hydroxymethylpyrazine-2-one) in the seeds. The testa contains arachidoside, leucocyanadin, and leucodelphinidin.

Of greatest concern is possible contamination of damaged or spoiled seeds with the teratogenic, carcinogenic aflatoxins. Two principal toxins, aflatoxins B and G, and their less toxic dihydro derivatives, aflatoxins B_2 and G_2, are formed by mould (e.g., *Aspergillus flavus*), and there is no satisfactory way to remove the toxins from feed and foods (however, peanut oils are free of aflatoxins because of alkaline processing). LD_{50} for aflatoxin for sensitive organisms may be less than 1 mg/kg body weight.

According to the U.S. National Academy of Sciences (NAS, 1973), 'Aflatoxin B_1 appears to be the most potent hepatocarcinogen known.' Rats receiving only 15 ppm aflatoxin in the diet have high cancer incidence. Arachin, with four antigens, and conarachin, with two antigens, have also been reported.

The plant is an annual, ascending (Guaranian and sequential Peruvian) to somewhat longer-lived ascending, decumbent, or prostrate (Bolivian and Amazonan), geocarpic, glabrate to hirsute herb with upright main or n axes. The two principal, n + 1 order, vegetative axes arise in the axils of the alternately arranged cotyledons (cataphylls).

The first two nodes (or sometimes three) of every vegetative branch are also subtended by cataphylls. The taproot connects four series of spirally arranged lateral roots abundantly branching and usually heavily supplied with nodules. Root tips are without epidermis and without hairs. The leaves are stipulate, pinnate with two opposite pairs of leaflets, alternately arranged in a 2/5 phyllotaxy on the n axis; distichous on n + 1 and higher order branches. The flowers are pea-like, enclosed between two bracts — one simple, subtending a very short peduncle; the other bifid, subtending the pedicel. The flowers are sessile but appear to be stalked after growth of a tubular hypanthium just before anthesis. The ovary is surrounded by the base of the hypanthium (perigynous), on the distal end of which are inserted two calyx lobes, one awl-like opposite the keel and the other broad and four-notched opposite the back of the standard. The petals are orange, yellow, cream or rarely white; they are inserted between the calyx lobes and the fused bases of the anther filaments (staminal column).

The standard is orange with veins marking the more yellow central face or brick red by extension of the red-veined area. Wings are yellow, or yellow at base and orange apically, to brick red; the keel is colourless to faintly yellow, clasping the staminal column and bending at right angles with it about halfway along its length. Stamens number 10, sterile filaments usually two, anthers eight (sometimes nine, rarely 10) — four globose, uniloculate, alternating with four oblong, three of which are biloculate and one, opposite the standard, uniloculate. The tip of the ovary bears 1–5 ovules, grows out between the floral bracts, bringing with it the dried petals, calyx lobes and hypanthium and creating a unique floral structure — the peg. The peg quickly turns down toward the soil and thrusts its tip (with its ovules) several centimetres into the soil where the tip turns horizontally and develops into the pod.

The fruit is an indehiscent legume up to 10 cm long; seeds number one to five, from smaller than 1 × 0.5 cm to 3.5 cm × 1.5 cm weighing less than 0.2 g to more than 2.0 g.

The testa is thin — pink, red, purple, tan, brown, yellow, white or red and white, pink and white, brown and white, purple and white, or marked with small purple dashes or splashes on a base colour. Flowering may be in fewer than 30 days and at more than 40 days. Fruit matures in 90–150+ days. It is self-pollinating, occasionally outcrossed by bees (Duke, 1981).

With 15–70 species, *Arachis* has its centre of diversity in the Mato Grosso of Brazil. Most species are diploid (2x = 2n = 20).

Annual species are characteristic and tolerant of semi-arid areas, whereas perennials are suited to humid high-rainfall areas. Peanuts are quite tolerant of acid soils and aluminium, requiring a minimum of lime for acceptable yields (Duke, 1982).

More than 4000 entries in the germ-plasm bank in the United States have arisen from the Guaranian (Spanish, Valencia, Natal Common, Barberton, Manyema, Tatu, Pollachi and numerous other locally named cultivars), the Bolivian and Amazonan (Virginia bunch, Virginia and Georgia runners, Matevere, Overo, Mani Pintado), and Peruvian (Tingo Maria, Chinese) gene centres and their extensions into North America, Africa, Europe and Asia.

Their classification is:

	A. hypogaea L. (1753)	
	Subsp. *hypogaea* Krap. & Rig.(1960)	
Alternative:	Bolivian and Amazonan	var. *hypogaea* Krap. (1968)
	Coastal Peruvian	var. *hirsuta* Kohler (1898)
	Subsp. *fastigiata* Waldron (1919)	
Sequential:	Peruvian Selva and Guaranian	var. *fastigiata* Krap. (1968)
	Guaranian	var. *vulgaris* Harz (1885)

Cultivars are distinguished botanically by pod and seed. In addition to the cultivated peanut, there are wild *Arachis* species known to be cross-compatible with cultivated peanuts and known to possess resistance to pests and diseases, including early and late leaf spot and spider mites. Among resistant cultivars are Schwarz 21, which is resistant to slime disease (caused by *Pseudomonas solanacearum*); Tarapota and PIs 314817 and 315608, which are resistant to rust (caused by *Puccinia arachidis*); NC 3033, resistant to black rot from *Cylindrocladium crotalariae*; IRHO numbers 56−369 and H32, resistant to rosette virus; Valencia PIs 337394F and 337409, resistant to *Aspergillus flavus*; Tarapota and PI 109839, resistant to early leaf spot (caused by *Cercospora arachidicola*); NC 2, resistant to stem rot from *Sclerotium rolfsii*; PIs 295233 and 290606, resistant to lesion nematode, *Pratylenchus brachyurus*; and Natal Common and Kumawu Erect, resistant to root knot nematode, *Meloidogyne arenaria*. Cultivars resistant to insects include Southeastern Runner 56-15, resistant to fall armyworm, *Spodoptora frugiperda*; NC 6, resistant to the southern corn rootworm, *Diabrotica undecimpunctata howardi*; Spancross to leaf feeding; and NC 10247, NC 10272, NC 15729 and ·NC 15745, resistant to the potato leafhopper, *Empoasca fabae*.

Assigned to the South American and African centres of diversity, peanut is reported to exhibit tolerance to drought, frost, low and high pH, heat, laterite, limestone, sand, smog, savanna, and ultraviolet rays (Duke, 1981). Now widely cultivated in warm countries throughout the world, the peanut was introduced in pre-Columbian times to the West Indies and Mexico, in early post-Columbian times to Africa and eastern Asia and during the colonial period to Atlantic North America (Duke, 1981).

Ecologically, it is suitable for the tropics, sub-tropics and warm temperate regions, grown from 40°S to 40°N. It thrives with 5 dm water during the growing season, with most moisture needed in the middle third of the season. It grows best on light, friable sandy loams but will grow in heavier soils.

Ranging from Cool Temperate Moist through Tropical Thorn to Wet Forest Life zones, peanut is reported to tolerate annual precipitation of 3.1−41.0 dm (mean of 162 cases was 13.8 dm), annual mean temperatures of 10.5−28.5°C (mean of 161 cases was 23.5°C), and pH of 4.3−8.7 (mean of 90 cases, 6.5) (Duke, 1981).

Commercial peanuts are propagated from seed. Virginia-type (alternately branched) peanuts have a dormancy; Spanish Valencia types (sequentially branched) have little or no seed dormancy. The seedbed should be prepared, either flat, or widely ridged.

Seed is often treated with antifungal dressing before planting. In advanced agriculture, peanuts are often mechanized in monoculture. In many countries they are cultivated by hand, sometimes in mixed culture. The spacing and seed rate vary with growth rate, habit and production methods. Stands of 250,000 plants/ha are sought in machine-drilled planting. For types planted by hand, however, much lower seed rates are used. Weeds are controlled by cultivation and by pre- and post-planting applications of selective herbicides.

Applied early, nitrogen usually results in large responses by short-season cultivars in semi-arid regions of West Africa. Phosphorus is added on tropical red earths but not necessarily on temperate sandy soils receiving P in a rotation. The roots and fruits absorb nutrients, and in the pegging zone calcium is essential for high yield of large-podded, alternate types. Seeds produced on Ca-deficient soil have poor germination and poor seedling growth. On the red soils of Africa, sulphur may be beneficial (Duke, 1981).

Although flowering may commence in 30 days, 80–150 days or more are required for fruit maturation. Hand-harvested plants are pulled up and turned over on the ground, stacked or placed on racks to cure. Pods are picked and allowed to dry in piles up to 5 cm deep on trays or are spread in the sun. In fully mechanized harvesting, the pulling, inverting and windrowing of the plants are a single operation. Pods are removed by combine machines and elevated into baskets attached to the combine or blown directly into trailing 'drying wagons' that are towed, when full, to drying stations where warm or ambient air is forced through the load of peanuts. In Argentina the combines pick and shell the pods in one operation so that the crop is marketed as dried seeds instead of dried pods. Woodruff (1981) reported experimental yields up to 7000 kg/ha, but commonly yields are 400–1500 kg/ha. The shelling percentage is 75–80 for sequential types and 60–80 for alternate types.

World production in 1986–87 was 21.3 million t (Table 5). Production in Africa 4.696 million t; and in North and Central America, 1.829 million t (USA = 1.627 million t). India (4.5 million t) and China made up most of Asia's output (FAO, 1988b). Production dropped by 12 per cent in China from 1985 but was still second largest on record. Output increased in India by 7 per cent. Gains in Senegal (33 per cent), Sudan (67 per cent) and Nigeria (17 per cent) reflected improved rainfall in the Sahel (FAO, 1988a).

Bogdan (1977) reported dry-matter yields of 4.5, 5.1, 3.9 and 2.8 t/ha respectively, 87, 94, 101, and 108 days after sowing. Such yields could be trebled in areas of the tropics where three crops could be grown annually. Ratnam (1979) found harvest indices of 20–47 per cent in bunch types, 12–31 per cent in semi-spreading types, and 10–22 per cent in spreading types. These percentages suggest that dry matter is 2–10 times as high as conventional seed yields, with potential use as fodder or fuel. Woodruff (1981) noted that maximum U.S. yields may be 6500–7000 kg/ha associated with 9000–10,000 kg dry matter for hay, soil enrichment or energy production and 300–400 kg N-fixing roots/ha.

Table 5. Regional and national groundnut production in 1986 (IFPRI/USDA data) (compiled by J. A. Wightman *et al.*, authors of chapter 5)

Region or country	Production		Produc-tivity	% world
	1000s ha	1000s t	(t/ha)	production
Asia	13031	15278	1.17	68
China	3502	6295	1.80	28
West Africa	2568	2472	0.96	11
East and Southern Africa	884	613	0.69	3
Latin America	543	691	1.27	3
Developed world	913	2030	2.22	9

Peanut residues include the total haulm, often calculated from a harvest index of 1:2. The shell is estimated to constitute 35−48 per cent of the total weight of the harvested peanut, the skin (testa) 4 per cent of the seed or 'nut' (Wu Leung *et al.*, 1972). However, in India, the husks are considered to represent 20−32 per cent of the weight, averaging 30 per cent. Husks are largely crude fibre (to 60 per cent), lignin and pentosans.

Peanut oil can be made on the farm with a sheller, a press, and a little time to let the gum settle to the bottom of the tank, although in 1981, Harwood concluded, 'Peanuts are an unlikely candidate for on-farm production of vegetable oil.' The rationale was that peanuts have to be dehulled before being pressed, and the hulls present a disposal problem. My question was why not use them to fuel dehulling.

Harwood added that peanuts should be segregated into edible and low-grade nuts to obtain full value from the crop. These processes are performed in large plants and are not amenable to small on-farm production. Furthermore, peanut oil was more expensive than cottonseed and soybean oil over a 15-year period.

Cajanus cajan (L.) Millsp. Fabaceae

Nutritious and wholesome, pigeon peas are popular as food in many developing countries. The green seeds (and pods) serve as a vegetable. Ripe seeds are a source of flour, used split as dhal in soups or eaten with rice. Dhal contains as much as 22 per cent protein, depending on cultivar and location. Tender leaves are used rarely as an herb or eaten like spinach. Ripe seeds may be germinated and eaten as sprouts.

Plants produce forage quickly and can be grown as a perennial for animal feed or green manure. They are often grown as shade for seedling trees or vanilla; as cover; or occasionally as hedge. Common names, besides pigeon pea, include gandul, red gram, Congo pea, gungo pea, no-eye pea, and pois de Angola. In Thailand and north Bengal, pigeon pea serves as host for the scale insect that produces lac or sticklac. In Madagascar the leaves are used as food for the silkworm. Dried stalks serve as fuel, thatch and basketry (Duke, 1981).

Pigeon pea has been widely used in folk medicine. My colleague and I (Duke and Wain, 1981) found evidence of its use as a treatment for bronchitis, ciguatera, colds, colic, convulsions, cough, diarrhea, dysentery, flu, headache, jaundice, leprosy, parturition, sore throat, stroke, swelling, tumours, urticaria, vertigo and worms. It is regarded by some as an antidote to poisoning (from eating fish or cassava). It is used as an astringent, expectorant, and sedative.

In India and Indonesia (Java), the young leaves are applied to sores, and the Indochinese claim that powdered leaves help one expel gallstones. In Argentina, a leaf decoction is prized for treatment of skin irritations, particularly of the genitals. Floral decoctions are used for bronchitis, coughs, and pneumonia. Chinese shops sell dried roots as an alexeritic, anthelminthic, expectorant, sedative, and vulnerary. Leaves are also used for toothache, mouthwash, sore gums, and dysentery. Scorched seed, added to coffee, is said to alleviate headache and vertigo. Fresh seeds are said to help males control incontinence of urine, whereas immature fruits are believed to relieve liver and kidney ailments (Morton, 1976; Duke, 1981).

Analysis of dhal (without husk) gave percentages of moisture, 15.2; protein, 22.3; fat (ether extract), 1.7; mineral matter, 3.6; carbohydrate, 57.2; Ca, 9.1; and P, 0.26; carotene (evaluated as vitamin A) was 220 IU/100 g and vitamin B_1, 50 IU/100 g. Sun-dried seeds of *C. cajan* are reported to contain (per 100 g) 345 kcal (1444 kJ), 9.9 per cent moisture, 19.5 g protein, 1.3 g fat, 65.5 g carbohydrate, 1.3 g fibre, 3.8 g ash, 161 mg Ca, 285 mg P, 15.0 mg Fe, 55 μg beta-carotene equivalent, 0.72 mg thiamine, 0.14 mg riboflavin, and 2.9 mg niacin (Table 6). Immature seeds of *C. cajan* are reported to contain, per 100 g, 117 kcal (490 kJ), 69.5 per cent moisture, 7.2 g protein, 0.6 g fat, 21.3 g total carbohydrate, 3.3 g fibre, 1.4 g ash, 29 mg Ca, 135 mg P, 1.3 mg Fe, 5 mg Na, 563 mg K, 145 μg beta-carotene equivalent, 0.40 mg thiamine, 0.25 mg riboflavin, 2.4 mg niacin, and 26 mg ascorbic acid. Of the total amino acids, 6.7 per cent is arginine, 1.2 per cent cystine, 3.4 per cent histidine, 3.8 per cent isoleucine, 7.6 per cent leucine, 7.0 per cent lysine, 1.5 per cent methionine, 8.7 per cent phenylalanine, 3.4 per cent threonine, 2.2 per cent tyrosine, 5.0 per cent valine, 9.8 per cent aspartic acid, 19.2 per cent glutamic acid, 6.4 per cent alanine, 3.6 per cent glycine, 4.4 per cent proline, 5.0 per cent serine.

Table 6. Composition of 100 g of the edible portion of raw pigeon peas (*Cajanus cajan*) (USDA 1986)[*].

Nutrient (unit)	Amount in 100 g, edible portion		
	Mean	Standard error	Number of samples
Proximate			
Water (g)	10.59	0.380	28
Food energy (kJ)	1436		
Protein (N x 6.25) (g)	21.70	0.315	41
Total lipid (fat) (g)	1.49	0.105	23
Carbohydrate, total (g)	62.78		
Crude fibre[b] (g)	3.12	0.960	13
Ash (g)	3.45	0.053	28
Minerals			
Calcium (mg)	130	7.724	18
Iron (mg)	5.23	0.367	30
Magnesium (mg)	183	17.121	14
Phosphorus (mg)	367	30.430	18
Potassium (mg)	1392	23.534	9
Sodium (mg)	17	1.407	4
Zinc (mg)	2.76	0.260	9
Copper (mg)	1.057	0.036	9
Manganese (mg)	1.791	0.138	9
Vitamins			
Ascorbic acid (mg)	0.0		
Thiamine (mg)	0.643	0.060	11
Riboflavin (mg)	0.187	0.015	12
Niacin (mg)	2.965	0.363	12
Pantothenic acid (mg)	1.266	0.057	8
Vitamin B_6 (mg)	0.283	0.041	12
Folacin (μg)	456.0	15.181	8
Vitamin B_{12} (μg)	0.0		
Vitamin A (IU)	28	2.344	8
Lipids			
Fatty acids			
Saturated, total (g)	0.330		
16:0 (g)	0.307		
18:0 (g)	0.024		
Monounsaturated, total (g)	0.012		
18:1 (g)	0.012		

Nutrient (unit)	Amount in 100 g, edible portion		
	Mean	Standard error	Number of samples
Polyunsaturated, total (g)	0.814		
18:2 (g)	0.778		
18:3 (g)	0.035		
Cholesterol (mg)	0.0		
Amino acids			
Tryptophan (g)	0.212		14
Threonine (g)	0.767		28
Isoleucine (g)	0.785		28
Leucine (g)	1.549		28
Lysine (g)	1.521		28
Methionine (g)	0.243		26
Cystine (g)	0.250		19
Phenylalanine (g)	1.858		19
Tyrosine (g)	0.538		26
Valine (g)	0.937		28
Arginine (g)	1.299		26
Histidine (g)	0.774		26
Alanine (g)	0.972		24
Aspartic acid (g)	2.146		24
Glutamic acid (g)	5.031		24
Glycine (g)	0.802		24
Proline (g)	0.955		23
Serine (g)	1.028		24

[a] The 100-g measure is slightly less than equal to ½ cup (102 g), a measure more common in cooking.
[b] Insoluble dietary fibre as determined by the neutral detergent fibre method: 13.5 g/100 g.

As is the case for most legumes, methionine, cystine, and tryptophan are the limiting amino acids in *C. cajan*. The oil of the seeds contains linolenic (5.7 per cent), linoleic (51.4 per cent), and oleic (6.3 per cent) acids and is 36.6 per cent saturated fatty acids. Seeds are reported to contain trypsin inhibitors and chymotrypsin inhibitors. Fresh green forage is 70.4 per cent moisture, with percentages of 7.1 for crude protein, 10.7 for crude fibre, 7.9 N-free extract, 1.6 for fat, 2.3 for ash. The whole plant, dried and ground, contains 11.2 per cent moisture, 14.8 per cent crude protein, 28.9 per cent crude fibre, 39.9 per cent N-free extract, 1.7 per cent fat, and 3.5 per cent ash (Duke, 1981).

The plant is a perennial woody shrub, mostly grown as an annual. The stems are strong, growing to 4 m and branching freely; the root system is deep and extensive, to about 2 m, with a taproot. Leaves alternate, pinnately trifoliolate, stipulate; stipels are small, subulate; leaflets lanceolate to elliptic, entire, acute apically and basally, penninerved, resinous on lower surface and pubescent, to 15 cm long and 6 cm wide. Inflorescences develop in terminal or axillary racemes in the upper branches of the bush. The flowers are multi-coloured with yellow predominant; red, purple, and orange occur in streaks or fully cover the dorsal side of the flag. The flowers are zygomorphic. The pods are compressed, with two to nine seeds separated from each other by slight depressions.

The pods do not shatter in the field. The seeds are lenticular to ovoid, with diameters to 8 mm. About 10 seeds weigh 1 g. Germination is crypto-cotylar (Duke, 1981).

There are many cultivars; they differ in height; habit of growth; colour of flowers, pods, and seeds; maturation; etc. Perennial types assume a tree-like appearance, yield well the first year but not later; they are suitable forage, cover, shade and hedge plants. Annual (weak perennial) types are small and are grown as field crops, mainly cultivated for their seeds.

Native to India (Duke, 1981) or Africa, pigeon pea has evolved different strains in Africa. These were brought to the New World in post-Columbian times. As is the case with *Arachis* spp., truly wild *Cajanus* has never been found, existing mostly as a remnant of cultivation. In several places *Cajanus* sp. persists in the forest. The closest wild relative, *Atylosia cajanifolia* Haines, has been found in some localities in east India; other *Atylosia* spp. are found scattered throughout India, and a group of endemic *Atylosia* species grow in North Australia.

In Africa *C. kerstingii* grows in the dry belts of Senegal, Ghana, Togo, and Nigeria. Pigeon peas occur throughout the tropical and sub-tropical regions, as well as the warm temperate regions (such as North Carolina) from 30°N to 30°S (Duke, 1981).

Pigeon pea is remarkably drought resistant, growing in areas with as little as 65 cm annual rainfall, even producing seed profusely. The crop matures early and pest damage is minimized. With a few exceptions, cultivars are photoperiod sensitive, with short days decreasing time to flowering. Under humid conditions, pigeon pea tends to produce luxuriant vegetation, and rain at flowering causes defective fertilization and permits attack by caterpillars. Annual precipitation of 6–10 dm is most suitable, with moist conditions for the first 2 growing months and dry conditions for flowering and harvest. Although pigeon pea grows best at 18–29°C, some cultivars tolerate 10°C under dry conditions and 35°C under moist conditions. The plant is sensitive to waterlogging and frost.

It will grow in all types of soils, with well-drained medium to heavy loams being best. Some cultivars tolerate salinity (6–12 mmhos/cm). Ranging from Warm Temperate Moist to Wet through Tropical Desert to Wet Forest Life zones, pigeon pea has been reported to tolerate precipitation of 5.3–40.3 dm/year (mean for 60 cases, 14.5 dm/year), and pH of 4.5–8.4 (mean for 44 cases, 6.4) (Duke, 1981).

Seeds are best planted in hills or on ridges of well-prepared soil where water does not collect; in pure stands, the rate is about 9–22 kg/ha for rows, but sometimes seed is broadcast. Seeds germinate in about 2 weeks. Quite frequently (in India) pigeon pea is grown in mixtures with other crops or in alternate rows (from one to three of a kind) with 3–10 rows of sorghum, groundnuts, sesame, cotton, pineapples, millets or maize. For pure crops, pigeon pea should be sown 2.5–5 cm deep in rows 40–120 cm by 30–60 cm. When sown as a mixture, it is sown in rows 1.2–2.1 m apart, with the space depending on the associated crop. Producers may plant three or four seeds in each hill, later thinning to two plants per hill.

Plants show little response to fertilizers; in fact, mixed plantings with millet in India showed a negative response to N. For the first month, pigeon pea shares the intercultivation of the main crop. In the tropics, phosphoric acid, 20–100 kg/ha, is recommended. Sulphur, with or without P, can markedly increase seed yield and nitrogen fixation.

Early cultivars start podding in 12 weeks but don't mature before 5–6 months. Late cultivars require 9–12 months. The crop may be ratooned for forage or allowed to persist for 3–5 years. Seed yields drop considerably after the first year, and disease build-up may reduce stand. In India, pigeon peas are sown in June–July. In north India, medium and late cultivars are common; they flower in January and yield a first crop in March–April. Early and medium cultivars flower in October–November, yielding in December–January. Very early cultivars have not been widely accepted.

In East Africa, the crop is harvested in June–July. In the Caribbean areas, green pods are harvested for home consumption or canning, local people having developed dwarf cultivars with more uniform pod maturity. The crop is mowed and threshed with a combine harvester.

Depending on cultivar, location and time of sowing, flowering occurs as early as 100 days and as late as 430 days. In the first harvest, one may have to pick the pods by hand, whereas at maturity the whole plant can be chopped with a sickle and left to dry in the field before being collected for threshing. Threshing is by wooden flails or trampling on floors. Grain is then cleaned by winnowing. Mechanical threshing and seed cleaning are possible.

Commercial dhal is prepared by either a dry or wet method. The dry method involves preliminary sun-drying for 3 or 4 days, followed by partial splitting of the grains with a stone mill. Partially split seeds are treated with vegetable oil and stored. Sesame oil is used for storage of less than a month (coconut oil has been used successfully in Sri Lanka), and for longer storage, castor oil is used. The seed coat absorbs the oil and becomes easier to split for dhal. The pigeon peas are split in half and are separated from the seed coats by sieving and winnowing. The dry method produces perfect half globes that soften uniformly in cooking and command a high price. From 40 kg of seeds, 18 kg of clean good-quality dhal is extracted. In the wet method, pigeon peas are allowed to soak in water for about 6 h, then are drained and mixed with finely sieved soil (2 kg soil to 40 kg of seeds). The mixture is heaped during the nights and spread in the sun to dry during the day; normally a couple of days is sufficient. Impurities are then removed, and the seed is split in half on a stone mill. About 31 kg of dhal is milled from 40 kg of seed by the wet method. Oil is not used for wet preparation of the dhal and is not added before sale of dhal prepared by either method. At home, oil (1 kg/40 kg dhal) may be added for preservation, but the dhal as such is not kept for longer than 2–3 months (Duke, 1981).

Green-pod yields are 1–9 t/ha. Dried-seed yields reach 2.5 t/ha but average 600 kg/ha. India's pigeon pea production, 1.818 million t from 2.54 million ha in 1975 was more than that of any other country. At the time, pigeon pea was being cultivated commercially (for canning) in the Dominican Republic, Trinidad, Puerto Rico, and the U.S. (Hawaii); in Africa, farmers in Kenya, Malawi, Tanzania and Uganda grow it mostly for home consumption. Elsewhere in the tropics it is a crop of kitchen gardens and hedges more than a staple food crop. However, in virtually every tropical country, it contributes valuable vegetable protein to the diet.

In 1975, Asia led world production, 1.845 million t, averaging 706 kg/ha; Africa produced 70,000 t, averaging 406 kg/ha; North America produced 41,000 t, averaging 1415 kg/ha; and South America produced 4000 t, averaging 449 kg/ha. In 1981, average yield of pigeon pea was 684 kg/ha in the developing world and 2222 kg/ha in the U.S., the only developed country producing large amounts.

Experimental yields suggest a straw factor of three for phytomass calculations. Biomass yields of 7 t/ha have been reported from Florida and 12 t/ha in Cuba. The woody stalks (2 t/ha) are used as fuel in India (NAS, 1981), the spindly stalks being used for cooking fuel as they are in Malawi. Historically, stalks were employed to make charcoal in gunpowder.

Glycine max (L.) Merr. Fabaceae

Synonyms for *Glycine max*, or soybean, are *Dolichos soja* L., *Phaseolus max* L., and *Soja hispida* Moench. The uses are many, as soybeans are one of the world's most important sources of oil and protein. Unripe seeds are eaten as a vegetable, and dried seeds eaten whole, split or sprouted. Processed, they give soy milk, a valuable protein supplement in infant feeding and a source of curds and cheese. Soy sauce is made from the mature fermented beans, and soy is an ingredient in other sauces. Roasted seeds are used as a coffee substitute. The highly nutritious sprouts are readily consumed in Asia. Seeds yield an edible, semi-drying oil, used as salad oil and for manufacture of margarine and shortening.

The oil is used industrially in paint, linoleum, oilcloth, ink, soap, insecticide, and disinfectant. Lecithin phospholipids, obtained as a by-product of the oil industry, are used as a wetting and stabilizing agent in the food, cosmetic, pharmaceutical, leather, paint, plastic, soap, and detergent industries.

Soy meal is rich protein for livestock and is, thus, increasing in demand. Meal and soybean protein are used in the manufacture of, among others, synthetic fibre, adhesives, textile sizing, waterproofing, and fire-fighting foam.

Flour prepared from the whole beans is full fat (with about 20 per cent oil); that from mechanically expressed meal is low fat (5–6 per cent oil); and that from solvent-extracted meal is defatted (about 1 per cent oil). The flour is used in baked goods and other food products and in extending cereal flour and meat products.

The vegetative portions of the plant are used as silage, pasture or fodder and, at times, as green manure. The straw can be used to make paper, stiffer than that made from wheat straw.

Chinese herbalists suggest that soybean aids functioning of the bowels, heart, kidney, liver, and stomach. A decoction of the root is said to be astringent. The meal and flour, with their low contents of starch, are used to prepare foods for people with diabetes.

Soybean diets are valued for acidosis, and soybean oil, with its high proportion of unsaturated fatty acids, is recommended, like safflower and poppyseed oil, to combat hyper-cholesterolemia. Commercial grades of natural lecithin, often derived from soybean, are reported to contain a potent vasodepressor. Lecithin in a lipotropic agent as well as being a prime source of choline. Soybean is listed as a major starting material for preparation of sitosterol and stigmasterol. Stigmasterol is a key starter for industrial synthesis of steroidal hormones.

Raw seeds of *G. max* have been reported to contain, per 100 g, 139 kcal (582 kJ), 68.2 per cent moisture, 13.0 g protein, 5.7 g fat, 11.4 g carbohydrate, 1.9 g fibre, 1.7 g ash, 78 mg Ca, 158 mg P, 3.8 mg Fe, 0.40 mg thiamine, 0.17 mg riboflavin, 1.5 mg niacin, and 27 mg ascorbic acid (Table 7). Sprouts contain, per 100 g edible portion, 62 kcal (260 kJ), 81.5 per cent moisture, 7.7 g protein, 1.8 g fat, 8.0 g total carbohydrate, 0.7 g fibre, 1.0 g ash, 52 mg Ca, 58 mg P, 1.1 mg Fe, 30 mg Na, 279 mg K, 25 mg beta-carotene equivalent, 0.19 mg thiamine, 0.15 mg riboflavin, 0.8 mg niacin, and 10 mg ascorbic acid. Dried yellow seeds are reported to contain 400 kcal

(1674 kJ), 10.2 per cent moisture, 35.1 g protein, 17.7 g fat, 32.0 g carbohydrate, 4.2 g fibre, 5.0 g ash, 226 mg Ca, 546 mg P, 8.5 mg riboflavin, and 2.2 mg niacin. The mineral composition (percentage on fresh-weight basis) is reportedly 2.0 K, 0.38 Na, 0.22 Ca, 0.0081 Fe, 0.0012 Cu, 0.24 Mg, 0.59 P, 0.02 Cl, 0.0032 Mn, 0.406 S, 0.0022 Zn, and 0.007 Al, with I, Mo, B, Ni, and Si in trace amounts (CSIR, 1956). Green feed of soybean contains 12.56 per cent protein, 23.7 per cent fibre, 52.1 per cent N-Free extract, 2.2 per cent ether extract, 1.9 per cent CaO, 0.57 per cent P_2O_5, 1.4 per cent MgO, and 2.4 per cent K_2O.

The hay contains 15 per cent crude protein, 29.1 per cent fibre, 42.6 per cent N-free extract, 1.3 per cent ether extract, 12.0 per cent total ash, 2.9 per cent CaO, 0.60 per cent P_2O_5, 1.2 per cent MgO, 0.3 per cent Na_2O, and 2 per cent K_2O. Soybean straw contains 16.0 per cent moisture, 7.4 per cent protein, 2.0 per cent either extract, 28.3 per cent N-free extract, 26.1 per cent fibre, and 10.2 per cent ash. Nutritional analyses of dozens of soybean products appear in the food composition table for use in East Asia (Wu Leung et al., 1972).

A bushy, rather coarse annual herb, soybean has stems up to 1.8 m tall, sometimes vine-like, terete toward the base, angled and sulcate to subquadrangular above, grey brownish or tawny, hirsute to pilose with pale hairs. The leaves are pinnately trifoliolate, their petioles 2–20 cm long, from subterete and sparsely pilose or glabrescent to strongly angled, sulcate and hirsute, the rachis 0.5–3 cm long, the stipules broadly ovate, abruptly acuminate, 3–7 mm long, conspicuously nerved, more or less strigose.

The leaflets are membranous and, like the leaves, are broadly ovate. They are sub-orbicular, oval or elliptic-lanceolate, 3–14 cm long × 2.5–10 cm wide, the terminal seldom being appreciably larger than the lateral. The leaflets are sparsely silky-strigose on both surfaces or glabrate above, strigose-velutinous below, the petiolules being 1.5–4 mm long, densely hirsute.

The stipels are narrowly lanceolate to setaceous, 1–3.5 mm long, bracts from broadly to narrowly lanceolate 4.5–5.5 mm long, several-nerved, strigose; the racemes are axillary, irregular, often leafy, and very short, 10–35 mm long. The peduncle and pedicels are often reduced and concealed by a densely hirsute vesture, the flowers sometimes single or paired in the lower axils. Glabrescent pedicels are 0.25–3 mm long; the calyx 5–7 mm long, setose to appressed-hirsute or strigose, with sub-equal teeth, the upper pair generally united to above the middle.

The bracteoles are setaceous, appressed, setose, 2.5–3.25 mm long. The corolla is white, pink, greenish blue, violet or purple, 4.5–7 mm long, and the standard is sub-orbicularobovate to sub-reniform, emarginate, and somewhat longer than the narrowly oblong wings, which exceed the keel, porrect or somewhat upturned near the apex.

Table 7. Composition of 100 g of the edible portion of raw soybeans (*Glycine max*) (USDA, 1986)[a]

Nutrient (unit)	Amount in 100 g, edible portion		
	Mean	Standard error	Number of samples
Proximate			
Water (g)	8.54	0.142	433
Food energy (kJ)	1742		
Protein (N x 5.71) (g)	36.49	0.205	454
Total lipid (fat) (g)	19.94	0.183	364
Carbohydrate, total (g)	30.16		
Crude fibre[b] (g)	4.96	0.787	138
Ash (g)	4.87	0.092	190
Minerals			
Calcium (mg)	277	5.268	71
Iron (mg)	15.70	0.741	78
Magnesium (mg)	280	9.190	49
Phosphorus (mg)	704	11.330	82
Potassium (mg)	1797	28.702	56
Sodium (mg)	2	1.084	5
Zinc (mg)	4.89	0.073	60
Copper (mg)	1.658	0.029	60
Manganese (mg)	2.517	0.099	58
Vitamins[c]			
Ascorbic acid (mg)	6.0		3
Thiamine (mg)	0.874	0.039	50
Riboflavin (mg)	0.870	0.196	21
Niacin (mg)	1.623	0.303	32
Pantothenic acid (mg)	0.793	0.189	6
Vitamin B_6 (mg)	0.377	0.065	6
Folacin (μg)	375.1		
Vitamin B_{12} (μg)	0.0		
Vitamin A (IU)	24		3
Lipids			
Fatty acids			
Saturated, total (g)	2.884		
14:0 (g)	0.055		
16:0 (g)	2.116		
18:0 (g)	0.712		
Monounsaturated, total (g)	4.404		
16:1 (g)	0.055		

Table 7 Continued

Nutrient (unit)	Amount in 100 g, edible portion		
	Mean	Standard error	Number of samples
18:1 (g)	4.348		
Polyunsaturated, total (g)	11.255		
18:2 (g)	9.925		
18:3 (g)	1.330		
Cholesterol (mg)	0.0		
Phytosterols (mg)	161		
Amino acids			
Tryptophan (g)	0.530		61
Threonine (g)	1.585		148
Isoleucine (g)	1.770		132
Leucine (g)	2.972		132
Lysine (g)	2.429		156
Methionine (g)	0.492		162
Cystine (g)	0.588		137
Phenylalanine (g)	1.905		132
Tyrosine (g)	1.380		127
Valine (g)	1.821		132
Arginine (g)	21.831		131
Histidine (g)	0.984		131
Alanine (g)	1.719		126
Aspartic acid (g)	4.589		126
Glutamic acid (g)	7.068		126
Glycine (g)	1.687		127
Proline (g)	2.135		141
Serine (g)	2.115		142

[a] The 100-g measure is just larger than the amount (93 g) of soybeans in ½ cup, a common measure in cooking.

[b] Insoluble dietary fibre as determined by the neutral detergent fibre method: 12.5 g/100 g.

[c] Alpha-tocopherol is present: 0.85 mg/100 g.

The pod is oblong, sub-falcate, pendant, 25–75 mm long × 8–15 mm wide, coarsely hirsute or setose, the bristly hairs being up to 2.5 mm long, yellowish-brown. Seeds, two or three per pod, are ovoid to sub-spherical or irregularly rhomboidal, 6–11 × 5–8 mm, greenish cream or greyish olive to reddish black, smooth, the caruncle scalelike, membranous, erect or appressed, about one-third to one-half the width of the hilum.

Soybean plants vary markedly, and many cultivars have been developed, bred for resistance to diseases, for flowering-time control, climatic and edaphic conditions or oil and protein content. Agricultural or extension agents should be consulted for the best local cultivar. Thirty-six trivial variants have been described as subspecies and varieties, and many horticultural cultivars have been developed. Several germ-plasm collections of soybean are described in Hill (1976), and good cultivars for the tropics have been listed in Singh *et al.* (1987). Assigned to the China–Japan centre of diversity, soybean is reported to exhibit tolerance to aluminium, bacteria, disease, frost, fungi, hydrogen fluoride, high and low pH, heavy soil, insects, laterites, limestone, mycobacteria, nematodes, variable photoperiod, pesticides, smog, smut, and viruses.

Soybean is widely cutivated, not known in the wild state. It is believed to be a cultigen derived from *Glycine ussuriensis*, reported to grow in China, Japan, Korea, USSR, and Taiwan.

Though a sub-tropical plant, soybean is now cultivated from the tropics to 52°N. In the U.S., its greatest development is in the corn belt. I observed it as one of the more frequent cultivars at 47°N in Nan Char, People's Republic of China. It does not survive where heat is excessive or winters are severe. It is a short-day plant, requiring 5 dm water during the growing season.

Soybean grows best on fertile, well-drained soils but does tolerate a range of soil conditions. Soybean soils must contain specific nitrogen-fixing bacteria, although recently developed cultivars have promiscuous nodulation (Singh *et al.*, 1987). When grown on the same land for 2–3 successive years, soybeans increase in yield.

The crop is suited to dry zones, to low or mid-country wet zones, or to irrigated land. Soybeans will grow better than many crops on infertile or poorly drained soil. Many high-latitude cultivars do poorly at low latitudes. Ranging from Cool Temperate Moist to Wet through Tropical Very Dry to Wet Forest Life zones, soybean has been reported to tolerate annual precipitation of 3.1–41.0 dm (mean of 108 cases, 12.8), annual mean temperatures of 5.9–27°C (mean of 108 cases, 18.2°C), and pH of 4.3–8.4 (mean of 98 cases, 6.2).

The crop is propagated by seed and requires thorough soil preparation, with a deep loose seedbed. Most growers prefer ploughing in fall or early spring rather than immediately before planting.

Weeds should be destroyed by light disking, harrowing or with cultivators, immediately before soybean is planted. Soil temperatures and day length determine the best time to plant seeds (at or after corn planting in many areas).

Full-season cultivars, which take most of the growing season to mature, produce highest yields when planted with or soon after corn. Rate of seeding varies with the area: in the northern U.S., narrow rows, 46–68 cm wide, produce the highest yields, whereas in the southern U.S., little advantage can be gained from planting rows closer than 90 cm.

Often, soybeans are planted with machines designed for other crops but adapted for soybeans by special plates. They are sometimes planted with a drill in which all the feed cups are covered except those needed for row planting. A row planter provides uniform depth of seed (should be 2.5-5 cm). Although seeding rate depends on the cultivar, the size of seed, the width of row and the germination, a good rate is 1 seed/2.5 cm of row. Close spacing encourages rapid growth of soybeans and aids in weed control, but spacings closer than 2.5 cm may increase lodging. Excessive lodging reduces yields and causes difficulty in harvesting.

Often, seeds are treated against soil-borne diseases, and treatment can be any time before planting, even in the preceding fall at harvest. Soybeans need inoculation with a commercial culture of nitrogen-fixing bacteria unless the bacteria are known to be in the soil or the cultivar is a promiscuous nodule producer. IITA has developed promiscuous soybeans with superior agronomic characters. Soybean bacteria live in the soil a number of years, and some farmers do not inoculate the soil if nodulated soybeans have been grown there in the previous 4–5 years. In the absence of nodulation, soybeans require nitrogen fertilizer for maximum yields. Soybeans fit well into many rotations, with corn, small grains or other legumes; or in rotation with cotton, corn or rice. They may be planted after early potatoes and vegetables, after winter grain or when grass, clover or row crops have failed.

Fertilizer needs vary with the soil and the cropping system; on soils of low fertility, fertilizers increase yields; however, fertilizer containing potash is injurious to germination when in direct contact with the seed. Fertilizer may be applied in bands 5–7 cm to the side and 5 cm below the seed; or soil and fertilizer may be mixed but 2.5 cm must be left between fertilizer and seed. Broadcast fertilizer should be ploughed under. Soybeans are more acid tolerant than other legumes but will respond to lime applications on acid soils.

Weed competition is serious and may reduce yields by 50 per cent. For example, in Taiwan, a hand-weeded crop yielded twice that of a weedy control (1600 vs 800 kg/ha), with alachlor (2 kg/ha), chloramben (2 kg/ha), linuron (0.25 kg/ha), and nitrolen (3 kg/ha) also doubling yields. Early cultivation (even before soybeans have emerged) prevents weeds from becoming established ahead of the soybeans. Both rowed and drilled soybeans can be cultivated effectively with a rotary hoe, drag harrow, or weeder. Soybean plants are easily injured by cultivating equipment just before and during emergence from the soil. After emergence, stem breakage is a risk if one is cultivating during the hot part of the day. Row-cultivating equipment is used for final cultivation. Soybeans are usually not grown under irrigation, at least in the U.S. A good crop usually requires about 50 cm of water and, in most areas where soybeans are grown, moisture is adequate. Soybeans tolerate dry soil before they bloom but not during the pod-filling stage. Row or flood irrigation may be used on land that has been leveled and prepared for it. Heavy, infrequent irrigations usually give better results and require less labour than do frequent light irrigations. Time between irrigations depends on the soil and weather. Double cropping of soybeans — usually by alternating with a small grain crop such as barley or wheat — has increased in warmer regions of the U.S. Typically two crops are obtained yearly, the small grain being seeded in the fall and harvested in spring. Immediately after harvest, soybeans are seeded. Both conventional ploughing and 'no-till' planting in the small grain stubble are widely used. Technological improvements in planting equipment, better herbicides, and early maturing cultivars of small grains have contributed to the increased use of double cropping.

All seeds on a soybean plant mature at essentially the same time. Maturity of the seed is accompanied by a rapid dropping of the leaves and drying of the stems. Harvest losses during combining may be 10−20 per cent, and special care is needed when seed for planting is harvested mechanically. As seed moisture drops below 12 per cent, mechanical injury increases and reduces subsequent germination. The combine should be adjusted frequently during the day so that the cylinder speed threshes but does not crack seed.

Storage should be in clean, dry bins, with the moisture content of individual loads not exceeding 11 per cent when storage is for 1 year and not exceeding 10 per cent for longer storage.

Excessive moisture encourages mould and spoilage. If the soybeans are kept dry, they will not deteriorate appreciably for a year or more. Viability deteriorates rapidly if seed is stored beyond the first planting season following harvest.

Soybeans make a versatile emergency crop for forage because they are adapted to a wide range of planting dates. They can supplement (not substitute for) alfalfa, clover or other hay crops. Soybean hay is difficult to cure, and loss of leaves and spoilage during curing may reduce quality, although many types of soybeans are good forage, with fine stems and small, dark seeds. At a rate of 136−204 kg seed/ha, soybean cultivars can equal other forage cultivars in quantity and quality of hay, being suitable for cutting from the time the pods begin to form until the seeds reach full size. A widely used guide in harvesting soybean hay is to cut during the first favourable weather after the seeds are half developed. Soybean hay is often left in the swath a couple of days to cure and then raked into small rows. Unless drying conditions are good, the windrows need turning before baling. A roller-crusher attachment on the mower will hasten the curing because crushed stems lose moisture more rapidly than intact stems. Soybeans require 75−200 days to mature, depending on cultivar and region.

Soybean hay yields average 5 t/ha and beans, about 1700 kg/ha. High-yielding cultivars, adapted to the locale and grown under favourable conditions, will yield more than twice the average. Some farmers have produced yields of more than 3400 kg/ha. In Taiwan, TK-51 irrigated with 200 t water/ha yielded 3.1 t beans/ha and 7.6 t dry matter compared with 2.8 t beans and 7.1 t dry matter for the control.

World production of soybeans was 89.9 million t in 1984, an increase of 55 per cent since 1976 (Singh et al., 1987). Total area under cultivation of soybean grew to 52.1 million ha during the same period, and average yields increased. The U.S. produced more than half, with Brazil contributing about 20 per cent and China, another 10 per cent. Africa produced 200,000 t, with an average 660 kg/ha (Singh et al., 1987). In 1986–87, world production reached 98.7 million t (FAO, 1988a). U.S. output fell by 7.5 per cent, whereas production in Latin America grew 13 per cent and area under soybean increased by 2 per cent. China increased production 12 per cent in 1986–87 to 12.116 million t (FAO, 1988b), increasing area to 8.4 million ha. Production in the U.S. was 51.245 million t. In Africa, production rose to 234,000 t and productivity to 737 kg/ha (FAO, 1988b).

On a per-kg cost basis, soybeans are a cheap source of protein. The use of soybean protein in the form of concentrates, isolates, and textured protein for human consumption offers a solution to the world's protein needs.

In 1979, the lowest yield was 150 kg/ha in Tanzania, the international average being 1660 kg/ha and a world high of 2525 kg/ha in Egypt (FAO, 1980).

Other figures for yields (Duke, 1981), showing bean:straw ratios of 1700:5000, 3100:7600 and 2800:7100 kg/ha, suggest a straw factor of 2.5, the chaff factor estimated at 1. In 1981, I reported the global average N fixation for soybeans to be 100 kg/ha, about half that of cowpea (Duke, 1981).

Maximum daily growth rate of soybean is 27 g/m^2 for an efficiency of 4.4 per cent (percentage utilization of solar radiation). Maximum growth averaged over the growing season is considerably lower. With production of 8.9 t/ha, soybean converts solar energy at an efficiency of only 0.16 per cent (one-tenth that of napier grass) if averaged over the whole year (Boardman, 1980). (Tropical sugar cane shows an efficiency of 1.0 per cent, cassava 0.8 per cent.)

In the tropics, more than one crop is possible annually, and in temperate regions, hot-weather soybeans can follow cool-weather crops of alfalfa, peas, or wheat. According to my phytomass files (Duke et al., 1987), annual productivity for various Glycine spp. ranges from 1 to 20 t/ha. Studying energy output-to-input ratios of 11 oilseeds, Goering (1981) found soybean to be highest (at 4.6) among unirrigated crops. Some irrigated crops had ratios of less than 1.0. Of the 11 vegetable oils, soybean oil was cheapest and was available in the greatest domestic quantity (Goering, 1981). The gross heating value of the oils was 87–89 per cent of no. 2 diesel fuel. Eight parts of soybean oil were emulsified with two parts 190-proof ethanol, with five parts of 1-butanol as emulsifier. The microemulsions performed as well as diesel fuel and were able to start a cold engine (Goering, 1981).

Disease-resistant cultivars of soybeans have been developed and are available for production in most areas (Singh *et al.*, 1987). Their use is the most effective means of reducing losses from diseases. Also available are cultivars that resist the development of root-knot and cyst nematodes.

Phaseolus vulgaris L. Fabaceae

The common bean, called also caraota, feijão, French bean, kidney bean, haricot, field bean, poroto, snap or string bean, frijol, and wax bean, is the most widely cutivated of all beans in temperate regions and is widely cultivated in semi-tropical and tropical regions. In temperate regions, the green immature pods are cooked and eaten as a vegetable. Immature pods are marketed fresh, frozen or canned, whole, cut or julienne style. Mature ripe beans, variously called navy beans, white beans, northern beans, or pea beans, are widely consumed.

In lower latitudes, dry beans furnish a large portion of the protein needs of families. In some parts of the tropics leaves are used as an herb, and, to a lesser extent, the green-shelled beans are eaten. In Java, young leaves are eaten as a salad. After beans are harvested, the straw is used for fodder.

Beans are said to be used to treat acne, diabetes, burns, diarrhea, dropsy, dysentery, eczema, hiccups, itch, rheumatism, sciatica, and tenesmus. They are reputed to improve functioning of the heart and kidney and to have properties as a depurative, diuretic, emollient and resolvent.

Beans are highly nutritious, a relatively low-cost protein food. Green snap beans contain 6.2 per cent protein, 0.2 per cent fat, and 63 per cent carbohydrate (Table 8). The vitamin contents (mg/100 g) of dried beans are thiamine, 0.6; riboflavin, 0.2; nicotinic acid, 2.5; and ascorbic acid, 2.0. Analysis of dried beans from another source yielded (mg/100g): Na, 43.2; K, 1160; Ca, 180; Mg, 183; Fe, 6.6; Cu, 0.61; P, 309; S, 166; and Cl, 1.8. Beans also contain I (1.4 μg/100 g), Mn (1.8 mg/100 g), arsenic (0.03 mg/100 g).

Raw immature pods of green and yellow or wax snap beans are reported to contain, per 100 g, 32 and 27 kcal (134 kJ and 113 kJ), 90.1 and 91.4 per cent moisture, 1.9 and 1.7 g protein, 0.2 g fat, 7.1 and 6.0 g total carbohydrate, 1.0 g fibre, and 0.7 g ash, respectively. Raw pods of kidney beans contain (per 100 g edible portion) 150 kcal (628 kJ), 60.4 per cent moisture, 9.8 g protein, 0.3 g fat, 27.8 g total carbohydrate, 2.3 g fibre, 1.7 g ash, 59 mg Ca, 213 mg P, 3.6 mg Fe, 10 μg vitamin A, 0.38 mg thiamine, 0.12 mg riboflavin, 1.5 mg niacin, and 7 mg ascorbic acid.

Table 8. Composition of 100 g of the edible portion of raw beans (*Phaseolus vulgaris*) (USDA, 1986)[a]

Nutrient (unit)	Amount in 100 g, edible portion		
	Mean	Standard error	Number of samples
Proximate			
Water (g)	11.75		86
Food energy (kJ)	1393		
Protein (N x 6.25) (g)	23.58		102
Total lipid (fat) (g)	0.83		108
Carbohydrate, total (g)	60.01		
Crude fibre[b] (g)	6.23		34
Ash (g)	3.83		85
Minerals			
Calcium (mg)	143		71
Iron (mg)	8.20	0.595	90
Magnesium (mg)	140		69
Phosphorus (mg)	407		66
Potassium (mg)	1406		67
Sodium (mg)	24		55
Zinc (mg)	2.79	0.212	68
Copper (mg)	0.958		64
Manganese (mg)	1.021		68
Vitamins			
Ascorbic acid (mg)	4.5		1
Thiamine (mg)	0.529		53
Riboflavin (mg)	0.219		53
Niacin (mg)	2.060		48
Pantothenic acid (mg)	0.780	0.022	32
Vitamin B_6 (mg)	0.397	0.007	32
Folacin (mμg)	394.1	13.422	32
Vitamin B_{12} (mμg)	0.0		
Vitamin A (IU)	8	1.083	22
Lipids			
Fatty acids			
Saturated, total (g)	0.120		
16:0 (g)	0.106		
18:0 (g)	0.014		
Monounsaturated, total (g)	0.064		
18:1 (g)	0.064		

Nutrient (unit)	Amount in 100 g, edible portion		
	Mean	Standard error	Number of samples
Polyunsaturated, total (g)	0.457		
18:2 (g)	0.178		
18:3 (g)	0.279		
Cholesterol (mg)	0.0		
Phytosterols (mg)	127		
Amino acids			
Tryptophan (g) .	0.279		
Threonine (g)	0.992		
Isoleucine (g)	1.041		
Leucine (g)	1.882		
Lysine (g)	1.618		
Methionine (g)	0.355		
Cystine (g)	0.256		
Phenylalanine (g)	1.275		
Tyrosine (g)	0.664		
Valine (g)	1.233		
Arginine (g)	1.460		
Histidine (g)	0.656		
Alanine (g)	0.988		
Aspartic acid (g)	2.852		
Glutamic acid (g)	3.595		
Glycine (g)	0.920		
Proline (g)	1.000		
Serine (g)	1.282		

[a] A cup of beans is equal to 184 g.
[b] Insoluble dietary fibre as determined by the neutral detergent fibre method: 10.4 g/100 g.

Whole seeds cooked contain 141 kcal (590 kJ), 68.0 per cent moisture, 5.9 g protein, 5.7 g fat, 17.9 g total carbohydrate, 1.1 g fibre, 2.5 g ash, 46 mg Ca, 120 mg P, and 1.9 mg Fe. Raw leaves contain (per 100 g) 151 kJ, 86.8 per cent moisture, 3.6 g protein, 0.4 g fat, 6.6 g total carbohydrate, 2.8 g fibre, 2.6 g ash, 274 mg Ca, 75 mg P, 9.2 mg Fe, 3230 μg beta-carotene, 0.18 mg thiamine, 0.06 mg riboflavin, 1.3 mg niacin, 110 mg ascorbic acid.

After harvest, plants can be fed to cattle, sheep, and horses. They are roughage when fed with good hay and are comparable to corn and sorghum fodder in nutritive value. After pod removal, silage may be prepared from green vines. The dehydrated meal made from the vines is comparable to alfalfa meal as a vitamin supplement for chicks, although meal from vines with mature leaves is inferior to that from younger plants.

The roots are reported to cause giddiness in human beings and animals, and the seeds — like other legumes — are reported to contain trypsin and chymotrypsin inhibitors. Also Haidvogl *et al.* (1979) reported toxic effects from eating only a few raw beans (*P. vulgaris*) or dried beans (*P. coccineus*). The report was about three boys, 4–8 years old, who rapidly showed symptoms of poisoning, notably sickness and diarrhea. Phasin, a toxalbumin destroyed by cooking, was considered responsible. All boys had normal aminotransferase values, and parenteral treatment with fluid and electrolytes led to complete recovery in 12–24 h.

Phaseolus vulgaris is highly polymorphic; it is an annual herb, erect and bushy, 20–60 cm tall, or twining with stems 2–3 m long; the germinating bean has a taproot, but adventitious roots usually emerge 1–2 days after germination and dominate the taproot, which remains 10–15 cm long. The leaves alternate, are green or purple, trifoliolate, stipulate, and petiolate, and have a marked pulvinus at the base. Leaflets are ovate, entire; acuminate, 6–15 cm long, 3–11 cm wide. Lax, axillary racemes have few flowers (12), which are zygomorphic, variegated, white, pink, or purplish, ca 1 cm long. The pods are slender, green, yellow, black, or purple, cylindrical or flat, 8–20 cm long, 1–1.5 cm wide; seeds 4–6–(12), usually glabrous, sometimes puberulent, with a prominent beak; white, red, tan, purple, grey or black, often variegated, reniform, oblong or globose, up to 1.5 cm long, endosperm absent; 100 seeds weigh 10–67 g, depending on cultivar. Germination is phanerocotylar. More than 14,000 cultivars are recorded; the major repository and distributor is CIAT (Centro Internacional de Agricultura Tropical) in Cali, Colombia (chapter 3). In the United States, they are grouped mainly into early maturing bush types and later pole types. Dry-shelled beans are grouped into four types: red kidney beans, 1.5 cm or more long, important in Latin America; medium field beans, 1–1.2 cm long, pinkish buff with brown spots, grown extensively in the United States, called pinto beans; marrow beans, 1–1.5 cm long, as Yellow Eye; and pea or navy beans, 8 mm or shorter, grown extensively in California.

In Latin America and Africa, regional preferences are strong for seed-coat colour and brilliance. Consumers in Venezuela and Guatemala favour black-seeded beans; in Colombia and Honduras, red; in Perú, cream or tan; in Brazil, black or tan.

Growth form in *P. vulgaris* and other *Phaseolus* spp. depends on number of nodes produced (oligonodal vs polynodal) and internode length (long vs short). Three definite forms are produced for cultivation: polynodal with long internodes — climber; polynodal with short internodes — indeterminate dwarf; and oligonodal with short internodes — determinate dwarf. Two leaf-size grades can also be distinguished in combination with these. With the range of seed sizes and shapes plus testa colours, the possible range of distinct types is enormous. A snap bean cultivar, Mild

White Giant, is reportedly tolerant to 'adverse conditions'; OSU 2065, Purley King (British pea bean requires temperature of 12–13°C at soil depth of 10 cm), and SRS 1884 to cool weather; Royalty to cold and wet soil; Longval to drought; Alabama Al, Ashley Wax, Choctaw, Cooper Wax, Logan, and Longval, to heat; and Pacer to short season.

Among dry beans, the cultivar Criolla is reportedly tolerant to heat and tropical conditions, and Bonita and Borinquen have also been cited as suited to tropical conditions. Assigned to the Middle and South American centres of diversity, common bean is reported to exhibit tolerance to aluminium, bacterial disease, drought, herbicide, hydrogen fluoride, high and low pH, laterite, manganese, peat, variable photoperiod, smog (SO_2), virus, and water excess. Pathogen tolerances were surveyed in Horsfall *et al.* (1972).

Just over a decade ago Nabham and Felger (1978) wrote:

> Perhaps the most significant event in recent bean breeding is Honma's interspecific cross, *P. vulgaris* × *P. acutifolius*, accomplished via tissue culture. This hybrid transferred the tepary's tolerance to *Xanthosoma phaseoli*, the causal agent of common bean blight, to the Great Northern cultivar of *P. vulgaris*. Honma had been unable to find a useful level of tolerance in other beans, and progeny from his interspecific hybrid made possible the development of blight tolerance in other *Phaseolus* cultivars around the world.

Other *Phaseolus* species of importance are the tepary bean, *P. acutifolius* A. Gray; the scarlet runner, *P. coccineus* L., and the lima bean, *P. lunatus*.

Common beans are native to the New World, probably central Mexico and Guatemala. They were taken to Europe by the Spaniards and Portuguese who also took them to Africa and other parts of the Old World. Now they are widely cultivated in the tropics, sub-tropics and temperate regions. Roughly 30 per cent of world production is from Latin America. They are less popular in India where other pulses are preferred.

Beans tolerate most environmental conditions in tropical and temperate zones but do poorly in very wet tropics where rain causes disease and flower drop. Rain is undesirable when dry seeds are harvested. Frost kills the plant. There are both short-day and day-neutral cultivars, and some black-seeded cultivars will grow well in standing water.

However, most grow best in well-drained, sandy loam, silt loam or clay loam soils, rich in organic content; they are sensitive to concentrations of Al, B, Mn, and Na. In soils with pH <5.2, Mn toxicity may be a problem. In calcareous soils, zinc deficiencies can be serious, and in sandy acid soils, Mg and Mo deficiencies may arise. At EC (conductivity) 1500 (EC of saturation extract), garden bean yields are decreased by 10 per cent; at EC 2000, by 25 per cent; and at EC 3500, by 50 per cent. French or snap beans seem more sensitive to Na than many other cultivars. Temperatures lower than -5°C are harmful at germination; -2°C at flowering; and -3° at fruiting, although some cultivars withstand short frosts as low as -3°C. The optimal monthly temperature for growth is 15.6−21.1°C, the maximum ca 27°C, the minimum ca 10°C. Blossom-drop is serious above 30°C and can completely prevent seed set above 35°C. Beans are traditionally a sub-tropical or temperate crop. In the tropics they are normally found in montane valleys (800−2000 m), and few beans are grown in the hot humid tropics where cowpeas fare better. Ranging from Boreal Moist to Wet through Tropical Very Dry to Wet Forest Life zones, common bean is reported to tolerate annual precipitation of 0.9−42.9 dm (mean of 217 cases, 12.8), annual mean temperatures of 5.7−28.5°C (mean of 216 cases, 19.3), and pH of 4.2−8.7 (mean of 144 cases, 6.4).

In temperate areas, seed should be planted about the same time as corn, when soil has become warm. Germination is rapid in soil warmer than 18°C. In pure stands, bush cultivars yield well at 30 × 30 cm spacings, but wider spacing facilitates weeding. Pole beans are usually planted 4−6 seeds in hills spaced about 1 m apart at a seeding rate of nearly 80 kg/ha. Seed rates are 20−115 kg/ha, depending on cultivar, seed size, and width of row; Red Kidney, Marrow, and Yellow Eye at 75−100 kg/ha; Pea Beans, Black Turtle Soup, at 30−40 kg/ha; in rows about 70−75 or 80 cm apart. Some pole beans are sown at rates as low as 25 kg/ha. Seed of good quality is essential for production of dry beans. The crop is susceptible to diseases and to damage from mechanization, frost and wet weather. With a corn, bean or beet drill with removable plates, beans are usually planted 5−8 cm deep − deep enough to give good coverage and sufficient moisture to promote fast germination and growth. Plants should be cultivated to control weeds, but hoeing late in the season can injure the roots, which extend between the rows just beneath soil surface. Inoculation of seed with nitrogen-fixing bacteria is unnecessary, but beans should be rotated with other crops to maintain high yields and quality and to reduce the hazard of diseases that survive in the soil or on plant refuse in the soil. In the tropics, beans are often interplanted with crops such as coffee, corn, cotton, sweet potatoes, and little or no fertilizer is employed, although the plant does respond to nitrogen. Barnyard manure (up to 25 t/ha) is recommended, and in the U.S., nitrogen and phosphate are applied.

Irrigation is beneficial in semi-arid regions, with sprinkling overhead preferred to flooding. Cultivars are often sown in mixtures. In Latin America, about 70 per cent of the beans are interplanted with corn. Grown alone, they are planted at 200,000−250,000 plants/ha in 50-cm rows with 5−10 cm between seeds. Bush beans are planted 30 × 30 or 50−60 × 5−10 cm, the latter permitting easier cultivation. Latin American bean production is mainly on marginal soil, nearly always with P deficiency, commonly with N problems as well; neither fertilizer nor the credit to obtain it is readily available.

Beans mature quickly, and green beans may be harvested 4−6 weeks after sowing. In early snap bean cultivars, harvest begins in 7−8 weeks, 1−2 weeks after flowering. Beans should be picked every 3–4 days. Bush beans mature over a short time; pole beans continue to bear for a long time. Dry beans should be harvested when most pods are fully mature and have turned colour.

To minimize shatter, harvesters should not shake the vines. The cutter consists of two broad blades set to cut two adjacent rows about 5 cm below the ground. Then prongs pull plants from both rows into one windrow in wet weather; plants are forked into field stacks ca 1.3 m in diameter and 2–3 m high that are supported by a centre stake.

In the Third World, beans are usually harvested by hand or manually gathered and windrowed. Plants are pulled, dried, and threshed; sometimes beans are hand-shelled.

Yields vary widely with cultivar, culture and region. In 1987, FAO (1988b) projections for world production of dry beans were 14 million t dry beans, an average of 526 kg/ha. Developing countries were projected to produce 11.6 million t.

The largest producer among developed countries was the United States, with 1.193 million t. India had the largest output (in 1986, 3.789 million t) and Brazil was second with 2.219 million t. Africa produced 1.8 million t and Asia 6 million t, with Latin America contributing most of the remainder. World production of green beans was 3.642 million t, with productivity being 6621 kg/ha. Of the total, Asia and Europe accounted for 1.254 million t and 1.204 million t respectively.

In contrast with what one expects in cereals, CIAT researchers (CIAT, 1977) suggested in dry beans 'large vegetative structures [lead] to increased yields [at least among plants that do not succumb to] lodging'. Hence the more bean, the more biomass residue.

'Increased dry matter production [correlates with yield] ($r = 0.96$) and a relatively constant harvest index ($r = 0.28$) ....' In Pornillo Sintético at CIAT, the harvest index (the ratio of seed yield to total dry matter) was 52–62 per cent, averaging 57 per cent, with highest yields of 4.1 t/ha associated with total dry matter of 7 t/ha, indicating a maximum residue of about 3 t/ha (CIAT, 1977).

Adams (1980) and Sandsted (1980) tabulated energy inputs in dry bean and snap bean production. In Michigan without irrigation, dry beans yielded 1176 kg/ha, equivalent to 4.1 million kcal (17.1 million kJ) at inputs of 3.1 million kcal (13.1 million kJ) − 720,000 kcal (3 million kJ) for machinery, 863,106 kcal (3.6 million kJ) for fuel, 643,500 kcal (2.7 million kJ) for N, 168,000 kcal (703,000 kJ) for P, 89,600 kcal (375,000 kJ) for K, 952 kcal (3984 kJ) for lime, 179,320 kcal (750,606 kJ) for seeds, 34,423 kcal (144,089 kJ) for insecticides, 391,647 kcal (1.6 million kJ) for herbicides, 38,258 kcal (160,142 kJ) for transportation, and 3036 kcal (12,708 kJ) for seed-treatment chemicals. The yield of irrigated dry beans was 2147 kg/ha in California, equivalent to 7.3 million kcal (30.7 million kJ), barely more than inputs (6.97 million kcal or 29.2 million kJ). These positive energetic returns (1.31 and 1.05 output to input) compare with a negative ratio for snap beans (0.345).

Experimental yields of dry beans can exceed 5.5 t/ha (bush beans). At CIAT, bush bean yields of 4.5 t/ha and trellis bean yields of 5.8 t/ha have been reported for a growth cycle of 100–200 days. Association with corn, however, reduces yields to about 2 t/ha (Duke *et al.*, 1987).

Vigna unguiculata (L.) Walp. subsp. *unguiculata* Fabaceae

Cowpea (crowder pea, black-eyed pea, southern pea) is cultivated for the seeds, shelled green or dried, and for the pods and leaves, consumed as green vegetables or used for pasturage, hay, ensilage, or green manure.

In West Africa, the vines are at times grown chiefly for the edible leaves, and many cultivars, if cut regularly, continue to produce leaves. Leaves are boiled, drained, sun-dried and then stored for later use. The tendency of indeterminate cultivars to ripen fruits over a long period makes them more amenable to subsistence than to commercial farming, which makes use of erect and determinate cultivars suited to monoculture.

In the U.S., green seeds are sometimes roasted like peanuts. The roots are eaten in Sudan and Ethiopia. Scorched seeds are occasionally used as a coffee substitute. Penduncles are a source of fibre in Nigeria. When used for silage, cowpea is usually mixed with corn or sorghum. The crop is useful as green manure, and leafy prostrate cultivars reduce soil erosion.

My colleague and I (Duke and Wain, 1981) have suggested elsewhere that the species is astringent, diuretic and tonic. It has a folk reputation as being a treatment for adenopathy, biliousness, burns, diarrhea, dysentery, dysuria, fistula, jaundice, leprosy, measles, nausea, nephrosis, neuralgia, thirst and tumours, mostly in China and India.

Cowpeas are sacred to the Hausa and Yoruba tribes and are prescribed for sacrifices to abate evil and to pacify the spirits of sickly children. Hausa and Edo tribes use cowpeas medicinally, one or two seeds ground and mixed with soil or oil to treat stubborn boils.

Raw, mature seeds typically contain ca 11.4 per cent moisture, 338 kcal (1415 kJ), 22.5 g protein, 1.4 g fat, 61.0 g total carbohydrate, 5.4 g fibre, 3.7 g ash, 104 mg Ca, 416 g P, 0.08 mg thiamine, 0.09 mg riboflavin, 4.0 mg niacin, and 2 mg ascorbic acid/100 g (Table 9).

Results at IITA, based on several thousand distinct cultivars, have suggested an overall average of 23–25 per cent protein, with potential for perhaps 35 per cent. The proteins consist of 90 per cent water-insoluble globulins and 10 per cent water-soluble albumins. Though much variation occurs, cowpeas, like most food legumes, are deficient in cystine, methionine, and tryptophan. Total sugars range from 13.7 to 19.7 per cent. They include 1.5 per cent sucrose, 0.4 per cent raffinose, 2.0 per cent stachyose, 3.1 per cent verbascose. Starch may vary from 50.6 to 67.0 per cent with 20.9−48.7 per cent amylose and 11.4−36.6 per cent amylopectin. Immature pods contain 85.3 per cent moisture, 47 kcal (197 kJ), 3.6 g protein, 0.3 g fat, 10.0 g total carbohydrate, 1.8 g fibre, 0.8 g ash, 45 mg Ca, 52 mg P, 1.2 mg Fe, 170 μg vitamin A, 0.13 mg thiamine, 0.10 mg riboflavin, 1.0 mg niacin, and 22 mg ascorbic acid/100 g. Tender shoots, raw, contain 89 per cent moisture, 30 kcal (125 kJ), 4.8 g protein, 0.3 g fat, 4.4 g total carbohydrate, 1.8 g ash, 73 mg Ca, 106 mg P, 2.2 mg Fe, 0.35 mg thiamine, 0.18 mg riboflavin, 1.1 mg niacin, and 36 mg ascorbic acid/100 g. The hay contains, per 100 g: 9.6 per cent moisture, 18.6 g crude protein, 23.3 g crude fibre, 2.6 g fat, 34.6 g N-free extract, and 11.3 g ash. Digestibility is improved when seeds are ground to a powder.

Seeds contain a trypsin inhibitor, a chymotrypsin inhibitor and a cyanogen in concentrations of ca 2 mg/100 mL extract. Cooking improves the nutritive value, perhaps because the activity of trypsin inhibitors and the amount of other toxins are decreased by heat.

Cowpea is an annual herb, erect or sub-erect (to 80 cm or more tall), spreading glabrous. The taproot is stout with laterals near the soil surface, the roots being associated with large nodules. Stems are usually procumbent, often tinged with purple. The first leaves above the cotyledons are simple and opposite; subsequent trifoliolate leaves alternate, the terminal leaflet often bigger and longer than the two asymmetrical laterals. The petiole is stout and grooved, 5−15 cm long. Leaflets are ovoid−rhombic, entire or slightly lobed, with an acute apex; they are 6.5−16 cm long, 4−11 cm wide, and the later leaflets are oblique.

The inflorescence is axillary, with two to four flowers crowded near tips on short curved peduncles, 2.5−15 cm long; the calyx is campanulate with triangular teeth, the upper two teeth connate and longer than the rest. The corolla is dull white, yellow or violet, with standard keel, 2−3 cm in diameter, truncate; the stamens are diadelphous, and anthers uniform; pods are curved, straight or coiled. Seeds, 2−12 mm long, are globular to reniform, smooth or wrinkled, predominantly red, black, brown, green, buff or white.

The seeds may be one colour or spotted, marbled, speckled, eyed or blotched (5−30 g/100 seeds, depending on cultivar). Germination is phanerocotylar. The crop flowers in early summer; fruits mid and late summer, depending on the cultivars' sensitivity to photoperiod and temperature and the prevailing conditions.

The most extensive collection of germ plasm (and literature) is at IITA (more than 15,000 accessions in 1989).

Table 9. Composition of 100 g of the edible portion of raw cowpeas (*Vigna unguiculata*) (USDA, 1986)[a]

Nutrient (unit)	Amount in 100 g, edible portion		
	Mean	Standard error	Number of samples
Proximate			
Water (g)	11.95	0.391	82
Food energy (kJ)	1408		
Protein (N x 6.25) (g)	23.52	0.205	147
Total lipid (fat) (g)	1.26	0.036	139
Carbohydrate, total (g)	60.03		
Crude fibre[b] (g)	4.58	0.249	65
Ash (g)	3.24	0.038	91
Minerals			
Calcium (mg)	110	11.803	47
Iron (mg)	8.27	0.246	59
Magnesium (mg)	184	7.012	45
Phosphorus (mg)	424	11.904	46
Potassium (mg)	1112	40.025	44
Sodium (mg)	16	1.681	39
Zinc (mg)	3.37	0.167	46
Copper (mg)	0.845	0.030	48
Manganese (mg)	1.528		42
Vitamins			
Ascorbic acid (mg)	1.5		1
Thiamine (mg)	0.853	0.031	197
Riboflavin (mg)	0.226	0.008	204
Niacin (mg)	2.075	0.094	189
Pantothenic acid (mg)	1.496	0.058	166
Vitamin B_6 (mg)	0.357		17
Folacin (μg)	632.6	41.904	17
Vitamin B_{12} (μg)	0.0		
Vitamin A (IU)	50.0		1
Lipids			
Fatty acids			
Saturated, total (g)	0.331		
12:0 (g)	0.001		
14:0 (g)	0.003		
16:0 (g)	0.254		
18:0 (g)	0.053		
Monounsaturated, total (g)	0.106		

Nutrient (unit)	Amount in 100 g, edible portion		
	Mean	Standard error	Number of samples
16:1 (g)	0.004		
18:1 (g)	0.088		
20:1 (g)	0.001		
22:1 (g)	0.012		
Polyunsaturated, total (g)	0.542		
18:2 (g)	0.343		
18:3 (g)	0.199		
Cholesterol (mg)	0.0		
Phytosterols (mg)			
Amino acids			
Tryptophan (g)	0.290		
Threonine (g)	0.895		
Isoleucine (g)	0.956		
Leucine (g)	1.802		
Lysine (g)	1.591		
Methionine (g)	0.335		
Cystine (g)	0.260		
Phenylalanine (g)	1.373		
Tyrosine (g)	0.760		
Valine (g)	1.121		
Arginine (g)	1.629		
Histidine (g)	0.730		
Alanine (g)	1.072		
Aspartic acid (g)	2.840		
Glutamic acid (g)	4.454		
Glycine (g)	0.971		
Proline (g)	1.057		
Serine (g)	1.178		

[a] A cup of cowpeas is equal to 167 g; a half cup, 84 g.
[b] Insoluble dietary fibre as determined by the neutral detergent fibre method: 7.6 g/100 g.

Cowpea varieties in the U.S. are grouped as 'crowder peas', 'black-eyed', and 'cream'. The first have seeds that are black, speckled, brown or brown-eyed, crowded in pods, usually globose (Brown Crowder being a good variety in Puerto Rico). The second (grown extensively in California, the southeast U.S. and Puerto Rico) have seeds that are white with a black eye around the hilum, not crowded in pod, whereas the cream type have cream-coloured seeds, not crowded in pods and are intermediate between crowder and black-eyed types such as Purple Hill, with deep purple mature pods and buff or maroon-eyed seeds. The leaves of forage cultivars like New Era are sometimes used also for human consumption.

Assigned to the African and Hindustani centres of diversity, cowpea is reported to exhibit tolerance to aluminium, drought, high and low pH, heat, laterite, nematodes, poor soil, shade, slope, virus, weeds, and wilt. Most cultivars cannot tolerate waterlogging. Subspecies include the catjang and the yardlong bean or asparagus bean.

The genus includes *V. aconitifolia* (Jacq.) Marechal, the moth bean; *V. angularis* (Willd.) Ohuri and Ohashi, azuki bean; *V. mungo* (L.) Hepper, black gram; *V. radiata* (L.) Wilczek, mung bean; *V. umbellata* (Thunb.) Ohwi and Ohashi, rice bean; and *V. vexillata* (L.) A. Rich., a tuber-forming species, the zombi pea (Martin, 1984).

The cowpea is ancient in Africa and Asia, and widespread in Africa, spreading by way of Egypt or Arabia to Asia and the Mediterranean. It is now widely cultivated throughout the tropics and sub-tropics. Wild and cultivated forms readily cross. Steele (1972) has agreed with earlier writers that the centre of origin is solely Ethiopian, with subsequent evolution prodominantly in the ancient farming systems of the African savanna.

Cowpea thrives on many kinds of soil, from highly acid to neutral; it is less adapted to alkaline soils. The crop will grow and yield in infertile soils but responds to P fertilization. It can withstand considerable drought and a moderate amount of shade but is less tolerant of waterlogging than soybean. Some plants are indeterminate in growth and continue to grow until killed by frost. In the tropics, such indeterminate plants may be weak perennials and continue growing as long as conditions are favourable. In some determinate types, the later flower initiation, the higher up the stem it is, the more flowers, and the greater the ultimate seed yield. Dry-matter production, seed yield, and root nodulation are reduced in photoperiods shorter than 12 h 13 min. Differences of as short as 12 min can affect flowering and seed yield. Cowpeas are short-day, warm-weather plants, sensitive to cold and killed by frost. They can be grown with less rainfall and under more adverse conditions than *P. vulgaris* or *P. lunatus*. Over a range of 21°C day/16°C night to 36°C day/31°C night, dry-matter production was greatest at 27°C day/22°C night. Night temperatures strongly affect many phases of the life cycle, and differences in day temperature during reproductive growth markedly affect crop duration and yield. Cultivars differ substantially in environmental responses.

Ranging from Warm Temperate Thorn to Moist through Tropical Thorn to Wet Forest Life zones, cowpea is reported to tolerate annual precipitation of 2.8–41.0 dm (mean of 54 cases, 14.2), annual mean temperatures of 12.5–27.8°C (mean of 54 cases, 22.1), and pH of 4.3–7.9 (mean of 46 cases, 6.2).

Seeds remain viable for several years. Germination is epigeal. Seeds should be planted after danger from frost is past. For production of hay or seed, crop should be sown early but for green manure and pasture it may be seeded late. Rate of seeding varies with method: when planted in rows, 10–40 kg/ha; when broadcast, 90 kg/ha. When grown for seed, cowpea is often planted in rows; when used for forage or green manure, it should be broadcast. For hog feed or silage, cowpeas are planted with corn, either at the same time or at the last cultivation of corn. In rows, cowpeas are spaced 5–7.5 cm apart, the rows being 75–90 cm apart.

Two or more cultivations are necessary to control weeds. The equipment used for corn is satisfactory, and cultivation should stop when plants begin to flower. In the U.S., 600–1000 kg/ha of a 4-8-8 NPK fertilizer is sometimes applied in bands 5 cm below seeds at planting. Cowpeas are usually rainfed, rarely irrigated. For weed control, amines of 2, 4-D and MCPA are said to be effective pre-emergence sprays. Also, trifluralin at 0.56–1.12 kg/ha just before sowing is said to give good control.

Cowpeas respond slightly to K application up to 45 kg/ha. Calcium ions in the soil aid inoculation, so application of lime (1 t/ha) is recommended in the U.S. where seed is more important than hay. Superphosphate recommendations are 112–224 kg/ha in the U.S. Sulphur can limit seed production and protein synthesis. Molybdenum recommendations are 20–50 g/ha, and Mn, Cu, Zn, and B are essential, in very small quantities, for effective nodulation and seed yield increases. The cowpea symbiosis has genetic potential for large seed yields; cowpea–*Rhizobium* associations should require only nominal amounts of fertilizer N, if any.

Early maturing cultivars produce in 3 months, giving pods in 50 days; late cultivars take 240 days to mature. The crop ripens unevenly, and the proper time for harvesting is difficult to determine. Usually, flowers and green and ripe pods occur on the vines at the same time. The crop is cut for seed when one-half to two-thirds of the pods are ripe. Harvesting may be by hand, by a special harvester or by self-rake reapers. For hay, the crop is cut when most of the pods are fully developed, and the first ones have ripened. If cut too early, the hay is difficult to cure; if cut too late, stems are long and woody and seed and leaves shatter badly. Any ordinary mowing machine can be used.

Yields vary with cultivar, climate, soil, and culture. In the tropics, yields of 400–600 kg dried beans/ha are common; in the U.S., 1000–1500 kg/ha, up to 3000 kg/ha for black-eyed peas in California.

Hay yields are about 5 t/ha. World production in 1981 was estimated at 2.27 million t, with Africa accounting for two-thirds of the total (Singh and Rachie, 1985). Two countries — Nigeria and Niger — produce 850,000 t and 271,000 t annually or about half the world output. The U.S. is the only developed country producing large amounts (60,000 t).

The estimated annual nitrogen fixation is 73–354 kg/ha, with a global average of 198 kg/ha (double that of soybeans) (Duke *et al.*, 1987). Cowpea is the second most important pulse in tropical Africa and in tropical America, especially Venezuela and Brazil.

In dry and humid areas, cowpeas are almost entirely self-pollinated. Some out-crossing (10–15 per cent) probably always occurs, with ants, flies, and bees as the main vectors. Flowers open early in the morning, close by noon, and fall off the same day. Pollen is sticky and heavy.

Insect Pests of Food Legumes
Edited by S. R. Singh
©1990 John Wiley & Sons Ltd.

1

Insect Pests of Cowpea

S. R. SINGH[a], L. E. N. JACKAI[a], J. H. R. DOS SANTOS[b] and C. B. ADALLA[c]

[a]*International Institute of Tropical Agriculture, Ibadan, Nigeria*
[b]*Universidade Federal do Ceará, Centro de Ciências Agrarias, Fortaleza, CE, Brazil*
[c]*University of the Philippines, Los Baños, College of Agriculture, Laguna, Philippines*

Introduction

Cowpeas, *Vigna unguiculata* Walp., also known as black-eye peas or southern peas, are cultivated in a range of ecologies and cropping systems in the tropics. However, the crop is most commonly grown in dry areas along with millet and sorghum.

Like other grain legumes, cowpeas are infested by insect pests during growth and in storage (Phelps and Oosthuizen, 1958; Appert, 1964; Saxena, 1971; Raheja, 1973, 1976a; Kayumbo, 1975; Agyen-Sampong, 1978; Khamala, 1978; Singh and Allen, 1979, 1980; Singh and Taylor, 1978; Singh and van Emden, 1979; Singh, 1980, 1985; Santos *et al.*, 1982; Neves *et al.*, 1982b; Singh *et al.*, 1983; Daoust *et al.*, 1985; Faleiro and Singh, 1985; Mariga *et al.*, 1985; Singh and Jackai, 1985; Jackai and Daoust, 1986; Santos and Quinderé, 1988). In general the pest problem is more serious in Africa (Table 1.1 and Figures 1.1–1.2) than in Asia or Latin America.

Yields often increase several-fold when monocrop cowpeas are protected from pests by insecticide applications (Booker, 1965; Farrell and Adams, 1967; Taylor, 1968; Koehler and Mehta, 1972), and, in general, cowpeas suffer more damage as a monocrop than as a mixed crop, which is the traditional method of cultivation.

Table 1.1. Insect pests of cowpeas: their relative importance and distribution

Scientific name	Plant parts damaged[a]	Distribution and pest status[b]		
		Africa	Asia	Latin America
ORTHOPTERA				
Acrididae				
Catantops spissus (Walker)	W	O	O	Y
Chrotogonus trachypterus (Blanch.)	W	Y	O	Y
Oxya japonica (Thunberg)	W	O	O	Y
Schistocerca flavofasciata (de Geer)	W	O	O	S
Schistocerca pallens (Thunberg)	W	O	O	S
Gryllidae				
Acheta assimilis Fabricius	W	S	O	S
Gryllotalpa sp.	W	O	O	O
Pyrgomorphidae				
Zonocerus variegatus (Linnaeus)	W	O	Y	Y
THYSANOPTERA				
Thripidae				
Caliothrips phaseoli Hood	L	Y	O	S
Megalurothrips sjostedti (Trybom)	F	M	O	Y
Sericothrips occipitalis Hood	L	S	O	Y
Thrips tabaci Linderman	F	Y	S	S
HEMIPTERA				
Coreidae				
Anoplocnemis curvipes (Fabricius)	P	S	O	Y
Anoplocnemis phasiana Fabricius	P	Y	N	Y
Clavigralla elongata Signoret	P	S	Y	Y
Clavigralla gibbosa (Spinola)	P	Y	S	Y
Clavigralla horrens Dolling	P	Y	S	Y
Clavigralla shadabi Dolling	P	M	Y	Y
Clavigralla tomentosicollis Stal.	P	M	Y	Y
Crinocerus sanctus (Fabricius)	P	Y	Y	M
Leptoglossus sp.	P	Y	Y	S
Riptortus sp.	P	O	S	Y
Riptortus dentipes (Fabricius)	P	M	O	Y

Scientific name	Plant parts damaged[a]	Distribution and pest status[b]		
		Africa	Asia	Latin America
Miridae				
Creontiades pallidifer Walker	LFP	Y	S	Y
Creontiades rubrinervis (Stal.)	LFP	Y	Y	S
Horcianosinus signoreti (Stal.)	LFP	Y	Y	O
Ragmus importunitas Distant	LFP	Y	S	Y
Pentatomidae				
Acrosternum sp.	P	S	S	S
Aspavia armigera (Fabricius)	P	S	O	Y
Edessa meditabunda (Fabricius)	P	Y	Y	S
Nezara viridula Linnaeus	P	O	S	S
Piezodorus guildinii (Westwood)	P	O	O	S
HOMOPTERA				
Aleyrodidae				
Bemisia tabaci (Gennadius)	L	O	S	O
Aphididae				
Aphis craccivora Koch	LFP	M	M	M
Aphis fabae Scopoli	L	O	O	O
Aphis gossypii Glover	L	O	O	O
Myzus persicae (Sulzer)	L	Y	Y	O
Picturaphis brasiliensis Moreira	L	Y	Y	O
Cicadellidae				
Amrasca kerri Purthi	L	Y	N	Y
Empoasca biguttula (Shiraki)	L	Y	N	Y
Empoasca dolichi Paoli	L	N	Y	Y
Empoasca kraemeri Ross and Moore	L	Y	Y	M
Empoasca signata Haust	L	O	Y	Y
COLEOPTERA				
Bruchidae				
Acanthoscelides clandestinus (Mots)	D	Y	Y	O
Acanthoscelides obtectus (Say)	D	Y	O	O
Bruchidius atrolineatus Pic	D	S	Y	O
Callosobruchus analis (Fabricius)	D	O	O	S
Callosobruchus chinensis (Linnaeus)	D	O	M	O
Callosobruchus maculatus (Fabricius)	D	M	M	M
Callosobruchus rhodesianus Pic	D	O	Y	Y
Zabrotes subfasciatus (Boheman)	D	Y	Y	O

Table 1.1 Continued

Scientific name	Plant parts damaged[a]	Distribution and pest status[b]		
		Africa	Asia	Latin America
Chrysomelidae				
Cerotoma arcuata (Olivier)	LFP	Y	Y	S
Cerotoma ruficornis (Olivier)	LFP	Y	Y	M
Diabrotica balteata LeConte	LFP	Y	Y	S
Diabrotica speciosa (Gremar)	LFP	Y	Y	M
Longitarsus manilensis Weise	L	Y	S	Y
Madurasia obscurella Jacoby	L	Y	M	Y
Medythia quaterna (Fairmaire)	L	S	Y	Y
Ootheca bennigseni Weise	L	S	Y	Y
Ootheca mutabilis (Sahlberg)	L	S	Y	Y
Coccinellidae				
Epilachna similis (Thunberg)	LP	O	Y	Y
Epilachna varivestis Mulsant	LP	Y	Y	O
Epilachna vigintioctopunctatà (Fabricius)	LP	Y	S	Y
Epilachna philippinensis (Dieke)	L	Y	S	Y
Curculionidae				
Alcidodes leucogrammus (Erichson)	LS	S	Y	Y
Aracanthus sp.	LP	Y	Y	O
Chalcodermus aeneus (Boheman)	P	Y	Y	Y
Chalcodermus bimaculatus Fiedler	P	Y	Y	M
Pantomorus glaucus (Perty)	LP	Y	Y	O
Piezotrachelus varius Wagner	P	N	Y	Y
Promecops sp.	LP	Y	Y	O
Nematocerus acerbus Faust	L	O	Y	Y
Lagriidae				
Chrysolagria viridipennis (Fabricius)	L	O	Y	Y
Lagria villosa Fabricius	L	O	Y	O
Meloidae				
Coryna apicicornis (Guerin)	F	O	Y	Y
Coryna hermanniae (Fabricius)	F	O	Y	Y
Mylabris amplectens Gerstaecker	F	O	O	Y
Mylabris farquharsoni Blair	F	O	Y	Y
Mylabris pustulata (Thunberg)	F	Y	O	Y
LEPIDOPTERA				
Arctiidae				
Amsacta sp.	LW	S	O	Y

Scientific name	Plant parts damaged[a]	Distribution and pest status[b]		
		Africa	Asia	Latin America
Gracillariidae				
Acrocercops caerulea Meyrick	L	Y	S	Y
Acrocercops phaeospora Meyrick	L	Y	S	Y
Acrocercops sp.	L	S	S	Y
Hesperiidae				
Urbanus sp.	L	O	O	O
Urbanus proteus (Linnaeus)	L	Y	Y	S
Lycaenidae				
Euchrysops cnejus (Fabricius)	LP	Y	O	Y
Euchrysops malathana (Boisduval)	LP	O	Y	Y
Thecla jebus (Godt.)	LP	Y	Y	O
Lymantriidae				
Euproctis innonata (Walker)	LF	O	O	Y
Euproctis scintillans (Walker)	LF	Y	O	Y
Euproctis similis (Moore)	LF	Y	O	Y
Noctuidae				
Agrotis ipsilon (Hufnagel)	SW	O	S	S
Agrotis subterranea (Fabricius)	SW	Y	Y	S
Heliothis armigera (Hübner)	LFP	O	N	Y
Heliothis zea (Boddie)	LFP	Y	Y	S
Mocis latipes (Fabricius)	SW	Y	Y	S
Spodoptera eridania (Cramer)	LP	Y	Y	S
Spodoptera frugiperda (Smith & Abbot)	LP	Y	Y	S
Spodoptera latifascia (Walker)	LP	Y	Y	S
Spodoptera littoralis (Boisduval)	LP	S	S	Y
Spodoptera ornithogali (Guenee)	LP	Y	Y	S
Olethreuthidae				
Cydia ptychora (Meyrick)	PD	S	S	Y
Cydia tricentra (Meyrick)	PD	Y	S	Y
Pyralidae				
Elasmopalpus lignosellus (Zeller)	S	Y	Y	M
Etiella zinckenella (Treitschke)	P	O	S	O
Hedylepta indicata (Fabricius)	L	Y	S	S
Maruca testulalis (Geyer)	FP	M	M	S

Table 1.1 Continued

Scientific name	Plant parts damaged[a]	Distribution and pest status[b]		
		Africa	Asia	Latin America
DIPTERA				
Agromyzidae				
Liriomyza congesta (Becker)	L	O	Y	Y
Liriomyza sativa Blanchard	L	Y	Y	N
Liriomyza trifolli (Burgess)	L	O	Y	Y
Melanagromyza obtusa (Malloch)	S	Y	M	Y
Ophiomyia phaseoli (Tryon)	S	S	M	Y

[a]Plant parts: R = roots; S = stems and peduncles; L = leaves; F = flower buds and flowers; P = green pods and seeds; D = dry grains; W = whole plant.

[b]Pest status: M = major; N = minor; S = sporadic; O = of no importance; Y = not known.

The pest complex includes leafhoppers, beanflies, aphids, flower bud thrips, pod borers, pod-sucking bugs and bruchids (Table 1.1). The peak activity of important pests of cowpeas in Africa and the estimated yield losses caused by these pests are indicated in Figures 1.1 and 1.2. Cowpea aphids, legume bud thrips, legume pod borer and pod-sucking bugs are major field pests in Africa. In Asia, cowpea aphids, leafhoppers, pod borers and beanflies are important. In Latin America, cowpea aphids, leafhoppers, beetles *(Cerotoma* sp., *Diabrotica* sp. and *Chalcodermus* sp.) are important; also legume pod borer and various pod bugs are often reported as sporadic pests in Asia and Latin America. Bruchid, *Callosobruchus maculatus* (Fabricius) is a major pest in storage throughout the tropics.

PEST CONTROL STATUS

Aphids and leafhoppers can be controlled by the cultivation of resistant varieties. A high level of resistance to these pests has been identified. Moderate levels of resistance to beanfly have been reported, but no concentrated efforts have been made for the development of resistant varieties. Several systemic insecticides applied as foliar sprays or granules applied to the soil appear to be effective. At present, insecticides are the best means of controlling lepidopteran pests, beetles and pod bugs.

Cowpea varieties with moderate levels of resistance to bruchids have been developed. However for long-term storage, supplementary insecticide application or fumigation is necessary.

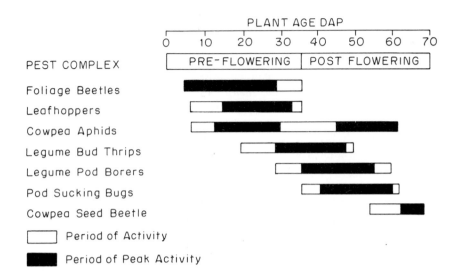

Figure 1.1. Selected pests of cowpeas in Africa and the periods of plant growth when they are active (DAP = days after planting) (adapted from Singh, 1980)

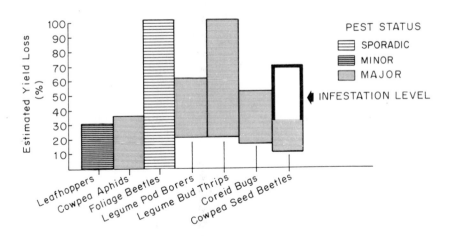

Figure 1.2. Estimated yield losses and pest status of selected cowpea pests in Africa (adapted from Singh, 1980)

In the West African savanna, cowpeas cropped with sorghum or millet are often planted far apart and are for the dual purposes of grain and fodder. The farmers do not apply any insecticide. Often, the yields from grain are low (about 200 kg/ha), with those from fodder being about 6000 kg/ha. The income from the fodder supplements that from the low grain yield. Early maturing cowpea planted with cereal with the first rains often escapes the peak activity of the major pests, but severe pest problems are noticed on monocrop cowpeas planted when the rains have been well established. Therefore cowpeas cultivated for grain purposes as a monocrop require insecticide protection for higher yields. A strategy for control of the cowpea pests in monocrops was proposed by Jackai et al. (1985).

The biology, bionomics and control of insect pests of cowpeas on a regional basis have been reported elsewhere (Singh, 1980, 1985; Daoust et al., 1985; Singh and Jackai, 1985), as has the pest status for cowpeas grown in many tropical countries (Singh et al., 1978b). Most recently, Jackai and Daoust (1986) briefly reviewed cowpea pests, and their information complemented that provided by Singh and van Emden (1979). This paper is an attempt to collate all the available information on cowpea insect pests in the tropics.

Orthoptera

ACRIDIDAE

Several grasshoppers have been recorded on cowpeas in Africa, Asia and Latin America. Many are of no importance unless populations are large. They feed on leaves, young stems and green pods. They are polyphagous and will infest cowpeas that happen to be present. Some of the common species found on cowpeas are *Catantops spissus* (Walker) and *Oxya japonica* (Thunberg) in Africa and Asia; *Schistocerca flavofasciata* (de Geer) and *Schistocerca pallens* (Thunberg) on all three continents; and *Chrotogonus trachypterus* (Blanch.) in Asia.

GRYLLIDAE

Gryllids, or common crickets, have been reported in isolated patches as pests of cowpeas. In Africa, they are often reported as a pest in Botswana and Tanzania; in Latin America, they have been reported as sporadic pests in the dry regions. The commonest species found infesting cowpeas are *Acheta assimilis* Fabricius (syn. *Gryllus assimilis* Fabricius) and *Gryllotalpa* sp. Crickets are nocturnal.

These pests cut young seedlings and feed voraciously on the entire plant. They lay eggs in the soil, with nymphs emerging after hatching. Both the nymphs and the adults do damage.

It is not easy to control crickets; they attack in large numbers throughout the life of the crop. If applied late in the evening, some of the insecticides effective against grasshoppers will work, and use of insecticide baits with rice bran or wheat has been recommended (Metcalf *et al.*, 1962).

PYRGOMORPHIDAE

In West Africa, cowpeas grown under irrigation during the dry season are sometimes attacked by elegant green grasshoppers, *Zonocerus variegatus* (Linnaeus). The early instars are gregarious and feed on foliage and green pods and sometimes do extensive damage to the crop. Grasshoppers lay eggs in the soil in capsules. Nymphs hatch and feed on various crops including grasses. Control of grasshoppers is best obtained by insecticide application. Several insecticides including gammalin, endosulfan, fenitrothion and monocrotophos are effective.

Thysanoptera

THRIPIDAE

Several species of thrips are found infesting cowpea leaf buds, flower buds and flowers in the tropics, but only a few are important (Okwakpam, 1967; Salifu, 1986).

Legume bud thrips, *Megalurothrips sjostedti* (Trybom) synonym *Taeniothrips sjostedti* (Trybom), is perhaps the only economically important pest and is a major pest of cowpea in Africa. Losses caused by this pest range from 20 to 100 per cent (Ingram, 1960; Singh and Taylor, 1978; Singh and Allen, 1980; Ezueh, 1981a).

The biology of this pest was studied in detail by Salifu (1986). He found that development from egg to adult totalled about 19 days. Adults prefer to lay eggs in the macroscopic flower buds of racemes. Eggs are also laid in the calyx tissue of the flowers. He found four developmental stages, consisting of two larval instars, a prepupa and a pupa stage. Adults are shiny black and are easily noticed on the flowers where they feed on pollen. The population dynamics and flight activity have been studied by Taylor (1969). The nymphs and adults feed on flower buds and can completely suppress flower production. The racemes of severely infested plants do not have any flower buds; they turn brown, dry up and fall off.

Cowpeas grown for grain yield suffer more damage than do cowpeas cultivated for fodder. In fact, for fodder production, thrips susceptibility may be advantageous as the cowpea plant may continue to produce foliage in the absence of flower and pod production. Cropped with sorghum, millet or cassava, cowpea consistently has been observed to have reduced thrips populations. The reduction may reflect shading from the other crops, a change of environment, a barrier effect or build-up of natural enemies on the accompanying crops.

Generally under heavy rains, thrips populations are low. The population increases under dry conditions or drought stress that normally follows the late growth stage of the crop. In several tests the early maturing cowpeas ER-1 and ER-7, which are susceptible to thrips in greenhouse tests, escaped thrips infestation when planted in the field and, thus, appeared resistant (Nangju *et al.*, 1979a,b). In the West African savanna where cowpeas are cropped with millet or sorghum, farmers normally plant an early maturing cowpea with the first planting of cereal. This cowpea is a determinate type and is grown for grain. Later, larger areas are planted with varieties of cowpeas that are photosensitive and are for dual purposes: fodder and grain, mostly harvested as fodder. In this way farmers in the savanna perhaps avoid or minimize the thrips damage.

It is easy to control this pest with insecticide applications during the flower bud and flowering period. Two or three applications may be necessary, depending on the time to plant maturity. Cypermethrin, methomyl and monocrotophos are effective.

Host-plant resistance has been researched extensively at the International Institute of Tropical Agriculture (IITA) for the last 15 years. A germ plasm collection of about 12,000 cowpea cultivars has been screened in the field for resistance to thrips. Simple techniques were developed to ensure uniform and high infestation in the field (Singh, 1980), and sampling methods were developed (Salifu and Singh, 1987). These included planting dwarf pigeon pea cultivars all around the field about 30 days before planting the test material. Along the borders *Crotalaria juncea* was planted at the same time to serve as a trap crop for legume pod borer, thus reducing the pod borer populations on cowpeas. The behaviour of legume pod borer on *Crotalaria* sp. has been documented elsewhere (Jackai and Singh, 1981). The test cultivars were planted in single rows, and known susceptible checks were planted every 10th row. The cowpeas were planted in September, as thrips populations are normally high during October—November at IITA.

At about 35 days after planting, endosulfan was sprayed at the rate of 200 g a.i./ha to ensure that legume pod borer populations did not interfere with legume bud thrips infestation. Plants were rated for thrips resistance at 45 and 55 days after planting. Cultivars with the least thrips damage were further tested in replicated field trials for confirmation.

The screening identified one accession, TVu 1509, as moderately resistant (Singh, 1977a). This accession has poor agronomic characters so breeders at IITA crossed it with several cultivars including Ife Brown, a locally improved variety. From this cross, TVx 3236, which combines moderate thrips resistance with high yield, was selected (Singh, 1980).

TVx 3236 has been released in several countries in Africa (Singh and Ntare, 1985; Singh, 1987) and was mentioned by Summerfield *et al.* (1985) as one of IITA's most productive varieties because of its popularity among African farmers. The mechanism of resistance in TVx 3236 has been studied by Roesingh (1980) and Salifu *et al.* (1988a,b) who indicated that resistance to thrips derives from a combination of low-level antibiosis and non-preference.

The physical basis for ovipositional non-preference appears to be associated with reduced air spaces in the calyx tissue of TVx 3236. Roesingh (1980) found that the parenchyma cells of the calyx in the resistant cultivar were closely packed, and he concluded this was the basis for antibiosis. He also concluded that the larvae were probably unable to pierce their way out and were unable to feed effectively in the compact tissue.

Very little research has been conducted on the biological control of this pest, although *Orius* spp. (Hemiptera: Anthocoridae) have been found to prey on legume bud thrips (Salifu, 1986) and on *Frankliniella* sp. (Letourneau and Altieri, 1983).

Trials conducted at IITA with cowpeas planted as a mixed crop with cassava consistently had fewer legume bud thrips than did cowpeas in monocrops.

Jackai *et al.* (1985) prepared an algorithm to represent schematically a pattern for control measures that would benefit from the varietal characteristics, cropping practices and other components of the overall system. The future strategy for control of this pest will involve combining thrips resistance, mixed cropping and minimal applications of insecticide.

In Africa, foliage thrips, *Sericothrips occipitalis* Hood, are found on cowpea seedlings during drought stress, causing malformed, distorted leaves with light yellow patches sometimes confused as signs of viral infection or leafhopper damage. These thrips are dark brown, the adults and nymphs both feeding in the leaf buds.

The foliage thrips population declines markedly with the onset of rains, and under normal crop-growing conditions the foliage thrips are not noticed. They are often found on seedlings in greenhouses or in irrigated plots during the dry season. Rarely do their populations increase enough in the field to cause economic losses.

Insecticides effective against legume bud thrips are also effective in controlling foliage thrips. Granular application of systemic insecticides in soil such as carbofuran has been found effective.

Thrips tabaci Linderman has been recorded on cowpeas in Asia and Latin America but is not economically important. Daoust *et al.* (1985) reported it as an occasional pest in Brazil. In Asia, *Thrips* spp. have been reported to cause damage to cowpea seedlings cultivated in rice fallows mostly during drought stress. Ruhendi and Litsinger (1979) reported that cowpea fields with long rice stubble suffered less thrips damage than did similar plantings in high-tillage plots without stubble.

Caliothrips phaseoli Hood, which is a minor pest of beans in Latin America, has occasionally been reported to infest cowpeas in Brazil (Santos and Quinderé, 1988). The signs of damage and chemical control measures are similar to those for foliage thrips.

Hemiptera

Coreidae

Several species of coreids infest cowpeas at the podding stage. They are sporadic, and sometimes large enough numbers infest pods to cause severe loss of grain yield. These pod bugs have a wide host range, infesting cultivated legumes and several wild hosts. During podding of cowpea, pod bugs migrate continuously from their wild hosts to the cowpeas. The adults and also in some species the nymphs suck sap from the green pods, causing premature drying of the pods and lack of normal seed formation (Materu, 1970; Singh and Jackai, 1985). The relationship of pod age to damage by pod bugs has been mentioned by Khaemba and Khamala (1981).

Clavigralla tomentosicollis Stal., synonym *Acanthomia tomentosicollis* Stal., is a major pest of cowpea in Africa. It is medium sized, hairy, and grey. Nymphs form large colonies on cowpea pods and peduncles and are not easily disturbed. Both adults and nymphs do serious damage. Adults are not strong fliers; they live 100–150 days. Eggs are laid in batches of 10–70 and, on average, about 200 eggs are laid by each female. The instars are each about 2 days except the last, which is about 6 days. The nymphal period totals about 14 days (Egwuatu and Taylor, 1977; Singh and Taylor, 1978)

Jackai and Singh (1988) have mentioned the methods utilized in field screening. A large number of cowpea accessions have been screened at IITA, and several have been shown moderate levels of resistance when pod-sucking bugs are at low or moderate densities. These include TVu 1, TVu 1890, TVu 3164, TVu 3198 and TVu 3199. Tough pod wall and pod hairs have been considered as factors involved in cowpea resistance to pod bugs (Chiang and Jackai, 1988; Chiang and Singh, 1988).

A technique using dry cowpea seed has been developed for rearing *C. tomentosicollis* nymphs and adults (Jackai, 1989) and has enabled IITA staff to produce large populations for screening purposes. Jackai (1984) studied the feeding behaviour of *C. tomentosicollis* and found the information useful in development of a screening technique. Dry seed and excised fresh pods are used to measure the developmental profile of the insect on a given food source, and a fresh pod test measures the level of seed damage.

By utilizing the technique, IITA scientists identified an excellent source of resistance in wild *Vigna*. The resistance derives from characters of the seeds as well as the pods, and some genotypes appear to have both types of resistance.

Clavigralla shadabi Dolling, synonym *Acanthomia horrida* (Germar), and *Clavigralla elongata* Signoret are the other two *Clavigralla* species commonly found in Africa on cowpeas. Both adults and nymphs feed on cowpea pods. *Clavigralla shadabi* is common in West Africa, whereas *C. elongata* is found mostly in East and Southern Africa. These two species of pod bugs are smaller than *C. tomentosicollis*. *Clavigralla shadabi* is distinguished from *C. elongata* by its spiny dorsal thorax, and *C. elongata* is distinguished by its long cylindrical body. The two pests have similar biology, the adults of both species living from 40 to 80 days. Eggs are laid singly, about 250 eggs per single female, and they hatch in about 6 days. There are five nymphal instars, and the total nymphal period is about 20 days (Singh and Taylor, 1978).

Clavigralla gibbosa (Spinola) and *Clavigralla horrens* Dolling have been reported from India as sporadic pests of cowpeas and other food legumes (Nair, 1975). The adults and nymphs suck the sap from green pods which shrivel.

Crinocerus sanctus (Fabricius) and *Leptoglossus* sp. have been reported from Latin America, the former a major pest mainly in Brazil and the latter in Mexico (Daoust *et al.*, 1985; Santos and Quinderé, 1988). The adults and nymphs suck the plant sap from shoots, young leaves and green pods resulting in serious loss of grain yield (Araújo *et al.*, 1984).

Riptortus dentipes (Fabricius) is a major pest of cowpea in Africa, the adults invading cowpea fields from adjacent areas. The adults are strong fliers and are elongated, light brown, with whitish-yellow lines on the side of their body. Fertilized females have a large black abdomen. Their life span is about 10–20 days. Eggs are laid in small batches, 5–15 eggs, with an average female laying about 50. The eggs hatch in about 6 days, and there are five nymphal instars, the first four lasting about 3 days each and the last about 6 days (Aina, 1975b). Control of this pest is difficult because of reinvasion from adjacent areas. Endosulfan, dimethoate and fenitrothion are reasonably effective (Singh and Jackai, 1985). Egg parasites have been observed when the pod bugs are reared in screen cages in the field at IITA.

Other *Riptortus* spp. have been reported from Asia as a sporadic pest of cowpea, but damage to cowpeas is less than to other grain legumes (Nair, 1975).

Anoplocnemis curvipes (Fabricius) is found throughout Africa. It is a sporadic pest and sometimes can do major damage to cowpeas (Aina, 1975a). It has a wide host range, including leguminous trees. The adults are black, fairly large and are strong fliers. Aina (1975c) and Ochieng (1977) studied the biology of this pest in Nigeria. The eggs, which are dark grey, are laid on leguminous trees or wild host plants in batches, normally in a chain. Each batch contains 10–40 eggs, and a single female normally lays 6–12 batches. The eggs hatch in 7–11 days. There are five nymphal instars, and the early instars resemble ants. The total nymphal period is about 30–60 days, depending on the host plant and weather conditions. Adults live up to 84 days. Ochieng (1977) reported egg parasites and observed eggs on the leaves of maize planted as a mixed crop with cowpea. Seldom are eggs laid on cowpea. Endosulfan, fenitrothion and methyl parathion are effective against this pest.

Another species, *Anoplocnemis phasiana* Fabricius, has been reported from Asia infesting cowpeas and other grain legumes (Nair, 1975; Singh and van Emden, 1979).

MIRIDAE

Creontiades rubrinervis (Stal.) and *Horcianosinus signoreti* (Stal.) have been reported from Brazil infesting cowpea leaves, flower buds and young pods (Santos and Quinderé, 1988). They are not deemed serious pests of cowpeas.

Creontiades pallidifer Walker and *Ragmus importunitas* Distant have been reported as feeding on cowpeas in India (Nair, 1975). Chemical control is similar to that for other pod bugs.

PENTATOMIDAE

Green stink bug, *Nezara viridula* Linnaeus, is common in the tropics but is not a serious pest of cowpea. It is much more important as a pest of soybeans, although it appears to cause serious losses of cowpea in the United States (Nilakhe *et al.*, 1981a; Schalk and Fery, 1982). Several cowpea cultivars have been screened for resistance to green stink bug (Nilakhe *et al.* 1981b; Nilakhe and Chalfant, 1982). The biology of *N. viridula* varies a great deal with host plant and climatic conditions (Wilson and Genung, 1957; Corpuz, 1969). Adults are greenish and lay eggs on the underside of the leaves. The entire life cycle takes 30–60 days (Schmutterer, 1969). The adults suck the sap from pods, causing premature drying and hindering seed formation. The bugs also inject a fungus *Nematospora coryli* into the developing seeds, which contributes additional damage (Wilson and Genung, 1957).

Aspavia armigera (Fabricius) is a sporadic pest of cowpeas in Africa.

Adults are dark brown with large scutellum and three white or orange angular spots. Several species are known, but *A. armigera* is by far the commonest, its eggs frequently being found on cowpea (Singh and Jackai, 1985). The adults and nymphs feed on cowpea pods by sucking the sap. Signs of damage are similar to those from other pod-sucking bugs.

In Latin America, *Piezodorus guildinii* (Westwood), *Edessa meditabunda* (Fabricius) and *Acrosternum* sp. are reported as sporadic pests and sometimes cause serious damage to cowpea pods, with the result being major losses of grain yield (Jackai and Daoust, 1986; Santos and Quinderé, 1988).

Control of the pentatomid bugs is similar to that for other pod bugs, the application of several insecticides being effective, including endosulfan, dimethoate and diazinon. Synthetic pyrethroids are generally not effective.

Homoptera

ALEYRODIDAE

Whiteflies, *Bemisia tabaci* (Gennadius), are found all over the tropics. They are important mainly as a vector for virus diseases on grain legumes. Very rarely is damage by direct feeding observed on cowpeas, although Faleiro and Singh (1985) reported whiteflies as a minor pest of cowpea in India. The whitefly is easily controlled by the application of systemic insecticides such as phosphamidon, fenthion and dimethoate.

APHIDIDAE

The black cowpea aphid, *Aphis craccivora* Koch, is considered one of the most important pests of cowpeas in Africa, Asia and Latin America (Bernabe, 1972; Faleiro and Singh, 1985; Singh, 1985; Singh and Jackai, 1985; Santos and Quinderé, 1988). In West Africa, during the last 10 years, aphid populations have continuously increased, and major losses to this pest have been observed. In Asia, it has been reported as a major pest from India, the Philippines, Thailand, Sri Lanka and Nepal. In Latin America, frequent aphid outbreaks have been reported from Brazil.

The biology of this pest has been extensively studied (Waghray and Singh, 1965; Dorge *et al.*, 1966; Bernardo, 1969; Radke *et al.*, 1972; Ansari, 1984). It varies with weather conditions, soil fertility, soil moisture and host plant. The adults live from 5 to 15 days and have a fecundity of over 100. Daily progeny production may vary from 2 to 20. A generation can be completed within 10–20 days, and there are four nymphal instars. The damage is caused by both adults and nymphs.

The pests primarily infest the seedlings and suck the sap, the result being stunted plants with distorted leaves. In extreme cases of heavy infestation combined with drought, the seedlings die. Aphids also infest the plant at later stages. They do not appear to cause any damage to foliage, but heavy infestation of flowers and pods can reduce yield. An indirect and often more serious damage is through transmission of aphid-borne viruses (Bock and Conti, 1974).

At IITA a major effort has been under way to develop aphid-resistant cowpea lines. Selected cowpea germ plasm in the "genetic diversified nursery" was screened in the greenhouse, and selected lines were also tested in the field. TVu 36, TVu 408, TVu 410, TVu 801 and TVu 3000 were identified as resistant (Singh, 1977b, 1978, 1980).

Singh and Jackai (1985) have described the methods utilized in screening. In the greenhouse, test materials were planted in wooden trays 54 × 40 × 11 cm filled with soil to 8 cm. The materials were planted in single rows — six rows, 40 cm long, 9 cm apart. The distance between plants was 4 cm. A row of a locally improved variety, Prima, was included as a susceptible check. Later, after identification of resistant lines, a resistant check row was also included. When the plants were about 10 days old, each was infested with five fourth-instar aphids by a camel's hair brush from an aphid culture maintained in the greenhouse. The infested trays were then introduced into cages (wooden frames covered with saran mesh) kept in the greenhouse. The dimensions of the cages were 140 × 81 × 66 cm. About 15 days after infestation, the plants were rated for aphid damage on a scale of 1–5. Plants rated as 1 were almost immune to aphid damage, and those rated 5 were highly susceptible and died within 15 days after infestation. Lines scoring 1 or 2 were tested at least twice. The resistant plants were transplanted in pots and were challenged again at flowering and podding.

The segregating plant populations were also screened in the greenhouse. Field screening was conducted only during the dry season, which is December–February in Nigeria, when aphid populations peak at IITA. The materials were planted as five row plots, 1 m apart and 3 m long, with a susceptible check every 10th row. Application of DDT on the cowpea seedlings increased aphid populations and resulted in uniform aphid infestations (Don-Pedro, 1980).

Cowpea aphids are easily controlled by the use of aphid-resistant varieties. The cowpea lines identified at IITA as resistant were tested against the aphid populations from several locations in Africa and Asia (Chari *et al.*, 1976; Dhanorkar and Daware, 1980; Karel and Malinga, 1980; Singh, 1980; MacFoy and Dabrowski, 1984; Ofuya, 1988). At Wye College, England, C.J. Hodgson is testing the reaction of cowpea aphid-resistant lines to aphid populations from the different regions in the tropics. Ansari (1984) found that antibiosis was the mechanism responsible for resistance (Table 1.2).

Table 1.2. Mechanism of resistance to *Aphis craccivora* Koch, IITA (adapted from Ansari, 1984).

Cultivar	Resistance	Fecundity[a]
TVu 36	Antibiosis	0
TVu 408	Antibiosis	0
TVu 410	Antibiosis	0
TVu 801	Antibiosis	0
TVu 3000	Antibiosis	0
Prima	Susceptible	481
Ife Brown	Susceptible	386

[a]Fecundity of five 1-day-old aphids in 14 days.

Genetic studies have revealed that a single dominant gene controls resistance (Singh and Ntare, 1985). A large number of aphid-resistant lines have been developed (Singh, 1987), and the best are in international yield trials. These lines are IT83S-728-5, IT83S-728-13, IT83S-742-2, IT83S-742-11, IT84E-1-108, IT84S-2246-4, IT85D-3577, IT87S-1390, and IT87S-1394. They need no insecticide protection against aphids.

Several insecticides are effective against aphids. For example, soil application of carbofuran granules gives good control at the seedling stage, and foliar applications of phosphamidon, dimethoate and pirimicarb are effective (Sarup *et al.*, 1961; El-Sebae and Saleh, 1970; Singh and Allen, 1980). In nature, aphid populations often are controlled by parasites, predators, fungal diseases, and adverse weather (Saharia, 1980; Jang and Yun, 1983; Singh and Jackai, 1985; Ofuya, 1986;). When weather conditions become favourable, however, aphid populations increase quickly.

Aphis fabae Scopoli and *Aphis gossypii* Glover also infest cowpea plants occasionally but are of no economic importance except in their role as vectors of viruses.

Myzus persicae (Sulzer) and *Picturaphis brasiliensis* Moreira have been reported from Latin America but are not considered a pest of cowpea.

CICADELLIDAE

A complex of leafhopper species infests cowpeas in the different regions (Singh and van Emden, 1979). In general leafhoppers are a serious pest of cowpeas in Latin America and parts of Asia but not in Africa (Parh, 1983a).

Empoasca dolichi Paoli, which is found in West Africa and parts of East Africa, rarely causes economic damage to the crop. The cowpea varieties grown on farms appear to be resistant to this pest (Singh, 1980).

The different leafhopper species infesting cowpea have similar biology (Singh and van Emden, 1979). Mostly females are found, and they reproduce parthenogenetically. They lay eggs in the leaf veins on the underside of the young leaves; when populations are dense, eggs are also laid in the stems of young seedlings. The number of eggs varies by species and host plant. On average, 50–150 eggs are laid by a single female. Depending on temperature, they hatch within 5–9 days. Five nymphal instars are found, with a nymphal duration of about 7–10 days. Adults live from 30 to 50 days (Parh and Taylor, 1981).

Leafhoppers are seedling pests and during drought can seriously damage the crop (Raman *et al.*, 1978). Both adults and nymphs infest leaves and suck the plant sap from the underside. The leaves yellow and begin cupping. Frequently, however, severe damage occurs without reduction in yield.

Leafhoppers are active insects, easily disturbed, and are particularly mobile during the warm part of the day. When the temperature is high, for instance during bright sunshine, leafhoppers hide in the bordering grasses. Population counts on plant surfaces should be taken early in the day when the hoppers are present on the plant and are less mobile (Singh, 1980).

Leafhoppers on cowpeas are easy to control. Several insecticides are effective, and a single insecticide application is often sufficient. Some of the more effective insecticides are chlorpyrifos, methomyl, entrimfos and dimethoate (Singh and Allen, 1979).

Resistance to damage by *E. dolichi* has been extensively studied at IITA (Singh, 1980). A world germ plasm collection of about 4000 cowpea cultivars has been screened, with initial tests being done in the field. Test material was planted in late September because the peak leafhopper populations appear in early October in southern Nigeria.

Fifteen days before the plantings, susceptible cowpea cultivars were planted at the border of field plots to ensure adequate leafhopper populations. Test cultivars were then planted 1 m apart in single rows 5 m long, with susceptible cultivars planted every 10th row as a check. The checks enabled researchers to rate the test cultivars for resistance and served as indicators for evaluating the leafhopper populations.

When the test cultivars were about 15 days old, the leafhopper-susceptible border rows were uprooted, and the tall uncut grass around the field was also cut. These activities concentrated the build-up of leafhopper population across the plot area. The test cultivars were rated visually for apparent field resistance at 30 days after planting. Cultivars rated as resistant were further tested for resistance in replicated field trials and later in greenhouse tests.

Four cultivars, TVu 59, TVu 123, TVu 662 and TVu 1190E, were rated as resistant (Singh, 1977b). TVu 1190E was identified as a single plant from an original collection, TVu 1190, from eastern Kenya. The parent, TVu 1190, is susceptible to leafhoppers and its seeds are brown. In contrast, TVu 1190E seeds are large and reddish and besides having a high level of resistance to leafhoppers are resistant to multiple diseases and to root-knot nematode, *Meloidogyne incognita* (Singh *et al.*, 1975a). Designated VITA-3, it also proved resistant to the *Empoasca* complex in international cooperative field trials conducted in Nigeria and Ghana in West Africa, Kenya and Tanzania in East Africa, in India and in Brazil (Singh, 1980). The mechanism of resistance in VITA-3 is tolerance (Table 1.3) and is being used extensively in the cowpea-breeding programs at IITA.

Tolerance, as defined by Painter (1951), is the ability of the plant to grow and reproduce or to repair injury despite supporting a population approximately equal to that damaging a susceptible host. The mechanism of resistance in TVu 59, TVu 123 and TVu 662 was found to be antibiosis (Table 1.3), which is the tendency to prevent, injure or destroy (insect) life (Painter, 1941, 1951).

Studies have indicated more than 40 per cent yield loss among cultivars susceptible to leafhoppers; in resistant VITA-3 and TVu 123, yield loss was less than 7 per cent (Singh and Allen, 1980). In most field trials, VITA-3 yield is depressed by application of insecticides that protect against leafhopper infestation (Raman *et al.*, 1978; Singh, 1978; Parh, 1983b).

Table 1.3. Mechanism of resistance to *Empoasca dolichi*, IITA (adapted from Raman *et al.*, 1980)

Cultivar	Resistance	Fecundity[a]
TVu 59	Antibiosis	12.1a
TVu 123	Antibiosis	10.3a
TVu 662	Antibiosis	8.0a
VITA-3	Tolerance	68.8b
Prima	Susceptible	59.3b

[a]Fecundity of 28 female adult leafhoppers in 14 days. Numbers followed by the same letter do not differ significantly at the 5 per cent level.

Amrasca signata Haust is reported from parts of East Africa — Ethiopia, Sudan and Egypt — and other species of *Amrasca* have been reported from Kenya, Tanzania and Uganda (Singh, 1980).

The signs of damage to cowpea seedlings are similar to those from other leafhoppers. These species can be considered as being of neglible importance as only rarely is their damage noticed.

Amrasca kerri Purthi and *Empoasca biguttula* (Shiraki) are reported from Asia as minor pests of cowpeas. Faleiro and Singh (1985) reported significant damage by *A. kerri* in India during dry weather with moderate populations of leafhopppers. They also observed that most cowpea varieties supported moderate levels of leafhoppers throughout growth, without any reduction in yield. Sagar and Mehta (1982) screened several cowpea varieties for resistance to *A. kerri*.

Empoasca kraemeri Ross and Moore, also known as green leafhopper, is a major pest of cowpeas in Latin America especially during the hot, dry months (Gonzales, 1960; Ramalho, 1978; Leite Filho and Ramalho, 1979; Oliveira and Araújo, 1979; Moraes *et al.*, 1980, 1982; Magalhaes and Silva, 1981; Neves *et al.*, 1982b; Santos and Quinderé, 1988). The signs of damage are similar to other leafhopper damage on cowpeas. The greatest damage is done when the populations peak a few days before flowering and continue throughout grain formation (Ramalho and Ramos, 1979; Moraes and Oliveira, 1981). If populations are controlled at about 8 and 15 days following germination, yield increases of up to 250 per cent have been obtained (Moraes and Ramalho, 1980). VITA-3 was reported as susceptible to *E. kraemeri* and Pitituba as resistant (Moraes, 1982). Since the mechanism of resistance in VITA-3 is tolerance whereby large populations of leafhoppers are found on the plant even though there is no loss in yield, sometimes it can be confused as being susceptible.

Coleoptera

Bruchidae

Several species of bruchids have been identified as pests of cowpeas (Southgate 1958, 1964; Booker, 1967; Raina, 1970; Wightman and Southgate, 1982; Santos and Quinderé, 1988). *Callosobruchus maculatus* (Fabricius) is the most important storage pest of cowpeas throughout the tropics (El-Sawaf, 1954; Schalk and Rassoulian, 1973; Akingbohungbe, 1976; Singh and Allen, 1980; Singh *et al.*, 1980; Caswell, 1981; Oliveira and Santos 1983; Oliveira *et al.*, 1984). In Nigeria alone, yield losses caused by this pest in storage are estimated at US\$ 30 million each year (Caswell, 1973).

Infestation often occurs in the field when pods near maturity (Prevett, 1961). Eggs are laid on the pods, but weevils prefer to enter inside the pods through holes made by other pests and lay eggs directly on the seed.

After the crop is harvested, the bruchids multiply and do considerable damage to stored cowpeas.

Utida (1954) described two morphological forms, the 'normal sedentary' found in storage and the 'active dispersing' forms found in the field. The density-dependent polymorphism in the adult has been studied (Utida, 1972; Messina and Renwick, 1985).

Howe and Currie (1964) studied the biology and reported that 35°C and 70 per cent relative humidity were ideal for oviposition. The females laid from 71 to 117 eggs, with an average 97 eggs. The adult life span was from 8 to 16 days and averaged 10 days. The eggs are glued on the top of the seed in storage; they are glossy and oval when fresh and hatch in about 3–5 days. The larvae penetrate the seed and do extensive damage by feeding inside. Four larval instars, each being from 2 to 4 days, are followed by a 2-day prepupal and a 5-day pupal stage (Carvalho and Machado, 1967; Osuji, 1982). After the pupal stage, adults emerge through an exit hole made by the larvae before pupation.

Owusu-Akyaw (1987) studied the biology of this pest at IITA. He found significantly more bruchid eggs laid on cowpea pods intercropped with maize than on cowpeas planted as a monocrop.

He observed that, of bruchid eggs laid on pods, a maximum 50 per cent were parasitized by *Uscana* sp. He also found differences in pod-wall resistance to bruchid and reported that varieties with a tough pod wall suffered the least damage. In a series of papers, Santos and colleagues (Santos and Vieira, 1971; Santos, 1971, 1976; Bastos, 1973a,b, 1974d,f; Santos and Bastos, 1977; Santos *et al.*, 1977a, 1978a,b, 1979, 1981) reported the biology, damage, yield losses and control of *C. maculatus* from Brazil. Schoof (1941) studied the effect of different relative humidities on the biology of *C. maculatus*, and Singh *et al.* (1980) studied the change in the developmental behaviour of *C. maculatus* and *C. chinensis*.

The damage is done by larvae feeding inside the seed. Often, farm storage for 6 months is accompanied by about 30 per cent loss in weight with up to 70 per cent of the seeds being infested and virtually unfit for consumption (Singh and Jackai, 1985).

At IITA, in 1974, studies were initiated to identify resistance to bruchids in cowpea. By screening a world germ plasm collection of about 12,000 accessions, researchers identified TVu 2027 as moderately resistant and the mechanism of resistance was found to be antibiosis resulting in larval mortality (Singh, 1977b, 1978, 1980).

The method for screening has been detailed elsewhere (Singh and Jackai, 1985), but, briefly, 40 seeds of each accession at about 13 per cent moisture were held in a plastic box 5 × 5 × 2 cm. Three pairs of 1-day-old bruchids were introduced into the box and were left for 24 h for egg laying. The adults were removed the next day.

Bruchid cultures were maintained in Kilner jars that had mesh lids. A filter paper dipped in Kelthane® MF was kept between the mesh layers to prevent mite infestation of the bruchid culture. The infested boxes and the bruchid culture were kept in a room at about 28°C and 70–80 per cent relative humidity. Five days after infestation, when the eggs had hatched and were easily visible, egg count was made. If any seeds had no eggs, they were removed. Adult emergence normally starts about 20 days after infestation. On susceptible varieties, large numbers of adults emerge within 3–4 days. On resistant lines, the percentage of adults that emerge is reduced, delayed and staggered (Table 1.4).

Table 1.4. Adult bruchid emergence in a resistant line, TVu 2027, and in a susceptible variety, Ife Brown (Singh, 1989, unpublished, IITA)

	% adult emer- gence	Emergence pattern (no. of adults/days after infestation)																
		23	24	25	26	27	28	29	30	31	32	33	34	35	36	37	38	39	40
TVu 2027	25.0	0	1	1	1	2	1	1	0	0	0	1	0	0	1	0	0	0	0
Ife Brown	80.0	6	12	6	4	0	0	0	0	0	0	0	0	0	0	0	0	0	0

The genetics of bruchid resistance in cowpea have been studied by Redden et al. (1983) and Adjadi et al. (1985) who observed that two recessive genes are required in the homozygous condition to confer resistance to bruchid. The F_1 hybrid was susceptible and F_2 segregated into a ratio of 15 susceptible to 1 resistant. Cowpea breeders working in close collaboration with entomologists at IITA have been able to incorporate resistance from TVu 2027 into several advanced breeding lines (Singh, 1987).

TVu 2027 appears to be resistant to C. maculatus populations from different geographical regions, with resistance being exhibited in testing with bruchid populations from Brazil, Nigeria and the Southern Republic of Yemen (Dick and Credland, 1986). Also, Ndlovu and Giga (1988) found TVu 2027-derived breeding lines as moderately resistant to Callosobruchus rhodesianus Pic. Other comparisons of resistance to C. maculatus have been undertaken by Vir (1982).

The resistance to bruchids in TVu 2027 was investigated by Gatehouse et al. (1979). They concluded that resistance derived from an elevated level of cowpea trypsin inhibitor (CpTI). Gatehouse and Boulter (1983) also showed that the level of CpTI within the cowpea seeds correlated with the resistance to insect infestation. Hilder et al. (1987) isolated and cloned the CpTI gene, introducing the possibility that the resistance can be incorporated into other crops for control of other insect pests.

Barfoot and Connett (1989) have indicated the market potential for the cowpea gene. However some researchers feel that the trypsin inhibitor alone does not account for bruchid resistance in cowpea, indicating need for further investigations. Birch *et al.* (1986) have focused on the significance of para-aminophenylalanine in *Vigna* as a seed defence against bruchids, and Nwanze and Horber (1976) concluded that the seed coats of cowpea affect oviposition and larval development of *C. maculatus.*

Giga and Smith (1981, 1983) and Southgate (1978) indicated the geographical distribution, bionomics and importance of bruchids on cowpeas. *Callosobruchus chinensis* (Linnaeus) is commonly found in Asia and parts of East Africa and is a serious pest of cowpea in storage (Avidov *et al.*, 1965; Appelbaum *et al.*, 1968; Bato and Sanchez, 1972; Faleiro and Singh, 1985). Its biology is similar to that of *C. maculatus.*

Bruchidius atrolineatus Pic is a field pest mostly found in West Africa (Booker, 1967; Huignard *et al.*, 1984) and also reported from Latin America. Essentially, this pest damages dry seeds in the pods in the field. Of all the bruchids (Table 1.1) infesting cowpeas, *B. atrolineatus* is the only one that does not continue to damage cowpea seeds in storage (Southgate, 1978).

Callosobruchus rhodesianus Pic is found in Africa and *Callosobruchus analis* (Fabricius) is reported from Africa, Asia and Latin America. Extensive studies on the biology, damage and control of *C. analis* have been conducted (Bastos, 1965a,b, 1967, 1968, 1969a,b, 1970; Oliveira, 1971). *Acanthoscelides clandestinus* (Mots), *Acanthoscelides obtectus* (Say) and *Zabrotes subfasciatus* (Boheman) are reported from Latin America (Constantino, 1956; Southgate, 1978; Jarry and Bonet, 1982; Santos and Quinderé, 1988). Varietal resistance to different bruchids in cowpea has been studied by Chandola *et al.* (1970).

Several methods for cowpea storage are used in rural environments of the tropics, the commonest being dry seeds in earthen pots. Many farmers mix the seed with materials such as neem leaves, sand, and chillies (Jotwani and Sircar, 1967; Su *et al.*, 1972; Taylor, 1975; Pandey *et al.*, 1976, 1986; Su, 1976, 1977; Swamiappan *et al.*, 1976; Ali *et al.*, 1983; Ivbijaro, 1983; Messina and Renwick, 1983; Pereira, 1983). In the drier regions of Africa, cowpeas are often stored in pods. For small farmers who produce limited amounts of dry cowpea seeds, mixing the seed with groundnut oil, about 5 mL/kg of seed proves practical and effective as protection against infestation (Singh *et al.*, 1978a).

Insecticides effective against *C. maculatus* (Abdel-Wahab *et al.*, 1975; Abbassy and Abdel-Rahim, 1981; Hussain and Abdel-Aal, 1982) include malathion, permethrin or pirimiphos-methyl (dusting of cowpeas stored in bags or kept in airtight containers) and phostoxin (fumigating of cowpeas stored in airtight containers). Phostoxin is effective against the eggs and larvae inside the seed and does not have any residue. Large-scale storage is in proper facilities with fumigants (Bastos, 1974d; Caswell and Akibu, 1980).

CHRYSOMELIDAE

In Africa, chrysomelid beetles are foliage feeders and to some extent also feed on flowers. Some of these beetles are vectors for viruses. In general they are sporadic and, unless populations are unusually high, do not cause losses of yield by direct feeding (Singh and Jackai, 1985).

Cowpea leaf beetle, *Ootheca mutabilis* (Sahlberg) is the commonest foliage beetle. Another related species *Ootheca bennigseni* Weise has been frequently observed in East Africa. Ochieng (1977) studied the biology and bionomics of *O. mutabilis* in Nigeria. He observed that eggs are laid in the soil (about 60 eggs/egg mass), and the total number of eggs laid by a single female varies from 200 to 500. Eggs are elliptical, light yellow and translucent, are held together in a mass by a sticky substance secreted by the female; they hatch in about 13 days. The larvae develop in the soil, and there are three larval instars. The first and second instars last about 6 days each, and the third lasts about 18 days followed by a prepupal stage, which lasts about 5 days. The pupal stage is about 16 days. The life cycle of this pest is greatly affected by the season and ranges from 60 to 250 days.

In southern Nigeria, where the rainfall is bimodal, during the second season, adults undergo obligatory diapause. After emergence they remain inactive in the soil for almost 60 days while reproductive parts are not fully developed and they are incapable of flight. Adults are normally shiny, light brown or orange; however light-black or brown adults are also found. They are about 6 mm long, oval and can live up to 3 months.

The damage is done by the adults, feeding between veins on the leaves. Dense populations can totally defoliate cowpea seedlings, resulting in the death of the plant. The larvae feed on the cowpea roots but seldom cause serious damage (Singh and Taylor, 1978). The adults cause indirect damage by transmitting cowpea yellow mosaic virus (Bock, 1971; Allen *et al.*, 1981).

Striped foliage beetle, *Medythia quaterna* (Fairmaire) synonym *Luperodes lineata* (Kars), is 3–4 mm long, so is smaller than *O. mutabilis*; it is striped longitudinally with white and light-brown markings. It is found mostly in the forest zone of West Africa. Compared with *O. mutabilis,* this pest has rather limited distribution. The biology is not fully known, but egg, larval and pupal stages are found in the soil (Singh and Jackai, 1985). The adults attack young cowpea seedlings by feeding on newly emerged leaves, mostly at the margins, and can completely defoliate and kill the plants. The adults are also vectors of cowpea yellow mosaic virus. Control of these beetles is best obtained by foliar application of endosulfan, methomyl and chlorpyrifos. A single application is often sufficient.

Leaf beetle, *Madurasia obscurella* Jacoby, commonly known as galerucid beetle, is reported as a major pest of cowpea from India (Gupta and Singh, 1981; Faleiro *et al.*, 1986). The adults feed on plant foliage and, when the populations are high, cause considerable damage to cowpea seedlings. They are nocturnal in habit and hide under debris and loose soil by day (Saxena, 1978). Extensive studies on control of this pest were conducted by Saxena *et al.*, (1971). They found basal applications of systemic insecticides, phorate, disulfoton and aldicarb as granules in the soil at planting time gave good control for 3–4 weeks. *Longitarsus manilensis* Weise has been reported from the Philippines (Esquerra and Gabriel, 1969).

The different chrysomelid species infesting cowpeas in Latin America have been reviewed by Daoust *et al.* (1985) and Santos and Quinderé (1988) (Table 1.1). *Diabrotica speciosa* (Olivier) and *Cerotoma arcuata* (Olivier) [synonym *Andrector arcuata* (Olivier)] are predominant in Brazil (Castro *et al.*, 1975; Haji, 1981). *Cerotoma arcuata* is a brown beetle with black head and two black dots at the base of each elytra (Costa *et al.*, 1978). *Diabrotica speciosa* is smaller (0.5 cm long) than *C. arcuata* and has a shiny green body and a brown head. It has three yellow spots on each of the elytra, sometimes giving the whole beetle a yellowish-green appearance. The adults of these beetles feed on foliage and can cause serious losses. The larvae of *D. speciosa* also feed on the roots and cause severe damage (Santos and Quinderé, 1988).

In Central America and the Caribbean, *Cerotoma ruficornis* (Olivier) and *Diabrotica balteata* LeConte are predominant (Risch, 1976). Their biology is similar to that of the other chrysomelids in Latin America. The adults feed on foliage, and the larvae damage roots and nodules, with resultant reductions in yield. In addition these beetles are highly efficient vectors of cowpea mosaic viruses (Valverde *et al.*, 1978; Costa *et al.*, 1981). They can be controlled by foliar insecticides such as endosulfan as well as by systemic insecticide granules mixed in the soil at planting.

COCCINELLIDAE

Several species of the genus *Epilachna* are distributed throughout the world and are pests of various grain legumes (Singh and van Emden, 1979). They are not serious pests of cowpeas, generally preferring to feed on beans. The Mexican bean beetle, *Epilachna varivestis* Mulsant, is occasionally found on cowpeas in Latin America (Garcia and Sosa, 1973), *Epilachna similis* (Thunberg) has been reported on cowpeas from Africa (Halteren, 1971), and *Epilachna vigintioctopunctata* (Fabricius) has been reported as a sporadic pest of cowpea in Asia (Koyama, 1950; Srivastava and Katiyar, 1972). *Epilachna philippinensis* Dieke has been reported from the Philippines (Esquerra and Gabriel, 1969). Adult *Epilachna* beetles are copper-coloured with black spots.

The biology differs little by species. Eggs are laid in clusters on the underside of the leaf. The larvae are initially aggregated and later disperse while feeding on the leaves. Adults also feed on the foliage. Since they are not a serious pest of cowpea, very little work has been done on *Epilachna* sp. in relation to cowpea. Foliar applications of several insecticides, including endosulfan, and soil applications of carbofuran and phorate granules appear to provide control.

CURCULIONIDAE

Striped bean weevil [*Alcidodes leucogrammus* (Erichson)], pod weevil [*Piezotrachelus varius* Wagner, synonym *Apion varius* Wagner] and *Nematocerus acerbus* Faust are the three weevils commonly reported on cowpeas from Africa. *Alcidodes leucogrammus* is a sporadic pest of cowpea (Booker, 1965). When the populations are high, it can cause serious damage. The adults, which are 7–9 mm long, dark brown with white markings on the elytra, feed on the leaves and lay eggs on the stem. The larvae tunnel and feed inside the stem, causing stunted growth; later the stem splits and the plant dies. Pupae are found inside the stem (Phelps, 1956). Several insecticides are effective against this pest, including endosulfan, methomyl and monocrotophos (Singh and Jackai, 1985).

Piezotrachelus varius is a minor pest of cowpea, seldom being numerous enough to cause economic damage. The adults are small, 3 mm long, shiny black with a long slender snout. Eggs are laid in the green pods, and the larvae feed and pupate inside the seed. The tiny black weevils emerge when the pods are dry, the life cycle totalling about 20 days. This pest is easy to control: a single application of any foliar insecticide including endosulfan and methomyl. *Nematocerus acerbus* is a large dark brown or blackish weevil. Adults feed on cowpea foliage but do not cause any significant damage.

In Latin America, cowpea curculio is considered a major pest of cowpea (Arant, 1938; Aciole, 1971; Vieira *et al.*, 1975; Neves 1982a,b,c). The species status is unclear, having been reported in much of the earlier literature as *Chalcodermus bimaculatus* Fiedler and more recently as *Chalcodermus* sp. or *Chalcodermus aeneus* (Boheman) (Daoust *et al.*, 1985). Reports about cowpea curculio in the USA have always referred to the pest as *C. aeneus*. Daoust *et al.* (1985) compared cowpea curculio specimens from Brazil that were cited as *C. bimaculatus* with museum specimens of *C. aeneus* and did not find any external differences that would distinguish one species from the other.

Chalcodermus bimaculatus adults are black, about 0.55 cm long, with large widely spread depressions on head, elytra, thorax and femurs (Vieira and Santos, 1974).

The biology and control of this pest have been extensively studied (Bastos and Aguiar, 1971; Bastos, 1974a,b,d,e,f; Bastos and Assunçao, 1975;

Santos and Oliveira 1978b; Quinderé and Barreto, 1982). Adults typically attack developing green pods; infestation is reduced as pods near maturity. Adults perforate pods with their rostrum, and females deposit eggs through the holes on the young developing seeds. The spots are easily recognized and are prominent on the pods. Pods shrivel and dry prematurely. Larvae, upon hatching within 2–3 days, penetrate the seeds where they remain until they reach the fifth instar. Fully developed larvae drop from pods onto the ground, move into the soil 1–6 cm deep where they pupate. Pupation lasts about 13 days under optimal conditions, the entire life cycle taking about 30 days. Santos and Bastos (1977) calculated the production losses in terms of seed weight, which quantifies the direct production losses. In addition are qualitative losses in acceptability of seed for consumption and in the germination capacity (Cuthbert and Fery, 1975b; Vieira *et al.*, 1975).

Extensive research on control of *C. aeneus* has been conducted in the USA, with development of chemical methods and host-plant resistance (Hetrick, 1947; Middlekauff and Stevenson, 1952; Dupree and Beckham, 1955; Chalfant and Canerday, 1972; Chalfant and Gaines, 1973; Chalfant, 1985). Factors thought to be related to resistance of *C. aeneus* have been studied (Cuthbert and Davis, 1972; Chalfant *et al.*, 1972; Cuthbert *et al.*, 1974; Ennis and Chambliss, 1976; Rymal and Chambliss, 1976; Grundlach and Chambliss, 1977; Fery and Cuthbert, 1978, 1979; Chambliss and Rymal, 1982), with the most important being 'pod-wall factor', which inhibits the perforation of the pods by adults, and the 'oviposition non-preference factors' (Cuthbert and Davis, 1972). Cowpea lines CR 17-1-13, CR 18-13-1 and CR 22-2-21 have relatively high resistance to *C. aeneus* (Cuthbert and Fery, 1975a). The first line, similar to Ala 963-8, has pod-wall factor resistance and the other two have resistance through non-preference.

Another cultivar Carolina Cream has also been cited as resistant (Fery and Dukes, 1984). According to Cuthbert and Fery (1979), if farmers were to plant even moderately resistant cultivars instead of curculio-susceptible ones, the populations of *C. aeneus* would decrease enough to make the use of insecticides more efficient.

Chalfant (1972, 1976, 1985) has indicated that toxaphene, methyl parathion and permethrin are effective against *C. aeneus* in the USA. We feel the research done in the USA is relevant to control of cowpea curculio in Latin America.

Daoust *et al.*, (1985) reported *Pantomorus glaucus* (Perty) as a pest of cowpea from Brazil. This species of weevil defoliates cowpea and is not a serious pest. Another curculionid mentioned as a pest of no economical importance is *Aracanthus* sp. It is supposed to be the same as *Promecops* sp. (Moraes, 1981).

The adults feed on leaf borders, biting and removing semi-circular edges of the leaves similar to damage caused by leaf cutter ants of the genus *Atta*

(Cavalcante *et al.*, 1979; Santos and Quinderé, 1988). Adults are dark brown, about 0.5 cm long, with a very short snout. They hide during the day in the soil. The biology of this pest is not known. Any of the foliar insecticides used for the control of other curculionids should be effective.

LAGRIIDAE

Lagria villosa Fabricius and *Chrysolagria viridipennis* (Fabricius) are two lagriids often found feeding on cowpea foliage in Africa. The feeding damage is characterized by circular holes on the leaves. *Lagria villosa* is larger than *C. viridipennis* and is blackish whereas *C. viridipennis* is bluish. They do not cause any significant losses in grain yield by direct feeding and are easy to control by a single insecticide application.

MELOIDAE

Several species of blister beetles have been reported from Africa; the commonest ones associated with cowpea are *Mylabris farquharsoni* Blair, *Mylabris amplectens* Gerstaecker, *Coryna hermanniae* (Fabricius), and *Coryna apicicornis* (Guerin). From Asia, *Mylabris pustulata* (Thunberg) and *M. amplectens* have often been reported.

Blister beetles are easily recognized by their characteristic brightly coloured elytra with broad black, yellow, or red bands. They are 15–28 mm long, often appear in large numbers, and cause serious damage to flowers. The beetles mostly visit flowers that are open for just a day, and this habit, combined with the mobility of the beetles, makes control with insecticides difficult (Singh and van Emden, 1979). The life history of blister beetles is rather complex; the larvae undergo hypermetamorphosis, and each larval instar is different. Eggs are laid in the soil where larvae and pupae are usually found. The adults are strong fliers, and populations are denser on cowpea intercropped with maize than on monocrops, the hypothesis being that maize tassels attract them (Singh and Jackai, 1985).

Lepidoptera

ARCTIIDAE

Hairy caterpillar, *Amsacta* sp., is a major pest of cowpea in Senegal (Ndoye, 1978). It has not been observed in other parts of Africa. In Senegal, Ndoye (1978) observed that the female moths lay eggs on young cowpea seedlings on the underside of the leaf in clusters of 100–500. The eggs hatch in 2–4 days, and the young caterpillars feed on the seedlings. Third and fourth instars are voracious feeders, often destroying entire cowpea fields. The pupa diapause in the dry season in the soil, and adults emerge with the onset of the rains. It is not easy to control this pest.

GRACILLARIIDAE

Leaf miners, *Acrocercops caerulea* Meyrick and *Acrocercops phaeospora* Meyrick, have been reported as sporadic pests of cowpea in India (Saxena, 1978) and Southeast Asia. The tiny moths lay eggs on leaf surfaces. Eggs hatch within 1−2 days, and the tiny larvae mine the surface of the leaves, producing blister-like lesions. Rarely do their populations become dense enough to cause any economical damage; however, recently, in both East and West Africa, sporadic and heavy infestation by leaf miner on cowpea has been observed. Singh and Merrett (1980) reported infestation from Tanzania, and, during 1988 and 1989, cowpea fields in southern Nigeria were often found infested with leaf miners. It is easy to control this pest with foliar insecticides (Price and Dunstan, 1983). Saxena (1978) observed varietal differences in infestation by leaf miners.

HESPERIIDAE

Urbanus proteus (Linnaeus), synonym *Eudamus proteus* (Linnaeus), has been reported from Brazil and other parts of Latin America as a sporadic pest of cowpea. The adult moths are chestnut coloured and lay eggs singly on the upper leaf surface. The spherical, whitish eggs measure about 1 mm in diameter and take about 5 days to hatch. The distinctive larvae have well-developed reddish heads from which the common 'match head' is derived. The larvae make shelters by rolling leaves and fastening the borders with silk strands. The larval period lasts about 3 weeks and the pupal period about 2 weeks (Santos and Quinderé, 1988). In parts of Brazil where the populations of this pest are low, a hymenopterous parasite *Apanteles* sp. has been frequently observed (Moraes, 1981). This pest is easily controlled by a single application of foliar insecticide such as endosulfan, methyl parathion or synthetic pyrethroids.

LYCAENIDAE

Euchrysops cnejus (Fabricius) [synonym *Catochrysops cnejus* (Fabricius)], *Euchrysops malathana* (Boisduval) and *Thecla jebus* (Godt.) have occasionally been found infesting cowpeas. *Euchrysops cnejus* has been reported from Asia. Sporadic outbreaks of this pest have been reported from India (Banerjee and Pramanick, 1964), and *E. malathana* has been observed in West Africa.

Thecla jebus has been reported from Brazil (Santos and Quinderé, 1988). The adults are bluish butterflies and are very active in the fields. Eggs are laid on flowers and leaf buds. Larvae feed on vital parts of the flower and eat the developing grain. They can be easily controlled by various insecticides including endosulfan and monocrotophos (Saxena, 1978).

LYMANTRIIDAE

Euproctis scintillans (Walker), *Euproctis similis* (Moore) from Asia and *Euproctis innonata* (Walker) from Asia and Africa have been reported as occasional pests of cowpea with no economical importance. The moths, which are yellowish, lay eggs in masses of 8–10, mostly on the underside of leaves, and cover them up with hairs. The hairy larvae are gregarious in the beginning. Subsequently they disperse, entering the buds and flowers and sometimes causing serious damage. The flower buds are preferred to young leaves, and one larva damages more than one flower. The entire life cycle is completed within 25–30 days (Nair, 1975). Several insecticides are effective against this pest, and one application provides control.

NOCTUIDAE

There are three cutworms that have been reported as pests of cowpea, although other species may also be involved. *Agrotis ipsilon* (Hufnagel) is the commonest, having been reported from Africa, Asia and Latin America. It is not a serious pest of cowpea in Africa but is sporadically found doing serious damage to cowpeas in Asia and Latin America. *Agrotis subterranea* (Fabricius) and *Mocis latipes* (Fabricius) have been reported as sporadic pests of cowpeas from several parts of Latin America (Santos and Quinderé, 1988). The cutworms reportedly feed on the plants and cut the plants at their roots. The pests are gregarious and migratory, and large populations can move through and destroy entire fields.

The biology and bionomics of *A. ipsilon* have been described by Nair (1975). The comparative biology of *A. ipsilon*, *A. subterranea* and *M. latipes* has been reported by Santos and Quinderé (1988). In general the species are similar in their biology.

Eggs are laid in batches of 30–50 on the underside of leaves, on parts of stem lying close to the ground or in wet and muddy soils. The adults prefer to lay eggs in shady places. As many as 300–1000 eggs are laid per female, depending on the cutworm species and the local climate. Eggs hatch in 2–10 days, depending on the temperature. The young larvae feed on fallen leaves or on leaves touching the soil, moving, as they grow older, to other parts of the plants. The full-grown larvae are about 4–5 cm long and mostly dark brown. During the day, they remain hidden under soil and come out to feed at night. The larvae coil and feign death when touched. Pupation takes place in soil and varies from 10 to 40 days, depending on the season. The total life cycle takes about 30–90 days. It is difficult to control cutworms. Inspection of field bunds for the presence of early instars is recommended because control at this stage is possible with insecticides applied to the soil (Santos and Quinderé, 1988). The later instars are difficult to control. Keeping fields free of weeds and leaving bare strips of earth between cowpea fields are recommended, as the caterpillars, after they have destroyed a crop, migrate in great numbers to adjacent areas.

African bollworm, *Heliothis armigera* (Hübner) [synonym *Helicoverpa armigera* (Hübner)], is reported from Africa and Asia (Srivastava, 1964; Agpad-Verzola and Cortado, 1969; Robertson, 1973; Nair, 1975; Akingbohungbe, 1982). American bollworm, *Heliothis zea* (Boddie), is reported from Latin America (Daoust *et al.*, 1985; Santos and Quinderé, 1988).

Heliothis armigera is a sporadic pest and, in recent years, has been increasingly observed infesting cowpeas in regions where maize is cultivated or cowpea is cultivated as a mixed crop with maize (Singh and van Emden, 1979). The bollworm species have similar biology; they are polyphagous and attack many crops. The larvae feed on leaves, flower buds, flowers and green pods and can cause serious damage to the crop. The larvae of early instars make a hole in the pod and move inside to feed on the grains. The older larvae feed on the grain from outside the pod and can be easily detected (Singh and Jackai, 1985). Adult moths are greyish brown. The female lays eggs singly, mostly on tender leaves, flowers and shoots. The eggs hatch in about 3–8 days. There are six larval instars, and the larval period can last from 14 to 35 days, depending on weather conditions. The larvae have characteristic longitudinal markings on each side of their body and are often dark brown or green. Pupation occurs in the soil, about 40 mm deep. In the tropics, the pupal period lasts from 9 to 16 days (Swaine, 1969; Schoonhoven and Cardona, 1980). For effective control, insecticide should be applied when the larvae are at an early stage of development. Endosulfan, chlorpyrifos, monocrotophos, methomyl and cypermethrin are effective against this pest (Sharma and Kaul, 1970). Several larval parasites have also been recorded (Reed, 1965; Robertson, 1973).

There are several species of *Spodoptera* that have been found on cowpeas (Monte, 1934; Srivastava, 1964; Nair, 1975; Singh and van Emden, 1979; Silva and Magalhaes, 1980; Nogueira, 1981).

Egyptian leaf worm [*Spodoptera littoralis* (Boisduval), synonym *Prodenia litura* (Fabricius)] has been reported as a sporadic pest from Asia and Africa. It is a serious pest of cowpea in Egypt. The biology of this pest has been detailed elsewhere (Singh and van Emden, 1979).

The adult moth is brownish and lays eggs on the underside of young leaves in clusters of 50–250, normally covered by hairy scales from the body of the female. Each female lays about 4–8 egg clusters, so the number of eggs can total 2000. The early instar larvae are greenish with black dots on the abdomen or sometimes only on the first and last abdominal segment. The older larvae are brown, with five pale-yellow or greenish longitudinal lines along the body with black spots laterally on each segment. The older larvae hide in the soil by day but are active, voracious feeders in the night, cutwormlike in habit. Depending on climatic conditions, the larval period can vary from 15 to 30 days. Pupation takes place in the soil and lasts about 10 days when there is no winter diapause.

Santos and Quinderé (1988) have reported *Spodoptera latifascia* Walker, *Spodoptera frugiperda* (Smith & Abbot), *Spodoptera ornithogali* (Guenee) and *Spodoptera eridania* (Cramer) as sporadic pests of cowpea causing serious damage in some parts of Brazil. The *Spodoptera* species are polyphagous and attack a wide range of crops. Primarily, they are defoliators but also bore inside green pods or feed inside the pod from the outside. When large numbers are present, complete crop loss is possible within a short time. It is comparatively easy to control early instar larvae, but not the older instars. Insecticides — endosulfan, methomyl, chlorpyrifos and cypermethrin — are effective. Parasites appear to play a role in keeping the pest populations at low levels, and in Egypt a polyhedrosis virus is effective (Kamal, 1951; Abul-Nasr, 1956; Robertson, 1973).

OLETHREUTHIDAE

Cowpea seed moth, *Cydia ptychora* (Meyrick) [synonym *Laspeyresia ptychora* (Meyrick)], has been reported as a sporadic pest of cowpea from Africa and Asia (Le Pelley, 1959; Srivastava, 1964; Halteren, 1971; Nair, 1975; Singh and Taylor, 1978; Akingbohungbe *et al.*, 1980, Ezueh, 1981b). A related species *Cydia tricentra* (Meyrick) has been reported as a pest of cowpea in southern India (Nair, 1975). The biology of *C. ptychora* has been studied by several scientists (Taylor, 1965; Perrin and Ezueh, 1978; Ezueh and Taylor, 1981; Olaifa and Akingbohungbe, 1981). The adult moths are characteristically cylindrical, small and grey.

On average, each female lays about 45 eggs during its life span of about 5 days. Eggs are flat and oval, approximately 0.5 mm long. White and translucent when laid, they become reddish when the embryo matures and can be easily seen. Eggs are normally laid on the green pods at the point of attachment. Incubation is 3 days. There are five larval instars, and the larval period lasts about 12 days. The first instar larvae enter the pod and stay inside, feeding on the developing seeds and do extensive damage. Sometimes, under moist conditions, damage to the seed continues even after harvest.

Early instars are white, whereas the later ones are pink to dark red. Mature larvae leave the pods to pupate in the soil. After about 5−6 days, adults emerge, mate, and deposit eggs on new plants in the early evening hours to complete the cycle.

Endosulfan and cypermethrin applied during the pod-filling stage are effective in control of this pest (Singh and Jackai, 1985). Varietal differences in the susceptibility of cowpea have been reported by Perrin (1978).

PYRALIDAE

The lesser cornstalk borer, *Elasmopalpus lignosellus* (Zeller), is a major pest of cowpea in Brazil (Daoust *et al.*, 1985). It is widespread in Latin America and attacks many cultivated plant species.

The biology of this pest has been studied on many crops. On cowpeas, the life cycle and parasite complex have been investigated by Leuck (1966), Stone (1968), and Lima *et al.* (1984). The adult moth lays eggs on the plants or on plant residues in the soil near the plants. The eggs hatch in about a week, attack the stems of cowpea seedlings at the soil surface or slightly below.

Larvae quickly bore into the cortical region of the plant and tunnel up the stem (Chalfant, 1985). As larval development proceeds, plant stems begin to rot, and foliage becomes yellow. Soon thereafter plants die and fall over (Daoust *et al.*, 1985).

Normally, plants more than 20 days old are not susceptible to attack by lesser cornstalk borer larvae (Santos *et al.*, 1977b). Larvae form only one channel inside stems and do not stay inside the stems. A small shelter made of webs, soil and other materials is formed at the opening of the gallery, and larvae frequent these shelters.

The most severe attacks are found in areas with sandy soils (Santos *et al.*, 1977b) and recently cleared areas (Moraes and Ramalho, 1980). Therefore, the lesser cornstalk borer causes stand losses, and hence yield losses, mainly in dry areas with sandy soils (Daoust *et al.*, 1985).

It should be possible to control the borer by soil insecticides and foliar applications during the seedling stage.

Lima bean pod borer, *Etiella zinckenella* (Treitschke), has a fairly wide distribution. It has been reported from several parts of Africa, Asia and Latin America (Wolcott, 1933; Abul-Nasr and Awadalla, 1957; Le Pelley, 1959; Srivastava, 1964; Santos and Oliveira; 1978a; Subasinghe and Fellowes, 1978; Santos and Lopes, 1979).

The biology of this pest has been studied by Singh and Dhooria (1971). The adult is a tiny moth that lays eggs on the growing tips of the plant, on flowers, or on developing pods (Nair, 1975). The first-instar larvae penetrate the pods and feed on the developing seeds.

The mature larvae emerge from the pod and pupate in the soil for 7–10 days, depending on the moisture in the soil (Singh and Dhooria, 1971). Control is easy early in the podding stage by the application of endosulfan, methomyl, or cypermethrin (Saxena *et al.*, 1969). In Brazil, Santos and colleagues (Santos and Oliveira, 1978a; Santos and Lopes, 1979) have evaluated several cowpea varieties for resistance and have found differences in susceptibility to this pest in field trials.

Leaf roller, *Hedylepta indicata* (Fabricius) [synonym *Omiodes indicata* (Fabricius)] has been reported on cowpea in Asia and Latin America (Nair, 1975; Santos and Quinderé, 1988) but is not an economically important pest of cowpea. The caterpillars roll the leaves or pull many leaves together, feeding on the leaves until only the midrib remains to conceal them. Thereafter they move to fresh leaves.

Several foliar insecticides are effective against this pest. The grain yields of cowpea are not reduced by the damage from this insect.

Legume pod borer, *Maruca testulalis* (Geyer), is an important pest of cowpea and has a very wide distribution in Africa, Asia and Latin America (Hambleton, 1935; Scott, 1940; Fontanilla, 1959; Srivastava, 1964; Taylor, 1964, 1978; Booker, 1965; Forsyth, 1966; Halteren, 1971; Nair, 1975; Singh and Taylor, 1978; Moraes and Ramalho, 1980; Neves *et al.*, 1982a; Jackai and Singh, 1983a; Daoust *et al.*, 1985; Singh and Jackai, 1985, 1988; Santos and Quinderé, 1988).

In 1988, Singh and Jackai reviewed the work done on *M. testulalis*. The most serious damage by the larvae is to flower buds and flowers. The larvae also do extensive damage to green pods, and the early generations infest peduncles and tender parts of the stem. The characteristic sign of larval feeding is webbing of flowers, pods and leaves with frass often noticeable on pods and shoot tips (Singh and van Emden, 1979).

Severe losses in yield (20–80 per cent) have been reported (Taylor, 1964, 1968; Taylor and Ezedinma, 1964; Jerath, 1968; Ayoade, 1969; Oei-Dharma, 1969; Nyiira, 1971; Koehler and Mehta, 1972; Roberts and Chipeta, 1973; Moraes and Ramalho, 1980; Singh, 1980; Okeyo-Owuor *et al.*, 1983; Araújo *et al.*, 1984).

The biology of this pest has been studied extensively (Djamin, 1961; Akinfenwa, 1975; Usua, 1976; Taylor, 1978; Jackai, 1981a,b; Okeyo-Owuor and Ochieng, 1981; MacFoy *et al.*, 1983; Valdez, 1989). The adult moth is dull white, with light-brown markings on the forewings and at the edges of the hindwings. The female moth lays up to 200 eggs on flower buds, flowers and tender leaves (Jackai, 1981b). Eggs hatch in 2–3 days, and there are five larval instars. Young larvae feed on tender plant stems, terminal shoots and peduncles during vegetative growth and on flowers and pods as plants mature (Singh and Taylor, 1978; Singh, 1980; Jackai, 1981a; Jackai and Daoust, 1986).

Older pod borer larvae are highly mobile, feeding continuously on flowers and newly formed pods. They cause severe damage throughout the reproductive cycle of the crop (Jerath, 1968; Singh, 1980; Okeyo-Owuor and Ochieng, 1981; Jackai and Daoust, 1986). The larval period varies from 8 to 14 days, depending on the climatic conditions. The larvae are active at night. During the day, they hide in flowers, pods, stems and the soil beneath plants. The late larval instars can be easily identified by the characteristic black dots on their body (Usua and Singh, 1979). Pods located within the leaf canopy on short peduncles or those touching other plant parts are more heavily infested and are more severely damaged. Full-grown larvae drop from flowers or pods onto the soil and pupate beneath the plant under leaf debris (Singh and Taylor, 1978; Usua and Singh, 1979). Adults emerge after 5–10 days and have a life span of 5–15 days (Taylor, 1967; Jerath, 1968).

Pathogenic organisms, parasites and predators of *M. testulalis* were studied by Otieno *et al.* (1981) and by Usua and Singh (1978). Several insecticides including methomyl, endosulfan and cypermethrin are effective against this pest (Lee, 1965; Jerath, 1968; Singh and Allen, 1980; Jackai, 1983).

Screening for pod-borer resistance was initiated at IITA in 1974, but progress was slow both in the field and in the mesh house because the levels of infestation either were not uniform or were too low. Several simple cultural methods were developed to assist in building uniform and higher infestation (Singh, 1980), and researchers screened 2800 accessions from the world germ plasm collection. Judged by the damage to stem and peduncles, TVu 946 and TVu 4557 were identified as less susceptible or moderately resistant to legume pod borer in the field. Both these cultivars have additional characters that make them less susceptible to flower and pod damage: they possess abnormally long peduncles that keep the pods, about two per peduncle, well over the plant canopy at a wider angle than normal farm varieties (Singh, 1980).

The seeds of TVu 946 are small, and the pods provide a sandpaper-like covering, the result being a much higher level of resistance than characterizes TVu 4557. The resistance in TVu 4557 is partly attributable to the hard, solid stem and peduncles as well as the angle at which pods are suspended.

The pods are kept apart from each other and are pointed toward the ground (Singh, 1980; Singh *et al.*, 1975b). These characters are at least some of the reasons for the reduced susceptibility to legume pod borer. Cowpea varieties with hollow stems and peduncles and with pods that are held below the plant canopy or touching each other suffer severe damage (Singh, 1980). The methods for screening for resistance to pod borer and the mechanism of resistance in TVu 946 have been further studied (Jackai, 1982; Dabrowski *et al.*, 1983; Otieno *et al.*, 1984).

An artificial diet for rearing *M. testulalis* was developed at IITA by Jackai and Raulston (1982, 1988) (Table 1.5) and has greatly assisted in screening for pest resistance. Prior to this, scientists at the International Center of Insect Physiology and Ecology (ICIPE) had systematized the rearing of this insect on a natural diet (Ochieng and Bungu, 1983). The artificial diet utilizes cowpea seed flour as well as ground green pods.

Field populations of the pod borer are regularly introduced in the laboratory culture to circumvent any negative effects of loss in genetic vigour often associated with long-term insect cultures.

At IITA more than a million larvae are reared per month. The insects produced are adequate for field infestation and laboratory studies of behaviour and host-plant resistance. At present a camel-hair brush is being used to initiate infestation, and research is in progress to develop a method that is less laborious and at least as accurate.

Laboratory and screenhouse evaluations have always been an integral component of work on host-plant resistance. Methods in current use at IITA involve dual-choice arena tests (DCAT) as well as no-choice damage assessment and developmental profile tests.

The DCAT is a 72-h study of the level and intensity of attack exhibited by 7–8-day-old larvae (Jackai, 1978, unpublished). The larvae are confined in a round plastic container (the arena) with a concentric arrangement of four 4-cm pod segments (with fully formed seed), the test line being alternated with a check, either susceptible or resistant. At the end of 72 h, the following are recorded:

- Feeding ratio (FR) — the number of pod segments attacked as a fraction of the whole, viz 0/4, 1/4...4/4;

- Feeding intensity (FS) — the extent/severity of attack estimated on a scale of 1–4, with 1 = little or no feeding with only a trace of frass, if any; 2 = initiation of tunnelling or boring into the pod with signs of some feeding; 3 = moderate tunnelling (up to ca 50 per cent of the pod contents eaten) with frass production; 4 = extensive tunnelling (>50 per cent of seeds eaten); production of abundant frass. Each pod segment is scored separately, and the scores are averaged for each line.
- Feeding index (FI) — computed as FR × FS, an overall estimate of the insect's feeding preference. A t-test of feeding indices provides a comparison between the test line and the control in each dual choice.

- Preference Ratio (PR) — computed by the method of Kogan and Goeden (1970), a comparison of performance by any number of test lines with a specific control. With a minimum value of zero and a maximum of 2, PR = 2 (F_1 test plant)/(F_1 check + F_1 test plant).

This procedure has been extensively used in screening wild cowpea relatives as well as other genotypes of special interest.

Diptera

AGROMYZIDAE

Beanfly, *Ophiomyia phaseoli* (Tryon) [synonym *Melanagromyza phaseoli* Tryon], is the most important dipteran that attacks cowpea (Wickramasinghe and Fernando, 1962; Srivastava, 1964; Nair, 1975; Hammad, 1978; Subasinghe and Fellowes, 1978; Singh and van Emden, 1979). It is a major pest of cowpea in Asia and is reported as a sporadic pest in some parts of East Africa and Egypt.

Table 1.5. Composition of artificial diet for rearing *Maruca testulalis* (adapted from Jackai and Raulston, 1988)

Ingredient[a]	Amount in diet
H_2O (for boiling agar)	2000 mL
Cowpea flour	400 g
Pod powder (cowpea)	50 g
Wheat germ	127.2 g
Wesson salt mix	42.4 g
Ascorbic acid	25 g
Aureomycin (5 per cent active ingredient)	11g
Methyl-parahydroxybenzoate	6.32 g
Sorbic acid	3.84 g
Agar	59.2 g
Sugar	60 g
KOH (4 M)	22 mL
Choline chloride (15 per cent)	29.6 mL
Acetic acid (25 per cent)	50 mL
Formaldehyde (10 per cent)	26 mL
Vitamin suspension[b]	30 mL
H_2O (for blending)	2000 mL

[a]Above ingredients are for approximately 4.0 L of diet.
[b]Contains the following vitamins per 100 mL of suspension in water: calcium pantothenate 1.2 g; niacin 0.6 g; riboflavin 0.3 g; folic acid 0.3 g; thiamine hydrochloride 0.15 g; pyridoxine hydrochloride 0.15 g; biotin 0.01 g; and B_{12} 0.0006 g.

The adult is a minute insect, about 2 mm long and shiny black (Abul-Nasr and Assem, 1966a). Infestation begins as soon as the plants germinate, and most plants are attacked within 7–10 days after germination. The fly oviposits mostly on the upper surface of the leaves. Eggs hatch in 3–4 days, and the larvae behave like leafminers, penetrating underneath the epidermis of the leaf, through the leaf midrib and leaf stalk, to the stem near the ground or near the petiole of older leaves where they pupate. In young plants, they may pupate in the root zone (Otanes and Quesales, 1918; Hassan, 1947; Lall, 1959; Agrawal and Pandey, 1961; Pandey, 1962; Abul-Nasr and Assem, 1968a). Leaves of infested plants have characteristic irregular lines made by the penetrating larvae. The leaves turn yellow and later fall off. The plants are stunted and yellow before they finally die. In most cases, the stem is swollen below the ground level; it cracks and turns brown. The plants that survive have a marked reduction in yield (Hassan, 1947; Ho, 1967; Abul-Nasr and Assem, 1966b).

Several insecticides are effective against beanfly (Lall, 1959; Ho, 1967; Abul-Nasr and Assem, 1968b; Davis, 1969; Abdel-Salam et al., 1972; Babu and Rajasekaran, 1981), and cultural practices such as adjusting the planting date and rotating crops reportedly reduce beanfly populations. Also a large number of parasites have been reported on beanfly (Abul-Nasr and Assem, 1968a; Greathead, 1975). Development of beanfly-resistant varieties is a good possibility (Singh and van Emden, 1979; Guled, 1988).

Pod fly, *Melanagromyza obtusa* (Malloch) [synonym *Agromyza obtusa* Malloch] has been reported as a major pest of cowpea from India (Nair, 1975). The biology of this pest appears to be similar to that of *O. phaseoli*.

From Brazil, *Liriomyza sativa* (Blanchard) has been reported by Santos and Quinderé (1988) as damaging cowpea seedlings. Moraes et al. (1981) reported differences in varietal reaction to *L. sativa*.

Liriomyza congesta (Becker) and *Liriomyza trifolli* (Burgess) have been reported from Egypt (Hammad, 1978).

Development of Pest-Control Strategies

Insect pests are major constraints to cowpea production in Africa. Losses caused by pests vary from 20 to almost 100 per cent (Singh and Allen, 1980). During the past several years, efforts have been made at several major national institutes and at IITA to develop a sound pest-control strategy. Control of cowpea pests by use of insecticides is not a problem. Several researchers have demonstrated several-fold increases in yield by insecticide protection. The yield increases by the application of insecticide have resulted in net profits to farmers, but adoption of this technology has been slow. There is a need to develop a sound pest-management strategy that will

Plate I. VITA-3 resistance to Empoasca *sp. (photo IITA)*

Plate II. TVu 3000 resistance to Aphis craccivora *(photo IITA)*

Plate III. Megalurothrips sjostedti *adult*
(photo IITA)

Plate IV. Megalurothrips sjostedti
damage to flower buds (photo IITA)

Plate V. TVx3236 moderately resistant to
Megalurothrips sjostedti *(photo IITA)*

Plate VI. Maruca testulalis *larvae (photo IITA)*

Plate VII. Maruca testulalis *damage (photo IITA)*

Plate VIII. Callosobruchus maculatus *adult (photo IITA)*

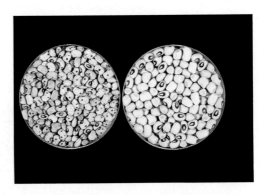

Plate IX. TVu 2027 resistance to Callosobruchus maculatus *(photo IITA)*

Plate X. Chalcodermus *sp. (photo reproduced by courtesy of*
Dr R. B. Chalfant, University of Georgia Research Station, USA)

Plate XI. Chalcodermus *sp. damage (photo reproduced by courtesy of*
Dr R. B. Chalfant, University of Georgia Research Station, USA)

minimize or eliminate insecticide application and that will be sustainable over a long period.

Cowpeas are essentially cultivated for dry seeds, leafy vegetables and green pods for consumption. In many dry regions, cowpeas also are grown as fodder for cattle and have high value. Many farmers, particularly in Asia, grow the crop for green manure, ploughing it into the soil. Therefore, pest-control strategies have to vary according to the intended use, the cropping system, ecology, storage period and market value. A strategy that would work for a traditional crop grown in West Africa mixed with millet or sorghum is very different from one suitable for a large-scale monocrop cultivated for dry grain.

Whatever the focus of the strategy, it must call for as few inputs as possible to minimize the risk of growing cowpea. Most farmers in Africa consider cowpea risky because they do not have the means available to control pests chemically. Pest-control strategies have to be based on an understanding of the physiology of the cowpea plant since this is the foundation for manipulation of the pest-control tactics.

The indeterminate cowpea plant has the capacity to grow and produce over a much longer period than most determinate varieties and is, hence, probably a more desirable plant type for subsistence farming. The longer period of growth enables the indeterminate type to compensate for damage to reproductive and vegetative parts as long as moisture is not a limiting factor. In most of Africa where cowpea is traditionally grown, moisture is limiting. For these areas, varieties with medium maturity that produce flowers longer than do the short compact determinate varieties would be ideal.

Chaturvedi *et al.* (1980) summarized the compensatory limits of determinate and indeterminate cowpea. Ezedinma (1973) found that medium-maturity cowpea can withstand early defoliations as severe as 50 per cent, without reductions in grain yield, although flowering sometimes was slightly delayed. Yield was affected only when there was insufficient moisture or when temperature was too high.

The critical period when leaf area is essential for yield production was during flowering and immediately afterward (Sinha and Savithri, 1978; Wien and Tayo, 1978). Indeterminate cultivars that produced excess leaf area suffered the least from defoliation during this period. Extra-early varieties and determinate cultivars, which produce little vegetative growth after flowering, suffered losses in yield (Wien and Tayo, 1978). However, in both the plant types, rapid growth in the 2–3 weeks at or near flowering provided some natural insurance for the cowpea plant (Sinha and Savithri, 1978).

Also, the cowpea produced an overabundance of flowers, with about 80 per cent being lost by abscission and only a few setting fruit (Sinha and Savithri, 1978). Ojehomon (1968) reported that only the first formed flower buds and flowers produced fruits and when these flower buds and flowers were removed, the flowers that subsequently developed and would have otherwise dropped, produced fruits (Sinha and Savithri, 1978).

Ojehomon (1970) and Wien and Tayo (1978) mechanically removed all flowers from cowpea plants for 10 consecutive days after flowering with no reduction in seed yield. Flower removal had to be continued for as long as 14–20 days before measurable yield losses occurred. In their experiments they did not use any extra-early determinate cowpeas.

Wien and Tayo (1978) demonstrated that continual removal of pod material is only slightly detrimental if it occurs at a stage when the plant can still compensate for the tissue that has been removed. In their experiments with pod cutting, halving the pods in the thin green stage did not reduce yield significantly. Removal of half the pods on each peduncle 2 weeks after flowering also had no effect on yield. If pods were cut after the seeds had filled but before pod senescence, yield was reduced, presumably because the plants could no longer compensate fully for the lost reproductive tissue once leaf senescence had started. Therefore, crop protection at this late stage of plant growth could be vital (Singh, 1980). The inheritance of yield components and their correlation with yield in cowpea has been mentioned by Aryeetey and Laing (1973).

Table 1.6. The effect of plant part removal or damage on cowpea plant (adapted from Singh, 1980)

Damage	Plant response	Effect on grain	Reference
Seedling defoliation	Tolerance	No effect on yield; sometimes delays maturity	Ezedinma, 1973
Up to 50% defoliation at and after flowering	Susceptibility	Lowers yield	Sinha and Savithri, 1978; Wien and Tayo, 1978
Early flower removal	Tolerance	No effect on yield; delays maturity	Ojehomon, 1970; Wien and Tayo, 1978
Early green pod damage	Tolerance	No effect on yield; compensatory mechanism	Wien and Tayo, 1978
Ripe pod damage	Susceptibility	Lowers yield	Wien and Tayo, 1978

An understanding of the cowpea's compensatory limits (Table 1.6), complemented by a picture of the cowpea pest complex in relation to the phenologic characteristics of the crop (Figure 1.1) and a knowledge of the losses caused by the pest complex (Figure 1.2), suggests some components of an approach to integrated pest management.

Undoubtedly host-plant resistance has to play a major role in the strategy both for subsistence and for large-scale farming because of the complexity and the numbers of insect pests involved from seed germination to storage. Although all the problems cannot be solved by host-plant resistance, dependence on other control measures can be minimized, with host-plant resistance and judicious use of insecticides being the key components. The other important components of integrated pest management would be cultural and biological control.

Host-Plant Resistance

Host-plant resistance in relation to cowpea pest management has been reviewed elsewhere (Singh et al., 1978c; Jackai and Singh, 1983b; Singh 1983, 1987). Varieties have been selected for resistance to aphids and leafhoppers; these two pre-flowering pests can be controlled without any insecticide application. The level of resistance to aphids is very high, with few aphid progenies being able to survive on the improved cultivars and those that survive being unable to grow.

Among the pre-flowering pests, however, legume bud thrips and legume pod borer are most important. They do extensive damage to flower buds and flowers. Moderate resistance to thrips has been incorporated in improved varieties, but a higher level is needed. At present, the varieties need supplemental protection from insecticides, although the amount required is much less than for other varieties. The resistance to legume pod borer has to be incorporated in agronomically superior lines.

The resistance to post-flowering pests, which also include legume pod borer and the various pod bugs, has been difficult to identify. It appears few less-susceptible lines are present. The moderate level of resistance to *C. maculatus* does make a big difference in storage. The resistant cowpeas can be stored for almost twice as long as susceptible varieties.

IT84S-2246-4 is resistant to aphids, thrips and bruchids. IT82D-716 and IT84S-2231-15 are resistant to thrips and bruchids. IT83S-728-5, IT83S-742-11 and IT835-742-13 are resistant to aphids and thrips. Additional sources of resistance to bruchids are available, according to Birch et al. (1985), in wild and semi-cultivated cowpeas. Since neither cultivated nor wild cowpea has yet exhibited high levels of resistance to legume bud thrips, legume pod borer, pod bugs or bruchids, efforts were initiated at IITA to screen wild *Vigna* for resistance to these major pests (Tables 1.7–1.11).

Table 1.7. Wild *Vigna* accessions tested for resistance to cowpea aphids, *Aphis craccivora* Koch (Singh, 1989, unpublished, IITA)

| | Number of accessions | | | % |
Species	Tested	Resistant	Susceptible	Resistant
Vigna luteola	6	6	0	100
Vigna vexillata	26	22	4	85
Vigna angustifolia	1	1	0	100
Vigna recemosa	1	1	0	100
Vigna reticulata	3	3	0	100
Vigna oblongifolia	14	2	12	14

Table 1.8. Wild *Vigna* accessions tested for resistance to legume flower thrips, *Megalurothrips sjostedti* (Trybom) (Singh, 1989, unpublished, IITA)

| | Number of accessions | | | % |
Species	Tested	Resistant	Susceptible	Resistant
Vigna unguiculata subsp. *dekindtiana*				
var. *dekindtiana*	59	23	36	39
var. *pubescens*	6	3	3	50
var. *protracta*	7	3	4	43

In *Vigna unguiculata* subsp. *dekindtiana*, several accessions under var. *dekindtiana*, var. *pubescens* and var. *protracta* were found resistant to legume bud thrips, legume pod borer and pod bugs. Unfortunately, all the accessions tested for bruchid resistance were susceptible. Several accessions of *Vigna vexillata*, *Vigna oblongifolia* and *Vigna luteola* appear to have resistance to legume pod borer, pod-sucking bugs and bruchids. A major effort is currently under way at IITA in collaboration with Drs L. Monti, University of Napoli, Italy; P. Perrino, Germplasm Institute, Bari, Italy; and L. Murdock, Purdue University, USA, to obtain interspecific crosses and biotechnological transfers of resistant genes from the gene pool of wild *Vigna* to cultivated cowpeas.

Table 1.9. Wild *Vigna* accessions tested for resistance to pod borer, *Maruca testulalis* (Geyer) (Jackai, 1989, unpublished, IITA)

| Species | Number of accessions | | | % |
	Tested	Resistant	Susceptible	Resistant
Vigna unguiculata subsp. *dekindtiana*				
var. *dekindtiana*	21	20	1	95
var. *pubescens*	2	2	0	100
var. *protracta*	4	4	0	100
Vigna vexillata	5	5	0	100
Vigna oblongifolia	10	10	0	100
Vigna reticulata	1	1	0	100
Vigna macrosperma	2	2	0	100

Table 1.10. Wild *Vigna* accessions tested for resistance to the pod-sucking bug, *Clavigralla tomentosicollis* Stal. (Jackai, 1989, unpublished IITA)

| Species | Number of accessions | | | % |
	Tested	Resistant	Susceptible	Resistant
Vigna unguiculata subsp. *dekindtiana*				
var. *dekindtiana*	59	58	1	98
var. *pubescens*	7	5	2	71
var. *protracta*	8	7	1	88
Vigna luteola	3	3	0	100
Vigna vexillata	17	17	0	100
Vigna oblongifolia	16	16	0	100
Vigna reticulata	1	0	1	0
Vigna macrosperma	2	2	0	100
Vigna antillana	1	1	0	100
Vigna angustifolia	3	3	0	100

Table 1.11. Wild *Vigna* accessions tested for resistance to bruchids, *Callosobruchus maculatus* (Fabricius) (Singh, 1989, unpublished, IITA)

| Species | Number of accessions | | | % |
	Tested	Resistant	Susceptible	Resistant
Vigna unguiculata subsp. *dekindtiana*				
var. *dekindtiana*	64	0	64	0
var. *pubescens*	9	0	9	0
var. *protracta*	6	0	6	0
Vigna luteola	6	6	0	100
Vigna vexillata	27	27	0	100
Vigna oblongifolia	19	11	8	58
Vigna reticulata	6	3	3	50
Vigna racemosa	8	1	7	13
Vigna ambacensis	7	0	7	0
Vigna venulosa	2	0	2	0
Vigna comosa	1	0	1	0
Vigna kirkii	1	0	1	0
Vigna macroptilium	2	0	2	0

CULTURAL CONTROL

Jackai and Daoust (1986) have reviewed cultural control in detail and have indicated some conflicting and some consistent results. From their review and our own studies at IITA, we conclude that leafhopper populations increase after weeding or if fields are kept free of grasses and weeds. Aphids and leafhoppers generally are fewer on mixed than on monocrop cowpeas.

Populations of foliage beetle and flower thrips are generally lower on intercropped cowpea than on monocrop cowpea, particularly when the intercrop is cassava. In contrast, populations of legume pod borer, pod bugs and flower beetles are generally observed to be higher in mixed-crop cowpea than in the monocrop particularly when cowpeas are planted with maize (Amoako-Atta et al., 1983; Ezueh and Taylor, 1984). Cowpeas planted far apart and mixed with millet or sorghum seem to suffer fewer infestations than monocrop cowpeas.

In regions were cutworms are a problem, ploughed strips between cowpea fields reduce damage. Beanfly and leafhoppers infest the crop much more frequently during drought stress than during normal conditions.

Effects of planting dates and mixed cropping have been studied, although the findings have sometimes been contradictory (Gerard, 1976;

Kayumbo, 1977; Perrin, 1977; Taylor, 1977; Nangju et al., 1979b; Litsinger et al., 1980; Risch, 1980; Ezueh, 1982).

BIOLOGICAL CONTROL

Several entomologists (Bell and Hamalle, 1971; Olaifa, 1977; Usua and Singh, 1978; Kumar et al., 1980; Heong, 1981; Matteson, 1981, 1982; Otieno et al., 1981; Daoust et al., 1982, 1983, 1984, 1985; Don-Pedro, 1983; Jackai and Daoust, 1986; Sandana and Verma, 1986) have written about the role of biological control in cowpea, but there has been no clear evidence of a dominant role played by the parasites and predators of the major insect pests. In fact, the studies to date have been very limited. High levels of predation of aphids and parasitism of pod bug eggs have been observed, and large numbers of parasites and predators have been reported as attacking legume pod borer larvae. Predators have also been found on legume bud thrips. How these observations can be put to the advantage of farmers who grow cowpeas is as yet unclear and should be systematically investigated.

CHEMICAL CONTROL

Many researchers have reported insecticides that are effective against pests of cowpea (Farrell and Adams, 1966, 1967; Dupree, 1970; Mehta and Nyiira, 1973; Santos et al., 1973; Ramasubbaiah and Lal, 1975; Attri and Lal, 1976; Ezueh, 1976; Raheja, 1976b; Verma and Lal, 1976, 1978; Dina, 1977, 1979; Dutta and Lal, 1980; Price et al., 1983; Oladiran and Oso, 1985; Faleiro et al., 1985, 1986). It is clear from the research conducted at IITA and elsewhere that most insecticides are effective against only certain groups of pests. DDT and carbaryl applications usually result in increased aphid and mite populations, while reducing leafhopper and other lepidopteran pests. Monocrotophos application reduces flower thrips populations but at times fails to control legume pod borer populations. Monocrotophos was found to be highly toxic to legume pod borer parasites. Synthetic pyrethroids, when applied alone on cowpea, have practically no effect on aphid and pod bug populations. Therefore, for effective control of post-flowering pests, synthetic pyrethroids have to be mixed with other insecticides such as endosulfan or dimethoate.

INTEGRATED PEST MANAGEMENT

The systems of integrated pest management (IPM) for cowpea grown by subsistence farmers in Africa have to differ markedly from those designed for the monocrop cowpea grown in advanced countries. In Africa, cowpea is mostly cultivated as a mixed crop with a range of cereals and is cultivated either for dry grain or for fodder and grain. It is one of many hosts for most of the insects that attack it, and the abundant alternative hosts maintain pest populations throughout the year. The farmers rarely apply insecticides, except possibly in storage.

Researchers seeking to develop IPM for cowpea in Africa are hindered by the lack of information on occurrence, behaviour, and peak of activity of the insect pests and have little information on the effects of companion crops.

In the USA, the only advanced country where cowpea is grown on a large scale, researchers focused their attention on IPM at least partly because the use of pesticides had become extensive and excessive in many areas. One of their major aims was to develop tactics to reduce insecticide application; they encouraged the scouting of crops for the presence of insect pests and they determined thresholds of insect populations above which insecticide was needed.

The scope for these methods in Africa is minimal at present; emphasis for IPM has to be on other control measures in the field. The development of insect-resistant varieties is paramount, although potential exists for use of biological control agents and cultural practices. Adjustment in the dates of planting certainly has promise in moderating insect attacks on cowpea in some ecologies.

Already, cowpea lines with resistance to aphids, leafhoppers, thrips and bruchids have been developed and have superior agronomic characters. They should be made available to farmers, as they represent a great blessing where no chemical protection is provided for crops.

Some progress has been made toward an understanding of biological and cultural control and even toward an understanding of the interaction between biological agents and cultural practices. For example, Ochieng (1977) reported that eggs of the pod bug *A. curvipes,* which attacks cowpea but does not lay eggs on it, were parasitized when laid on maize but often escaped parasitism when laid on alternative hosts.

Also, early maturing cowpea consistently escapes heavy infestation and damage when planted along with cereal early in the season in the moist savanna. Farmers have taken advantage of this finding and many now grow an extra crop of cowpea for dry grain. Late in the season, they plant a dual-purpose cowpea.

More than a decade ago, the potential for the development of IMP systems for cowpea was being discussed (Singh *et al.,* 1978c). Later Jackai and Daoust (1986) schematically presented a model of integrated pest management in the southwestern part of Nigeria. This model relied heavily on insect-resistant varieties but included cultural control (mixed-crop cowpea) and judicious use of insecticides (Agyen-Sampong, 1976; Assa, 1976; Bindra and Sagar, 1976; Nangju *et al.*, 1979a; Ta'Ama, 1983). Advanced cowpea lines with moderate levels of resistance to 2–3 insect pests have been reported (Singh, 1987). There is a need to develop several lines incorporating the resistance already identified and to continue the search for resistance to other post-flowering pests.

The Food and Agriculture Organization of the United Nations and the United Nations Environment Programme have long supported IPM activities, and recently ICIPE has been actively pursuing IPM in Africa as has IITA. A concerted, collaborative effort is needed.

Insect Pests of Food Legumes
Edited by S. R. Singh
©1990 John Wiley & Sons Ltd.

2

Insect Pests of Soybean in the Tropics

L. E. N. JACKAI[a], A. R. PANIZZI[b], G. G. KUNDU[c] and K. P. SRIVASTAVA[c]
[a]International Institute of Tropical Agriculture, Ibadan, Nigeria
[b]Centro Nacional de Pesquisa de Soja (CNPSo), Empresa Brasileira de Pesquisa Agropecuária (EMBRAPA), Londrina, Paraná, Brazil
[c]Division of Entomology, Indian Agricultural Research Institute, New Delhi, India

Although primarily a temperate crop in the past, soybean, *Glycine max* (L.) Merrill, has great potential in tropical Africa, Latin America and Asia (Kolavalli *et al.*, 1987). In the lowland tropics of Africa alone, an estimated 145 million hectares could be cropped with soybeans. The growing of soybeans in Africa dates back to the early 1800s when missionaries are thought to have introduced the crop (Mayo, 1945). Since then, soybeans have spread with some success to most African countries.

In the past 20 years, soybean has also gained ground in Latin America, the major producing countries being Brazil, Argentina and Paraguay. Most of the cultivars in Latin America were introduced from the United States, but Brazil, which has become a leading producer in the world, is now a key source of improved cultivars for neighbouring countries. The major production zone in South America is 15–30°S (Val, 1985).

Soybean was first introduced in Brazil in 1914 (Rio Grande do Sul), and the first commercial fields were established in 1931. The area under the crop expanded rapidly because of soybean's high profitability and its amenability to double-cropping with wheat (Val, 1985). Bonato (1981) grouped soybean production in Brazil under traditional, expanding and potential regions depending on the area cultivated and the level of technology applied. The traditional region comprises the states of Paraná, São Paulo, Rio Grande do Sul and Santa Catarina and was responsible for 90 per cent of national production in 1975.

The expanding region is the centre of the country and accounts for 27.2 per cent of national production. The technology used here has been developed in Brazil. The potential region is the area between 0° and 10°S.

In Paraguay, soybean was introduced as early as 1921 and is now mainly a crop for export, with 70 per cent being exported as grain and 30 per cent being processed internally. Similarly, most of the production in Argentina is for export, and the area under the crop has grown markedly in recent years. In fact, in all the Latin American countries with a history of soybean production — including Chile, Uruguay and Bolivia — production has increased sharply in recent years.

The spread of soybean in Africa, however, has been checked by a series of constraints, both biological and socio-economic (Singh and Rachie, 1987). This is true in other parts of the tropics as well but to a much lesser extent than in Africa. The major biological constraints to production in the tropics are insect pests, diseases and edaphic conditions (including rhizosphere), with the most severe pest problems being in areas where the crop has been grown the longest (Panizzi et al., 1977a; Kogan 1981; Talekar, 1987). The socio-economic problems have been reviewed by Kolavalli et al. (1987), Weingartner (1987), and Sun et al. (1987).

This chapter addresses the constraints posed by insect pests, which are considered by most authorities to be the largest impediment to increasing production of soybeans worldwide. The reader interested in the other constraints, particularly as they apply to tropical environments, may consult Singh et al. (1987).

Insect pests are a particular problem in Southeast Asia where the crop has been cultivated for several hundred years; insects also are a growing problem in South America where production has expanded at a phenomenal rate; soybean in Africa is still reasonably free of serious problems caused by insect pests.

However, the distinction between regions is one of magnitude of severity more than of species diversity. For example, the southern green stink bug is present wherever soybeans are grown but attains devastating levels in Brazil, the USA, and in Asia (Table 2.1).

In some cases niches are occupied by related (either by taxon or behaviour) species in different areas — e.g., the Bihar hairy caterpillar, *Diacrisia obliqua* synonym *Spilosoma obliqua* (Walker), which is notorious as a defoliator on soybeans in India but is almost unknown in other parts of Asia, Latin America and Africa (Kogan and Turnipseed, 1987).

Outside India, in West and Northeast Africa, soybean is host to another defoliator, *Spodoptera* spp. (known by several common names) and a complex of loopers/semiloopers (in Southern Africa — especially Zimbabwe). Occasionally, a unique pest occurs in an area (e.g., the girdle beetle in India) and causes damage that has not been seen anywhere else.

In most cases it is only a matter of time until the problem is far from unique, as insects spread with relative ease within and between countries and regions.

Traditionally, soybean has not had serious infestations during storage. As a result, reviews on soybean entomology — for example, Turnipseed and Kogan (1976) and Kogan and Turnipseed (1987) — often make little or no mention of storage pests. However, given the right environment, a number of storage insects will, and do, attack soybean in storage.

A number of cosmopolitan and generalist feeders (in stored products) have been reported on soybean by various workers. Some constitute a real threat to sustainability, whereas many may simply have been fortuitously associated with the crop. Studies on developmental profiles of the various pests would provide a reliable basis for predicting the type and nature of association.

Coleoptera

Coleoptera includes several defoliators as well as pests that attack seedlings and roots. Extensive studies have been conducted on the biologies of the major species found on soybeans (Turnipseed and Shepard 1980; Kogan, *et al.*, 1980).

Many of the defoliators are highly polyphagous, the early species being beetles mainly in the family Chrysomelidae *(Diabrotica* spp.; flea beetles; *Cerotoma* spp.), Coccinellidae *(Epilachna* spp.) or Lagriidae *(Lagria* sp. and *Chrysolagria cuprina)*. *Epicauta atomaria* (Meloidae), and *Phaedonia indica*, which is important in Indonesia, also feed on foliage. However, except in the USA where *Epilachna varivestis* and *Cerotoma trifurcata* are important pests, defoliation by Coleoptera is generally sporadic and has not been systematically documented.

In Nigeria, a number of beetles, especially *Barombiella humeralis* (synonym *Barombia humeralis*) (Laboulbene), *Medythia quaterna* (F.), *Ootheca mutabilis* (Sahlberg), *Nematocerus acerbus* Faust, and *Alcidodes dentipes* F. have been reported (Ezueh and Dina, 1979) but are minor pests.

Coleopterans skeletonize soybean or create round bullet-type holes, with feeding damage only occasionally producing irregular holes or serrated margins. The damage is clearly distinguishable from that by lepidopteran and orthopteran defoliators (Kogan *et al.,* 1980).

Soybeans, like other legumes, are tolerant to injury, particularly defoliation. Losses of up to 30 per cent in leaf area before pod development do not negatively affect grain yield (Wien and Tayo, 1978; Turnipseed and Kogan, 1976; Kogan and Turnipseed, 1987). However, soybeans are less able to withstand damage to their stems (particularly in the seedling stage).

Table 2.1. Insect pests on soybean in the tropics, their feeding sites and status[a]

ORDER/family Scientific name	Feeding site	Pest status			References
		Africa	Asia	Latin America	
COLEOPTERA					
Anobriidae					
Lasioderma serricorne (Fab.)	Flour	O	O	Y	Srivastava *et al.*, 1973; Williams, 1986; Bhattacharya, 1988
Bostrichidae					
Rhizopertha dominica (Fab.)	Seed	Y	O	Y	Kapoor, 1964; Bhattacharya and Pant, 1969
Bruchidae					
Callosobruchus chinensis (L.)	Flour	Y	O	Y	Srivastava and Bhatia, 1959; Pandey et al., 1976; Panizzi and Slansky, 1985a
C. maculatus (Fab.)	Flour	O	O	Y	Srivastava *et al.*, 1973; Williams, 1986; Bhattacharya, 1988
C. rhodesianus (Pic)	Flour	O	O	Y	Srivastava *et al.*, 1973; Williams, 1986; Bhattacharya, 1988
Tenebrionidae					
Tribolium castaneum (Hbst.)	Seed	N	O	Y	Kapoor, 1964; Bhattacharya and Pant, 1969
T. confusum (du Val)	Flour	O	O	Y	Srivastava *et al.*, 1973; Williams, 1986; Bhattacharya, 1988
Dermestidae					
Trogoderma granarium (Everts)	Seed	Y	O	M	Kapoor, 1964; Bhattacharya and Pant, 1969

ORDER/family Scientific name	Feeding site	Pest status Africa	Asia	Latin America	References
Chrysomelidae					
Cerotoma arcuata (Olivier)	Foliage	N	Y	Y	Turnipseed and Shepard, 1980; Kogan *et al.*, 1980
C. ruficornis (Olivier)	Foliage	N	Y	N	Turnipseed and Shepard, 1980; Kogan *et al.*, 1980
C. trifurcata (For.)	Foliage	N	N	M	Turnipseed and Shepard, 1980; Kogan *et al.*, 1980
Diabrotica speciosa (Gremar)	Foliage	N	Y	N	Turnipseed and Shepard, 1980; Kogan *et al.*, 1980
Coccinellidae					
Epilachna varivestis Mulsant	Foliage	N	N	M	Turnipseed and Shepard, 1980; Kogan *et al.*, 1980
Lagriidae					
Chrysolagria cuprina (Thomson)	Foliage	N	Y	N	Turnipseed and Shepard, 1980; Kogan *et al.*, 1980
Lagria villosa Fab.	Foliage	N	N	N	Turnipseed and Shepard, 1980; Kogan *et al.*, 1980
Lamiidae					
Obereopsis (Oberea) brevis (Swed.)	Stem	Y	M	Y	Singh and Singh, 1966; Gangrade *et al.*, 1971
Meloidae					
Epicauta maginata (Fab.)	Foliage	Y	M	Y	Turnipseed and Shepard, 1980; Kogan *et al.*, 1980
Phaedonia inclusa (Stal.)	Foliage	Y	M	Y	Turnipseed and Shepard, 1980; Kogan *et al.*, 1980

Table 2.1 Continued

ORDER/family Scientific name	Feeding site	Pest status Africa	Asia	Latin America	References
DIPTERA					
Agromyzidae					
Melanagromyza dolichostigma de Meijere	Foliage	N	M	Y	Greathead, 1968; Spencer, 1973; Talekar, 1987
M. sojae (Zehntner)	Foliage	N	M	Y	Greathead, 1968; Spencer, 1973; Talekar, 1987
Ophiomyia centrosematis de Meijere	Foliage	N	M	Y	Greathead, 1968; Spencer, 1973; Talekar, 1987
O. phaseoli (Tryon)	Foliage	N	M	Y	Greathead, 1968; Spencer, 1973; Talekar, 1987 ICRISAT, 1976a,b; Lateef and Reed, 1983
Anthomyiidae					
Delia platura (Meigen)	Seedlings, pods	Y	M	Y	Gujarati *et al.*, 1971; Chaudhary *et al.*, 1976
Hylemyia cilicrura (Meigen)	Seedlings, pods	Y	M	Y	Gujarati *et al.*, 1971; Chaudhary *et al.*, 1976
Platystomatidae					
Rivellia apicallis (Hendel)	Roots	Y	O	O	Eastman and Wuensche, 1977; Eastman, 1980; Kumar Rao and Sithanantham, 1989
R. basilaris (Wiedermann)	Roots	Y	O	Y	Eastman and Wuensche, 1977; Eastman, 1980; Kumar Rao and Sithanantham, 1989
R. quadrifasciata (Macquart)	Roots	Y	O	O	Eastman and Wuensche, 1977; Eastman, 1980; Kumar Rao and Sithanantham, 1989
Rivellia sp.	Roots	N	Y	Y	Jackai *et al.*, 1985
HEMIPTERA					
Alydidae					
Megalotomus parvus (Westwood)	Pods, seeds	Y	Y	M	Panizzi, 1988a
Riptortus clavatus (Thunberg)	Pods, seeds	M	M	Y	Ezueh and Dina, 1979; Talekar, 1987
R. dentipes (Fab.)	Pods, seeds	N	M	Y	Ezueh and Dina, 1979; Talekar, 1987; Taylor, 1978

ORDER/family Scientific name	Feeding site	Pest status			References
		Africa	Asia	Latin America	
R. linearis (F.)	Pods, seeds	M	M	Y	Ezueh and Dina, 1979; Talekar, 1987; Pflucker, 1981
Coreidae					
Anoplocnemis curvipes	Pods, seeds	O	Y	Y	Ezueh and Dina, 1979
Cletus spp.	Pods, seeds	O	O	Y	Kashyap and Adlakha, 1971
Leptoglossus zonatus	Pods, seeds	O	Y	O	Panizzi, 1988
Lygaeidae					
Chaliops spp.	Leaves, shoots, buds, pods	Y	O	Y	Lal, 1974
Pentatomidae					
Acrosternum acuta Dallas	Pods, seeds	M	Y	Y	Jackai and Singh, 1987
A. acuminata	Pods, seeds	M	Y	Y	Turnipseed and Kogan, 1976
A. armigera	Pods, seeds	M	Y	M	Jackai and Singh, 1987
Aspavia armigera (Fab.)	Pods, seeds	M	Y	Y	Ezueh and Dina, 1979; Jackai and Singh, 1987
Euschistus heros (Fab.)	Pods, seeds	Y	Y	M	Kogan and Turnipseed, 1987
E. servus (Say)	Pods, seeds	Y	Y	M	Kogan and Turnipseed, 1987
Nezara antennata (Scott)	Pods, seeds	Y	N	Y	Kobayashi, 1959; Todd and Herzog, 1980
N. viridula (L.)	Pods, seeds	M	M	M	Jackai and Singh, 1987; Talekar, 1987; Turnipseed and Kogan, 1987
Piezodorus guildinii (Westw.)	Pods, seeds	M	Y	M	Ezueh and Dina, 1979; Panizzi and Slansky, 1985b
P. hybneri (Gmelin)	Pods, seeds	Y	Y	N	Panizzi and Slansky, 1985a
P. punctiventris	Pods, seeds	N	Y	Y	Kogan and Turnipseed, 1987

Table 2.1 Continued

ORDER/family Scientific name	Feeding site	Pest status			References
		Africa	Asia	Latin America	
HOMOPTERA					
Cicadellidae					
Amrasca biguttula (Shiroki)	Foliage	Y	M	Y	Litsinger et al., 1978; Kogan et al., 1980
Asymmetrasca decedens (Paoli)	Foliage	O	O	Y	Hammmad, 1978
Balclutha hebe (Kirk.)	Foliage	O	O	Y	Hammmad, 1978
Empoasca christiani (Dworakowska)	Foliage	M	Y	M	Rahman, 1975; Parh, 1979
E. dolichi Paoli	Foliage	O	Y	O	Rahman, 1975; Parh, 1979
E. fabae (Harris)	Foliage	N	Y	O	Singh and van Emden, 1979
E. kerri (Pruthi)	Foliage	Y	M	M	Saxena, 1978
E. kraemeri (Ross & Moore)	Foliage	N	Y	M	Singh and van Emden, 1979
E. signata Haust	Foliage	O	O	Y	Hammad, 1978
Orosius sp.	Foliage	O	O	Y	Hammad, 1978
Scaphytopius acutus (Say)	Foliage	Y	Y	O	Granada, 1979; Helm et al., 1980
ISOPTERA					
Termitidae					
Macrotermes sp.	Stem	N	N	Y	Malaka, 1972
Odontotermes sp.	Stem	N	N	Y	Malaka, 1972
LEPIDOPTERA					
Arctiidae					
Spilosoma (Diacrisia) obliqua (Walker)	Foliage	Y	M	Y	Bhattacharya and Rathore, 1977; Deshmukh et al., 1977
Geometridae					
Scopula remotata (Guenee)	Foliage	Y	M	Y	Gujarati et al., 1973

ORDER/family Scientific name	Feeding site	Pest status Africa	Pest status Asia	Pest status Latin America	References
Noctuidae					
Anticarsia gemmatalis (Hübner)	Foliage	Y	Y	M	Guagliumi, 1966; Posada et al., 1970; Corseiul and Redaelli, 1977; Herzog and Todd, 1980
Heliothis armigera (Hübner)	Foliage, pods, seeds	M	M	Y	Srivastava, 1964; Agpal-Verzola and Cortado, 1968; Robertson, 1973; Nyiira, 1978; Buckmire, 1978; Tsedeke et al., 1982
H. virescens (Fab.)	Foliage	Y	N	M	Reed and Pawar, 1982
H. zea (Boddie)	Foliage	N	Y	M	Turnipseed and Kogan, 1976; Kogan and Turnipseed, 1987
Spodoptera exempta (Walker)	Foliage	N	Y	Y	Rose et al., 1988
S. exigua (Hübner)	Foliage	Y	M	Y	Bhattacharya and Rathore, 1977, 1980
S. littoralis (Boisd.)	Foliage	M	M	N	Kamal, 1951; Hammad, 1955, 1978; Gangrade et al., 1975; Shaheen, 1977; Jackai and Singh, 1987
S. litura (Fab.)	Foliage	Y	M	Y	Bhattacharya and Rathore, 1977, 1980
Chrysodeixis acuta (Walk.)	Foliage	N	Y	O	Taylor, 1980
C. chalcites (Fab.)	Foliage	N	Y	O	Taylor, 1980
Pseudoplusia includens (Walker)	Foliage	Y	Y	M	Turnipseed and Kogan, 1976; Ramiro, 1977; Herzog, 1980
Trysanoplusia orichalcea (Walker)	Foliage	M	M	Y	Bhattacharya and Rathore, 1977, 1980; Taylor, 1980; Talekar, 1987
Pyralidae					
Elasmopalpus lignosellus (Zeller)	Stem	Y	M	M	Corseuil and Terhorst, 1965; Pacheco, 1970; Rizzo, 1972; Turnipseed, 1973
Ephestia cautella (Walker)	Flour, seeds	Y	M	Y	Chaudhary and Bhattacharya, 1976; Saxena, 1976
Etiella zinckenella (Treitschke)	Pods, flowers	O	M	Y	Naito et al., 1983; Talekar, 1987

Table 2.1 Continued

ORDER/family Scientific name	Feeding site	Pest status Africa	Asia	Latin America	References
Hedylepta indicata (Fab.)	Foliage	M	M	M	Ezueh and Dina, 1979; Chyan *et al.*, 1984; Kogan and Turnipseed, 1987
Lamprosema diemminalis (Guenee)	Foliage	Y	O	Y	Bhattacharya and Rathore, 1977
L. indicata (Fab.)	Foliage	Y	M	Y	Rejesus, 1976; Sepswasdi, 1976; Sachan and Gangwar, 1980
Maruca testulalis (Geyer)	Foliage, flowers, pods	O	O	O	Rejesus, 1976; Ezueh and Dina, 1979
Plodia interpunctella (Hübner)	Flour, seeds	M	M	Y	
Tortricidae					
Cydia fabivora (Meyr.)	Shoots, axils	Y	Y	M	Willie, 1946; Corseuil *et al.*, 1974; Kogan and Turnipseed, 1987
C. nigricana (F.)	Pods, seeds	Y	Y	N	Turnipseed, 1975; Foerster, 1978
C. pychora (Meyr.)	Pods, seeds	O	O	M	Nanne Roe, 1968; Singh, 1977; Singh and Jakhmola, 1983
Epinotia aporema (Wals.)	Foliage, stem	Y	Y	M	Clarke, 1954; Ferreira, 1980

[a]Pest status: M = major; O = occasional; N = minor; and Y = not yet reported.

The stem is the feeding site of the girdle beetle, which only recently has demanded attention and is described briefly here.

The coleopteran pests of roots and nodules are *Cerotoma arcuata*, which is known to occur in Central and South America,and a closely related species *Cerotoma trifurcata* in North America (Kogan and Turnipseed, 1987).

Coleoptera also encompasses several species of insects well known for their attacks on tropical legumes in storage. However, few of the classic storage pests thrive on soybean, particularly intact soybean (Kapoor, 1964; Bhattacharya and Pant, 1969). Only when the physical environment of the grain is altered, for example, through increased relative humidity, does soybean suffer damage from storage pests. Although samples of soybeans, from different parts of Nigeria, have been found infested with *Callosobruchus maculatus* and *Lasioderma serricorne*, the likelihood is that the condition (especially the seed coat) of the whole grain was altered and thus permitted infestation.

Studies conducted in India (Srivastava, 1973) with *Trogoderma granarium* and *C. maculatus* confirm the vulnerability of seeds in altered conditions. Normally *Tribolium confusum*, *Tribolium castaneum*, *Lasioderma serricorne*, *C. maculatus* and *C. rhodesianus* will infest soybean only after it has been processed into flour (Williams, 1986; Bhattacharya, 1988); however, they could inflict heavy damage in stores of flour (Chaudhary *et al.*, 1972; Srivastava, 1973).

Other studies in India (Srivastava and Bhatia, 1959) indicated that *Callosobruchus chinensis* (Linnaeus) strongly prefer soybean over other legumes for oviposition — a finding that was later confirmed by Pandey *et al.* (1976) who also showed satisfactory adult emergence.

Recently, the Nigerian Stored Products Research Institute in Ibadan and the Rivers State University of Science and Technology in Port Harcourt launched studies in collaboration with IITA because of increasing reports of infestation of soybean in storage. The work is likely to gain impetus as the area under soybean is rapidly expanding in Nigeria and other countries in Africa.

Because of the low levels of infestation on soybean in storage in most countries, little is done to control storage pests. Other problems are more critical, and conventional storage methods are often relied upon. Common sense indicates that at present the best control of storage pests is host-plant resistance, and where adequate levels of resistance are available, there is generally no reason to rely on toxic synthetic chemical products. The choice of varieties makes a difference. For example, in tests with *T. granarium*, some soybean varieties enabled the insect to develop better than did others, and the percentage of adults emerging was highly variable — 11 per cent for Bragg and 82 per cent for Ankur.

Other control methods such as the use of natural enemies and cultural control have not been given much attention to date, and the release of biological control agents in flour storage is likely to be resisted.

LAMIIDAE

Girdle beetle, *Obereopsis brevis*, synonym *Oberea brevis*, is medium-sized when adult, with very long antennae. The anterior half of the elytra is a deep brown, while the posterior half is black. The larva is polyphagous and has been reported on cowpea, bittergourd, chillies and soybean in central India where it appears to have become a key pest (Singh and Singh, 1966; Gangrade *et al.*, 1971).

The females make girdles (or rings) around the petiole or stem and drill into the plants, subsequently inserting their eggs singly in these holes. Each female makes 3–4 girdles and lays up to 72 yellowish eggs that measure 1.25–2.25 mm across and hatch in 3–8 days (Gangrade, 1974). The larval period takes 10–13 days, with full grown larvae being 18–20 mm long (Battacharya and Rathore, 1977). The entire life cycle takes 40–70 days, depending on environmental conditions.

Bhattacharya and Rathore (1977) reported that the girdles are always in pairs, and they hypothesized that the girdles serve to adjust the moisture content in the pith for the egg. The authors based their conclusion on the absence of eggs in newly made girdles, which were presumably still too moist.

Girdling by the female beetle leads initially to drying of the trifoliolate along the margins. If the region of attack is on the main stem, all the leaves and the shoot above the girdled area eventually dry up.

Larvae feed inside the stem making it hollow. Infested parts wither and dry. The extent of damage is highly dependent on the plant stage attacked, but an attack during the seedling stage could cause 75 per cent plant mortality and could reduce yield by as much as 85 per cent.

Even though plants older than 1 month old may not die from the attack, they usually suffer yield reductions of about 60–70 per cent (Battacharya and Rathore, 1977) with additional losses resulting from lodging (Battacharya and Rathore, 1980).

Control

Only the use of insecticides has provided any relief from *O. brevis* infestation. Endosulfan, dimethoate and methyl dymeton are currently recommended (Battacharya and Rathore, 1980).

Diptera

Among Diptera are only a few of the many different pests of soybean, but the species can be devastating because of the stages at which they attack the crop. By far, the most important pest of the early vegetative (seedling) phase of soybeans in Asia is the complex of agromyzid flies.

Similarly, because infestation of roots or planted seed can reduce plant stand establishment and nodulation (number and intensity), soil-inhabiting dipterans along with termites are probably the most damaging of the pests that live in the soil for all or most of their life cycle. Many other insect pests inhabit the soil, usually as pupae or hibernating forms, but cause damage only to above-ground plant parts.

AGROMYZIDAE

Agromyzid flies show a distinct preference for young seedlings (from a few days after emergence to 4 weeks old) and exhibit behavioural differences by species. According to Talekar (1987) there are eight known species, the most destructive being *Ophiomyia phaseoli* (Tryon), *Ophiomyia centrosematis* (de Meijere), *Melanagromyza sojae* (Zehntner), and *Melanagromyza dolichostigma* de Meijere.

The beanfly or stemfly has also been reported on soybean in Africa (Greathead, 1968; Spencer, 1973) where the main host plant appears to be *Phaseolus* bean (Greathead, 1968). It has not been reported from Latin America (Kogan and Turnipseed, 1987). Damage results from the activity of the larvae, which tunnel through foliar veins and other epidermal or cortical plant tissues.

The small, shiny blue-black adults of *O. phaseoli* lay up to 300 eggs during their life time on young leaves. They usually make many punctures but deposit eggs in only a few. After 2−4 days, larvae hatch and bore sideways beneath the epidermis into the nearest vein. They work their way into the stem through the petiole. By the second instar, larvae have begun to bore down the stem. Variations in the direction of initial larval movement have been reported (Greathead, 1968; Talekar, 1987), but the insect always ends up in the stem.

Feeding is on the cortical layers at ground level of young plants but may extend to other parts such as the taproot, killing the plant (Bhattacharya and Rathore, 1977; Talekar 1987). The larval period lasts about 10 days, and the pupal period about 6−7 days, depending on location and weather conditions (van der Goot, 1930; Hassan, 1947; Taylor, 1958; Greathead, 1968).

Before pupation, which usually takes place at ground level, the larva forms a thin semi-transparent 'window', which facilitates exit of the adult fly. A generation is completed at 21°C on potted plants in 27–31 days, followed by a 2-day pre-oviposition period (Greathead, 1968).

The life cycle of *M. sojae* differs from that of *O. phaseoli* only in the site where larval feeding takes place. The former feeds mostly in the inner cortex (pith), whereas *Ophiomyia* spp. appears to feed sub-epidermally.

Like *Ophiomyia* species, *Melanagromyza* species lay their eggs on leaves but, unlike their relatives in *Ophiomyia*, they prefer the underside of the leaf. *Melanagromyza sojae* deposits its eggs in the lower mesophyll, whereas *M. dolichostigma* does so on the pubescent undersurface of expanded leaves (Spencer, 1973).

Ophiomyia centrosematis lays its eggs in the hypocotyl and stem in East Africa (Greathead, 1968), but in Taiwan Lee (1976) reported having observed oviposition in leaf tissue. The locations of the observations are sufficiently dissimilar for the species to have evolved different behavioural patterns (May, 1958). Other differences have been reported from Asia (AVRDC, 1985). For example, *O. centrosematis* is said to pupate close to the surface of the leaf rather than forming a window for adult emergence. Details of the life cycles of the other species of beanflies can be found in Moutia (1945), Greathead (1968), Spencer (1959, 1961), Lee (1976) and Talekar (1987). Adults of all species feed on sap from leaves or cotyledons.

Characteristic signs of infestation include yellowing and wilting of the first leaves (Taylor, 1958), reduced vigour and capacity to accumulate dry matter (AVRDC, 1985), eventually leading to the drying of seedlings and the death of the plants.

Feeding punctures leave small yellowish spots on the leaves. Entire plantings can be destroyed in highly infested areas, such as Indonesia and Thailand (Sepswasdi, 1976). If plants survive the initial attack, their stems may rupture at ground level where they swell with the pressure of larvae and pupae (Taylor, 1958). In Africa, estimates of yield losses caused by agromyzids are more than 50 per cent for field beans (Taylor, 1958), and in Asia 31–72 per cent (Bhattacherjee, 1980; AVRDC, 1981). The host range of beanflies includes several wild leguminous plants, which are thought to serve as permanent reservoirs of the pest.

Control

Beanflies attack while the plant is becoming established, so good control of this pest is paramount. Although even 100 per cent infestation may not cause complete loss of yield, the level of control of beanflies often determines how much a crop will be worth.

Chemical: At present, chemicals are the most reliable method to control beanfly infestation, and in many instances insecticides are used as prophylaxis. Traditionally, botanicals, such as nicotine, and several inorganic products, such as arsenic and Bordeaux mixture, as well as oil sprays (van der Goot, 1930) were used. Then in the early part of this century a vast number of synthetic insecticides were introduced.

Organochlorides such as DDT dominated the picture but were eventually restricted and, in some cases, completely banned because of the hazards they posed to the environment. Later, seed treatments with dusts or emulsions of aldrin, dieldrin and endrin were reported to be effective (Taylor, 1959; Walker, 1960; Wikramasinghe and Fernando, 1962).

Present restrictions on the use of highly persistent organochlorides have left the control of beanflies to carbamates and organophosphates, which do not always provide satisfactory protection for the crop. However, applying systemic insecticides in furrows at, or soon after, planting has proved effective (Roongsook *et al.*, 1973; Hussein, 1978) as have foliar applications of monocrotophos, dimethoate and omethoate (500 g a.i./ha) at 3, 7, 14, 21 and 28 days post germination (AVRDC, 1985).

A sludge of endosulfan mixed with seed before planting has also shown promise in applications on *Phaseolus* beans in Zambia (Stuart Irwin, entomologist, formerly at Msekera Agricultural Research Station, Chipata, Zambia, 1987, personal communication), but the efficacy is dependent on the weather conditions. A recently introduced carbamate, carbosulfan, may provide good control of beanfly but poses a health hazard in areas where leaves are consumed (Jackai *et al.*, 1988). In many cases, germination is slightly impaired by seed dressings but the advantage from control of beanflies is undisputable (Walker, 1960).

Host-plant resistance: High levels of resistance to *M. sojae* have been identified in wild soybean (*Glycine soja*) germ plasm at AVRDC (Talekar, 1987), but attempts to transfer this resistance into agronomically acceptable genotypes have not been successful.

The backcrosses turned out to be susceptible, leading Talekar (1987) to conclude that the resistance was of no practical value. Ten *G. soja* and two *Neonotonia wightii* accessions exhibited good resistance to *M. sojae*, and IC 18734, an accession collected from Himachal Pradesh, India, has been reported as being resistant to *O. phaseoli* (Kundu and Goswani, 1985), but no accessions have yet been identified as resistant to the biotype of *O. phaseoli* that occurs in Indonesia.

Efforts at developing resistant varieties will probably continue and, with time, yield good results. Several sources of resistance have been reported for cowpea (IITA, 1986), and work on the identification of genetic resistance in *Phaseolus* sp. is well under way in the joint programme between Centro

Internacional de Agricultura Tropical and the Southern African Development Coordination Conference (SADCC) in that region.

The relative ease with which insecticides can be obtained and the ignorance of the identity of this species complex have combined to limit the progress in breeding for resistance, particularly in Africa.

Paradoxically, one of the most detailed studies on beanflies was that by Greathead (1968) conducted in Tanzania.

Natural enemies: In the absence of any good sources of resistance to beanfly, biological control is worth pursuing along the lines established by Greathead (1968) in East Africa and van der Goot (1930) in Indonesia.

High rates of parasitism among beanflies in East Africa were reported by Greathead (1968) and may account for differences in infestation among the countries. For example, in regions where beanfly occurs, the level of severity varies widely, with Zambia, Tanzania, Uganda and Ethiopia probably being the most infested countries and Rwanda, Zimbabwe and Kenya being much less so. Also, it is conceivable that parasite–predator activity has checked the expansion of beanfly across Africa. Clearly, the relationships between natural enemies and the beanfly are not well enough understood, as experiences to date have been mixed. Biological control was attempted without success on Madagascar and Mauritius but is reported to have been successfully deployed in Hawaii where the beanfly was accidentally introduced in the 1960s. *Opius melanagromyzae* and *O. importatus* were imported from Uganda (Davis, 1970) and apparently prevented build-up of beanfly.

Cultural: Traditional farming practices such as planting patterns, crop combinations and crop-residue management can contribute to cultural control of insect pests, but the effects of cultural control are not always, or easily, predictable, as the underlying principles involve rather complex interactions of biotic and abiotic factors (Jackai and Daoust, 1986).

In Java, intercropping of soybean with eggplant (*Solanum melongena*) and yambean (*Pachyrrhizus erosus*) reportedly reduced infestation by *O. phaseoli*, the scientist concluding that the cover provided by the companion crop partially hid the soybean and, therefore, made it less accessible to the insect (van der Goot, 1930). According to Talekar (1987), extensive field trials with 58 crops as companions to soybean at AVRDC (1981a,b) did not show any such effects on *M. sojae*.

Manipulating the date of planting introduces temporal asynchrony between insect and host plant and seems to reduce beanfly infestation on *Phaseolus* beans in Zambia (J. Kannaiyan and S. Sithanantham, pathologist and entomologist respectively, FAO Legume Project, Msekera Agricultural Research Station, Chipata, Zambia, 1988, personal communication).

However, socio-economic considerations and the exigencies of the weather often dictate what is planted, and when. Pest infestation has never been the deciding factor in agronomic practices among farmers.

ANTHOMYIIDAE

Kogan and Turnipseed (1987) have listed one dipteran seed pest of soybean, *Delia platura*, synonym *Hylemyia platura* (Meigen) — the seed corn maggot — which occurs in several parts of Asia, including India where it is classifies as a major pest, particularly in Delhi, Jabalpur, Pantnagar and Khasi Hills.

This pest appears to cut across climatic zones, having been reported in temperate (USA, China, Japan) as well as tropical countries.

Another species, *Hylemyia cilicrura*, also attacks germinated seeds and seedlings in India, and along with *D. platura*, has been recorded on plants in several families — pea, maize, onion, potato, curcubits, buckwheat, alfalfa, lima bean, and azuki bean.

The maggots of these species feed on seed embryos and reduce germination. Even if infested seeds germinate, they often cannot unfold the cotyledons above the ground and they die prematurely (Gujarati *et al.*, 1971). If opened, the cotyledons are partly eaten and turn brownish (Chaudhary *et al.*, 1976).

The adult is a small yellowish-grey fly, which shows increased activity before rain. Females lay elongated whitish eggs on, or near, the seeds. The eggs hatch within a week. Tiny whitish-yellow maggots with a pointed head, curved mandibles and a thick, rounded posterior feed singly or in groups inside the seed, which becomes swollen with moisture. Larvae (maggots) become fully grown within 2 weeks and pupate either in the damaged seed or in the soil. Pupae are red- to dark-brown. Adults emerge after 1 week, with the entire life cycle lasting 4—5 weeks.

Control

Chemical: Granular formulations have played a prominent role in the chemical control of the seed corn maggot. Carbofuran, disulfoton, carbaryl, trichlorphon, aldicarb and dimethoate are widely used at about 1.0 kg a.i./ha applied in the furrow at planting. Sometimes, emulsifiable concentrates of carbaryl, endosulfan, quinalphos and dimethoate are sprayed on the seed before the furrow is covered or before the seed is planted. Another option is to treat seed with carbofuran (Bhattacharya and Rathore, 1977). Most of these insecticides give satisfactory control and no adverse effect on seed germination has been detected. Gujarati *et al.* (1971) found phorate granules the most effective.

Host-plant resistance: A number of exotic soybean varieties have shown reduced damage by the seed corn maggot under Indian conditions — Merit, Clark 63, Adelphia, Harosoy-63 and Portage (Bhattacharya and Rathore, 1977). More emphasis is expected to be placed on varietal evaluation in areas where this pest is becoming serious. Screening is conducted after the seeds are planted: a portion of the furrow, about half a metre long, is opened and the seed examined for signs of infestation or damage. The variety Merit had an infestation level of about 16 per cent, whereas highly susceptible genotypes (e.g. Chippewa) suffered up to 41 per cent infestation.

PLATYSTOMATIDAE

Rivellia quadrifasciata (Macquart), the nodule fly, was first reported in the southern USA in 1975 (Eastman and Wuensche, 1977) on soybean and a *Rivellia* species may have been responsible for an infestation of soybean nodules observed in Niger Republic in Africa (Jackai *et al.*, 1985). Closely related species, *Rivellia apicallis* Hendel, *Rivellia basilaris* Wiedermann and *Rivellia angulata*, have been reported from a number of countries in Asia (Bhattacherjee, 1977; Kumar and Sithanantham, 1989).

The life cycle of *R. quadrifasciata* has not been fully studied; however Eastman (1980) has provided some basic information that should be useful in recognizing this insect and the damage it causes.

Eggs are about 1 mm long and shaped like rice grains. Larvae have posterior spiracles located on russet-coloured, sclerotized stigmatic plates with two thorn-shaped protuberances. Pupation takes place in the soil (Eastman and Wuensche, 1977). The adult is about 5 mm long and has wings marked with four black bands. The thorax is black, and the abdomen reddish-yellow (Namba, 1956).

The larvae consume the contents of soybean nodules and, hence, reduce the plant's capability to fix nitrogen (Newsom *et al.*, 1978) and its growth and seed yield.

Plants grown in sand or sandy loams seem to have higher infestation (Eastman, 1978), and this characteristic lends some support to the possibility that *Rivellia* sp. was responsible for damage of nodules in Niger where soils are of this type (Jackai *et al.*, 1985).

Hemiptera

In contrast to other cultivated legumes, soybean is attacked by few insects that damage solely the flowers. However, during the plant's reproductive phase it is liable to attack by pod pests. The two major orders encountered worldwide on soybean pods are Hemiptera and Lepidoptera. The hemipterans are mainly stink bugs: *Nezara viridula, Piezodorus* spp. and *Aspavia* sp. Others are *Riptortus* spp. (Alydidae), *Anoplocnemis curvipes* (Coreidae), etc.

Nezara viridula, the southern green stink bug, has been reported from Asia (Talekar, 1987); South America (Turnipseed and Kogan, 1987) and Africa (Jackai and Singh, 1987); the green stink bug, *Acrosternum* spp. from Africa, South America (Turnipseed and Kogan, 1976; Jackai and Singh, 1987); the brown stink bug, *Euschistus servus* and *E. heros* from Latin America (Kogan and Turnipseed, 1987); *Piezodorus guildinii* from Africa (Ezueh and Dina, 1979) and Latin America (Panizzi and Slansky, 1985a,b); and *Piezodorus hybneri, Riptortus linearis, R. clavatus*, and *R. dentipes* from Africa (Ezueh and Dina, 1979) and Asia (Talekar, 1987). *Megalotomus parvus* has been observed in Brazil (Panizzi, 1988a), and *Aspavia armigera* has been reported in Africa (Ezueh and Dina, 1979; Jackai and Singh, 1987). A wide range of other Hemiptera have been reported on soybean (Table 2.1); those considered important on more than a local scale are described in this chapter.

A careful look at the literature clearly indicates that *N. viridula* is the most cosmopolitan and economically most important species worldwide (Todd and Herzog, 1980; Panizzi and Slansky, 1985a; Todd, 1989). This is probably the reason that research on stink bugs is advanced, especially in the USA, Brazil and Japan. Nevertheless, these pests remain one of the most intractable and ricalcitrant problems in agriculture. They are found practically everywhere soybean is grown in both tropical and other regions. They insert their stylets (mouth parts) into developing pods and suck sap from the seeds. This injury results both in reduction (shrivelling, abortion) and deformation of seeds (Todd and Herzog, 1980). Feeding damage on the mature pods and seeds causes mainly a reduction in the quality of seed.

Besides robbing the plant of its juices, the stink bugs inject histolytic enzymes that are essential for their digestion of the food (Miner, 1966, 1972) and, during feeding, transfer pathogenic organisms (Daugherty *et al.*, 1964). It is the combination of these factors that results in the damage often associated with hemipteran pests.

In some regions, stink bugs and other Hemiptera cause extensive damage, with up to 60 per cent reduction in yields (Jackai *et al.*, 1985); more commonly, yield losses are in the range of 15−30 per cent (Daugherty *et al.*, 1964; Miner, 1966).

ALYDIDAE

Riptortus linearis is widespread in Asia where it probably is as important as *R. clavatus*, a closely related species. In Africa, *R. dentipes* has received some attention (Ezueh and Dina, 1979; Jackai *et al.*, 1985), with IITA (1988) documenting its dominance among (more than half of) the pod-sucking bugs occurring on soybean during both planting seasons in Gandajika, Zaire. *Riptortus linearis* is reported to attack soybean as well as some Solanaceae and Convolvulaceae (Talekar, 1987), laying eggs on the underside of leaves and on pods (Kalshoven, 1981). According to work done in Indonesia by Kalshoven (1981), it takes 3 weeks for nymphs to go through five instars, with an adult lifespan of 4–47 days (Tengkano and Soehardjan, 1985).

Damage by *Riptortus* species is generally considered to be more serious per unit time than that of other pod bugs. However, as far as can be ascertained from the literature, no work has been done to substantiate this allegation.

PENTATOMIDAE

The southern green stink bug, *N. viridula*, is probably the most studied pentatomid because of its worldwide distribution and importance as a pest of several crops. In fact, when people talk about 'stink bugs', they normally are referring to *N. viridula*. In Latin America, the southern green stink bug has been reported from Argentina (Bosq, 1937), Uruguay (Ruffinelli and Piran, 1959), Brazil (Lima, 1940; Corrêa-Ferreira *et al.*, 1977); in Africa it has been reported from Nigeria (Ezueh and Dina, 1979; Jackai *et al.*, 1985); Zaire (IITA, 1988); Zambia and Zimbabwe.

Talekar (1987) reported that it is the most important pod pest in Asia. Some workers believe that it originated in Southeast Asia because of the extreme variation in the species from that region (Yukawa and Kiritani, 1965; Kiritani, 1970). It could have spread on the wind to various countries (Distant, 1980), as it has been reported landing on ships close to mainlands (Asahina and Turuoka, 1970). According to Todd and Herzog (1980), the earliest report of *N. viridula* on soybean was by Hoffman (1935). Kiritani *et al.* (1965) listed 145 plant species in 32 families as being hosts of *N. viridula*. Other authors (Todd and Herzog, 1980) have given a list of host plants in 18 families with more than 40 plant species (Table 2.2).

The host range of this insect is obviously wider than has been reported, especially as many tropical host plants (particularly wild species) have not been adequately documented. Other lists of host plants are available from Brazil (Silva *et al.*, 1968) and Argentina (Rizzo, 1968). Leguminous species appear to be the preferred hosts. The phytophagous nature of stink bugs has been reviewed by Todd (1989), and the host range in the tropics is extremely wide, as the populations of the pest are not tempered by the effects of winter as they are in temperate climates.

Table 2.2. Host plants of hemipteran pests of soybean

Pest	Host plant		
	Family	Common name	Scientific name
Nezara viridula	Amaranthaceae	Amaranth	*Amaranthus* sp.
	Chenopodiaceae	Lambsquarter	*Chenopodium* sp.
	Compositae	Sunflower	*Helianthus annus*
	Cruciferae	Cabbage	*Brassica oleracea* capita
	Cruciferae	Cauliflower	*B. oleracea* var. botrytis
	Cruciferae	Collard	*B. oleracea* var. viridis
	Cruciferae	Mustard	*Brassica* sp.
	Cruciferae	Radish	*Raphanus sativus*
	Cruciferae	Turnip	*Brassica rapa*
	Cucurbitaceae	Cucumber	*Cucumis sativus*
	Cucurbitaceae	Squash	*Cucurbita* sp.
	Cyperaceae	Nutsedge	*Cyperus esculentus*
	Euphorbiaceae	Castor bean	*Ricinus communis*
	Gramineae	Corn	*Zea mays*
	Gramineae	Rice	*Oryza sativa*
	Gramineae	Sugar cane	*Saccharum officinarum*
	Gramineae	Wheat	*Triticum* sp.
	Juglandaceae	Pecan	*Carya illinoensis*
	Leguminosae	Bean	*Phaseolus* sp.
	Papilionaceae	Beggarweed	*Desmodium* sp.
	Papilionaceae	Clover	*Trifolium* sp.
	Papilionaceae	Cowpea	*Vigna unguiculata*
	Papilionaceae	Crotalaria	*Crotalaria* sp.
	Papilionaceae	Peanut	*Arachis hypogaea*
	Papilionaceae	Peas	*Pisum sativum*
	Malvaceae	Cotton	*Gossypium hirsutum*
	Malvaceae	Okra	*Abelmoschus esculentus*
	Passifloraceae	Passion flower	*Passiflora incarinata*
	Phytolaccaceae	Pokeweed	*Phytolacca decandra*
	Polygonaceae	Sorrel	*Rumex* sp.
	Rosaceae	Peach	*Prunus persias*
	Rosaceae	Blackberry	*Rubus* sp.
	Rosaceae	Wild plum	*Prunus* sp.
	Rutaceae	Grapefruit	*Citrus paradisi*
	Rutaceae	Lemon	*C. limon*
	Rutaceae	Lime	*C. aurantifolia*
	Rutaceae	Orange	*Citrus* sp.
	Solanaceae	Eggplant	*Solanum melongena*

Pest	Host plant		
	Family	Common name	Scientific name
N. viridula	Solanaceae	Pepper	*Capsicum* sp.
	Solanaceae	Potato	*Solanum tuberosum*
	Solanaceae	Tobacco	*Nicotiana tabacum*
	Solanaceae	Tomato	*Lycopersicum esculentum*
	Vitaceae	Wild grape	*Vitis* sp.
	Lauraceae	Cassia	*Cassia* sp.
Piezodorus guildinii	Leguminosae	Alfalfa	*Medicago sativa*
	Leguminosae	Green bean	*Phaseolus vulgaris*
	Leguminosae	Crotalaria	*Crotalaria lanceolata*
	Leguminosae	Peanut	*Arachis hypogaea*
	Leguminosae	Cowpea	*Vigna unguiculata*
	Leguminosae	Indigo	*Indigofera* spp.
Euschistus heros	Leguminosae	Bean	*Phaseolus* sp.
	Euphorbiaceae	Wild poin-settia	*Aeschynomere rudis* *Euphorbia heterophylla*
Riptortus linearis	Solanaceae	Eggplant	*Solanum melongena*
	Solanaceae	Tobacco	*Nicotiana tabacum*
Aspavia armigera	Leguminosae	Cowpea	*Vigna unguiculata*
	Gramineae	Rice	*Oryza sativa*
Acrosternum sp.	Leguminosae	Cowpea	*Vigna unguiculata*
	Gramineae	Rice	*Oryza sativa*

Besides various legumes (soybean, cowpea, *Crotalaria*, cassia), corn, rice, citrus, turnip, beet, raddish, tobacco, numerous weeds, coffee, senna and okra have been reported as hosts (Drake, 1920; Todd and Herzog, 1980; Jones and Sullivan, 1982; Hammond, 1983; Negron and Riley, 1987) (Table 2.2). These other hosts enable the pest to survive when soybean is not available for colonization.

Stink bug damage is similar across species; differences result only from possibly the range and the nature of the histolytic enzymes present in the saliva of the insects (Miles, 1972). As the severity of damage by stink bug increases, qualitative changes in soybean oil are observed. Linoleic, palmitic, stearic and oleic acids increase whereas linolenic acid decreases (Todd *et al.*,

1973). Protein content increases and oil content decreases (Miner, 1961, 1966).

The life cycle of *N. viridula* has been studied in environments around the world, and differences are minor. Adults mate soon after emergence and become sexually mature shortly thereafter. The female begins egg-laying about 3 weeks after emergence, depositing the eggs in tight, regularly shaped clusters that are firmly glued together. She lays about 4–6 egg masses, each consisting of 42–113 eggs (Singh, 1973). Incubation takes 4–6 days, with eggs becoming deep yellow and eventually bright orange at eclosion (Todd, 1989). Newly hatched nymphs tend to remain aggregated and on their egg shells. No feeding takes place during this instar (Bowling, 1980). Hatching and moulting seem to be highly synchronized during this stage (Lockwood and Story, 1986). The nymphs move away from the egg shells during the second instar; they, however, remain strongly aggregated on the fruiting structures of the soybean plant. The second instar accounts for the highest nymphal mortality (Panizzi and Rossini, 1987) and is the stage at which feeding begins. During this stage the extent to which the nymphs disperse depends on the availability of food. Sometimes, the nymphs form smaller clusters. Pre-imaginal dispersal peaks during the fourth and fifth instars, when the stink bug population spreads by walking (Panizzi *et al.*, 1980; Schumann and Todd, 1982).

Mortality is again quite high during the fifth and final instar, especially as the insect moults into an adult. All stink bug species have five instars (Todd and Herzog, 1980). Keys to *N. viridula* and *N. antennata* and descriptions of various instars have been provided by Kobayashi (1959). Male and female adults look alike, but females are slightly bigger. The females also feed more than males do because they have a higher nutritional requirement (for reproduction) (Lockwood and Story, 1986). For the same reason, the nutritional status of the last nymphal stadium is critical (Todd, 1989).

Under most conditions, development of *N. viridula* takes 21–27 days on most legumes, and the life cycle is completed in about 63 days (Singh, 1973; Harris and Todd, 1980; Konje, 1988). The time increases with decreases in temperature, and the rate of development is affected by aggregation, as is the mortality (Kiritani, 1964; Kiritani and Kimura, 1965, 1966). Aggregation appears to provide some protection from predators (Lockwood and Story, 1986).

Other pod-sucking pentatomids associated with soybean include the stink bugs *Piezodorus hybneri* in Asia, *Piezodorus guildinii* in the Americas and Africa; *Euschistus heros* occurring in South America and possibly in Central America (Panama) (Rolston, 1974). In Africa *Aspavia armigera*, *Aspavia* spp. and *Acrosternum* sp. have been reported on soybeans (Ezueh and Dina, 1979; Jackai and Singh, 1987). All of these genera contribute substantially to the losses.

Piezodorus guildinii has been expanding its focus and increasing in importance during the last decade and a half. In South America, it is considered the most widely distributed species on soybean.

In Colombia and Peru, it is the commonest pentatomid species (Waldbauer, 1977; Irwin *et al.*, 1981), and in Argentina it is an important pest of alfalfa (Fraga and Ochoa, 1972).

Piezodorus guildinii is a neotropical pentatomid found from the southern USA to Argentina. It has been reported also from Africa where it occurs mainly during periods of reduced rainfall.

The pest has a wide host range, about 40 plant species so far reported (Panizzi and Slansky, 1985a). Its preference, however, is for legumes, and wild leguminous species serve as hosts when crops are not available (Hallman, 1979; Panizzi and Slansky, 1985b); soybean, alfalfa and bean (*Phaseolus vulgaris*) seem to be the preferred cultivated plants.

Damage to the crop by *P. guildinii* is similar to that by *N. viridula*. Nymphs aggregate on, or near, egg shells, and early instars are strongly gregarious, dispersing as they get older (Panizzi *et al.*, 1980). *Piezodorus guildinii* is more mobile than *N. viridula*, and females of both species disperse farther than males in soybean fields (Costa and Link, 1982). Characteristics of nymphs and adults of *P. guildinii* have been described and illustrated by Fraga and Ochoa (1972); Galileo *et al.*, (1977) and Grazia *et al.*, (1980), working in South America. No biological studies of *P. guildinii* on soybeans in Africa have been published, but the insect is important.

Piezodorus hybneri has been reported from Asia in Thailand, Korea, Taiwan and Japan but is thought to be less important than other stink bug species. Satayavirut (1981) reported that the females lay cylindrical eggs in double rows on leaves. After 4 days (20°C; 70 per cent RH), the eggs hatch into nymphs that go through five instars of about 18 days. The same author reported that adults live an average 32 days and lay 207 eggs in Thailand.

Euschistus heros occurs in several countries of South America and in Panama (Rolston, 1974). In Brazil, it is the third most important member of the complex of pentatomid pests (Panizzi, 1985). However, the host range of *E. heros* appears to be more restricted than that of the other pentatomids.

Common bean, *Aeschynomere rudis* and soybean appear to be the principal hosts; however, the insect has recently been reported to feed and reproduce on a weed (*Euphorbia heterophylla*) common in soybean fields in certain areas (A. R. Panizzi, 1988, unpublished). Information on its biology under field and laboratory conditions is available (Grazia *et al.*, 1980; Villas Bôas and Panizzi, 1980) despite the limited attention accorded to it in the past.

Aspavia armigera is important only in Africa where it has been reported to occur in the east–central and western regions (Jackai and Singh, 1987). It is often one of the early colonizers of soybean fields but is soon outnumbered by other stink bugs and by alydids, e.g. *R. dentipes*. Not much research has been conducted on this pest because of its lesser importance on major crops. It feeds and reproduces on soybean, cowpea and rice (Olagbaju, 1988).

Aspavia armigera causes damage similar to that caused by *N. viridula* and other members of the pod-sucking bug complex, and exclusion studies conducted in the laboratory at IITA show that it can cause substantial damage at high populations (Konje, 1988). Other studies in Nigeria have shown that *A. armigera* prefers the humid forest zones where it occurs with *N. viridula* and *Acrosternum* sp. It seems to be replaced by *P. guildinii* in the guinea savanna (IITA, 1983).

Eggs are oval and are laid singly on different parts of the soybean plant. In the laboratory, the pest prefers cottonwool or gauze for oviposition. On cowpea, incubation lasts about 5 days, and there are five nymphal instars that total 18−25 days (Olagbaju, 1988).

No biological studies have been conducted on soybean, but results would probably be similar.

Using museum specimens, IITA scientists have reported three different morphological forms, some of which may be different species, although this has not been verified.

Aspavia acuminata Montadon has three predominant dorsal spots and thoracic spines pointed dorso-anteriorly; *Aspavia acuminata* sp. nr. *albidomaculatus* looks like *A. acuminata* but is larger and has stiffer spines that are curved slightly dorso-posteriorly.

The commonest form is *A. armigera*, which has the 'standard' spine structure − straight and pointed laterally − from which others are thought to have deviated.

A lot of work has been done on the nature of damage caused by Hemiptera found on soybean, particularly *N. viridula*. Several workers (e.g., Daugherty *et al.*, 1964; Miner and Wilson, 1966) have shown that damaged seeds contain less oil and more protein and fat than intact seeds.

The insects inject hystolytic enzymes when they penetrate the pod with their stylet (Miner, 1966), and the enzymes liquefy the seed contents, enabling the insects to feed.

Procedures for rearing a number of these species on dry seeds in the laboratory have been developed (Corrêa-Ferreira, 1985; Jackai, 1989).

Overall seed damage by Hemiptera is generally correlated to the number of punctures (Jackai, 1984), but Jensen and Newsom (1972) have pointed out that the location of punctures is more important than the numbers.

For example, a puncture in the radicle−hypocotyl axis prevents germination even though several punctures elsewhere on the seed may not even affect germination. Any damage to seeds greatly reduces their aesthetic value and consequently their marketability. The effects on nutritional, agronomic (seed viability) and economic (marketing) characteristics are all closely associated, making hemipteran damage particularly important.

Control

Chemical: The commonest approach to control of stink bugs is chemical sprays, and it is also generally the most efficacious. However, it does not have to be the only approach. Difficulty in the control of *N. viridula* lies mainly in the wide host range of this insect, and spraying targeted only at the desired crop often has to be repeated to kill new colonizing adults.

In Asia where the stink bug is an acute problem, insecticides recommended include DDT (May, 1958), even though various tests have found it no longer effective (Mitchell, 1965; Miyazaki and Sherman, 1966; Swaine, 1969). Apparently the insect developed resistance to DDT as was shown in Hawaii (Miyazaki and Sherman, 1966). Other organochlorides found effective in Asia include gamma BHC and dieldrin; in Africa endosulfan has been used with good results (IITA, 1982).

Among organophosphates, methyl parathion is recommended for use in Brazil (Corseuil *et al.,* 1974); in West Africa monocrotophos and dimethoate are used and, more commonly, a mixture of dimethoate and cypermethrin (Sherpa Plus®), which was developed for use on cowpea, has proved effective against stink bugs and defoliators on soybean. Other groups of insecticides such as carbamates and synthetic pyrethroids on their own have been reported to give good results (Table 2.3) in some countries (Mitchell, 1965; Swaine, 1969; AVRDC, 1982). Control of *P. guildinii, E. heros, Riptortus* spp., *A. armigera* and others is similar to that for *N. viridula* (Corseuil *et al.,* 1974). However, in Brazil, *P. guildinii* is known to be more susceptible to carbaryl than to methyl parathion, while the reverse is true for *N. viridula*. Endosulfan effectively controls both species (Gazzoni, 1978). Differential susceptibility to insecticides may also exist for other species.

Biological: Like other arthropod pests, the pentatomids have their share of natural adversaries that constrain population expansion, with both insects and diseases playing some role in biological control. Other animal taxa (e.g. reptiles, birds and mammals) also have contributory roles (Slansky and Panizzi, 1987; Panizzi and Rossini, 1987). Several programmes on the control of *N. viridula* with parasitoids have been labelled as successes (DeBach, 1962; Clausen, 1978; Caltagirone, 1981), and as many as 52 parasitoids have been recorded from *N. viridula* (Jones, 1988), although many may have been incidental (Table 2.4). The parasitoids used most successfully in the control of *N. viridula* have been those that attack eggs, *Trissolcus basalis* and *Telenomus mormideae* (Figure 2.1) (Corrêa-Ferreira, 1986; Todd, 1989).

Table 2.3. Insecticides currently being used to control insect pests of soybean

Insect	Insecticide	Dosage (g a.i./ha)
Beanflies (*Ophiomyia phaseoli, O. centrosematis, Melanagromyza sojae, M. dolichostigma*)	Aldrin[a]	-[b]
	Dieldrin[a]	-[b]
	Endrin[a]	-[b]
	Chlordane[a]	-[b]
	Dimethoate	500
	Omethoate	500
Leafhoppers (*A. biguttula, E. kerri, E. christiani, E. dolichi, E. signata, Asymmetrasca decedens*)	Toxaphene[a]	400
	Carbofuran	400
	Carbaryl	-[b]
Elasmopalpus lignosellus	Carbofuran	-[b]
	Carbosulfan	-[b]
	Diazinon	-[b]
Epinotia aporema, Cydia fabivora	Monocrotophos	400
	Chlorpyrifos-ethyl	-[b]
Pseudoplusia includens	Methomyl	500
	Monocrotophos	500
Semiloopers (*Trysanoplusia arichalcea, Chrysodeixis chalcites, C. acuta*)	Trichlorphon	500
	Endosulfan	750
	Fenvalerate	100
	Cypermethrin	150
Spodoptera sp.	Endosulfan	750
	Cypermethrin +	50 +
	dimethoate	250
Stink bugs (*Nezara viridula, Piezodorus guildinii, Euschistus heros*)	Carbaryl[c]	800
	Endosulfan[d]	437
	Fentrothion	500
	Phosphamidon	600
	Metamidophos[d]	300
	Methyl parathion[e]	480
	Trichlorphon	750
	Gamma BHC[a]	-[b]
	Dieldrin[a]	-[b]
	Endosulfan	750
	Cypermethrin +	35 +
	dimethoate	250

Table 2.3 continued

Insect	Insecticide	Dosage (g a.i./ha)
Heliothis spp.	Methomyl	500
	Methyl parathion[f]	750
	Carbaryl	500
H. armigera	Cypermethrin	100
Etiella zinckenella	Carbaryl	-[b]
	Azinphosmethyl	-[b]
	Mexacarbate	-[b]
	Triazophos	-[b]
	Fenvalerate	100
	Quinalphos	400
Cydia ptychora	Dimethoate	400
	Phosphamidon	-[b]
	Chlorpyrifos-ethyl	-[b]
	Methomyl	500
Delia platura, Hylemyia cilicrura	Carbofuran	100
	Disulfoton	1000
	Carbaryl	1000
	Trichlorfon	1000
	Aldicarb	1000
	Dimethoate	1000
	Quinalphos	30
Anticarsia gemmatalis	*Baculovirus anticarsia*	50[g]
	Bacillus thuringiensis	500[h]
	Carbaryl	192
	Diflubenzuron	15
	Endosulfan	175
	Prophenophos	100
	Thiodicarbe	70
	Trichlorfon	400
Pseudoplusia includens	Carbaryl	320
	Endosulfan	437
	Methyl parathion	300
	Chlorpyrifos-ethyl	-[b]
E. aporema	Metamidophos	300
	Methyl parathion	480

a Use of this insecticide has been banned in Brazil.
[b]Highly variable rates of application.
[c]Recommended for *P. guildinii* only.
[d]Recommended for *N. viridula* and *P. guildinii*.
[e]Recommended for *N. viridula* and *E. heros*.
[f]Most effective for *H. zea*.
[g]50 larval equivalent.
[h]Dosage of the commercial product with 16.109 IU (international units).

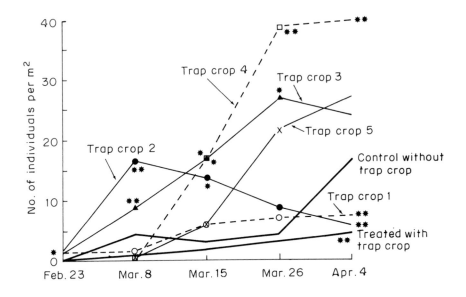

Figure 2.1. Effects of parasitoids on stink bugs with and without a trap crop.

Also, dramatic results have been obtained with parasites especially the tachinid flies *Trichopoda pennipes* and *Trichopoda pilipes*. In Brazil, the commonest tachinid in soybean fields is *Eutrichopodopsis nitens*; in Argentina, *Trichopoda giacomellii*, *T. gustavoi*, and *T. nigrifrontalis*; in Uruguay, *Trichopoda* spp. and in Chile, *Ectophasiopsis arcuata* (Jones, 1988). *Trissolcus basalis* is probably the most important parasitoid associated with *N. viridula*.

According to a recent review of parasitoids of *N. viridula* (Jones, 1988), early nymphal stages of the pest are generally not heavily attacked by parasitoids, but the last two instars are vulnerable to *Trichopoda* spp. Jones (1988) listed 13 species of tachinids that attack adult *N. viridula*.

In Africa, little work has been done on the biological control of *N. viridula*, but one of us (L.E.N.J.) has observed egg parasites at several locations (Jackai, unpublished). Natural enemies are believed to contribute toward keeping the *N. viridula* populations low in the savanna of Nigeria where soybean is cultivated. In support of this belief, experiments conducted in Zaria, northern Nigeria, showed no yield differences between insecticide-protected and unprotected plots.

Table 2.4. Entomopathogens, parasites and predators of the major pests of soybean in the tropics

Host ORDER/species	Stage attacked	Parasites, predators, entomopathogens		
		Order	Family	Species
COLEOPTERA				
Cerotoma sp.	Adult beetles	Moniliales	Moniliaceae	*Beauveria bassiana*[a]
Diabrotica sp.	Adult beetles	Moniliales	Moniliaceae	*B. bassiana*
DIPTERA				
M. phaseoli	Larvae	Hymenoptera	Pteromalidae	*Chlorocytes* sp.
M. sojae	Pupae	Hymenoptera	Pteromalidae	*Sphegigaster brevicornis, S. longicornis*
O. phaseoli	Larvae	Hymenoptera	Eulophidae	*Tetrastichus* sp.
	Larvae	Hymenoptera	Braconidae	*Opius melanagromyzae, O. importatus*
HEMIPTERA				
Acrosternum sp.	Eggs	Hymenoptera	Scelionidae	*Telenomus mormideae*
E. heros	Eggs	Diptera	Tachinidae	*Trissolcus basalis, T. scuticarinatus, Neorileya* sp.
	Eggs	Hymenoptera	Encyrtidae	*Ooencyrtus* sp.
	Eggs	Hymenoptera	Scelionidae	*T. mormidaeae, Telenomus* sp.
N. viridula	Eggs	Hymenoptera	Formicidae	*Solenopsis invicta*
	Eggs	Hymenoptera	Sclenopidae	*T. basalis, T. brochymenae, T. hullensis, T. scuticarinatus, Neorileya* sp.
	Adult flies	Diptera	Tachinidae	*Trichopoda pilipes, T. pennipes, Eutrichopodopsis nitens*
	Last 2 larval instars	Diptera	Tachinidae	*Trichopoda giacomellii, T. gustavoi*
	Eggs	Hymenoptera	Encyrtidae	*Amyotea malabarica, Ectophasiopsis arcuata, Ooencyrtus submetallicus*

Parasites, predators, entomopathogens

Host ORDER/species	Stage attacked	Order	Family	Species
N. viridula	Eggs	Hymenoptera	Scelionidae	*Telenomus podisi, T. mormideae*
P. guildinii	Eggs	Hymenoptera	Scelionidae	*T. basalis*
	Adults	Diptera	Tachinidae	*E. niens*
	Nymphs	Hemiptera	Pentatomidae	*Tynacantha marginata*
	Larvae	Hymenoptera	Encyrtidae	*Litomastix truncatellus*
	Eggs	Hymenoptera	Scelionidae	*Telenomus* sp. *T. mormideae*
HOMOPTERA				
E. kerri	Eggs	Moniliales	Moniliaceae	*Hirsutella guyana*[a]
LEPIDOPTERA				
A. gemmatalis	3rd instar larvae	Coleoptera	Carabidae	*Callida* sp., *Calosoma argentatus, Lebia* sp.
	Larvae	Diptera	Tachinidae	*Jurinella salla, Patelloa similis, Euphorocera* sp.
	Larvae	Hemiptera	Lygaeidae	*Geocoris* sp.
	Larvae	Hemiptera	Ichneumonidae	*Euphoropsis perdistinctus, Microcharops bimaculata*
	Larvae	Hemiptera	Nabididae	*Nabis* sp.
	Larvae	Hemiptera	Pentatomidae	*Podisus* sp., *Podisus nigrispinus, T. marginata*
	Eggs	Hymenoptera	Trichogram-matidae	*Trichogramma pretiosum*
	Larvae	Moniliales	Moniliaceae	*Nomuraea rileyi, Entomophthora* sp. [a]
C. acuta	Larvae	Hemiptera	Nabididae	*Nabis* sp.
	Larvae	Hymenoptera	Braconidae	*Apanteles* sp. nr. *inctusus*
	Eggs	Hymenoptera	Chalcidae	*Brachymeria* sp.
	Larvae	Hymenoptera	Eulophidae	*Euplectrus chapadae, E. epiplemae*

Table 2.4 Continued

| | | Parasites, predators, entomopathogens | | |
Host ORDER/species	Stage attacked	Order	Family	Species
C. ptychora	Larvae	Hymenoptera	Braconidae	Apanteles sp., Braunsia sp., Phanerotoma sp.
S. obliqua	Larvae	Hemiptera	Pentatomidae	Cantheconidae furcellata
Epinotia aporema	Eggs, larvae	Hymenoptera	Braconidae	Apanteles sp.
	Larvae	Diptera	Tachinidae	Nemorilla ruficornis
	Larvae	Hymenoptera	Braconidae	Agathis sp., Chelonus sp.
E. zinckenella	Eggs	Hymenoptera	Trichogrammatidae	Philomacroploea pleuralio
H. indicata	Eggs	Diptera	Tachinidae	P. similis, Hemisturmia carcelioides
	Larvae	Diptera	Tachinidae	N. ruficornis
	Larvae	Hymenoptera	Braconidae	Agathis sp., Bracon hellulas, Macrocentrus sp.
	Larvae/pupae	Hymenoptera	Chalcididae	Brachymeria sp., Spilochalcis sp.
	Larvae	Hymenoptera	Ichneumonidae	Eiphosoma minense, Pimpla golbachi
H. armigera	Larvae	Coleoptera	Coccinellidae	Coccinella sp.
	Larvae	Diptera	Tachinidae	E. perdistinctus
	Eggs, larvae	Diptera	Tachinidae	Carcelia sp., Eriborus sp., Exorista fallax, Palexorista laxa
	Larvae	Hemiptera	Anthocoridae	Orius sp.
	Larvae	Hemiptera	Pentatomidae	Podisus maculiventris
	Larvae	Hemiptera	Reduviidae	Sycanus indagator
	Eggs, larvae	Hymenoptera	Braconidae	Apanteles sauros, Bracon brevicornis, Chelonus inanitus,
	Eggs, larvae	Hymenoptera	Braconidae	Microplitis demolitor, M. rufiventris
	Eggs	Hymenoptera	Trichogrammatidae	Trichogramma sp.
	Eggs, larvae	Neuroptera	Chrysopidae	Chrysopa carnea
M. testulalis	Larvae	Hymenoptera	Braconidae	Apanteles sp., Braunsia sp., Phanerotoma sp.

Parasites, predators, entomopathogens

Host ORDER/species	Stage attacked	Order	Family	Species
S. exigua	Larvae	Hymenoptera	Braconidae	Zela sp.
	Larvae	Hymenoptera	Eurytomidae	Eurytoma sp.
	Larvae, pupae	Hymenoptera	Ichneumonidae	E. perdistinctus
S. litura	Eggs, larvae	Coleoptera	Carabidae	Calosoma chlorostictum
	Eggs	Coleoptera	Staphylinidae	Paederus alfierii, Peritus sp.
	Larvae	Diptera	Tachinidae	Actia palpalis, A. nigritula, Trachina larvarum
	Larvae	Hemiptera	Anthocoridae	Orius albidipennis
	Eggs	Hemiptera	Anthocordiae	Orius laevigatus
	Larvae	Hymenoptera	Braconidae	Apanteles sp., Zela chlorophthalina, Z. nigricornis
	Pupae	Hymenoptera	Chalcididae	Chonomorium eremita
	Larvae	Hymenoptera	Ichneumonidae	Eulimnerium xanthostoma
	Eggs	Hymenoptera	Scelionidae	Telenomus hawaii, T. spodoptera
	Eggs	Hymenoptera	Trichogrammatidae	Trichogramma evanescens, T. minutum, T. spodoptera
	Eggs, larvae	Neuroptera	Chrysopidae	Chrysopa vulgaris
	Eggs, larvae	Neuroptera	Chrysopidae	Helicomitus festivus
S. latifascia	Larvae	Diptera	Tachinidae	P. similis
	Larvae	Hymenoptera	Ichneumonidae	M. bimaculata

A number of reports have shown that insecticides are not essential for control of stink bugs in most countries of Africa and Asia, and biological control should be pursued. For example, in Hawaii, *N. viridula* was controlled by natural enemies imported from other countries — *T. basalis* from Australia and *T. pennipes* from the West Indies (Davis, 1961, 1967; Davis and Krauss, 1963).

Predators do not seem to be as important as parasitoids in regulating populations of *N. viridula*. However, egg and nymphal predators have been identified by Ragsdale *et al.* (1979) using enzyme-linked immunosorbent assays (ELISA), and reports from Louisiana, USA, showed that insects and spiders in 6 orders and 19 families preyed on *N. viridula* (Stam, 1978; Stam *et al.*, 1987). *Solenopsis invicta* was cited as the most important egg predator during the vegetative stages of soybean, grasshoppers becoming important during the reproductive phase. Even though these predators are nonspecific in their food habits, they can contribute much to control.

In India, a predatory bug, *Amyotea malabarica* (Fab.) has been observed on nymphs and adults of *N. viridula* (Singh, 1973), but key-factor analysis has shown that parasitism at the egg stage accounts for the majority of total mortality of *N. viridula* from the egg to the third-instar stage (Kiritani, 1964, 1965).

The use of entomopathogens in the control of *N. viridula* appears to have reasonable potential but has not been systematically evaluated. Diseases caused by *Beauveria bassiana*, *Metarrhizium anisopliae* and *Entomophthora* sp. have been recorded among several hemipteran pests of soybeans in Latin America (Panizzi and Slansky, 1985a). Use of such agents for control of stink bugs deserves to be investigated more widely in future.

Host-plant resistance: The potential for genetic resistance to stink bugs, particularly the southern green stink bug, has received much attention over the years (Jones and Sullivan, 1979; Gilman, *et al.*, 1982). The results of research have not been commensurate with the effort, mainly because stink bugs have a wide host range and their nutritional ecology makes them elusive.

Low levels of resistance were reportedly found in a number of plant introductions (PI) in the USA after extensive germ plasm screening (Turnipseed and Sullivan, 1976; Hartwig and Kilen, 1989): PI 171451, PI 227687 and PI 229358. A breeding line, ED 73-371, has also been reported as having a low level of resistance.

The stink bug exhibited relatively high mortality, protracted pre-imaginal development and low weight gain on the resistant cultivars compared with performance on commercial varieties (Jones and Sullivan, 1978). PI 227687 showed resistance to *N. viridula* and other stink bugs in tests conducted in Nigeria (IITA, 1981) and Taiwan (AVRDC, 1984).

Recently, PI 171444 has been shown to possess higher levels of resistance to *N. viridula* than have been described for other genotypes (Gilman *et al.*, 1982; Kester *et al.*, 1984; IITA, 1988). This accession has also shown resistance to *R. clavatus* in Asia (Talekar, 1987).

Moderate levels of field resistance to *N. viridula* have been reported for a few soybean breeding lines in Nigeria (Jackai *et al.*, 1988) — probably phenetic resistance (Norris and Kogan, 1980) as well as antixenosis and host-evasion particularly in early maturing genotypes. Kester *et al.* (1984) have suggested these factors as an explanation for the field resistance of PI 229358.

In addition, workers in Brazil have reported that Chi-Kei, n. IB and IAC 74-2832 suffer little seed damage (Panizzi *et al.*, 1981) from stink bug, the amount of damage appearing to be inversely related to seed number. As the number of seeds damaged per day by hemipterans is relatively constant, genotypes with a greater number of pods and, therefore, seeds per plant generally suffer less overall seed damage (Panizzi *et al.*, 1986).

These findings are in line with results from a programme on small-seeded soybean in São Paulo State of Brazil (Rosseto *et al.*, 1981, 1986, 1989; Lourenção and Miranda, 1987), although not all genotypes with large seeds (and therefore fewer pods and seeds per plant) necessarily suffer higher levels of damage than do small-seeded ones. Other characters such as pod-wall thickness may confer resistance to *N. viridula* and other hemipteran pod pests.

Little is known about host-plant resistance to the 'lesser' Hemiptera — for reasons related to economics. Presumably, with increased interest in trying to study the dynamics of the overall cropping system and with better understanding of the complex interrelationships among pests and the ecosystem, more attention will be given to this group in future.

Cultural: A variety of agronomic manipulations (or cultural practices) are known to alter the population profiles of stink bugs in several ways, although they may not reduce populations below damage thresholds (Glass, 1975). Cultural control, in general, causes no undesirable ecological consequences and is highly compatible with other pest-control tactics.

Soybean producers have manipulated date of planting and have used trap cropping (a variant of sorts of intercropping) with some success in a number of countries. Modifying the date of planting creates temporal asynchrony between insect pest and host plant, as does the use of early maturing (or in some instances late maturing) varieties.

The use of early maturing cultivars in Brazilian agriculture has been intensified recently as a means to escape stink bug infestation (Kobayashi and Cosenza, 1987). The amount of insecticide use has dropped as a result (Panizzi, 1985).

Planting soybean early has been shown to limit damage by stink bugs in Paraná state, Brazil (Panizzi *et al.*, 1979), but Schumann and Todd (1982) reported no significant differences between yields from soybean planted early and late. The reports are a reminder that many factors affect performance of a cultivar, including the type and relative abundance of wild hosts in the vicinity.

Trap crops have been tested in the management of stink bugs on soybean and have proved effective when their use is synchronized across a region or locality. Two generalized models for successful trapping have been suggested elsewhere (Jackai, 1983):

- In model 1, both the trap and the main crops are almost equally attractive to the pest, and the trap crop is planted so that it matures first.

- In model 2, the trap crop is distinctly more attractive to the pest than is the main crop and is planted so that it matures at the same time as the main crop, serving as a preferred host.

In both models, the pest is killed on the trap crop by insecticides or, if possible, by mechanisms inherent in the trap crop such as allelochemicals. In most trap cropping attempted to date, the insecticides were sprayed only on the trap (Figure 2.2) (Panizzi, 1980a; IITA, 1982; Kobayashi and Cosenza, 1987).

Trap cropping may not be appropriate for use by smallholders (Jackai, 1983) but seems promising for medium- to large-scale growers.

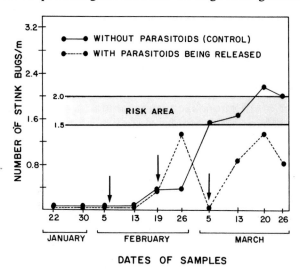

Figure 2.2. Numbers of stink bugs on soybean used as a trap crop on the margins of a main soybean crop; the count was taken just before the trap crop was sprayed (from Corrêa-Ferreira, 1986).

Recently, Kobayashi and Cosenza (1987) showed that stink bugs (particularly *N. viridula*) tend to maintain the highest densities of their population 4–5 m away from the border of a soybean field (towards the centre) and that this knowledge, coupled with an understanding of the plant age at which infestation occurred, could be used to render trap crops more appropriate and successful. They planted about 5 per cent of a soybean field with a suitable trap (a soybean variety) along the marginal areas and sprayed it whenever the stink bug population exceeded the threshold that the trap crop could support. In this configuration, the main crop, variety Cristalina, suffered about 29 per cent seed damage compared with 40 per cent without the trap crop. Similarly, in an earlier study conducted in Nigeria, a trap crop formed 10–20 per cent of the soybean field and, when sprayed with endosulfan, controlled stink bugs quite well, the main crop giving grain yields superior to those from unprotected soybean and similar to those from a fully protected monocrop (IITA, 1981). The researchers who carried out the study did not, however, attempt to understand the colonization pattern (horizontal distribution in the field) or time of colonization *vis-à-vis* the crop phenology.

Homoptera

CICADELLIDAE

Leafhoppers may be found on soybean leaves as long as these structures remain green; when they attack during the early vegetative stage of the plant, they can be particularly devastating. The damage they do can generally be recognized by the presence of browning on the leaf margins followed by 'cupping' (i.e. upward and inward curving) and 'blistering' of the leaves. The disease-like appearance is referred to as hopperburn; it can result in drying and eventually death of the leaves (Smith and Poos, 1931). Heavy infestations can stunt growth and even kill the plants (Ogunlana and Pedigo, 1974a), but usually these insects do not cause economic damage (Ogunlana and Pedigo, 1974b; Turnipseed and Kogan, 1976).

The host range of leafhoppers appears to be vast; Kogan *et al.* (1980) gave an account of the most commonly reported host plants and their associated species in North America where such studies have been extensive. Elsewhere, little systematic work has been conducted. In Africa and South America, the genus *Empoasca* is predominant, and *Empoasca kerri* has been reported from India (Saxena, 1978), but in Southeast Asia the predominant species seems to be *Amrasca biguttula*, which appears to attack all cultivated legumes (Litsinger *et al.*, 1978). *Empoasca christiani* and to a lesser extent *Empoasca dolichi* are the commonest species in Africa (Raman *et al.*, 1978; Parh, 1983).

Species less frequently encountered include *Empoasca signata*, *Asymmetrasca decedens*, *Orosius albicinctus* and several *Balclutha* species, all reported mainly from Egypt. It is not always clear which of these species have been recorded on soybean as they are reported on legumes in general (Hammad, 1978).

Smith (1978) reported that in Brazil leafhoppers cause serious damage mainly on crops grown in sandy soils where the poor water-retention capacity predisposes plants to drought stress and easy destruction by leafhoppers. The predominant species in Latin America is *Empoasca kraemeri* and occasionally *Empoasca fabae,* which is better known from North America (Singh and van Emden, 1979).

In West Africa, conditions of drought during early vegetative growth are often associated with severe leafhopper damage, and this appears to hold true in other regions as well. The extent to which soybeans (or other crops) are colonized and damaged by leafhoppers is affected by trichome type, density and orientation (Wolfenbarger and Sleesman, 1963; Broersma *et al.*, 1972; Pillemer and Tingey, 1976; Turnipseed, 1977). Glabrous soybean varieties therefore tend to be more severely damaged.

The life history and the biology of most leafhopper species are similar. The females lay between 80 and 142 eggs in veins on the underside of young leaves or on the petioles or stems of young seedlings, according to studies of *E. dolichi* and *E. christiani* with cowpea (Parh, 1983) and with *Phaseolus* (Wilde *et al.*, 1976). The eggs hatch in about 9 days, and nymphs go through five instars in 10 days. The nymphs, like the adults, tend to feed on the underside of leaves, sucking sap from the mesophyll and moving sideways when disturbed. During hot days the adults are found in tall grasses along the bunds of the fields with soybeans (Singh and van Emden, 1979).

A detailed account of the North American species, *E. fabae*, has been given by Helm *et al.* (1980). *Scaphytopius fuliginosus* Osborn, is the only leafhopper to date that has been associated with the transmission of a disease (Helm *et al.*, 1980), the reports being about a disease called 'machismo' in Colombia (Granada, 1979).

Control

Leafhoppers can be controlled in a variety of ways, but the use of insecticides and resistant varieties seems to be the commonest. The use of disease organisms has also been shown to have potential (Wraight and Roberts, 1987).

Chemical: Many growers use systemic insecticides (Table 2.3), which have been extensively researched in control of leafhoppers, especially in the USA.

Systemic organophosphates and carbamates such as toxaphene, monocrotophos at 400 g a.i./ha (Singh, 1978) and carbofuran are very effective in controlling leafhoppers (Jackai *et al.,* 1988). Both granular formulations and emulsifiable concentrates have been associated with good results, but, in the Philippines, Litsinger *et al.* (1978) suggested that granular formulations are preferable. Other products with mainly contact activity such as carbaryl have also been shown to be effective.

Host-plant resistance: Resistance of soybeans to damage by leafhoppers is well established and seems to be based mainly on the presence of hairs (Singh *et al.,* 1971; Broersma *et al.,* 1972; Ogunlana and Pedigo, 1974b; Helm *et al.,* 1980). The degree of pubescence and the orientation, type and structure of the hairs determine the level of resistance (Pillemer and Tingey, 1976; Norris and Kogan, 1980). In the tropics, not much research has been conducted into resistance of soybean to leafhopper presumably because of the presence of other pests that are considered more important and the general limitation on resources.

Cultural: Successful use of cultural practices to suppress leafhopper populations has been reported in the Philippines. Litsinger and his associates (1978) evaluated the effects of planting soybean in rice stubble, 20, 40 and 60 cm long, and found that stubble 40 and 60 cm long substantially reduced infestation by *A. biguttula*. Broadcasting of soybean through rice stubble is common in Southeast Asia and is now considered a cheap and effective method of controlling leafhoppers. This practice also reduces populations of of other pests.

Biological: Little information is available on the use of natural enemies or entomopathogens for the control of leafhoppers on soybeans anywhere in the tropics. However, given the role of parasites in the control of leafhoppers on rice in the Philippines and elsewhere in Asia, there is good reason to believe that natural enemies are at work wherever leafhoppers are present but do not constitute a serious problem.

In a recent study conducted in Brazil, a pathogen (*Hirsutella guyana*) of *E. kerri* was identified on cowpea and has been named as being responsible for epizootics. Thus, this pathogen could be used against the pest in the soybean agro-ecosystem.

Isoptera

Termites are important soil arthropods in the African savanna (Sands, 1962, 1965; Malaka, 1972), where they create mounds and eat stems and branches of cowpea, soybean, maize and other crops.

Their distribution within a field is usually spotty, but, wherever they are present, more than 25 mounds of various sizes can be found per hectare. Crops do not grow well on levelled termite mounds, and even when mounds are not formed the insects can completely destroy the vascular system of plants (usually late in plant growth).

Plants that have been attacked dry up or lodge, manifesting signs similar to those of vascular diseases. Infested plants can be pulled from the ground with little or no force.

Examining the root system and stem, one can find whitish, succulent insects, but termite damage is insidious and may be quite advanced before it is detected (Ohiagu, 1985).

No estimates of termite damage on soybean are available, as no studies have ever been conducted. Moreover, the species causing damage on soybean have not been described but are likely the same as those on cowpea or maize grown in contiguous ecological zones or in the same fields.

In West Africa, some of the key species attacking food crops, including soybean, are *Macrotermes lepidus* and *Odontotermes* spp.

Producers can generally avoid termite damage by changing fields or bypassing spots with mounds; although levelling the mounds is believed to suppress termite activity, the practice is of doubtful value since the queen termite has to die to stop or significantly reduce activity in a termite colony. Persistent insecticides control termites (Malaka, 1972), and Malaka (1972) has outlined several other methods used in Nigeria.

Lepidoptera

Some of the most important phytophagous insects associated with soybean belong to the order Lepidoptera. Species of importance vary slightly between regions, but some species have become key pests everywhere soybean is grown (Table 2.1). Because of the cosmopolitan importance and indisputable notoriety of lepidopteran defoliators on soybean, a few will be described in some detail in this section; however many defoliators have very restricted distribution and are not discussed here. These include some *Spodoptera* spp., the geometrid *Scopula remotata* (Gujarati *et al.*, 1973), *Maruca testulalis* in the Philippines (Rejesus, 1976), Nigeria (Ezueh and Dina, 1979), Colombia (Zenner-Polania, entomologist, Colombia, 1989, personal communication), Brazil, Solomon Islands and Micronesia.

Some Lepidoptera found on soybean leaves also feed on reproductive structures — on pods more often than on flowers. *Heliothis armigera* and several species of *Spodoptera* are probably the most important pod and foliage feeding Lepidoptera in the tropics. Others such as *Cydia ptychora* and *Etiella zinckenella* feed almost entirely on the fruits.

In temperate Asia, an important pest of soybean pods is the soybean pod borer *Leguminivora glycinivorella*, which appears to be restricted to Japan and Korea and has not been reported from any tropical country. Rarely do pests strictly of flowers cause economic damage.

ARCTIIDAE

Anticarsia gemmatalis (Hübner), velvet bean caterpillar, is the most important defoliator in the western hemisphere (Turnipseed and Kogan, 1976) and has been extensively studied, especially in the USA (Ford *et al.*, 1975). A more recent review of its biology and sampling procedures has been given by Herzog and Todd (1980).

In Latin America, this pest has been reported in Venezuela (Guagliumi, 1966), Colombia (Posada *et al.*, 1970), Brazil (Corseuil and Redaelli, 1966), and Argentina (Rizzo, 1971).

In Brazil *A. gemmatalis*, locally known as 'lagarta da soja', causes serious defoliation wherever soybean is grown in the country (Panizzi *et al.*, 1977a). Peak populations occur in January in the northern states and February in the south (Corrêa-Ferreira *et al.*, 1977). Light trap collections show a peak density in December and January (Silveira Neto *et al.*, 1973).

Larvae are usually greenish and striped but vary from brown to almost black, particularly in the last instar and under crowded conditions (Anazonwu and Johnson, 1986; Fescemyer and Hammond, 1986). Their distribution in the plant appears to be clearly demarcated according to age.

Small larvae are found mainly in the lower plant parts and move upwards as they grow older (Ferreira and Panizzi, 1978); they move downwards again as they prepare for pupation, which takes place in the soil at the base of the plant and lasts about 10 days (Turnipseed and Kogan, 1976). This insect is not reported as a pest in other regions of the world.

Spilosoma obliqua, synonym *Diacrisia obliqua*, (Walker) is a polyphagous pest — called the 'Bihar hairy caterpillar' in India where it causes havoc on soybeans. It reportedly also feeds on other legumes, maize and jute (Deshmukh *et al.*, 1977). Ninety host plants have been recorded for this pest (Bhattacharya and Rathore, 1977), but there are probably many that are unknown.

The adult is yellowish brown with black dots on the anterior margin of the forewings. Its abdomen is pink with black dots on the dorsal and lateral planes.

Females lay 500–1500 eggs, in batches of 400–750 on the leaf surface (Bhattacharya and Rathore, 1977). The eggs are initially pale green and darken before hatching (3–7 days during August–September and 11–15 days later in the year).

Larval development is highly dependent on temperature and relative humidity, but there are 5–6 larval instars that last about 20–30 days. Pupation takes 10–15 days in a cocoon. The life cycle averages 164 days at 15°C but becomes shorter as temperature increases up to 35°C when no development occurs (Singh and Gangrade, 1977). The Bihar hairy caterpillar feeds gregariously during the first three larval instars, with the yellow (third) instars migrating to other plants. Because of the large amounts of foliage consumed, the later instars disperse. Defoliation by *S. obliqua* has been shown to cause losses of about 15 per cent of pods and more than 80 per cent of pod weight. These losses are however quite variable in different varieties (Kundu, 1984).

NOCTUIDAE

Spodoptera spp. have been reported on soybeans, especially in Africa and Southeast Asia. For example, *Spodoptera littoralis* Boisd. has been reported as a serious pest of soybean in Egypt (Hammad, 1955, 1978) where high losses have been recorded during early infestations (Kamal, 1951; Shaheen, 1977). It is also known to occur in Nigeria where increasing damage to soybean foliage has been observed by one of us (L.E.N.J.). Formerly, *S. littoralis* was a dry season pest that sometimes attacked main season soybean just prior to senescence. Recently, there has been increasing concern that *S. littoralis* is feeding earlier in plant growth and may become a pest of significance in future. In September and October 1988, there was an outbreak of a related species, *Spodoptera exempta* (Walker), at several places in Nigeria. Normally this species prefers graminaceous plants (Rose *et al.*, 1988) and so restricts itself to cereals and grasses. However, the pitch-black larvae of this species were found on soybean at various sites and caused some damage. This observation underscores the caution that has been sounded before — that the spectrum of pests of soybean in Africa is bound to expand with increasing cultivation of the crop.

Female *S. littoralis* lays several hundred eggs in masses on the underside of leaves. The eggs are usually protected from environmental stresses including natural enemies (Kamal, 1951) by silk webbing and scales from the body of the female. Larvae hatch in a few days after eggs are laid. Young larvae show a tendency to remain aggregated but disperse as they get older. Larvae of *S. littoralis* are voracious feeders, quite often causing complete skeletonization of leaves. They are nocturnal feeders but may be seen feeding on the plants during the early morning hours. Normally, they hide in debris during the day and become active again at dusk. Even though this pest has been classified as minor in certain locations (Ezueh and Dina, 1979), it is the most important defoliator of soybean in West Africa and is bound to become more important with expansion of soybean production on the continent.

In Asia, particularly the Indian subcontinent, *Spodoptera litura* (Fabricius) and *S. exigua* (Hübner) are reported to be important soybean pests (Bhattacharya and Rathore, 1980). These are as polyphagous as *S. littoralis*, attacking plants such as cabbage, cotton, tomato, and several other crops in a wide range of families (Gangrade, 1974).

Females of both *S. litura* and *S. exigua* have a tremendous oviposition potential, often laying well over 1500 eggs per female on the lower epidermis. *Spodoptera litura* lays 1000–2000 eggs in batches that are covered by a buff of coloured hairs (Bhattacharya and Rathore, 1977). Eggs are protected as previously described, and larval behaviour is quite similar to that of *S. littoralis*, epecially with regard to aggregation of early instars and voracious feeding by older larvae.

There are 5–7 instars, depending on temperature (fewer at higher temperatures). Total larval duration is 14–20 days in *S. litura* and 12–17 days in *S. exigua*. Pupation takes place in the soil or debris on the ground and lasts for 6–10 days, the entire life cycle taking 4–5 weeks at 27°C in both species (Bhattacharya and Rathore, 1977).

Fully grown caterpillars measure 20–30 mm long and are tawny-brown, with rows of yellow–green dorso-lateral stripes and white lateral bands. *Spodoptera exigua* larvae measure about 25 mm long and have white longitudinal stripes.

Heliothis armigera is widely distributed in the tropics and sub-tropics. It is reported as a serious pest on chick-peas and pigeon peas in India (Srivastava, 1964); on common bean in Asia and East Africa (Agpal-Verzola and Cortado, 1968; Robertson, 1973; Nyiira, 1978; Tsedeke *et al.*, 1982). In Thailand this insect constitutes one of the most intractable problems on soybean (Arunin, 1978). The extreme polyphagy of this pest probably accounts for the notorious status it has earned and the difficulty experienced in developing sustainable control methods against it. However, despite the impressive list of host plants, only a few are of economic importance.

There appears to be some confusion in the literature about the distribution of *H. armigera* and *Heliothis zea* (Singh and van Emden, 1979; Singh, 1983). The two pests do not overlap geographically. In general, *H. zea* seems to be restricted to the USA (Kogan and Turnipseed, 1987), whereas *H. armigera* is found from Cape Verde Islands, through Africa, Asia and Australia to the Pacific Islands, and from Germany in the north to New Zealand (Reed and Pawar, 1982). *Heliothis armigera* also occurs in the Caribbean (Buckmire, 1978). Another species, *H. virescens*, the tobacco budworm, is commonly found on cotton in the Americas and in the West Indies (Reed and Pawar, 1982).

Other *Heliothis* species of lesser importance are known to occur in several areas (Srivastava, 1964; Agpal-Verzola and Cortado, 1968; Robertson, 1973; Arunin, 1978; Buckmire, 1978).

In some accounts, *H. armigera* has been classified as a defoliator (Talekar, 1987); however, both foliage and pods are often damaged by this pest, and the most critical damage to soybean is on pods.

The adult is a medium-sized yellowish-brown moth with distinct dark spots on the forewings. The hindwings are lighter and span about 40 mm. According to Bhattacharya and Rathore (1980), the female lays well over 1200 yellow–green eggs singly on leaves. After 3–8 days (Singh and van Emden, 1979; Talekar, 1987), the eggs hatch into larvae that quickly take up the colour of the foliage on which they feed. Larvae go through a series of colour changes as they get older — green, yellow, brown of various shades or a combination of these. *Heliothis armigera* larvae generally have three lateral stripes — a pale white, a much darker band and a light band on each side of the body. In Zimbabwe, variations from this general pattern have been reported (Anonymous, 1981). Mature larvae are big and chunky, measuring about 30 mm long. The larval period in Zimbabwe takes 16–35 days (Anonymous, 1981); in India it takes 20–25 days (Bhattacharya and Rathore, 1980).

There are normally six larval moults, although seven have been recorded in Zimbabwe during the cold season (Pearson and Darling, 1958). Pupation takes place in an earthen cell about 35–80 mm underground. A report from Zimbabwe (Anonymous, 1981) indicated that some pupae take 14–21 days, whereas others (long-term) overwinter (up to 6 months).

Adults have a pre-oviposition period of 1–4 days and lay eggs for about 5 days in India and for 10–25 days in South Africa depending on the season. An average 730 eggs (range 480–1600 eggs) are laid, usually on the underside of the leaf along the mid-rib. Eggs are nearly spherical with a flattened base.

Young larvae feed on tender foliage (usually the upper leaf epidermis — Patel *et al.*, 1974) or on flowers and flower buds (Jayaraj, 1982). The location of larval feeding may depend on the availability of sites or on the pest's geographical race.

Damage by *H. armigera* to pods of soybean is easily recognized: the holes are round and are on the locules where seeds are found. Similar damage is found on cowpea where it is more dramatic because of the longer pods (Singh and van Emden, 1979). Larvae feed on the seeds with only their head inside the pod; hardly ever does the entire larva enter the pod. This means the pest is an easy prey; nevertheless, damage to pods and seeds can be extensive as several pods can be damaged by one larva (Singh and van Emden, 1979).

PLUSIINAE

The soybean looper/semilooper complex involves a number of species within the family Plusiinae. Some seem to be restricted to certain regions, but because of inaccurate or incomplete taxonomic information it is difficult to ascertain whether or not the reports from different countries truly involve different species. Only the most important of the species are discussed here.

The soybean looper, *Pseudoplusia includens*, synonym *Plusia oo* (Walker), is the commonest plusiine occurring on soybean in the Americas (Turnipseed and Kogan, 1976). In a number of countries, for example Brazil, it causes substantial crop losses (Ramiro, 1977). Damage occurs mainly to the lower leaves, which may be completely skeletonized.

Larvae are green, with light stripes running the length of the body. There are five larval instars on soybean, although more have been recorded on other hosts (for example, peanuts — Jackai, 1978). The larval period lasts 13−20 days.

Pupation occurs in a silken cocoon attached to the soybean plant and lasts for about 7−14 days. Pupae are light green at first but later become dark. The life cycle and other aspects of the biology of *P. includens* have been reviewed by Herzog (1980).

Soybean semilooper, *Plusia orichalcea*, synonym *Trysanoplusia orichalcea* (Walker), occurs in Africa and Asia and appears to have filled the niche occupied by *Pseudoplusia includens* in the Americas. It is the predominant plusiine found on soybean in Zimbabwe and India (Bhattacharya and Rathore, 1980; Taylor, 1980). In Indonesia, a closely related species is encountered (Talekar, 1987).

The adults are medium-sized moths with mottled brown forewings. Two other semiloopers found in Zimbabwe (*Chrysodeixis chalcites* and *C. acuta*) have similarly coloured forewings. However, each forewing of *P. orichalcea* has a conspicuous wedge-shaped golden patch whereas the forewings of the other two species have two small, distinct silvery or golden spots, forming the semblance of a disjointed figure '8' (Taylor, 1980).

Pre-oviposition is 3−5 days in *P. orichalcea*. Adults lay tiny, creamy yellow or pale-green eggs, about 0.5 mm in diameter, singly on the undersurface of leaves or on the stem.

Small, whitish to pale-green larvae with black spots at the bases of the setae hatch from the eggs after 3−4 days. These soon become green, presumably because of the plant food.

Altogether there are five or occasionally six larval stages; the first stadium is about 3 days, the second is 1 day, and the rest are about 3 days each. *Chrysodeixis chalcites* has six, occasionally seven, instars. When full grown, larvae measure about 35 mm. The pupae are dark brown.

In Zimbabwe, the egg, larval and pupal stages take 3−4, 14−21 and 7−10 days, respectively, giving a total of 24−35 days' generation time (Anonymous, 1981). During cool months, generation time is extended. Adults live for only 2−5 days (Bhattacharya and Rathore, 1977). Normally, there are several generations a year, but only two of these are passed on soybean.

Taylor (1980) reported the host range of semiloopers to include — in addition to soybean — cowpea, cotton, alfalfa (lucerne), velvet bean, groundnut, potato and a wide variety of garden and ornamental plants. Damage gradually increases from selective feeding on the lower epidermis by newly hatched larvae to voracious eating of leaf tissue, skeletonizing plants. Young pods are eaten occasionally. Bhattacharya and Rathore (1977) reported that larvae feed singly on leaves, perhaps as a means of efficient resource allocation among members of the population. This behaviour is not likely to be manifested by young larvae.

PYRALIDAE

The lesser cornstalk borer, *Elasmopalpus lignosellus* (Zeller), is a stem feeder of considerable importance in Brazil where it is known as 'broca do colo da soja'. It is widely distributed in the Americas, from the southern USA, south to Mexico, Brazil and Argentina (Corseuil and Terhorst, 1965; Pacheco, 1970; Turnipseed, 1973; Rizzo, 1972). In Brazil *E. lignosellus* is reported mainly in the south where soybean is mostly grown; however considerable damage occurred during the first year of cultivation in the Cerrados of central Brazil (Panizzi *et al.*, 1977a). This pest has not been reported in the African or Asian tropics.

Elasmopalpus lignosellus is polyphagous, with a host range comprising non-leguminous as well as leguminous plants (Corseuil and Terhorst, 1965). Although there are no detailed studies on the host associations of *E. lignosellus*, Busoli *et al.* (1977) concluded that plants in the Gramineae family were *E. lignosellus'* preferred hosts.

This insect attacks soybean seedlings, inflicting severe damage, particularly during periods with sub-optimal rainfall or in sandy soils (Turnipseed and Kogan, 1976; Eastman, 1980). Entire stands have been known to be ravaged by *E. lignosellus*.

Mature larvae of this insect are about 16 mm long, bluish-green with transverse bands. The moths are brownish grey, the female having almost black forewings (Eastman, 1980).

Larvae bore into the stems of the young plants generally at ground level. At the point of penetration, the insect weaves a shelter of soil and plant debris to form the characteristic 'earthen shelter' attached to the stem. Seedlings usually die from *E. lignosellus* attack, and older plants lodge or become weak as a result of the girdling of the stems (Turnipseed and Kogan, 1976; Smith, 1978). Further information on the biology is provided by Sauer (1939) and Corseuil and Terhorst (1965).

A number of lepidopteran pyralid larvae cause damage to soybean by folding or rolling the leaves. They are quite widely distributed but are of minor economic importance (Table 2.1). However, because of their wide distribution and therefore potential for becoming serious pests, the more important species are discussed here.

Lamprosema indicata, synonym *Nacolela indicata* (Fab.), is found in India (Sachan and Gangwar, 1980), Thailand (Sepswasdi, 1976), Philippines (Rejesus, 1976), and probably other countries of Asia. A related species *Lamprosema diemminalis* has also been reported in India (Bhattacharya and Rathore, 1977).

Lamprosema indicata is creamy yellow to light brown and has oblique wavy black lines, whereas *L. diemminalis* is yellowish brown with both pairs of wings covered with black blotches. Adults of *L. indicata* lay up to 400 eggs singly or in batches of 5–20 on the leaf. The eggs hatch in 7–8 days. The larvae feed on the epidermal layers of leaves, which they fold, presumably to provide protection from environmental stresses. All six larval instars and the pupal period are spent within the folded leaves and occasionally in fallen leaves. However, not more than two larvae beyond the third instar tend to be found within a folded leaf. Larval duration is 22–28 days, and pupation takes 5–15 days, the entire life cycle taking up to 48 days (Kapoor *et al.,* 1972; Sepswadi, 1976).

Damaged leaves have a silvery-brown papery look and are noticeable from a distance. Several may be webbed together. Even though damage is heaviest, and therefore most obvious, during the latter part of crop growth, attack starts much earlier. The highest infestation recorded from India is 72–95 per cent of plants, which resulted in only 9.2 per cent loss of yield (Gangwar and Thakur, 1988). This is hardly surprising since the maximum number of folds per plant is three or four, harbouring 1–11 of the pests.

Leafroller, *Hedylepta indicata,* synonym *Omiodes indicata* (Fabricius) causes the same kind of damage as *L. indicata.* However, it is more widely distributed, having been recorded as a pest of soybean in Nigeria (Ezueh and Dina, 1979), Japan, Korea, Taiwan, Philippines (Chyan *et al.,* 1984) and Thailand. Kogan and Turnipseed (1987) also reported it in Latin America.

Females lay eggs, up to 466, on the upper epidermis where the larvae will feed when they hatch. Larvae roll the leaflet and feed inside the roll. Several leaves may be stuck together. There are five instars, lasting about 14–15 days. Pupation takes up to 16 days and occurs within the rolled leaflet. Heavy infestations are noticeable from a distance and, if they occur during the early vegetative phase or during pod filling, will affect yield (Chyan *et al.,* 1984). The host range of *H. indicata* is known to include several crops, among which is cowpea.

Etiella zinckenella (Treitschke) − the lima bean pod borer − has a cosmopolitan distribution and a wide host range. Among the plants attacked are mung bean, cowpea, green gram and pigeon pea in India (Srivastava, 1964); common bean in the Philippines and Puerto Rico; and soybean in Australia, Brazil and Nigeria (Smith, 1978; Turner, 1978; Ezueh and Dina,

1979). Cowpea, pigeon pea and lima bean are important hosts in Africa (Le Pelley, 1959; Abdul-Nasr and Awadalla, 1957).

It is probably the most important borer of soybean pods in most of the Asian tropics (Naito *et al.*, 1983; Talekar, 1987). A different species, *Etiella hobsoni* is found in Indonesia (Naito *et al.*, 1983). Only one case of infestation of soybean by *E. zinckenella* has been reported in Africa (Ezueh and Dina, 1979) but its presence elsewhere on the continent should not be ruled out.

The existence of biotypes has been suggested as the possible reason for its presence on crops other than soybean in the USA. Similarly, in Africa, it occurs mainly on cowpea. In Asia it is a major pest of soybean but not common bean — the reverse of the situation in the USA.

Damage by *E. zinckenella* results from the larvae boring into pods and flowers (Kobayashi, 1976a). Up to 80 per cent pod damage has been reported in Indonesia, but only 10–15 per cent in Taiwan (Talekar, 1987). Young seeds are destroyed in the process. A brown spot on the pod usually indicates the point of larval entry, and a larger hole is left where the mature larva escapes to pupate in the soil (Talekar, 1987). Feeding marks are rough and the injured pod contains large, round fecal pellets (Kobayashi, 1976a). Pods often rot away as a result of the accumulation of these. Blossoms are also infested and serve as oviposition substrates along with pods and growing tips (Barroga, 1969; Singh and Dhooria, 1971).

The moth is brownish grey with a white stripe along the leading edge of the narrow forewings (wingspan is 20–27 mm) (Hill, 1975). It is easily attracted to light traps.

Females lay 60–200 white oval eggs (0.6 mm long), singly or in batches of 2–12 (Kobayashi, 1976b). Oviposition takes place on the young pods, the calyx or the leaf stalks. After a highly variable incubation (3–16 days), eggs hatch into small yellowish-grey larvae. According to Talekar (1987), these larvae move about on the pod, spin a web, bore into the pod and begin feeding on developing seeds. Several larvae may thus enter the pod, but, because of cannibalism, only one or two survive.

Insufficient food supply in the pod causes larvae to migrate to other pods. After five larval instars, which take about 20 days, larvae measuring about 15 mm long form a cocoon and pupate in the soil at the base of the plant. Pupation is highly dependent on temperature and can take anywhere from 1 to 9 weeks (Hill, 1975), although some records give a pupal period of 8–10 days in India (Barroga, 1969; Singh and Dhooria, 1971; Kobayashi, 1976b).

Ephestia cautella (Walker), known as the almond moth, and *Plodia interpunctella* (Hübner), the Indian meal moth, infest stored soybeans and are well known as storage pests on crops such as rice, sorghum, maize, and peanuts (Bhattacharya and Rathore, 1977). *Ephestia cautella* is said to be the most important pest of stored soybean in India (Chaudhary and Bhattacharya, 1976; Saxena, 1978), also attacking stored grains such as wheat, maize and green gram.

Larvae develop on whole soybean in about 52 days and on soybean flour in 36 days. Furthermore, adult emergence was only 3 per cent on whole bean compared with 87 per cent on flour (Bhattacharya and Rathore, 1977). Development takes longer (up to 63 days) on some soybean varieties as well as other hosts, e.g. green gram and *Phaseolus* beans.

Like *E. cautella, P. interpunctella* (Hübner) infests a wide range of stored products, webbing together the infested material (flour or grain) and contaminating the storage with feces.

The adult moth has distinct wing coloration: the front and base of the forewings are mottled greyish-brown and the space between is a light greyish-white, resembling a dirty white band across the anterior portion of the folded forewings. The hindwings are uniformly greyish-white.

The females lay 40–350 or more minute, white oval eggs (Metcalf *et al.*, 1962), singly or, less often, in small clusters. Incubation varies but is usually within a few days to a week. Larvae become fully mature in about 2 weeks, sometimes considerably longer (Metcalf *et al.*, 1962). Pupation takes place within a silken cocoon on the surface of the produce. The entire life cycle normally takes about 4–6 weeks.

Plodia interpunctella has recently been reported infesting large quantities of stored whole soybean in Nigeria (J. and F. Thackway, director of human resources and spouse, IITA, 1988, personal communication). Samples from these stocks were reared under laboratory conditions at IITA, and the adults were subsequently identified at the Nigerian Stored Products Research Institute in Ibadan (by Dr. T. Falomo).

TORTRICIDAE

Epinotia aporema, synonym *Eucosma aporema* (Walsingham) — the shoot and axil feeder — has been reported from Latin America and the southern United States (Clarke, 1954).

In Brazil it occurs from Rio Grande do Sul in the south to Goiás in the central region (Ferreira, 1980). As the common name implies, the larva feeds on soybean shoots and axils. Its host range includes legumes such as groundnuts (peanuts), alfalfa, peas and clover (Montero, 1967; Morey 1972; Biezanko *et al.*, 1974). *Epinotia aporema* is considered an important soybean pest, albeit with restricted distribution in Argentina and Brazil and possibly elsewhere in that region.

Eggs are light yellow and oval. Larvae are initially yellowish green with shiny black heads and prothoracic shield; they become pale brown as they get older, progressing through five instars. The adults are small, brown moths with silver spots on their wings (Ferreira, 1980). Several generations can occur in one year, depending on location and date of planting (Gazzoni and Oliveira, 1979).

Cydia fabivora, synonym *Laspeyresia fabivora* (Meyrick), feeds on vegetative parts and floral buds, preferring tender buds and young leaflets during the early larval instars (Ferreira, 1980). Its distribution is uncertain, as it has frequently been incorrectly identified, closely resembling *E. aporema* (Turnipseed and Kogan, 1976). It has been reported on soybeans in Peru (Willie, 1946) and Brazil (Corseuil *et al.*, 1974) but undoubtedly also occurs in other Latin American countries. Its life cycle is similar to that of *E. aporema*.

Also like *E. aporema*, *C. fabivora* causes stunting of the plant and reduction in yield. Late-maturing and late-planted varieties suffer the greatest damage from these pests.

In Africa and Asia, the niche occupied by these pests in the Americas appears to have been occupied by *Maruca testulalis* (the cowpea pod borer) (Dina, 1981; Kogan and Turnipseed, 1987), *Hedylepta indicata* and *Lamprosema indicata* (Rejesus, 1976; Arunin, 1978; Ezueh and Dina, 1979). During the 1988–89 cropping season in Brazil, severe attacks of *M. testulalis* were reported from many areas of the country. Whether these attacks represent the advent of another serious pest of soybean in that country remains to be seen.

This group of pests is of potentially enormous economic importance in soybean cultivation, but populations hardly ever reach levels that call for control measures. There is, nonetheless, a need for continued efforts to monitor their populations.

Cydia ptychora, synonym *Laspeyresia ptychora* (Meyr.), is commonly known as the cowpea seed moth in Africa but becomes an important pest of soybean if the conditions are right (Singh, 1977a). It is found infesting pods of cowpea in East and West Africa (Le Pelley, 1959; Taylor, 1965; Halteren, 1971). A different species has been reported on pigeon pea in East Africa (Le Pelley, 1959), and an unidentified species has been reported on common bean in South America (Nanne Roe, 1968). *Cydia ptychora* is also known to attack mung bean, green gram, pigeon pea and soybean in Sri Lanka (Singh, 1977b) and has recently been reported on soybean in Madhya Pradesh in India (Singh and Jakhmola, 1983). The closely related species *Cydia fabivora* found in Brazil occupies a different niche; *Cydia nigricana* attacks field peas in Europe.

Considerable work has been done on this pest on cowpea, particularly in Nigeria (Taylor, 1969; Perrin and Ezueh, 1978; Ezueh, 1981; Olaifa and Akingbohungbe, 1981a,b, 1982; Ofuya and Akingbohungbe, 1988). Damage by pod-infesting *Cydia* spp. is similar on different host plants.

'Guesstimates' of losses caused by *C. ptychora* on soybean have little or no empirical data to back them up. The only available information on potential losses from *C. ptychora* infestation puts the pod and seed damage at a minimum of 4 per cent and a maximum of 95 per cent for a crop planted in July in India and nil for soybean planted at any other time (Kumar *et al.*, 1981). There are reports of heavy infestations of *C. ptychora* on stored soybean in Africa (Singh, S.R., 1980, personal communication), so it appears the infestation was not recognized in the field.

Cydia ptychora is a tiny, pale-brown moth that lays its eggs on cowpea peduncles and pods nearing maturity. Its behaviour is probably similar on soybean. The first-instar larvae enter the pod where they remain until ready to pupate. Several seeds are damaged as the insect feeds, forming irregular, dry fecal pellets that are retained within the pod. Early instars are creamy white but turn pink to bright red as they get older. Soybean pods infested by *C. ptychora* usually have sealed entry holes that give the impression of clogged pinholes. Soybeans left unduly long in the field after they are ready for harvest are prone to heavy damage from *C. ptychora* infestation. A similar situation has been reported by Jones and Jones (1974) for other crops that are harvested dry rather than fresh. Because of this, *C. ptychora* is generally regarded as 'a pest of negligence'.

When an infested crop is carried into storage where humidity is optimal for the insect to continue development, severe damage results. This is true as well for other legumes. Damaged seeds are glued together with the insect's frass by means of silky threads.

Control

In general, lepidopteran defoliators can be controlled by a single approach, although one must take into account differences in individual species, especially their resistance to insecticides. A wide range of control measures has been reported.

Chemical: Different chemicals have become popular in different parts of the world (Table 2.3) — the popularity presumably reflecting both the biophysiology of the predominant pests and the relative marketing aggressiveness of the chemical companies.

For example, insecticides are the main tactic used for *E. lignosellus* control. Applied to the soil or as a seed treatment, carbofuran and carbosulfan have shown good activity against stem feeders on other crops and should therefore be effective in controlling *E. lignosellus* on soybean. Diazinon has been recommended for use in seriously infested areas (Turnipseed, 1975) such as in Brazil.

Also, in Brazil, carbaryl is recommended for the control of

A. gemmatalis while monocrotophos and chlorpyrifos-ethyl are used against *E. aporema* and *C. fabivora* (Turnipseed, 1975; Foerster, 1978). Despite the efficacy of these and other products available in the Brazilian market, there is an increasing trend towards a reduction of pesticide use on soybean. Broad-spectrum insecticides are no longer recommended except in rare cases and the use of microbial insecticides (e.g. *Bacillus thuringiensis*) and insect-growth regulators (e.g. diflubenzuron) is on the increase.

The rationale is easy to understand. Panizzi *et al.* (1977b) reported resurgence of stink bugs, *A. gemmatalis* and *Plusia* species in several soybean fields after the application of a mixture of methyl parathion and methomyl as a result of the harmful effects of these products on natural enemies. Similar observations have been made on other insects (Panizzi and Ferreira, 1980).

Pseudoplusia includens is easily controlled with several insecticides (Table 2.3), but in Latin America methomyl and monocrotophos (both at 500 g a.i./ha) are recommended where the pest poses an urgent or serious problem (Kogan, 1976). The Plusiinae found in Zimbabwe do not constitute a serious threat to soybean and are controlled using other means.

For best results, insecticide applications to control semiloopers must be at the onset of infestation because early instars are easier to kill than older ones. Monocrotophos, trichlorphon and endosulfan are registered in Zimbabwe for use in controlling semiloopers. A number of other products such as carbaryl and some synthetic pyrethroids are also effective. Scouting for larvae is recommended before embarking on a spraying programme.

The literature on the lepidopteran pests' development of resistance to insecticides is disturbing, with well-documented accounts for several *Spodoptera* spp. in Egypt and Asia (Talekar, 1987).

Heliothis zea has also developed resistance to some recommended insecticides probably because cotton, which is also attacked by this pest, is heavily treated with insecticides (Turnipseed, 1983). The pest may soon develop resistance to the synthetic pyrethroids, too, as these are increasingly being used on soybean (and cotton). The insecticide-resistant *H. zea* population may originate from an area quite different from where resistance to insecticides was identified (Turnipseed, 1983).

Among the insecticides used against *Heliothis* spp. are methomyl, methyl parathion and carbaryl, with methomyl proving to be most effective against *H. zea* in the southeastern USA (Turnipseed *et al.*, 1974). Endosulfan has been used to control *H. armigera* on beans in East and Southern Africa (Swaine, 1968), and in Zimbabwe it is registered for use against *H. armigera*, loopers and aphids on soybean (Wessels, 1978). However, recent results of field tests on common bean in Ethiopia showed that endosulfan is probably no longer effective (Tsedeke and Adhanom, 1980). The pyrethroid, cypermethrin, sprayed at 100 g a.i./ha, has been recommended as a substitute.

The development of insecticide resistance in insect pests in the tropics is favoured by the rapid turnover of generations. However, where there are no indications of resistance to insecticides, e.g., in West Africa, *Spodoptera* species and other insect pests can still be controlled using a wide range of insecticides including monocrotophos, endosulfan and insecticide cocktails such as cypermethrin and dimethoate (Sherpa Plus®). Other products have also been used satisfactorily.

Several insecticides are used in the control of *Cydia* spp. However, because larvae are concealed within the pods, insecticides are likely to be effective only before the larva enters the pod.

Systemic insecticides have been suggested (Ezueh, 1976a), but their efficacy is questionable if experience with chemical control of another pod borer, *Maruca testulalis*, is any indication (Jackai, 1983). Other products with different modes of action (e.g., contact) can be effectively used but require proper timing (Perrin and Ezueh, 1978).

In fact, many of the commonly used chemicals are effective against this pest, including dimethoate, phosphamidon, chlorpyrifos-ethyl (Taylor, 1965; Ezueh, 1976b).

Many products effective in reducing damage by *C. ptychora* may be doing so by killing the adults and eggs during general management of other pests, as in cowpea (Perrin and Ezueh, 1978).

For the control of *Etiella* spp., tests conducted in California, USA (Stone, 1965), and in Taiwan (AVRDC, 1982b) have shown that carbaryl, azinphos-methyl, mexacarbate, monocrotophos, triazophos, fenvalerate and quinalphos are all satisfactory, but the extensive host range of this pest makes reliance solely on chemical control impracticable. Also triazophos and carbaryl cause phytotoxicity, and Talekar *et al.* (1977) have reported that chemical residues may be translocated into the seeds, thereby raising serious concerns about the hazards to consumers.

Biological: Biological control of soybean pests seems to have great potential in areas of the world where insecticide use is minimal such as Africa south of the Sahara. However, because of the relative newness of the crop in this region, not enough studies have been conducted.

Elsewhere, both insects and entomopathogens have been extensively used for the control of a number of Lepidoptera found on soybean (Table 2.4), with parasites as well as predators playing a major role.

A detailed account of attempts to control *S. litura*, an important defoliator of soybean in Egypt, is given by Kamal (1951) who advocated biological control of the pest because of the unsatisfactory long-term results obtained from insecticides.

Kamal (1951) reported that egg predators reduced *S. litura* up to 60 per cent and predation of young larval instars an average 34 per cent during

June and August. This period coincided with peak infestation and peak predation. Apparently, a complex of predators was responsible and included coccinellids *Coccinella* sp., *Cheilomenes* sp., *Scymnus* sp., ants, mantids, Neuroptera *(Chrysopa* sp.) and spiders. Kamal subsequently studied in detail the biology of *Coccinella undecimpunctata* L., which feeds on aphids as well as mealybugs and eggs and young larvae of *S. litura*. This predator also is reported to feed on nectar from cotton blossoms. Pressure by hyperparasites, — including a braconid *Dinocampus coccinellae*, *Tetrastichus coccinellae* and a pteromalid, *Eupteromalus* sp. — somewhat reduced the efficiency of C. undecimpunctata. *Paederus alfierii, Peritus* sp. (egg predators), the carabid larval and nymphal predator *Calosoma chlorostictum chlorostictum*; the egg predators *Orius albidipennis* Reut. and *O. laevigatus* Fieb. (Anthocoridae); *Chrysopa vulgaris* Schn., *Helicomitus festivus* Ramb (Neuroptera) (egg and larval predators) have been described by Kamal (1951).

In addition to predatory insects, a large number of indigenous parasites have been reported on *S. litura*, e.g., *Tachina larvarum* L. (larval parasite), *Actia palpalis* Will. (larval parasite), *Eulimnerium xanthostoma, Zela chlorophthalina, Z. nigricornis, Trichogramma evanescens, T. minutum* and *Chonomorium eremita*, a parasite of *S. litura* pupae.

Even though the individual contribution of each of these natural control agents may be small, their collective impact can be considerable — an estimated 32 per cent in summer and up to 75 per cent during the winter (Kamal, 1951). Many of these species are not specific to *S. litura*; therefore their value as biological control agents can be vast. However, the levels of attack on *S. litura* are still inadequate for control. As a result, a number of exotic parasites have been introduced to augment local agents. Among these were *Actia nigritula, Microplitis demolitor, Telenomus hawaii, Telenomus spodoptera* mainly from Southeast Asia.

In India, one dipteran species and a braconid parasite (*Apanteles* sp.) as well as a pentatomid bug, *Cantheconidea furcellata* have been reported from *S. litura*, but no effort appears to be under way to encourage biological control. Eight hymenopteran parasites have also been recorded on *Lamprosema indicata* (Bhattacherjee, 1976).

Among predatory species, *Calosoma argentatus granulatum* is abundant (Heinrichs *et al.*, 1979; Turnipseed, 1980) and can consume as many as 91 *A. gemmatalis* larvae daily, whereas other carabids such as *Callida* spp. and *Lebia* spp. consume about 8 and 5 larvae, respectively (Corrêa-Ferreira and Moscardi, 1985).

Chrysodeixis acuta, which causes up to 50 per cent loss in grain yield in India (Singh, 1987), has been reported to be parasitized by a number of hymenopterans (Table 2.4).

Parasites of *Heliothis* sp. have been studied extensively in several countries (King *et al.*, 1982; Habib, 1973; Yen, 1973; Ibrahim, 1980) (Table

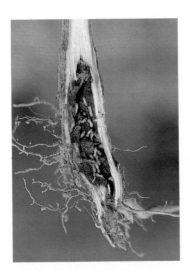

Plate I. Termite damage (photo IITA)

Plate II. Nezara viridula *adults (photo IITA)*

Plate III. Nezara viridula *damage (photo IITA)*

Plate IV. Riptortus dentipes *(photo IITA)*

Plate V. Spodoptera *sp.* *(photo IITA)*

2.4). In India, *Campoletis chlorideae* is the most important, and *Microplitis demolitor* has been reported to be the major parasite in Australia (King *et al.*, 1982). In Egypt, *Apanteles* spp. and *Microplitis rufiventris*, *Chelonus inanitus*, *Bracon brevicornis* and *Barylypa humeralis* are the most effective (Ibrahim, 1980). In India, five reduviids attack *Heliothis* (Rao, 1974), the most promising being *Sycanus indagator*. Others, including spiders, have been reported (King *et al.*, 1982), and *A. flavipes* has been reported to attack larvae of *S. obliqua* (Muthukrishnan and Senthamizhselvan, 1988).

Even though the use of natural enemies through augmentation or other techniques has been shown to be beneficial, results are often inconsistent and economically unattractive because of the logistics of production.

In this respect, *Trichogramma* spp. (parasite) and *Chrysopa* sp. (predator) are more promising than other natural enemies (Morrison *et al.*, 1978). There is also some evidence that use of hemipteran predators, such as *Podisus maculiventris*, in *Heliothis* management is feasible (Lopez *et al.*, 1976).

Despite the suggestion that biological control of *E. zinckenella* is promising because of the pest's occurrence throughout the year on some host plants, there is a dearth of information. In fact, according to Kobayashi (1976a,b), only one parasitic hymenopteran, *Philomacroploea pleuralio* has been reared from *E. zinckenella* larvae from Taiwan and Japan. Research is needed on the potential not only for parasitic control but also for pressure by entomopathogens of this species.

This is also true for *E. lignosellus* as there are no direct records of any natural enemy activity on this pyralid on soybean. Nevertheless, Sauer (1946) and Silva *et al.* (1968) reported a braconid (*Macrocentrus muesebecki*), an ichneumonid (*Pristomerus* sp.) and a tachinid (*Plagiprospherysa* sp.) as parasites of *E. lignosellus* on other crops.

On field peas in Canada, exotic parasites were released against the pea moth (*Cydia* sp.) (Cameron, 1938; Wishart, 1943 cited in Perrin and Ezueh, 1978), and many of the larval parasitic genera reported on the legume pod borer, *Maruca testulalis* have also been observed on *C. ptychora*. These include the braconids *Braunsia* sp., *Apanteles* sp., *Phanerotoma* as well as unidentified ant and lizard species (Perrin and Ezueh, 1978). The level of control achievable with natural enemies is not known and needs to be examined within the context of an integrated strategy for control of this insect.

Bacterial and viral diseases (entomopathogens) have been used for the control of *Spodoptera* species in Egypt (Abdul-Nasr, 1956) and the Bihar hairy caterpillar, *S. obliqua*, during the rainy season in India. In Zimbabwe, farmers have for several years practised the control of the semilooper complex (*P. orichalcea*, *C. chalcites* and *C. acuta*) using preparations of polyhedrosis virus collected from diseased larvae.

Farmers have been trained to collect the diseased larvae every season and store the samples for use during the next season (Anonymous, 1981). Virus-infected larvae continue to feed for some time before they die; therefore the virus should be introduced into the insect population early during crop development (Taylor, 1980). The same or a similar virus has been reported in Zambia (T. Tonga, extension agronomist, Zambia Seed Company, 1986, personal communication) and in Egypt (Abdul-Nasr, 1956).

These so-called microbial insecticides also play a major role in the control of soybean defoliators in Latin America. For example, a nuclear polyhedrosis virus of *A. gammatalis* (AgNPV) has been used in Brazil (Moscardi and Corso, 1981; Moscardi, 1983). This virus causes the black disease known locally as 'doença preta', which greatly reduces larval populations of *A. gemmatalis* when applied at 50 larval equivalents/ha. The use of AgNPV in Brazil started in 1980–81 and currently covers 500,000 ha. It is projected to exceed 1.5–2.0 million ha before the turn of the century (Moscardi, in press).

Another entomopathogen of *A. gemmatalis*, the fungus *Nomuraea rileyi*, causes what is referred to locally as the white disease. Field epizootics of *N. rileyi* have been reported in several states of Brazil (Corrêa *et al.,* 1977) and are probably quite widespread in South America. Because of its rapid progress, this disease keeps larval populations of *A. gemmatalis* from causing economic damage. This is particularly true in the wet season and in closely planted soybean where high humidity favours disease spread (Panizzi, unpublished). The combination of AgNPV and *N. rileyi* may eventually eliminate the need for insecticides to control *A. gemmatalis* (Moscardi and Ferreira, 1985). Other entomopathogens of minor importance have been reported. For example, fungi in the genus *Entomophthora* attack *A. gemmatalis, P. includens* and related species; *Beauveria* sp. (probably *bassiana*) attacks chrysomelids, *Diabrotica* and *Cerotoma*, as well as other soybean pests (Panizzi *et al.,* 1977a). Carner (1980) has published the range of entomopathogens and methods for sampling disease incidence.

Host plant resistance: A great effort has been made during the last two decades to develop soybean varieties resistant to arthropods. Leadership has often been provided by researchers in developed countries, particularly the USA (Turnipseed and Kogan, 1976; Turnipseed and Sullivan, 1976). However, no commercial varieties are as yet available with adequate levels of resistance to defoliators (Kogan and Turnipseed, 1987). Only very recently, have reports (Hartwig and Kilen, 1989) suggested that some new varieties with good levels of resistance to a number of soybean pests will soon be available. A breeding programme in Mississippi, USA, has promising results, mainly from PI 229358, which is resistant to the soybean looper, *P. includens, A. gemmatalis, H. virescens* and *H. zea* (Table 2.5).

Table 2.5. Soybean varieties with resistance to various pests

Variety/accession	Pest species	Nature of resistance
N4582, N3498, N2980, N3697, N3008		_[a]
Glycine soja	M. sojae	_[a]
Neonotonia wightii	M. sojae	_[a]
IC 18734	M. phaseoli	_[a]
PI 229358	P. includens, A. gemmatalis, H. virescens, H. zea	_[a]
	R. clavatus, N. viridula, Stink bugs	Antixenosis
PI 171444	S. littoralis	Antibiosis, antixenosis
	P. includens, R. clavatus, N. viridula	Antixenosis
JS-72-44	S. obliqua	Tolerance
MACS-128	S. obliqua	Tolerance
JS-78-81	L. indicata	Tolerance
JS-73-22	L. indicata	Tolerance
JS-72-185	L. indicata	Tolerance
JS-72-20	L. indicata	Tolerance
JS-71-5	L. indicata	Tolerance
JS-78-67	L. indicata	Tolerance
UPSM 391	S. obliqua	Tolerance
UPSM 398	S. obliqua	Tolerance
UPSM 495	S. obliqua	Tolerance
UPSM 509	S. obliqua	Tolerance
UPSM 930	S. obliqua	Tolerance
PI 171451	Stink bugs	_[a]
PI 227687	N. viridula	Antixenosis, antibiosis
ED 73-371	Stink bugs	Phenetic, antixenosis, antibiosis
ED 73-355	Stink bugs	Phenetic, antixenosis
Chi-Kei	N. viridula	Tolerance
IAC 74-2832	N. viridula	Tolerance
IAC 78-2318	Defoliators	Tolerance
Merit	D. platura, H. cilicrura	_[a]
Clark 63	D. platura, H. cilicrura	_[a]
Adelphia	D. platura, H. cilicrura	_[a]
Harosoy-63	D. platura, H. cilicrura	_[a]
Portage	D. platura, H. cilicrura	_[a]
IAC 100 (PI 518756)	Stink bugs	Many small seeds
TGx 713-09D	Stink bugs	Phenetic, tolerance
TGx 307-048D	Stink bugs	Phenetic, tolerance

[a]Not determined or else not provided in the literature.

Also, recently some work at IITA in Nigeria has produced encouraging results in the development of soybean varieties resistant to *S. littoralis* (Ojo, 1988), the commonest defoliator of soybean in Africa. The source of resistance is PI 171444, which had been identified earlier as resistant to a number of pests including *H. zea* in the USA (Gilman *et al.*, 1982; Turnipseed and Sullivan, 1976). This plant introduction is also resistant to some hemipteran pod pests and is thought to combine two types of resistance to *S. littoralis*: antibiosis (resulting in reduced pupal size and elevated mortalities) as well as non-preference (antixenosis) for feeding (Ojo, 1988). The IITA programme has used this accession in breeding for insect resistance and has launched studies of inheritance.

In India, JS-72-44 (Guarav) has been reported as having resistance to *S. obliqua*. However, the level of resistance and how useful it is in breeding programmes are as yet unclear. Another variety, MACS-128, that was infested by *S. obliqua* suffered only 8.42 per cent grain loss compared with 42 per cent loss in a more susceptible variety, DS-178, which was only about half as infested (5 per cent vs 9 per cent infestation in MACS-128). These findings suggest tolerance in MACS-128. A number of genotypes with resistance to the leaf folder, *L. indicata*, have been reported by Srivastava and Srivastava (1988). These are JS-78-81, JS-73-22, JS-72-185, JS-72-20, JS-71-5 and JS-78-67.

No resistant genotypes have been reported for any of the Plusiinae, in Asia or Africa, possibly because no serious screening has been done. However, in Latin America, IAC 78-2318 has been reported as having multiple resistance to several pests of soybean, including defoliating caterpillars (Lourenção and Miranda, 1987).

Also, PI 171444 has been shown to be resistant to the soybean looper *P. includens* in the USA (Kester *et al.*, 1984). The major difficulty in finding good sources of resistance to soybean defoliators lies in the polyphagy of many of the pests. Bhattacharya and Rathore (1977), for example, listed as many as 29 families that are fed on by *S. obliqua*, and many are wild hosts and span a wide taxonomic range.

Studies were conducted under natural field conditions by Bhattacharya and Rathore (1977), and the results indicated great variations in responses to feeding damage caused by defoliators at the different growth stages of close to 2000 germ plasm lines. Most of the accessions had scores higher than 6 for damage on a scale of 1−9. Among the accessions receiving damage ratings of 4 or lower were UPSM 391, UPSM 398, UPSM 495, UPSM 509 and UPSM 930, all of which matured within 100 days. The exact nature of resistance was not investigated, but the authors conjectured that tolerance was the mechanism. Further studies have been carried out, and Bragg (U.S. introduction), Hampton, UPSS 38, UPSM 57, Kalimpong and UPSM 120 were selected as potentially resistant.

Screening conducted at AVRDC has identified seven accessions that are moderately resistant to *E. zinckenella* in Taiwan, but all seven proved susceptible in Indonesia where the pod borer population is much higher (Talekar and Chen, 1983). These results underline the need for controlled testing where the pest population can be manipulated such that one can predict pest densities that defy the mechanism of resistance. Also, the results may reflect differences in pest species — a reminder that species should be properly identified before resistance studies become extensive.

Small-seeded varieties with many pods suffer less damage from *E. zinckenella* (r = -0.81**) than do large-seeded cultivars (Talekar, 1987) and, because of their late maturity, escape the peak infestation of the insect.

Tests performed with *E. cautella* in India indicated several varieties of soybean that reduced adult emergence and depressed pupation (JS-3, UPSM-20, Clark 63, UPSS-29, UPSS-57, Harosoy-63, Semmes, UPSS-46, Lee, Hardee, Davis and UPSM-57) (Bhattacharya and Rathore, 1977). It is also well-established that whole grain is generally less susceptible than flour of the same soybean variety. This general wisdom has led to the obvious speculation that the seed coat acts simply as a physical barrier, but other factors are important, according to experiments by Bhattacharya and Rathore (1977).

Little, if any, work has been done on resistance of soybeans to *C. ptychora*, and efforts should be made to screen both cultivated and wild genotypes to identify useful sources of resistance. Planting early maturing varieties or manipulating the date of planting would go a long way towards reducing infestation and damage by *C. ptychora*. Also, prompt harvesting and processing of mature soybean would minimize infestation and reduce losses in storage.

Cultural: Date-of-planting manipulation is also effective in the control of some soybean defoliators. Using Clark 63 and Harosoy-63 and various dates of planting in India, for example, Bhattacharya and Rathore (1977) were able to show significant differences in the populations of *S. litura*, *P. orichalcea* and *S. obliqua*. These differences were also reflected in grain yield. The crop planted on 27 February yielded much better than crops planted on 17 February and 8 March. The poor yields were not a reflection solely of pest attacks (e.g. the March planting was destroyed by monsoon rains), but the 27 February planting exhibited a lower prevalence of pests at the test location.

Manipulation of planting date has also been shown to work for *A. gemmatalis* and *Plusia* spp. More larvae of these pests were collected on early soybean planted in narrow rows than on soybean planted later at wider spacings between rows in Paraná state of Brazil (Panizzi *et al.*, 1979) (Figure 2.2).

In Egypt, hand-picking egg masses of *S. litura* every day was recommended to farmers as a method of cultural control for this pest. Careful studies on the effect of egg removal on natural enemies, however, indicated that picking egg masses once every 3 days was more favourable than removing the masses every day because it allowed the beneficial fauna to survive (Kamal, 1951).

Early planting and proper weed control help reduce *E. lignosellus* problems (Dietz *et al.*, 1976) as does careful management of crop residues. Although no specific information is available on *E. lignosellus*, the increasing use of zero-tillage is likely to increase the incidence of this pest in the field as it does for other crop pests. Similarly, little information is available about effects of cultural practices in the control of *Cydia* spp. on soybean, and intercropping experiments involving other legumes and cereals conducted in different countries have been either inconclusive or contradictory in their effects on the species (Perrin and Ezueh, 1978). Nevertheless, knowledge gained from cowpea pests suggests some advantage from intercropping legumes with cereals. This system warrants increased attention for researchers who are seeking methods to improve pest control in peasant agriculture where no other control measures are consciously practised.

Integrated Pest Management

Where soybean pests have been a serious threat to production, insecticides have played the major role in their control in the past. However, current recommendations show a distinct effort aimed at reducing the insecticide component of pest-management practices, particularly in the USA and Brazil (Turnipseed and Newson, 1989; Kogan and Turnipseed, 1987; Gazzoni and Oliveira, 1979). The change reflects an increased understanding of the interactions between insect pests and their environment − the total agro-ecosystem. Studies on economic damage levels and how these are impinged upon by biological, cultural, and chemical control as well as by varietal resistance have made possible some successful programmes in integrated pest management (IPM) in Brazil (Turnipseed, 1975; Kogan *et al.*, 1977; Panizzi *et al.*, 1977a; Kogan and Turnipseed, 1987; Kobayashi and Cosenza, 1987), following examples that have been established in the USA (Turnipseed and Newsom, 1983; Kogan and Turnipseed, 1987). Elsewhere in the tropical world such programmes are yet to be developed or fully adopted.

IPM is a concept that was first advanced by Stern and his colleagues (1959) and has had a strong following ever since (Pedigo *et al.*, 1986). As pointed out by Flint and van den Bosch (1981) in their book *Introduction to Pest Management*, the dependence on insecticides for the control of pests has given rise to pest resurgence, secondary outbreaks, resistance to insecticides as well as contamination often worse than the original pest.

To minimize the side-effects of pest control is the *raison d'être* of IPM — the judicious use of pest-control tactics that can be applied in a compatible manner, with as little disruption of the natural balance of the ecosystem as possible and in an economically sound fashion.

By implication, insecticide use needs to be drastically reduced while more advantage is taken of other tactics including habitat modification (or cultural control), beneficial organisms and plant resistance.

Obviously, the stockpiles of information on individual methods of control are sufficient to enable the formulation of good IPM programmes in most countries. However, the 'magic' that insecticides can, and do, perform coupled with their relative ease of acquisition and the total lack of enforcement of regulatory controls make growers reluctant to adopt IPM packages, which involve new tasks such as monitoring of pest levels. Also, the lack of technical personnel who have sufficient commitment and know-how to assist growers has militated against the development and use of IPM.

In Africa, where the pest problem on soybean is negligible compared with that elsewhere or on other crops (such as cowpea), sound control programmes can be developed and used in a way that avoids the problems encountered from heavy reliance on insecticides in countries like Brazil and the USA.

Along these lines, some initial work has been conducted in Zimbabwe (Taylor and Kunjeku, 1983). Scientists determined economic thresholds for the semilooper, *T. orichalcea* and concluded that farmers should not apply insecticides unless pest densities during pod development reached 15.7 larvae/m of row or, during bean development, 7.6 larvae/m of row.

However, the authors did not mention, and therefore presumably did not investigate, how their findings on application of insecticides could be integrated with current efforts in biological control of semiloopers in Zimbabwe. Farmers in the country have been trained in the production and use of nuclear polyhedrosis virus to control semiloopers (Anonymous, 1981), and, one would think, could combine in an efficient way, insecticidal control (based on economic threshold levels) with biological control with entomopathogens.

This example clearly illustrates how disjointed research work on soybean pests in Africa and elsewhere in the tropics has been and, for the most part, continues to be. The programme at IITA has centred on the development of resistant genotypes (Jackai *et al.*, 1988) but currently includes plans to investigate the role of beneficial organisms in the soybean agro-ecosystem, to integrate the use of natural control with the use of resistant varieties and then subsequently to add insecticide use where the population of stink bugs (the major pest species) gets out of hand.

Naturally, it will take several years for full-scale IPM programmes to be developed, but the awareness and impetus needed are now in place. The urgency of the effort is clear as the pest problem on soybean in West Africa already appears to be more serious than that in Southern Africa and is likely to increase (both in diversity and in intensity) as soybean production expands.

In Egypt, where *S. littoralis* is reported to be an important pest problem on soybean (Kamal, 1951), much work has gone into investigations of insecticides, entomopathogens (Hassan and Moewed, 1973, 1974a,b; Moawed, 1980), and beneficial insects (Kamal, 1951). The biology of the pest and damage thresholds have also been studied. With this data base, one is still unable to find reports of a well-articulated and functional IPM programme on soybean in Egypt. The wherewithal is there, and all that is now required is the formulation of a compatible and economic integration of the individual tactics.

Similar examples can be drawn from other tropical countries and are much more numerous than are cases in which IPM programmes have been developed. Nevertheless, efforts in Brazil can serve as a model.

The major insect pests of soybean in Brazil are two defoliators — *A. gemmatalis* and *P. includens* — and stink bugs. A number of control methods have been developed over the years for each pest, major as well as minor or localized. Before IPM packages began being developed, farmers depended almost exclusively on insecticides, which were used often in excessive amounts and, sometimes, despite being banned. This situation gradually changed with the introduction of an IPM programme. A look at the design and outcome is worthwhile.

The Brazilian Programme

Several paired fields were selected for the pilot programme in 1975. The fields measured 10–30 ha each and were selected on each of nine farms in Rio Grande do Sul and Paraná states. One field in each pair was subjected to management practices of local farmers and the other to that of an IPM scheme that consisted of:

- weekly scouting (monitoring) of pest populations and the prevalence of *N. rileyi* virus on *A. gemmatalis*;
- estimation of plant defoliation and growth;
- establishment of economic thresholds based on level of defoliation, pest density and plant-growth stage;
- use of minimum effective rates of insecticides when populations and levels of injury exceed the threshold.

In the first year of the programme, insecticide use was reduced by 78 per cent on the IPM fields without any real differences in grain yield compared with farmer-treated fields (Kogan *et al.*, 1977).

In subsequent years, the programme was expanded with results similar to those of 1975 and was adopted by the national soybean research centre at EMBRAPA. The same year, the first technical bulletin of the research centre — *Insetos da Soja no Brazil* — was published. This bulletin contained photographs and descriptions of major pests and the damage they cause, natural enemies and recommendations on judging economic thresholds (Panizzi *et al.*, 1977a).

By 1980, the programme involved more than 200,000 farmers in an area of 2.5 million ha, resulting in a net reduction of about 60 per cent in insecticide usage and a savings of $10/ha on chemicals alone (Oliveira, 1979).

Obviously, the programme involved training of extension personnel to carry out scouting, strong support from government and cooperation by chemical companies; it also incorporated frequent evaluation and, where necessary, modification, which is implicit in any good IPM programme if it is to continue to be applicable.

In 1980, the Brazilian IPM programme revised its recommendations about threshold levels and target pests. One new pest, the shoot and axil borer, *E. aporema*, was added, and the threshold was to be when 25–30 per cent of the growing points showed signs of attack. Threshold levels for other pests are (Figure 2.3):

- Defoliators: 30 per cent defoliation and presence of 20 larvae/m of row during the vegetative phase or 15 per cent defoliation and presence of 20 larvae/m from onset of flowering to pod-filling.
- Seed suckers: 2 stink bugs/m from start of pod-setting to end of pod-filling for soybean that is meant for processing or 1 stink bug/m during the same period if the beans are meant for use as seed.

No insecticide treatment is recommended during maturation.

The use of AgNPV to control *A. gemmatalis* (Moscardi and Corso, 1981) has been added as a component of the overall programme and has rendered the program even more attractive to growers. To maintain the momentum, the Brazilians are planning to concentrate now on the training of extension personnel at all levels.

Another success in IPM in Brazil was reported by Kobayashi and Cosenza (1987) who conducted a study between 1983 and 1985 in the Cerrados. They integrated *Trissolcus mitsukurii* introduced from Japan with indigenous species such as *T. basalis* and *T. mormideae*, early maturing varieties and 'trap soybean', greatly reducing insecticide applications.

The study exemplifies the kind of understanding needed to formulate a reliable IPM programme, and the results illustrate how location- and time-specific the programmes are, particularly in relation to economic thresholds, natural enemy guilds and changes in pest structure and status.

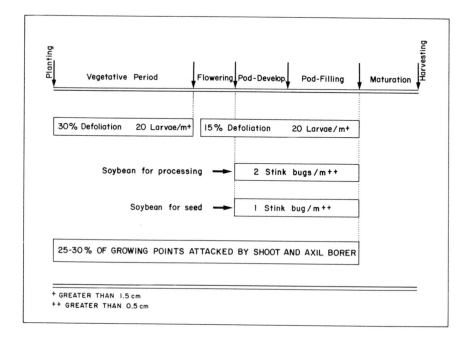

Figure 2.3. Economic injury levels currently being used in Brazil for IPM of defoliators, stink bugs and shoot and axil borers.

The authors found, for example, that the stink-bug complex changed with time after initial cultivation of the crop. Noctuids, stink bugs and chrysomelids attacked soybean, respectively, 1–2 years, 3–4 years, and 5–6 years after the onset of production.

Also, parasitism of the stink bugs was generally much lower where insecticide was sprayed on the crop more than twice, particularly when the sprayings were at pest densities below the threshold. The authors' target was to obtain stable, rather than high, yields as a step towards sustainable agriculture.

They tested the efficacy of early maturing soybeans, on the one hand, to escape (and hence minimize) damage by stink bugs and, on the other hand, to serve as a trap crop. For the latter, the early maturing variety was planted along the margins of the field in well-defined areas equal to about 5 per cent of the total. Insecticide was applied only to the trap crop and only when the density of stink bugs bigger than 5 mm surpassed 2 bugs/m^2 (soybean for seed) or 4 bugs/m^2 (soybean for processing).

Thus, only 5 per cent of the total area received insecticide, and the impact on natural enemies was significantly reduced (Kobayashi and Cosenza,

1987). The level of stink bug damage in the late-maturing variety with the trap was always less than in that without the trap.

A number of other IPM programmes on soybean have been tried in South America in places such as Argentina (J. C. Gamundi, entomologist, Estación Experimental Agropecuária Oliveiros, Argentina, 1988, personal communication); Peru (Irwin *et al.*, 1981); Bolivia and Paraguay (Panizzi, 1986) and Uruguay (I.C. Corso, personal communication). Others have been reported in temperate China for pod borers (Kogan and Turnipseed, 1987). To date, South America, particularly Brizil, has taken the lead in this important aspect of soybean protection; however, much remains to be done to ensure the adoption of such methods on a wide scale.

The merits of an IPM programme are numerous and easily repay the efforts in developing, implementing and sustaining one. The set of conditions that underpin successful programmes (Flint and van den Bosch, 1981) are by now quite obvious:

- an understanding of the biology of the crop or resource in relation to its environment;
- an identification of the key pests and an understanding of their biologies and interrelationship with, and effects on, the plants — signs of damage, loss in productivity, critical stage of attack, etc.;
- an identification of factors that contribute to natural control as well as those that favour the pest;
- a clarification of concepts, methods and materials for control (permanent suppression or temporary restraint);
- a system of re-evaluation for adjustment of methods and focus to keep pace with the pest status — in space and time.

Because of the great diversity in local conditions and pests, individuals designing IPM packages should:

- direct control measures at the weakest link in the pest's life cycle;
- as much as possible use methods that conserve and augment the natural mortality factors that characterize the ecosystem;
- if possible, attempt to diversify the ecosystem;
- build-in a continuous pest-monitoring system.

Concluding remarks

Much research remains to be done on soybean pests in several parts of the tropics. Exemplary work has been reported from the USA and Brazil, but even in these countries scientists and farmers alike find themselves confronted with new problems every year.

Pests and their control must be viewed as a dynamic system, sometimes at equilibrium within the ecosystem, but more often in a state of flux, where the equilibrium has been disrupted by agricultural and other human activities.

Our knowledge and understanding of the entire system, not the pests alone, must be increased if we are to develop and implement practicable IPM systems for soybean. Basic studies of pests on the one hand and of ecological frameworks on the other are the building blocks for a sound IPM programme. Government support and community involvement are essential for their success.

In Africa and other regions where the cultivation of soybean is relatively new, the data base on soybean pests is small but the opportunity great for the design of systematic, reliable and location-specific IPM programmes. Time is on the side of plant protection scientists working on this crop in such areas, but time does not wait! The successes elsewhere have indicated the components and framework that can be adopted and modified to suit local circumstances. Although at present in Africa, pests of soybean are not serious, the experience in Latin America, Asia and the southern USA is a reminder that the challenge is real and the solution sometimes elusive.

We wish to acknowledge gratefully several colleagues who made contributions during the preparation of this chapter. We depended heavily on the work of N.S. Talekar (1987) of AVRDC and that of Bhattacharya and Rathore (1977) in compiling the information from Asia and elsewhere. Also, our secretarial staff worked hard to get the manuscript ready on time, and we salute them. We express very special appreciation to Eyoanwan Inang for her assistance in the final preparation of this chapter.

Insect Pests of Food Legumes
Edited by S. R. Singh
©1990 John Wiley & Sons Ltd.

3

Key Insects and Other Invertebrate Pests of Beans

Cesar Cardona[a] and Ashok K. Karel[b]

[a]Centro Internacional de Agricultura Tropical (CIAT), PO Box 6713, Cali,
Colombia
[b]Moi University, PO Box 3900, Eldoret, Kenya

Many species of insects and other invertebrate pests affect common or dry
beans (*Phaseolus vulgaris* L.) before and after harvest (Ruppel and Idrobo,
1962; Singh and van Emden, 1979; Schoonhoven and Cardona, 1980; Karel
et al., 1981; Cardona *et al.*, 1982a; Karel, 1984a; King and Saunders, 1984)
(Table 3.1). The few that have been recognized as economically important
(Table 3.2) are often found in complexes that attack every part of the bean
plant (Figure 3.1), including the seeds in storage.

This chapter updates the literature on bean pests with emphasis on pest
ecology, non-chemical control methods and species regarded as major pests
of *P. vulgaris* in Africa and tropical America, the largest bean-producing
regions of the world.

Some of the major invertebrate pests of beans are cosmopolitan in
distribution (Table 3.2). Examples of these are bruchids, bean aphids,
whitefly, the green stink bug, and *Maruca testulalis* Geyer. Others have
regional importance and have not been recorded elsewhere. Examples are the
pod weevil, the Mexican bean beetle, and, to a lesser extent, the seedcorn
maggot. Perhaps the most striking difference between the insect faunas of the
new and old worlds is that the beanfly complex (*Ophiomyia* spp.), by far the
most important pest of beans in Asia, Africa, and Oceania, has not so far
been recorded in the Americas.

The economic impact of insect damage varies widely between and within
regions depending on area, season, cultivar, planting date, and cultural
practices. For example, losses caused by leafhoppers during dry seasons in
Latin America can be as high as 80 per cent, whereas during wet seasons

Table 3.1.   **Scientific name, status and distribution of insect pests attacking dry beans**

Scientific name	Plant parts damaged[a]	Africa	Asia	Americas	Oceania
ORTHOPTERA					
Gryllidae					
Acheta assimilis Fabricius	L,S			N	
THYSANOPTERA					
Thripidae					
Caliothrips braziliensis (Morgan)	L,F			N,S	
Caliothrips fasciatus (Pergande)	L,F			N	
Caliothrips phaseoli (Hood)	L,F			N	
Frankliniella dampfi Priesner	F	N,S			
Frankliniella insularis (Franklin)	L,F			N	
Frankliniella williamsi (Hood)	L,F			N	
Megalurothrips sjostedti Trybom	F	M,S			
Taeniothrips nigricarnis	F	N	N		N
Sericothrips sp.	L,F			N	
HEMIPTERA					
Coreidae					
Anoplocnemis curvipes F.	P	N			
Clavigralla schadabi Dolling	P	N			
Clavigralla tomentosicollis Stal.	P	N			
Riptortus dentipes F.	P	N			
Riptortus pilosus	P		M		
Riptortus servipes F.	P				N
Cydnidae					
Cyrtomenus bergi (Froeschner)	R			N,S	
Miridae					
Lygus hesperus Knight	P			N,S	
Pentatomidae					
Acrosternum marginatum P.de Beauv	P			N,S	
Edessa rufomarginata (de Geer)	P			N	
Euschistus bifibulus (P.de Beauv)	P			N,S	
Nezara viridula Linnaeus	P	N	N	N	N
Piezodorus guildinii (Westwood)	P			N,S	
Piezodorus pallescens	P	N			
Thyanta perditor (F.)	P			N,S	

Scientific name	Plant parts damaged[a]	Distribution and status[b]			
		Africa	Asia	Americas	Oceania

Scientific name	Plant parts damaged[a]	Africa	Asia	Americas	Oceania
HOMOPTERA					
Aphididae					
Aphis craccivora Koch	L,F,P	N	N	N	N
Aphis fabae Scopoli	L,F,P	M	M	N	
Aphis gossypii Glover	L,P	N		N	
Myzus persicae (Sulzer)	L	N	N		
Tetraneura nigriabdominalis (Sasaki)	L			N	
Aleyrodidae					
Bemisia tabaci (Gennadius)	L	N	N	M	N
Tetraleurodes acadiae (Quaintance)	L			N	
Trialeurodes abutiloneus (Haldeman)	L			N	
Trialeurodes vaporariorum (Westwood)	L			M	
Cicadellidae					
Agallia sp.	L			N	
Austroasca spp.	L				N
Carneocephala spp.	L			N	
Empoasca dolichi Paoli	L	N			
Empoasca fabae (Harris)	L			M	
Empoasca kraemeri Ross & Moore	L			M	
Empoasca lybica Le Berg	L	N			
Empoasca spp.	L			N	
Oncometopia sp.	L			N	
Tylozygus fasciatus Walker	L			N	
COLEOPTERA					
Bruchidae					
Acanthoscelides obtectus (Say)	G	M	M	M	
Callosobruchus chinensis (Linnaeus)	G	N	N		
Callosobruchus maculatus (Fabricius)	G	N	N	N	
Zabrotes subfasciatus (Boheman)	G	M	M	M	
Chrysomelidae					
Acalymma spp.	L			N	
Cerotoma facialis Erickson	L,F,P,R			M	
Cerotoma ruficornis (Olivier)	L,F,P,R			M	
Cerotoma salvini Baly	L,F,P,R			N	
Colaspis spp.	L,F			N	
Disonycha glabrata (F.)	L			N	

Table 3.1 Continued

Scientific name	Plant parts damaged[a]	Distribution and status[b]			
		Africa	Asia	Americas	Oceania
Diabrotica sp.	L,F,P,R			N	
Diabrotica balteata	L,F,P,R			M	
Gynandrobrotica sp.	L			N	
Luperodes quaternus Fairmaire	L	N			
Maecolaspis sp.	L			N	
Ootheca bennigsenni Weise	L	M			
Ootheca mutabilis Sahlberg	L	M			
Systena s-littera L.	L			N	
Coccinellidae					
Epilachna mexicana Guerin	L			N	
Epilachna varivestis Mulsant	L,P			M	
Epilachna sp.	L			N	
Curculionidae					
Alcidodes leucogrammus Erichson	S	N			
Apion aurichalceum Wagner	P			N,S	
Apion godmani Wagner	P			M	
Meloidae					
Coryna sp.	F	N			
Epicauta spp.	L,F	N	N	N	
Lytta spp.	L,F			N,S	
Mylabris sp.	F	M	M		
Scarabeidae					
Phyllophaga spp.	R			S	
Phyllophaga menetriesi (Blanchard)	R			S	
LEPIDOPTERA					
Arctiidae					
Estigmene acrea Drury	L			S	
Estigmene columbiana Roths.	L			N	
Hesperiidae					
Urbanus proteus (Linnaeus)	L			N	
Noctuidae					
Agrotis ipsilon (Hufnagel)	L,R,S	S	S	S	S
Autoplusia egena Guen.	L			N	
Heliothis armigera (Hübner)	L,P	S	S		S
Heliothis virescens (F.)	P			M,S	
Heliothis zea (Boddie)	P			S	
Pseudoplusia includens (Walker)	L			N	

Scientific name	Plant parts damaged[a]	Distribution and status[b]			
		Africa	Asia	Americas	Oceania
Spodoptera eridania (Cramer)	L			N	
Spodoptera exigua (Hübner)	L,F			N	
Spodoptera ornithogali (Guenee)	L			N	
Trichoplusia ni (Hübner)	L,P			S	
Olethreutidae					
Epinotia aporema (Walsm.)	L,S,P			M,S	
Pyralidae					
Elasmopalpus lignosellus (Zeller)	S			S	
Etiella zinckenella (Treitschke)	P	S	S	S	S
Omiodes (=Lamprosema) indicata (Fabricius)	L	N	N	N	
Maruca testulalis (Geyer)	P	M	M	M,S	M
DIPTERA					
Agromyzidae					
Liriomyza huidobrensis (Blanchard)	L			M,S	
Liriomyza sativae Blanchard	L			N,S	
Liriomyza trifolii Burgess	L	N	N		
Melanagromyza phaseolivora Spencer	L,S			N	
Melanagromyza sp.	P			N	
Ophiomyia centrosematis de Meijere	S	M	M		M
Ophiomyia phaseoli (Tryon)	S	M	M		M
Ophiomyia spencerella Greathead	S	M	M		M
Anthomyiidae					
Delia platura (Meigen)	R,S	N		M,S	

OTHER INVERTEBRATE PESTS

ARACHNIDA ACARINA
Tarsonemidae

Polyphagotarsonemus latus (Banks)	L,P	N	N	M,S	

Tetranychidae

Eotetranychus lewisi (McGregor)	L			N	
Oligonychus sticneyi (McGregor)	L			N	
Tetranychus cinnabarinus Boisduval	L	N		N	
Tetranychus desertorum Banks	L			N	
Tetranychus ludeni (Zacher)	L			N	
Tetranychus telarius L.	L			N	

Table 3.1 Continued

Scientific name	Plant parts damaged[a]	Distribution and status[b]			
		Africa	Asia	Americas	Oceania

GASTROPODA PULMONATA
Limacidae
Limax maximus L.   L   N

Veronicellidae
Vaginulus plebeius (Fisher)   L   N   ?   M,S

[a]Plant parts: R = roots; S = stems and peduncles; L = leaves; F = flower buds and flowers; P = green pods and seeds; G = dry grains.

[b]Pest status: M = major; N = minor; S = sporadic; O = of no importance; Y = not known.

Table 3.2. Major insect pests of dry beans in tropical areas of the world

Scientific name	Common name	Nature of damage and remarks
THYSANOPTERA		
Megalurothrips sjostedti Trybom	Flower thrips	Suck sap from flower buds and flowers; can be serious in hot, dry weather in Africa; are minor pests in the Americas
HOMOPTERA		
Aphis fabae Scopoli	Black bean aphid	Suck sap from leaves, stem, flowers, and pods; act as vectors of diseases in Africa; are a minor pest in the Americas
Bemisia tabaci (Genn.)	Whitefly	Suck sap from leaves; are minor pest in Asia and Africa; a major vector of virus diseases in Latin America
Empoasca kraemeri Ross & Moore	Leafhopper	Suck sap from leaves, petioles and pods; are the most important insect pest of beans in the Americas; not present in Africa or Asia
COLEOPTERA		
Acanthoscelides obtectus (Say) and *Zabrotes subfasciatus* (Boheman)	Bruchids	Attack seed in storage

Scientific name	Common name	Nature of damage and remarks
Ootheca bennigseni Weise	Leaf beetle	Adults feed on foliage; act as virus vector in Africa; not reported in the Americas
Cerotoma facialis Erickson and *Diabrotica balteata* LeConte	Leaf beetles	Adults feed on foliage; act as virus vectors; larvae feed on roots and root nodules; main chrysomelid species in the Americas
Epilachna varivestis Mulsant	Mexican bean beetle	Adults and larvae feed on foliage; are major pest in the U.S., Mexico, and parts of El Salvador; not reported elsewhere
Apion godmani Wagner	Pod weevil	Larvae feed on developing seeds within the pod; are major pest in Mexico and Central America; not reported elsewhere
LEPIDOPTERA		
Maruca testulalis (Geyer)	Legume pod borer	Larvae feed on flower buds, flowers, green pods; a major pest of legumes in Asia and Africa; a minor pest in the Americas
DIPTERA		
Delia platura Meigen	Seedcorn maggot	Larvae feed on germinating seeds and seedlings; important in certain areas of the Americas but not in Africa or Asia
Liriomyza spp.	Leaf miners	Larvae mine the foliage; minor pests in Africa; increasingly important in the Americas
Ophiomyia phaseoli Tryon, *O. spencerella* Greathead, and *O. centrosematis* de Meijere	Beanflies	Larvae bore into the stems of seedlings; the most important pest of beans in Africa, Asia and Oceania; not reported in the Americas

they average 22 per cent (CIAT, 1975). The beanfly complex in Africa and Asia is responsible for losses that vary from slight to 100 per cent (Karel and Matee, 1986), and pod weevils in Central America can destroy 9–80 per cent of the crop (Salguero, 1983). Bruchids attacking beans in storage cause losses of 30–73 per cent in Africa (Khamala, 1978) and 13–35 per cent in Latin America (Schoonhoven and Cardona, 1980). Given such variability, we dare not discuss the mean yield losses caused by insects.

Damage is not expressed only in yield reductions caused by insects. In Central America, where beans are grown mainly on small farms, slugs affect

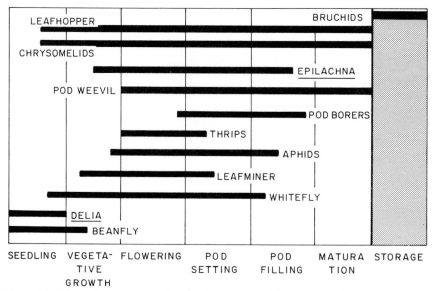

Figure 3.1. Time of occurrence of major insect pests of beans according to crop phenology

half a million farms annually (Andrews, 1983) and have become a serious socioeconomic problem. Bruchid damage also affects smallholders' economies: fear of bruchid damage forces farmers to sell their produce as soon as possible, even when supply is high and prices are low (Schoonhoven, 1976).

Bean cropping systems and bean control tactics differ widely in Africa, Asia and the Americas, with the latter ranging from sophisticated, large-scale applications of granular insecticides in Latin America, to occasional insecticidal applications on small farms. In much of Africa, Asia and Latin America, however, farmers rely on natural mortality factors to suppress insect populations.

Mixed cropping is common throughout the tropics. This has been found to reduce pest incidence and damage. Still, it must be combined with other protective measures to optimize yields, and literature from studies in several African countries suggests that large yield increases can be obtained with effective insect control (Karel and Ndunguru, 1980).

Other cultural practices can also reduce insect populations. Shifting of planting dates helps to reduce pressure from leafhoppers, bean pod weevil, seedcorn maggot, beanflies and other insects, but it has limited application in areas where rainfall distribution governs planting dates. Also, weeding, land preparation, and burning of residues help control cutworms, white grubs, slugs, and other insect pests.

Frequent fallow periods and short growing seasons seem to undermine biological control in beans, although efforts in biological control, to date, have been minimal. Apart from the introduction and release of larval parasites of the Mexican bean beetle and the use of *Bacillus thuringiensis* Berliner to control lepidopteran foliage feeders in Latin America, there have been no attempts to mass-rear, mass-release, or manipulate parasites or predators of bean pests. Nevertheless, research in this area, as well as in the possible use of insect pathogens, must continue.

Progress has been made in identifying cultivars with genetic resistance to leafhoppers, bruchids, pod weevil, Mexican bean beetle, beanfly, mites, and pod borers. The research must maintain its impetus to minimize pesticide applications. Most national research programmes have updated chemical control recommendations, and valuable information on economic injury levels and critical periods of control has recently been published. This will help researchers and others formulating recommendations on integrated pest management (IPM) for which host-plant resistance is the foundation. The overall aim should be to increase the profitability of the crop with due regard to protection of the environment. Recent examples of how to carry out IPM in beans are provided by Pohronezny *et al.* (1981), Andrews (1984), and Karel and Schoonhoven (1986).

In the following pages the most important insect pests of beans are discussed systematically under each order. Mites and slugs are not insects but are included because of their economic importance in certain areas.

Orthoptera

GRYLLIDAE

The common cricket, *Acheta assimilis* F. (syn. *Gryllus assimilis* F.), has been recorded as a minor pest of beans in several areas of the Americas (King and Saunders, 1984). A polyphagous species, this insect attacks seedlings of maize, rice, beans, soybeans, and other crops. The life cycle has been described by Wille (1943), Metcalf *et al.* (1962) and King and Saunders (1984). Eggs are creamy white, 2 mm long and banana-shaped. Oviposition occurs in the soil. Nymphs are black or brown, feed initially on organic matter and then on seedlings. Adults are dark brown or black, with quadrate head and thorax, long antennae and abdominal cerci. Both nymphs and adults are active at night, cutting the stems and feeding on roots and leaves of bean seedlings. Still, the damage is not usually important. If necessary, crickets can be controlled by means of a mixture of wheat or rice bran, molasses, and an insecticide such as carbaryl or trichlorphon (Metcalf *et al.*, 1962; Sifuentes, 1978).

Thysanoptera

THRIPIDAE

Thrips are pests of beans in several countries of tropical America, Asia and Africa. In South America, *Caliothrips braziliensis* (Morgan), *Frankliniella* sp., and *Sericothrips* sp. have been recorded (Posada *et al.*, 1970; Rossetto *et al.*, 1974). In Central America, King and Saunders (1984) list *C. fasciatus* (Pergande), *C. phaseoli* (Hood), *F. insularis* (Franklin), and *F. williamsi* (Hood). All of these are regarded as minor pests of the crop.

In dry, hot weather, *C. braziliensis* causes some damage to cotyledonary and first true leaves of early planted crops, but most plants recover from this damage. In older plants, thrips feed on leaves, flowers and petioles. Female *C. braziliensis* insert the eggs into leaves, petioles, and stems. In laboratory studies at CIAT, eggs of this species hatched in 5−6 days. First-instar larvae developed in 1−2 days, and the second lasted 4−5 days. The pupae lasted 2−3 days. Longevity and fecundity of adults have not been studied.

Flower thrips, *Megalurothrips sjostedti* Trybom (syn. *Taeniothrips sjostedti*), are important in Africa (Ingram, 1969b; Taylor, 1969; Nyiira, 1973; Annecke and Moran, 1982). Other thrips recorded in Africa include *Taeniothrips nigricarnis* and *Frankliniella dampfi* Priesner (Ingram, 1969b; Schmutterer, 1969; Karel *et al.*, 1981).

Observations on the biology of *M. sjostedti* were made by Ingram (1969b). Females (1 mm long and shiny black) lay eggs in flower buds. Two larval instars seem to occur, and pupation takes place in the soil. The entire cycle from egg to adult emergence probably requires 10−14 days. Both nymphs and adults damage bean flowers. If weather is dry and the infestations are high, flower buds will not open and flowers may not set pods (Karel *et al.*, 1981). Injury is characterized by feeding punctures on the base of flower petals and stigma, distortion, malformation, and discoloration of flowers.

In general, chemical control of thrips is rarely needed. Karel *et al.*, (1981) and Karel and Mughogho (1985) reported that control of flower thrips in Africa can be achieved by spraying with monocrotophos or cypermethrin. However, Ingram (1969a) had previously found that chemical control of thrips did not improve seed yield.

Not much is known about the natural enemies of bean thrips. At CIAT, in Colombia, nymphs and adults of *Orius tristicolor* (White) have been observed preying on *C. braziliensis* and *Sericothrips* sp. Virtually nothing has been published on the resistance of bean cultivars to thrips.

Hemiptera

COREIDAE

Spiny bugs, *Clavigralla schadabi* Dolling (syn. *Acanthomia horrida* Germar) and *C. tomentosicollis* Stal. (syn. *A. tomentosicollis* Stal.) are the two most common coreid bugs infesting beans and other legumes in Africa. Clavigralla hystricoides (syn. *A. hystricoides*) has been noted in Tanzania (Bohlen, 1978).

Adult *Clavigralla* spp. measure 7−10 mm long. The body is covered with conspicuous hair and the prothorax presents two spines, hence the common name. The prothoracic spines project anteriorly in *C. schadabi* and *C. hystricoides*. In *C. tomentosicollis*, the spines are smaller and project laterally. *Clavigralla schadabi* is grey and smaller than *C. tomentosicollis*, which is hairy and brown. The smallest is *C. hystricoides*, which is black (Karel, 1984a).

Materu (1968) studied the biology and population dynamics of *C. schadabi* and *C. tomentosicollis* in Tanzania. Females lay as many as 200 eggs, in batches of 10−70, which hatch in 6 days. There are five nymphal instars over a total 28−35 days. Nymphs and adults are usually sluggish and often feed together on a single pod. Bugs suck sap from developing seeds and cause dimpling in the seed coat as well as browning and shrivelling of seeds and pods. Insecticides such as endosulfan, dimethoate and monocrotophos have been found to control these bugs effectively (Swaine, 1969; Nyiira, 1978). However, Matteson (1982) reported that bug populations could be increased as a result of sprays.

Several species of *Riptortus*, known as coreid bugs, can sometimes cause severe damage to bean plants by sucking sap from green pods *Riptortus dentipes* F. is the most common of these species. Others are *R. tenuicornis* Dall. and *R. longipes* Dall. (Le Pelley, 1959; Forsyth, 1966). Adults are slender, about 17 mm long, and light brown with white or yellow lines on the sides of the body. They are strong fliers and usually choose to oviposit on legumes other than beans and on weeds. As the adults visit beans from alternative hosts, control is difficult and requires repeated applications of the same insecticides as are effective against *Clavigralla* spp.

The giant coreid bug, *Anoplocnemis curvipes* F., a major pest of cowpea and pigeon pea in tropical Africa, is regarded as a minor pest of beans, feeding on young pods or shoots and causing an appearance like dieback.

PENTATOMIDAE

Pentatomid damage is caused primarily by adults and nymphs sucking sap from young pods. Feeding punctures cause necrosis, resulting in pod spotting and deformation, yellowing and premature drying of pods, and lack of seed formation. In general, pentatomids are regarded as minor pests of beans.

Several species occur in Latin America. According to King and Saunders (1984), the green stink bug, *Acrosternum marginatum* (Palisot de Beauvois), is found in Central America, Mexico, the Caribbean and parts of South America. Other pentatomids reported in the Americas are *Edessa rufomarginata* de Geer, *Euschistus bifibulus* (Palisot de Beauvois), *Padaeus trivittatus* Stal. and *Thyanta perditor* (F.). The cosmopolitan and polyphagous bugs *Nezara viridula* (L.) and *Piezodorus guildinii* (Westwood) are not regarded as being economically important in common beans (Swaine, 1969; Costa *et al.*, 1980, 1981; Karel *et al.*, 1981).

Homoptera

APHIDIDAE

Several Aphididae attack common beans. In general, direct damage is not important, but their ability to transmit bean common mosaic virus makes them important economic pests. Species common on beans in the Americas are *Aphis gossypii* Glover, *A. craccivora* Koch, *A. spiraecola* Patch, *A. fabae* Scopoli, *Tetraneura nigriabdominalis* (Sasaki), *Myzus persicae* (Sulzer), and *Brevicoryne brassicae* (L.) (Zaumeyer and Thomas, 1957; Costa and Rossetto, 1972; Schoonhoven and Cardona, 1980; Becquer and Fernandez, 1981). In Africa and Asia, *A. fabae* and *A. craccivora* seem to cause greater losses than they do in the Americas.

Remaudière *et al.* (1985b) regard *A. fabae* as the main species. In the tropics, this is a parthenogenetic species that feeds on several other legume crops (Remaudière *et al.*, 1985a). Apterous forms appear when food is abundant and climatic conditions are optimal. Alates appear when food is in short supply and there is overcrowding. Winged adults may invade bean fields soon after crop emergence but preflowering is the stage at which damage to the plants is critical (Khaemba and Ogenga-Latigo, 1985). The life cycle takes 11–13 days, and adults live for 6–15 days. Apterous forms are found in colonies around the stem, growing points and leaves.

Chemical control is effective (Swaine, 1969; Karel *et al.*, 1981). However, insecticide applications may destroy effective natural enemies, several of which have been released in Burundi (Autrique and Ntahimpera, 1986). Pirimicarb, a selective aphicide, has been recommended. In Latin America, where resistance to bean common mosaic virus has been incorporated in common beans, chemical control of aphids is not needed.

Resistance of beans to *A. fabae* has been studied by de Fluiter and

Ankersmit (1948) and by Rose *et al.* (1978) but has not been explored in Africa.

ALEYRODIDAE

The sweetpotato whitefly, *Bemisia tabaci* (Gennadius), a major vector of virus diseases in Latin America, is a minor pest of beans elsewhere. Other aleyrodids found on beans in tropical America are *B. tuberculata* Bandar, *Tetraleurodes acaciae* (Quaintance), *Trialeurodes abutiloneus* (Haldeman), and *Trialeurodes vaporariorum* (Westwood). The group exhibits host-correlated variation (Mound, 1963) and different races (Bird and Maramorosch, 1978).

Bemisia tabaci is polyphagous (Russell, 1975) and is a vector of such important virus diseases as bean golden mosaic virus and bean chlorotic mottle (Gamez, 1971). Mechanical damage is not important so the insect is a major pest only in areas where virus transmission occurs, namely Central America, parts of Mexico, the Caribbean, Brazil, and Argentina (Costa, 1965; Gamez, 1971; Blanco and Bencomo, 1981; Cardenas, 1982).

Russell (1975) summarized the biology of *B. tabaci*: females lay 25–32 eggs singly or in groups on the undersurface of bean leaves where the egg pedicle is inserted. Immature stages also occur on the undersurface of leaves. The egg-to-adult cycle is completed in about 3 weeks. These figures are similar to those reported for cotton (Butler *et al.*, 1983).

Planting for extended periods favours build-up of whiteflies so that later plantings are affected more than early ones (Alonzo, 1975). Soybeans act as a transitional host for whitefly infestations (Costa, 1975), so a narrowing of the time devoted to planting and elimination of soybeans have been proposed as control measures but have not been widely adopted.

Virtually nothing is known about resistance of bean cultivars to *B. tabaci* (Berlinger, 1986). Some preliminary work (Boica and Vendramin, 1986; CIAT, unpublished results) suggests that variability exists. Resistance to bean golden mosaic virus has been shown to be an economic method of control (Aldana *et al.*, 1981; Rodriguez, 1983), eliminating the need to control the vector.

Prospects for biological control of *B. tabaci* do not seem bright (Gerling, 1986). In areas where cultivars susceptible to bean golden mosaic virus are planted, there is the need to control whitefly infestations by means of insecticides. Granular insecticides such as carbofuran, aldicarb and phorate applied at planting time are effective (Mancia *et al.*, 1973a; de Bortoli and Giacomini, 1981).

CICADELLIDAE

Leafhoppers, mainly *Empoasca* spp. are widely distributed in tropical and subtropical bean-growing areas. *Empoasca lybica* Le Berg and *E. dolichi* Paoli are minor pests of the crop in Africa (Karel, 1984a), whereas *E. kraemeri* Ross & Moore is the most important and widely distributed pest of beans in sub-tropical and tropical America, from Florida in the United States to Central and South America (Ross and Moore, 1957; Schoonhoven and Cardona, 1980; Oliveira *et al.*, 1981). *Empoasca fabae* (Harris), an important pest in North America, has been reported in Central America (King and Saunders, 1984), but several workers question its presence south of the United States (Ross and Moore, 1957; Schoonhoven *et al.*, 1985). Other minor species of *Empoasca* in Latin America are listed by Ruppel and DeLong (1956), Bonnefil (1965), Langlitz (1966), and Schoonhoven *et al.*, 1985).

The biology of *E. kraemeri* was studied by Wilde *et al.* (1976) who found that eggs are inserted into leaf blades, petioles, leaf veins, and stems, with 50−82 per cent of the eggs located in petioles (Gomez and Schoonhoven, 1977). Eggs hatch in 8−9 days, and the five nymphal instars are completed in 8−11 days. Adults are distinctly green; they live an average of 62 days. Females lay an average 107 eggs, and the sex ratio is usually 1:1. In Brazil, Leite and Ramalho (1979) observed a 3-day preoviposition period and a shorter adult lifespan.

Leafhopper attacks begin at the seedling stage and can continue through several generations till the crop is mature. Damage is caused by nymphs and adults feeding in phloem tissue. The result is leaf curling and chlorosis (hopper burn), stunting, and severely reduced yields or, in many cases, complete crop loss. Attacks and damage are more severe during dry, hot weather and are aggravated by poor soil conditions or insufficient soil moisture (Schoonhoven and Cardona, 1980). Yield losses are high when populations are dense at early stages of growth and flowering. Damage occurring after pod set does not significantly affect yields (Schoonhoven *et al.*, 1978a).

Planting dates have a significant impact on leafhopper populations. In El Salvador, Miranda (1967) obtained yields of 1182 kg/ha when beans were planted at the end of the wet season, but only 121 kg/ha when beans were planted in the middle of the dry season. Likewise, leafhopper populations become dense at CIAT in Palmira, Colombia, when beans are planted in hot, dry weather.

Besides planting dates, cultural practices can be manipulated to reduce leafhopper populations. Consistently, lower *E. kraemeri* populations occur on beans planted in association with maize (CIAT, 1977; Hernandez *et al.*, 1984), sugar cane (Garcia *et al.*, 1979) and other crops. Weed cover has also been found to reduce leafhopper populations (CIAT, 1976; Altieri *et al.*, 1977), but weed competition is such that no yield advantage is obtained when weed cover is used to suppress leafhopper populations (Schoonhoven *et al.*, 1981; Andow, 1983). Mulching with aluminium foil and rice straw significantly reduces adult leafhopper colonization, possibly as a result of increased light reflection, but this method of control has serious economic and practical limitations (Cardona *et al.*, 1981; Wells *et al.*, 1984). Andrews *et al.* (1985) showed that plastic mulches are economically feasible in the production of snap beans but advised against their use for dry beans.

Several natural enemies of *E. kraemeri* have been recorded in the Americas. Among them, the egg parasite *Anagrus* sp. (Hymenoptera: Mymaridae) ranks as the most important (CIAT, 1980; Pizzamiglio, 1979). Although parasitism can be as high as 80 per cent under field conditions, it cannot keep leafhopper populations below economically damaging levels (Gomez and Schoonhoven, 1977). Other natural enemies include the trichogrammatid *Aphelinoidea plutella* (Girault), the mymarid egg parasite *Polynema* sp. and the dryinid *Agonatopus* sp. (Pizzamiglio, 1979). The parasitic fungi *Hirsutella guyana* and *Erynia radicans* (Brefeld) were found in Brazil by Ghaderi (1984). *Erynia radicans* has also been recorded in Colombia (Schoonhoven *et al.*, 1985) and Honduras (Caballero and Andrews, 1985). In general, it is considered that biological control of *E. kraemeri* in the Americas is not feasible because of the seriousness of damage by the leafhopper and the aggressiveness of the pest.

Host-plant resistance to *E. kraemeri* may be the most promising method of control. It has been extensively studied at CIAT where more than 18 000 accessions have been screened. Initial screenings are based solely on visual scoring of damage (leaf distortion and yellowing) recorded 25, 35 and 45 days after planting. Intermediate and resistant materials are rescreened in replicated nurseries in which a visual estimate of pod setting is also made. The differences in yield from insecticide-protected and unprotected plots are then evaluated.

To date, 3–4 per cent of the 18 000 *P. vulgaris* accessions evaluated have been classified as resistant. Most of these are small-seeded, black or cream-coloured, indeterminate bush beans (Galwey, 1983). Large-seeded, red and white beans are more susceptible. Higher levels of resistance have been found among *P. acutifolius* (tepary beans) and *P. lunatus* L. (lima beans) (Lyman and Cardona, 1982).

Mechanisms of resistance to *E. kraemeri* have been the subject of several studies. Wilde and Schoonhoven (1976) did not find antibiosis or definitive signs of antixenosis and concluded that tolerance was the main mechanism. Additional research (CIAT, 1982) suggested that tolerance was manifested by reduced damage, higher leaf-area index, and higher pod setting. Later, in both free- and no-choice tests, ovipositional antixenosis was detected for several cultivars (Kornegay *et al.*, 1986, 1988). The tolerance and antixenosis defence mechanisms seem to be inherited according to an additive-dominance genetic model (Kornegay and Temple, 1986).

In general, breeding for resistance to *E. kraemeri* has been complicated by the lack of high levels of resistance in dry beans, lack of diversity in resistance responses, the quantitative nature of inheritance (Galwey and Evans, 1982a) and strong genotype–environment interactions (Galwey and Evans, 1982b; Kornegay et al., 1986; Schoonhoven et al., 1985). The process has proved most difficult in large-seeded beans. Nevertheless, a recurrent selection programme has been successful in diversifying mechanisms of resistance (Kornegay et al., 1986, 1988). Some of the leafhopper-resistant lines have been consistently outstanding, yield well under heavy pressure from insects and have wide adaptation in Latin America (Schoonhoven et al., 1985). Progress will be expedited when barriers to crossing P. vulgaris with other species are overcome (Galwey et al., 1985).

In areas where resistant bean cultivars are not available, there is the need to control the leafhopper by chemical means. Several insecticides such as monocrotophos, methamidophos, dimethoate and granular carbofuran are effective (CIAT, 1974, 1976; Murguido, 1983). Economic injury can be produced by two to three nymphs/leaf in susceptible varieties and four to five in resistant cultivars (CIAT, 1976, 1982). Andrews (1984) recommended that spraying be instituted when one adult per plant is found at the seedling stage. Two nymphs per leaf or two adults per plant are critical population levels between the two-leaf stage and pod setting. Higher populations can be tolerated during and after pod filling.

Coleoptera

BRUCHIDAE

Most of the 28 species of insects listed by Schoonhoven (1976) as occurring on stored beans are not economically important. Besides *Callosobruchus chinensis* (L.), which causes some damage in Africa, the two most universal and important pests in storage are the Mexican bean weevil, *Zabrotes subfasciatus* (Boheman) and the bean weevil, *Acanthoscelides obtectus* (Say).

The economic importance of bruchids has not been well documented. McGuire and Crandall (1967) estimated 35 per cent of losses occurred from storage in Central America but did not specify whether losses were caused solely by insects or by other factors. In Brazil and Colombia, losses have been estimated at 13 and 7 per cent, respectively. Figures as high as 73 per cent have been calculated in Kenya (Schoonhoven, 1976; Khamala, 1978).

There are some important biological and ecological differences between these bruchids. *Zabrotes subfasciatus* glues the eggs to the testae of beans and does not usually attack in the field. In contrast, *A. obtectus* scatters the eggs among stored seeds or oviposits on maturing pods in the field. Also, *Z.*

subfasciatus is a tropical species, whereas *A. obtectus* is more sub-tropical, well adapted to the cooler environments, for example, the highlands of the tropics.

Otherwise, the life history of these bruchids is quite similar (Howe and Currie, 1964). Larvae of both species feed inside the seed and moult four times before pupation. After pupation, the adult may remain in the cell for several days before pushing the 'window' prepared by the last instar larva to facilitate adult emergence. Adults mate and oviposit soon after emergence and usually do not eat.

Zabrotes subfasciatus females are larger than males and can be differentiated by the presence of four characteristic cream-coloured spots on the elytra. Males are entirely brown. At CIAT, where colonies are maintained at 28°C and 75−80 per cent RH, females lay an average 36 eggs and live 13 days. The egg stage lasts 5−6 days, larval development takes 14 days and the pupal stage takes 6−7 days. Sex ratios are usually 1:1.

Acanthoscelides obtectus adults are brown, and the sexes can be recognized only under the microscope by differences in the genitalia. At 26°C and 75−80 per cent RH, females live 14 days and lay an average 45 eggs. Eggs hatch in 6−7 days, and the larval−pupal development takes 23 days. There are four larval instars. Sex ratios are 1:1.

Bruchids can be controlled by several means. Farmers traditionally use mixtures of grain with inert materials such as sand, crystalline silica, bentonite, magnesium carbonate, laterite dust, and ashes from fireplaces (CIAT, 1975; Schoonhoven, 1976; Standaert *et al.*, 1985). Black pepper has also been successfully used against *A. obtectus* (Lathrop and Keirstead, 1946).

Storing beans in the pod is practised by some farmers to reduce *Z. subfasciatus* infestations, as eggs deposited on pod walls hatch but the larvae cannot penetrate. This method cannot, however, be used against *A. obtectus*, since this species attacks in the field, ovipositing on mature pods (Labeyrie and Maison, 1954; Menten and Menten, 1984). Labeyrie (1957) clearly demonstrated that storing beans unshelled or delaying harvest considerably increases *A. obtectus* attacks and damage.

Vegetable oils effectively control bruchids. Schoonhoven (1978) found that oil from cotton, peanut, soybean, oil palm, or maize was efficient at 5−10 mL/kg of seed. Likewise, neem-seed oil has been found effective in Africa (Kiula and Karel, 1985). Unrefined oils can be used (Hill and Schoonhoven, 1981).

Chemical control of bruchids is effective with well known insecticides such as malathion, pyrethrins, pirimiphos-methyl, and fenitrothion (Salas and Ruppel, 1959; McFarlane, 1970; CIAT, 1975; Ruppel *et al.*, 1981). For large volumes of seed, the fumigants aluminium phosphide and methyl bromide are extensively used.

Extensive work on resistance of beans to bruchids has been conducted at CIAT in Colombia, and other countries (Ramalho *et al.*, 1977; Oliveira *et al.*, 1979; Menten and Menten, 1984) in Latin America. Resistance levels in cultivars are low, Schoonhoven and Cardona (1982) concluding that no acceptable levels of resistance were present in the 6000+ cultivars tested against *Z. subfasciatus*. Similarly, no adequate levels of resistance were detected among more than 10 000 cultivars tested with *A. obtectus*.

However, high levels of resistance to both species of Bruchidae were identified among non-cultivated, small-seeded wild forms of *P. vulgaris* of Mexican origin (Schoonhoven *et al.*, 1983; CIAT, 1984). These genotypes can easily be crossed with cultivars. Resistance derives from antibiosis expressed as reduced oviposition, high mortality of late first-instar and early second-instar larvae, lengthy larval development, reduced progeny weight and reduced fecundity of emerging females (Schoonhoven *et al.*, 1983; Cardona *et al.*, 1989).

A new lectin-like protein, called arcelin, present only in resistant wild accessions, was identified by Osborn *et al.* (1986) and postulated as the factor responsible for resistance to *Z. subfasciatus*. Further work indicated that arcelin expression was governed by a single mendelian gene that could easily be transferred into cultivated genotypes by means of backcrosses (Harmsen *et al.*, 1987). Following characterization and purification of arcelin (Osborn *et al.*, 1988a), the purified protein was tested by means of 'artificial' seeds. At a concentration of 10 per cent in the seed, arcelin conferred high levels of resistance against *Z. subfasciatus* but not against *A. obtectus* (Osborn *et al.*, 1988b).

Work is under way to transfer genes for arcelin into cultivated beans and to determine the effect of this protein on human nutrition. At present, lines with desirable commercial characteristics and high levels of resistance to *Z. subfasciatus* have been developed (Cardona and Posso, 1987; CIAT, 1988).

Resistance to *A. obtectus* is also being sought but progress has been hampered by the lack of understanding about factors responsible for resistance. A heteropolysaccharide was postulated by Gatehouse *et al.* (1987), but the hypothesis needs further research.

CHRYSOMELIDAE

Chrysomelid beetles are among the most widely distributed pests of beans (Ruppel and Idrobo, 1962; Singh and van Emden, 1979; Schoonhoven and Cardona, 1980; Passoa, 1983; King and Saunders, 1984). Prevalent genera are *Diabrotica* and *Cerotoma* in Latin America and *Ootheca* in Africa. Other genera are *Epitrix*, *Systena*, *Colaspis*, *Maecolaspis*, *Gynandrobrotica*, *Chalepus*, *Nodonota*, and *Chaectonema* (Schoonhoven and Cardona, 1980). The striped foliage beetle, *Luperodes quaternus* Fairmaire, is a minor pest of beans in Africa (Schmutterer, 1969). This review concentrates on the banded cucumber beetle, *Diabrotica balteata* LeConte, the bean beetle, *Cerotoma facialis* Erishson and the foliage beetles *Ootheca bennigseni* Weise and *O. mutabilis* Sahlberg as these are the most damaging species.

Chrysomelids affect beans in three ways: larvae damage roots and root nodules; adults feed on foliage at all crop stages; and adults may act as vectors of viral diseases (Gamez, 1972). Sometimes adults also feed on flowers and young pods.

Diabrotica balteata is highly polyphagous, having been recorded on 32 host plants. Of these, beans and maize are hosts for larvae and adults, although larvae do not survive well on bean roots (Gonzalez *et al.*, 1982). Adults readily feed on bean foliage but prefer to oviposit on soil in which young maize plants are growing (Young and Candia, 1962). Females undergo pre-oviposition, which varies from 5–12 days in Colombia (Gonzalez *et al.*, 1982) to 4–8 days in Mexico (Young and Candia, 1962). Eggs are laid singly or in clusters of as many as 12 eggs in soil cracks or beneath plant debris. A female can lay up to 800 eggs and lives an average 37 days. Eggs hatch in 5–6 days, and there are three larval instars, which together last 14 days. Pupation occurs in a cell in the ground (Pitre and Kantack, 1962) and lasts 6–7 days. The sex ratio is 1:1.

The biology of *C. facialis* is similar. Females live 52 days, undergo a 5–12 day pre-oviposition, and lay an average 532 eggs. The egg lasts 6 days, there are three larval instars (totalling 10–11 days), and the pupae last 6–7 days. The sex ratio is 1:1 (Gonzalez *et al.*, 1982).

Most damage by *D. balteata* and *C. facialis* occurs during the seedling stage. Adult and larval damage at different population levels and crop-growth stages was evaluated by Cardona *et al.* (1982b). In greenhouse studies, significant damage and leaf-area reduction were detected when plants were infested 1, 4 and 7 days after planting. Plants, 14 days or older, did not show significant reduction in leaf area. Under field conditions, mixed and pure populations of these chrysomelids caused yield reductions at infestation levels of two to four adults per plant during early growth stages and, to a lesser extent, during flowering. No significant damage occurred at other growth stages.

Adult *O. bennigseni* are shiny light brown or orange beetles, 6 mm long. Eggs are elliptical, yellow and translucent, laid in the soil in masses of 40–60. A female can lay from 200 to 400 eggs. Eggs hatch in 11–14 days. Larvae develop in the soil, and there are three instars lasting altogether 40–45 days. Pupation lasts 14–20 days. The life cycle of *O. mutabilis* (Ochieng, 1977) is similar.

Ootheca spp. adults feed on leaves by making holes in the interveinal regions. Heavy infestations reduce photosynthetic activity and can cause seedling death (Karel *et al.*, 1981). Flowers occasionally are attacked. Bean seed yield losses from *O. bennigseni* range from 18 to 31 per cent in Tanzania (Karel and Rweyemamu, 1984).

Intercropping of beans can reduce chrysomelid populations (Risch, 1980; Hernandez *et al.*, 1984). A few natural enemies have been identified, but their efficiency seems to be low. No sources of resistance to *D. balteata* or *C. facialis* have ever been identified in Latin America. Karel (1985b) and Karel and Rweyemamu (1985) have identified genotypes with moderate to high levels of resistance to *O. bennigseni* in Tanzania.

When natural control is not effective and populations reach economically damaging levels, sprays with carbaryl, methomyl or malathion are effective. In Latin America, Cardona *et al.* (1982b) recommended limiting sprays to the early stages of crop growth or to the initial flowering when more than two adults are found per plant.

COCCINELLIDAE

The Mexican bean beetle, *Epilachna varivestis* Mulsant, is a pest of beans (Turnipseed and Kogan, 1976) in the United States, Mexico, parts of Guatemala, Honduras and El Salvador with the most serious losses being in Mexico. It has not been reported elsewhere but has been cited as a pest of cowpea and lima bean in El Salvador (Mancia and Roman, 1973). Other host plants include runner beans, mung bean, urd bean, and beggarweed (Turner, 1932; Wolfenbarger and Sleesman, 1961; Augustine *et al.*, 1964).

Damage is caused by both larvae and adults, which feed on leaves mainly but also stems and pods when populations are high. Larvae scrape the leaf tissue, compress it and then swallow the juices. As a result, leaves look skeletonized, and there is a severe reduction in photosynthetic capacity of the plant. Damage is more serious at early stages of crop growth and mature larvae are more damaging than adults (Turner, 1935).

In Central America pre-oviposition lasts 7−15 days. Eggs are yellow to orange and are laid, in batches of 36−54, on the undersurface of leaves (Mancia and Roman, 1973). Eggs last 6 days, and there are four larval instars, which are completed in 15−16 days. The prepupa lasts 2 days, and the pupal stage 6−7 days. Pupation occurs on leaves, and pupae are found attached to the undersurface of leaves. Adults are copper coloured, with 16 black spots on the elytra. They live 4−6 weeks. Elmore (1949) reported that in the United States adults hibernate, often gregariously, in woodlands and debris. In tropical conditions, the beetle may have four generations from May to November (Mancia and Roman, 1973). The life cycle on soybeans is similar (Mellors and Bassow, 1983). However, Hammond (1984) found that development on dry beans took 16 per cent less time than on soybeans.

Some cultural practices may help in reducing Mexican bean beetle

Plate I. Bemisia tabaci *adult (photo CIAT)*

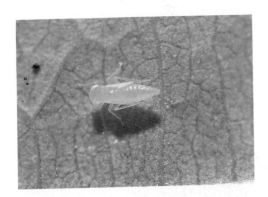

Plate II. Empoasca kraemeri *nymph (photo CIAT)*

Plate III. Empoasca kraemeri *damage (photo CIAT)*

Plate IV. Diabrotica balteata *adult* *(photo CIAT)*

Plate V. Epilachna varivestis *larvae* *(photo CIAT)*

Plate VI. Apion godmani *oviposition (photo CIAT)*

Plate VII. Apion godmani *damage (photo CIAT)*

Plate VIII. Agrotis ipsilon *damage (photo CIAT)*

Plate IX. Liriomyza *sp. damage (photo CIAT)*

populations. Removal of plant debris and deep ploughing are recommended. According to Turner (1935), damage by beetles is decreased at low planting densities. Mixed cropping of maize and beans also reduces beetle populations (Sanchez, 1977; Martinez, 1978). Companion plantings were studied by Latheef and Irwin (1980) who found fewer beetles on beans bordered by French marigold than on other beans, but the benefits were overshadowed by allelopathic effects of marigold on beans.

Several natural enemies of the Mexican bean beetle have been reported in the literature. Predators include the coccinellids *Coleomegilla maculata* de Geer and *Hippodamia convergens* Guerin-Meneville and the pentatomids *Podisus maculiventris* (Say) and *Stiretrus anchorago* (F.) (Waddill and Shepard, 1975). The ectoparasitic mite *Coccipolipus epilachnae* Smiley, which sucks hemolymph from the underside of elytra of adult beetles, was observed in El Salvador (Smiley, 1974) and introduced into the United States (Schroder, 1979) as a promising natural enemy. Subsequently, Cantwell *et al.* (1985a) and Hochmuth *et al.* (1987) concluded that the mite did not have a significant effect on the adult, as parasitized beetles behaved normally, consumed the same amount of food as non-parasitized individuals, and did not show a significant reduction in their reproductive capacity or longevity, apparently because the pest has an inherent ability to tolerate some loss of hemolymph.

The best known natural enemy of Mexican bean beetle is the eulophid larval parasite, *Pediobius foveolatus* (Crawford), which has been effectively used to control the pest on soybeans in the United States (Stevens *et al.*, 1975). This parasite was introduced into Mexico and became established in 3 years (Carrillo, 1977), but there does not seem to be a recent evaluation of its effectiveness. Carrillo (1977) also reports that the tachinid *Aplomyiopsis epilachnae* (Aldrich) can parasitize up to 70 per cent of larvae.

The bacterium *Bacillus thuringiensis* Berliner controls larvae under laboratory and field conditions (Cantwell and Cantelo, 1982). Cantwell *et al.* (1985b) later reported that sprays of this bacterium combined with liberation of the parasite *P. foveolatus* effectively control the pest.

Studies on resistance of dry beans to Mexican bean beetle have produced inconsistent results. Wolfenbarger and Sleesman (1961) did not observe resistance in the *P. vulgaris* accessions they evaluated. However, Campbell and Brett (1966) found variability, reported as resistant accessions that had previously been rated as susceptible, and showed that egg number, egg masses and adult weights were significantly reduced when beetles were reared on resistant cultivars. In Mexico, Montalvo and Sosa (1973) classified several bean cultivars as resistant. Others were reported by Raina *et al.* (1978). However, the literature includes no evidence of these materials' being used in a breeding-for-resistance programme. The mechanisms of resistance to this pest seem to be a combination of antibiosis and non-preference, the latter reflecting reduced sugar contents in resistant genotypes (Lapidus *et al.*, 1963; Arevalo, 1977; Jones *et al.*, 1981). Recent work on resistance to Mexican bean beetle has concentrated on improving screening methods and knowledge of host–plant interactions (Raina *et al.*, 1980; Wilson, 1981).

In the absence of resistant varieties, it is necessary to control the beetle by chemical means. Carbaryl, malathion and methyl parathion are still effective (Cadena and Sifuentes, 1969). Hagen (1974) obtained an effective 10-week control with granular applications of disulfoton, carbofuran, phorate, aldicarb, and fensulfothion at planting. The effectiveness of pyrethroids was reported by McClanahan (1981). Zungoli *et al.* (1983) found that the chitin inhibitor, diflubenzuron, gave adequate control with no apparent effect on the main parasite, *P. foveolatus*. Action thresholds of 25 adults/ha (Cadena and Sifuentes, 1969) or 1–1.5 larvae/plant (Michels and Burkhardt, 1981) have been established.

CURCULIONIDAE

The pod weevils *Apion godmani* Wagner and *A. aurichalceum* Wagner are the two most important curculionids affecting beans. *Apion godmani* is a serious pest in Mexico and parts of Central America, namely Guatemala, El Salvador, Honduras, and northern Nicaragua (McKelvey *et al.*, 1951; Schoonhoven and Cardona, 1980; Salguero, 1983). It does not occur in coastal areas and is most damaging at high altitudes. *Apion aurichalceum*, less important than *A. godmani*, is found in the highlands of Mexico (McKelvey *et al.*, 1951) and Guatemala (Salguero, 1983). Other less important species within the genus *Apion* are reported by McKelvey *et al.* (1947) and Mancia (1973b).

In Mexico, Sifuentes (1978) estimated 50 per cent yield loss, and Guevara (1962) reported as much as 80 per cent damage. Salguero (1983) estimated 17 per cent damage on average in the central–western plateau of Guatemala and 9–60 per cent in the southeastern plateau. Mancia (1973a) observed as much as 94 per cent loss in El Salvador, while seed damage in Honduras has ranged from 1 per cent in resistant varieties to 85 per cent in susceptible genotypes (CIAT, unpublished results). *Apion aurichalceum* is less important, possibly as a result of its ovipositional habit: the female lays some 35 eggs in the distal part of the pod, larvae develop in one or two seeds, and the remaining seeds escape infestation (McKelvey *et al.*, 1951).

Adults of *A. godmani* are black weevils, about 3 mm long; they usually appear before flowering and cause light, non-economic feeding damage to leaves and flowers. The female oviposits on newly formed pods during the day, by chewing a small hole in the mesocarp, usually above the developing seed, and inserting a white, semi-translucent egg. Second-instar larvae bore into the mesocarp of the pod wall and feed on developing seeds, leaving the hilum intact. Usually one larva develops per seed, but three to five have been found during heavy infestations with a maximum of seven per seed and 28/pod. Pupation takes place within the pod, near the damaged seed. Adults emerge from the pods at harvest or soon thereafter (McKelvey *et al.*, 1947; Mancia, 1973b).

Mancia (1973d) found that the egg stage lasted 5 days, the three larval instars 16 days and the prepupa and pupa 2 and 9 days, respectively. Adults lived from 10 days to nearly a year, mated several times, underwent a 10-day pre-ovipositional period and laid a maximum of 392 eggs per female. In Mexico, McKelvey *et al.* (1951) reported a longer larval period of 21 days and four larval instars. The egg-to-adult period in Mexico lasted 42−56 days, and adults lived an average of 3 months. A shorter egg-to-adult cycle of 28−30 days was calculated by Salguero (1983) in Guatemala. The insect disappears during the dry season, but survival sites have not been located.

Several larval parasites of *A. godmani* and *A. aurichalceum* have been reported — among them, the braconids *Triaspis* sp. and *Bracon* sp. in Mexico, El Salvador and Guatemala (McKelvey *et al.*, 1951; Mancia, 1973b; Salguero, 1983; Perez, 1985). In addition, Perez (1985) reported the pteromalids *Pteromalus* sp. and *Zatropis* sp. the eupelmid *Cerambycobius* sp. and the eurytomid *Eurytoma* sp. in Mexico. The efficiency of these natural enemies, and of the fungus *Metarrhizium* sp., which was detected attacking adults in Guatemala (Salguero, 1983), has not been evaluated.

Host-plant resistance to *A. godmani* has been the object of several studies. McKelvey *et al.* (1951) identified several Mexican accessions as resistant, as did Guevara (1962) and colleagues (Guevara *et al.*, 1962), and Medina and Guerra (1973). From these studies and the intensive screening conducted in El Salvador by Mancia (1973d), high levels of resistance were confirmed in accessions (Mexico 1290, Amarillo 154, Negro 150, Puebla 152, lines 12 and 17 Salvador).

These sources of resistance were used in a breeding project that identified highly resistant lines: damage to less than 10 per cent of pods and less than 2 per cent of seeds (CIAT, 1982). Resistant lines with better adaptation to Mexican and Central American conditions have been used in crosses to recover resistance through transgressive segregation (Beebe, 1983). Simultaneously, new parents of Mexican origin were identified. As a result, well-adapted resistant lines of acceptable seed size and colour are available at present (CIAT, 1988).

Chemical control of the pod weevil is still important. Monocrotophos, methamidophos, methomyl, methyl parathion and carbaryl are effective (Mancia *et al.*, 1973b). Carbofuran is also effective (Mancia, 1973a). Sprays are most effective when made applied 6 days after flower initiation and again 7 days later (Mancia *et al.*, 1974).

MELOIDAE

Adults of *Epicauta* spp. and *Lytta* spp. are occasional pests of beans in Central America, feeding on flowers and foliage (King and Saunders, 1984). In Africa, a number of blister beetles or flower beetles that belong to the genera *Mylabris* and *Coryna* may be important (Le Pelley, 1959; Schmutterer, 1969; Hall, 1985).

These beetles are recognized by the bright colours on the elytra, with broad black, yellow, or red bands. They are about 15−35 mm long and are strong fliers; they lay eggs in the soil where larvae and pupae develop. Beetles are difficult to control and may cause serious damage by devouring flowers. Repeated applications of insecticides and picking are recommended.

SCARABEIDAE

According to Schoonhoven and Cardona (1980), as well as King and Saunders (1984), white grubs of the genus *Phyllophaga* are minor pests of beans in the Americas. *Phyllophaga menetriesi* (Blanchard) is described by King and Saunders as the most important species of the group in Central and South America.

Damage from these insects is usually confined to small scattered areas; plant losses are not usually high but, on occasion, are locally devastating.

White grubs feed on roots and the result is yellowing of leaves. Losses can be reduced by proper land preparation and weed control or, if there is a history of previous attacks, by incorporation of granular insecticides.

Lepidoptera

ARCTIIDAE

The saltmarsh caterpillar, *Estigmene acrea* (Drury), is widespread in the Americas, mainly attacking cotton, lettuce, and sugar beets, and, though commonly found on beans, is not a major pest of this crop. Other hosts include maize, vegetables, soybean, sesame, tobacco, and several weeds (Young and Sifuentes, 1959).

Biological studies on this species have been carried out by Stevenson *et al.* (1957) and Young and Sifuentes (1959). Adult moths lay egg masses with as many as 1000 eggs. Larvae are initially gregarious and then solitary and develop in 17−19 days. They are covered with setae.

Pupation takes place on the soil in plant debris. Control of this insect is rarely needed.

HESPERIIDAE

The bean leafroller, *Urbanus proteus* (L.) (syn. *Eudamus proteus*) is widely distributed from the United States (Quaintance, 1898) to Brazil (Freitas, 1960) and Chile (Diaz, 1976). This is a minor pest of beans that has been the object of several studies. In Florida, Greene (1971a) calculated that economic damage occurs when leaf area of more than 725 cm^2/plant is destroyed. Yield is reduced when fourth-instar larvae are more numerous than 26/plant. More than four, fifth-instar larvae per plant would also be economically important. However, these populations are rarely seen, possibly because only 4 per cent of the individuals reach the fifth instar.

The adult butterfly lays one to six eggs per leaf on the lower surface. Larvae fold the leaf margin and feed and pupate within the fold. Larvae can be recognized by their three dorsal longitudinal lines and large red-brown head capsules. In Colombia, van Dam and Wilde (1977) found that the egg hatches in 4 days, while larval and pupal development takes 23 and 11 days. Findings by Greene (1971b) in Florida and by Diaz (1976) in Chile were similar. Chemical control of this insect has not been necessary.

NOCTUIDAE

Noctuids affecting beans include the well known and widely distributed cutworm *Agrotis ipsilon* (Hufnagel), polyphagous foliage feeders like *Pseudoplusia includens* (Walker), *Trichoplusia ni* (Hübner) and *Spodoptera* spp. as well as several species within the *Heliothis* complex (Table 3.1). This review will concentrate on the most important group, the *Heliothis* complex.

In Africa, Asia and Oceania, the so-called American bollworm, *Heliothis armigera* Hübner, is an important pest of beans (Swaine, 1969; Nyiira, 1973; Karel, 1984a, 1985d). The common name is a misnomer as the species is not present in the Americas where *H. virescens* (F.) and *H. zea* (Boddie) cause sporadic but severe damage (Schoonhoven and Cardona, 1980).

Larvae feed on pods and at high population levels can be devastating, destroying several seeds in a pod. Secondary rotting may destroy any remaining seeds. Karel (1985d) reported losses in seed yield as heavy as 20 per cent.

The bionomics of these species is, in general, similar. Adults are stout-bodied, nocturnal moths that lay eggs singly on growing points and leaves. Larvae undergo six larval instars that last from 14 to 30 days. Pupation occurs in the soil, lasting from 10 to 14 days (Swaine, 1969) in Africa and from 9 to 16 days in Latin America (Schoonhoven and Cardona, 1980). There are several generations per growing season.

Several natural enemies of *Heliothis* spp. on beans have been reported in Africa (Reed, 1965; Karel, 1981) and in Latin America (King and Saunders, 1984). Chemical control of older larvae may be difficult. Along with carbaryl, endosulfan, and monocrotophos, pyrethroids such as cypermethrin are recommended to control young larvae (Swaine, 1969; Karel 1984b, 1985d). A nuclear polyhedrosis virus was tested on beans in Australia (Rogers *et al.*, 1983) and compared favourably with the pyrethroid fenvalerate.

OLETHREUTIDAE

Epinotia aporema (Walsm.) attacks beans in Latin America and is important in Peru (Wille, 1943) as well as in Chile (Brucher, 1941). This insect can also attack faba beans, chick-peas, soybeans, alfalfa, and lentils (Wille, 1943).

Females lay an average of 100 eggs in four to eight masses during 1−2 weeks. The egg stage lasts 4−7 days (Wille, 1943; Ripa, 1981). There are five larval instars, which together are completed in 14−22 days. Pupation occurs in a cocoon on leaves or on the ground and lasts 14−16 days. Adults live 15−22 days and are active at night.

Larvae damage beans by feeding on or in terminal buds, stems, and pods. They weave their excrement together and push it out of the feeding canals. The insect may also cause flower damage and abortion. Stems and buds can be deformed and pod damage may be severe.

A few natural enemies, namely the egg parasite *Trichogramma* sp. and the tachinid larval parasite *Eucelatoria* sp., have been found (Wille, 1943; Ripa 1981). Some work on resistance to *E. aporema* has been done in Peru (Avalos, 1982), but breeding for resistance has not been attempted. Adequate chemical control is available with aminocarb, parathion, carbaryl, and fenvalerate (Torres, 1968; Avalos, 1977).

PYRALIDAE

Four main pyralids attack beans: the lesser cornstalk borer − *Elasmopalpus lignosellus* (Zeller) − the lima bean pod borer − *Etiella zinckenella* (Treitschke) − *Omiodes indicata* (F.) and the legume pod borer − *Maruca testulalis* (Geyer). Of these *M. testulalis* is present in Africa, Asia, and the Americas, whereas the others have regional importance in the Americas.

Lesser Cornstalk Borer

Elasmopalpus lignosellus is widespread in Central and South America but is most serious in Brazil (Costa and Rossetto, 1972) and Peru (Avalos and Lozano, 1976). It is a polyphagous insect that feeds on beans, sugar cane, cotton, sorghum, rice, peanuts, cowpea and several weeds. Females lay eggs singly on leaves, stems, or in the soil. Larvae last 13−26 days, and there are six larval instars. Pupation occurs in the soil (Leuck, 1966). Damage is caused by larvae, which enter the stem just below the soil surface and tunnel upward. Attacks usually occur when plants are 10−12 cm high with two leaves. Damaged plants look flaccid and wilt or lodge (Salinas, 1976).

Work on resistance, albeit preliminary, did not reveal variability (Avalos and Lozano, 1976). Some species of Braconidae, Ichneumonidae, and Tachinidae are larval parasites (Leuck and Dupree, 1965; Salinas, 1976), but their efficiency has not been evaluated. Clean fallowing and heavy irrigation are practices recommended for control, together with the application of granular insecticides at planting (Campos, 1972).

Lima Bean Pod Borer

Etiella zinckenella occurs in the United States (Stone, 1965), Mexico, parts of Central America, the Caribbean (King and Saunders, 1984) and Brazil (Ramalho *et al.*, 1978), but not much is known about its economic importance, attacks being sporadic and only occasionally damaging.

Eggs are laid on flowers and pods. Larvae are yellow, green, or pink with red−brown dorsal lines. The pest can feed on flowers but prefers to act as a pod borer, sometimes causing the damaged flowers and small pods to abort. Pupation occurs in the pod or in the ground (Stone, 1965).

Chemical control of this borer is difficult and should be directed to small larvae before they perforate pods (King and Saunders, 1984). Some work on resistance was carried out in Brazil by Ramalho *et al.* (1978) who detected variability in terms of infested pods and damaged seeds.

Omiodes indicata

Though common in Latin America, *O. indicata* is a minor pest of beans (Ruppel and Idrobo, 1962; King and Saunders, 1984). Females oviposit on the lower surface of leaves, laying an average of 330 eggs. Hatching occurs in 4 days, and the green larvae develop in 11 days. Larvae weave leaves together, feed on the parenchyma and pupate within this package. Natural control is usually sufficient, chemical control being recommended only if 33 per cent or more defoliation occurs at flowering (de Bortoli, 1980).

Legume Pod Borer

Maruca testulalis, a major pest of legumes in Asia and Africa (Taylor, 1978;

Singh and van Emden, 1979), is a minor pest of beans in the Americas (Schoonhoven and Cardona, 1980; King and Saunders, 1984). It is one of the most important post-flowering insects affecting beans in East Africa (Karel *et al.*, 1981), Karel (1985d) estimating yield losses in Tanzania at more than 30 per cent.

The biology of *M. testulalis* has been extensively studied in Africa (Taylor, 1967, 1978; Jackai, 1981). Eggs are round to oval, yellow and translucent, with reticulate sculptures on the thin and delicate chorion. They are laid singly on flower buds, flowers, and young leaves of bean plants and hatch in 2−3 days. Larvae are whitish with dark spots on each side of the body forming dorsal longitudinal rows. The five larval instars last 8−14 days. The prepupae last 1−2 days, and pupation takes place in a double-walled pupal cell under leaf debris. The pupal period lasts 5−15 days, and the complete life cycle from egg to adult emergence varies from 18 to 35 days. Adult moths live for 5−7 days.

Damage to flower buds and flowers can be serious. Larvae feed also on green pods, and early instars can attack peduncles or tender parts of stems. Larvae web together flowers, pods, and leaves. Frass is often present on pods (Singh and van Emden, 1979).

Chemical control is effective with cypermethrin, carbaryl, endosulfan, fenitrothion, and monocrotophos (Singh and Allen, 1979; Karel *et al.*, 1981; Karel, 1985d). For Latin America, King and Saunders (1984) established an action threshold of one damaged pod per two plants. Although host-plant resistance offers potential in the control of legume pod borer, screening for resistance in beans has not been done.

Diptera

AGROMYZIDAE

Leaf miners

Leaf-miner damage is caused by the maggot, which destroys the palisade tissue of leaves by making serpentine tunnels called mines. The mines reduce photosynthetic area, thereby reducing yield, and render leaves unacceptable for consumption as a green vegetable.

A number of species of leaf miners occur on beans in Latin America, including the cosmopolitan and polyphagous species *Liriomyza huidobrensis* (Blanchard) and *L. sativae* Blanchard (Spencer, 1973). Other species in the Americas include *Melanagromyza phaseolivora* Spencer in Ecuador and *Japanagromyza* sp. in coastal areas of Peru. In Africa, *L. trifolii* (Burgess) is regarded as a minor pest of beans and other legumes (de Lima, 1979) though it can be important on beans in Egypt (Hammad, 1978) and Mauritius (Fagoone and Toory, 1983) *Liriomyza sativae* and *L. trifolii* also occur in Guam (Schreiner *et al.*, 1986).

Liriomyza sativae has a short life cycle, 24−28 days, annually completing several generations. This species is particularly important in Venezuela, especially when young plants are attacked. The insect is usually regulated by natural enemies such as braconids, eulophids, and pteromalids (Spencer, 1973), but it can become a problem when insecticides are used indiscriminately (Schreiner *et al.*, 1986).

Liriomyza huidobrensis is an important pest in certain areas of Ecuador, Peru, Colombia, and Brazil, usually as a result of misuse of insecticides. The life cycle has been studied by Espinosa and Sanchez (1982) in Ecuador: the egg stage lasts 2−3 days; the larval stage 7−9 days, the pupae 5−7 days, and adults 3−6 days. There are several generations per year. In Brazil, Prando and da Cruz (1986) calculated the duration of the egg, larval and pupal stages as 2, 6, and 8 days, respectively. Females lived 11 days and the males 4 days. The mean number of eggs per female was 133.

Liriomyza trifolii is polyphagous — a native of the southeastern United States that has spread rapidly to many areas of the world (Schreiner *et al.*, 1986). Its life cycle on beans is about 21 days, and therefore several generations can develop in one season (Katundu, 1980).

Chemical control of leaf miners is difficult. Insecticides can provoke high populations and outbreaks, resulting in defoliation and significant yield losses (Spencer, 1973). The pyrethroids permethrin, fenvalerate, and cypermethrin are recommended (Espinosa and Sanchez, 1982), although cases of resistance to several insecticides have been reported (Schreiner *et al.*, 1986). Preliminary work on bean resistance to *L. trifolii* has been initiated in Africa (Fagoone and Toory, 1983).

Beanflies

Beanflies, which are key pests of beans in Africa, Asia, and Oceania, are known by several common names such as stemfly, bean stem maggot, stemborer, stem miner, bean stem miner, snap beanfly and soybean leafminer.

Karel (1985a) has summarized the literature on beans with a detailed bibliography, and Greathead (1968) published the most comprehensive work on beanflies, detailing virtually all aspects of their life. Other major texts are those of Swaine (1969), Spencer (1973), Greathead (1975), Talekar and Chen (1986), and Karel (1985a).

The taxonomy of the group, based upon the morphology of the ovipositor in the female and aedeagus in the male, was in disarray until recently. In this review, names adopted by Spencer (1973) will be utilized. The major species affecting beans are *Ophiomyia phaseoli* Tryon (syn. *Melanagromyza phaseoli*), *O. spencerella* (Greathead) (syn. *Melanagromyza spencerella*), and *O. centrosematis* (de Meijere). Minor species are *O. recticulipennis* Singh and Ipe in India (Rao and Rao, 1977), *Melanagromyza dolichostigma* de Meijere in Java and Taiwan (Spencer, 1973), and *M. sojae* (Zhnt.) in Taiwan (AVRDC, 1982).

Taxonomic confusion has led to false identifications and interpretations in the literature. For example, Spencer (1973) considers the *M. sojae* (Zhnt.) reported from Uganda to be synonymous with *O. phaseoli*. Likewise, *O. centrosematis* may have been considered as *O. phaseoli*; and *O. spencerella*, not *O. phaseoli* as reported by Walker (1960), was probably responsible for the oviposition on stems.

Ophiomyia phaseoli occurs in tropical and sub-tropical areas of Africa, Asia and Oceania. It is a major pest of beans and several other legumes, breeding also on safflower and black nightshade. References on host plants of this and other species are provided by Talekar and Chen (1986) and Karel (1985a). Greathead (1968) regarded *O. spencerella* as more important than *O. phaseoli* in certain areas of East Africa, and recent evidence from international screening (CIAT, unpublished results) tends to support this view. *Ophiomyia centrosematis*, the least important of the species in the complex, occurs on several hosts in Australia, tropical and sub-tropical Asia and East Africa (Greathead, 1968; Spencer, 1973; Lee, 1976; Singh *et al.*, 1979).

What follows is an attempt to summarize the wealth of information on the biology of beanflies provided by Greathead (1968) and other authors. *Ophiomyia phaseoli* oviposits on the surface of leaves, mainly the upper surface (van der Goot, 1930; Abul Nasr, 1977). The adults puncture foliage to feed, and the female uses some of the holes for oviposition (Greathead, 1968; Davies, 1969; Swaine, 1969). Karel (1985a) reported that eggs of this species are laid in 10−15 per cent of the punctures made. *Ophiomyia spencerella* rarely oviposits on leaves, laying its eggs in the stem but, mainly, in the hypocotyl. *Ophiomyia centrosematis* prefers to lay eggs in the stem. Eggs are visible from the outside only when tissues are clarified.

Eggs (0.3 mm in length, 0.1 mm in diameter) of beanflies are smooth, white, and oval. In the case of *O. phaseoli*, Karel (1985a) reported that females lay an average 70 eggs, whereas Agrawal and Pandey (1961) recorded a mean of 33, and Otanes (1918), a mean of 200.

The eggs of *O. phaseoli* hatch in 2−4 days. Newly emerged larvae are transparent to yellowish white. They tunnel through the leaf tissue to a nearby main vein or the mid rib and then to the petiole where they usually moult into the second instar. They then mine to a branch or upper part of the stem and moult again. Third instars bore down the stem. Larvae of *O.*

spencerella feed and tunnel within the stem down into the root and return to pupate in the stem just above the soil surface (Greathead, 1968) or sometimes in the root (Ho, 1967). Both *O. spencerella* and *O. centrosematis* feed extensively in the hypocotyl and taproot before pupation.

Mature larvae are 2.5 mm long; they have black rasping hooks as mouthparts and yellow—white prothoracic and anal spiracles (Ho, 1967; Greathead, 1968; Talekar and Chen, 1986). According to Greathead (1968), *O. phaseoli* has 8.4±1.2 pores in posterior spiracles, whereas *O. spencerella* has an average 9.9±1.2 and *O. centrosematis*, an average 3. These openings on the posterior spiracles continue during the pupal stage. The total larval period in warm climates is 8—10 days (Karel, 1985a).

Pupae are barrel-shaped, about 5.5 mm by 2.2 mm. Those of *O. phaseoli* are translucent yellow—brown; *O. centrosematis*, translucent red— and yellow—brown; and *O. spencerella*, characteristically black. The pupal stage lasts 7—9 days (Greathead, 1968; Swaine, 1969).

Adults are shiny black and undergo a premating period that lasts 3 days (Greathead, 1968; Babu 1978). Females mate once (Lall, 1959) and lay eggs 2—4 days later. Adult males and females live 11 and 8—12 days respectively.

The total cycle from egg to adult emergence varies from an average 20 days in warm weather to 42 days in cooler environments (Karel, 1985a). Agrawal and Pandey (1961) reported 8—9 generations annually in India, whereas van der Goot (1930) counted up to 14 in Java, Indonesia.

Damage from adults is insignificant (Rogers, 1979), the major damage occurring at the seedling stage as a result of larval feeding. A considerable portion of the stem is eaten, and the stem is later ruptured by puparia. Roots can also be severely affected. As a result, plants are weakened, stunted and may die. *Ophiomyia phaseoli* causes heavy mortality (Otanes, 1918; Ho, 1967; Greathead, 1968; Swaine, 1969; Karel and Matee, 1986), and recent evidence indicates that *O. spencerella* can be equally or more damaging in certain highlands of Africa (Autrique, 1987).

Damage is pronounced in dry weather, under poor soil conditions, and in late plantings. Plants can recover if they show the ability to produce adventitious roots. However, losses of 100 per cent in yields of beans have been recorded from Africa (Wallace, 1939).

Adjusting planting dates and rotating crops reduce beanfly populations and damage (Karel *et al.*, 1981; Karel and Materu, 1983; Mohamed and Karel, 1986). Earthing-up (hilling) is often recommended because it helps the plant to produce adventitious roots that, in turn, help recovery of the plant.

Many braconids, cynipids, eulophids, eupelmids, eurytomids, and pteromalids have been found parasitizing *Ophiomyia* spp. (e.g., Greathead, 1968; Talekar and Chen, 1986), but none seems to be efficient in reducing beanfly populations below levels causing major losses in tropical regions. Success in controlling *O. phaseoli* was achieved in Hawaii following introduction of the braconid *Opius importatus* Fischer (Greathead, 1975).

Several insecticides, including dimethoate, endosulfan, monocrotophos, cypermethrin and pyrethrum have been reported effective for beanfly control (Swaine, 1969; Karel *et al.*, 1981; Matee and Karel, 1984; Karel and Matee, 1986). Seed dressing with endosulfan, controversial as the recommendation may be in the context of African culture, is highly efficient in the control of beanfly (Autrique, 1987; Lays and Autrique, 1987).

Development of resistant cultivars is promising as a means of control, but sustained research is needed. Reports on resistance have been put out by, among others, Moutia (1945), Rogers (1974, 1979), CIAT (1981), Lin (1981), Abate (1983a,b), as well as Karel (1985c) and colleagues (Rwamugira and Karel, 1984; Karel and Maerere, 1985; Msangi and Karel, 1985; Mushobozy and Karel, 1986). A little is known about tolerance and antibiosis (Rwamugira and Karel, 1984; Mushobozy and Karel, 1986), but much research is still needed for one to draw conclusions. A small breeding-for-resistance programme is under way in Africa. Initial results have not been encouraging, but the possibility is that better levels of resistance will be found among parents and breeding lines than have been detected so far (CIAT, unpublished results).

ANTHOMYIIDAE

The seedcorn maggot, *Delia platura* (Meigen) (syn. *Hylemyia cilicrura* Rond.), is a bean pest in Chile, Mexico, and parts of the United States and Canada. It has been reported also in Central America (King and Saunders, 1984) and Brazil (Hohman, 1980). *Delia florilega* (Zetterstedt), a closely related species, is found in the northeastern United States (Kim and Eckenrode, 1987). There has been some confusion about the taxonomy of this group as the genus has been named *Delia*, *Phorbia* and *Hylemyia*. Maize, beans, potatoes, beets, tobacco, peas, lima beans, and some vegetables are host plants of the seedcorn maggot.

The biology of the species has been studied by Miller and McClanahan (1960), Harris *et al.* (1966), and Hohman (1980), among others. Adults resemble house flies, and females oviposit near seeds or plants in the soil. Larvae attack bean seeds or seedlings and pupate in the soil. Eggs are white and last for 2−8 days (Harris *et al.*, 1966), depending on temperature (Sandsted *et al.*, 1971). The pupa lasts 9−12 days, and there can be as many as three generations during one bean crop. The first generation seems to be the most damaging (Montecinos *et al.*, 1986).

Damage by *D. platura* ranges from a few holes in the first true leaves to complete destruction of the growing point. Vea *et al.* (1975) concluded that 5−10 maggots/seed were required to reduce stands of kidney, lima, and snap beans. Subsequently, Vea and Eckenrode (1976b) determined that a 25 per cent loss of the first pair of unifoliate (cotyledonal) leaves reduces yield in snap beans by 11–48 per cent. Losses are substantial when maggots feed on the growing points. Plants look stunted and 'baldheaded', and most die.

Shallow planting in warm, moist soils can hasten emergence of plants and, thus, limit the at-risk period (Sandsted *et al.*, 1971). Montecinos (1982) recommended late plantings in Chile. Biological control was found to be ineffective (Miller and McClanahan, 1960).

Resistance of beans to seedcorn maggot has been implied in reports of materials with low levels of damage (Guevara, 1969; Vea and Eckenrode, 1976a; Hagel *et al.*, 1981), but success in breeding for resistance has been negligible. In fact, Hagel *et al.* (1981) concluded that materials rated as resistant benefited substantially from protection provided by treatment with chlorpyriphos.

Dieldrin seed dressing was for many years the standard treatment to control seedcorn maggot on beans and other crops. As this product was banned in many countries and as the insect developed high levels of resistance to chlorinated hydrocarbons, recent research has focused on alternatives. Seed dressing with chlorpyriphos has been recommended by Gould and Mayor (1975), Crowell (1976), Ruppel (1982), and Montecinos *et al.* (1986). Diazinon seed dressing and granular applications of carbofuran, fonophos, and phorate are also effective (Eckenrode *et al.*, 1973; Ruppel, 1982; Montecinos *et al.*, 1986).

Other Invertebrate Pests

ARACHNIDA: ACARINA

Tarsonemidae

The tropical mite, *Polyphagotarsonemus latus* (Banks) is a minor pest of beans in Africa (Hill, 1975) and the Americas (Schoonhoven *et al.*, 1978b). A polyphagous species, it occasionally causes serious damage, especially in areas of Brazil (CIAT, 1975).

It is small and green; its life cycle short, with egg, larva, pseudopupa, and adult stages together lasting only 6–7 days in Brazil (Flechtman, 1972), 4–5 in Colombia (Schoonhoven *et al.*, 1978b) and about 7 in Africa (Hill, 1975). Males live 12 days; females, 15 days, laying an average 48 eggs (Schoonhoven *et al.*, 1978b).

Polyphagotarsonemus latus attacks beans that have flowered, sucking sap from young leaves and pods. Mite-damaged leaf edges roll up and take on a shiny appearance. Undersurfaces of leaves may turn purple. Young leaves turn yellow to gold and become deformed, whereas pods become brownish. The signs are at times mistaken for mineral deficiencies or damage by virus.

Sulphur, endosulfan, dicofol, and omethoate (Schoonhoven *et al.*, 1978b) control the pest, whereas dimethoate seems to stimulate it (Harris, 1969).

Tetranychidae

In general, tetranychid mites are minor pests of beans. In Latin America, *Tetranychus desertorum* Banks has a wide host range (Nickel, 1960). Other species include *T. telarius* L. (syn. *T. cinnabarinus* Boisduval), *T. urticae* Koch, *T. ludeni* (Zacher), *Eotetranychus lewisi* (McGregor), *Oligonychus sticneyi* (McGregor), and *O. yothersi* (McGregor) (Andrews and Poe, 1980; King and Saunders, 1984). In Africa, *T. telarius* (Hill, 1975; Khamala 1978; Nyiira, 1978) and *T. urticae* (Nyiira, 1978) have been recorded.

Spider mites attack when beans near physiologic maturity so they rarely influence seed yield.

GASTROPODA PULMONATA

Veronicellidae (slugs)

In general, slugs are minor pests of beans in Africa, Asia and Latin America. However, they have become a serious problem in Honduras, parts of Nicaragua and small regions of Mexico (Andrews and Dundee, 1986). Of the several species reported, *Vaginulus plebeius* (Fischer) [syn. *Sarasinula plebeia* (Fischer)] is by far the most important. The taxonomy of the group is in complete disarray, and, according to Andrews (1983), there is no certainty about the correct identification of this pest. In the absence of better information, we use the name *V. plebeius* for this review.

Vaginulus plebeius was first reported in 1967 in El Salvador (Mancia, 1973c). Since then, it has superimposed its range of distribution on that of other species. According to Andrews (1983), up to 500 000 Central American subsistence farmers suffer losses caused by slugs every year.

Slugs are hermaphroditic, and self-fertilization in *V. plebeius* is common. An individual may lay as many as 80 eggs in masses under plant debris or in soil cracks. Eggs are oval, translucid, and they hatch in 20−24 days at 27°C. Young resemble adults and reach maturity in 2−5 months (Mancia, 1973c). Slugs live 12−18 months and grow 5−7 cm long. According to Andrews and Lema (1986), one generation takes 8 weeks, and there may be two generations per year in Honduras.

Damage from the young slugs is apparent, as whole leaves, except for veins, are consumed. Older slugs consume entire seedlings as well as leaves. Pods can also be attacked. Econcmic injury occurs at 1 slug/m^2 or 1 slug trapped/night (Andrews and Barletta, 1985).

Ridding fields and field borders of weeds and plant debris, burning crop residues, proper land preparation and draining fields are recommended methods of control (Mancia, 1973c; Andrews, 1983). Chemical control is most effective with baits prepared with metaldehyde, although the residual effect of such baits is short, especially under wet conditions (Mancia, 1973c; Crowell, 1977).

Future Strategy for Control

Chemicals are still the commonest method of controlling bean pests; however, insecticides, effective as they may be, bring adverse effects well discussed in entomological literature. Moreover, insecticides are too expensive and are unavailable to the bulk of subsistence farmers in Africa, Asia, and Latin America. Hence, a priority for research should be to find alternatives that preserve the natural control agents of existing and potential pests. If insecticides are required, they should be applied only when needed as part of effective and economical control of bean pests.

The use of natural enemies requires attention despite difficulties posed by the short growing cycle of the crop and the extended fallows. Recent efforts like the introduction of exotic aphidiids into Burundi (Autrique *et al.*, 1985) to assist native parasites in reducing bean aphids should be encouraged.

Future control methods must emphasize simple cultural practices that support biological control and host-plant resistance strategies.

Much progress has been made in identifying sources of resistance and in understanding resistance mechanisms. What is still lacking is a sustained effort to develop cultivars combining such resistance with other desirable traits.

The aim should be to integrate different control tactics into simple recommendations that can be implemented by bean farmers.

Insect Pests of Food Legumes
Edited by S. R. Singh
©1990 John Wiley & Sons Ltd.

4

Insect Pests on Pigeon Pea

S. S. LATEEF and W. REED[a]

[a]International Crops Research Institute for the Semi-Arid Tropics (ICRISAT),
Patancheru 502 324, Andhra Pradesh, India

Pigeon pea, *Cajanus cajan* (L.) Millsp., is grown commercially in India and
in a few other countries in Asia, Africa (particularly in the East), the
Caribbean, Latin America and in Australia. It is grown as a "backyard" or
hedge crop throughout the tropics and sub-tropics and is a major source of
protein in several countries. The seed is harvested mainly when mature but
sometimes green. The plants are used for fodder, fuel, basket-making and
construction.

In farmers' fields pigeon pea is commonly grown as an annual, intercropped with cereals, fibre crops and other legumes. It is also grown as a
perennial, particularly in hedges.

More than 200 species of insects have been recorded as pests on pigeon
pea in India, but only a few cause economic losses and are common over
large areas (Table 4.1).

Most economic damage is caused by pests that feed on the flowers and
pods. Tests have shown that the plant can compensate for defoliation during
the vegetative stage so damage at earlier stages reduces seed yield little.
Studies at ICRISAT by Sheldrake and Narayanan (1977) showed the removal
of 50–75 per cent of the leaves throughout the reproductive phase resulted
in only slight and statistically insignificant reduction in seed yield.

Pigeon pea has been reported to produce an overabundance of buds and
flowers, of which about 80 per cent are shed (Narayanan and Sheldrake,
1975). To determine the role played by pests in flower and pod shedding on
this crop, staff at ICRISAT rated and recorded the damage caused by insects
in the shed flowers and pods from six cultivars, which were grown on deep

Table 4.1. Insect pests on pigeon pea [*Cajanus cajan* (L.) Millsp.]

ORDER/Scientific name	Family	Portion of plant attacked[a]	Pest status, 0-5[b]	Pests reported from countries	References
COLEOPTERA					
Acalymma bivittatum (Fab.)	Chrysomelidae	L	1	C. America	Saunders *et al.*, 1983
Acanthoscelides (*Bruchus*) *obtectus* (Say)	Bruchidae	D	1	Pandemic	Joplin, 1974
A. zeteki King.	Bruchidae	D	3	Caribbean	Buckmire, 1978
Adoretus caliginosusbicolor Br.	Scarabaeidae	R, L	1	India	Davies and Lateef, 1975; ICRISAT, 1976a
A. stoliczkae Ohs.	Scarabaeidae	R, L	1	India	ICRISAT, 1976a
Alcidodes collaris (Pasc.)	Curculionidae	G	2	India	Panchabhavi *et al.*, 1972; Davies and Lateef, 1975; Nair, 1975; ICRISAT, 1976a
				Bangladesh	Kabir, 1978
A. fabricii (F.)	Curculionidae	G	1	India	Nair, 1975; ICRISAT, 1976a
Apate monachus F.	Bostrychidae	S	1	Nigeria	ICRISAT 1976a; Egwuatu and Taylor, 1977a
				C. America	Saunders *et al.*, 1983
Apion amplum Fst.	Apionidae	P	2	Kenya	ICRISAT, 1977
A. benignum (Faust)	Apionidae	P, D	3	India	Davies and Lateef, 1975; Lateef and Reed, 1983
A. clavipes Gerst.	Apionidae	P, D	3	India	ICRISAT, 1976a; Sinha and Yadav, 1983
				Bangladesh	Anon.,1964
A. ripicola Hartm.	Apionidae	P, D	1	E. Africa	Le Pelley, 1959
A. ugandanum Wagn.	Apionidae	P, D	1	Kenya	LePelley, 1959

ORDER/ Scientific Name	Family	Portion of plant attacked[a]	Pest status, 0-5[b]	Pests reported from countries	References
Apogonia sp.	Scarabaeidae	R, L	1	India	ICRISAT, 1976a
Atactogaster dejeani Fst.	Curculionidae	L	1	India	ICRISAT, 1976a
Aulacophora foveicollis Lucas	Chrysomelidae	L, F	3	India	Nair, 1975
				Kenya	Le Pelley, 1959
A. africana Weise	Chrysomelidae	L, F	3	Kenya	Khamala *et al.*, 1978
Barombiella humeralis (Lab.)	Chrysomelidae	L, F	3	Nigeria	Egwuatu and Taylor 1977a; Singh and Taylor, 1978
Callosobruchus analis (F.)	Bruchidae	P, D	4	India	Nair, 1975; Reed *et al.*, 1989
C. chinensis (L.)	Bruchidae	P, D	4	India	Srivastava, 1964; Davies and Lateef, 1975; Nayar *et al.*, 1976; Sangappa and Balaraju, 1977
				Bangladesh	Kabir, 1978
				Caribbean	Buckmire, 1978
C. maculatus (F.)	Bruchidae	P, D	4	India	Davies and Lateef, 1975
= *Bruchus quadrimaculatus* F.				Caribbean	Buckmire, 1978; Joplin, 1974
C. maindroni Pic.	Bruchidae	P, D	2	India	ICRISAT, 1976a
C. theobromae (L.)	Bruchidae	P, D	4	India	Ayyar, 1963; Srivastava, 1964; Davies and Lateef, 1975; Nayar *et al.*, 1976
Cantharis setacea Cast.	Cantharidae	S	0	India	Srivastava, 1964; Davies and Lateef, 1975; Nayar *et al.*, 1976
Carpophilus dimidiatus F.	Nitidulidae	D	3	Nigeria	Egwuatu and Taylor, 1977a
				Kenya	Khamala *et al.*, 1978
Caryedon serratus (Oliver)	Bruchidae	D	3	C. America	Saunders *et al.*, 1983
Cathartus quadricollis Guen.	Silvanidae	D	3	Nigeria	Egwuatu and Taylor, 1977a
Chalcodermus angulicollis (F.)	Curculionidae	L	1	Caribbean	Buckmire, 1978

Table 4.1 Continued

ORDER/ Scientific name	Family	Portion of plant attacked [a]	Pest status, 0-5 [b]	Pests reported from countries	References
Cheilomenes spp.	Coccinellidae	L	1	India	Reed et al., 1989
Colobodes dolichotis M.	Cantharidae	S	0	India	Subramanian and Venugopal, 1959; Nayar et al., 1976; ICRISAT, 1976a
Coryna apicicornis Guen.	Meloidae	F	3	Kenya Tanzania	ICRISAT 1977; Khamala et al., 1978 Le Pelley, 1959
Cryptocephalus castaneus	Cryptocephalidae	L	1	Peru	Pflucker, 1981
Cyrtozemia cognata Marshall	Curculionidae	L	1	India	Pal, 1972
Deiradolcus cajanus Alam	Curculionidae	P	3	Bangladesh	Anon., 1964
Demarchus pubipennis Jacoby	Chrysomelidae	L	1	India	Odak et al., 1968; Davies and Lateef, 1975; Nayar et al., 1976
Dereodus denticollis Boh.	Curculionidae	L	1	India	ICRISAT, 1976a
Diaprepes abbreviatus (L.)	Curculionidae	L	1	Caribbean	Schotman, 19886
Diphaulaca n. sp.	Halticidae	L	1	Trinidad	Barrow, 1968
Epicauta albovittata Gestro	Meloidae	L	2	Kenya	Khamala et al., 1978
Epilachna spp.	Coccinellidae	L	1	India Kenya	Nair, 1975 Khamala et al., 1978; Okeyo-Owuor, 1978
Episomus humeralis Chev.	Curculionidae	L	1	Bangladesh	Anon., 1964
E. lacerta (F.)	Curculionidae	L	1	India	Davies and Lateef, 1975; Nayar et al., 1976; Ayyar 1963
Gnathopastoides rouxi Cast.	Meloidae	F	1	India	Nair, 1975
Gonocephalum depressum F.	Tenebrionidae	G	1	India	Davies and Lateef, 1975; ICRISAT, 1976a
G. dorsogranosum Frm.	Tenebrionidae	G	2	India	ICRISAT, 1976a

ORDER/ Scientific Name	Family	Portion of plant attacked [a]	Pest status, 0-5 [b]	Pests reported from countries	References
G. elongatum F.	Tenebrionidae	G	1	India	Davies and Lateef, 1975; ICRISAT, 1976a
G. simplex F.	Tenebrionidae	G, R	1	Kenya	Khamala et al., 1978; Okeyo-Owuor, 1978
Gyponychus quinquemaculatus Hust.	Curculionidae	L	1	Kenya	Le Pelley, 1959
Hypolixus truncatulus (F.)	Curculionidae	R, L	1	India	ICRISAT, 1976a
Indozocladius (Ceutorhynchus) asperulus (Faust.)	Curculionidae	F	3	India	Fletcher, 1914; Davies and Lateef, 1975 Nayar et al., 1976; ICRISAT, 1976a
Lachnosterna (Holotrichia) consanguinea Blanchard	Scarabaeidae	L, R	1	India	Bindra and Singh, 1971b
L. jamaiceansis	Scarabaeidae	L, R	1	Pandemic	Joplin, 1974
Luperodes spp.	Chrysomelidae	G, L	1	India	ICRISAT, 1976a; Lal et al., 1981
Luperus puncticollis Jac.	Chrysomelidae	L	1	India	ICRISAT, 1976a; Nayar et al., 1976
Madurasia obscurella Jac.	Chrysomelidae	L	1	India	Verma and Pant, 1975
Monolepta signata Ol.	Chrysomelidae	L	1	India	Davies and Lateef, 1975; Nair, 1975
Mylabris amplectens Gerst.	Meloidae	F	4	Tanzania	Le Pelley, 1959
M. aptera Gerst.	Meloidae	F	1	Kenya Tanzania	Khamala et al., 1978 Le Pelley, 1959
M. balteata Pall.	Meloidae	F	1	Kenya	Le Pelley, 1959
M. dicincta Bertoloni	Meloidae	F	1	Tanzania	Le Pelley, 1959
M. farquharsoni Bla.	Meloidae	F	5	Kenya Kenya	Khamala et al., 1978 Khamala et al., 1978
M. hypolachna Gestro	Meloidae	F, P	3	Nigeria Kenya	Egwuatu and Taylor, 1977a Okeyo-Owuor, 1978

Table 4.1 Continued

ORDER/ Scientific name	Family	Portion of plant attacked [a]	Pest status, 0-5 [b]	Pests reported from countries	References
M. oculata var, tricolor Gerst.	Meloidae	F	3	Zimbabwe	Rowe, 1980
M. phalerata (Pallas)	Meloidae	F	3	India	Lal et al., 1981
M. pustulata (IThunb.)	Meloidae	F	4	India	Srivastava, 1964; Davies and Lateef, 1975; Nayar et al., 1976; Joplin, 1974
				Bangladesh	Anon., 1964
				Sri Lank	Subasinghe and Fellowes, 1978
				Thailand	Isaravurak and Potan, 1988
M. seminigra Voigt.	Meloidae	F	5	Kenya	Le Pelley, 1959
				Nigeria	Egwuatu and Taylor, 1977a
Myllocerus discolor var. variegatus Boh.	Curculionidae	L	1	India	Nayar et al., 1976
M. maculosus Desb.	Curculionidae	L	0	India	Nayar et al., 1976
M. undecimpustulatus Faust	Curculionidae	L	2	India	ICRISAT, 1976a
M. transmarinus maculosus Desb.	Curculionidae	L	1	India	ICRISAT, 1976a
Nematocerus spp.	Curculionidae	L	1	India	Reed et al., 1989
				E. Africa	Khamala et al., 1978; Okeyo-Owuor, 1978
Oberea brevis Swed.	Cerambycidae	S	2	India	Singh et al., 1978
Onthophagus gazella (F.)	Scarabaeidae	R, L	1	India	ICRISAT, 1976a
Opatroides punctulatus Brull.	Tenebrionidae	L	1	India	ICRISAT, 1976a
Oxycetonia versicolor (F.)	Scarabaeidae	F	1	India	ICRISAT,1976a
Pachnoda cordata (Drury)	Scarabaeidae	F	5	Nigeria	Egwuatu and Taylor, 1977a
Peltotrachelus juvencus (Fst.)	Curculionidae	L	1	India	ICRISAT, 1976a
Phyllobius spp.	Curculionidae	L	1	India	ICRISAT, 1976a; Lateef and Reed, 1983
Podagrica spp.	Chrysomelidae	L, F	1	E. Africa	Khamala et al., 1978; Okeyo-Owuor, 1978
				Nigeria	Egwuatu and Taylor, 1977a

ORDER/Scientific name	Family	Portion of plant attacked [a]	Pest status, 0-5 [b]	Pests reported from countries	References
Promecops sp.	Curculionidae	L	1	Caribbean	Buckmire, 1978; Schotman, 1986
Specularius sulcaticollis (Pic.)	Bruchidae	D	1	Kenya	Southgate and McFarlane, 1979
S. erythraeus (Pic.)	Bruchidae	D	1	Kenya	ICRISAT, 1977; Southgate and McFarlane, 1979
Sphenoptera laplumei Kerr	Buprestidae	S	2	Nigeria	Egwuatu and Taylor, 1977a
S. perotetti Gl.	Buprestidae	S	2	India	Srivastava, 1964; Davies and Lateef, 1975; Nayar et al., 1976
S. indica Laporte and Gorg.	Buprestidae	S	2	India	ICRISAT, 1976a; Reed et al., 1989
Sternocera laevigata Ol.	Buprestidae	S	0	India	ICRISAT, 1976a
Systates sp.	Curculionidae	L	1	Kenya	Khamala et al., 1978
Tanymecus indicus Fst.	Curculionidae	L	1	India	Srivastava, 1964
Tribolium castaneum (Hbst.)	Tenebrionidae	D	1	India	Khare et al., 1966
				Caribbean	Buckmire, 1978
Zurus aurivilianus	Curculionidae	L	1	Peru	Pflucker, 1981
DIPTERA					
Dasyneura lini Barnes	Cecidomyidae	F	1	India	Nair, 1975
Melanagromyza chalcosoma Spencer	Agromyzidae	P	5	E. Africa	ICRISAT, 1982b
				Nigeria	Singh and Taylor, 1978
M. (Agromyza) obtusa (Mall.)	Agromyzidae	P	5	India	Fletcher, 1914; Ahmad, 1938; Davies and Lateef, 1975; Nayar et al., 1976; Lal et al., 1981; Kabir, 1978
				Bangladesh Sri Lanka	Subasinghe and Fellowes, 1978; Thevasagayam and Canagasingham, 1961

Table 4.1 Continued

ORDER/ Scientific name	Family	Portion of plant attacked[a]	Pest status, 0-5[b]	Pests reported from countries	References
				Thailand	Isaravurak and Potan, 1988
				Kenya	Le Pelley, 1959; Khamala et al., 1978; Okeyo-Owuor, 1978
				Uganda	Joplin, 1974
Ophiomyia centrosematis (deMeijere)	Agromyzidae	S	2	India	ICRISAT, 1976a,b; Lateef and Reed, 1983
Ophiomyia sp.	Agromyzidae	R, S	1	Kenya	Khamala et al., 1978
				Nigeria	Singh and Taylor, 1978
Rivellia angulata Hendel	Platystomatidae	R	3	India	Siddappaji and Gowda, 1980; Sithanantham et al., 1981b
HEMIPTERA					
Acanthomia brevirostris Stål = *Clavigralla scuellaris* (Westw.)	Coreidae	F, P	1	E. Africa	Joplin, 1974
A. horrida (Germar)	Coreidae	P	3	E. Africa	Khamala et al., 1978
				Nigeria	Egwuatu and Taylor, 1977a
Acanthomia sp.	Coreidae	P	3	Sierra Leone	Taylor, 1978
				Tanzania	Materu, 1971
Aconophora concolor	Membracidae	L	1	Peru	Pflucker, 1981
A. femoralis Stål	Membracidae	L	1	C. America	Saunders et al., 1983
Acrosternum accutum Dall.	Pentatomidae	P	1	Kenya	Khamala et al., 1978
A. graminea (Fabr.)	Pentatomidae	L	0	India	ICRISAT, 1976a
A. marginatum (Palisto de Beauvois)	Pentatomidae	L	1	C. America	Saunders et al., 1983
Aethus indicus Westw.	Cydnidae	S, L	0	India	ICRISAT, 1976a

ORDER/ Scientific name	Family	Portion of plant attacked [a]	Pest status, 0-5 [b]	Pests reported from countries	References
Agnoscelis nubila Fb.	Pentatomidae	F, P	0	India	Davies and Lateef, 1975; Nair, 1975; ICRISAT, 1976a
A. pubiscens Thunb.	Pentatomidae	F, P	1	Kenya	Khamala et al., 1978
Anoplocnemis curvipes (F.)	Coreidae	P	4	Nigeria	Egwuatu and Taylor, 1977a; Singh and Taylor, 1978
A. phasiana Fb.	Coreidae	L, F, P	1	E. Africa India	Le Pelley, 1959; Khamala et al., 1978 Fletcher, 1914; Davies and Lateef, 1975; Nair, 1975
Anoplocnemis spp.	Coreidae	L, F, P	1	Kenya E. Africa Sierra Leone	Okeyo-Owuor, 1978 Okeyo-Owuor, 1978 Taylor, 1978
Aphis cardui L.	Aphididae	L, F, P	1	India	Srivastava, 1964; Davies and Lateef, 1975
A. citricola van der Goot	Aphididae	L, F, P	1	C. America	Saunders et al., 1983
A. craccivora Koch.	Aphididae	L, F, P	1	India E. Africa Trinidad	Srivastava, 1964; Davies and Lateef, 1975 Khamala et al., 1978 Laurence, 1971
A. gossypii Glov.	Aphididae	L, F, P	1	India	Ghosh, 1981
A. medicaginus Kle	Aphididae	L, F	1	India	Kadam and Patel, 1972
Aphis sp.	Aphididae	L, F, P	1	Kenya Caribbean	Khamala et al., 1978 Buckmire, 1978
Bemisia tabaci (Genn.)	Aleyrodidae	L	1	India Kenya	Atwal, 1976 Khamala et al., 1978

Table 4.1 Continued

ORDER/ Scientific name	Family	Portion of plant attacked [a]	Pest status, 0-5 [b]	Pests reported from countries	References
Bolbonata corrugata Fowler	Membracidae	L	1	C. America	Saunders et al., 1983
Calcoris angustatus Leth.	Miridae	F	0	India	Davies and Lateef, 1975
Campylomma livida Reut.	Miridae	F	3	India	ICRISAT, 1976b; Lateef and Reed, 1983
Centrococcus insolitus (Gr.)	Pseudococcidae	S, L	0	India	Nair, 1975; Atwal, 1976; Nayar et al., 1976
Cerococcus catenorius (Heinrich)	Coccidae	S	1	Brazil	Heinrich, 1966
Ceroplastes spp.	Coccidae	S	1	Uganda Peru	Le Pelley, 1959 Pflucker, 1981
Ceroplastodes cajani Mask.	Coccidae	S	1	India	Srivastava, 1964; Davies and Lateef, 1975; ICRISAT, 1976a; Nair, 1975
Cicadella spectra Dist.	Cicadellidae	L	1	India	ICRISAT, 1976a; Nayar et al., 1976; Lateef and reed, 1983
Clastoptera variabilis	Cercopidae	L, S	1	Peru	Pflucker, 1981
Clavigralla gibbosa Spinola	Coreidae	F, P	5	India Bangladesh Thailand	Srivastava, 1964; Bindra and Singh, 1971; Davies and Lateef, 1975; Nair, 1975 Anon., 1964 Isaravurak and Potan, 1988
C. scutellaris (Westw.)	Coreidae	F, P	5	India	ICRISAT, 1976a,b
C. spinofemoralis Shir. = *C. horrens* (Dohrn)	Coreidae	F, P	3	India	Srivastava, 1964; Bindra and Singh, 1971; Nayar et al., 1976; ICRISAT, 1976ab
C. (Acanthomia) tomentosicollis Stål	Coreidae	F, P	5	E. Africa Nigeria	Le Pelley, 1959; Khamala et al., 1978 Egwuatu and Taylor, 1977a, 1979
Cletus signatus Walk.	Coreidae	F, P	4	India	ICRISAT, 1976a
C. fuscescens Walk.	Coreidae	F, P	4	E. Africa	Khamala et al., 1978
Coccidohystri insolita (Green)	Pseudococcidae	L, F, P	2	India	Patel et al., 1985

ORDER/ Scientific name	Family	Portion of plant attacked [a]	Pest status, 0-5 [b]	Pests reported from countries	References
Coccus alpinus De Lotto	Coccidae	S	1	Kenya	Khamala *et al.*, 1978
C. elongatus Sign.	Coccidae	S	3	Uganda	Le Pelley, 1959
C. hesperidum L.	Coccidae	S	0	India	Nayar *et al.*, 1976
C. longulum (Doug.)	Coccidae	S	0	India	Nayar *et al.*, 1976
Coptosoma cribraria F.	Plastaspidae	L, F	1	India	Ayyar, 1963; Srivastava, 1964; Nair, 1975; Davies and Lateef, 1975; Nayar *et al.*, 1976
C. nazirae At.	Plastaspidae	L, F	0	India	Ayyar, 1963; Davies and Lateef, 1975; Nayar *et al.*, 1976
C. siamicus F.	Plastaspidae	P	1	Bangladesh	Anon., 1964
Coridus janus (Fab.)	Pentatomidae	L	0	India	ICRISAT, 1976a
Corythucha gossypii F.	Tingidae	L	1	Caribbean	Buckmire, 1978
Creontiades pallidifer Wlk.	Miridae	F	1	India	Srivastava, 1964; Davies and Lateef, 1975
C. pallidus (Ramb.)	Miridae	F	3	India	ICRISAT, 1976a; Lateef and Reed, 1983
Cyclopelta siccifolia Westw.	Pentatomidae	F, P	0	India	Fletcher, 1914; Davies and Lateef, 1975; Nair, 1975; Nayar *et al.*, 1976
Dactynotus ambrosiae (Thomas)	Aphididae	F, P	1	C. America	Saunders *et al.*, 1983
Deraeocoris fulleberni	Miridae	F, P	1	Kenya	Okeyo-Owuor, 1978
Dismicoccus brevipes (Cockerell)	Pseudococcidae	R	0	India	Rajagopal *et al.*, 1982
				Tanzania	Le Pelley, 1959
Dolycoris indicus (Stål)	Pentatomidae	F, P	4	India	ICRISAT, 1976a,b; Davies and Lateef, 1975; Nair, 1975
Drosicha stebbingi Gr.	Margarodidae	S	0	India	Srivastava, 1964; Davies and Lateef, 1975; Nair, 1975; Nayar *et al.*, 1976
Dysdercus cardinalis Gerst.	Pyrrhocoreidae	F, P	1	Kenya	Khamala *et al.*, 1978
D. koenigi (Fab.)	Pyrrhocoreidae	F	1	India	ICRISAT, 1976a

Table 4.1 Continued

ORDER/ Scientific name	Family	Portion of plant attacked [a]	Pest status, 0-5 [b]	Pests reported from countries	References
D. fabae (Harris)	Cicadellidae	L	3	India	Davies and Lateef, 1975
				Puerto Rico	Baquero, 1980
				Caribbean	Buckmire, 1978
				Peru	Pflucker, 1981
D. nigrofasciatus Stal.	Pyrrhocoreidae	P	1	Kenya	Khamala *et al.*, 1978
Edessa meditabunda (F.)	Pentatomidae	F, P	1	Caribbean	Buckmire, 1978; Schotman, 1986
Empoasca binotata Pruthi	Cicadellidae	L	1	India	Srivastava, 1964; Davies and Lateef, 1975; Nair, 1975; Nayar *et al.*, 1976
E. fabalis Delong	Cicadellidae	L	1	Trinidad	Laurence, 1971
E. kerri Pruthi	Cicadellidae	L	1	India	Atwal, 1976; Singh and Singh 1978a,b
E. lybica De Berg	Cicadellidae	L	1	Kenya	Khamala *et al.*, 1978
Enchenopa monoceros	Membracidae	L	1	Peru	Pflucker, 1981
Erythroneura cajanae sp. n.	Cicadellidae	L, S	1	Bangladesh	Ahmed, 1971
Eurybrachys tomentosa Fb.	Eurybrachydae	L	1	India	Nair, 1975; Nayar *et al.*, 1976
Eurystylus sp.	Miridae	F	3	India	ICRISAT, 1976a,b
Ferrisia virgata (Cockerell)	Pseudococcidae	L, S	1	India	Gautam and Saxena, 1986
Graptostethus rufus Distant	Lygaeidae	P	0	Nigeria	Egwuatu and Taylor, 1977a
G. servus (Fabr.)	Lygaeidae	P	0	India	Fletcher 1914; Davies and Lateef, 1975; Nair, 1975
Gampsocoris pulchellus (Dallas)	Neididae/ Berytidae	L	0	India	Singh and Patel, 1968
Homoeocerus indus Dist.	Coreidae	S	1	India	ICRISAT, 1976a
Hyalymenus tarsatus (Fab.)	Alydidae	L	1	C. America	Saunders *et al.*, 1983

ORDER/ Scientific name	Family	Portion of plant attacked[a]	Pest status, 0-5[b]	Pests reported from countries	References
Icerya purchasi Mask.	Coccidae	S	1	Kenya	ICRISAT, 1977; Khamala et al., 1978; Joplin, 1974
				Peru	Pflucker, 1981
Inglisia bivalvata Gr.	Coccidae	S	1	India	Nair, 1975; Nayar et al., 1976
I. conchiformis Newst.	Coccidae	S	1	Uganda	Le Pelley, 1959
Jacobiasca lybica (de Beryeven)	Cicadellidae	L	1	Africa	Reed et al., 1989
Laccifer lacca (Kerr) = Tachardia lacca (Kerr)	Coccidae	S	1	India	Srivastava, 1964; Davies and Lateef, 1975; Nair, 1975; Nayar et al., 1976
Laccifer longispina Misra	Coccidae	S	1	India	Teotia, 1964; Nair, 1975
Lecanium longulum D.	Coccidae	S	1	India	Ayyar, 1963; Srivastava, 1964; Davies and Lateef, 1975; Nair, 1975
L. hesperidum L.	Coccidae	S	1	India	Nair, 1975
Leptocentrus obliquis W.	Membracidae	L	0	India	Nayar et al., 1976
L. taurus (Fab.)	Membracidae	L	1	Bangladesh	Kabir, 1978
Leptocoris sp.	Coreidae	F	1	India	ICRISAT, 1976a
Leptoglossus australis (Fab.)	Coreidae	P	1	Kenya	Khamala et al., 1978
L. phyllopus (L.)	Coreidae	L, F	1	C. America	Saunders et al., 1983
L. zonatus (Dallas)	Coreidae	L, F	1	C. America	Saunders et al., 1983
Lygaeus panduras Scop.	Lygaeidae	L	0	India	Fletcher, 1914; DAvies and Lateef, 1975
Lygus spp.	Miridae	L	1	Uganda	Le Pelley, 1959
Macrosiphum nigrinectaria Theo.	Aphididae	L	1	E. Africa	Le Pelley, 1959
Margarodes niger Gr.	Margarodidae	S	0	India	Srivastava, 1964; Davies and Lateef, 1975; Nair, 1975; Nayar et al., 1976

Table 4.1 Continued

ORDER/ Scientific name	Family	Portion of plant attacked[a]	Pest status, 0-5[b]	Pests reported from countries	References
M. papillosus Gr.	Margarodidae	S	0	India	Srivastava, 1964; Davies and Lateef, 1975; Nair, 1975; Nayar et al., 1976
Membracis albolimbata Fowler	Membracidae	L	1	C. America	Saunders et al., 1983
M. mexicana Guerin	Membracidae	L	1	C. America	Saunders et al., 1983
Menida histrio Fab.	Pentatomidae	F, P	0	India	Davies and Lateef, 1975
Mirperus jaculus Thunb.	Alydidae	P	3	Nigeria / Kenya	Egwuatu and Taylor, 1977a / Khamala et al., 1978
M. torridus Westw.	Alydidae	P	3	Nigeria	Egwuatu and Taylor, 1977a
Myzus persicae Sulzer	Aphididae	L,F,P	1	India	Read et al. 1989
Neurocolpus mexicanus Dist.	Miridae	P	3	C. America	Saunders et al., 1983
Nezara viridula (L.)	Pentatomidae	F, P	3	India / Bangladesh / E. Africa / Nigeria / C. America / Sierra Leone / Caribbean	Davies and Lateef, 1975 / Anon., 1964 / Khamala et al., 1978 / Egwuatu and Taylor, 1977a; Singh and Taylor, 1978 / Buckmire, 1978; Saunders et al., 1983 / Taylor, 1978 / Schotman, 1986
Nipaecoccus vastator (M.)	Pseudococcidae	S	0	India	Nayar et al., 1976
Oncaspidia pilosicollis	Coreidae	P	3	Nigeria	Egwuatu and Taylor, 1977a
Otinotus oneratus W.	Membracidae	S	2	India	Srivastava, 1964; Davies and Lateef, 1975; Nair, 1975; Nayar et al., 1976
Oxycarenus sp.	Lygaeidae	P	1	India	Davies and Lateef, 1975
O. hyalinipennis Costa	Lygaeidae	S, L, D	3	Kenya	Khamala et al., 1978

ORDER/ Scientific name	Family	Portion of plant attacked [a]	Pest status, 0-5 [b]	Pests reported from countries	References
O. laetus K.	Lygaeidae	S	1	India	Davies and Lateef, 1975
Oxyrachis tarandus F.	Membracidae	S	2	India	Srivastava, 1964; Paramanik and Basu, 1967; Davies and Lateef, 1975; Nayar et al., 1976
Piezodorus guildinii (Westwood)	Pentatomidae	F, P	1	C. America	Saunders et al., 1983
P. hybneri (Gmelin)	Pentatomidae	F, P	1	India	ICRISAT, 1976a
				E. Africa	Okeyo-Owuor, 1978
P. pallescens Germ.	Pentatomidae	L	1	Kenya	Le Pelley, 1959; Khamala et al., 1978
Planococcus citri Riso.	Pseudococcidae	S	1	India	Nayar et al., 1976
				New Guinea	van Velson, 1961
P. kenyae Le Pelley	Pseudococcidae	S, F	1	Kenya	Le Pelley, 1959; Khamala et al., 1978
Poophilus costalis Walk.	Aphrophoridae	S	1	India	ICRISAT, 1976a
P. torrenus Walk.	Aphrophoridae	S	1	Kenya	Khamala et al., 1978
Pseudococcus filamentosus Ckll.	Coccidae	S	1	India	Nair, 1975
Ptylus grossus (Fab.)	Cercopidae	S	1	Kenya	Le Pelley, 1959
Riptortus dentipes F.	Coreidae	P	3	Nigeria	Egwuatu and Taylor, 1977a
R. fuscus F.	Coreidae	F	0	India	Srivastava, 1964; Davies and Lateef, 1975; Nair, 1975; Nayar et al., 1976
R. linearis F.	Coreidae	F	1	India	Srivastava, 1964; Davies and Lateef, 1975; Nair, 1975; Nayar et al., 1976
R. pedestris (Fabr.)	Coreidae	P, F	1	India	Srivastava, 1964; Nair, 1975; Nayar et al., 1976
				Bangladesh	Anon., 1964
Saissetia hemisphaerica Targ.	Coccidae	S	1	Peru	Pflucker, 1981
S. neglecta Delotto	Coccidae	S	1	Puerto Rico	Gaud and Tuduri, 1977

Table 4.1 Continued

ORDER/Scientific name	Family	Portion of plant attacked [a]	Pest status, 0-5 [b]	Pests reported from countries	References
S. oleae Bernard	Coccidae	S	0	India	Nair, 1975; Nayar et al., 1976
Sitobion nigrinectaria Theo.	Aphididae	L, P, F	3	E. Africa	Odebiyi, 1981
Spilostethus sp.	Lygaeidae	S	0	India	ICRISAT, 1976a
Taylorilygus vosseleri (Popp.)	Miridae	L, S, P	3	Kenya	Khamala et al., 1978; Reed et al., 1989
Thyanta perditor (Fab.)	Pentatomidae	P	1	C. America	Saunders et al., 1983
Tricentrus bicolor Dist.	Membracidae	S	0	India	Nayar et al., 1976
Tylopelta sp.	Membracidae	L	1	C. America	Saunders et al., 1983
Urentius euonymous Dist.	Tingidae	L	1	Pandemic	Joplin, 1974
Vanduzea segmentata (Fowler)	Membracidae	L	1	C. America	Saunders et al., 1983
HYMENOPTERA					
Bruchophagus mellipes Gaham	Eurytomidae	D	0	India	Nayar et al., 1976
Ceratina binghami Ckll.	Apidae	L, F	1	India	Nayar et al., 1976
Megachile anthracina S.	Megachilidae	L	1	India	Srivastava, 1964; Davies and Lateef, 1975;
				Bangladesh	Nayar et al., 1976
					Anon., 1964
M. disjuncta F.	Megachilidae	L	1	India	Srivastava, 1964; Davies and Lateef, 1975;
					Nayar et al., 1976; Nair, 1975
Megachile sp.	Megachilidae	L	1	India	Ayyar, 1963; Lateef and Reed, 1983
Solenopsis geminata F.	Formicidae	R	1	India	Nair, 1975; Nayar et al., 1976
Tanaostigmodes cajaninae La Salle	Tanaostigmatidae	P	3	India	ICRISAT, 1976a; Lateef et al., 1985

ORDER/ Scientific name	Family	Portion of plant attacked [a]	Pest status, 0-5 [b]	Pests reported from countries	References
ISOPTERA					
Allondotermes sp.	Termitidae	S	2	Kenya	Khamala *et al.*, 1978
Ancistrotermes sp.	Termitidae	R	1	Nigeria	Egwuatu and Taylor, 1977
				Kenya	Khamala *et al.*, 1978
Odontotermes parvidens H.	Termitidae	S	2	India	Srivastava, 1964; Davies and Lateef, 1975; Nair, 1975; Nayar *et al.*, 1976
				Bangladesh	Anon., 1964
Microtermes sp.	Termitidae	R, S	2	India	Reed *et al.*, 1989
				E. Africa	Khamala *et al.*, 1978; Okeyo-Owuor, 1978
				Nigeria	Egwuatu and Taylor, 1977
LEPIDOPTERA					
Acanthoplusia orichalcea (F.)	Noctuidae	L	0	India	Davies and Lateef, 1975; ICRISAT, 1976a
Acherontia styx W.	Sphingidae	L	0	India	Davies and Lateef, 1975; ICRISAT, 1976a
Adisura atkinsoni (Moore)	Noctuidae	F, P	3	India	Srivastava, 1964; Saxena 1974; Davies and Lateef, 1975; ICRISAT, 1976a
A. marginalis Walk.	Noctuidae	F, P	3	India	Davies and Lateef, 1975; ICRISAT, 1976a,b; Thontadarya *et al.*, 1982
A. stigmatica Warr.	Noctuidae	F, P	3	India	ICRISAT, 1976a,b
Agrotis ipsilon (Hufn.)	Noctuidae	S, L	1	Kenya	Joplin, 1974; Khamala *et al.*, 1978
				India	Atwal, 19076
A. segetum (Shiff)	Noctuidae	S, L	1	Kenya	Khamala *et al.*, 1978; Okeyo-Owuor, 1978
				India	Atwal, 1976

Table 4.1 Continued

ORDER/ Scientific name	Family	Portion of plant attacked [a]	Pest status, 0-5 [b]	Pests reported from countries	References
Amsacta albistriga Walk.	Arctiidae	L	0	India	Srivastava, 1964; Davies and Lateef, 1975; Nayar et al., 1976
A. collaris Hamps = *Estigmene lactinea*	Arctiidae	L	1	India	Davies and Lateef, 1975
A. moorei B.	Arctiidae	R, S	1	India	Srivastava, 1964; Davies and Lateef, 1975; Nayar et al., 1976
Anarsia accrata Meyr.	Gelechiidae	L	0	India	Nair, 1975
A. ephippias (Meyr.)	Gelechiidae	L	0	India Bangladesh	Saxena, 1974; Nair, 1975; Srivastava et al., 1977 Anon, 1964
A. exallacta Meyr.	Gelechiidae	L	0	India	Nair, 1975
A. omoptila Meyr.	Gelechiidae	L	0	India	Nair, 1975
Ancylostomia stercorea (Zell.)	Pyralidae	F, P	1	Tanzania Trinidad Peru Caribbean	Bennet, 1960; Laurence, 1971; Buckmire, 1978 Laurence, 1971 Korytkowski and Torres, 1966 Schotman, 1986
Anticarsia gemmatilis	Noctuidae	L	1	India	ICRISAT, 1976a
A. irrorata F.	Noctuidae	L	0	India	Nair, 1975; ICRISAT, 1976a
Anuga multiplicans Walk.	Noctuidae	L	0	India	ICRISAT, 1976a
Aproaerema modicella D. = *Stomopteryx subsecivella*	Gelechiidae	L	1	India	Nayar et al., 1976; ICRISAT, 1976a
Atteva fabriciella Swed.	Yponomeutidae	L	0	India	ICRISAT, 1976a
Automeris sp.	Saturniidae	L	1	Peru	Pflucker, 1981
Azazia rubricans (Boisduval	Noctuidae	L	0	India	Davies and Lateef, 1975; ICRISAT, 1976a

ORDER/ Scientific name	Family	Portion of plant attacked [a]	Pest status, 0-5 [b]	Pests reported from countries	References
Brachyacma palpigera Wals.	Gelechiidae	L	0	Caribbean	Schotman, 1986
Caloptilia (Gracillaria) soyella van Dev.	Gracillariidae	L	1	India	Ayyar, 1963; Srivastava, 1964; Davies and Lateef, 1975; Nayar dt al., 1976
Caloptilia sp.	Gracillaridae	L	1	Caribbean	Schotman, 1986
Catephia mosara Swinh.	Noctuidae	L	0	India	ICRISAT, 1976a
Catochrysops strabo (F.)	Lycaenidae	F, P	3	Kenya	Khamala et al., 1978
				India	Nayar et al., 1976; Lal et al., 1981; Lateef and Reed, 1983
Chorizagrotis auxiliaris (Grote)	Noctuidae	F, P	0	Pandemic	Joplin, 1974
Chrysodeixis chalcites Esp.	Noctuidae	L	0	India	Davies and Lateef, 1975
Corcyra cephalonica St.	Galleriidae	D	1	India	Joshi, 1976
Cyphosticha coerulea Meyr.	Gelechiidae	L	0	India	Davies and Lateef, 1975; Nair, 1975
Dasychira basalis Wlk.	Lymantriidae	L	1	Uganda	Le Pelley, 1959
D. georgiana Fawcett	Lymantriidae	L	1	Uganda	Le Pelley, 1959
D. (Olene) mendosa Fab.	Lymantriidae	L	0	India	Davies and Lateef, 1975; Nayar et al., 1976; Varma and Mangalasain, 1977
D. plagiata Walk.	Lymantriidae	L	0	Uganda	Le Pelley, 1959
Digama hearseyana Moore	Arctiidae	L	0	India	ICRISAT, 1976a
Elasmopalpus rubedinellus (Zell.)	Phycitidae	P	4	Caribbean	Joplin, 1974
				Peru	Korytkowski and Torres, 1966
Etiella zinckenella (Treits.)	Phycitidae	P	3	India	Fletcher, 1914; Davies and Lateef, 1975; ICRISAT, 1976a; Nayar et al., 1976
				Bangladesh	Kabir, 1978
				Sri Lanka	Subasinghe and Fellowes, 1978
				C.America	Carlos, 1975; Saunders et al., 1983

Table 4.1 Continued

ORDER/Scientific name	Family	Portion of plant focus[a]	Pest status, 0-5[b]	Pests reported from countries	References
				E. Africa	Le Pelley, 1959; Khamala et al., 1978
Euchrysops (Catochrysops) cnejus (F.)	Lycaenidae	F, P	3	India	Fletcher, 1914; Srivastava, 1964; Bindra and Jakhmola, 1967; Davies and Lateef, 1975; Kapadia, 1975; Lal *et al.*, 1981
E. malathana Boisd.	Lycaenidae	P	3	Nigeria	Egwuatu and Taylor, 1977a
				Uganda	Le Pelley, 1959
Eucosma melanaula Meyr.	Tortricidae	L	0	India	Nair, 1975; Nayar *et al.*, 1976
Euproctis dewitzi Grunb.	Lymantriidae	L	1	Uganda	Le Pelley, 1959
E. fraterna Moore	Lymantriidae	L	0	India	Fletcher, 1914; Davies and Lateef, 1975; Nair, 1975; Nayar *et al.*, 1976; Atwal, 1976
E. hargreavesi Coll.	Lymantriidae	L	1	Uganda	Le Pelley, 1959
E. lunata Walk.	Lymantriidae	L	0	India	Davies and Lateef, 1975
E. producta Walk.	Lymantriidae	L	1	Uganda	Le Pelley, 1959
E. subnotata Walk.	Lymantriidae	L, F	3	India	Lateef and Reed, 1983
Euproctis sp.	Lymantriidae	S	1	Kenya	ICRISAT, 1976a; Khamala *et al.*, 1978
Exelastis atomosa (Wals.)	Pterophoridae	F, P	4	India	Fletcher, 1914; Davies and Lateef, 1975; Nayar et al., 1976; Lal *et al.*, 1981
				E. Africa	Le Pelley, 1959; Joplin, 1974; Khamala *et al.*, 1978
				Bangladesh	Anon., 1964
				Sri Lanka	Subasinghe and Fellowes, 1978
E. crepuscularis Meyr.	Pterophoridae	F, P	3	Uganda	Le Pelley, 1959
Fundella cistipennis (Dyar)	Pyralidae	F, P	3	Caribbean	Schotman, 1986

ORDER/Scientific name	Family	Portion of plant attacked[a]	Pest status, 0-5[b]	Pests reported from countries	References
F. pellucens Zeller	Pyralidae	F, P	3	C. America / Caribbean	Buckmire, 1978; Saunders et al., 1983 / Schotman, 1986
Glyphodes bivitralis Guen.	Pyraustidae	L	0	India	Nayar et al., 1976
Grapholita (Cydia) critica (Meyr.)	Tortricidae	L, F, P	4	India	Fletcher, 1914; Srivastava, 1964 Paramanik and Basu, 1968; Davies and Lateef, 1975; Nayar et al., 1976; Lal et al., 1981
				Bangladesh	Anon., 1964; Kabir, 1978
				Thailand	Isaravurak and Potan, 1988
Helicoverpa (Heliothis) armigera (Hüb.)	Noctuidae	L, F, P	5	India	Bindra and Jakhmola, 1967; Reddy 1973; Davies and Lateef, 1975; ICRISAT, 1976a,b; Lal et al., 1981
				Bangladesh	Kabir, 1978
				Australia	Wallis et al., 1979
				Sri Lanka	Subasinghe and Fellowes, 1978
				E. Africa	Le Pelley, 1959; Khamala et al., 1978
				Sierra Leone	Taylor, 1978
				Thailand	Isaravurak and Potan, 1988
= Heliothis obselata Fab.	Noctuidae	F, P	1	India	Fletcher, 1914; Srivastava, 1964; Atwal, 1976
= Heliothis rama sp. n.	Noctuidae	F, P	4	India	Bhattacherjee and Gupta, 1972
Helicoverpa punctigera (Wallengren)	Noctuidae	F, P	4	Australia	Reed et al., 1989
Helicoverpa (Heliothis) zea (Boddie)	Noctuidae	L, F, P	5	North America	Killinger, 1968
				Caribbean	Schotman, 1986
				C.America	Saunders et al., 1983

Table 4.1 Continued

ORDER/ Scientific name	Family	Portion of plant attacked [a]	Pest status, 0-5 [b]	Pests reported from countries	References
Heliothis virescens (F.)	Noctuidae	F, P	4	Caribbean	Schotman, 1986
				Pandemic	Joplin, 1974
				Pto Rico	Carlos, 1975
				Peru	Korytkowski and Torres, 1966; Pflucker, 1981
				Trinidad	Buckmire, 1978
				C.America	Saunders et al., 1983
				US Virgin Islands	Snow et al., 1974
Herse convolvuli L.	Sphingidae	L, F	0	India	Davies and Lateef, 1975
Hyposidra talaca Walk.	Geometridae	L	0	India	ICRISAT, 1976a
Lampides (Cosmolyce) boeticus (L.)	Lycaenidae	F, P	3	India	Srivastava, 1964; Davies and Lateef, 1975; Nayar et al., 1976; Lal et al., 1981
				E. Africa	Le Pelley, 1959; Joplin, 1974
Leguminivora (Cydia) ptychora (Meyr.)	Tortricidae	L	2	India	Nair, 1975; ICRISAT, 1976a,b; Khamala et al., 1978; Le Pelley, 1959
				E. Africa	
				Nigeria	Perrin, 1976
Marasmarcha liophanes Meyr.	Pterophoridae	F, P	0	India	Chari and Patel, 1967; Davies and Lateef, 1975
Margaronia bivitralis Guen.	Pyralidae	F, P	1	India	Nair, 1975
Maruca testulalis (Geyer.)	Pyralidae	L, F, P	4	India	Fletcher, 1914; Saxena, 1974; Davies and Lateef, 1975; Patel and Singh, 1977; Lal et al., 1981
				Sri Lanka	Subasinghe and Fellowes, 1978; Thevasagayam and Canagasingham, 1961
				Thailand	Isaravurak and Potan, 1988
				Nigeria	Egwuatu and Taylor, 1977a; Singh and Taylor, 1978

ORDER/Scientific name	Family	Portion of plant attacked [a]	Pest status, 0-5 [b]	Pests reported from countries	References
				Bangladesh	Anon., 1964
				E. Africa	Khamala et al., 1978; Le Pelley, 1959
				C. America	Saunders et al., 1983
				Sierra Leone	Taylor, 1978
				Fiji	Anon., 1980
				Caribbean	Schotman, 1986
Mythimna separata Walk.	Noctuidae	L	0	India	ICRISAT, 1976a
Nacoleia vulgalis Gn.	Pyralidae	F, P	0	India	Nair, 1975
Nanaguna breviuscula Wlk.	Noctuidae	P	1	India	Nair, 1975; Patnaik et al., 1986
Neostauropus (Stauropus) alternus (Walk.)	Notodontidae	L	0	India	Srivastava, 1964; Siddappaji et al., 1974; Davies and Lateef, 1975; Nayar et al., 1976
Pardasene virgulana (Mab.)	Noctuidae	P	4	Kenya Uganda	Le Pelley, 1959 Khamala et al., 1978
Pelopidas mathias F.	Hesperiidae	L	0	India	ICRISAT, 1976a
Pingasa ruginaria G.	Geometridae	L	0	India	Ayyar, 1963; Nair, 1975; Davies and Lateef, 1975; Nayar et al., 1976
Porthesia (Euproctis) scintillans W.	Lymantriidae	L	0	India	Puttarudraiah, 1947; Srivastava, 1964; Davies and Lateef, 1975; Nayar et al., 1976
Psalis pennatula F.	Lymantriidae	L	0	India	ICRISAT, 1976a
P. securis	Lymantriidae	L	0	India	Davies and Lateef, 1975
Rapala iarbus F.	Lycaenidae	L, F	0	India	ICRISAT, 1976a

Table 4.1 Continued

ORDER/ Scientific name	Family	Portion of plant attacked[a]	Pest status, 0-5[b]	Pests reported from countries	References
Sphenarches anisodactylus Walk.	Pterophoridae	F, P	1	India Sri Lanka Ivory Coast Kenya	Davies and Lateef, 1975; ICRISAT, 1976a,b; Subasinghe and Fellowes, 1978; Bigot and Vuattoux, 1981; Okeyo-Owuor, 1978
S. caffer Zell.	Pterophoridae	F, P	3	India Nigeria Sri Lanka Trinidad	Davies and Lateef, 1975; Nair, 1975; Joplin, 1974; Atwal, 1976; Egwuatu and Taylor, 1977a; Thevasagayam and Canagasingham, 1961; Schotman, 1986
Spilosoma (Diacrisia) obliqua (Walk.)	Arctiidae	L, F	3	India Bangladesh	ICRISAT, 1976a; Atwal, 1976; Kabir, 1978
Spodoptera exigua Hüb.	Noctuidae	L, F	1	India Kenya	ICRISAT, 1976a; Atwal, 1976; Okeyo-Owuor, 1978
Spodoptera litura Fab.	Noctuidae	L, F	1	India	Nair, 1975; ICRISAT, 1976a; Atwal, 1976
S. littoralis B.	Noctuidae	L, F	1	Nigeria	Singh and Taylor, 1978
Spodoptera sp.	Noctuidae	L, F	1	Caribbean	Schotman, 1986
Streblote siva Lef.	Lasiocampidae	L	0	India	ICRISAT, 1976a
Syntomis passalis F.	Syntomidae	L, F	2	India	ICRISAT, 1976a; Nair, 1975
Thosea aperiens Walk.	Cochlidiidae	L	0	India	David and Santhanaraman, 1964; Nayar et al., 1976
Trichoplusia ni Hb.	Noctuidae	L	1	India	ICRISAT, 1976a; Atwal, 1976
Trichopilus congrualis Wales	Pterophoridae	F, P	0	India	Savalia, 1971
Utetheisa lotrix (Cram)	Arctiidae	L	1	Pandemic	Joplin, 1974

ORDER/Scientific name	Family	Portion of plant focus[a]	Pest status, 0-5[b]	Pests reported from countries	References
ORTHOPTERA					
Acanthacris ruficornis F.	Acrididae	L	1	Uganda	Le Pelley, 1959
Catantops erubescens Walk.	Acrididae	L, S	1	India	Davies and Lateef, 1975
Chrotogonus spp.	Acrididae	L, S	1	India	Davies and Lateef, 1975
Colemania sphenerioides (Bol.)	Acrididae	L, S	3	India	Fletcher, 1914; Davies and Lateef, 1975; Lateef and Reed, 1983
Cyrtacanthacris tatarica (L.)	Acrididae	L, S	2	India	Davies and Lateef, 1975
				Kenya	Khamala *et al.*, 1978
Eyprepocnemis alacris (Serville)	Acrididae	L, S	2	India	Davies and Lateef, 1975
Gryllus bimaculatus Deg.	Gryllidae	R, G	1	Kenya	Khamala *et al.*, 1978; Okeyo-Owuor, 1978
Patanga succincta (L.)	Acrididae	L, S	2	India	Davies and Lateef, 1975
Pyrgomorpha bispinosa Walk.	Pyrgomorphidae	L, S	1	India	Davies and Lateef, 1975
Zonocerus variegatus (L.)	Pyrgomorphidae	L	3	Nigeria	Egwuatu and Taylor, 1977a
THYSANOPTERA					
Caliothrips indicus Bagnall	Thripidae	F	0	India	Atwal, 1976; Lal *et al.*, 1981
Dolichothrips varipes Bagnall	Thripidae	F	0	India	Davies and Lateef, 1975; Joplin, 1974
				Sri Lanka	Thevasagayam and Canagasingham, 1961
Frankliniella insularis (Frank.)	Thripidae	F	3	Trinidad	Pollard and Elie, 1981
F. schultzei (Trybom)	Thripidae	L	0	India	Satpathy *et al.*, 1979
				Kenya	Khamala *et al.*, 1978

Table 4.1 Continued

ORDER/ Scientific name	Family	Portion of plant attacked [a]	Pest status, 0-5 [b]	Pests reported from countries	References
F. sulphurea (Schmutz)	Thripidae	F	0	India	Vaishampayan and Singh, 1969; Yadav *et al.*, 1974; Davies and Lateef, 1975
Leucothrips theobromae	Thripidae	F	1	Peru	Pflucker, 1981
Liothrips sp.	Phoethripidae	L, F, P	1	Peru	Pflucker, 1981
Megalurothrips usitatus (Bagn.)	Thripidae	F	3	India	ICRISAT, 1976a; Nayar *et al.*, 1976; Lateef and Reed, 1983
Megalurothrips (Taeniothrips) distalis (Karny) = *T. nigricornis* (Schmutz)	Thripidae	F	1	India / Bangladesh	Yadav, 1967; Nair, 1975; Lal *et al.*, 1981; Vaishampayan and Singh, 1969; Davies and Lateef, 1975; Lateef and Reed, 1983 / Anon., 1964
Megalurothrips (Taeniothrips) sjostedti (Tryb.)	Thripidae	F	3	Nigeria / Sierra Leone / Kenya	Egwuatu and Taylor, 1977a; Singh and Taylor, 1978; Taylor, 1978 / Khamala *et al.*, 1978
Thrips hawaiiensis (Morgan)	Thripidae	F	0	India	Nayar *et al.*, 1976
Thrips tabaci Lind.	Thripidae	F	0	E. Africa	Schmutterer, 1969; Okeyo-Owuor, 1978

[a] Pest attacks G = germinating seeds and seedlings; R = roots/nodules; S = stems; L = leaves; F = buds and flowers; P = pods; D = dried and stored seeds.

[b] Pest status 0 = is of little or no importance (casual pest); 1 = causes little damage to plant (leaf blotches, sap sucking etc); 2 = causes occasional seedling/plant damage; 3 = is occasionally serious, sporadic or of local importance; 4 = is common, causes widespread concern; 5 = is serious, widely distributed, causes heavy economic losses.

black soil (Vertisol) and on shallow red soil (Alfisol). They found that the majority of the shed flowers had no detectable damage but that more than half of the shed pods, particularly from the Vertisol, were damaged by pests, so insect damage appears to contribute to pod shedding.

Sheldrake *et al.* (1979) showed also that removal of early flowers from pigeon pea plants had little or no effect on final grain yield. This ability of pigeon pea to compensate for losses complicates assessment of losses caused by pests. However, some attempts have been made to assess yield losses caused by pod borers in pigeon pea (Lateef, 1977; Reed, 1983).

Not much has been published about how growth habit, duration and flowering of pigeon pea cultivars influence pest damage levels. In our studies at ICRISAT, we noted that pest damage differed considerably with growth habit and duration of the cultivars. The determinate, clustering types, particularly of short- and medium-duration, suffered most from lepidopteran borer attack. The indeterminate, medium- and long-duration cultivars had more damage from podfly (Lateef and Reed, 1980).

If all or most of the first flush of flowers and pods are lost, then the plant will produce more flushes, and the yield may be as good as normal. Some pigeon pea cultivars can compensate for early losses much better than others. The reports about losses caused by pests emphasize that the range is wide because of the number of pests and the variation by location, year and cultivar.

In India, Argikar and Thobbi (1957) reported 0.3−19.6 per cent pod loss caused by *Exelastis atomosa* (Walsingham); Gangrade (1963, 1964) recorded 27−100 per cent pod damage and 11−87 per cent seed loss from podfly damage in five pigeon pea cultivars in Madhya Pradesh. In the same state, Odak *et al.* (1967) recorded that the podfly *Melanagromyza obtusa* Malloch damaged 34−64 per cent of pods in four cultivars and that the seed damage ranged from 13.5 per cent to 33.2 per cent. The damage by *Helicoverpa armigera* (Hübner) and *E. atomosa* was considerably lower. Srivastava *et al.* (1971) reported from Kanpur that podfly damage to pods of various cultivars was 8−29 per cent.

Bindra and Jakhmola (1967) reported a high correlation (r = 0.97) between podfly incidence and seed damage in pigeon pea in Madhya Pradesh. They further reported that the podfly damage to seeds was 6−10 per cent by weight and that other pests, including *H. armigera*, caused only 1−4 per cent loss. However, Davies and Lateef (1978) reported 5−85 per cent pod damage by lepidopteran pests in cultivars of various maturities, with *H. armigera* being the most damaging pest in Andhra Pradesh.

In Africa published assessments of pigeon pea losses are few. In Tanzania, Materu (1970) reported that more than 50 per cent of pigeon pea seeds were disfigured and unmarketable because of pod bug attack. In Uganda, Köhler and Rachie (1971) recorded 5 per cent seed damage by *H.*

armigera. Okeyo-Owuor (1978) assessed losses in pigeon peas in Kenya using data from pesticide trials. He attributed 13 per cent seed loss to lepidopteran borers and 11 per cent seed loss to the podfly, *Melanagromyza* sp.

The distribution, damage signs, description, biology and control of the important pests of the different orders of the class Insecta are discussed in the following.

Coleoptera

APIONIDAE

The pod weevil, *Apion clavipes* Gerst., is regarded as a major pest of pigeon pea in some areas (Sinha and Yadav, 1983) including Bangladesh (Anon., 1964); *Apion benignum* (Faust) is occasionally found in southern India. In Kenya, *Apion amplum* Faust was found infesting pigeon pea in farmers' fields (ICRISAT, 1977). Elsewhere, these weevils are relatively uncommon.

The creamy white larvae damage the green seeds in the pods, but damage is usually noticed only after the adults emerge by cutting their way out of the pod. The beetles also chew small holes in leaflets and flowers. The adults are small black weevils. There do not appear to be any published reports on the biology of these pests. Pesticides, including dimethoate, monocrotophos and the synthetic pyrethroids can be used to control these pests.

BRUCHIDAE

The bruchid, *Callosobruchus maculatus* F. is common on pigeon pea and some other grain legumes worldwide, both in pods in the field and in stored seed. Other species, including *Callosobruchus analis* (F.) and *Callosobruchus chinensis* (L.) are also found in the stored seed.

The matured and dried pods are attacked on the plant; the round exit hole through the pod wall and the white eggs on the pod wall are easily seen. Infested stored seed can also be recognized by the eggs and the round exit holes.

The dull brown beetle (3 mm) lays its eggs on pods or seeds. The white larva burrows into the pod or seed through the base of the egg and then feeds and develops into a pupa inside the seed, from which the adult emerges through a neat cylindrical hole. A generation takes 4 weeks or more, depending on temperature. In the Caribbean, the eggs of *C. chinensis* on pigeon pea hatched in 4–6 days; larval period lasted up to 21 days, pupal period 7–10 days; and the life cycle was completed in 32–37 days (Schotman, 1986).

This pest infests pigeon pea pods nearing maturity (Ghosh, 1937; Raina, 1972; ICRISAT, 1977; Sangappa and Balaraju, 1977), so the pods should be harvested as soon as they mature, and the seed should be sun-dried before being placed in clean, beetle-proof containers (metal, wood, earthenware or plastic). Fumigation with a range of chemicals has been reported to control infestations in stores. Also, a thin coating of edible oils can be used to prevent build-up of bruchids in stored seeds (ICRISAT, 1976b; Sangappa, 1977).

Raghupathy and Rathnaswamy (1970) screened several varieties of pigeon pea for resistance to *C. chinensis* but had little success. The possibility of utilizing bruchid-resistant varieties for large-scale production is remote.

BUPRESTIDAE

The stem borer *Sphenoptera indica* Laporte and Gorg. (jewel beetle) is fairly common but sporadic in central and southern India, feeding on several legumes, including pigeon pea and groundnut. *Sphenoptera laplumei* Kerr has been reported to cause stem damage to pigeon pea in Nigeria (Egwuatu and Taylor, 1977a).

The larvae tunnel in the stem above and below ground. A prominent gall forms around the stem at ground level, but similar galls are found when other insects, including weevil larvae, feed on the stem. Young plants wilt and die, but older plants may survive and produce normal numbers of pods.

The white, legless larvae grow 20 mm long or longer, with a characteristic bulb at one end that is formed from the head and thorax. Pupation takes place in the tunnel in the root or stem. The adult beetle is dark but iridescent, with a jewel-like reflection that gives the common name to this beetle. Little is known of its biology and control. Burning old infested stems may reduce attacks in the next season.

COCCINELLIDAE

The coccinellids, commonly referred to as ladybird beetles, are small and usually brightly coloured, with darker spots. The *Epilachna* spp. are herbivorous, but *Cheilomenes* spp. nymphs and adults are predatory on small insects, including aphids. In the absence of prey, *Cheilomenes* spp. adults will chew holes in leaves, possibly to obtain moisture.

CHRYSOMELIDAE

The chrysomelids are generally shiny, metallic beetles; *Podagrica* spp. are flea beetles, so called because they can jump long distances.

CURCULIONIDAE

The stem weevils, *Alcidodes fabricii* (F.) and *Alcidodes collaris* (Pasc.) are common in central and southern India. Young plants are girdled by the adult so the upper portions of the plants wilt and dry; also, the stems may break. The adult beetle (6 mm long) of *A. fabricii* is dark red–brown with white longitudinal stripes, and *A. collaris* is black with white bands on the elytra.

The eggs are laid singly in holes made in the stem by the beetle and covered with stem fibre. The white larvae bore into the stem. A swelling or gall is formed near the point of entry. The stem may break at these points. The life cycle takes about 35 days in south India (Nair, 1975). These pests seldom merit control measures. They may kill a few young plants, but neighbouring plants grow to fill the spaces.

Leaf-damaging weevils *Myllocerus* spp. and *Phyllobius* spp. are widespread in India on pigeon pea and several other host plants. *Nematocerus* spp. and *Systates* spp. have been reported from Africa. Other genera and species of weevils are also reported to feed on pigeon pea leaves.

The adult weevils chew the leaflets, generally at the margins, so the edges look ragged. The larvae feed in the soil on organic matter, including plant roots. The adults of *Myllocerus undecimpustulatus* Faust (5 mm) have 11 small black spots on their ash-grey bodies (hence the locally common name of ash weevil). The white larvae are found in the soil.

Damage to pigeon pea has not been regarded as meriting separate control measures. However, on other crops, particularly on some varieties of cotton, *M. undecimpustulatus* is a major pest in some localities, and insecticides including monocrotophos have been recommended for its control.

The bud weevil, *Indozocladius asperulus* Faust, is widely distributed in peninsular India. Both grubs and adult weevils cause damage to buds and flowers. The small (2 mm), greyish-green weevil thrusts its eggs into the buds where white larvae develop singly. Full-grown grubs drop to the ground and pupate in the soil. The life cycle is completed in 10–22 days, averaging 14.5 days during January–February in south India (Govindan *et al.*, 1977). In severe attacks, the numbers of flowers are substantially reduced. In Karnataka, India, 10–80 per cent infestation was observed in pigeon pea (Govindan *et al.*, 1977). This pest can be controlled effectively by insecticides, like dimethoate and endosulfan. A larval parasite, *Diaparsis* sp. (Hym.: Ichneumonidae) has been reported by Naik *et al.* (1979).

MELOIDAE

The blister beetles *Mylabris pustulata* Thunb. and other *Mylabris* spp. are widespread and common in India. Several species of *Mylabris* and *Coryna* have been recorded from pigeon pea in Africa. The adult beetles feed on the flowers and can greatly reduce the numbers of pods that are set.

Mylabris pustulata (25 mm) is one of the larger species, with very obvious black and red coloration on the adult. Other genera and species of blister beetles vary in size but most have conspicuous coloration. Their name is derived from the blisters that are produced on human skin by the exudate (containing cantharidine) that they produce when disturbed. Little is known of the life history, but the larvae of most species feed upon insects in the soil and so are generally beneficial.

In locations where large areas are cropped with pigeon pea, the blister beetles are diluted across the crop and cause little damage. However, when flowering corresponds with the time that adults are common (from August to October in southern India), most flowers in small plots will be eaten, and crop losses may be substantial. The beetles can be controlled manually by crushing, for they are slow moving. Gloves and other protective clothing should be worn. Few insecticides are effective against these beetles, but synthetic pyrethroids give reasonable control.

Several genera of beetles, other than weevils, have been reported feeding on pigeon pea leaves in India and in Africa. A few of these deserve mention.

SCARABAEIDAE

Lachnosterna (Holotrichia) spp. are larger beetles, of importance because their larvae (often referred to as white grubs) cause considerable damage to a range of crops by feeding on roots. The adults are active after sunset.

Adoretus spp. are brightly coloured, shiny beetles, their larvae feed on roots. These beetles are seldom, if ever, present in large enough populations to cause extensive damage to pigeon pea and so do not merit specific control measures. The tests conducted by Bindra and Singh (1971b) showed that the sprays of fenitrothion (0.05 per cent) and of carbaryl (0.1 per cent) provided the best control of adults on plants.

Diptera

AGROMYZIDAE

Stemfly, *Ophiomyia phaseoli* (Tryo), is common in Africa, Asia and Australasia, feeding in the stems of several legumes, including pigeon pea; *Ophiomyia centrosematis* (de Meijere) has been reared from pigeon pea stems at ICRISAT but may be rare on this crop.

The upper portions of infested young plants wilt, and the plants may die. Close examination of the stem at the base of the wilted portion will reveal a larva or puparium.

The shiny black fly, which is 2 mm long, lays its eggs on the upper surfaces of leaves. The white larvae tunnel down leaf veins into the stem where they feed and pupate. The *O. phaseoli* flies mate 2–6 days after emergence, and eggs are laid 2–4 days after mating. The egg-laying capacity of a female varies from 14 to 64. Egg period lasts 2–4 days. Larval period is 9–12 days in November and December and 6–7 days in March and April in northern India. The pupal period is 5–9 days in March–April and 18–19 days in November–December. Adult life is 8–22 days for females and, on average, 11 days for males (Nair, 1975). This pest is seldom found in large enough numbers in pigeon pea to be of concern, but it is a major pest in other legumes, including beans. On those crops, systemic soil insecticides such as phorate have been recommended for control.

The podfly, *Melanagromyza obtusa* Malloch, is a widespread and major pest of pigeon pea in Asia and extends to Australasia. Reports of this species in Africa are probably erroneous, for there it is replaced by *Melanagromyza chalcosoma* Spencer, which is common in the pods of other legumes as well. In north and central India, up to 100 per cent of pods have been recorded as being infested by *M. obtusa* with 87 per cent seed loss (Gangrade, 1963; Vishakantaiah *et al.*, 1973). Surveys in India, 1975–81, indicated a mean pod damage of 20.8 per cent in 359 fields sampled in north India where long-duration cultivars were grown; 22.3 per cent in 446 fields sampled in central India where medium- and long-duration pigeon pea were grown; and 11.1 per cent in 443 fields sampled in south India where short- and medium-duration cultivars were grown (Lateef and Reed, 1983).

There are no obvious signs of podfly attack until the fully grown larva chews a hole (about 1 mm in diameter) in the pod wall, leaving a "window" through which the fly emerges after pupation in the pod. Damaged seeds are of no value.

The small black fly lays about 80 minute white eggs through the pod wall. After 2–3 days, the white legless larvae (3 mm) hatch and feed for 5–6 days inside the green seeds. Two or more larvae of *M. chalcosoma* often develop in one seed, but usually only one larva of *M. obtusa* develops in a seed. The brown puparium is formed inside the pod but outside the seed. The pupal period lasts for 8–9 days. Adult life lasts 3–6 days (Nair, 1975). A generation takes about 22 days under optimal conditions.

As all stages of development are inside the pod, only systemic insecticides such as dimethoate and monocrotophos are effective against these pests; insecticides such as endosulfan will give some protection by killing the adults. A closed season during which no pigeon pea pods are available will reduce infestation, and, conversely, extending the time that pods are available by mixing cultivars of differing durations will allow several generations to develop and should be avoided. Some pigeon pea genotypes are particularly susceptible to egg laying, so the selection of resistant cultivars may be possible (Sithanantham *et al.*, 1981b). Intensive screening of more than 9000 pigeon pea accessions at ICRISAT has revealed a number of resistant sources such as ICP 7050-E1, ICP 6977, ICP 10531-E1, ICP 7941-E1, ICP 7946-E1, and ICP 8102-5-S1-EB (Lateef *et al.*, 1986). These selections have been used in crosses by breeders at ICRISAT and at different national centres in India, both to intensify the resistance and to combine it with other desirable traits including disease resistance. The lines developed should result in increased yields with little or no pesticide application.

The larval parasites, *Euderus lividus* (Ashm) (Hym.: Eulophidae) (Ahmad, 1938), *Euderus agromyzae* Gang. (Hym.: Eulophidae) (Nair, 1975), and *Eurytoma* sp. (Hym.: Ormyridae) (Sithanantham, 1987) have been reported parasitizing *M. obtusa* larvae and pupae in India.

PLATYSTOMATIDAE

Rivellia angulata Hendel has been recorded only in India, reportedly attacking the nodules on pigeon pea roots (Siddappaji and Gowda, 1980; Sithanantham *et al.*, 1981a). However, similar damage has been reported from Africa, and other species are known to attack nodules on several legumes in the Americas, Africa and Australasia. The larvae penetrate and hollow out the nodules, feeding upon the active, nitrogen-fixing portions. Heavy attacks, usually in Vertisols, have resulted in the destruction of more than 90 per cent of the nodules. The plants may show yellowing, typical of nitrogen deficiency, and reduced growth. The flies, which have black bands on their wings, lay their eggs on the plants and on the soil. The larvae disperse to the root nodules where they feed and grow. The full-sized cream-coloured larva is 10 mm long. Pupation is in the soil. A generation can be completed in about 4 weeks. No control measures can be recommended. Large doses of insecticides to the soil have given poor control of this insect, and such treatment is obviously uneconomic. The addition of nitrogen fertilizer to the soil will probably alleviate the deficiency resulting from nodule damage.

Hemiptera

ALEYRODIDAE

Whitefly, *Bemisia tabaci* (Genn.), is very common and widely distributed, being found on many host plants across the Americas, Europe, Africa, and

Asia. On pigeon pea in India, whitefly is of importance as the vector of a virus that causes yellow mosaic disease.

The adults are very small (1 mm) with white, wax-powdered wings. Eggs are laid on the undersurface of leaflets. The first instar nymph crawls about on the leaflet surface until it finds a suitable site for feeding. It then remains at that site, feeding by sucking. It grows into a flat, oval-shaped, scale-like 'puparium' fringed by wax filaments. A generation can be completed in fewer than 30 days.

Whiteflies have not been recorded as being sufficiently damaging on pigeon pea to merit control measures, even though the yellow mosaic disease is fairly common in post rainy season India. Several insecticides, including dimethoate and monocrotophos, are reported to control this insect.

APHIDIDAE

Several species of aphids have been reported from pigeon pea, but *Aphis craccivora* Koch is the commonest both in Asia and in Africa. The colonies of aphids can be seen on the young stems, leaflets and pods. One sign of infestation is twisted young leaves of seedlings, and growth is severely affected by heavy infestations. In larger plants, heavy infestations can cause wilting.

Aphis craccivora damages groundnuts most but is common on several legumes, including pigeon pea. The adults are black and shiny, up to 2 mm long, and some are winged. The nymphs are similar to the adults but smaller, with a light wax cover that makes them look grey or dull. The life cycle of the aphid from egg to adult averages 8.3 days. The reproductive life of the adult lasts 6.7 days, during which 14–17 offspring are produced per female (Nair, 1975).

Aphis fabae Scop. are similar, but the adults are less shiny and dark brown–green rather than black.

Myzus persicae (Sulzer) and *Macrosiphum* spp. on pigeon pea are generally green. All of these aphids can produce a new generation in a week, so infestations build up very quickly.

Aphid colonies on pigeon pea seldom thrive for long, probably because of natural enemies. Also, rains reduce infestations. Several systemic insecticides, including dimethoate and monocrotophos, give adequate control.

CICADELLIDAE

Jassids have been recorded from pigeon pea in most areas where the crop is grown. They are not easily identified to the species level. In India, *Empoasca kerri* Pruthi is the species most commonly reported from pigeon pea and other legumes. *Jacobiasca lybica* (de Beryeven) has been reported from pigeon pea in Africa and *Empoasca fabae* (Harris) from the Americas and Caribbean.

The attacked leaflets become cup-shaped and yellow at the edges. Heavy attacks result in the leaflets' turning red–brown with subsequent defoliation and stunting. These small green insects (2.5 mm) feed by sucking on the leaflets. They are found on both upper and lower leaf surfaces. The adults fly when disturbed. The nymphs resemble the adults but have no wings and run sideways when disturbed. The eggs are inserted on the underside of leaflets in veins. A generation can be completed in 2 weeks under optimal conditions. Heavy infestations, sufficient to cause yield loss, have been seen in northern India and in Kenya.

In Puerto Rico typical Witches' broom occurs when leafhoppers, *E. fabae*, colonize field plants (Baquero, 1980). These hoppers are the vectors of *Mycoplasma*-like organisms, which were found to be associated with a bushy canopy disease of *C. cajan*. (Vakilli and Maramorosch, 1974).

Several insecticides, including dimethoate and endosulfan, have been found to give adequate control of this pest.

COCCIDAE

Several species, genera and families of scale insects are known to feed upon the stems of pigeon pea in Africa and Asia. The scale-like insects are obvious on the stems and sometimes on the leaves. In general, they are not major pests when pigeon pea is grown as an annual but commonly build up and kill plants that are kept as perennials. In Asia, one species, *Laccifer lacca* (Kerr), whose secretion provides the commodity lac, is sometimes cultivated on pigeon pea but mainly on *Acacia* spp.

The young nymphs are mobile and can be spread by wind; the adult females are sedentary and usually found in colonies. Scales are often protected from their numerous natural enemies by ants, which feed upon the exudates from the scales. *Ceroplastodes cajani* Mask. is the commonest scale on pigeon pea in India. Many species of scales are found on pigeon pea in eastern Africa where most plants are long-duration genotypes and are frequently ratooned or left to grow for more than a year. *Icerya purchasi* Mask., a polyphagous species, is one of the most colourful scales found on this plant.

The other coccids associated with pigeon pea are *Saissetia oleae* Ber., *Lecanium longulum* D., *Lecanium hesperidum* L., *Inglisia bivalvata* Gr., *Pseudococcus filamentosus* Ckll., *Centrococcus insolitus* Gr., *Margarodes niger* Gr., *Drosicha stebbingi* Gr. and *Laccifer lacca* K.

Scale insects can be controlled directly by the use of systemic insecticides. Alternatively, destruction of the ants will rapidly result in a build-up of many natural enemies that will control the scales.

The mealybugs (pseudococcids) *Ferrisia virgata* (Cockerell), infesting pigeon pea and *Dismicoccus brevipes* (Cockerell) infesting rhizobium nodules of pigeon pea, have also been recorded in India.

COREIDAE

Of the coreids, *Anoplocnemis* spp. and *Riptortus* spp. are found on several hosts in Africa and Asia, but *Clavigralla gibbosa* Spinola is the most important pod-sucking bug on pigeon pea in India and *Clavigralla (Acanthomia) tomentosicollis* (Stal.) is the most important in Africa. *Clavigralla scutellaris* (Westw.) is common in Africa and Asia. Other coreids are also occasionally found on this crop.

All of these bugs, and others, suck the developing seeds through the pod wall. The seeds become shrivelled with dark patches, will not germinate and are not acceptable as human food.

The adults of *Anoplocnemis* spp., which are mainly dark, are the largest (30 mm) of these bugs. *Riptortus* spp. (18 mm) are mainly brown, and *Clavigralla* spp. are brown−grey. *Clavigralla scutellaris* (12 mm) is the largest in its genus and is broader than *C. gibbosa* and *C. tomentosicollis*, both of which are about 10 mm long.

The biology and bionomics of *C. gibbosa* were studied in detail in India by Bindra (1965), Gangrade (1961), Kapoor (1966), Singh and Patel (1968), Choudhary (1969), Bindra and Singh (1971a) and Nawale and Jadhav (1980). In Africa, Egwuatu and Taylor (1977b, 1979) and Materu (1970, 1971) have studied the biology, population dynamics and losses caused by *C. tomentosicollis* and *Acanthomia horrida*. These bugs lay their eggs in clumps of 5−15 on the leaf and pod surfaces. The young nymphs, which feed by sucking green tissue, are usually found in groups. The large nymphs and adults can feed on seed through pod walls. A generation takes 4 weeks or more, according to temperature. The female of *C. gibbosa* lays up to 437 eggs. Incubation varies from 3 to 20 days. The nymphal development takes 8−31 days, depending on prevailing temperatures. The adults live for 1−2 months, 4−6 generations, being observed in a year (Bindra, 1965). Similar information has been reported for *C. gibbosa* by Nawale and Jadhav (1980).

Insecticides, particularly those with some systemic action such as dimethoate and monocrotophos, are usually effective in controlling these pests. In East Africa some pigeon pea genotypes have been reported as being resistant to the sucking bugs (Paul A. Omanga, pulse breeder, National Dryland Farming Research Station, Katumani, Machakar, Kenya, 1982, personal communication), so screening for resistance may be productive.

The egg parasitoids, *Hardronotus antestiae* Dodd (Bindra, 1965) and *Gryon* sp. (Lateef and Reddy, 1984), have been recorded as effective control agents. A reduviid bug preys on the eggs of *C. gibbosa*. Also, Rawat *et al.* (1969) have recorded a predatory mite *Bachartia* sp. (Erythraeidae: Acarina) on *C. gibbosa*. Egwuatu and Taylor (1977b) reported observing the egg parasitoid *Gryon gnidus* Nixon (Hym.: Scelionidae) on *C. tomentosicollis* in Nigeria.

MEMBRACIDAE

The cow bugs, *Otinotus oneratus* W. and *Oxyrachis tarandus* F., are common in central and southern India. The bugs suck the sap from green stems. Heavy infestations can result in the formation of corky calluses, wilting and reduced plant vigour. The grey–brown adults (7 mm long), which have thorn-like projections on the thorax, lay their eggs on the stems. The nymphs exude a liquid that is utilized by ants, which in return help to protect the bugs from natural enemies. The cow bug derives its name from the habit of providing 'milk' to the ants. No specific control measures are recommended. Insecticides used to control the major pests, particularly dimethoate, will reduce the populations of this minor pest. *Centrodora* sp.nr. *mumtazi* Hayat (Hym: Aphelinidae) was found parasitizing the eggs of *Oxyrachis* sp. in India (Lateef and Reddy, 1984).

MIRIDAE

Several species of mirid bugs reportedly suck the buds and other young tissues of pigeon pea. *Taylorilygus vosseleri* (Popp.) is one in East Africa, but this species is more damaging on cotton. *Campylomma* spp., *Creontiades pallidus* (Ramb.) and *Eurystylus* sp. are common on pigeon pea in India.

The bugs suck the vegetative and flowering buds and may cause deformation of the leaves and abortion of flower buds.

Campylomma spp. are small green, elongate, ovoid bugs, the adults being about 2 mm long. *Creontiades pallidus* are larger — the adults, about 8 mm long. *Eurystylus* spp. and *T. vosseleri* are brown and about 4 mm long. All insert their eggs into the soft tissue of the plants. The nymphs feed by sucking green tissue. A generation of these bugs can generally be completed in as little as 2 weeks.

Large populations of these bugs can lead to the abortion of many flower buds. However, the plants produce far more buds than are required so only in rare cases will yield be reduced by these insects. It is unlikely that specific control measures are required for these bugs, as they are susceptible to most of the insecticides that are used to control the major pests.

PENTATOMIDAE

The pentatomid bugs *Nezara viridula* (L.), *Piezodorus hybneri* (Gmelin) and *Piezodorus pallescens* Germ. in Africa, *Piezodorus guildinii* (Westwood) in Central America and *N. viridula* and *Dolycoris indicus* (Stål.) in India are common on several legumes and other hosts. Several other genera of Pentatomidae are also occasionally found on pigeon pea throughout the tropics and sub-tropics.

The nymphs and adults suck the sap from the vegetative and floral parts and from the developing seeds, leaving the seeds unsuitable for consumption. The common insecticides used against other pests control these bugs.

Hymenoptera

MEGACHILIDAE

Leaf cutter bees (*Megachile* spp.) are distributed throughout the tropics. They cut neat, semi-circular portions from the leaflets of pigeon pea and carry them to nests in the soil, in rotten wood or in crevices of structures. The adult bees, which are a range of colours and sizes, are important pollinators of pigeon pea. *Megachile* spp. are not social insects like honey bees but are 'solitary', each female forming its own nest and laying eggs in it. The larvae are fed on the green leaf tissue.

Damage has never been reported to be extensive enough to merit control measures.

TANAOSTIGMATIDAE

Tanaostigmodes cajaninae LaSalle, the pod wasp, is widely distributed on pigeon pea in India, is common on research stations, but is rare in farmers' fields. It attacks very young pods, which either do not grow or develop only at the locules not attacked. The exit hole made by the emerging wasp is smaller than that of the podfly. The small wasp (2 mm) lays translucent, flattened, oval eggs (measuring 0.8 × 0.4 mm) on the flower and young pod. The white legless larva (2.5 mm) feeds on the young seed and inner pod wall. The larval period lasts 8–10 days at ca 25°C. Pupation occurs in the pod locule. The pupal period is 5–7 days, and adults survive up to 7 days (males) and 9 days (females). A generation is completed in less than 3 weeks. Observations on the ICRISAT research farm have indicated that *T. cajaninae* larvae from the field are substantially parasitized. The torymid parasites, *Paraholaspis* sp. and *Senegalella* sp., have been recorded from this pod wasp (Lateef and Reddy, 1984; Lateef *et al.*, 1985).

This insect is a pest on research stations where a range of cultivars are grown and thus extend the time that pods are available. Under such conditions, the pest builds up over many generations in each year. Also, pesticides such as endosulfan appear to control the natural enemies but not the pests. Restriction of the range of durations of cultivars growing in an area will reduce this pest to a rarity. Systemic pesticides such as dimethoate will reduce populations.

Isoptera

TERMITIDAE

The termites, *Odontotermes* spp. and *Microtermes* spp., are common throughout the tropics and sub-tropics. At times, they cause wilting and death of young plants; the telltale sign is a hole in the stem, just below the soil surface. When the stem and roots are split, small white termites (*Microtermes* spp.) are seen in tunnels. The stems of some large plants are coated or 'sheeted' with earth, underneath which the termites (*Odontotermes* spp.) feed. Termites often attack plants that are damaged or dying as a result of disease or mechanical injury. It is unusual for healthy pigeon pea to be attacked. Termites are social insects that form colonies, usually in chambers below the soil surface. The workers, which are seen in and on plants, collect plant material to stock the 'fungus gardens' (food stores) in some of the chambers. The workers are small (4 mm) and soft white-bodied but with a brown head. The soldier caste, which protects the colony, has a larger head and well-developed mandibles. The queen, which is cosseted in one of the underground chambers, can grow to several centimetres, with most of the body consisting of a distended abdomen.

Seed treatment with aldrin or HCH is recommended in areas where plant damage is common. In areas where the termites form large mounds that hinder cultivation, the occupants of the nests can be poisoned by a drenching with solutions of these insecticides. In general, however, adequate cultivation and rapid growth of healthy plants result in little termite damage.

Lepidoptera

ARCTIIDAE

The polyphagous arctiids are widely distributed in Asia and Africa. They feed upon the leaves, buds and flowers of many plants including pigeon pea.

On pigeon pea, the larvae feed upon the leaves and inflorescences, causing obvious damage. *Amsacta* spp. and *Spilosoma obliqua* are commonly known as 'hairy caterpillars', for they are densely covered with long hairs. The hairs of these and other caterpillars can cause skin rashes and other allergies so caution in handling them is advised. Populations of these larvae on pigeon pea are seldom great enough to merit pesticide use. However, there are occasional reports of severe defoliation, particularly by *Amsacta* spp. Several insecticides, including endosulfan, normally give adequate control.

GELECHIIDAE

Aproaerema modicella D. is a leaf-mining caterpillar that damages pigeon pea and soybean but more so groundnut. It is the larva of a micromoth. The larva mines the leaves, producing pale-brown patches along the mid-ribs. After a week of life within the leaves, the larvae come out, web together two or more leaflets as a home within which they can live and feed. The leaves wither. The life cycle of the pest totals about 3 weeks. This pest can be controlled by spraying with systemic insecticides.

Anarsia ephippias Meyr. is a small brown caterpillar that webs together the top shoots and feeds from within the webs (Srivastava *et al.*, 1977). *Anarsia acerata* Meyr. infests pigeon pea in southern India. In northern India, *Anarsia exallacta* Meyr. webs together and destroys the top leaves of pigeon pea. These pests infest pigeon pea in small numbers so chemical protection is not required.

GRACILLARIDAE

The leaf roller, *Caloptilia soyella* van Dev., gets its common name from the habit of the green larva: it rolls up the leaflets from the tips and lives within the fold. The folded portion is skeletonized and it dries up. The larva pupates within the leaf fold. No economic loss is caused by this pest. It is parasitized by *Asympiesilla indica* G.

LYCAENIDAE

The blue butterflies, *Lampides boeticus* (L.) and *Catochrysops strabo* F. are widely distributed in Asia. *Lampides boeticus* is common in East Africa as well. Larvae are found on several cultivated and wild legumes. The larvae chew leaves, buds, flowers and pods. The small, blue eggs, which are beautifully sculpted, are laid singly on buds, leaves and green pods. Each female lays about 30–120 eggs, which hatch in 4–7 days. The larvae (12 mm) are green, oval and flattened. The larval period lasts 9–27 days. Pupation takes place in plant debris, on the plant or on the soil; pupae are green and live 7–19 days. Adults live for 2–6 days, a generation being completed in about 3–8 weeks (Pandey *et al.*, 1978).

Although the butterflies are common, and they lay very many eggs on pigeon pea, relatively few larvae are found on the crop, possibly because natural enemies reduce their numbers. Control specifically for these insects is seldom if ever required, but they are controlled incidentally when pesticides such as endosulfan are applied to control major pests.

A larval parasitoid, *Hesperencyrtus lycoenephila* (Risbec) (Hym.: Encyrtidae) and *Lampides crassipes* Cam. (Hym.: Ichneumonidae) were recorded from *Listrodromus boeticus* (L.) in India (Bhatnagar and Davies, 1979). In Sri Lanka, Subasinghe and Fellowes (1978) have recorded *Tetrastichus ayyari* (Eulophidae), *Brachymeria lasus* (Chalcididae) and *Aploma metallica* (Tachinidae) parasitizing *L. boeticus* larvae.

LYMANTRIIDAE

Tussock caterpillars, *Porthesia (Euproctis) scintillans* W. are larvae of a yellowish moth, which lays eggs in masses of 8–10, mainly on the lower surface of pigeon pea leaves and covers them up with hairs.

The hairy caterpillars are gregarious; they feed on buds and flowers. In south India, incubation lasts for about 5 days, the larval period 15 days and the pupal period 10 days (Nair, 1975).

Euproctis subnotata Walk. caterpillars are brown, 2 cm long, with prominent tufts of hair on their body. The hairs of these and other caterpillars can cause skin rashes. Populations on pigeon pea seldom merit pesticide use.

Apanteles inclusus Ratz. (Hym.: Braconidae) reportedly parasitizes *E. subnotata* larvae (Lateef and Reddy, 1984).

NOCTUIDAE

Helicoverpa armigera (Hübner) is widely distributed on more than 180 cultivated and uncultivated host plants (Manjunath *et al.*, 1985) in the tropics and sub-tropics but not in the Americas where it is replaced by *Helicoverpa zea* (Boddie) and *Heliothis virescens* (Fab.). In Australia, both *Helicoverpa punctigera* (Wallengren) and *H. armigera* attack pigeon pea in farmers' fields.

Helicoverpa spp. and *Heliothis* sp. are of great importance, for they destroy many buds, flowers and pods. If flowers and pods are not available, they feed on leaflets. Severe damage during the vegetative stage delays flowering, and in India up to 95 per cent pod damage has been observed. ICRISAT surveys of pigeon pea in India have shown generally high levels of pest-caused losses.

Table 4.2. Damage to pods of pigeon pea by lepidopteran borers in samples from farmers' fields in India, 1975-81 (Lateef and Reed, 1983)

Zones	Fields sampled (no.)	Pods damaged (%)
Northwest (short-duration)	49	29.7
North (long-duration)	359	13.2
Central (medium- and long-duration)	446	24.3
South (short- and medium-duration)	443	36.4

Lepidopteran borers, mainly *H. armigera*, have caused severe damage to pigeon pea in northwest, central and south zones (Table 4.2). The trials conducted at ICRISAT during 1975−76 with cultivars of determinate and indeterminate growth habits, representing different maturity groups, showed that the pest status of the lepidopteran pod borers was considerably affected by days to flowering of the cultivars. Damage caused by *H. armigera* to pods of short- and medium-duration cultivars was high, particularly to those of determinate (pod cluster) habit (Lateef and Reed, 1980).

The susceptibility of the determinate types was confirmed in other trials, in which cultivars that were segregating for plant habit were compared (Table 4.3). In all the cultivars, the determinate types were more heavily attacked by *H. armigera*, and more pods survived until harvest on the indeterminate types.

The *H. armigera* moth lays its small white, beautifully sculpted eggs, usually singly, on the upper and outer surfaces of leaves, flowers, pods and stems. The female moth is generally extremely prolific and lays well over 1000 eggs; an average of 730 eggs per female was recorded in south India (Jayaraj, 1982). The eggs hatch in 3−7 days, and the young larva feeds by scraping green tissue. Older larvae chew voraciously into buds, flowers and pods, leaving characteristic round holes; they are highly cannibalistic. The large larvae (27 mm) have a wide range of colours, including yellow, green, pink, brown and black but all have characteristic light and dark stripes along each side. The larval period is completed in 14−38 days.

Table 4.3. Pod borer damage on determinate and indeterminate segregants of pigeon pea cultivars of different maturities grown without insecticide on Alfisol and Vertisol blocks at ICRISAT, 1975-76

Parent cultivar	Growth habit[a]	Alfisol		Vertisol	
		Pods on 40 plants	Borer damage (%)	Pods on 40 plants	Borer damage (%)
Short-duration					
Pusa Ageti	D	3017	64.5	5221	76.2
	I	8953	25.9	8086	41.9
Medium-duration					
ICP 7050	D	11259	23.3	5431	49.0
	I	17582	12.1	13511	21.1
Long-duration					
ICP 6365	D	3242	25.4	4750	42.9
	I	8047	15.5	8449	27.1
SE ± (m)		± 2.00		± 2.09	

[a]D = determinate; I = indeterminate.

Pupation is normally in the soil or in plant debris and is completed in 6−12 days. During winter months, extended pupation (up to 2−3 months) was observed in a small portion of pupae. Under favourable conditions, a generation can be completed in just over 4 weeks. There can be 5−7 generations of the pest in a year. The moths are predominantly nocturnal.

In Tanzania, Reed (1965) recorded a reduction in number of eggs laid by a female of *H. armigera* from 1226 in March−May to 198 in June−July 1962. The incubation, on average, was 2.78 days in March, and the larval period 21.1 days, with the total larval period ranging from 30 to 171 days. He also noticed a small but progressively increasing proportion of pupae entered diapause.

The tobacco budworm, *Heliothis virescens* (Fab.), is the most damaging pest of pigeon pea in Central America. This pest also attacks many other crops including tobacco, cotton, tomato, beans and sweet potato.

The newly hatched larvae feed on the leaves, buds, flowers and pods. Later, they bore into the pods and feed on the developing seeds.

The eggs are laid singly on buds, flowers and young pods. They hatch in 3 days. The fully grown larva leaves the pod, falls to the ground and pupates in the soil. The larval period lasts for about 22 days, and the pupal period averages about 18 days. The total life cycle is about 43 days (Schotman, 1986).

When pigeon pea is planted in backyards or on field plot borders, usually no control measures are attempted. In pure stands or when intercropped, the pigeon pea can benefit from several contact insecticides and synthetic pyrethroids, which give good control of the pest.

Several parasitoids have been recorded on *H. virescens* in Central America (Schotman, 1986), including the egg parasite *Trichogramma fasciatum* Perk. (Trichogrammatidae) and larval/pupal parasites such as *Bracon* spp. (Braconidae), *Parasierola* sp. (Bethylidae), and *Archytas pilvintris* Wulp. Predators mentioned are *Chrysopa* sp. (Chrysopidae) and *Polistes barbadensis* Richards (Vespidae).

Lablab podborer, *Adisura atkinsoni* Moore, is widely distributed in southern India. It is a major pest of *Dolichos lablab* and is often found in low numbers on pigeon pea. Two other species, *Adisura marginalis* Walk. and *Adisura stigmatica* Warr., are occasionally also found on pigeon pea.

Eggs are laid on flowers and on very young pods. Incubation lasts 3 days, and the larval period 14–15 days. The larvae bore into buds, flowers and green pods.

The green larva (15 mm) is very similar to *H. armigera* and is often confused with it in the field. It can be distinguished by its brown lateral stripes. Pupation is in the soil and lasts 11 days. The moth has yellow–brown forewings and white hindwings. A generation is completed in about 4 weeks.

This insect seldom, if ever, becomes numerous enough on pigeon pea to merit separate control. Insecticides used to control other major pests such as endosulfan will incidentally control this insect. The caterpillars of *A. atkinsoni* are parasitized by *Microbracon lefroyi* D. and G., *Bracon hebetor* S., *Bracon brevicornis* Wes., *Carcelia evolans kockiana* Tns., *Hymenobostnina* sp. and *Enicospilus* sp., whereas *Palexorista* sp., *Enicospilus heliothidis* Vie, and *Diadegma* sp. have been recorded attacking the caterpillars of *A. stigmatica* (Bhatnagar and Davies, 1979).

Other noctuids infesting pigeon pea are *Agrotis ipsilon* (Hufn.), *Agrotis segetum* (Shiff), *Azazia rubricans* (Bois.), *Catephia mosara* (Swinh.), *Chrysodeixis chalcites* (Esp.), *Mythimna separata* Walk., *Nanaguna breviuscula* Wlk., *Pardasene virgulana* (Mab.), *Spodoptera litura* Fab. (in Asia), *Spodoptera littoralis* B. (in Africa) and *Trichoplusia ni* Hb.

Components of Pest Management

The use of cultivars resistant to the major pest complexes in each area would be a significant step towards successful pest management (Reed *et al.*, 1980).

At ICRISAT, several sources of resistance to *H. armigera* in pigeon pea have been identified, and now the work is in progress to incorporate disease resistance and high-yielding characters in the pest-resistant material.

The pigeon pea genotypes that have proved resistant are ICP 1903-E1, ICP 1811-E3, ICP 10466-E3, ICP 5036-E2, and ICP 3615-E1. Lines bred for *H. armigera* resistance are ICPX 77303, ICPL 84060, ICPL 87088, ICPL 87089 ICPL 187-1, and PPE 45-2.

In studies at ICRISAT on the mechanisms of resistance to *H. armigera*, most of the resistant genotypes exhibit oviposition non-preference. A low level of antibiosis has also been demonstrated in some selections (Lateef *et al.*, 1987).

The sowing of resistant cultivars at the optimal time by all farmers in an area promises to be the major component in any pest-management strategy. The pest populations would be diluted across the crop area, with minimal opportunities to build up by dispersing from early to late-sown crops (Lateef, 1977; Reed *et al.*, 1980).

Preliminary studies in India on the effects of mixed cropping and intercropping of pigeon peas with cereals and other legumes (Satpathy *et al.*, 1979) showed that population levels for pests, parasites and predators all depended on the crop mix and differed from levels in monocrop pigeon pea (Bhatnagar *et al.*, 1982). The careful selection of compatible crops with non-additive pests, but whith the common parasite and predator complexes, may result in lower, more stable pest attacks.

Manipulation of sowing dates and maturity periods also promises to have profound effects on *Helicoverpa* spp. attacks (Pandit, 1965), particularly if all farmers in an area synchronize the sowings.

Also, a number of parasitoids have been detected on various pests of pigeon pea (Table 4.4) so it may be possible to increase the native parasitoid populations by breeding them in laboratories and releasing them in fields to boost populations early in each season. Nuclear polyhedrosis virus (NPV), which kills *Helicoverpa*, is another possibility for use on farmers' fields (Sanap and Deshmukh, 1988).

Successful control of pod borers has been achieved in India with insecticides, including synthetic pyrethroids and endosulfan. However, considerable resistance to insecticides has been reported in *Helicoverpa* sp. in areas where spraying has been intensive. Now, farmers need suitable tactics for insecticide management. Insecticides should be applied only when needed, when pest populations exceed the economic threshold.

The thresholds vary by area, and local entomologists must calculate them after appropriate experimentation. Insecticides can keep the crops relatively pest free, but questions must be asked whether prophylactic or scheduled application does more damage than good in the long run and how many applications are appropriate.

Table 4.4. Natural enemies of *Helicoverpa armigera* in India and Sri Lanka (Achan *et al.*, 1968; Rao, 1968; ICRISAT, 1976a; Subasinghe and Fellowes, 1978; Bhatnagar and Davies, 1979; Sithanantham and Reed, 1980; Bhatnagar *et al.*, 1982; Sithanantham, 1987)

Type and species of natural enemy	Family
INDIA and SRI LANKA	
Egg parasitoid	
Trichogramma chilonis Ishii	Trichogrammatidae
Egg predator	
Chrysopa sp.	Chrysopidae
Larval parasitoid	
Apanteles ruficrus Hal.	Braconidae
Bracon (Microbracon) brevicornis Wesm.	Braconidae
Chelonus sp.	Braconidae
Microplitis sp. nr. *pallidipes*	Braconidae
Rogas sp.	Braconidae
Atractodes sp.	Ichneumonidae
Ecphoropsis perdistinctus	Ichneumonidae
Campoletis chlorideae Uchida	Ichneumonidae
Enicospilus sp. nr. *zyzzus* Chiu	Ichneumonidae
Eriborus argenteopilosus Cam.	Ichneumonidae
Diadegma sp.	Ichneumonidae
Eucelatoria sp.	Tachinidae
Carcelia illota Curran	Tachinidae
C. kockiana Tns.	Tachinidae
Goniophthalmus halli Mesnil	Tachinidae
Drino (Prosturmia) inberbis	Tachinidae
Exorista fallax	Tachinidae
Larval predator	
Delta spp.	Eumenidae
Clubiona sp.	Clubionidae
Neoscona theis	Araenidae
Polistes olivaceus de Geer	Vespidae
Ropalidia marginata Lepeltier	Vespidae
Thomisus sp.	Thomisidae
Nematode parasite	
Ovomermis albicans Sieb.	Mermithidae
Larval pathogen	
Nuclear polyhedrosis virus (NPV)	

Limitations on use of new, effective insecticides are that most farmers of the semi-arid tropics lack the financial resources and technical know-how for successful pesticide application and for maintenance of the equipment. Most farmers have to be content with what remains of the crops after the pests have taken their share. Disadvantages of insecticides are well known: although effective in the immediate objective of killing pests, they usually also:

- are highly toxic to human beings and animals;
- persist in the environment;
- kill the natural predators and parasites of insect pests; and
- lead to resistant strains of both insects and mites.

Researchers must seek strategies that enable farmers in the semi-arid tropics to harvest more from their land without investing heavily in sprayers and insecticides that cause pollution and environmental disruption.

PYRALIDAE

Podborer, *Ancylostomia stercorea* (Zell.), is common in East Africa, the Caribbean and Central America. The moths are 9 mm long with a wing span of 19 mm. Forewings are burnished gold, marked with four minute dark spots. Hindwings are hyaline, with the apical margin fringed. A pair of dark lines run close and parallel to the fringe. A small, dark streak runs in the middle of the hindwing, with a black band on the margin of the hindwing.

Eggs are ovate, cream-coloured, later turning pink. They hatch in 5–7 days. Larvae are green, sparsely covered with setae; their mandibles are dark brown; and two black dots can be found on either side of the first thoracic segment. The larval period lasts 17–25 days. Pupae are obtect, dark brown when mature. Pupation extends up to 14 days, the life cycle being completed in 37–47 days under Caribbean conditions (Schotman, 1986).

Another pyralid pest of pigeon pea in the Caribbean is *Fundella pellucens* Zell., which completes its life cycle in 32–44 days.

These pests can be controlled by contact insecticides, and several parasites have been observed on larvae of *A. stercorea* and *F. pellucens*. Examples are *Bracon cajani*, *Apanteles* sp., *Goniozus* sp. and *Phanerotoma bennetti*. An egg parasite of *F. pellucens*, *T. fasciatum*, was also recorded in the Caribbean.

Lima bean podborer, *Etiella zinckenella* Treitschke, is widely distributed on several legumes throughout the tropics and semi-tropics. This larva is generally found in maturing and dried pods. Infestations build up at the end of the pigeon pea season, particularly when temperatures are high.

White elliptical eggs are laid in small groups on developing pods. A female lays 47–178 eggs, which hatch in 5–6 days. The young larvae are green but later turn red. They feed inside the pod, reaching a length of

14 mm. The larval period lasts 10–13 days; pupation is in the soil and is 9–20 days, depending on prevailing conditions. The moth has grey forewings, with a white costal margin; the hindwings are pearly translucent. A generation can be completed in 4 weeks under favourable conditions (Singh and Dhooria, 1971).

The lima bean podborer is generally a minor pest on pigeon pea and seldom merits specific control.

Bhatnagar and Davies (1979) listed several braconids that parasitize larvae of *E. zinckenella* in India, including *Bracon hebetor* Say and *Phanerotoma hendecasisella* Cam.

The cowpea podborer, *Maruca testulalis* (Geyer), is common on legume species throughout the tropics and sub-tropics.

The larva webs together leaves, buds and pods and feeds inside the webs. The yellow, oval eggs are laid in small batches, commonly on terminal buds. The larva (14 mm) is white–yellow with rows of conspicuous black spots on the dorsal surface but the spots are not clearly seen on the yellow–green prepupae. Pupation is in the web or in a silk cocoon on the ground. A generation can be completed in less than 3 weeks in optimal conditions. This is a major pest of pigeon pea and other grain legumes in many areas of Africa and in central India. The webs protect the larvae from contact insecticides, so careful application is required. Several insecticides, including endosulfan, will kill the larvae. The pest is particularly destructive on determinate-type pigeon pea, and considerable differences in plant susceptibility have been reported.

A braconid, *Phanerotoma hendecasisella* Cam., was reported to be a major parasite of *M. testulalis* larvae and could be used effectively as a biocontrol agent in India and Sri Lanka (Subasinghe and Fellowes, 1978; Lateef and Reddy, 1984).

PTEROPHORIDAE

The plume moths, *Exelastis atomosa* (Walsingham) and *Sphenarches anisodactylus* Walk., are widely distributed in Asia and in East Africa, but in India, *S. anisodactylus* is commoner on lablab bean than on pigeon pea.

The green, oval and minute eggs of *E. atomosa* are laid singly on buds and young pods. These hatch in 3–4 days. The larva (14 mm) is green or brown, spindle-shaped and covered with short spines and larger hairs. It chews into buds, flowers and pods. The larval period lasts 25–30 days.

The pupa, which looks like the larva, is usually found on the pod surface. Pupation lasts 3–7 days. The adult has brown, plume-like wings. A generation can be completed in about 4 weeks.

Exelastis atomosa can be particularly numerous on pigeon pea planted after the rainy season and is generally an important pest. It can easily be

Plate I. Anoplocnemis *sp. adult*
(photo ICRISAT)

Plate II. Aphis craccivora *on pods*
(photo ICRISAT)

Plate III. Mylabris pustulata *adult*
(photo ICRISAT)

Plate IV. Lampides boeticus *adult*
(photo ICRISAT)

Plate V. Euproctis subnotata *caterpillars*
(photo ICRISAT)

Plate VI. Helicoverpa armigera *larva*
(photo ICRISAT)

Plate VII. Helicoverpa armigera *pod damage*
(photo ICRISAT)

Plate VIII. Helicoverpa armigera *resistant cv.*
PPE-45-2 and susceptible cv. T-21 (photo ICRISAT)

Plate IX. Melanagromyza obtusa *maggots and puparium*
(photo ICRISAT)

controlled by several insecticides including endosulfan. It has several natural enemies, and these may prevent it from building up.

Several larval parasites have been reported from India by Bhatnagar and Davies (1979), Lateef and Reddy (1984), and Sithanantham (1987) and from Sri Lanka by Subasinghe and Fellowes (1978). The commonest on *E. atomosa* are *P. hendecasisella*, *Apanteles paludicolae* Cam. (Hym.: Braconidae), *Diadegma* sp. (Hym.: Ichneumonidae) and *Tropimeris monodon* Boucek (Hym.: Chalcididae). In Sri Lanka on *S. anisodactylus*, *A. paludicolae* and *T. monodon* were recorded.

TORTRICIDAE

Grapholita critica (Meyr.), formerly known as *Eucosma critica*, is common throughout pigeon pea-growing areas of India, and *Leguminovora ptychora* (Meyr.) is common on several legumes, including pigeon pea, in East Africa. Pigeon pea leaflets are webbed together with silk, and the larva feeds within the web. As the web often includes the terminal bud, further growth of the shoot is prevented. Infestations start at the seedling stage and may persist to the reproductive stage of the crop when the larvae feed inside flower buds and in young pods.

Grapholita critica is a small brown moth that lays about 100 eggs on the leaf buds and young leaves. Eggs hatch in 3 days. The larva is cream–yellow and grows to about 10 mm before pupating in the web. The pupal period lasts 4–6 days. Although leaf webbers make young pigeon pea crops look very untidy, they seldom cause noticeable yield loss. The plants produce side shoots to compensate for the loss of terminal buds and so produce bushier plants. If insecticides are not used, many parasites and predators soon bring this pest under control. As the larvae inside the webs are well protected from contact insecticides, a systemic insecticide (e.g., monocrotophos) or one with some fumigant action (e.g., dichlorvos) is required. The larvae are parasitized by *P. hendecasisella*, *Apanteles taragamae* Vier., *Goniozus* sp., and *Elasmus albopictus* Craw.

Orthoptera

ACRIDIDAE

Many genera and species of grasshoppers and locusts have been recorded as feeding on pigeon pea. In Africa, *Zonocerus variegatus* (L.) and *Schistocerca* spp. are common and in India, *Catantops erubescens* Walk., *Colemania sphenerioides* Bol., *Cyrtacanthacris tatarica* (L.), and *Patanga succincta* (L.) are known to cause substantial damage to pigeon pea plants. Most of them feed on the leaflets and seldom reduce yields, although outbreaks of locusts result in complete defoliation and failure of most species of plants including pigeon pea. One grasshopper that causes unusual damage to pigeon pea is *C. erubescens*, which girdles branches of the plant, causing them to wither and die. No control measures are normally required, for the densities of these insects seldom reach economic thresholds.

GRYLLIDAE

The cricket, *Gryllus bimaculatus* Deg., is known to cause substantial damage to pigeon pea roots and seedlings in Kenya.

Thysanoptera

THRIPIDAE

Several genera and species of thrips have been recorded from pigeon pea. In India the commonest species appears to be *Megalurothrips usitatus*, which feeds in the flowers. In East Africa, other species of *Megalurothrips* are common on pigeon pea and are regarded as being of some importance.

Heavy infestations of thrips can lead to bud and flower drop. Rawat *et al.* (1969b) found a reduction of 36 per cent in pod formation in unprotected pigeon pea in India, and *Frankliniella insularis* Schmutz infestation caused 47 per cent reduction in pod set of pigeon pea in Trinidad (Pollard and Elie, 1981). In India, Yadav *et al.* (1974) noted two species of thrips, *Frankliniella sulphurea* Schmutz and *Taeniothrips nigricornis* Schmutz, visiting flowers of pigeon pea, when the buds began to unfold and deserted them only after the initiation of pod development. Significant differences were noticed in the development of pods in relation to different levels of thrips populations. A moderate population of thrips (23–150 per 100 flowers) was found beneficial to fertilization and pod setting. The black adults (1 mm) and nymphs of *M. usitatus* are easily seen with the naked eye, particularly when they are on yellow flower petals. A generation can be completed within 4 weeks. Studies at ICRISAT showed that the mean incubation was 5.6 days, the mean nymphal period, 10.7 days and the adult longevity, 14.1 days (Pawar and Srivastava, 1985). Thrips in India seldom build up enough on pigeon pea to cause substantial damage. In most cases, insecticides used to control major pests (e.g., endosulfan for *Helicoverpa* control or dimethoate for podfly control) will incidentally reduce the thrips populations.

We gratefully acknowledge assistance from colleagues at ICRISAT in the preparation of this chapter.

Insect Pests of Food Legumes
Edited by S. R. Singh
© 1990 John Wiley & Sons Ltd.

5

Pests of Groundnut in the Semi-Arid Tropics

J. A. WIGHTMAN, K. M. DICK, G. V. RANGA RAO, T. G. SHANOWER, and
C. G. GOLD[a]

[a]*International Crops Research Institute for the Semi-Arid Tropics (ICRISAT),
Patancheru, Andhra Pradesh 502324, India*

Arachis hypogaea L. (groundnut or peanut), which originated in the eastern
slopes of the Andes, among the headwaters of the Amazon, is now mainly
grown in Asia, especially in India and China. Other key zones include
Southern and West Africa, although production in the latter, especially in
Nigeria, has fallen considerably as a result of climatic and political changes.
North Carolina, Georgia, and other southern states in the U.S. are the
leading producers in the developed world. Groundnuts are also grown in
Australia, mainly in Northeast Queensland, where the industry is
comparatively small but scientifically important because the crop is grown
in a dry environment comparable to much of the semi-arid tropics. Thus,
much of the information generated by the sophisticated (well-funded)
scientific and extension services in Australia is applicable to the farms of
the developing world.

Insect pests of groundnuts were first extensively reviewed by Feakin
(1967, revised 1973); later Smith and Barfield (1982) listed 356 taxa then
known to be associated with the crop and discussed the control of groundnut
pests largely from the point of view of the developed world. More recently,
Wightman and Amin (1988) briefly discussed pests of groundnuts grown in
the semi-arid tropics, and Amin (1988) reviewed the Indian situation. The
pattern of pests on Western-style farms was discussed by Wightman (1989).
These texts, together with internal documents from ICRISAT, have provided
much of the background for this chapter.

In this chapter, we have supplemented and updated these works rather than replaced them. A major source of information has been a 5-month survey of groundnut fields carried out by one of us (J.A.W.) in Africa and India, the results of which are being finalized for publication.

Groundnuts (*Arachis* spp.), which are a valuable source of dietary protein (ca 35 per cent), vitamins, and minerals and contain 45–50 per cent high-quality oil, are unusual legumes in that the seeds grow underground. Fertilization activates an intercalary meristem in the base of the ovary. This results in the production of a stalk-like structure, the gynophore or peg, that grows downward and into the soil, carrying the presumptive germinal tissue in the tip. The ovules grow and turn into pods holding usually two, but sometimes three or four, seeds. The duration of a crop can be as short as 90 days, as in the case of some Spanish bunch cultivars grown in India, or can extend to about 150 days (e.g., Valencia and runner types popular in parts of Southern Africa where the summer rains last 4 months or so). Groundnut can be grown in the arid and semi-arid parts of the tropics because it tolerates high temperatures in its canopy and extended periods of low moisture in the soil.

The crop is vulnerable to four cohorts of insects:
- non-viruliferous foliage feeders;
- viruliferous foliage feeders (virus vectors);
- invertebrates living in the soil; and
- those that feed on the harvested and stored pods and kernels.

Of these, the virus vectors and soil insects are the most insidious — the former, because a small number of an otherwise harmless population can cause considerable yield losses, and the latter, because they are seldom detected before they have caused considerable damage. Soil-inhabiting insects can attack the pods, the roots or both, and the crop as a whole when it is drying in the sun after harvest. Pod feeders, even when they do not reduce yields to any extent, increase the risk of aflatoxin contamination caused by the invasion of *Aspergillus flavus* (McDonald, 1966; McDonald and Harkness, 1968). Root invaders can kill the plants or markedly reduce yields, particularly on drought-prone farms with light soils (as in central Zimbabwe and Senegal) where the plants need extensive systems of fine roots to survive.

As farmers commonly sell part of their crop soon after harvest, they avoid the problems involved in maintaining the quality and economic value of the product during storage. These problems are then faced by market traders, oil millers and exporters. One of the main causes of deterioration of stored groundnuts is insect infestation. Attack by postharvest insect pests results in a reduction both in the overall quantity of kernels and in the quality of the oil. Insect infestation also generates heat and moisture within silos or stacks of groundnuts, thereby increasing the risk of fungal attack and the attractiveness of the product to other insects.

More than 100 species of insect are capable of infesting stored groundnuts (Redlinger and Davis, 1982). A majority of these are only occasional pests or can survive on groundnut kernels only after more destructive species have altered the environment, e.g., by increasing the moisture in the kernels. A number of species are important pests of shelled groundnuts, particularly when many of the kernels are broken during decortication (Duerden and Cutler, 1957). These species are found also in stocks of in-shell groundnuts, feeding on kernels that are exposed as a result of mechanical damage to pods during harvesting, drying or transport. As few species are able to penetrate intact pods, storage in this form reduces the number of species likely to cause significant losses.

The importance of postharvest insect pests and the degree to which their control by insecticide application is warranted largely depend on how the groundnuts in stock will ultimately be used. In some tropical regions, groundnuts being stored prior to local processing for oil extraction may be protected sufficiently by a combination of initial drying, in-shell storage and good storage management. However, groundnuts intended for seed supply or for export are often shelled soon after harvest so that imperfect or damaged kernels can be discarded (Rouzière, 1986). If prolonged storage is necessary after shelling, then more rigorous control procedures are almost certainly required.

To reduce the susceptibility of groundnuts to insect and fungal attack during storage, producers commonly leave them to dry in windrows or loose stacks until moisture content is below 7 per cent (Blatchford and Hall, 1963).

As new stocks can be cross-infested from crop residues, stores should be swept clean and material from the previous harvest removed and burned before they are refilled. If the store or container is known to have held stocks infested by pests such as *Elasmolomus sordidus*, then it is advisable to apply an organophosphorous insecticide, preferably as a wettable powder, to the interior surfaces of the store after it has been cleared (Table 5.1). In areas where groundnuts are stored in gunny, the sacks should be checked for live insects, including pupal cocoons, before they are refilled. To ensure against survival of the pests, one can roll the sacks together and place them in a sealed oil drum with a single phosphine tablet for 5–10 days.

Since infestation of clean groundnut stocks will usually begin in the surface layers of a stack or bulk, the application of an insecticide spray or dust provides some measure of protection, particularly against such pests as *E. sordidus*, which will come in contact with the insecticide throughout its life cycle. Sacks of pods can be sprayed with any of the insecticides recommended for residual application to store walls (Table 5.1). Spraying each layer while a stack is being constructed is more effective than applying a single treatment once the stack is completed but involves greater expenditures both of insecticides and of labour.

Table 5.1. Chemical control measures for protection of stored groundnuts*

Control operations	Insecticide common name and formulation	Application rate of whole product with specified a.i. concentration
Space treatment of empty stores	Dichlorvos: resin strips fog or aerosol	1 strip/30 m^3 12 mL (5 g a.i./L)/m^3
Application of insecticidal spray to interior surfaces of stores or to sacks of pods	Malathion (wp)	500 g 25% a.i. in 5 L water/100 m^2
	Fenitrothion (ec)	200 mL 50% a.i. in 5 L water/100 m^2
	Chlorpyriphos-methyl (ec)	200 mL 50% a.i. in 5 L water/100 m^2
	Pirimiphos-methyl (ec)	100 mL 50% a.i. in 5 L water/100 m^2
	Iodofenphos (wp)	300 g 50% a.i. in 5 L water/100 m^2
	Bromophos (wp)	400 g 50% a.i. in 5 L water/100 m^2
	Permethrin (ec)	40 mL 50% a.i. in 5 L water/100 m^2
	Deltamethrin (wp)	50 g 50% a.i. in 5 L water/100 m^2
Direct application of spray to surface layer of pods in bulk storage	Malathion (wp)	250 g 50% a.i. in 5 L water/100 m^2
	Fenitrothion (ec)	100 mL 50% a.i. in 5 L water/100 m^2
	Chlorpyriphos-methyl (ec)	100 mL 50% a.i. in 5 L water/100 m^2
	Iodofenphos (wp)	150 mL 50% a.i. in 5 L water/100 m^2
	Bromophos (wp)	220 mL 50% a.i. in 5 L water/100 m^2
Admixture of insecticidal dust with pods	Malathion	250 g 4% a.i./t
	Fenitrothion	400 g 4% a.i./t
	Pirimiphos-methyl	400 g 4% a.i./t
	Bromophos	500 g 4% a.i./t

Control operations	Insecticide common name and formulation	Application rate of whole product with specified a.i. concentration
Fumigation of bagged or bulk stocks of pods or kernels under gastight sheeting	Methyl bromide (gas)	60-70 g/t for 48 h (increase dosage by 50% for control of *Trogoderma*)
	Phosphine (solid aluminium phosphide)	3-5 g/t for 7 days (3-5 tablets or 15-25 pellets)
Fumigation of small quantities of pods or kernels e.g. in polythene sacks or oil drums	Phosphine (solid aluminium phosphide)	0.4-0.6 g/100 kg for 7 days (2-3 pellets)

[a] a.i. = active ingredient; ec = emulsifiable concentrate; wp = wettable powder.

In parts of West Africa, where heaps of pods are stored in the open air, insecticides can be applied as a spray or dust to the surface of these heaps. However, as trading and movement of groundnut stocks take place, the surface layer of pods will be disrupted and the efficacy of surface treatments reduced.

The ideal is to add phosphine (1 g/m^3, equivalent to 5 tablets or 25 pellets/t) to the groundnuts as the store is filled (FAO, 1985). Phosphine can also be used to treat small quantities of groundnuts, e.g., seed supplies placed in airtight containers. One pellet (0.6 g) placed on top of groundnuts in polythene-lined sacks should give satisfactory control of insect infestation (Proctor and Ashman, 1972). Oil drums, sealed with aluminium tape or strips of polyurethane foam, can be used for the same purpose.

Research on appropriate methods of managing the pests of groundnuts in the developing world is carried out by several agencies besides the national research programmes of the many countries that grow groundnut. ICRISAT, which is near Hyderabad in peninsular India, is invested with a global responsibility for promoting groundnut production. It maintains a collection of the world's groundnut and wild species and has the capacity to carry out an extensive crossing programme each season. Through these facilities, it supports national programmes and international research organizations by supplying them germ plasm, breeding lines, or populations.

Its Legumes Entomology Unit is concentrating on the development of integrated pest management (IPM) for the small farmers of the semi-arid tropics, in part, by carrying out basic research that is beyond the scope of some national programmes. The international collaborators include scientists in the Peanut Collaborative Research Support Program (PCRSP) of the United States Agency for International Development (AID) who are currently active in Burkina Faso, Philippines, and Thailand (Campbell, 1986) and who are also able to supply entomologically important germ plasm.

The U.K.-based Overseas Development and Natural Resources Institute (ODNRI) arranges for entomologists to work with ICRISAT scientists on problems such as termite control and the mechanisms of host-plant resistance.

Cooperation with the Australian Centre for International Agricultural Research and with the Food and Agriculture Organization of the United Nations (FAO) has led to IPM training workshops in Asia. In other words, a range of research on groundnut pests is in progress around the world, and we have been able to draw on it — though many of the results are as yet unpublished — in the preparation of this chapter.

Orthoptera

Grasshoppers are often conspicuous in groundnut fields because they are large and can fly when disturbed. They can sometimes be seen feeding on the young, unfolded leaves and are, thus, responsible for the symmetric holes found on opened leaflets. Feeding caterpillars, in contrast, tend to attack the leaves later, leaving behind randomly distributed holes.

There are no reports of yield losses caused by grasshoppers, although fields of the crop have probably been destroyed by plague locusts (*Locusta migratoria*, *Scistocerca gregaria*, and *Cyrtacanthacris septemfasciata*, etc.) along with any other crops that are in the path of a swarm. Examples of non-damaging grasshoppers are *Zonocerus elegans* and *Pyrgomorpha granulata*, which are both common in Africa.

In groundnut fields in Southern Africa, plants missing from around holes in the ground inhabited by crickets and mole crickets indicate that seedlings have been attacked. However, once established, groundnut plants seem to be safe from these insects, even the large bush crickets (75 mm long) such as *Brachytrupes membranaceus* that are common some years in countries like Botswana.

Researchers can, with patience, find stick insects in groundnut crops, and mantids (many species) were sufficiently abundant on groundnut in parts of Malawi to have deserved a rating of 'important predators'.

Dermaptera

EARWIGS

Earwigs damage groundnuts in India where *Euborella stali* is the major earwig pest and in Israel where *Annisolabis* sp. bores holes in pods (Cherian and Basheer, 1940; Melamed-Madjar *et al.*, 1970; Palaniswamy, 1977). Cherian and Basheer in 1940 indicated that *E. stali* and *A. annulipes* are synonymous, the former having precedence.

Earwigs lay eggs in clusters in the soil where, in southern India, they incubate for 7−11 days. Under laboratory conditions, the females lay 20−140 eggs (n = 5). There are five nymphal instars. The adults can live for 2−3 months (Cherian and Basheer, 1940). On the ICRISAT farm, we find that they are commonest on Vertisols.

Their pod-boring results in either mouldy seeds, premature germination or the rejection of consignments at the wholesale market. The extent and intensity of damage are not known because wire-worms, false wire-worms, ants, termites and millepedes can cause similar damage. As the culprits usually have disappeared by harvest time, when the damage is discovered, there is scope for confusion. However, Amin (1988) found that earwigs can damage up to 65 per cent of the pods of a crop.

Dry formulations of insecticides such as aldicarb, carbofuran, phorate, chlordane and DDT (Melamed-Madjar *et al.*, 1970; Padmanabhan *et al.*, 1973; Palaniswamy, 1977) have been recommended for control but none is particularly effective. This information was presumably oriented toward farmers who have 'earwig hotspots' because none of the authors indicated how to predict an attack.

Isoptera

TERMITES

Termites are often misnamed 'white ants'. The reason presumably is that their soil mounds or termitaria are confused with ant hills, the denizens of which have no taxonomic relationship with termites but share the characteristics of a complex social or caste system and a largely subterranean existence. Termites are as much a part of the tropics and sub-tropics as drought and mango trees. They also have as much influence on the landscape in that they remove dead plant material from the soil surface, using it as cement in termitaria that can be seen all over Africa, Australia, and Asia.

Their importance as pests and as soil movers is recognized in a number of reviews: Verma and Kashyap, 1980 (emphasis on India); Lee and Wood, 1971; Harris, 1961, 1969. There is also an extensive bibliography of the termite literature (Ernst and Araújo, 1986). Ruelle (1985) gives a concise account of the termites of Southern Africa.

There are nine families of Isoptera, two of which are relevant to our understanding of the groundnut fauna. Termitidae is the most important. It contains 80 per cent of the species of this order, including economically important genera such as *Microtermes, Odontotermes, Macrotermes* and *Trinervitermes*, together with the soldierless termites that were consistently found 10–20 cm below the soil surface under groundnut plants in the moister parts of Southern Africa (J.A.W.). This last group eats organic matter in the soil and probably has no economic importance. The Hodotermitidae (harvester termites) includes *Hodotermes mossambicus*, which attacks groundnut plants in many parts of Africa.

Termites are pests of groundnut crops mainly in Africa, although they also create problems for farmers in India. A special survey of groundnut insects, especially those living in the soil (Table 5.2), indicates *Microtermes* and *Odontotermes* are the genera most likely to cause yield losses, although others are implicated. Termites do not figure highly in the relevant literature from Southeast and East Asia, presumably because the termite's way of life is not compatible with rice farming (groundnut is often grown in rice fallow in Asia). Termites do not seem to be part of the groundnut fauna in Australia or in South America, either.

Biology

With few exceptions, termite colonies consist of members of four castes: primary reproductives, supplementary reproductives, soldiers, and workers. The reproductives produce eggs and are larger than the other castes. The 'queen' can be 5 cm long, her abdomen being crammed with ovarioles that produce millions of eggs over many years. The flying termites that are a common sight at dusk after the first showers of the rainy season are new reproductives seeking mates. After finding a suitable site, they mate and initiate a new colony. The supplementary reproductives take over whenever a king or queen dies.

Soldiers and workers are sterile and have no wings or flight muscles. The soldiers have large, heavily sclerotized heads. They protect the colony from predators, usually with powerful mandibles, which in the case of *Macrotermes* spp. are strong enough to draw blood from a person's hand. The nasute soldiers, e.g., those of *Trinervitermes* spp., eject a sticky substance from the pointed front of their pear-shaped head when they are disturbed.

Table 5.2. The distribution of termites associated with the groundnut crop[a]

Species	Location	Reference
ASIA		
Coptotermes formosanus	China	Verma and Kashyap, 1980
Odontotermes sp.	Thailand	J.A.W.
Odontotermes obesus	South Asia	Roonwal, 1979
O. brunneus	India	Reddy and Sammaiah, 1988
Trinervitermes biformis	India	Feakin, 1973
	Sri Lanka	Roonwal, 1979
Microtermes thoracalis	India	Smith and Barfield, 1982
M. obesi	South Asia	Roonwal, 1979
EAST AFRICA		
Eremotermes nanus	Sudan	Feakin, 1973
Macrotermes bellicosus	Sudan	Feakin, 1973
M. subhyalinus	Sudan	Verma and Kashyap, 1980
Odontotermes nilensis	Sudan	Feakin, 1973
O. anceps	Kenya	Smith and Barfield, 1982
Microtermes thoracalis	Sudan	Feakin, 1973
M. lepidus	Sudan	Hebblethwaite and Logan, 1985
SOUTHERN AND SOUTH AFRICA		
Microtermes sp.	Zambia	J.A.W.
	Malawi	J.A.W.
	Zimbabwe	J.A.W.
	Botswana	J.A.W.
Microcerotermes sp.	Malawi	J.A.W.
Odontotermes sp.	Tanzania	Feakin, 1973
	Malawi	J.A.W.
	Zambia	J.A.W.
O. badius	South Africa	Feakin, 1973
O. latericius	South Africa	Feakin, 1973
O. lacustris	Malawi	J.A.W.
O. bomaenis	Zambia	J.A.W.
O. amanicus	Malawi	J.A.W.
O. kibarensis	Zimbabwe	J.A.W.
O. transvaalensis	Malawi	J.A.W.
	Zimbabwe	J.A.W.
	Botswana	J.A.W.

continued

Table 5.2 continued

Species	Location	Reference
O. rectanguloides	Zimbabwe	J.A.W.
O. latericus	Zambia	J.A.W.
O. montanus	Malawi	J.A.W.
Ancistrotermes latinotus	Zaire (Congo)	Feakin, 1973
	Malawi	J.A.W.
	Zimbabwe	J.A.W.
	Zambia	J.A.W.
Allodontotermes sp.	Malawi	J.A.W.
A. morogorensis	Tanzania	Smith and Barfield, 1982
A. tenax	Zimbabwe	J.A.W.
	Zambia	J.A.W.
Nasutitermes sp.	Malawi	Smith and Barfield, 1982
Pseudoacanthotermes sp.	Malawi	J.A.W.
P. militaris	Malawi	J.A.W.
	Zambia	J.A.W.
Trinervitermes sp.	Malawi	J.A.W.
Hodotermes mossambicus	Malawi	J.A.W.
Macrotermes sp.	Malawi	J.A.W.
M. falciger	Malawi	J.A.W.
M. ?natalensis	Malawi	J.A.W.
	Zambia	J.A.W.

WEST AFRICA

Species	Location	Reference
Amitermes evuncifer	Nigeria	Feakin, 1973
Microcerotermes sp.	The Gambia	Feakin, 1973
Hodotermes mossambicus	Senegal	Smith and Barfield, 1982
Odontotermes vulgaris	Senegal	Appert, 1966
Ancistrotermes crucifer	The Gambia	Feakin, 1973
O. smeathmani	Nigeria	Johnson *et al.*, 1981
Microtermes sp.	Nigeria	Feakin, 1973
	The Gambia	Feakin, 1973
	Niger	Lamb, 1979
M. lepidus	Nigeria	Johnson and Gumel, 1981
M. subhyalinus	Nigeria	Perry, 1967
M. parvulus	Senegal	Appert, 1966
Trinervitermes geminatus	Senegal	Feakin, 1973
T. obenerianus	Senegal	Verma and Kashyap, 1980

SOUTH AMERICA

Species	Location	Reference
Syntermes sp.	Brazil	Smith and Barfield, 1968

[a] This table adds to the lists of previous reviews; 'J.A.W.' signifies data from the unpublished survey records of J. A. Wightman.

There are often two sizes of soldiers. Even though sterile, some have rudimentary reproductive organs and are recognizable as males or females. When collecting termites for identification, one should seek soldiers rather than workers because workers of different species are not clearly distinguishable. They are pale, sterile individuals of both sexes; they vary in size and aggregate to perform all the duties not carried out by the soldiers and reproductives — building and maintaining nests, finding and hauling food, and, most importantly in the case of the Macrotermitinae (Termitidae), tending fungal gardens.

Termites primarily feed on organic matter, but some, and these are the pest species, feed in or on live plants. The workers digest their food completely, including lignin, with the assistance of the symbiotic protozoa that are in their gut. They supply the other castes, either with a watery secretion from the mouth, which the reproductives receive, or anally (soldiers). There are many variations on this theme.

Many of the termites that are found in groundnut fields construct gardens of fungi of the genus *Termitomyces*. The fungus is cultured on the fresh faeces of the workers and forms part of the diet of the colony.

Like most soil insects, termites are influenced by the soil moisture. This was shown on a macro scale by Johnson *et al.* (1981), who derived a relationship between annual rainfall (x) and the percentage of groundnut stands with taproots invaded by *Microtermes* spp. (y) whereby:

$$y = (24493/x) - 20.6$$

Their data showed that, in those areas of Nigeria where the annual rainfall is more than 800 mm, less than 10 per cent of stands are attacked. On a smaller scale, Wheatley *et al.* (1989) showed that the number of termites (*M. obesi*) attacking wooden pegs was strongly influenced by soil moisture. Most of the attacked pegs were in soil with moisture of $10-13$ per cent where the field capacity of this Alfisol was 18.3 per cent and the wilting point 12.0 per cent.

Generally soil insects are regarded as beneficial to agricultural systems because of their role in the comminution of organic matter. However, termites use the organic matter efficiently, moving it through several members of a colony before plastering it into the wall of their nest. Thus the nutrients that were once potentially available for recycling are locked up until the nest collapses.

If termites have a beneficial role, it is aeration of the soil as they tunnel and build galleries underground. In times of flood, these tunnels presumably permit the rapid percolation of water.

Damage and Economic Importance

On a world basis, termites vie with white grubs as the 'worst field pest' of groundnut because of the damage they do and the difficulties in stopping them from doing it. Termites can:

- kill plants by boring into the root, sometimes via the lesion made by a white grub, but usually of their own volition, e.g., *Microtermes* spp. in many parts of the world, but especially in dry conditions, particularly at the end of the growing season. *Ancistrotermes* sp. and *Nasutitermes* sp. in Malawi appear to behave in the same way as *Microtermes* (J. A. Wightman, personal observation), as does *Amitermes evuncifer* in Nigeria (Sands, 1962);

- cover plants in a thin layer of soil (sheeting) to protect the workers from solar radiation and perhaps predators while they remove the stems and leaves from within the sheeting, e.g., *Odontotermes* spp.;

- 'fell' the stems and lower branches of the plant by chewing through just a few millimetres of the stem where it abuts the crown (*Macrotermes* spp. mainly but sometimes *H. mossambicus*). The effect is similar to that of beavers chopping down pine trees to construct a dam. The termites form sub-colonies at the base of the plant, complete with exits guarded by soldiers and with several ventilation chimneys. They proceed systematically along the row, sometimes cutting all of the stems on a plant but more often about half of them. They are usually most active along the sides of a field. The damage they cause can go unnoticed because the dead stems are removed by other species of termites within a few days and the branches of the depleted plants, when there are some, spread out and hide the damage;

- remove the soft corky tissue from between the fibrous 'veins' of the pods (*Microtermes* spp. in Africa and, seemingly, *Odontotermes* spp. in India). This process of scarification does not have much effect on yield and does not apparently influence the value of the product on the local market but it does permit infection by fungus, including *A. flavus*. This fungus produces a powerful carcinogen (aflatoxin) as a metabolic by-product (McDonald and Harkness, 1968);

- bore the pods and remove the kernels (again, mainly *Microtermes* spp., which also cut through the pegs) (Johnson *et al.*, 1981); and

- deplete the crop as it is drying in the field (*Odontotermes* spp.), Burrell *et al.* (1965) reporting up to 30 per cent damage of pods.

The later the harvest the greater is the level of termite damage and the level of aflatoxin contamination. For example, in experiments carried out in northern Nigeria, there were no toxic samples in groundnuts harvested in a crop 162 days old, but after 176 days, kernels from broken gleanings had medium to very high levels of aflatoxin. Termite damage, which was 4–38 per cent (average 18 per cent) in all picked pods, averaged 60 per cent in gleanings (McDonald and Harkness, 1968). Drying procedures were tested but did not improve the results except in the wet season. Placing pods on a mat to dry so that they could be moved under cover at night and when it rained did help (Burrell *et al.*, 1965; McDonald and Harkness, 1966).

Separating the influence of the activities of individual species on crop yields is difficult. The most extensive research in this field was by Johnson *et al.* (1981) and Johnson and Gumel (1981) in Nigeria between 1977 and 1979. Damage to the foliage (under soil sheeting) by *Odontotermes* sp. did not result in more than 5 per cent yield loss. Most of the crop loss was attributed to *M. lepidus*, which attacked the pods (boring and scarifying) and killed plants outright by invading the taproots. Its worst attacks during the 3 years were in the sudan savanna where it caused 8–41 per cent losses in yield. This zone was a commercial groundnut-growing area.

McDonald and Harkness (1966) were perhaps the first to link termite damage with aflatoxin incidence in northern Nigeria. Gleanings, which are the section of the crop most likely to be eaten by the farm family, had up to 100 per cent incidence.

The incidence — and the importance of scarification as the cause — of infection with *A. flavus* was also the subject of a special study by Johnson and Gumel (1981). They found that root damage by *M. lepidus* was related to the incidence of scarified pods. Again, in the sudan savanna of Nigeria, in unhealthy stands, where taproot penetration had taken place, 44–88 per cent of the pods were scarified. This percentage compares with 8–32 per cent scarification in healthy stands. Despite the high level of scarification in the farmers' fields, the incidence was only 5 per cent in samples from the local markets.

The implication is that scarified pods were retained by the farming families either for eating or for seed. As 85–91 per cent of the scarified pods were infected by fungus but only 5 per cent by *Aspergillus* spp., the extent of the risk of aflatoxin-induced cancer to which the families were exposed is hard to determine. However, it was clearly present.

In an earlier survey in Nigeria by Broadbent *et al.* (1968), 400 kernels were examined from each of 73 markets. The kernels from 31 were less than 1 per cent mouldy, from 14 were 1–2 per cent mouldy and the remainder were 2–5 per cent mouldy. *Aspergillus flavus* was found 16 times, with other species being considerably more abundant.

In view of the importance of fungi in the life of termites, it is not surprising that they are contaminated with fungi. However, experimentation has indicated that they are not directly responsible for introducing *Aspergillus* spp. into groundnut pods (Johnson and Gumel, 1981).

In Botswana, although the groundnut crop is small compared with that of Nigeria in its heyday, the problems are similar. At Sebele Research Station, Gabarone, 5–40 per cent of the plants were killed by termites (*Microtermes* sp.) depending on the location within the research area. In one experiment, plants from seeds that had not received any insecticidal treatment had 64 per cent sound pods. Of the remainder, about 15 per cent were perforated by termites, 11 per cent scarified, and 10 per cent totally destroyed. Seed treatment with an insecticide (carbaryl) did not improve matters. This means that only 50 per cent of the potential crop was worth harvesting. A. Mayeux considered the situation to be worse in other parts of Botswana (extracted from an ICRISAT internal report entitled 'Effects of soil insects on groundnut yields in Zambia and Botswana', J. A. Wightman, Jan. 1988).

Also, one of us (J.A.W.) encountered a crop that had been totally destroyed by *Microtermes* sp. in the south of Malawi, in an area experiencing intense late-season drought. All fields sampled in this vicinity had up to 10 per cent plant mortality caused by termites. *Macrotermes* sp. activity caused 12 per cent reduction of pods on plants (number of plants examined was 1200 of 80 000) growing on a study plot at Chitedze Agricultural Research Station in Malawi (ICRISAT internal report 'An evaluation of five insecticides for the control of foliage and soil insects in a groundnut crop in Malawi and some effects of soil insects on yield parameters', J. A. Wightman and A. S. Wightman, Jan. 1988).

Similarly, in India, reports reviewed by Verma and Kashyap (1980) indicated 5–50 per cent mortality in the Nimar tract of Madhya Pradesh, accompanied by 8–23 per cent pod damage and, in western Rajastan, 10–45 per cent damage by termites was recorded.

Sudhakar and Veeresh (1985) showed that the avoidable loss caused by termites to a groundnut crop, with and without insecticide application, was 51.2 per cent (year 1) and 50.2 per cent (year 2). Their study site was near Bangalore in Karnataka. At ICRISAT centre, Logan (1988) reported that 48.5 per cent of the untreated plants in an insecticide field trial carried out in rainfed conditions had been attacked by termites and that 5.5 per cent of the pods from these plants were scarified. The influence of termites on yield cannot, in this experiment, be separated from the damage caused by other soil insects, but the control of termites contributed to the 80 per cent improvement in yield in the more successful insecticide treatments.

Control

Insecticides: The routine application of cyclodiene insecticides to the soil of a groundnut field at 1–2 kg a.i./ha before sowing is the best way to prevent yield losses caused by termites. Dust, prill or granular formulations are the most effective. This method is not recommended, however, because these insecticides find their way into the kernel oil at contamination levels that are not acceptable under the FAO/WHO (World Health Organization) *Codex Alimentarius*.

There is no doubt that many other insecticides will kill termites if they come in contact with them. However, the conventional formulations of other insecticides do not persist long enough in tropical soils to protect the crop to the end of the growing season. It has already been shown that termites are mainly an end-of-season problem. The few termites present in a field early in the season may be controlled by an organophosphate or carbamate insecticide, but as soon as conditions are suitable later, the termites will invade the crop. Side dressings of such insecticides may be beneficial but can only be effective if rain falls at the right time and in the correct quantity to allow the insecticide to penetrate the soil without getting washed away.

It is suspected that the termite workers are able to separate their main galleries from insecticide-contaminated soil by lining them with soil sheeting deposited through their anuses. This may explain the comparative advantage of termites over the ants that occupy the same tract of insecticide-treated soil.

There is room for experimentation on this topic, as data collected in Malawi indicated that *Macrotermes* proliferated rapidly after the application of chlorpyriphos, perhaps because their ant predators had been killed (Wightman and Wightman, 1988, unpublished).

The need to protect insecticides from degradation in the soil has been answered in part by the development of a formulation consisting of plastic pellets that release the active ingredient for a predetermined period. Several of these slow- or controlled-release formulations controlled termites effectively when tested on the ICRISAT farm and near Bangalore in India.

Chlorpyriphos was particularly promising at the rate applied (5 kg a.i./ha), but we would not recommend furthering its use by farmers in semi-arid tropics because of the price and the residue in the kernels (Logan, 1988). In a field trial in Malawi this material protected the haulms of the harvested crop from nearly 20 per cent weight loss caused by the activities of *Odontotermes* spp. Farmers throughout Southern Africa were united in their conviction that termites can cause up to 50 per cent losses in pod weight at this stage.

Host-plant resistance: Amin *et al.* (1985) described the screening of 530 accessions for resistance to scarification by *Odontotermes* sp. As termites usually have an aggregated distribution within a field, the researchers attempted to increase and sustain the population by releasing adults collected from light traps, providing sawdust for them to eat during the dry season and cultivating shallowly during the afternoons (when termite workers seek cool soil strata).

Scoring damage on a 1–9 scale and noting the percentage of scarified pods, they found, over a period of three seasons, that NCAc 2243 tan, 2243 dark purple, 2240 dark purple, 2240 tan, 2242 and 2142, were highly resistant (these accessions were the result of irradiation of groundnut in experiments at North Carolina State University), as were NCAc 10033, 343, 17888, 2230, 1705, FESR 386 and the cultivar M 13. The implications of these data are being determined in field trials in Botswana, Burkina Faso, Malawi, and Niger.

Johnson *et al.* (1981) observed a certain amount of resistance in 'well established local varieties' grown in Nigeria, compared with improved lines. They also noted that the other key legumes in the area, bambara groundnut and cowpea, were not attacked by termites. They thought the findings reflected the indigenous nature of these two crops and the exotic status of groundnut in Africa. This observation may be valuable in future, as genetic engineering techniques develop.

Natural enemies: Termites in the soil are the natural prey of ants, perhaps because they occupy the same or similar niches. In any case, ants dominate the invertebrate predators' guild in many groundnut fields and reduce the levels of termite attack. This is illustrated by the results of an insecticide field trial in Malawi (Wightman and Wightman, 1988, unpublished) where the number of *Macrotermes* for every 10 m of row ranged from 11.5 (controlled-release phorate, 2 kg a.i./ha) to 79.0 (isofenphos granules, 2.5 kg a.i./ha) in the insecticide treatments, compared with 1.0 in the untreated control (SE = ± 12.6). These data were collected 13 weeks after sowing. They illustrate a detrimental effect of insecticides.

There are a number of vertebrates that prey on termites (anteaters, armadillos, echidna, and numbats), but their influence on groundnut production is not known. Birds are the main predators of the reproductives that swarm during the day and the night fliers are taken by bats. The wingless, nest-seeking prereproductives are a valuable food source for small rodents and insectivores.

Cultural: The relationship between late-season drought and termite attack suggests that crops harvested before drought are less vulnerable than those harvested later. This implies that farmers should sow a variety with a short growing season. This approach is also sound from the perspective of disease avoidance and the general agronomy of the crop.

Many farmers do not clear their fields of crop residues after harvest, but they could reduce the amount of food available to sustain termites through the dry season by incorporating residues into the soil, composting them off the field or, as a last resort, burning them. Mechanical cultivation, repeated each season might, in time, reduces the general population of termites.

Table 5.3. Termite damage to groundnut pods as influenced by mulches, ICRISAT centre, January-March 1989 (split pod design; data are means of 20 replicates)

	Percentage of pods with scarification[a]		Degree of damage[b]
Neem cake mulch	2	(0.02)	0.04
Ipomaea, mulch of chopped branches, leaves	7	(0.07)	0.14
Celosia mulch	17	(0.17)	0.38
Sunn hemp litter	59	(0.66)	1.69
Bare ground (control)	36	(0.37)	0.88
F value	132.6		
Pods on top of mulch	20	(0.21)	0.50
Pods mixed with mulch	28	(0.31)	0.75
F value	22.1		

[a] Figures in parentheses are arc-sine-transformed values of radians.
[b] Damage scored on a 0-4 scale where 0 = no scarification; 2 = 26-50 per cent; and 4 = 76-100 per cent of the surface of each pod scarified.

Experiments in Colombia have shown that sunn hemp (*Crotalaria juncea*) sown as an intercrop reduces the amount of damage caused by a burrowing bug, *Cyrtomenus bergi*, to cassava (Vargas, 1988); however intercropping groundnut with sunn hemp at ICRISAT centre did not reduce scarification or pod boring by *Odontotermes* sp.

An experiment carried out at ICRISAT showed that mulches had a profound influence on the level of damage caused to dry pods by termites (Table 5.3) (Gold *et al.*, 1989). Four mulches were compared: neem cake, sunn hemp litter, the weed *Celosia argentia*, and the chopped foliage and branches of another weed, *Ipomaea fistulosa*. The control treatment was bare ground. The *I. fistulosa* was included because of the observation that the leaves of this plant are not eaten by goats nor by any other mammal and, in our experience, by only one species of insect. Groundnut pods either were laid on the surface of the mulch or were admixed.

The data showed clearly that the pods were protected from termites (*M. obesi* and *Odontotermes* spp.) by the neem cake and by the chopped *I. fistulosa*. The *C. argentia* deterred termites slightly but not significantly, whereas the sunn hemp litter apparently attracted termites. The pods on the top of the mulch were less damaged than those that had been mixed with the mulch. The implication of these results is that a base of either neem cake or *I. fistulosa* can be used to protect piles of groundnut plants from termites when they are drying in the field. A further possibility is that the mulch would protect plants growing in the field, provided there is sufficient rain to carry the potentially insecticidal leachate into the soil. This is currently being tested.

Nigerian farmers' methods: Farmers are, of course, aware that termites reduce their groundnut yields and that there may be ways of preventing them from coming into the fields. In fact, Malaka (1972) surveyed farmers in part of Nigeria and asked them how, other than by the purchase and use of insecticides, they controlled termites. The responses were listed under 23 headings, including the hiring of drummers to drive them away and burying dead goats or fish viscera in the fields. Some other approaches were:

- sprinkling alum solution, kerosene, DDT sold for bedbug control, the liquid left after boiling locust bean seed, or the contents of expired cell batteries around the crops;
- pouring disinfectant or an infusion of *Sanseveria libericum* into nests;
- putting soldier ants into nests;
- removing the 'royal couple' from nests;
- burying cassava meal (fufu); and
- planting termite grass (*Vetiveria nigrotana*) around ornamentals and *Digitaria* sp., *Cymbopogon shoenanthus* and *Pennisetum purpureum* around farms.

Homoptera

APHIDIDAE

Aphis craccivora (syn. *A. laburnae, A. leguminosae*), the groundnut or cowpea aphid, is the aphid usually reported to be a pest of groundnut. The adults are black and shiny with brown legs. The cauda is prominent, and the cornicles are long, thin and black. It reproduces asexually throughout the year in the tropics. The nymphs are a dusty brown.

Biology

Hosts are mainly legumes, including a wide range of cultivated species, but the insect is not restricted to this family nor does it accept all legumes as a host. Srikanth and Lakkundi (1988) found that, in experimental conditions in Bangalore, south India, the aphid moved freely to field bean, blackgram, and cowpea, moved less often to green gram and groundnut, and avoided soybean and green pea entirely. In comparing the reproductive performance of *A. craccivora* on these hosts, they found that cowpea promoted higher growth and reproductive rates than did groundnut. They did not examine the possibility that rearing the parent colony on cowpea influenced the result.

A similar experiment was reported by Hamid *et al.* (1977) who also found that *A. craccivora* would not reproduce on soybean, reproduced poorly on green pea and horse gram but was well adapted to vetch and *Medicago hispida*. They found no reproducing colonies on soybean in an extensive survey of Pakistan. These authors ascribe importance to their observation that the species was attended by ants *Pheidole* sp. and *Momorium indicum* at 90 per cent of the sites visited.

These results and observations are in contrast with those of Highland and Roberts (1984) who compared the feeding preferences and reproductive rates of three species of aphid including *A. craccivora* (collected from the field in Virginia, USA), on four species of host plant. In a 'settling preference' test, soybean was preferred to groundnut, but cowpea and groundnut scored equally. Reproductive performance on groundnut was the same as on soybean, cowpea being superior in this test.

In other words, American and South Asian aphids of the same species differ in their response to host plants — a finding that indicates existence of biotypes in this species (Simon *et al.*, 1982).

A common pattern in the tropics is for *A. craccivora* to spend the dry or winter season on wild hosts such as *Medicago* spp., *Melilotus* spp., and *Trifolium* spp., as well as on volunteer growth of legume crops, including groundnut (Hamid *et al.*, 1977, writing about Pakistan). Evans (1954) lists more than 20 species of possible off-season hosts from Southern and East Africa, some of which may harbour virus.

Aphis craccivora disperses soon after the rains start. Farrell (1976a), working in Malawi, found that the main migratory flights are 5−6 weeks after the emergence of the earliest groundnut crop. In Hyderabad, India, the first colonies are found on groundnut 3−4 weeks after crop emergence in mid- to late July, 4−6 weeks after the start of the rainy season.

Damage and Economic Importance

This species has been found in most parts of the world between about 40°S and 40°N. It causes damage primarily as a vector of viruses, but it can injure plants by its feeding activity alone. It concentrates on the upper stems, in the flowers, and on the pegs. Plants that are heavily attacked early in the crop season become twisted, stunted and become covered in honeydew, which results in a sooty mould. Plants that are thus damaged are likely to be covered by their more robust neighbours. Feeding damage has been cited as the cause of yield loss in India (e.g., Bakhetia and Sidhu, 1976a) and West Africa (e.g., Mayeux, 1984). Such claims from India have not been accompanied by supporting data, but Mayeux (1984) stated that plants up to 7 weeks old can suffer as much as a 48 per cent loss in yield potential. After this time, the aphids disappear.

The ability of this and other species of aphid to transmit virus diseases is, however, the key to the damage it causes. The groundnut rosette virus (GRV) has been a major preoccupation among groundnut farmers and scientists in sub-Sahelian Africa since the mid 1920s, although the disease was diagnosed by Zimmerman as being caused by a virus as early as 1907. Storey and Bottomley (1928), working in South Africa, established that the vector was *Aphis leguminosae* (= *craccivora*) and was probably not a jassid. Their experiments were based on the collection of insects from infested plants in the field and on glasshouse tests. The techniques they adopted are still a model for contemporary virologists. The signs and characteristics of the virus complex have been described by Storey and Bottomley (1928). GRV is, in fact, a composite virus (Hull and Adams, 1968; Dubern, 1980), but this does not apparently influence considerations of the vector.

Aphids can transmit a virus in a persistent or non-persistent manner. For instance, with the persistent virus, GRV, a minimum of 4.5 h is required for acquisition and 3 min for inoculation. The latent period is 22.5 h or more. The insects retain the ability to inoculate plants with the virus, but no transovariolar transmission has been detected (Dubern, 1980, on a strain of GRV in Côte d'Ivoire). In contrast, *A. craccivora, A. solanella, Myzus persicae* and *Liaphis erysimi* retain the peanut stunt virus for only 30 min (*A. gossypii, A. solanum* and *Rhopalosiphum maidis* do not transmit this virus) (El Sadiq and Ahmed, 1986). *Aphis craccivora* does not transmit all groundnut viruses, according to Sreenivasulu *et al.* (1981). In a study of peanut green mosaic virus, *A. gossypii* and *M. persicae* transmitted the southern Indian strain non-persistently, but *A. craccivora* would not, despite repeated attempts.

A recently named affliction of groundnut in Southern Africa, groundnut streak necrosis disease (GSND), is transmitted, apparently in a non-persistent manner, by *A. gossypii* — transferring the sunflower yellow blotch virus from *Tridax procumbens* — which is a common weed in the Rift Valley. Also of relatively recent concern is the peanut stripe virus, which is now widespread in parts of Southeast Asia and was reportedly brought into the USA in seeds from the People's Republic of China. *Aphis craccivora* is known to be one vector, being able to transmit the disease after feeding on an infected plant for 1 min (Demski *et al.*, 1984a,b). Another potyvirus, peanut mottle, is also spread by *A. craccivora*, after 30−60 s feeding on an infected plant. *Myzus persicae* is a more effective vector (Paguio and Kuhn, 1976).

Control

Insecticides: Aphids are susceptible to most insecticides — a conclusion from David *et al.* (1965), Sundara Babu (1969), Bakhetia and Sidhu (1976b), and Thakkar *et al.* (1981) who wrote about *A. craccivora* in India and from Davies (1975) who reported for East Africa. However, their susceptibility does not mean that they are simple to control by chemical methods. They reproduce faster than their natural enemies, which tend to be susceptible to the same insecticides. The result is flare-ups by the aphids and the need for repeated applications at frequent intervals, unless selective aphicides such as menazon and pirimicarb are applied (Evans, 1954; Davies, 1975; Cameron *et al.*, 1983).

Davies (1975) found that a series of four foliar sprays of menazon reduced GRV incidence in rainfed conditions in Tanzania. However, the experiments were presumably carried out with estate or commercial production in mind because this procedure would probably not fit into the production pattern of the small-scale grower.

Host-plant resistance: Evans (1954) detected resistance to *A. craccivora* in several lines of the Mwitunde group of cultivars from the northwest of Tanzania in a series of field trials designed to seek resistance to GRV. Although the disease appeared in the crop initially, the secondary infestation, i.e., spread by aphids moving out from infestation loci initiated by immigrant alates, was restricted. This was reflected in the superior yields of the aphid-resistant genotypes.

In a screenhouse test in the Punjab, India, Brar and Sandhu (1975) found that spreading and semi-spreading plant forms promoted the rate of aphid population growth when compared with bunch types. Several genotypes appeared to have some resistance — AH 7983, AH 6279 and Faizpur.

Brar (1981), reporting a field experiment, also in the Punjab, India, found little difference among 43 genotypes, as far as their ability to support aphid population growth was concerned, but did demonstrate that the spreading varieties carried more aphids than semi-spreading and bunch forms. He apparently did not try to relate this to the relative number of growing points in the different plant-growth types.

Screenhouse tests at ICRISAT centre indicated that *Arachis chacoense*, *A. villosa*, *A. correntina* and *A. glabrata* exhibited high levels of resistance to *A. craccivora*. Progenies of interspecific hybrids of *A. hypogaea* with *A. chacoense* and *A. villosa* also showed high levels of resistance (Amin, 1985).

However, of the many genotypes tested, EC 36892 (ICG 5240) has been the most consistently resistant in southern India and in Malawi; it is, thus, the most promising source of resistance for breeding (Tables 5.4–5.6) (Padgham *et al.*, 1989).

Table 5.4. *Aphis craccivora* **from eight randomized plots at ICRISAT centre 20 days after emergence, rainy season, 1987**

	Mean	Minimum	Maximum	Log mean	Rank
NCAc 343	436.3	160	1058	2.64	4
EC 36892 (ICG 5240)	167.1	33	440	2.22	1
NCAc 2240	1376.7	956	2262	3.14	8
M 13	781.5	272	1230	2.89	7
ICGS 11	503.0	208	860	2.70	5
ICGS 44	376.5	126	466	2.58	3
JL 24	235.0	72	838	2.37	2
ZMB 2087	619.8	256	1034	2.79	6
SE ±	101.1			0.28	
CV	54			14	

The aphids in Asia appear to respond to the antibiosis differently from those in Africa (Table 5.7) — an indication of *A. craccivora* biotypes. Also, the data provide evidence of 'natural selection' by farmers, with Chalimbana, a cultivar popular in Malawi, performing well in Africa.

Host-plant resistance to a vector such as aphids has been demonstrated as protection against GRV infection (Table 5.7). The GRV level in EC

36892 remained low even under an abnormally heavy infestation by viruliferous aphids in a screening nursery up to about 40 days after emergence, by which time the virus has a reduced effect on crop yield.

Table 5.5. *Aphis craccivora* **at 11 days and 6 days after five apterous adults were placed on 20 potted plants 5 days after emergence in a glasshouse in Malawi**

	Aphids (no./plant)					
	At 11 days			At 6 days		
	Mean	± SE	Rank	Mean	± SE	Rank
EC 36892 (ICG 5240)	104.4	14.0	1	68.7	38.4	1
ICGM 620 (ICG 5725)	123.8	13.4	2	74.1	11.9	2
ICGM 493 (RG 1)	133.9	13.6	3	76.5	6.0	3
Chalimbana (ICGM 489)	165.1	16.2	4	88.1	8.1	4
RMP 40	177.3	16.0	5	90.4	12.1	5
RMP 93	193.7	17.7	6	102.6	16.4	6
NCAc 343 (ICGM 660)	200.7	20.8	7	-	-	-
Mani Pintar (ICGM 490)	217.1	19.0	8	116.1	11.7	8
RMP 19	242.1	23.4	9	-	-	-
ICGM 576 (RMP 12)	244.9	21.4	10	-	-	-
NCAc 17090 (ICGM 543)	266.3	15.4	11	-	-	-
ICGM 578 (RMP 91)	286.8	19.3	12	-	-	-
NCAc 2214 (ICGM 539)	293.0	24.5	13	116.3	12.8	9
ICGM 577 (RMP 89)	353.1	22.0	14	112.6	14.3	7

Table 5.6. Comparison of *Aphis craccivora* **numbers on five genotypes where the aphids were from Malawi and ICRISAT centre**

Genotype	Malawi			ICRISAT centre		
	Mean	RA[a]		Mean	RA[a]	
		1	2		1	2
EC 36892 (ICG 5240)	104	100	88	13	100	53
NCAc 343 (ICG 2271)	201	114	100	125	188	100
Chalimbana (ICGM 489)	167	110	97	253	215	115
Mani Pintar (ICGM 490)	217	116	101	213	209	111
NCAc 17090 (ICG 1697)	266	120	105	63	162	105

[a] RA = relative abundance with 1 = EC 36892, 2 = NCAc 343 as standards.

Table 5.7. Incidence of groundnut rosette virus (GRV) in 10 rows of a susceptible genotype (Malimba) with infected plants every 1.5 m, interspersed with 10 paired rows of an aphid-resistant genotype, EC 36892 (ICG 5240), and single rows of eight GRV-susceptible genotypes (lumped data) at Chitedze Agricultural Research Station, Malawi, 1987 (courtesy of Dr K. R. Bock)

Initial number of plants (12 June)	Virus incidence (%)			
	29 Jan	13 Feb[a]	12 Mar	13 Apr[b]
Malimba	487	49.9	69.6	81.3	99.3
EC 36892	248	8.1	13.7	31.8	43.9
Susceptibles[c]	262	30.9	69.5	82.1	97.8

[a]Plants infected after this time would lose little yield as a result of GRV.
[b]Adjusted for within-season plant mortality, this was the pre-harvest count.
[c]AH 138, Matimule Encarnado, AH 229, AH 134, AH 202, AH 188, AH 15714, and Morrumbene Castanho.

Natural enemies: There is no systematic study of the effectiveness of the natural enemies of *A. craccivora* as natural control agents. Farrell (1976b), writing of Malawian conditions in the mid 1960s, presented the most complete investigation. He concluded that the natural enemies reduce population densities only after the aphid population starts to decline toward the end of the season, as a result of the deterioration of the host. Coccinellid and syrphid larvae were the most numerous predators. *Aphidius colemani* (Braconidae) and *Psyllaephagus pulvinatus* (Encyrtidae) were found among the aphids after the population began to decline. Entomophagous fungi also appeared late in the season.

Booker (1963) also listed the coccinellid and syrphid larvae he found eating *A. craccivora*. Farrell's report is not in complete accord with J.A.W.'s observations in the farmers' fields around the research station where Farrell carried out his experiments, albeit some 20 years earlier.

Aphis craccivora does not tolerate high densities (Farrell, 1976b), but few plots with more than 50 aphids/plant were found in the heterogenous environment of the farmers' fields. On the other hand, coccinellids, syrphids and other potential predators were present on the plants in relatively high densities, i.e., one coccinellid or syrphid larva per aphid colony of about 20 individuals at the time of expected population build-up.

Table 5.8. *Arachis hypogaea* genotypes with some degree of resistance (*) to jassids *Empoasca fabae* (Ef), *E. kerri* (Ek), *Jacobiasca formosana* (Jf), thrips *Frankliniella schultzei* (Fz) and *F. fusca* (Ff), and termite *(Odontotermes* sp.) (t) scarification

Genotype identity		Ef	Ek	Jf	Fz	Ff	t	References[a]
AH 7729	ICG 1602			*				7
Benihandach		*						7
EC 36892	ICG 5240			*				7
EC 99219	ICG 589, 3569			*				7
FESR 386						*		1
GNLM[b]	ICG 2741			*	*			1,5,6
K 4				*	*			5,6
M 6-76	ICG 7446			*				7
M 13	ICG 156			*			*	1,5
M 57-72	ICG 7490			*				7
M 137-74				*				7
M 896-76 (1)				*				7
M 399-72	ICG 7490			*				7
NC 6	ICG 6429	*	*			*		2,4,7
NCAc 343	ICG 2271	*	*	*	*	*	*	1,2,3,4,5,6
NCAc 406	ICG 266	*	*					1,9
NCAc 489		*	*					1,9
NCAc 785		*	*					1,9
NCAc 1006				*				7
NCAc 1337	ICG 398			*				1
NCAc 1694				*				7
NCAc 1705	ICG 6764	*	*	*			*	1,5,6,9
NCAc 1741		*	*		*			6,9
NCAc 1787				*				7
NCAc 1807	ICG 7490			*				7
NCAc 2139	ICG 6826			*				7
NCAc 2142	ICG 2036	*	*	*	*			1
NCAc 2144	ICG 2307	*	*					1,6
NCAc 2154	ICG 5037			*	*			1,6
NCAc 2214	ICG 5040	*	*	*				1,6,9
NCAc 2230	ICG 5041	*	*	*				1,5,6,9
NCAc 2232	ICG 5042	*	*	*	*			1,5,6,9
NCAc 2240	ICG 5043	*	*	*	*			1,5,6,9
NCAc 2242	ICG 5044			*	*	*		1,5,6
NCAc 2243	ICG 5045	*	*	*	*			1,5,6,9

Table 5.8 continued

Genotype identity		Ef	Ek	Jf	Fz	Ff	t	References[a]
NCAc 2460	ICG 7803	*	*		*			1,9
NCAc 2462	ICG 2320				*			1
NCAc 2666	ICG 1660	*	*					1,9
NCAc 2700	ICG 411	*	*					1,9
NCAc 2772	ICG 2350	*						9
NCAc 10033						*		1
NCAc 10207	ICG 8314	*						3,4
NCAc 10211	ICG 5727	*						3,4
NCAc 10247	ICG 5681	*						3,4
NCAc 10272	ICG 5682	*						3,4
NCAc 10277	ICG 5683	*						3,4
NCAc 15729	ICG 5691	*						3,4
NCAc 15730		*						3,4
NCAc 15736		*						3,4
NCAc 15739	ICG 5731	*						3,4
NCAc 15744		*						3,4
NCAc 15745	ICG 8241	*						3,4
NCAc 16940	ICG 8099			*		*		5,6
NCAc 17888	ICG 6317	*					*	1,9
PI23442				*				7
RC44	ICG 8896	*						6
RMP 40							*	1
Thai numbers								
	207				*			8
	278				*			8
	309				*			8
	324				*			8
	329				*			8
	331				*			8
	807				*			8
	875				*			8
	950				*			8
	986				*			8
	1149				*			8
	1150				*			8
	1155				*			8
VRR 257	ICG 7113			*				5

[a] References are: 1 Amin *et al.*, 1985; 2 Campbell, 1986; 3 Campbell *et al.*, 1976; 4 Campbell *et al.*, 1977; 5 ICRISAT, 1982; 6 ICRISAT, 1983; 7 ICRISAT, 1984; 8 Sathorn Sirisingh and Manochai Keerati-Kasikorn, 1986; and 9 Prof. J. C. Wynne, personal communication, germplasm data base, North Carolina State University.

[b] GNLM = Gujarat Narrow Leaf Mutant.

A possible line of research is to plant perennial 'off-season' hosts of the aphid in unused land around the farms to sustain aphids and their natural enemies during the dry season in the vicinity where farmers need them after the crops are sown. However, one would have to be careful to make sure that such plants did not act as the reservoirs of the components of the GRV complex or of other crop virus diseases.

Commonly, in India and African groundnut fields, rain displaces aphids from groundnut plants (J.A.W., personal observation). Although many regain their feeding sites, some may become prey to predators living on the soil surface, such as carabids, spiders and ants. Also, periods of persistent rainfall increase the RH around the plants, thereby promoting the development of entomophilous fungi. Thus, a density-independent factor (rain) could be important in the natural control of aphids.

Cultural: There are two ways in which farmers can escape infestations by GRV-carrying aphids — close spacing and early sowing. These have been demonstrated in Nigeria by A'Brook (1964) and Booker (1963), in Malawi by Farrell (1976a,b), and in Uganda by Davies (1976). They were also referred to by Mayeux (1984) writing of West African conditions. Farrell (1976b) showed that the aphids reproduced less rapidly on closely spaced plants, suggesting a form of pseudoresistance induced by the physiologic state of the host.

Close planting should be possible at all stages of the season. However, early sowing may not always be possible because of other activities that compete for farmers' time, such as the sowing and weeding of the staple or of more important cash crops. J.A.W. found that the majority of the farmers that he surveyed in central Malawi and other parts of Southern Africa sowed within about a week of the start of the rainy season. This may account for the low incidence of GRV in this area. Farmers used wide spacing — in part to fit with the row spacing adopted for maize and tobacco but also to make their seed supply go further.

Farrell (1976c) found that intercropping groundnut with field beans *Phaseolus vulgaris* could reduce the rate of the spread of the virus through a crop. He noticed that the aphids became impaled on the recurved trichomes that are on the underside of the bean leaflets. He attributed the comparative slowness of secondary spread of virus to this resistance factor in the beans. However, he considered that an early sown, closely spaced, monocrop reduced the losses caused by GRV more effectively than intercropping with beans.

Several writers have pointed to the need for removing off-season volunteer growth from the vicinity of groundnut fields as a means of reducing the level of *A. craccivora* and GRV in susceptible areas (e.g., Evans 1954; Misari et al., 1980). The areas that apparently need most attention are river banks, the sides of drainage and irrigation canals and land irrigated for off-season crops. This seems reasonable, as it is likely that at least one of the components of the virus complex could overwinter in volunteers, although this has yet to be confirmed.

TETTIGOMETRIDAE

Weaving (1980), the origin of much of the following information on *Hilda patruelis*, commented that published literature on the family Tettigometridae is limited, and her observation is still true. As far as pests of groundnut are concerned, two species in this family deserve mention.

One is well known to groundnut growers in much of Africa — *H. patruelis*. This insect is sometimes called the groundnut planthopper, but the title is not particularly appropriate because it is mainly subterranean when living on the groundnut crop. This makes it more of a 'digger' than a 'hopper'. Rose (1962) and Taylor (1981) have provided further information about the species, and all three of these authors drew on observations made in Zimbabwe.

The other species, *Hypochthonella caeca* has no common name, is virtually unknown, and can be dealt with quickly. The only record of extensive damage caused by this insect was by Rose (1962), attributing to it the destruction of 70 per cent of a groundnut crop in Zimbabwe. However, as soil insects are not always considered when maladies of groundnut are diagnosed, its damage elsewhere may have gone unheralded. One of us (J.A.W.) found *H. caeca* under groundnut plants in central Zambia, in low numbers. It is white and about 3 mm long. The plants it lives on turn yellow and are stunted. It is attended by doryline ants. Rose stated that it causes similar damage to tobacco. As these two crops are common in rotations in Southern Africa, there is at least the potential for the build-up in population densities of this insect.

Biology

The eggs are silvery blue—mauve and are laid in rafts of 10—40 on the pods, pegs or upper roots of the plant, although sometimes they number more than 100/raft, as more than one insect may lay in the same place. The eggs are the most easily found stage. The period from oviposition to final moult is 37 days at 23°C and 74 per cent RH, the egg stage lasting 10 days at 20° and 12 days at 23°. In Tanzania, the life cycle lasts 6 weeks, according to Jepson (1948). The adults are mottled olive green, brown and cream and attain 3—4 mm in length. The nymphal stadia are similarly coloured. All stages have been well illustrated by Weaving (1980).

Hilda is oligophagous, some 42 host species having been listed in Zimbabwe. Roots of common and persistent weeds such as *Conyza sumatrensis*, *Bidens pilosa*, and *Tagetes minuta* become infested and allow the populations to survive through the dry season. The fleshy taproots of *C. sumatrensis* are particularly popular. The life cycle can be completed above ground on trees and ornamentals such as *Cassia*, *Hybiscus*, and *Protea*. The insect has been found on the root systems of, besides groundnut, soybean, sunflower, maize, sunn hemp and potato (Taylor, 1981).

Ant attendants palpate the nymphs with their antennae and receive honeydew from the anus. They build a network of galleries around the base of the plants. These probably allow hilda to move around in the soil among the roots, as neither the adults nor the nymphs have fossorial adaptations. The galleries are destroyed by heavy or persistent rainfall, despite efforts by the ants to repair them. This explains to some extent the 'local knowledge' in Southern Africa that associates hilda epidemics with dry seasons. Weaving's analysis of official records indicated that hilda outbreaks were most frequent in years when the rainfall was below average.

Damage and Economic Importance

Signs of damage by *H. patruelis* are often easy to see, although, because of its cryptic colouring and motility, the insect is not always easy to find. It lives on the roots of groundnut plants, just below the crown, and moves from one plant to another, usually along a row.

Infestation can be detected by the rapid wilting and death of plants around the periphery of fields and by the presence of small black ants, e.g., *Pheidole megacephala*, that tend hilda.

Weaving's (1980) literature review and J.A.W.'s survey indicate that hilda is found south of a line extending from Sudan in the east to Nigeria in the west. The presence of crops such as groundnut, sunflower, and cashew as well as of certain common weeds may be the factors determining its distribution.

Hilda is believed to inject toxin into host plants when it feeds (ICRISAT, 1985). The vascular tissues of the roots turn brown soon after attack, the leaves turn yellow, and the stems droop until they become prostrate.

Outbreaks of hilda are highly sporadic. J.A.W. found specimens throughout Southern Africa but found only one field (out of about 100) where it was a pest. This was in Malawi, and the plant mortality was so high that the farmer had abandoned the crop. Hilda had spread to other farms by the time of the survey and probably caused considerable damage in the 6−8 weeks remaining before harvest.

Extension officers in Malawi found that some farmers would not grow groundnut for up to 5 years after seasons in which hilda was epidemic. Farmers over large tracts of Tanzania that appeared to be suitable for groundnut production did not grow this crop because of the 'black ants'. It is possible that the ants attending hilda were blamed for crop failures. The region in question had many cashew trees, which are a favoured alternative host for hilda in the off season.

Control

Insecticides: Taylor (1981) was not positive about the feasibility of controlling hilda with insecticides. She stated that monocrotophos, the only insecticide registered in Zimbabwe for hilda control at that time, was erratic in controlling infestations. Estate farmers in Zimbabwe apply carbofuran granules before sowing as prophylaxis (J.A.W., unpublished) and spray insecticides on weeds edging fields. However, these activities are beyond the means of the smallholders, about whom we are most concerned.

In 1985, an unattributed article in *Kenya Farmer* recommended that aldrin or dieldrin be worked into the soil before sowing or that diazinon, fenthion or fenitrothion be sprayed onto the bases of plants. The advice is questionable, as insecticide application would be effective only if farmers could forecast outbreaks and the cyclodienes might leave residues in the kernels.

Host-plant resistance: We know of no report of host-plant resistance to this species, but hot spots in Tanzania would be a good choice if screening for resistance becomes necessary.

Natural enemies: Hilda eggs are parasitized by *Psyllechthrus oophagus* (Hymenoptera: Encyrtidae). During 15 months of testing, Weaving (1980) found that 56 per cent of all eggs were parasitized and that only 14 per cent of the egg batches contained no parasites.

Parasitism was lowest in July–August and in December–January. The former period coincided with a low rate of oviposition by hilda and the latter, with high rainfall. Observations by Mchowa and Mitumbili (1987) in Malawi concur with the low rate of parasitism in the early part of the growing season when farmers need some natural control of this pest. Research on the host–parasite system might be of benefit. The only known predator of hilda is a coccinellid, *Hyperaspis*, that was seen feeding on eggs laid on the stem of *Hybiscus*.

Cultural: No systematic research on the cultural control of this 'difficult' species has been carried out. The ability of the insect to live through the dry season on weeds points to the possibility that farm hygiene would reduce the risk of an infestation. Delaying groundnut planting until the rains are established may also help. In fact, the heavy attack J.A.W. encountered in Malawi was in a field sown in early November with some early showers. The farmer took a risk in the hope of getting high preseason prices for his crop. Several other farmers in central Malawi had done the same but had suffered small losses to hilda. The rest of the farmers sowed with the main rains in early December, and none had detectable infestations. It could be that the early sown crops became infested because the farmers provided a preferred host when other plants had not started growing or that planting coincided favourably with the phenological characteristics of the parasite. Much is left to learn about this species.

CICADELLIDAE OR JASSIDAE

Smith and Barfield (1982) listed 15 entries, including five genera, under the family Cicadellidae or Jassidae. *Empoasca* spp. predominated the list, and we can add *E. pruthi* from India (Amin, 1983) and *E. signata* collected (by J.A.W.) from near Harare, Zimbabwe, but apparently common on groundnut throughout Southern Africa where there are reportedly about 350 species of *Empoasca* (J.G. Theron in Scholtz and Holm, 1985).

Austroasca viridigrisea may be a groundnut pest in Australia but was not included in the list. The literature takes note of jassids because of the insects' widespread and often abundant appearance, although the information about their pest status is conflicting.

Biology

DeLong (1971) gave an account of the biology and ecology of leafhoppers in general. They are slender, small (3–5 mm), and yellow or green. The adults fly readily when disturbed. In fact, observers can estimate their density after a little experience, by noting how many are flushed out by a walk through the crop.

The nymphs are usually found on the underside of a leaf. The egg is embedded in the tissue of the host, usually in the leaf. Incubation does not extend beyond a week in the tropics. There are five nymphal instars in the species found on groundnut. They resemble the adult except for the absence of fully developed wings. The nymphal period is also relatively rapid, lasting 7–14 days, according to the season.

The females are, in general, relatively fecund, laying up to 300 eggs, the actual number depending upon the food quality of the host and the seasonal and climatic conditions, as well the survivorship of the female. Thus, the life cycle can be completed in 2–4 weeks in tropical conditions.

Wheatley *et al.* (1989) found that when groundnut plants were grown along a drought-gradient, jassids were most abundant where the hosts were least stressed. They were also found where leaf (canopy) temperatures were lowest, i.e., about 30°C as opposed to temperatures exceeding 45°C. This experiment was carried out in peninsular India after the rainy season.

Damage and Economic Importance

Empoasca spp. and their close relatives appear wherever groundnut crops are grown. *Austroasca* spp. are found in Queensland, Australia. *Cicadulina* spp. are found in Africa, and *Orosius* spp. and *Erythroneura tripunctula* have been recorded from Asia.

The damage caused by *Empoasca* spp. and closely related genera is easy to diagnose. The first sign is a whitening of the veins on the underside of the leaflet. Chlorosis then sets in, usually at the tip of the leaf, and moves down the blade, followed by necrosis, again starting at the tip. The crop can take on a scorched appearance as a result of the necrosis. This is called hopper burn and is probably produced by a salivary toxin. The toxin appears to be lacking in *Austroasca viridigrisea*, the (Australian) vegetable jassid, which stipples the leaves. The related lucerne jassid (*A. alfalfae*), which is also found in Australia, produces the conventional feeding signs (Turner, 1980).

The economic impact of jassids in groundnut crops is not easy to determine. From the practical point of view it is difficult to get a groundnut field with only jassids present so that experimental plots can be treated with insecticides to eliminate these insects alone. Reports, therefore, often lump data for the removal of both jassids and thrips. For example, Sivasubramaniam and Palaniswamy (1986) applied monocrotophos every 15 days to half their study plots. Jassids and thrips were the only insects present, and, in 1983, this gave a pod yield increase of 48.5 per cent (1.75 t/ha compared with 0.9 t/ha). In the protected plots, an average 2.3 jassids were found for every three leaflets and in the unprotected plots, 2.19, whereas thrips numbered, respectively, 2.11 and 2.98. The authors do not state whether the mean insect densities were for the whole season or were just one observation. In 1984, a repeat of the experiment showed a 19.6 per cent increase (1.27 t/ha to 1.58 t/ha) in pod yields from the protected plots (jassids, per three leaflets, numbered 2.06 in unprotected plots compared with 0.46 in protected plots, and thrips were 3.51 compared with 1.92). The data from the 1984 study are similar to those of Saboo and Puri (1978) who attributed a 40 per cent loss in pod yield to jassids and thrips.

These results are difficult to understand when one considers that complete defoliation by caterpillars to all but the young plants causes no more than about 10 per cent loss in yields of TMV 2, a cultivar that is susceptible to many pests but that is widely grown in peninsular India. Furthermore, ICRISAT data point to no more than a 10 per cent pod loss attributable to jassids (*E. kerri*) even at much higher densities. Similarly, Campbell (1986) indicated that, in an experiment carried out by Kollmer, 60 per cent of leaves had to be scorched before yield loss could be detected. Even when all leaves were scorched, the loss in yield was only about 15 per cent. These findings are also in line with those of Turner and Briar (1979) in Australia and Ellis (1984) in Canada. The possibility of a 'host-genotype-environment-pest biotype' interaction should not be excluded.

Control

Chemical: Experience at ICRISAT has been that any insecticide applied at rates lethal to aphids or small caterpillars also kills jassids.

Host-plant resistance: Smith *et al.* (1985) have described methods of evaluating the reaction of groundnut genotypes to jassids (*E. fabae*). They concluded that the proportion of jassid-damaged leaflets was the best indication of the loss in photosynthetic area as well as the host's reaction.

Many groundnut genotypes are resistant to jassids (Table 5.8), and some have been used in breeding programmes (ICRISAT, 1985, 1986, 1987, 1988). W. V. Campbell and J. C. Wynne working in North Carolina (North Carolina State University, personal communication to J.A.W.) found resistance to leafhoppers in hybrids, primarily C12 × C37, that resulted from their crosses of NC Bunch and PI 121067. NCAc 343, also known by the ICRISAT identity number of ICG 2271, is one. It has a wide spectrum of resistance to a number of pests, although its agronomic characters were considered to be sub-optimal when it was registered (Campbell *et al.*, 1971). NCAc 343 is a parent of NC 6, a large-seeded Virginia-type, that was bred for sustained high yield in the presence of pests, including *E. fabae*.

Wynne and Campbell also found resistance to jassids in mutants selected after the irradiation of NC 4. Examples include NCAc 1705, 2142, 2144, 2230, 2232, 2240, 2243, and 2462, which in some cases have resistance to other pests as well (Table 5.9; Campbell *et al.*, 1971, 1975, 1976; Prof. J. C. Wynne, 1989, personal communication).

Likewise, many *Arachis* spp. have resistance to jassids (Campbell and Wynne, 1980; ICRISAT, 1986, 1987). This 'wild' resistance will probably not be exploited, as genes for resistance are readily available in cultivated species and the pest is of doubtful importance. Even though jassids may not cause economic damage in groundnut, their presence may induce farmers to apply insecticides.

Resistance has been transferred from one continent to another by Campbell and colleagues in the USA and in Southeast Asia, and jassid resistance is now included in several genotypes with multiple pest resistance (Campbell *et al.*, 1986; Sathorn Sirisingh and Manochai Keerati-Kasikorn, 1986).

Much of the information available points to the surface structures of the leaves as being of prime importance in the mechanism of resistance. In particular, the trichome length, density, straightness and location are implicated as well as the thickness of the epidermis (Campbell *et al.*, 1976; Dwivedi *et al.*, 1986).

The genetic studies of Holley *et al.* (1985) and Dwivedi *et al.* (1986) indicated that the genes responsible for resistance to jassids have a high level of combining ability. In fact, one character, 'long trichomes on the leaf margins' was used by Dwivedi and co-workers to select for jassid resistance in the absence of the insects. Their work pointed to NCAc 2230 as the best parent to impart jassid resistance, despite the low yield potential of the cultivar.

However, Holley *et al.* (1985) concluded that the most resistant parents did not always produce the most resistant progeny and vice versa. They also pointed out that the direction of the cross can influence the results so one must investigate, or at least be aware of, maternal and reciprocal effects.

Natural enemies: DeLong (1971) indicated that, although jassids are parasitized by members of 12 insect families, parasitism probably has little influence on their population density. He indicated that pipunculids and dryinids (Hymenoptera) are prominent jassid parasites.

As with many small plant-eating insects, jassids living on groundnut are probably eaten by many general predators, such as lycosid spiders. However, DeLong commented that chrysopids and coccinellids have been seen to ignore jassids in favour of other prey.

Cultural: At ICRISAT, peak populations of jassids occur in the second month after sowing (September and late-December—early January). The pattern is characteristic of phytophagous insects on an annual crop where natural enemies eventually provide control, but the pattern may reflect immigration followed by emigration caused by a change in the quality of the host plant. If older plants are unfavourable as hosts to immigrating adult jassids, then early sowing may help avoid an attack.

In a general review, Andow (1983) found that 32 populations of nine jassid species increased in intercropped life systems with non-hosts, whereas two populations representing two species decreased. He found that 12 populations (five species) increased in cropping systems with multiple hosts, and none decreased. ICRISAT data showed that densities of *E. kerri* in groundnut intercropped with sunflower, sunn hemp and pearl millet were lower than in groundnut grown as a sole crop. We do not know the reason for this.

OTHER HOMOPTERAN FAMILIES

Smith and Barfield (1982) indicated that pseudococcids (mealybugs) and coccids (scale insects) have been taken from groundnut plants from all around the world, but we know little about their applied ecology on this crop. One of us (J.A.W.) found mealybugs on the stems and roots of plants in Southern Africa, including what may be the first record of *Phenacoccus solani* from Malawi. This species has previously been found in South Africa and Zimbabwe, but the individuals found in Malawi differed slightly in an important character. During the survey, the plants with mealybugs feeding on them seemed smaller than the average. However, it was too early in the season for effects on pod yield to be manifest and too brief an observation to rule out the possibility that the insects were seeking a biochemical milieu of plants stunted by less obvious factors.

Johnson and Gumel (1981) found that superficial pod damage was caused by the mealybug *Dysmicoccus* sp. in Nigeria. Also, J.A.W. observed membracids, *Oxyrachis* sp., feeding on the roots of dying plants near Gabarone, in Botswana.

Heteroptera

Most of the Heteroptera attacking groundnut plants belong to the families Coreidae and Pentatomidae. They include species conspicuous by virtue of their size, such as *Leptoglossus australis* and *Anoplocnemis curvipes*, or abundance, such as *Nezara viridula* and *Piezodorus* spp. They come under the general heading of 'tip wilters' because their feeding causes the growing points to bend. The significance of this damage is not known but is likely to be small.

Elasmolomus sordidus — synonym *Aphanus sordidus* (Fabricius) — is widespread in tropical Africa and India (Conway, 1976) and has been reported from Brazil (Slater, 1972). It attacks a number of oilseed crops and feeds on groundnuts while they are drying in the field and when in store. The adult is dark brown, approximately 10 mm long and 2 mm wide. In the field, females lay cylindrical eggs in the soil or on drying groundnut haulms, but in stores eggs are laid loosely among the groundnuts or in sacking.

The first-instar nymphs have a bright red abdomen, but later instars become progressively darker. The length of the life cycle and optimum conditions for development have not been established. All stages are highly mobile, but adults and the larger nymphs tend to be restricted to the surface layers of stacks or sacks because they are too large to penetrate into a bulk or sack of pods. All stages feed on kernels, by piercing the pod with their rostrum. Mould grows where the testa has been punctured, and intensive feeding eventually causes the kernels to shrivel. The free fatty acid increases in the oil, producing a rancid flavour (Gillier, 1970). When large populations build up in stores, the pods become covered in dark spots of faecal material.

Thysanoptera

Thrips seem to feed on groundnut plants throughout the geographical range of the crop. Smith and Barfield (1982) listed 18 species belonging to 7 genera but, strangely, left out *Megalurothrips*, which is commonly found in large numbers in the flowers of groundnut plants and many other legumes. None of the best represented genera — *Caliothrips*, *Frankliniella*, *Scirtothrips* and *Taeniothrips* — are restricted to any one continent. The identification of thrips is a task for experts, although Amin and Palmer (1985), Ananthakrishnan (1969), Dyadechko (1964) and Lewis (1973) are helpful in this respect.

  Scirtothrips dorsalis forms the bulk of the thrips fauna in groundnut fields (and in the air above them — according to ICRISAT suction trap data) in South and Southeast Asia. This species may be the vector of the yellow spot virus. Its feeding damage is conspicuous: brown lesions and severe distortion. It lives in the folded leaflets. *Scirtothrips aurantii* was found by J.A.W. on groundnut it Malawi but is normally thought of as a pest of citrus. *Frankliniella schultzei* is mainly a flower dweller and has been implicated as a vector of the tomato spotted wilt virus with *Frankliniella occidentalis* and *Frankliniella fusca*. *Thrips palmi* is probably the main vector of the tomato spotted wilt virus, with Thrips tabaci, both of which live mainly in the folded leaflets. *Caliothrips* species cause mottling on the leaf surface, but there is no information available about their economic importance. *Megalurothrips usitatus* is often (usually?) found in the flowers of legumes all over Asia, and J.A.W. found this species in flowers in Southern Africa.

Damage and economic importance

Wightman (1990), on reviewing the groundnut pests in Western agriculture, found that reports about the economic importance of damage caused by thrips (especially *F. fusca*) were strongly polarized. One set of data indicated that the economic burden of thrips on groundnut farmers in the state of Georgia was the huge cost of insecticides applied to kill them. However, since that time, a definitive study in North Carolina has shown that a yield loss will occur when there is more than 40% leaf damage in a crop up to 6 weeks after sowing (Turnjit and Campbell, personal communication, 1989) — i.e., when damage is severe among the young plants. This is pertinent information because the distortions caused by thrips to the foliage of young plants look serious, especially when temperatures are low so that the crop cannot outgrow the damage. This occurs in groundnut sown in winter under irrigation in India when it is suspected that the yield losses are small, especially when compared with the damage caused by thrips when they introduce a virus into a crop.

When tomato spotted wilt virus is introduced into groundnut, it causes bud necrosis disease. In the West this is mainly thought of as a crippling disease of tomatoes and ornamentals, but it also causes widespread death and stunting of groundnut in the USA, Australia and Asia. Even if the plant achieves maturity, the seeds are usually shrivelled and discoloured.

The role of thrips as vectors has been discussed by Reddy and Wightman (1988), and new research at ICRISAT, in conjunction with the British Museum of Natural History (unpublished), has shown that *T. palmi* is probably a major vector of the tomato spotted wilt virus in India.

Control

ICRISAT focuses on control measures to stem the spread of the tomato spotted leaf virus by regulation of the density of the vectors.

Chemical: Many insecticides will kill thrips, but relatively high doses are required to eliminate these tiny insects (Reddy and Wightman, 1988). In fact, following insecticide use, population explosions have been reported (Reddy and Wightman, 1988).

Natural enemies: Phytophagous thrips are preyed upon by a number of general predators, such as mirid and anthocorid bugs, as well as by predatory thrips. There are no data about the natural control agents, but the relative ease with which phytophagous species reproduce after insecticide application indicates that natural enemies regulate their densities.

Host-plant resistance: Despite great efforts by ICRISAT's virologists, little resistance to the tomato spotted wilt virus has been found in *A. hypogaea*. This does not mean that the breeders have been inactive in this area because many lines with resistance to thrips have been located and the appropriate genes incorporated into agronomically acceptable genetic backgrounds (Table 5.8). Many of the genotypes and hybrids with resistance to jassids are also resistant to thrips. Robut 33-1 (Kadiri 3) is a popular cultivar in southern India and Tanzania. It is a source for resistance to thrips and a parent to high-yielding lines such as ICGS 11 and ICGS 44.

Cultural: One method of reducing the risk of an outbreak of tomato spotted wilt virus is to phase the sowing of the crop in such a way that the seedling (i.e., the stage that is the most vulnerable to the virus) will not be exposed to an invasion of thrips. This implies the need for knowledge of flight periodicity of the species. Research at ICRISAT has shown that the prevalence of the virus increases as the planting date is delayed — both in the rainy and in the postrainy season. Furthermore, a densely sown crop is likely to have lower losses attributable to the virus than a widely spaced crop (Wightman and Amin, 1988).

Physical barriers across the prevailing wind also influence thrips' density. This can mean an intercrop that is not a host, such as sorghum, maize and millet or a row of trees.

Weeds harbour both the vectors and the virus; however, weed clearing operations in Australia succeeded in reducing the prevalence of the virus only to a limited extent (Saint-Smith *et al.*, 1972). Whether coordinated, selective weed destruction would have had the desired effect of reducing 'off-season' reservoirs is not clear.

Hymenoptera

Smith and Barfield (1982) listed Formicidae as the only hymenopteran family attacking groundnuts. Of the eight genera listed, only one, *Dorylus*, includes species causing extensive damage. *Dorylus orientalis* is found in peninsular and northeast India, Bangladesh, south China, Nepal (Terai), Sri Lanka, Burma, Thailand and the northern tip of the Malaysian peninsula. Another species of *Dorylus*, or perhaps the same one, was found for the first time by J.A.W. throughout Southern Africa underneath groundnut plants and damaging the pods.

The workers in this genus are almost totally subterranean and eyeless. They are light brown, 5–11 mm long (major workers) or 2.5–3 mm long (minor workers). They are polyphagous and cause damage to many root and tuber crops as well as to seedlings and to beehives, attacking the brood and stealing honey and pollen. The workers are said to eat other insects and earthworms. They make a 2-mm-wide hole in the distal end of groundnut pods and remove the contents. They leave little trace of their passage, whereas termites leave soil and most pod-boring beetle larvae leave frass.

The pods of plants growing in small plots at ICRISAT centre have been entirely destroyed by *D. orientalis*, and probably many other such instances have gone unrecorded in South Asia.

However, in Thailand the pest potential of this species has been realized and publicized by Manochai Keerati-Kasikorn and Preecha Singha (1986). These scientists found that attacks started 7 weeks after emergence, i.e., as soon as the pods started to form. Farmers in the area of north Thailand lost 15–48 per cent (mean, 32 per cent) of their crops as a result of this pest. Attempts to control it by using copra baits treated with insecticide were not successful.

J.A.W. has seen notches cut out of leaves by megachilid (leafcutter) bees, but this is probably of no economic importance.

Coleoptera

BRUCHIDAE

Caryedon serratus (Olivier), commonly referred to as groundnut borer, groundnut weevil, or groundnut bruchid, is found in many parts of the tropics, breeding on the seeds of common tree legumes such as *Cassia* spp., *Acacia* spp., *Bauhinia* spp., *Piliostigma* spp. and *Tamarindus indica*, as well as on harvested groundnuts (Davey, 1958). Synonyms are *Bruchus serratus* Olivier, *Bruchus gonagra* Fabricius, *Caryedon fuscus* (Goeze), and *Caryedon gonagra* (Fabricius).

In West Africa, *C. serratus* is recognized as a serious pest of groundnuts both in commercial storage (Pattinson and Thornton, 1965; Pointel *et al.*, 1979) and in farmers' seed stores (Conway, 1975). It also attacks groundnuts in commercial storage in India (Dick, 1987). Although it occurs in some parts of Central and South America (Johnston, 1986) and the Caribbean (USDA, 1976), it apparently does not infest stored groundnuts in these regions (Robert, 1985).

The adult is 4–7 mm long and reddish brown, with dark irregular markings on the elytra. It has prominent, compound eyes and can be easily distinguished from other storage pests by its broad hind femur, which bears a conspicuous comb of one large spine and 8–12 smaller ones.

Adult females attach their eggs singly to the pods. When the first instar larva hatches, it burrows directly through the pod wall and the seed coat to feed on the cotyledons. Larval development is completed within a single kernel. When mature, larvae may partially or completely emerge from the pod, leaving a characteristic round hole, approximately 3 mm in diameter. Larvae frequently migrate to the bottom of a stack or heap before pupating

(Conway, 1983; Dick, 1987). Damage caused by subsequent generations is commonly heaviest in this part of the stack.

The papery, ovoid cocoons are distinctive. Their discovery is often the first indication of infestation. Under optimal conditions (30–33°C and 70–90 per cent RH), the period from egg to adult emergence is approximately 40 days.

Infestation by *C. serratus* can begin in the field with the migration of adult beetles from wild hosts to newly harvested groundnuts. Alternatively, clean groundnut stocks can become infested when placed in stores containing infested residues from previous crops.

The relative importance of these two possible sources of infestation is unclear and would influence the efficacy of control procedures. In a country-wide survey in the Gambia, Conway (1975) found that 21 per cent of samples from windrows and 40 per cent from stacks drying in farmers' fields were already infested with *C. serratus*.

Although the mean level of infestation was low (0.1–2.0 per cent of pods in each sample), Conway concluded that field infestation was the main source of the bruchid populations found in groundnut stores. Other authors (Appert, 1954; Green, 1959) doubt the ability of *C. serratus* to migrate from wild hosts to the cultivated crop and consider crop residues to be the primary source of infestation.

In the Congo, Matakot *et al.* (1987) were unable to find a consistent relationship between the presence of *C. serratus* in storage and infestations in the field. They concluded that outbreaks of the pest originated chiefly from residual populations surviving in village stores. Their studies suggested that the size of bruchid populations is ultimately determined more by factors that influence the rate of population development than by the initial source of infestation.

Control

Chemical: In West Africa, lindane, malathion, bromophos, or iodofenphos dust are reportedly applied frequently to windrows to prevent infestation by *C. serratus* of groundnuts intended for seed supply or for the confectionary market (Conway, 1975; Deuse and Pointel, 1975; Gillier and Bockelee-Morvan, 1979).

In Senegal, bromophos dust (2 per cent a.i.), applied at a rate of 200 g/m^2 to the surface and base of large seccos, reportedly gives effective control of *C. serratus* (Pointel *et al.*, 1979). Small quantities of pods or kernels retained by farmers as seed can be protected by the admixture of insecticidal dust. However, insecticide should not be applied directly to groundnut kernels intended for consumption or oil expression.

Table 5.9. The survival of *Caryedon serratus* eggs and the subsequent F_1 generation on the groundnut pods of some advanced breeders lines (ICGV) and cultivars

Genotype	Egg survival (%)	F_1 prepupae and pupae (no./100pods)
ICGV 87204	18.7	6.9
ICGV 87354	22.0	10.4
TMV 2	28.7	10.0
2133	29.7	10.9
ICGV 86014	31.2	12.8
J 11	32.4	10.2
NCAc 343	32.5	12.8
ICGS 44	33.9	10.4
ICG (FDRS) 43	34.5	11.5
Robut 33-1	34.9	15.2
ICGV 86042	35.5	14.8
ICG (FDRS) 10	36.4	13.4
ICGS 11	39.9	10.8
M 13	39.9	16.5
ICGV 86016	40.1	15.7
ICGS 1	40.1	9.7
ICGV 86127	40.9	13.0
ICGV 86124	41.0	11.7
ICGV 86015	41.6	16.4
ICG (FDRS) 4	41.8	11.0
NCAc 17090	43.4	12.2
ICGV 86056	43.6	10.0
JL 24	52.4	17.2
ICGV 86055	55.6	13.2
ICGS 5	59.8	9.2
SE ±	12.5	3.3

If groundnuts are already infested with *C. serratus* when they are stored, then bruchid larvae may be present throughout a heap or stack and may have caused considerable damage before they are detected. In this situation, the only effective treatment is fumigation with methyl bromide or phosphine gas. Methyl bromide has been used extensively in West Africa to protect groundnut stocks (Gillier and Bockelee-Morvan, 1979). The recommended dosage for the control of *C. serratus* infesting groundnut pods and kernels is 60–70 g/t for 48 h (FAO, 1985). The number of times any one consignment of groundnuts can be fumigated is limited because inorganic bromide is retained in the oil of groundnut kernels (Feakin, 1973). Western countries, in general, and the USA, in particular, have now become concerned about bromide residues in foodstuffs. Also, repeated applications may reduce the germination potential of groundnuts kept for seed, particularly if the seeds' moisture content is above that recommended for safe storage (Redlinger and Davis, 1982).

Phosphine has certain advantages over methyl bromide in that it requires no special equipment for application and leaves no residues. However, effective treatment takes longer than with methyl bromide (5–10 days) and could disrupt routine stock movements.

Natural enemies: The larvae of *C. serratus*, particularly when feeding inside intact pods, are well protected from predators and parasites. However, final instar larvae often migrate within a store before pupating and are then vulnerable to attack by predators, such as the reduviid bug *Amphibolus venator* (Klug) (Howe and Freeman, 1955; Dick, 1987).

Caryedon serratus pupae are preyed on by prostimatic mites of the genus *Pyemotes* (Bruce and LeCato, 1979). Matakot *et al.* (1987) reported that parasitism of *C. serratus* pupae by *P. tritici* contributed to regulation of *C. serratus* populations in groundnut stores in Congo. Similarly, in Gambian stores, heavy mortality of *C. serratus* pupae was caused by *P. ventricosis* (Conway, 1975).

Host-plant resistance: To date, there have been no large-scale breeding programmes aimed at reducing the inherent susceptibility of groundnuts to attack by *C. serratus.* The lack of attention probably reflects the relative cost-effectiveness of insecticide applications, the limited geographical area in which this pest has been considered to be of major importance and the failure of entomologists and breeders to come together in a suitable place.

Opportunities to reduce susceptibility to *C. serratus* derive from genotypic variability in characteristics that affect oviposition on pods, larval penetration of the pod wall, and development of larvae in the kernels. Significant variation among genotypes has been demonstrated for a number of these characteristics (Table 5.9) (Mittal, 1969; P. Dobie, Overseas Development and Natural Resources Institute, 1986, personal communication).

BUPRESTIDAE

The larvae of *Sphenoptera indica (perotetti)*, jewel beetle, penetrate groundnuts below the crown and burrow through the central core of the root, thereby killing or stunting the plant. By the time they pupate (in the root cortex they have hollowed out), there is little vascular or pithy tissue remaining.

Jewel beetles are a rainy season pest at the ICRISAT farm. In one season we attributed 14 per cent plant mortality to this insect in a rainfed field and 8 per cent in a field that was irrigated whenever water was needed. The full range and the extent of damage caused by this species are not known. First-instar larvae have been found in groundnut pods at ICRISAT but this is considered to be rare. Experiments at ICRISAT showed that this species was controlled by a presowing treatment of chlorpyrifos at 4–5 kg a.i./ha.

CURCULIONIDAE

The only species of weevil that really concerns groundnut growers is the white-fringed weevil or railroad weevil, *Graphognathus leucoloma*. It is common in North America and is apparently still extending its range in Australia. J. Rogers (personal communication) indicated that it is currently causing losses to groundnut farmers in central Queensland.

The adults eat the foliage but it is the root-eating habits of the larvae that cause stunting and plant death. The species is parthenogenetic, each female laying 1000–2000 eggs during her long adult period. The host range is wide, including potatoes and several common pasture and forage legumes — *Trifolium* spp. and *Medicago* spp. — but, according to Feakin (1973), groundnut is a favoured host. Feakin also indicated that the application of a persistent insecticide at the time of sowing in fields with recent infestation gives satisfactory control in high-input cultivations.

Another weevil species that may reduce yields, this time in northern India, is *Myllocerus undecimpustulatus maculosus*, the ash or grey cotton weevil. The adults appear in the rainy season. They cause an irregular scalloping around the edge of groundnut leaflets. Brar and Sandhu (1975) reported marked resistance to this species in all the spreading genotypes they tested. AH 288, AH 8045, C 112, C 148, C 162, Karod 4-11, M 13, M 145, S 230, T 28, 1-2, and 4-6 were the least attractive to the adult weevils. Research may reveal that the larvae cause considerably more damage to their hosts than is suspected (Wightman, 1987).

Both Rose (1962) and Broad (1966) pointed to problems caused by the larvae of weevils in Zimbabwe, mentioning *Systates exaptus* and *Mesoleurus dentipes* specifically. Groundnut crops are believed to induce local increases in population densities, which endanger the following maize crop. These species feed on the roots and pods of groundnut plants.

J.A.W. found *Systates* spp. in Zimbabwe and Malawi, and *Diaecoderus* sp. in Malawi. Jepson (1948) reported plants being skeletonized by *S. articollis* in Tanzania. He also reported the 'yellowing and failure of a young plantation' as being associated with an attack by *Diaecoderus* sp. The yellowing is a sign of nitrogen deficiency and is a result of an attack on the nodules by the larvae. For example, it occurs when *Sitona* spp. attack legumes, including groundnut (Smith and Barfield, 1982; Wightman, 1987).

DERMESTIDAE

The khapra beetle, *Trogoderma granarium* Everts, is more tolerant of hot, dry conditions than many other storage pests and is commonest in the semi-arid areas of Africa, West Asia and northern India. It has not been recorded from Southeast Asia, South America, or Australia (Banks, 1977).

In some areas, such as northern Nigeria, where *T. granarium* has been a major obstacle to exporting groundnut, intensive programmes of fumigation have succeeded in reducing its importance (Halliday, 1967). In other regions, such as Somalia, it is still regarded as the most serious pest of stored groundnuts (Fenili *et al.*, 1983).

Adults are oval, 2–3 mm long, and dark brown with black mottling. Their dorsal surface is covered with fine hairs. They live for about 2 weeks and do not feed or fly. The larvae are straw-coloured and, from the fourth instar onward, have characteristic, dense tufts of hair on each abdominal and thoracic tergite. The bionomics of this species developing on groundnuts have not been rigorously examined in the laboratory, and optimal conditions for its development are still a matter for debate. Its common occurrence in hot, dry areas is generally attributed to its inability to compete with faster-breeding species in humid environments (Smith, 1963).

Larvae of certain strains enter diapause when subjected to adverse conditions such as extremes of temperature or population density. When almost mature, the pre-diapause larvae often leave their food supply to enter crevices in the storage structure where they may remain for many months (Burges, 1962, 1963). In this state, metabolic activity is low, and the larvae are extremely resistant to insecticides. Complete disinfestation is, therefore, difficult. Because of this, *T. granarium* is considered a most important pest by countries that import groundnuts, and the presence of even a few individuals is likely to result in the rejection of an entire groundnut consignment.

Methyl bromide is effective against all the main beetle pests of shelled groundnuts, although the dosage must be increased by 50 per cent to be effective against *T. granarium* (FAO, 1985). *Trogoderma granarium* is, however, as susceptible as most other species to phosphine, which should be applied at the same rates as those used for pyralid moths (Table 5.2).

Mattesia trogodermae has potential for the control of *Trogoderma* spp. (Schwalbe *et al.*, 1974). A commercial product would have to contain spores of a number of different pathogen species because they are relatively specific.

ELATERIDAE AND TENEBRIONIDAE

Wire-worms and false wire-worms

Wire-worms and false wire-worms can be dealt with together because the convergence of their evolution that led to their morphological similarity extends to their predilection for groundnut pods. There are problems with their identification. The larvae are pencil-shaped and can be up to 4 cm long. They are creamy white to brown. Their life cycles tend to be longer than those of white grubs, but little is known about their biology except that they damage groundnut pods by boring through the shell and eating the seeds. Only the adult lives aboveground. Both types of insect have been found damaging groundnut pods and the newly sown seed at ICRISAT centre, but their identity and that of other species in Asia are not known.

The adults of false wire-worm species in the genus *Gonocephalum* (e.g., *G. simplex*) are called dusty brown beetles. They are found throughout sub-Saharan Africa, and J.A.W. found large numbers associated with groundnut crops in a black soil area in the south of Malawi in December and January.

The larvae can clearly damage many pods during their long development, even though their density rarely exceeds 10/100 plants (Wightman, 1989). When their density is added to that of other pod borers (millepedes, termites, ants and white grubs), this cohort must destroy many pods during a cropping season. Central Malawi was particularly hard hit by this group of insects, with one for every two plants in some places.

Rust-red Flour Beetle

Among Coleoptera, the key pest of stored groundnuts is *Tribolium castaneum* from the family Tenebrionidae. Commonly known as the rust-red flour beetle, it is found throughout the tropics. The adults are 3−4 mm long, chestnut brown and have a life span of several months. They are strong fliers and are often the first insects to colonize new stocks of groundnuts.

The females lay their eggs in cracks in the testa or in holes in the kernels created by the adult while feeding. Thus, the first-instar larvae, which cannot penetrate an intact seed coat, are able to feed directly on the cotyledon.

The larvae are cylindrical, with two prominent 'horns' on the last abdominal segment. They create tunnels in the cotyledons as they feed and pupate within the kernels. Both adults and larvae feed on the eggs and pupae of other storage pests and are also strongly cannibalistic. Development from egg to adult takes about 32 days at 30°C and 90 per cent RH, but the period is doubled when the RH drops to 70 per cent.

Feeding by the adults and larvae creates a fine dust that contains less oil than whole kernels and has a much higher free fatty acid content (Davey *et al.*, 1959). Thus, the feeding of *T. castaneum* reduces the quality, as well as the quantity, of the oil produced.

Measures to prevent infestation of stores by *C. serratus* are effective also against *T. castaneum*, and phosphine treatment is recommended over methyl bromide because it leaves no residue.

Natural control has promise, as populations of *T. castaneum* released into large plywood bins containing 200 L of groundnut pods have been effectively suppressed by *X. flavipes*, introduced 7 days later (Press *et al.*, 1975). After 14 weeks, the predator had reduced *T. castaneum* populations to less than 10 per cent of control populations and had reduced the number of damaged kernels by 66 per cent. Also, laboratory studies suggest that a pathogen *Nosema whitei* controls *Tribolium* sp.

As with the other pests of stored groundnuts, there have been few studies of host-plant resistance to the beetles that commonly attack decorticated stocks. Mbata (1986) examined the susceptibility of some newly released Nigerian varieties to infestation by *T. castaneum*. Significant differences existed between genotypes, both in the time of development and in the number of F_1 adults produced.

Whether the adults were fewer because of differences in the number of eggs laid or in the mortality of immatures was not reported. The larvae of *T. castaneum* developed more quickly and more reliably on broken kernels than on whole kernels, probably because of both the marked oviposition preference of *T. castaneum* females for broken rather than whole kernels and the inability of first-instar larvae to damage intact groundnut kernels (Mathur and Kausal, 1984). The significant differences observed in development period on the broken kernels must however reflect differences in the suitability of the cotyledons as sources of nutrition.

MELOIDAE

Blister, pollen or flower beetles are large (up to 3 cm long) and conspicuous; they feed on the flowers of legume crops in all of Africa and in much of Asia. The genera include *Mylabris, Coryna* and *Epicauta*. The younger larvae (triungulins) feed in or on the eggs of locusts and grasshoppers and are, therefore, considered to be beneficial. The flower-eating habit of the adults probably has little influence on the yield of groundnut because the crop produces an excess of flowers, and the flowers are self-pollinated early in the day. Their bright or metallic colours are conspicuous so that their importance may be overestimated.

SCARABAEIDAE

White grubs share with termites the reputation of being among the most widespread and most serious field pests of groundnut in the developing world. In general, termites are most serious when rainfall is limited or badly distributed, particularly at the end of the growing season, whereas white grubs are most damaging when rainfall is adequate, especially early in the season when the plants are young (J.A.W., personal observation). In this chapter, we are most concerned with melolonthids and rutellines. Members of other sub-families have life systems oriented more towards dung and other forms of dead organic matter (Veeresh, 1978).

Biology

There is general agreement about the life cycle of these insects in the tropics, e.g., Broad (1966) for Southern Africa and Brar and Sandhu (1980a) for India. There are three larval instars that can be easily distinguished by the size of the head capsules. This stage feeds on the roots of hosts. Oligophagy is probably commoner than polyphagy. Depth of feeding, and therefore the type of roots, is determined by soil moisture, soil temperature and the amount of feeding activity of other white grubs (Wightman, 1972).

When the larva has reached its maximum size, it burrows well below its normal feeding zone and forms an earthen cell. It pupates within this cell and awaits the start of the next rainy season before it ecloses. The adults emerge at dusk and, in sequences and combinations that are species-specific, mate, feed on ground-level vegetation, and fly up to several hundred metres to feed on trees of selected species. The adults are active in the month or so following the 'planting rains'.

The eggs are white, oblate spheroids. They are found in clusters, 15 cm or more below the soil surface. The insects are not particularly fecund, each female producing 20–80 eggs. The eggs hatch as the groundnut reaches the late seedling stage, and the larvae sometimes feed on organic matter in the soil before they commence feeding on the roots.

This general picture does not tell the full story. For example, in Africa, J.A.W. found relatively large specimens (i.e., third-instar larvae measuring 2–4 cm long) in groundnut fields quite soon after sowing. This implies that they had overwintered, as is the case with *Rhopaea magnicornis* in Australia for instance (Gough and Brown, 1988). J.A.W. also found eggs and newly hatched larvae well into the growing season. These findings suggest that gaining an understanding of the bionomics of this taxon in Southern Africa will be complicated by the diversity of the species and the variation within species.

Table 5.10. White grubs associated with the groundnut crop[a]

Species	Location	References
Adoretus cribrosus	Zimbabwe	Smith and Barfield, 1982
A. umbrosus	Africa	Smith and Barfield, 1982
Adoretus spp. (up to 4)	Malawi, Zambia, Zimbabwe	J.A.W. J.A.W.
Anomala antiqua	Burma	Smith and Barfield, 1982
A. atrovirens	Indonesia	Smith and Barfield, 1982
A. phebeja	Africa	Smith and Barfield, 1982
Anomala spp. (up to 11)	Botswana, India, Malawi, Zambia, Zimbabwe	J.A.W. J.A.W. J.A.W.
Eulepida mashona	Africa	J.A.W.
Heteroligus claudius	Nigeria	J.A.W.
Heteronyx brevicollis	Australia	J.A.W.
Lachnosterna caudata	Australia	J.A.W.
L. (Holotrichia) consanguinea	India	J.A.W.
L. fissa	India	J.A.W.
L. serrata	India	Vereesh (1978)
Lepidiota sp.	Australia	Gough and Brown, 1988
Maladera sp.	Thailand	Sathorn Sirisingh, personal communication
Oxycetonia versicolor	India	Smith and Barfield, 1982
Podalgus (Crator) cuniculus	Africa	Smith and Barfield, 1982
Popillia japonica	China	Smith and Barfield, 1982
Rhopaea magnicornis	Australia	Smith and Barfield, 1982
Schizonycha africana	Africa (NE)	Smith and Barfield, 1982
S. fusca	Malawi	J.A.W.
S. straminea	Malawi	J.A.W.
Schizonycha spp. (up to 8)	Malawi	J.A.W.
Schizonycha spp. (up to 3)	Zimbabwe	J.A.W.
Trissodon (Isodon) puncticollis	Australia	J.A.W.
Trochalus sp.	Malawi	J.A.W.
Xylotrupes gideon	Burma	Smith and Barfield, 1982
?Sericini (tribe) (indet. 8 species)	Malawi, Zimbabwe, Zambia	J.A.W. J.A.W.

[a] This table adds to the lists of previous reviewers; J.A.W. signifies data from the unpublished survey records of J. A. Wightman.

Damage and Economic Importance

White grubs are found wherever groundnut crops are grown in the developing world (and in Australia). It is clear that many species are yet to be described. J.A.W.'s survey in Southern Africa accounts for about half of the current records (Table 5.10) and indicates the dearth of taxonomic back-up. Most of the larvae he collected were undescribed species belonging to three genera. They were most frequently recovered from sandy soil or well-tilled ferruginous loam, especially where rainfall was average or better than average. For example, white grubs were abundant in the red loams of central Malawi but were less frequent in the silts of the Luangwa Valley and in the light red soil near Chipata in Zambia (Table 5.11). In Zimbabwe, white grubs were not common in fields that had just come out of fallow or that had been converted from bush earlier in the season.

Table 5.11. White grubs detected during a survey of groundnut farms in Southern Africa, 1986, rainy season[a]

Country	Location	Number of fields	White grubs (no./100 plants)
Malawi	Mitundu	6	18.4
	Likundu	4	50.7
	Chileka	7	39.7
	Nsalu	3	76.1
Zambia	Choma	3	2.4
	Mumbwa	5	14.6
	Chipata	5	13.3
	Luangwa Valley	5	3.0
	Kabwe	3	19.2
Zimbabwe[b]	Masvingo	5	11.1
	Chilimanzi	4	7.5
	Manyene	4	37.3
	Mawere	6	33.3
	Wedza	6	45.4
	Chinhoyi	4	91.8

[a] Data collected by J. A. and A. S. Wightman
[b] Data for Zimbabwe are arranged with the southernmost (and, therefore, the driest) location first.

Similarly, in Australia, J. Rogers, working from central Queensland, was able to recognize 18 species living under local groundnut crops, although he has not yet determined their identity (personal communication). The point is that both Dr. Rogers and J.A.W. actually set out to look for these insects in the soil in groundnut fields so one can expect further such surveys will reveal many more species.

At present, Africa is the continent where white grubs are a widespread problem. This is in line with Veeresh's (1978) statement that only two species are important (sometimes very important locally) in India: *Lachnosterna (= Holotrichia) consanguinea* mainly in the light alluvial soils of northern India and *L. serrata* throughout the sub-continent.

There are also several records from Southeast and East Asia (Table 5.10). *Maladera* sp. is the most abundant white grub in north Thailand and another unidentified species has recently been found in northeast Thailand (Sathorn, personal communication).

White grubs sever fine roots, often close to the taproot of the groundnut, the result being elimination of a relatively large amount of water-absorbing area even when only a small amount of tissue is eaten. As the attacks come mainly during the late seedling stage, they can stunt or even kill the plant, particularly if soil moisture is limited. Often, examinations of older plants that have been attacked reveal distinct lesions on the taproots, which become entry points for *Microtermes* spp. and *Odontotermes* spp., as well as for fungal infections. White grubs also destroy pods at all stages of development.

There are many generalizations in the literature about the degree of damage caused by white grubs to groundnut crops, but few give specific data or attempt to relate insect number to damage. The most precise report came from Australia, where Gough and Brown's (1988) data showed one white grub (*Lepidiota* sp.)/3 m of row (about 15 plants) caused a loss of pods equal to 44 kg/ha.

Bakhetia (1983) showed, in experiments carried out at two sites in the Punjab in northern India during 2 years, that the avoidable loss caused to groundnut crops by *H. consanguinea* was from 29 per cent to 42 per cent. Bakhetia and Brar (1983) increased the yield of groundnut crops from 0.68 t/ha to more than 1.2 t/ha by using insecticides that ostensibly controlled white grubs, again in the Punjab. Similarly, in tests from Varanasi, in northern India, the best insecticide treatment (phorate 10G at 2.5 kg a.i./ha) reduced a population of 52 larvae/m^2 to 12/m^2 with a resultant improvement in yield of 300 kg/ha over a control plot yield of 775 kg/ha. Initially populations were about 4 larvae/plant (Janardan Singh and Paras Nath, 1985). In Tirupati, in southern India, a plot protected with phorate, at 1.5 kg a.i./ha yielded 1.72 t/ha compared with a mean control plot yield of 1.17 t/ha (Siva Rao *et al.*, 1984).

Table 5.12. Insecticides that have been recommended for the control of white grubs in groundnut crops

Location species	Insecticide	Rate[a] (kg a.i./ha)	Reference
India			
Holotrichia	Phorate 10G	1-3	Bakhetia, 1982a
consanguinea		1	Brar and Sandhu, 1980a,b
		2.5	Ram and Yadava, 1982; Vishwa Nath and Srivastava, 1981;
		1.5	Siva Rao *et al.*, 1984
		SC[a]	Ram and Yadava, 1982
	Carbofuran 3G	1-3	Bakhetia, 1982a
		1	Brar and Sandhu, 1980a,b,; Bakhetia *et al.*, 1982
		1.5	Siva Rao *et al.*, 1984
		SC	Bakhetia, 1982b; Ram and Yadava, 1982
	Isofenphos 5G	1-3	Bakhetia, 1982a
		1	Brar and Sandhu, 1980
		SC	Bakhetia, 1982b
	Quinalphos 5G	1	Bakhetia, 1982b
	Quinalphos 25EC	1	Bakhetia, 1982b
	Dazomet 10G	2.5	Vishwa Nath and Srivastava, 1981
	Heptachlor (10% dust)	2.5	Vishwa Nath and Srivastava, 1981
	Fensulfothion 5G	1	Bakhetia *et al.*, 1982
	Chlorpyriphos	SC	Bakhetia, 1982b
	Phoxim	SC	Bakhetia, 1982b
	Fenitrothion	SC	Bakhetia, 1982b
Africa			
Eulepida mashona	Dieldrin dust 2%		Broad, 1966; Rose, 1962
	Aldrin, endo-sulphan, and heptachlor (no details)		Rose, 1962
Australia			
Heteronyx spp.	Carbofuran	3	Rogers, personal communication

[a] SC = seed coating.

These data show that white grubs can have a marked influence on the yield of groundnut crops. However, they do not exclude the possibility that other insects were also exerting an influence on crop yield and that their influence had gone undetected. In fact, in a series of five experiments carried out in Malawi, dieldrin was applied to experimental plots, with resultant yields up to 60 per cent higher than control plots. Although white grub was implicated in some cases, clearly other soil organisms (especially termites) were also involved (Wightman, 1989).

Control

Chemical: A number of insecticides have been listed for the control of white grubs (Table 5.12). Carbamate and organophosphate, although they break down rapidly in tropical soils, should kill larvae before losing their potency. As the insects have only one generation per year (compared with continual invasion and reinvasion characteristic of termites), control can be effective by materials that remain active for a comparatively short period.

Host-plant resistance: No resistance to these insects has been confirmed.

Natural enemies: Brar and Sandhu (1980b) listed the natural control agents of white grubs in India. Microbial agents include the fungi *Aspergillus parasiticis, Beauveria bassiana,* and *Metarrhizium anisopliae*; the bacteria *Bacillus cereus, B. thuringiensis, Diplococcus* sp., *Clostridium* sp., and *Micrococcus* sp. Two scolid parasites, *Scolia aureipennis* and *Campsomeris callaris,* have also been reported. Predators include carabid larvae, toads, many bird species and mammals such as mongooses and pigs.

Cultural: There is scope for community action for reducing the general population of white grubs in a farming area when the beetles are above-ground in the evening to mate and feed. Brar and Sandhu (1980b) cited cases where literally millions of beetles have been destroyed. They also maintained that repeated ploughing, flooding and puddling reduce white grub densities.

SILVANIDAE

The merchant grain beetle — *Oryzaephilus mercator* (Fauvel) — and its sibling species *O. surinamensis* are found throughout the tropics. The two are difficult to distinguish morphologically, but *O. surinamensis* is generally associated with cereal products rather than oilseeds (Howe, 1956).

Oryzaephilus mercator is ecologically and behaviourally similar to *T.*

castaneum, although it is generally regarded as a less serious pest. The adults are 2.5–3.5 mm long with a distinctively ridged prothorax, bearing six large teeth on either side. The larvae are cylindrical and cream-coloured. They can be distinguished from *T. castaneum* larvae by the absence of 'horns' on the last abdominal segment. First-instar larvae cannot penetrate intact testae and must feed on exposed kernels of groundnut. Under optimal conditions (30–33°C and 70 per cent RH), the life cycle is completed in 28–35 days.

Infestation by these beetles is unlikely to begin in the field. Thus, the measures recommended for prevention of infestation of clean stocks by *C. serratus* and *E. sordidus* are appropriate, perhaps as a routine. Methyl bromide and phosphine are effective.

Both *Tribolium* and *Oryzaephilus* spp. are preyed on by *X. flavipes*. In small silos filled with groundnut pods, *X. flavipes* adults, released on the surface of the bulk, suppressed populations of *T. castaneum* and *O. mercator* introduced into the groundnuts at different depths from the surface (Press *et al.*, 1979). Dispersed populations of *O. surinamensis* and *T. castaneum* were successfully controlled by *X. flavipes* when the predator was released into a warehouse in which small quantities of culture media had been used to simulate debris from previous harvests (LeCato *et al.*, 1977).

In contrast to the relatively numerous studies that indicate the potential for control of moth pests by bacteria and viruses, there is little indication that stored-product Coleoptera can be similarly suppressed by these pathogens (Hodges, 1984). However, several protozoa are known to be pathogens of the beetle pests of groundnut. The results of laboratory trials have shown that *Nosema oryzaephili* has considerable potential for the control of *Oryzaephilus* spp. (Burges *et al.*, 1971).

OTHER COLEOPTERAN SPECIES

Other coleopteran species that occasionally infest stored groundnuts but rarely cause significant losses include *Tenebroides mauritanicus* (L.), *Lasioderma serricorne* (F.), *Latheticus oryzae* Waterhouse, *Cryptolestes* spp., *Alphitobius* spp., and *Carpophilus* spp. These minor pests are usually found in association with one or more of the major pests and appear to be successfully controlled by the same chemicals.

Lepidoptera

Defoliators, especially Lepidoptera, can cause such foliar damage that farmers apply insecticides because of concern about the appearance of the crop. We at ICRISAT believe that such injudicious use of insecticides has intensified pest problems. In 1980, Amin and Mohammad described the proliferation of insects, including Lepidoptera, that are rated as groundnut pests in India. The number of species, the intensity of attack and their geographical range have all increased.

In trying to work out how or why this happened, we have been led to consider changes in land management, particularly the introduction of irrigation schemes that have made possible the highly profitable cultivation of groundnut during the dry season. For instance, canals have been dug in northwestern India; the digging of wells and the purchase of pumps have been subsidized; and subsidized or free electricity has been made available to run the pumps in rural areas.

The agriculture, which was primarily dryland, has changed in some communities to continuous or relay-cropping of groundnut. One result is a build-up of lepidopteran insects, especially where cash surpluses have permitted the purchase of insecticides. A prime example is *Spodoptera litura*, which, 20 years ago, would not feed freely on groundnut but which has since become a major pest in key areas. Many successive generations have had access to groundnut crops so one presumes that local populations of the species have become adapted to this particular host. The start of the same process has recently been detected in our surveys of groundnut crops in coastal Andhra Pradesh, with *Helicoverpa* (= *Heliothis*) *armigera* being a potential new pest.

This is the background in which groundnut entomologists at ICRISAT centre have had to select the direction in which to orient their research, in the context of the needs of Asian groundnut growers (there are different problems in Africa). The main emphasis of the research is on two lepidopteran species — *S. litura* and *Aproaerema modicella*. It is not possible to give a full account of the results of the ICRISAT research because much is currently in progress.

ARCTIIDAE

Other lepidopteran species that damage groundnut include *Amsacta albistriga* (red hairy caterpillar) in southern India, *A. moorei* (hairy caterpillar) in northern and central India, and *Diacrisia obliqua* (Bihar hairy caterpillar) in northern India, Burma, China, and Bangladesh. Recently, Amin (1988) gave a full account of the hairy caterpillars. This group of Arctiidae are among the most feared insect pests, at least in India, because they can appear apparently from nowhere, just as crops are becoming established at the start of the rainy season. The moths eclose from the underground pupal cases within days of the first planting rains. Each female is capable of laying nearly 1000 eggs, usually in clusters. The 'hairy' larvae are cryptic, at least initially, so that farmers may not be aware that they have infested the field until it's too late to protect the crop. Fortuitously they usually have only one generation a year, and it lasts about 1 month in the tropical zone and a little longer in the north. This means farmers may be able to sow a second crop.

Amin indicated that egg parasites could be effective control agents. However, the sporadic and localized nature of the insects' appearance makes it difficult to carry out research on their control or to screen for host-plant resistance. If the diapause could be broken, screening with reared individuals would be possible and — if farmers expressed interest in obtaining cultivars with resistance — desirable.

GELECHIIDAE

The groundnut leafminer, *Aproaerema modicella*, is a serious pest of groundnut and soybean in South and Southeast Asia. It has been reported from India, Sri Lanka, Bangladesh, Burma, Thailand, Laos, Kampuchea, Vietnam, China, the Philippines, Indonesia and Malaysia (references in Mohammad, 1981; Islam *et al.*, 1983; Crowe, 1985).

In India, it has been called the most important pest of groundnuts (Amin, 1983). The literature on this pest was reviewed by Mohammad (1981), and we have relied heavily on that work for this text. By correspondence with the British Museum of Natural History, London, he made clear the synonymy of this species. *Anacampsis nerteria, Aproaerema nertaria, Stomopteryx nertaria, S. subsecivella,* and *Biloba subsecivella* are alternative names that have appeared in the literature this century, even quite recently.

Biology

Female moths deposit the small (ca 0.6 mm in diameter), white, oval eggs on the undersides of leaflets, often near the midrib but also on the petioles and stem. In experimental conditions they lay between 87 and 186 eggs, although one female laid as many as 473 (Cherian and Basheer, 1942; Gujrati *et al.*, 1973). Under field conditions typical of South Asia, eggs hatch in 3–4 days, but, at cooler temperatures, up to 8 days may be required (Kapadia *et al.*, 1982).

First-instar larvae are pale white or yellow with dark brown head capsules. The body may change to light green or brown in later instars. The feeding by early instars is discernible by the serpentine (sometimes blotch) mines. Later instars (third instar onwards) leave the mine. They then web together two halves of one leaflet or two or more leaflets to form a refuge from which they continue to consume epidermal and mesophyll tissue.

The number of larval instars is not clear: Kapadia *et al.* (1982) and Amin (1988) reported three, Gujrati *et al.* (1973) four, and Islam *et al.*

(1983) six. Research at ICRISAT, in which the head width of a cohort of larvae was checked daily, indicated that there are five instars with a Dyar's constant of 1.4 to 1.7.

The larval period lasts between 9 and 28 days in the field and is clearly dependent upon temperatures (Cherian and Basheer, 1942; Sandhu, 1978; Kapadia *et al.*, 1982). Pupation occurs within the webbed leaflets and lasts 3–10 days. This species appears sporadically, both within and between seasons.

Peak leafminer populations occur in Thailand in July and August (Campbell, 1983), although Mohammad (1981) reported that other researchers found heavy infestations during November and December, with only negligible numbers in March through July. The densest populations on groundnuts in Bangladesh are in March and April (Islam *et al.*, 1983). In India, peak leafminer populations occur at the end of the season following the rains — March–May (Amin and Mohammad, 1980). Leafminer populations can also build up in September and October, the end of the rainy season, especially in low-rainfall years (Amin, 1983). Seven generations on a single crop of soybean have been reported from China (Yang and Liu, 1966), although in India three or four generations are typical.

Conventional wisdom is that *A. modicella* is favoured by warm sunny days and that rainfall inhibits its proliferation. Wheatley *et al.* (1989) did not dispute the predilection for warm, sunny days but found no experimental evidence that rain slowed the build-up. They pointed to the possibility that chemical changes in the nutritional quality of the leaflets during drought stress favoured the development of the larvae.

All except one of the known host plants are legumes (Table 5.13). The exception is *Rhychosia minima* (Rubiaceae), a weed. Pigeon pea and alfalfa are two other crops, in addition to groundnut and soybean, that *A. modicella* attacks. Phisitkul (1985) attempted to rear groundnut leafminer on a variety of other plants — sunn hemp (*Crotalaria juncea*), winged bean (*Psophocarpus tetragonolobus*), yard-long bean (*Vigna sinensis* subsp. *sesquipedalis*), siratro (*Macroptilium atropureum*), hamata (*Crotalaria pallida*), and sword bean (*Canavalia gladiata*). The females oviposited on these plants at a much lower rate than on groundnut or soybean, and larvae were unable to complete their development. These findings indicated that the species has a limited host range among cultivated legumes: further research is needed to delimit the number of wild hosts.

Damage and Economic Importance

The groundnut leafminer larvae feed on leaves, thereby reducing the photosynthetic potential of the plant. At a certain population intensity, pod and haulm yields are reduced. As with other caterpillars, the older instars consume much more tissue than early ones. Islam *et al.* (1983) reported that a single larva will consume 175 cm^2 of leaf tissue, and, according to Jagtap *et al.* (1984), the groundnut leafminer and *A. craccivora*, together, were responsible for an average of 16 per cent loss in dry pod yield over 3 years, the loss being equivalent to 303 kg/ha. Reduction in the dry weight accumulation as a result of larval feeding also translates into reduced haulm yield. Significant increases have been observed when yields of insecticide-treated plants (plots) have been compared with those that received no insecticides (Sivasubramaniam and Palaniswamy, 1983; Rajput *et al.*, 1984, 1985). Using screen cages and artificial infestation, Tej Kumar and Devaraj Urs (1983) found that each additional per cent of infestation by the groundnut leafminer resulted in 1.2 per cent yield loss.

In Thailand, Sathorn Sirisingh and Manochai Keerati-Kasikorn (1986) provided complete insecticide protection from the groundnut leafminer and compared the results with those from other levels of protection. Yields of plants given a pre-sowing treatment of granules and five foliar sprays of monocrotophos were 1597 kg/ha compared with 747 kg/ha for unprotected controls. Among the controls, 660 leaflets/20 plants were damaged after 40 days. The plants that received just one application of monocrotophos 30 days after emergence gave 73 per cent of the yield of the full treatment.

Research at ICRISAT showed that the cultivar Robut 33-1 (Kadiri 3) can withstand considerable damage before exhibiting losses in yield (ICRISAT, 1986). This cultivar was grown under four insecticide regimens: dimethoate, at high and low rates; diflubenzuron; and dichlorvos were used (Table 5.14). The 'high' level of dimethoate far exceeded what was needed but represented what many farmers actually apply to their crops. The 'low' level of dimethoate was clearly adequate to protect the crop, and, in fact, as the heavy infestation of leafminer did not appear until pod filling, two sprays could have been dispensed with. There were low populations of *S. dorsalis* and *E. kerri* on the crop, but these were believed to have had little impact on yield. These data indicated that the economic threshold for this cultivar grown post rainy season for third generation only is between 30 and 70 larvae/plant. This is for plants that were close to harvest.

An exercise in simulation and dynamic programming by Dudley *et al.* (1989) indicated the degree of host-plant resistance given a range of parasitism levels. It also showed that if the pest attack became too severe, farmers would lose money if they harvested the crop.

Control

Most research on the groundnut leafminer has been directed at its control.

Table 5.13. Host plants of *Aproaerema modicella*, the groundnut leafminer

Host species	Reference
Arachis hypogaea	Maxwell-Lefroy and Howlett, 1909
Vigna radiata (= *Phaseolus aureus*)	Prasad *et al.*, 1971
Cajanus cajan	Bainbridge-Fletcher, 1914
Medicago sativa	Sandhu 1977, 1978
Psoralea corylifolia	Maxwell-Lefroy and Howlett, 1909
Inigofera hirsuta	Jai Rao and Thirumalachar, 1977
Vigna umbellata (= *Phaseolus calacaratus*)	·Jai Rao and Thirumalachar, 1977
Glycine soja	Vanhall, 1922 (in Mohammad, 1981)
Trifolium alexandrium	Thontadarya *et al.*, 1979
Teramnus labiolis	Das and Misra, 1984
Lablab purpureus	Das and Misra, 1984
Rhychosia minima	Srinivasan and Siva Rao, 1984
Boreria hispida	Srinivasan and Siva Rao, 1984

The goal of integrated pest management is to reduce the reliance on chemical control and instead emphasize cultural control, host-plant resistance and biological or natural control.

Chemical: Insecticides of all classes have been screened for activity against the groundnut leafminer. These chemicals have generally been applied to foliage, either as a liquid spray or as a dust, but some systemic insecticides have also been evaluated. Isofenphos applied as a granular formulation before sowing at 2 kg/ha in the furrow provided season-long protection from the groundnut leafminer on the ICRISAT farm.

Table 5.14. The effect of four insecticide regimens on the maximum number of groundnut leafminer larvae and groundnut yield (data are means of five replicates, 1984-85 post rainy season, ICRISAT farm)

Treatment[a]	Larvae (max./ plant)	Larval parasit- ism (%)[b]	Haulm yield (kg/ha)	Pod yield (kg/ha)
Dimethoate (8 × 400 g a.i./ha)	1.9	0	1880	1780
Dimethoate (3 × 200 g a.i./ha)	31.4	33.9	1640	1700
Diflubenzuron (3 × 250 g a.i./ha)	74.9	42.5	1420	1430
Dichlorvos (3 × 300 g a.i./ha)	67.9	50.0	1510	1580
Control (no spray)	85.0	61.0	1270	1150

[a] All insecticides in 350 L water/ha.
[b] One week before the crop was harvested.

No one has reported resistance among groundnut leafminers to any insecticide, although it is equally true that no tests have been reported despite the use of carbaryl and gamma-BHC (lindane) for more than 20 years and parathion for 10 years (Rajput et al., 1984; Ghule et al., 1987). Nearly all synthetic chemicals have proved effective in reducing populations of the pest or in increasing yields compared with unsprayed plots.

Host-plant resistance: The only cultivar in which host-plant resistance has been detected is M 13. However, resistance, including tolerance, to groundnut leafminer has been detected in several germ-plasm lines (ICRISAT, 1986), including spreading, Spanish bunch, and Valencia types. Resistance in soybean has been much less promising. In two trials that evaluated nearly 40 varieties, no differences in densities of groundnut leafminers were found (Mundhe, 1980; Shetgar and Thombre, 1984). Sathorn Sirisingh and Manochai Keerati-Kasikorn (1986) found that genotypes Colorado, Congo Red, M-gango, Tatu, and TMV 1 had high levels of resistance. A further 49 lines had moderate resistance.

Natural enemies and entomopathogens: Natural control by diseases, predators and parasitoids seems to play a large role in suppressing leafminer populations. At least three disease agents infect the larvae in India: nematodes, viruses and fungi (Oblasami et al., 1969; Kothai, 1974, in

Mohammad, 1981; Srinivasan and Siva Rao, 1986). The impact of these organisms on the population dynamics of groundnut leafminer has not been quantified, although they are often responsible for a high level of larval mortality.

The most important natural control agents are hymenopterous parasitoids, which have been studied in detail only in India. More than 30 parasitic Hymenoptera, including hyperparasites, have been reared from leafminer eggs, larvae and pupae. In southern India, nine parasitoid species are active during and after the rainy season, with parasitism highest from September to November and from February to March (Srinivasan and Siva Rao, 1986).

Eight parasitoid species have been recorded from northern India, six having been recovered in the rainy season (July–October) and four post rainy season (December–May). Two species were present in both seasons (Yadav *et al.*, 1987). Phisitkul (1985) reported two larval and two pupal parasitoids in northeast Thailand but at low levels. The parasitoids found on groundnut leafminer at ICRISAT centre included at least 10 species, some primary and some secondary. Preliminary results have indicated that early in the groundnut-growing season the parasitoid community is dominated by one or two species, with one usually accounting for more than 50 per cent of the total. Later, and especially at the end of the season, four or five species are present and no one species accounts for more than 35 per cent of the total.

Three states in India had evidence of peaks in parasitism up to 90 per cent (Khan and Raodeo, 1978; Srinivasan and Siva Rao, 1986; Yadav *et al.*, 1987). This high rate is in accord with our experience at ICRISAT. It supports our belief that farmers should use insecticides judiciously so that they do not interfere with the natural control of this species. ICRISAT data have demonstrated the influence of insecticides on the rate of parasitism (Table 5.14) and the potential for integrating natural control with insecticide application.

Cultural: We know virtually nothing about how cropping pattern and methods of cultivation influence the incidence of groundnut leafminer. The experiments that have been attempted at ICRISAT to help fill this void coincided with negligible leafminer populations.

However, an observation that has elicited interest is that leafminer populations were considerably lower on unweeded plots than on weed-free plots. This observation is being followed up, with studies on the levels of natural enemies in the weedy area. We have also observed that growing groundnut crops in a relay works against farmers. This practice is common where irrigation is available. In these circumstances, groundnut crops may overlap for up to 10 months of the year.

Although there is a chance that natural enemies will proliferate in such areas and exert natural control, farmers ofen interfere with this process by applying insecticides to kill groundnut leafminers or other species of insects at population levels well below the economic threshold. This results in flare-ups, exacerbated by the continuum of host pants made available to these insects by the cropping pattern.

Groundnut Leaf Webber

Groundnut leaf webber, *Anarsia ephippias*, is a gelechiid that causes concern to groundnut farmers in northern India (Bakhetia, 1976). It makes 'shot holes' in the leaves and webs the growing points. Every plant in a field on a university research farm in the Punjab was once found to be attacked. The life cycle lasts from 26 to 53 days.

A number of parasites, including a chalcid *Brachymeria* sp., attacked 24 per cent of the larvae in Bakhetia's study area. The caterpillars were killed by a range of insecticides, endrin and parathion being superior, although fenitrothion might be selected on grounds of safety.

Leaf Roller

Leaf roller, *Lamprosema abstitalis*, appears to have habits similar to *A. ephippias* but is found in north Thailand. It was part of a complex of Lepidoptera that was found in the experimental area of Schiller *et al.* (1982). The data indicated that, if insecticides were to be applied, best results were achieved in combinations with fungicides.

NOCTUIDAE

The tobacco cutworm or armyworm, *Spodoptera litura*, extends throughout Asia and Oceania, including New Zealand and Japan (to 45°S and N), but also Oman, Malagasy Republic, Mauritius and Colombia. It has 78 hosts of economic importance. Its range abuts that of *S. littoralis* 60° east of Greenwich (in Pakistan and Afghanistan). The genus has been and is known as *Prodenia* and the proximity of *S. litura* and *S. littoralis* may have led to references to *Prodenia 'littoralis'*.

Cotton leaf worm, *Spodoptera littoralis*, is found throughout Africa and the Middle East. It is usually a leaf eater of minor importance, but occasional flare-ups occur, for instance in Malawi in 1988. These may be associated with insecticide-caused outbreaks on other crops. This species shares many features with its Asian counterpart, including a pod-boring habit.

Biology

The female moth of *S. litura* lays batches of 200–1000 eggs in egg 'masses' on the leaflets, and she may lay 3–10 of them. She covers the eggs in silk webbing and her body scales, colouring the mass a golden bronze. Larvae hatch in about 3 days in the tropical zone. They are aggregated initially and then disperse, feeding largely by night and hiding at the base of the plant during the day. Fully grown larvae are 3–4 cm long.

The larvae have a greenish appearance but this can vary considerably. Key characteristics are the dark marks on the first abdominal segment and the light yellow line running the length of the body. Pupation takes place in the soil. The moths eclose after about 1 week. They may undergo a migratory flight before commencing oviposition. Flight activity is highest from dusk to about 2200 h. Their seasonal flight pattern is being monitored with pheromone traps, mainly in India but also in Burma, Nepal and Sri Lanka.

Information collected at ICRISAT centre has shown that, in the Hyderabad area, 12 peaks occur during the year, each one presumably indicating a new generation. This synchronization was not previously apparent. However, the monthly cycle is disrupted from February to May when activity of this species is greatest and overlapping of generations is apparent (Ranga Rao *et al.*, in preparation).

Damage

Spodoptera is primarily a defoliator. The first and second instars 'scratch' the leaf surface, a sign that more serious damage is to come. The older larvae strip the laminae from the leaflets. Under heavy population pressure, only the midribs remain. At this stage, the larvae leave the crop *en masse* to seek more food in neighbouring fields, hence the common name of armyworm. This species also takes on a pod-boring habit in the light soils of northern India. Presumably, when it seeks shelter during the day it is able to follow the pegs to the pods through the friable soil.

Several authors have judged the effect of defoliators on the yield of groundnut crops by ablation techniques (Enyi, 1975; Mercer, 1976; Santos and Sutton, 1983; Wilkerson *et al.*, 1984). We are not satisfied that this approach can simulate the effect of defoliating insects because it gives the plant an abrupt metabolic shock, especially in drought conditions. In contrast, defoliation by insects is gradual. We have, therefore, devised a method for working with *S. litura* at ICRISAT centre, releasing fourth-instar caterpillars into enclosures containing groundnut plants. During the final three instars, the larvae eat more than 95 per cent of their total consumption.

Table 5.15. Effect on pod yield of larvae of *Spodoptera litura* when introduced to a groundnut crop (TMV 2) at four densities and four growth stages at ICRISAT, 1986–87, post rainy season, and 1987, rainy season (data are means of five replicates)

Crop stage (days after emergence) Larvae (no./plant)	Post rainy season[a]		Rainy season[a]	
	Defoli- ation (%)	Yield loss (%)	Defoli- ation (%)	Yield loss (%)
Seedling (10)				
1	54 (47)	22 (22)	57 (49)	12 (14)
2	60 (51)	28 (29)	68 (56)	10 (12)
5	100 (90)	67 (56)	100 (90)	70 (57)
10	100 (90)	68 (56)	100 (90)	78 (62)
Flowering (30)				
1	40 (39)	18 (22)	15 (23)	9 (15)
2	46 (43)	18 (22)	53 (47)	11 (13)
5	72 (58)	49 (45)	65 (54)	11 (13)
10	88 (77)	61 (51)	72 (58)	11 (13)
Pegging (50)				
1	23 (29)	10 (12)	17 (25)	3 (6)
2	30 (33)	14 (18)	41 (40)	4 (7)
5	32 (34)	20 (21)	57 (49)	14 (16)
10	36 (36)	13 (14)	65 (54)	19 (26)
Pod formation (70)				
1	32 (34)	7 (9)	21 (27)	5 (8)
2	46 (42)	13 (14)	37 (37)	7 (9)
5	61 (52)	15 (18)	56 (49)	6 (9)
10	63 (52)	12 (16)	62 (52)	10 (18)
SE ±	(4)	(4)	(3)	(5)
CV (%)	15	35	12	5

[a] Data in parentheses are arc-sine transformations.

Although our research has not been completed, the effects of defoliation on yield are clearly seasonal, damage having a more serious effect in the postrainy season (December–April). The pattern is believed to occur because the plants are not able to outgrow the defoliation caused during the cool period (December–January) (Tables 5.15-5.17). The groundnut plant is clearly able to recover from complete defoliation at the seedling stage and from heavy defoliation later in development. A plant with 30 per cent defoliation looks doomed but can, in fact, recover. We have known farmers who spray insecticide on their crops when they find only one or two feeding notches on several plants.

Control

Chemical: If insecticides are to be applied for the control of this species on groundnut crops, they should be directed at the youngest larvae. At this stage, little or no defoliation would have occurred, and the small larvae can be killed with less insecticide (or at least lower concentrations) than can larger larvae. Farmers are often unsuccessful in their attempts to kill larvae that are approaching maximum size. Also, insecticides with a low environmental impact, such as diflurbenzuron, dichlorvos or lannate, would be sufficiently potent to kill small but not large larvae.

Our data, which, we stress, are subject to refinement, suggest that the most effective time for application is 6 days after 50 or more male moths are found in a pheromone trap for more than 3 nights or 2–3 days after crop inspection reveals more than three egg masses per metre of row.

Table 5.16. Yield losses in groundnuts when damage caused by *Spodoptera litura* occurs at different stages and for different periods in 1986–87, post rainy season, and 1987, rainy season. Fourth-instar larvae were introduced at a rate of two per plant to cultivar TMV 2 (means of five replicates)

Crop age when larvae introduced (days after emergence)	Post rainy season		Rainy season	
	Pod yield (g/plant)	Yield loss (%)[a]	Pod yield (g/plant)	Yield loss (%)[a]
10	9.7	28 (29)	4.8	10 (18)
30	10.7	18 (22)	5.0	11 (15)
50	11.3	14 (18)	5.6	4 (7)
70	12.7	13 (14)	5.2	7 (9)
10 + 30 + 50 + 70	6.5	50 (45)	2.3	56 (49)
30 + 50 + 70	11.6	16 (18)	5.0	10 (16)
50 + 70	15.0	2 (3)	5.7	3 (5)
No larvae (control)	13.4	–	5.4	–
SE ±	0.9	(4)	0.3	(5)
CV (%)	18	46	15	65

[a] Data in parentheses are arc-sine transformations.

Foliar sprays of many insecticides — endosulfan, carbaryl, fenvalerate, monocrotophos, etc. — have been recommended for the efficient control of *S. litura* (Ayyanna *et al.*, 1982) especially, if formulated with mineral oil (Onayama *et al.*, 1985). Neem preparations may also be effective as a larval growth retardant or as a moth repellent (Joshi and Sitaramaiah, 1979; Opender Koul, 1985). Difficulty in killing the large larvae still remains a major problem and may reflect deficiencies in the spray mixture or inefficient application.

However, reports of insecticide resistance in this species from both ends of Asia — China and India — serve as a warning. Ramakrishnan *et al.* (1984) found that larvae from Andhra Pradesh were resistant to malathion (5.7 fold), pyrethrum (14.7 fold), lindane (16.3 fold) and endosulfan (85.9 fold). The comparable data from China (Chou *et al.*, 1984) indicated variable levels of resistance, depending on location. The worst examples were resistance to fenvalerate (4.1 fold), permethrin 13.0 fold), mevinphos (63.0 fold) and carbofuran (79.0 fold). As this species spends the days at ground level, there is scope for attempting to control it with baits containing insecticides, but the results of such attempts are difficult to interpret.

Natural enemies: Spodoptera litura is found in many habitats, so it is not surprising that the literature abounds with references to natural control agents on a range of crops. G. V. Ranga Rao has listed, in an unpublished review, 118 species of parasites (including nematodes) and predators from Asia and the Pacific.

Among the egg parasites, *Trichogramma* spp. predominate, with reports by Chiu and Chiu in 1976 for China, Chu (1979) for Indonesia, Joshi *et al.* (1979) and Patel *et al.* (1971) for India. However, scientists and others who have attempted to induce natural control by mass-releasing egg parasites have not been particularly successful. The parasites are influenced by the host plant, and the whole operation seems to bear no relationship to the economics of pest control. Furthermore, there can be little to gain from exerting an extra control on a stage where natural mortality is already high.

Braune (1982) found that *Telenomus remus* achieved 54 per cent egg parasitism. He found an inverse relationship between egg mass size and per cent parasitism. The thickness of the mass was also important, most parasitism occurring among eggs on the top layer. Joshi *et al.* (1982) found that a 2 per cent neem extract did not repel *T. remus* when applied to the eggs. This points to the possibility of an integrated control scheme based on neem and egg parasites.

Larval and pupal parasites are more diverse and numerous than the egg parasites, especially among the braconids (54 per cent of the species), mainly *Apanteles* spp. and *Bracon* spp. The rest are tachinid flies (14 per cent) such as *Paribaea orbata*, ichneumonids (14 per cent), plus relatively few eulopids, chalcids, scelionids, encyrtids and muscids (Battu, 1977; Zaz and Kushwaha, 1983; Jayanth and Nagarkatti, 1984; Michael *et al.*, 1984; Rao and Satyanarayana, 1984; Jalali *et al.*, 1987; Sathe, 1987). The pupal stage seems to be relatively unaffected by parasites, perhaps because it is usually underground. The reports available do not indicate that the levels of larval parasitism are ever very high: they never approach those encountered with other lepidopteran species such as *A. modicella*. The nocturnal habits of *S. litura* may be involved.

Table 5.17. Effect of defoliation by *Spodoptera litura* on yield of six groundnut genotypes. Fourth-instar larvae were introduced in 1986–87, post rainy season, and 1987, rainy season (means of five replicates)

Crop stage (days after emergence) and genotype	Post rainy season[a]		Rainy season[b]	
	Defoli-ation (%)	Pod yield (g/plant)	Defoli-ation (%)	Pod yield (g/plant)
Seedling (10)				
ICGV 86031	86 (71)	10.0	100 (90)	4.5
ICG 5240	61 (52)	8.4	100 (90)	10.5
ICGV 86030	87 (74)	5.8	100 (90)	4.6
ICGV 86535	83 (75)	10.2	100 (90)	3.9
ICG 156	100 (90)	6.1	100 (90)	4.7
ICG 221	100 (90)	4.4	100 (90)	1.7
Flowering (30)				
ICGV 86031	58 (50)	11.7	45 (42)	9.2
ICG 5240	70 (57)	8.3	54 (47)	10.0
ICGV 86030	59 (51)	6.4	58 (50)	12.4
ICGV 86535	68 (55)	11.7	47 (43)	9.2
ICG 156	75 (61)	13.3	44 (41)	10.0
ICG 221	91 (76)	7.9	50 (45)	4.0
Pegging (50)				
ICGV 86031	37 (37)	15.0	64 (53)	10.8
ICG 5240	44 (41)	6.9	67 (55)	13.3
ICGV 86030	47 (44)	7.2	68 (56)	11.6
ICGV 86535	54 (48)	10.4	64 (53)	10.9
ICG 156	41 (39)	13.1	60 (51)	10.2
ICG 221	50 (45)	10.0	69 (56)	5.3
Pod filling (70)				
ICGV 86031	22 (30)	18.8	35 (36)	10.8
ICG 5240	11 (16)	14.5	24 (29)	12.0
ICGV 86030	14 (17)	12.2	36 (37)	12.3

Crop stage (days after emergence) and genotype	Post rainy season[a]		Rainy season[b]	
	Defoliation (%)	Pod yield (g/plant)	Defoliation (%)	Pod yield (g/plant)
ICGV 86535	12 (17)	12.8	26 (25)	9.6
ICG 156	28 (31)	17.1	38 (38)	12.5
ICG 221	18 (25)	12.8	39 (39)	5.4
Insect-free controls				
ICGV 86031	–	18.3	– 11.4	
ICG 5240	–	14.5	– 14.7	
ICGV 86030	–	11.1	– 11.1	
ICGV 86535	–	12.5	– 12.0	
ICG 156	–	17.9	– 10.4	
ICG 221	–	13.7	– 5.4	
SE ±	(7.3)	1.3	(4.0) 1.1	
CV (%)	(26.6)	19.4	(12.7)20.6	

[a] ICGV 86031 = GBPRS 312, ICG 5240 = EC 36892, ICG 86030 = GBPRS 66, ICGV 86535 = GBPRS 15, ICG 156 = M 13, and ICG 221 = TMV 2.
[b] Data in parentheses are arc-sine transformations.

Leaf damage caused by *S. litura* is rarely severe at ICRISAT centre, but we consistently have noted that damage is increased in areas where insecticides have been applied (Wightman and Amin, 1988). We have also found considerably less damage caused by *Spodoptera* sp. and other defoliators in farmers' fields where insecticides have not been applied.

Arthropod predators of *S. litura* abound. They include reduviids (Sitaramaiah *et al.*, 1975), pentatomids (Kapoor *et al.*, 1975; Pawar, 1976), predatory wasps (Nakasuji *et al.*, 1976), carabids and staphylinids (Chu, 1979). There are also some reports of spiders attacking *S. litura* (Kapoor *et al.*, 1975). Birds, such as cattle egrets, eat the larvae, and bats, frogs (J.A.W., personal observation), lizards (Bhanotar and Srivastava, 1985) are vertebrates that consume the moths. There appears to be no quantitative information about the role or efficiency of various natural enemies on the control of this species.

Noctuids appear to be susceptible to many diseases especially the cytoplasmic and nuclear polyhedrosis viruses (Asayama and Osaki, 1970). Although this has been known to be true for *S. litura* for some time, scientists in the national agricultural research services of the semi-arid tropics have not exploited the knowledge. The one exception was by Krishnaiah *et al.* (1985) who used two sprays of a virus suspension to kill *S. litura* on black gram in Andhra Pradesh. We hope that this kind of information will extend to other crops and that farmers will initiate such practices for themselves.

Bhatnagar *et al.* (1985) found that *S. litura* is parasitized by mermithid nematodes. In addition, they showed that the rate of parasitism was higher on black soils than on red soils. Kondo and Ishibashi (1984) provided information about the parasitism of this pest by *Steinernema* sp. in Japan. A number of bacteria and fungi, e.g. *Beauveria bassiana* and *Serratia marcescens*, attack *S. litura* larvae in nature (Zaz and Kushwaha 1983; Ansari *et al.*, 1987). However, this does not seem to have much applied significance.

Host-plant resistance: We do not know of many genotypes with resistance to *S. litura*, but our experiments have revealed that it exists at levels that can be exploited. Under laboratory conditions, more than half (56 per cent) *S. litura* died during the first instar when fed on ICGV 86031 (= GBPRS 312), whereas mortality on ICG 221 was only 12 per cent. The percentage of adults emerging from larvae fed on ICGV 86031 was 29, compared with 46 for those fed on ICG 221. Clearly, ICGV 86031 has resistance to the first-instar larvae and is tolerant to *Spodoptera* sp. attack in farmers' fields, although the efficacy can be influenced by the season (Table 5.17). The aphid-resistant genotype EC 36892 may also be resistant to *S. litura* (Table 5.17).

Cultural: Farmers sow castor plants in their groundnut fields to attract *Spodoptera* moths because they lay eggs preferentially on the leaves of the trap crop where they and the larvae are easy to find and destroy. Farmers in coastal Andhra Pradesh dig ditches around their fields to trap migrating larvae. The effects of such practices are not known.

Helicoverpa armigera

Helicoverpa (= *Heliothis*) *armigera* is found on all tropical and sub-tropical land masses, except the Americas, where other members of the genus cause problems. It has many common names including boll worm, pod borer, and gram borer — a reflection of its many hosts. It feeds primarily on flowers and fruits of the host but is known to eat groundnut foliage, causing signs of damage that are indistinguishable from those of *Spodoptera*.

In the cotton-growing areas of Andhra Pradesh, which are close to major groundnut-growing districts, pesticides have figured heavily in crop management (one could say 'pest mismanagement') in recent years and have led to insecticide-resistant *Helicoverpa* and severe crop losses caused by the pest. A spill-over to groundnut appears to be a result. J.A.W. observed this species on groundnut foliage in Botswana and Tanzania but only where insecticides had been applied. Jepson (1948) observed that groundnut is most likely to be attacked by this species when maize is included in the rotation.

Cut Worms

Cut worms, *Agrotis* sp., are found mainly in African groundnut fields around the bases of the plants, especially in districts where *Phaseolus* beans are grown. They feed at ground level and damage the crown and lower stems. The feeding itself probably causes little yield loss but affords an entry for fungal diseases and *Odontotermes* spp.

PYRALIDAE

The species of Lepidoptera that commonly infest stored groundnuts belong to the family Pyralidae and all have similar life cycles. The adult moths do not feed so they live for only 1–2 weeks. Females lay their eggs in cracks or grooves in the surface of groundnut pods or kernels.

The larvae either feed on the seed surface or tunnel into the cotyledons. They move freely through the groundnuts, contaminating them with a tough, silken fibre that eventually binds together kernels, frass and exuviae. This type of contamination is easily distinguishable from the fine dust that results from beetle infestation and may be economically more important than the weight loss caused by larval feeding.

Often the larvae leave the groundnuts to find pupation sites in the storage structures or in the sacking. The adult moths emerge, disperse throughout a store before mating on the surface of the stored product. Oviposition occurs chiefly in the surface layers of a bag or bulk of groundnuts. Thus, even though the larvae are mobile, heavy infestations are generally concentrated within the top 10–20 cm of a bulk store or the outside layers of a stack (TDRI, 1984).

The rice moth, *Corcyra cephalonica* (Stainton) Pyralidae (Gallariinae), has the ability to develop at low humidities (<20 per cent) and is more prevalent than the other stored-product caterpillars in the semi-arid tropics (Hodges, 1979). The adults are pale brown and 12–15 mm long when at rest. Females have long labial palps that point directly forward, whereas males have short inconspicuous palps.

Generally, the larvae are white except for the head capsule and prothoracic tergite, which are brown. On abdominal segments 3–6 and 10, there are well-developed pro-legs. The larval spiracles are characteristically thickened on their posterior rim. The setae arise from clear areas of cuticle surrounded by a dark ring. At 28°C and 70 per cent RH, the life cycle from egg to adult takes 40–50 days. Male moths emerge, on average, 1–2 days before females.

Like other lepidopteran species, *C. cephalonica* is generally regarded as a secondary pest of in-shell groundnuts, unable to penetrate sound pods (Table 5.18). However, in laboratory studies, larvae hatching from eggs laid on apparently sound pods penetrated the shell to feed on the kernels and chewed their way out of the pod once the food supply was exhausted (K. M. Dick, personal observation).

The tropical warehouse moth or almond moth — *Ephestia cautella* — is a pest of many stored commodities and is common throughout the tropics and sub-tropics. Its life cycle is similar to that of *C. cephalonica*.

The adults are 6–9 mm long at rest and greyish-brown, with an indistinct pattern on the forewings. The labial palps in both the male and the female point upwards. The larvae can be distinguished from those of *C. cephalonica* both by the spiracles, the rims of which are evenly thickened, and by the setae, which arise from dark brown spots on the cuticle. At 28°C and 70 per cent RH, the life cycle takes 40–50 days. Although this species is regarded as a secondary pest of in-shell groundnuts, populations increasing by a factor of 37 per cent monthly have been recorded in a warehouse containing groundnut pods (Hagstrum and Stanley, 1979).

The Indian meal moth, *Plodia interpunctella* (Hübner) Pyralidae (Phycitinae), seems to be most prevalent in cool areas of the tropics, e.g., highland regions. Its habits and life history are similar to that of the moth species already described. The adults are 8–12 mm long when at rest and are easily recognized by the markings on their forewings: the basal third is cream-coloured while the rest is reddish-brown. The labial palps point directly forward. The larvae are pale yellow and can be distinguished from those of other stored-product Pyralidae by the absence of any pigmentation at the base of the setae.

Under adverse conditions, e.g., extreme temperatures or high population densities, the life cycle of *P. interpunctella* may be prolonged by a larval diapause. During diapause, normal applications of insecticides, including fumigants, may prove ineffective.

Monitoring Infestation Levels

Although it is the larvae of lepidopteran pests that damage groundnuts, monitoring trap catches of adult moths is the most effective way of detecting low-density infestation. Pheromone traps now provide a cheap and simple alternative to light traps or suction traps for flying insects and have greatly increased the feasibility of monitoring moth populations in tropical stores. The sex pheromones released by all female Phycitinae have a chemical component that will attract males of *P. interpunctella* and *Ephestia* spp.

At least two designs — a funnel trap and a delta-shaped sticky trap — are commercially available for monitoring *P. interpunctella* and *E. cautella*. The addition of specific synergists increases the attractiveness of the pheromone to individual species while reducing its attractiveness to other Phycitinae. In *C. cephalonica*, both male and female moths release a pheromone (Singh and Sidhu, 1976); however, chemical communication between sexes appears to be less important in this species than in phycitine species.

Spangler (1987) has shown that, like other galleriine moths, male *C. cephalonica* produce ultrasonic pulses that affect the behaviour of both males and females. This ultrasonic communication may be more influential than pheromone emission and may thus prevent development of a trap based on pheromones for *Corcyra* sp.

Control

Insecticides: When groundnut stocks are stored immediately after drying, they probably have not yet been infested by pyralid moths. Infestation is a result of the movement of moths from infested stocks or crop residues to newly harvested material. To prevent this from occurring, one should treat stores the same way as for pests of in-shell groundnuts. Empty stores that can be made relatively gastight can be treated with dichlorvos, either in aerosol form (requires the use of an aerosol generator) or impregnated in strips of PVC. The latter act as slow-release dispensers and provide a cheap and convenient method of controlling moth populations in stores. Hung up in stores at a rate of 1 strip/30 m^3, these strips should control adult-moth populations for 12−14 weeks (Redlinger and Davis, 1982).

The possibility of replacing conventional insecticide applications with methoprene, an insect-growth regulator, has been examined in warehouse trials in the southern USA (Vick *et al.*, 1985). Used as a bulk treatment on in-shell groundnuts, methoprene reduced numbers of F_1 adult *E. cautella* to <10 per cent of those in an untreated control. However, it disrupts nothemal metamorphosis from the larvae to the pupae so did not eliminate damage to kernels by larval feeding (reduced a maximum of only 60 per cent). Nevertheless, the authors concluded that if methoprene were applied to uninfested stocks at the beginning of storage, it would prove a satisfactory alternative to conventional insecticides.

Fumigation of individual stacks within a warehouse is unlikely to eradicate the pest because adult moths resting on the walls of the storage structure will escape exposure to the fumigant and rapidly reinfest the stacks. If the structure can be made airtight, whole-store fumigation will be effective.

Natural enemies and entomopathogens: Parasitic wasps are common natural enemies of the moths throughout the tropics (Myers, 1929: Ayyar, 1934; Risbec, 1950; Rawnsley, 1959). Under optimum conditions, populations of parasites, such as *Bracon hebetor* Say, increase faster than their moth hosts — generation time is only half that of the host (Hagstrum, 1984), and several parasites can develop within a single host larva (Keever *et al.*, 1985). However, a rapid increase in parasite numbers is unlikely to occur without large numbers of unparasitized moth larvae.

If parasitic wasps were to control moth pests, their numbers would have to be augmented before large numbers of larval hosts become available. A number of laboratory and warehouse tests have been carried out to investigate the potential of this approach (Arbogast, 1984), and in laboratory cultures of *P. interpunctella*, a single introduction of *B. hebetor* reduced emergence of F_1 adults by 74 per cent (Press *et al.*, 1974). Semi-weekly releases of *B. hebetor* into a warehouse containing simulated crop debris infested with *E. cautella* resulted in more than 90 per cent reduction in emergence of adult moths, compared with predator-free, control populations (Press *et al.*, 1982).

Keever *et al.* (1986) augmented natural populations of *B. hebetor* and the predatory anthocorid bug *Xylocoris flavipes* in bulk stores of groundnuts, releasing the natural enemies from culture jars immediately after the warehouse was filled and every 2 weeks thereafter. Although the effect of the individual species could not be determined, the two together controlled moth populations better than conventional bulk treatment with malathion.

The ability of *X. flavipes* to survive on residual pest populations has also been demonstrated (LeCato *et al.*, 1977): the release of 30 pairs prevented increases for 14 weeks in a warehouse where populations of *E. cautella* were breeding on small quantities of culture medium left to simulate debris from the previous crop. In contrast, a predator-free moth population increased by a factor of 100 during the same period.

Although releases of parasites, such as *B. hebetor* and *X. flavipes*, suppress the numbers of adult moths in the F_1 generation, enough active larvae may survive to cause unacceptable damage to the kernels. A study on bulk, in-shell groundnuts indicated that populations of *E. cautella* and *P. interpunctella* adults were suppressed naturally by *B. hebetor* after 1–2 months. By this time, however, 10–12 per cent of the kernels had been damaged by moth larvae (Keever *et al.*, 1985).

One way that kernel damage could be reduced while larval parasites are establishing control is to release larval and egg parasites simultaneously. Brower (1984) demonstrated the potential use of egg parasites of the genus *Trichogramma* as biological control agents in groundnut stores. At monthly intervals, 200 eggs of *E. cautella* and *P. interpunctella* were released into a number of identical stores containing 200 kg of in-shell groundnuts. Simultaneously, moth eggs parasitized by *T. pretiosum* were placed in the stores, the number of eggs and the timing of the releases varying for different stores. Successful suppression of both moth species was obtained for up to

4 months, with release rates of 1000 parasitized eggs, three times each week.

Another natural enemy of phycitine moths in tropical stores is the mesostigmatan mite *Blattisocius tarsalis*. Both laboratory and warehouse studies have shown that in specific circumstances, *B. tarsalis* can control populations of *E. cautella* (Graham, 1970; Haines, 1981). Stored-product moths can be suppressed also by naturally occurring epizootics of *Bacillus thuringiensis* Berliner (Hagstrum and Sharp, 1975), and, currently, both dust and wettable powder formulations of *B. thuringiensis* can be obtained commercially (McGauhey, 1982). The bacillus provides effective control of *E. cautella* and *P. interpunctella* when applied either to the bulk store or to the surface layers of groundnuts; it persists under storage conditions, without a noticeable decrease in insecticidal activity, for at least a year (Arbogast, 1984).

At present, no viral formulations have been registered for use on stored groundnuts, because granulosis viruses (GV) such as *Plodia* GV are effective in controlling only single species of moth populations (Hunter *et al.*, 1973a) and, hence, are not alternatives to conventional insecticides. Nuclear polyhedrosis viruses isolated from *E. cautella* may prove more commercially exploitable as they have been shown to be almost as toxic to *P. interpunctella* (Hunter *et al.*, 1973b) as to *E. cautella*.

Host-plant resistance: Few studies have explored whether genotypes of groundnut vary in their susceptibility to attack by stored-product moths. Mbata (1987) carried out a number of experiments with *P. interpunctella* and newly released groundnut varieties in Nigeria. Adult females, given a choice of kernels of different varieties, showed significant oviposition preferences for certain of them.

Significant genotypic variation was also shown to exist in the developmental period from egg-hatch to adult emergence and the percentage survival to adult emergence of first-instar larvae. These differences were not related to the size or colour of the kernels. There was considerable variation in genotype responses in an experiment carried out at ICRISAT centre (Table 5.18) with a wide range of advanced breeding material, germ plasm and cultivars.

Similar results emerged in experimental studies of the susceptibility of selected Indian groundnut varieties to attack by *E. cautella* (Pandey *et al.*, 1977). In both studies, broken kernels were more susceptible to infestation than were whole kernels of the same variety. This indicates that the testa itself provides some measure of protection against first-instar larvae. Variability in characteristics of the testa may make some genotypes significantly more resistant to attack, although this possibility could be confirmed only by large-scale screening.

Table 5.18. The survival of late larval and pupal *Corcyra cephalonica* after one generation on the kernels of advanced groundnut breeding lines (ICGV), genotypes and cultivars (50 eggs were introduced to 50 g of kernels; data are the means of 20 replicates of each genotype)

Genotype	F$_1$ larvae and pupae (% survival)	Weight loss (g)
TMV 2	6.1	5.4
JL 24	6.6	7.2
ICGV 86056	10.3	7.4
M 13	17.9	11.9
ICGV 86015	16.0	12.4
ICGV 86014	24.7	13.0
ICGV (FDRS) 43	20.1	13.2
NCAc 343	23.0	13.9
ICG (FDRS) 10	20.3	14.9
ICGV 86042	20.8	15.2
ICGV 86016	26.7	17.0
2133	22.6	17.4
ICGV 86055	31.2	18.8
ICGV 5	30.6	18.8
ICGS 11	38.8	21.6
Robut 33-1	42.2	22.6
ICGS 44	39.4	22.8
ICGS 1	42.4	25.0
ICGV 86127	47.2	26.8
ICGV 86124	48.4	29.7
NCAc 17090	48.2	31.3
ICG (FDRS) 4	53.4	31.4
SE ±	6.8	3.3

Diplopoda

MILLEPEDES

Millepedes join the other key members of the soil fauna — white grubs and termites — as being among the most problematic and serious groundnut pests. As they are pod borers, their activity can lead to the invasion of the pod by soil fungi, including *Aspergillus flavus*, the source of aflatoxin.

The species that can be encountered in groundnut fields in West Africa — mainly Senegal — are (Demange, 1975):

- Stemmiuloidea: *Diopsiulus*
- Spirostreptoidea (= 'Iules'): *Graphidostreptus tumuliporus, Urotropis perpunctata, Peridontopyge conanci, Peridontopyge pervittata, Peridontopyge rubescens, Peridontopyge spinosissima, Peridontopyge trauni, Haplothysanus chapellei, Syndesmogenus mimeuri*
- Polydesmoidea: *Streptogonopus aethiopicus, Habrodesmus duboscqui, Sphenodesmus occidentalis.*

The iuliform species are cylindrical in section and can be 30 cm or so long and include the pest species. The polydesmids have a flattened section and are not groundnut pests, but their presence can lead to concern.

Distribution

A survey of the literature leads to the conclusion that millepedes are a West African problem. However, millepedes also contribute to pod loss in Southern Africa. Soil samples taken during J.A.W.'s survey showed that in some areas (central Malawi and east Zambia — especially in the silty soils of the Luangwa valley) there were more than 20 millepedes/100 plants. They appeared to be causing 5–10 per cent pod loss across Southern Africa as a whole.

Biology

This account is based on Demange (1975) and Gillon and Gillon (1979a,b). Millepedes avoid light and desiccation. This means that they live in the soil, in termitaria or under litter during the day. The nature of the shelter sought is somewhat species specific. For instance, *G. tumuliporus* aggregates at the bases of trees and in termite mounds but is not found in the open field. *Peridontopyge spinosissima* is most likely to be found under trees, and *P. rubescens* and *S. mimeuri* are rarely found in termitaria. However, these generalizations are subject to seasonal variation, as most species, *G. tumuliporus* being the exception, spend the dry season in the soil of the open field.

In a study by Gillon and Gillon (1979a), carried out in a groundnut-based system near Darou, Sine-Saloum, *P. rubescens* and *S. mimeuri* were the dominant species, the former accounting for one-third of the numbers and the biomass of millepedes. A finding by these authors (1979b) was that aestivation activity was essential in future population studies of this taxon. During the rainy season (July–October), most millepedes were in the top 10 cm of soil, but during the dry season, most were 23–30 cm deep and some as deep as 70 cm.

Another characteristic of millepedes is that they aggregate and migrate en masse over night. This means that a study of the relations between population density and pod damage would need to be on an extensive scale.

Damage and Economic Importance

Millepedes attack the pods from the time they are a swelling on the tip of the peg until the shell begins to harden. It is likely that their importance has been underestimated. Even though they only make a characteristic neat, round hole in the pod this results in the rapid decay of the pod and peg that will have disappeared by harvest. Their affinity for the soft pods probably is associated with Demange's (1975) observation that millepedes constantly seek a source of moisture. Groundnut pods provide water as well as a diet with a high nutrient content.

There are relatively few accounts of the degree of pod damage. Demange (1975) found that in northeast Nigeria damage by *Peridontopyge* sp. was localized and severe but was about 10 per cent over all. This may not sound like much, but at that time Nigeria ranked high among groundnut producers, at a national production of 600 000 t, and most of it came from this region.

A more recent groundnut pest-monitoring exercise in Bengou, Niger, showed that the millepede population built up when the pods started to form in mid-July. It 'increased dramatically' until the pods hardened when it declined leaving 39 per cent of the pods damaged. Millepedes were considered to be the most important biotic constraint to production (ICRISAT, 1988).

Control

Insecticides: There is no known method of controlling millepedes with pesticides (Wightman and Amin, 1988), although Appert (1966) found that fungicides repelled them.

In field tests of insecticides carried out in Malawi, J.A.W. found not even a suggestion that insecticides, such as dieldrin, chlorpyriphos and carbofuran, reduced millepedes. Plots treated with phorate had 2.5 times the millepedes found on control plots.

We do not know the reasons, but we can see several possibilities:

- Millepedes are not susceptible to insecticides because they are not insects; we could find no account of toxicologic effects of insecticides on millepedes in laboratory conditions.

- Large millepedes have to ingest or absorb a relatively large amount of insecticide to die compared with the amount that would kill the first instar of white grubs.
- They have a thick (calcified?) carapace that may protect them from absorption during contact with insecticides.
- Their mobility and their propensity to migrate suggests that the individuals in field is constantly changing and dead millepedes are being constantly replaced.

Several questions need to be answered about the possible use of toxins for controlling millepedes. If suitable toxins were identified and formulated for application prophylactically in 'hot spots', would they be made available by government agencies? Could farmers afford them? What would be their impact on the soil fauna such as predatory ants that keep termites and white grubs under some kind of control?

Natural enemies: Demange (1975) found that millepedes have a number of parasitic nematodes, protozoa and bacteria in their gut but gave not indication of their pathogenicity. he also pointed to the existence of parasitic flies and reduviid bugs that attack millepedes but, again, no specifics. Millepedes are able to defend themselves from attack with the secretions of their repugnatorial glands.

Host-plant resistance: No sources of host-plant resistance to millepedes have been identified.

Future Strategies for Control

To recommend suitable strategies for control of groundnut pests in the field, one would need to know more about the pests. The results of J.A.W.'s survey in Southern Africa indicate the depths of ignorance on this subject. Of the 40 or more white grub species collected, most had not been previously described as larvae. This collection was made from about 100 sites, mainly in Malawi, Zambia and Zimbabwe. The implication is that further surveys will turn up even more unknown species.

We believe similar surveys should be carried out in other parts of Africa and in most of Asia. We suggest that surveys concentrate on soil insects in Africa where defoliators are not a problem and on the whole fauna in Asia where both defoliators and soil insects reportedly cause losses. An exercise like this, though large, would define the nature, intensity and distribution of the problems we face. It should be regarded as a first step in an IPM programme.

We do not even know whether the soil insects have always been a problem but have been unheralded until recently because no one has looked for them. The problem may have been induced by the change to systems of permanent agriculture. J.A.W. had the impression that fewer insects were in soils that had been in fallow or that had been uncovered by shifting agriculture than were in soils cropped in a long-term rotation system. This impression should be tested because it implies that the cropping system induced the problem.

We know that white grubs, wire-worms and termites are pests of not only groundnuts but maize. We don't know whether some crop combinations of fallowing would reduce the prevalence of the pests.

We have reported resistance to termite scarification, but perhaps other sources of resistance — such as antibiotic substances in the roots — exist in some genotypes. We believe the wild *Arachis* species are a good place to begin a search because they have high levels of resistance to other pests. Also, the marked differences in the response of storage pests to the lines tested at ICRISAT indicate resistance that has yet to be exploited in the pods and seeds of *A. hypogaea*.

In Asia, the overuse of insecticides must be addressed. Researchers must establish the thresholds at which defoliators cause yield losses to groundnut crops and then ensure that colleagues in the extension service understand the implications. They — we — must also collect and collate data about insecticide resistance among groundnut pests in the field and in storage.

Groundnuts are a valuable cash crop, and insecticides are widely used to prevent losses during storage, particularly when stocks are intended for the confectionary trade. As a result, in many parts of West Africa, resistance to commonly used insecticides had developed more than 10 years ago (Deuse and Pointel, 1975; Gillier and Bockelee-Morvan, 1979). The development stimulated interest in alternative methods of protecting stored groundnuts, particularly in the southern USA, where insecticide use is most intense and the problem is most serious (Zettler, 1982).

A cheap and effective refuge trap, containing an oil-based food attractant, is commercially available for monitoring the three main beetle pests of shelled groundnuts (Barak and Burkholder, 1985). The efficiency and selectivity of this trap can be increased by the addition of genus-specific pheromone lures. A male-produced aggregation pheromone, which attracts *Tribolium* adults of both sexes, and a female-produced sex pheromone, which attracts adult male *Trogoderma* sp., are both commercially available (Chambers, 1987). An aggregation pheromone has been isolated in the genus *Oryzaephilus* but is not yet available for use in traps (Pierce *et al.*, 1984).

A number of studies have attempted to optimize pheromone application in the protection of stored groundnuts, e.g., by mass trapping (Reichmuth *et al.*, 1976) or by disrupting reproductive behaviour with pheromone-saturated air (Brady *et al.*, 1975; Sower and Whitmer, 1977). Recent research has

Plate I. Empoasca *sp. damage (photo ICRISAT)*

Plate II. Empoasca *sp. resistant and susceptible varieties
(photo ICRISAT)*

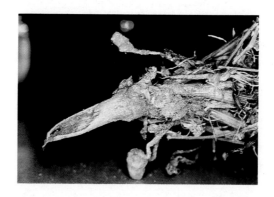

Plate III. Microtermes *damage (photo ICRISAT)*

Plate IV. Microtermes *damage over a large field (photo ICRISAT)*

Plate V. Spodoptera litura *larvae (photo ICRISAT)*

Plate VI. Spodoptera litura *resistant and susceptible varieties
(photo ICRISAT)*

Plate VII. Caryedon serratus *damage (photo ICRISAT)*

focused on the integration of pheromones with other methods of control. Pheromones can be used to lure insects to a pathogen such as the protozoan *Mattesia trogodermae*, which attacks populations of *Trogoderma glabrum* (Shapas *et al.*, 1977), and granulosis virus, which is effective against populations of *P. interpunctella* (Kellen and Hoffman, 1987). In both these cases, adult males, attracted to a pheromone source, became infected and subsequently spread the disease to females. The larvae of the F_1 generation became infected by consuming the cadavers of diseased adults. This system may be cheaper than spraying pathogens directly on to groundnut stocks but may require the use of more than one pheromone/pathogen source to control the range of species likely to be present.

Some studies have examined the compatibility of biological control agents with conventional control techniques. Most of the natural enemies of stored-product moths are susceptible to conventional insecticides (Haines, 1984). However, insecticides vary in their toxicity to parasitic Hymenoptera. Less toxic insecticides, such as permethrin, can be used without a reduction in effective control of moth larvae (Press *et al.*, 1981).

The timing of insecticidal applications is important. The toxic effect of insecticides on *Trichogramma*-parasitized eggs of *E. cephalonica* decreases with the increasing age of the eggs (Varma and Singh, 1987). First-instar larvae of *C. cephalonica* are more susceptible to malathion and pirimiphos-methyl than *B. hebetor*, but later instars are less susceptible than the wasps (Witethom, 1980). Thus, with the use of selective insecticides and the careful timing of applications, the adverse effects on natural enemies can be minimized. Similarly, insect pathogens may be used with conventional insecticides. For example, phosphine fumigations can be carried out without impairing the activity of *Plodia granulosis* virus (PGV) or *B. thuringiensis* (McGauhey, 1975). Hunter *et al.* (1975) have shown that bulk treatment with PGV and malathion provided better control of *P. interpunctella* in an almond nut warehouse than did either treatment alone.

Controlling or modifying the atmosphere in groundnut stores has been examined in both laboratory and warehouse trials. For instance, a nitrogen-compensated vacuum prevented insect infestation of groundnut kernels held as emergency seed supplies during 18 months of storage in Senegal (Rouzière, 1986). Gas mixtures containing 30–80 per cent carbon dioxide and 20 per cent oxygen, with any balance as nitrogen or air, are lethal to eggs of *E. cautella* exposed for 48 h, at 25°C (Bell, 1984). The admixture of carbon dioxide with phosphine or methyl bromide also increases the speed and efficiency of fumigations against *Tribolium* spp. and *Trogoderma* spp. (Desmarchelier and Wohlgemuth, 1984). Although controlled-atmosphere storage seems to offer a highly effective method of insect control, its use in the tropics would probably be limited by the need for bottled gases.

Much of the work on the integration of biological, physical and chemical control of groundnut pests has been carried out in the USA. Those strategies shown to provide acceptable levels of control should now be tested in tropical stores in areas such as West Africa where alternatives to conventional insecticides are most urgently required.

Insect Pests of Food Legumes
Edited by S. R. Singh
©1990 John Wiley & Sons Ltd.

6

Vectors of Virus and Mycoplasma Diseases: An Overview

G. Thottappilly[a], H. W. Rossel[a], D. V. R. Reddy[b], F. J. Morales[c], S. K. Green[d] and K. M. Makkouk[e]

[a]*International Institute of Tropical Agriculture (IITA), Ibadan, Nigeria*
[b]*International Crops Research Institute for the Semi-Arid Tropics (ICRISAT), Patancheru, Andhra Pradesh, India*
[c]*Centro Internacional de Agricultura Tropical (CIAT), Cali, Colombia*
[d]*Asian Vegetable Research and Development Center (AVRDC), Shanhua, Tainan, Taiwan*
[e]*International Center for Agricultural Research in the Dry Areas (ICARDA), Aleppo, Syria*

Among the numerous pathogens affecting legumes in the tropics, viruses are perhaps the major production constraint. Virus diseases were recorded in cultivated crops more than 300 years ago. However, little was known about their properties until the turn of this century. Now it is known that a virus is an infectious nucleoprotein capable of multiplying only in living cells. On the basis of signs, graft transmission, and size of entities, diseases caused by viruses can be distinguished from those induced by fungi, bacteria, and nematodes. Evidence of infectiousness through, for example graft transmission, is required to differentiate a virus disease from a physiologic disorder, and evidence of multiplication is necessary to distinguish disorders induced by toxins from diseases caused by viruses. For many years, 'yellows' type diseases were thought also to be caused by viruses because of the signs of infection, the transmission by vectors and the failure to isolate fungal or bacterial pathogens. Currently, most of these diseases are known to be caused by procaryotic microorganisms related to members of the Mycoplasmatales and Rickettsiales. In the past many attempts to isolate and cultivate these organisms failed, and their characterization is still difficult.

Doi *et al.* (1967) and Ishiie *et al.* (1967) were the first to propose that mycoplasma-like organisms (MLOs) were the causal agents of yellows diseases. They based their conclusions on electron microscopic observation of MLOs associated with diseased but not with healthy plants and on the remission of signs of disease following treatment with tetracycline. MLOs are pleomorphic microorganisms, bounded by a single unit membrane and devoid of cell walls. They contain ribosomal RNA and DNA in the form of a coil in the nuclear region. The presence of both RNA and DNA clearly distinguishes them from plant viruses. Penicillin, which interferes with bacterial cell-wall synthesis, has no effect on MLOs (Ghosh and Raychaudhuri, 1972).

To date, more than 80 different plant diseases caused by MLOs have been reported (Maramorosch *et al.*, 1970; Whitcomb and Davis, 1970; Davis and Whitcomb, 1971; Hull, 1971, 1972; Maramorosch, 1974; Grunewaldt-Stocker and Nienhaus, 1977; Tsai, 1979; Nienhaus and Sikora, 1979; Ploaie, 1981; Mandahar, 1987), and nearly all are associated with yellowing and stunting and sometimes signs of witches' broom. MLOs are confined to phloem tissues, from which they are acquired by homopterous insects (Whitcomb, 1972; Tsai, 1979; Sinha, 1984).

A few diseases previously regarded as being caused by MLOs were found to be caused by spiroplasmas — long, motile helical filaments, some of which have been cultured on artificial media (Davies and Worley, 1973).

Also, some of the 'yellows' diseases have been shown to be caused by rickettsia-like organisms (RLOs) (Maramorosch, 1974), which have cell walls like bacteria and are susceptible to penicillin. Although several diseases caused by MLOs have been reported from the tropics, hardly any diseases caused by spiroplasmas and RLOs are known to occur in the tropics.

Because of the similarities in insect transmission of some viruses and procaryotes, this chapter deals with vectors of both disease agents. Many virus diseases of plants, and probably all plant diseases caused by MLOs, are transmitted by insect vectors. The transmission of viruses and MLOs by invertebrates is of great interest to both the virologists and the entomologists.

There is considerable interest in understanding the relationships between vectors and viruses, especially viruses that have been shown to multiply in the vector. Such viruses can be regarded as both plant and animal viruses. Transmission by invertebrate vectors is usually a complex phenomenon involving the virus, the vector, the host plant, and the environment.

In this chapter we consider the insect groups that act as vectors of viruses and MLOs on tropical food legumes. The biologic transmission of several tropical legume viruses/mycoplasmas is still poorly understood. Therefore, in this review, besides listing some of the known vectors of these pathogens of tropical legumes, we give an overview of the relations between the vector and the virus or mycoplasma, citing examples. One of the main objectives is to stimulate more research on virus and mycoplasma diseases in the tropics and to obtain basic information on vectors as well as on their transmission characteristics — information that underpins effective strategies for control.

According to Harris (1981a), 381 species of animals have been reported to transmit plant viruses; of this group, approximately 94 per cent belong to the phylum Arthropoda and 6 per cent to the phylum Nematoda. Undoubtedly, insects constitute the largest group of arthropod vectors, and more than 70 per cent of all insect vectors of plant viruses belong to the order Homoptera, aphids (family Aphididae) being the most important.

In addition, leafhoppers (Cicadellidae), planthoppers (Delphacidae), treehoppers (Membracidae), whiteflies (Aleyrodidae), mealybugs (Pseudococcidae), beetles (Coleoptera) and thrips (Thysanoptera) are known vectors. In other arthropod groups, the mites (Acarina: Eriophyidae) are also transmit plant viruses.

This chapter complements relevant reviews by Sylvester (1962, 1969a, 1980, 1985); Maramorosch (1963, 1969); Sinha (1968, 1973, 1981, 1984); Watson (1972); Watson and Plumb (1972); Carter (1973); Gibbs (1973); Peters (1973); Harris (1977, 1978, 1979, 1980, 1981a,b, 1983); Pirone and Harris (1977); Nault and Rodriguez (1985); Morales (1986) as well as Nault and Ammar (1989). In addition, *Aphids as Virus Vectors* edited by Harris and Maramorosch (1977) and other books in the series (Harris and Maramorosch 1980, 1982; Maramorosch and Harris 1979, 1981) are excellent resources.

Selected literature on virus diseases of tropical legumes includes the publications of Goodman and Nene (1976); Raychandhuri and Nariani (1977); Galvez (1980); Gamez (1980); Galvez and Cardenas (1980); Nienhaus (1981); Allen (1983); Boswell and Gibbs (1983); Thottappilly and Rossel (1985, 1987); Rossel and Thottappilly (1985); Lin and Rios (1985); Mali (1986); Mali and Thottappilly (1986); Morales (1986); Buddenhagen *et al.* (1986); Reddy *et al.* (1986); Ansa *et al.* (1988) and Lima and Santos (1988).

Transmission

Plant viruses are unable to penetrate tissues of their plant hosts on their own. This process is often achieved through another organism — a vector — that carries the virus from an infected to a healthy plant. Transmission studies are essential to clarify how plant viruses are disseminated. Testing of trapped vectors on plants enables determination of the vectors' efficiency in transmission. A complete understanding of virus–vector relationships aids in the characterization of plant viruses and in the development of suitable control methods.

Mode of Transmission

Insect-transmitted plant viruses may be conveniently divided into three basic types, i.e. those transmitted in a non-persistent, semi-persistent or persistent manner (Watson and Roberts, 1939, 1940; Sylvester, 1956, 1969a; Garrett, 1973). Some virologists prefer to refer to viruses that are transmitted in a non-persistent manner as being stylet-borne (Kennedy et al., 1962; Pirone, 1969) or, more recently, as noncirculative (Harris 1977, 1979). Viruses transmitted in a persistent manner are called circulative. The persistent (circulative) viruses can be subdivided into propagative and non-propagative, depending on whether or not they multiply in the vector (Harris 1977, 1981b).

Non-persistent viruses are of considerable economic importance and are far more numerous than those transmitted in a persistent manner. Aphids are known to transmit several viruses in a non-persistent manner. Important features of non-persistent transmission are:

- The virus is acquired in a very short time by an insect that has probed, or fed on, an infected plant. An optimal time for acquisition of viruses ranges from a few seconds to a few minutes.
- The acquired virus is immediately transmissible to another plant.
- Within hours, the insect loses the ability to transmit the virus.
- Fasting before acquisition raises efficiency of transmission (Watson, 1972).

Fasting induces aphids to make a number of brief probes into a leaf, rather than a single, long probe, which is more typical of an aphid that has recently fed. Experiments have shown that non-persistent viruses are more readily acquired by the aphid during brief probes than during longer phloem-seeking probes. Because non-persistent viruses can be acquired and transmitted by the aphid during probes as brief as a few seconds, it is thought that the virus is taken from and inoculated into the epidermal cells of the leaf. The presence of these viruses in relatively superficial tissues correlates with the fact that the majority of non-persistent viruses are readily sap transmissible.

Semi-persistent viruses, such as beet yellows and parsnip yellow fleck, have transmission properties intermediate between non-persistent and persistent viruses. They resemble non-persistent viruses in that they do not circulate within the vector (Harris, 1977), but the vector retains the ability to transmit them for as long as 3–4 days. The virus may be acquired by the vector in as little as 30 min, but transmission is usually more efficient if the acquisition feeding time is several hours. Fasting by a vector before acquisition of the virus has no influence on the efficiency of transmission.

Persistent viruses are taken in by vectors, accumulate within them, enter the haemolymph by passing through the gut wall, reach the salivary glands, and are then transmitted to plants along with saliva as the vector feeds. These viruses are not transmitted immediately after acquisition but become transmissible only after a latent period. The transmitting ability of insects lasts for many days and is not lost during moulting. The percentage of infective insects increases proportionally with increase in length of acquisition feeding. Persistent viruses are generally not mechanically transmissible.

Some features of persistent or circulative viruses are:

* a long feeding time for acquisition — 6 h for efficient transmission;
* a latent period after the insect starts acquiring the virus until it is able to transmit the virus to a healthy plant;
* a long period in which the insect (having acquired the virus and completed the latent period) retains the ability to transmit the virus — several days, often throughout the insect's life;
* Retention of the virus through the moult (ecdysis) of the insect, a feature that is called transstadial passage.

Passage through the moult is an important criterion for distinguishing between non-circulative (non-persistent and semi-persistent) and circulative (persistent) viruses (Frazier, 1966; Harris, 1977, 1979). Only persistent viruses survive ecdysis and are transmitted by adults that acquire virus as nymphs.

Propagative viruses possess a prolonged latent period, which is presumably the time needed for them to multiply and to reach high enough concentrations to be transmissible (Black, 1959; Duffus, 1963, Maramorosch, 1964). Vector specificity of these viruses is a reflection of the intimate biological relationship (Sylvester, 1969b; Misari and Sylvester, 1983). Propagative viruses occur systemically and can be found in almost all body parts of a vector (Sinha and Chiykowski, 1969; Sylvester and Richardson, 1970; Harris, 1979). They follow a definite route and sequence as they spread through the body of a vector after acquisition. The virus adsorbs to the gut, which is generally a primary site of virus multiplication, passes into the haemolymph, is carried to salivary glands and is finally injected into healthy plants with saliva during feeding. Transovarial transmission has been demonstrated in several cases (Fukushi, 1969), and virus multiplication in the insect has been studied by several researchers using serological tests (Reddy and Black, 1966; Chang, 1977; Falk and Tsai, 1985; Nault and Gordon, 1988).

Persistent viruses usually show a high level of specificity in their vector relationship, in contrast to non-persistent viruses in which one virus frequently can be transmitted by more than one aphid species. Whether or not virus spread from particular sources leads to the development of an epiphytotic depends on numerous factors, including:

* the nature of the virus,
* the number of sources of infection,
* the distance between exposed and unexposed crops,
* the nature, life cycle and numbers of principal vectors,

- environmental factors favouring vector spread and virus multiplication in the host, and
- the crop's susceptibility.

The Major Vectors

APHIDS

Aphids constitute the largest group among plant virus vectors (Table 6.1). They are mostly soft-bodied insects from 1 to 7 mm long and are usually yellow, green, brown, red, or black. About 3800 species of aphids have so far been described (Eastop, 1973, 1977; Eastop and Hille Ris Lambers, 1976). Of the total described to date, 200 species have been recorded as vectors of plant viruses (Kennedy et al., 1962). The biology, feeding behaviour, speed with which they reproduce, and their worldwide distribution make them ideally suited for transmitting plant viruses (Hille Ris Lambers, 1972; Harris, 1977, 1981a). Many aphids are known to transmit more than 30 viruses each. *Myzus persicae* alone is a vector of more than 120 viruses. Furthermore, cucumber mosaic virus and many other viruses are transmitted by more than 60 aphid species.

Biology

Aphids possess a piercing and sucking apparatus to feed. Mouth parts consist of two pairs of stylets (mandibles and maxillae), a labium, a large slender rigid organ with a deeply concave anterior surface forming a channel for the stylets, and a labrum. The two pairs of stylets form a compact bundle that slides in the channel of the labium and constitutes the piercing organ. The piercing organ has two ducts formed by the interlocked maxillae. Through one, the anterior salivary duct, saliva is injected into the plant; through the other, the posterior food canal, sap is sucked from the plant. According to Forbes and MacCarthy (1969), the mean length of 75 single stylets of adult *M. persicae* was just under 500 μm.

Aphids secrete two types of saliva: a material that gels rapidly to form a salivary sheath and a non-gelating material that is water-soluble (Miles, 1959, 1968). The salivary sheath remains in the host tissue even after stylet withdrawal. Aphids as individuals are small and inconspicuous. But because of their high rate of multiplication they soon become very numerous and visible. The complex life cycle of aphids makes them very flexible and permits them to cope with environmental changes and other adverse conditions. Several generations are produced every year, and their fecundity is high.

Table 6.1. Some aphid vectors of viruses of leguminous crops in the tropics

Aphid Virus	Type of transmission	Key references
Aphis craccivora		
Cowpea aphid-borne mosaic/blackeye cowpea mosaic	Non-persistent	Bock, 1973; Atiri, 1984 Atiri *et al.*, 1984
Azuki bean mosaic	Non-persistent	Boswell and Gibbs, 1983
Cucumber mosaic	Non-persistent	Mali and Thottappilly, 1986
Peanut stripe	Non-persistent	Demski *et al.*, 1984
Bean common mosaic	Non-persistent	Kennedy *et al.* 1962
Bean yellow mosaic	Non-persistent	Iwaki, 1979
Beet western yellows	Persistent	Boswell and Gibbs, 1983
Soybean mosaic	Non-persistent	Irwin and Goodman, 1981; Suteri *et al.*, 1985
Peanut mottle	Non-persistent	Kuhn and Bock, 1975; Reddy *et al.*, 1978
Broad bean wilt	Non-persistent	Mali, 1986
Groundnut eyespot	Non-persistent	Dubern and Dollet, 1980
Peanut stunt	Non-persistent	Boswell and Gibbs, 1983
Groundnut rosette assistor	Persistent	Watson and Okusanya, 1967; Davis, 1972
Bean leaf roll (pea leaf roll)	Persistent	Thottappilly *et al.*, 1977b; Ashby, 1984; Johnstone *et al.*, 1984
A. fabae		
Cowpea aphid-borne mosaic	Non-persistent	Vidano and Conti, 1965
Bean common mosaic	Non-persistent	Kennedy *et al.*, 1962; Khaemba and Latigo, 1982
Bean yellow mosaic	Non-persistent	Kennedy *et al.*, 1962
Cucumber mosaic	Non-persistent	Kennedy *et al.*, 1962
A. gossypii		
Peanut green mosaic	Non-persistent	Sreenivasulu *et al.*, 1981
Cucumber mosaic	Non-persistent	Kennedy *et al.*, 1962
Beet western yellows	Persistent	Boswell and Gibbs, 1983
Peanut mottle	Non-persistent	Kuhn and Bock, 1975
Bean common mosaic	Non-persistent	Kennedy *et al.*, 1962
Cowpea aphid-borne mosaic	Non-persistent	Boswell and Gibbs, 1983
A. medicaginis		
Cowpea aphid-borne mosaic	Non-persistent	Boswell and Gibbs, 1983

Table 6.1 continued

Aphid Virus	Type of transmission	Key references
A. glycines		
Bean yellow mosaic	Non-persistent	Iwaki, 1979
Indonesian soybean dwarf	Persistent	Iwaki *et al.*, 1980
A. spiraecola		
Bean common mosaic	Non-persistent	Kennedy *et al.*, 1962
A. rumicis		
Bean common mosaic	Non-persistent	Mukhopadhyay and Chawdhury, 1986
Acyrthosiphon pisum		
Bean leaf roll		
(pea leaf roll)	Persistent	Thottappilly, 1969, 1970; Thottappilly *et al.*, 1977b
Cucumber mosaic	Non-persistent	Kennedy *et al.*, 1962
Legume yellows	Persistent	Duffus, 1979
Bean yellow mosaic	Non-persistent	Kennedy *et al.*, 1962
Alfalfa mosaic	Non-persistent	Kaiser, 1979
A. sebaniae		
Pea leaf roll	Persistent	Kaiser and Schalk, 1975
Hyperomyzus lactucae		
Peanut mottle	Non-persistent	Kuhn and Bock, 1975
Macrosiphum euphorbiae		
Cowpea aphid-borne mosaic	Non-persistent	Vidano and Conti, 1965
Beet western yellows	Persistent	Boswell and Gibbs, 1983
Bean yellow mosaic	Non-persistent	Kennedy *et al.*, 1962
Myzus persicae		
Cucumber mosaic	Non-persistent	Sharma and Varma, 1982; Pio-Ribeiro *et al.* 1978
Cowpea aphid-borne mosaic	Non-persistent	Vidano and Conti, 1965
Beet western yellows	Persistent	Boswell and Gibbs, 1983
Bean yellow mosaic	Non-persistent	Kennedy *et al.*, 1962
Bean leaf roll	Persistent	Thottappilly, 1969; Thottappilly *et al.*, 1977b
Peanut mottle	Non-persistent	Kuhn and Bock, 1975
Peanut stripe	Non-persistent	Xu *et al.*, 1983
Peanut green mosaic	Non-persistent	Sreenivasulu *et al.*, 1981
Azuki bean mosaic	Non-persistent	Boswell and Gibbs, 1983

Aphid Virus	Type of transmission	Key references
Broad bean wilt	Non-persistent	Mali, 1986
Soybean mosaic	Non-persistent	Lucas and Hill, 1980; Schultz _et al._, 1983
Bean common mosaic	Non-persistent	Mali, 1986; Zettler and Wilkinson, 1966
Aulacorthum (= Acyrthosiphon) solani		
Soybean dwarf	Persistent	Tamada, 1970, 1975; Damsteegt and Hewings, 1987
Bean leaf roll	Persistent	Thottappilly _et al._, 1977b
Legume yellows	Persistent	Duffus, 1979
Beet western yellows	Persistent	Boswell and Gibbs, 1983
Brachycaudus helichrysi		
Beet western yellows	Persistent	Boswell and Gibbs, 1983
Brevicoryne brassicae		
Beet western yellows	Persistent	Boswell and Gibbs, 1983
Rhopalosiphum padi		
Peanut mottle	Non-persistent	Kuhn and Bock, 1975

Aphids migrate when light and temperature conditions increase above certain thresholds. Most plant viruses are transmitted during the insects' active flight within and between crops or between secondary hosts and crops. Since the rate of development is affected by temperature, a daily 'double peak' of flight from the host plant is characteristic for many aphids in the temperate region. In the tropics, some species have only one peak of flight activity, and this may be in the morning or afternoon. _Aphis nevii_ flies mostly in the morning in the forest zone of Nigeria, whereas the banana aphid, _Pentalonia nigronervosa_, flies mainly in the afternoon. Aphids may travel several hundred miles under suitable conditions (Eastop, 1973).

Host Selection and Adoption

Aphids begin probing plants after alighting: they insert the tips of their stylets into a suitable area of host epidermis. Monophagous aphids select and feed on plants of related species, whereas polyphagous aphids are not fastidious and feed on a wide range of hosts. When an aphid probes a plant, it can behave in one of three ways, with major implications for epidemiology: it can become dissatisfied with the plant and leave; it may be satisfied, make further probes, and remain on the plant to feed perhaps throughout its life; or it can be satisfied, feed and reproduce but leave after a few hours, repeating this throughout life, producing isolated groups of nymphs on crops.

Aphis craccivora is an important pest of cowpea and other legumes in the tropics (Table 6.1), and it is known to transmit cowpea aphid-borne mosaic, cucumber mosaic, bean common mosaic, peanut stripe and peanut mottle viruses in a non-persistent manner. It transmits groundnut rosette assistor, beet western yellows and bean leaf roll viruses in a persistent manner. In the tropics, cucumber mosaic virus, which is widespread, is transmitted by several aphids including *A. craccivora*, *A. fabae* and *A. gossypii*.

Adult aphids are most commonly used in vector studies. However, nymphs, in general, are more efficient in transmitting viruses, both non-persistent (Thottappilly *et al.*, 1972, 1977a) and persistent (Bath and Chapman, 1968; Gill, 1970; Sugawara *et al.*, 1970; Tsai *et al.*, 1972; Tamada, 1975; Sylvester and Osler, 1977).

LEAFHOPPERS AND PLANTHOPPERS

Leafhoppers and planthoppers transmit several economically important viruses (Kisimoto, 1973) to food crops but they are of only minor importance to legumes (Table 6.2). They have sucking mouth parts and pierce tissues more rapidly and more destructively than do aphids.

Table 6.2. Leafhopper vectors of viruses and mycoplasma-like organisms of leguminous crops in the tropics

Vector Disease	Distribution	Reference
Empoasca fabae Pigeonpea witches' broom	Puerto Rico	Licha-Baquero, 1980
Orosius argentatus Bean summer death	Australia	Bowyer and Atherton, 1971
Scaphytopius fuliginosus Machismo disease of soybean	Mexico	Granada, 1979; Fletcher *et al.*, 1984
Scaphytopius acutus Bud proliferation of soybean	USA	Derrick and Newsom, 1984
Orosius sp. Witches' broom of soybean	India	Dhingra and Chenulu, 1983
? Legume witches' broom	Indonesia	Iwaki *et al.*, 1978

Leafhoppers, planthoppers and their Auchenorrhyncha relatives are collectively referred to as hoppers. The first report of planthopper transmission of a plant virus was by Kunkel (1922) who demonstrated that *Peregrinus maidis* was the vector of maize mosaic virus. Since 1930, much progress has been made on describing the role of leafhoppers and planthoppers as vectors of viruses (Nielson, 1968, 1979, 1985; Nault and Ammar, 1989). Until 1967, all plant pathogens transmitted by hoppers were thought to be viruses until leafhopper-transmitted MLOs were discovered (Doi *et al.*, 1967; Ishii *et al.*, 1967; Davis and Whitcomb, 1971). Later, scientists showed that hoppers also transmit spiroplasmas (Whitcomb, 1981).

Further, some diseases transmitted by hoppers have been shown to be associated with RLOs (Maramorosch *et al.*, 1975; Chiykowski, 1981) or xylem-limited bacteria (Purcell, 1979). Nearly all plant mycoplasmas are transmitted by hoppers (Tsai, 1979; Sinha, 1984).

WHITEFLIES

Whiteflies (order Homoptera, family Aleyrodidae) are second only to aphids in transmitting economically important virus diseases in the tropics (Varma, 1963; Costa, 1965, 1969, 1976; Costa *et al.*, 1983; Bird and Sánchez, 1971; Gamez, 1971; Nene *et al.*, 1972; Pierre, 1975; Bird and Maramorosch, 1975, 1978). Three species of whiteflies, *Bemisia tabaci, Trialeurodes vaporariorum* and *T. abutilonea* are known to transmit plant viruses (Muniyappa, 1980). About 1156 whitefly species are known worldwide (Mound and Halsey, 1978), and as detailed studies are undertaken, more species are likely to emerge as vectors of plant viruses. In sub-tropical and temperate countries, they particularly affect glasshouse-grown crops (Loebenstein and Harpaz, 1960; Costa, 1965; Duffus, 1965, 1975).

Many reviews have been published about plant viruses transmitted by whiteflies (Varma, 1963; Costa, 1969, 1976; Nene, 1973; Bird and Maramorosch, 1978; Galvez and Cardenas, 1980; Muniyappa, 1980). Whiteflies multiply to great numbers on the underside of leaves. Generally, female whiteflies are more efficient vectors than males (Anno-Nyako *et al.*, 1983). Viruses may be transmitted by whiteflies in a non-persistent (e.g. cowpea mild mottle virus) or, more commonly, a persistent manner (e.g. cowpea golden mosaic virus) (Muniyappa, 1980; Duffus 1987). *Bemisia tabaci* is by far the most important whitefly vector of legume viruses (Table 6.3). For example, several viruses such as cowpea golden mosaic, lima bean golden mosaic, horsegram yellow mosaic and African soybean dwarf viruses are transmitted by *B. tabaci* in a persistent manner, whereas only cowpea mild mottle virus is known to be transmitted in a non-persistent (Muniyappa and Reddy, 1983) or semi-persistent manner (Anno-Nyako, 1984, 1986).

Table 6.3. Whitefly vectors of viruses of leguminous crops in the tropics

Vector Virus	Type of transmission	Key references
Bemisia tabaci		
Bean golden mosaic	Persistent	Gamez, 1971; Goodman and Bird, 1978; Bird *et al.*, 1972, 1973
Cowpea golden mosaic	Persistent	Anno-Nyako *et al.*, 1983; Vetten and Allen, 1983; Ahmed, 1978
Cowpea mild mottle	Semi- persistent Non-persistent	Iwaki *et al.*, 1982 Anno-Nyako, 1984, 1986 Muniyappa and Reddy, 1983

Jalo bean angular
  mosaic (strain of
  cowpea mild mottle)
	Non-persistent	Costa *et al.*, 1983

Soybean crinkle leaf	Persistent	Iwaki *et al.*, 1983
African soybean dwarf	Persistent	Rossel *et al.*, 1982; Rossel, 1986
Mungbean yellow mosaic	Persistent	Nair and Nene, 1973a,b.; Honda *et al.*, 1983; Rathi and Nene, 1974
Horsegram yellow mosaic	Persistent	Muniyappa and Reddy, 1976; Muniyappa *et al.*, 1987
Euphorbia mosaic	Persistent	Costa, 1975
Lima bean golden mosaic	Persistent	Williams, 1975, 1976; Vetten and Allen, 1983
Bean dwarf mosaic	Persistent	Morales and Niessen, 1988b
Greengram yellow mosaic	Persistent	Murugesan and Chelliah, 1977
Urd bean yellow mosaic	Persistent	Ahmed and Harwood, 1973

THRIPS

Thrips, belonging to the order Thysanoptera, are known vectors of plant viruses (Sakimura, 1962, 1963; Best, 1968; Mound, 1973; Ananthakrishnan, 1980; Reddy and Wightman, 1988). They have been reported to transmit tomato spotted wilt, peanut yellow spot and tobacco ringspot viruses. Tobacco ringspot virus is transmitted by *Thrips tabaci* and peanut yellow spot virus by *Scirtothrips dorsalis*. Tomato spotted wilt virus has been shown to be transmitted by four species of thrips: *T. tabaci*, *Frankliniella fusca*, *F. occidentalis* and *F. schultzei*. Best (1968) detailed the relationship of the virus to its vectors and host plants.

Table 6.4. Beetle vectors of viruses of leguminous crops in the tropics

Vector Virus	Key references
Acalymma vittatum Cowpea severe mosaic	Boswell and Gibbs, 1983
Apion arrogans Broad bean mottle	Makkouk and Kumari, 1989
Apion vorax Broad bean mottle Broad bean strain Broad bean true mosaic	Cockbain, 1983 Cockbain, 1971 Cockbain, 1971
Chalcodermus bimaculatus Cowpea severe mosaic	Lima and Gonçalves, 1980
Cerotoma arcuata Cowpea severe mosaic	Costa _et al._, 1978; Costa and Batista, 1979 ; Ranjnauth _et al._, 1987
Cerotoma ruficornis Cowpea severe mosaic Cowpea chlorotic mottle Bean curly dwarf mosaic Bean mild mosaic Bean yellow stipple	Jensen and Staples, 1971; Valverde _et al._, 1978 Boswell and Gibbs, 1983 Hobbs, 1981 Hobbs, 1981 Morales and Gamez, 1989
Cerotoma trifurcata Southern bean mosaic Cowpea severe mosaic Blackgram mottle Cowpea chlorotic mottle Bean pod mottle	Walters and Henry, 1970 Boswell and Gibbs, 1983 Scott and Phatak, 1979 Hobbs and Fulton, 1979 Ross, 1963; Walters 1969
Cerotoma variegata Cowpea severe mosaic	Boswell and Gibbs, 1983
Colaspis flavida Broad bean mottle	Walter and Surin, 1973
Colaspis lata Bean pod mottle	Horn _et al._, 1970

Table 6.4 Continued

Vector
    Virus   Key references

Diabrotica adelpha
    Bean curly dwarf mosaic   Hobbs, 1981
    Bean rugose mosaic   Gamez, 1972a, b,

Diabrotica balteata
    Bean mild mosaic   Hobbs, 1981
    Cowpea severe mosaic   Boswell and Gibbs, 1983
    Bean pod mottle   Horn *et al.*, 1970
    Bean curly dwarf mosaic   Hobbs, 1981
    Cowpea chlorotic mottle   Boswell and Gibbs, 1983
    Bean rugose mosaic   Gamez, 1972a, b,
    Bean yellow stipple   Morales and Gamez, 1989

Diabrotica speciosa
    Cowpea severe mosaic   Costa *et al.*, 1981; Cupertino *et al.*, 1981

Diabrotica undecimpunctata
    Bean curly dwarf mosaic   Meiners *et al.* 1977
    Bean mild mosaic   Meiners *et al.* 1977
    Cowpea severe mosaic   Boswell and Gibbs, 1983
    Bean pod mottle   Horn *et al.*, 1970
    Cowpea chlorotic mottle   Hobbs and Fulton, 1979
    Broad bean mottle   Walters and Surin, 1973

Diabrotica virgifera
    Cowpea severe mosaic   Boswell and Gibbs, 1983

Epilachna varivestis
    Blackgram mottle   Scott and Phatak, 1979
    Southern bean mosaic   Boswell and Gibbs, 1983
    Cowpea severe mosaic   Boswell and Gibbs, 1983
    Bean mild mosaic   Meiners *et al.* 1977
    Bean curly dwarf mosaic   Meiners *et al.* 1977

Epicanta vittata
    Bean pod mottle   Patel and Pitre, 1971

Henosepilachna dodecastigma
    Urd bean leaf crinkle disease   Kolte and Nene, 1972
    (Blackgram crinkle virus)

Monolepta signata
    Blackgram mottle   Honda *et al.* 1982

Plate I. Medythia quaterna, *vector of cowpea yellow mosaic virus (photo IITA)*

Plate II. Ootheca mutabilis, *vector of among others cowpea yellow mosaic virus (photo IITA)*

Plate III. Bemisia *sp., vector of, among others,*
cowpea golden mosaic virus and cowpea mild mottle virus
(photo IITA)

Plate IV. Cowpea plant affected by cowpea
aphid-borne mosaic virus (photo IITA)

*Plate V. Cowpea plant affected by cowpea golden
mosaic virus (photo IITA)*

*Plate VI. Soybean plant affected by African soybean
dwarf virus (photo IITA)*

Plate VII. Groundnut plant affected by groundnut rosette virus (photo ICRISAT)

Plate VIII. Groundnut rosette virus resistant and susceptible varieties (photo ICRISAT)

Table 6.4 Continued

Vector Virus	Key references

Nematocerus acerbus
  Cowpea mosaic
  (Cowpea yellow mosaic)
	Whitney and Gilmer, 1974

Ootheca mutabilis
  Cowpea mosaic (= cowpea yellow)
  Cowpea mottle
  Southern bean mosaic
	Chant, 1959
	Shoyinka *et al.*, 1978
	Allen *et al.*, 1981

Paraluperodes quarternus
  Cowpea mosaic
  (Cowpea yellow mosaic)
	Whitney and Gilmer, 1974

Sitona lineatus var viridifrons Broad bean mottle	Borges and Louro, 1974

Tobacco ringspot virus is transmitted only by larvae, in contrast to tomato spotted wilt, which is acquired only by larvae but can be transmitted by both larvae and adults. The virus has been reported to be able to multiply while in the thrips vector (Reddy and Wightman, 1988).

BEETLES

For a long time, beetles have been recognized as vectors of plant viruses (Smith, 1924) and have now been shown to transmit about 45 different viruses (Table 6.4). According to Harris (1981a), at least 74 beetle species have been reported to be vectors in the families Chrysomelidae, Curculionidae, Meloidae, and Coccinellidae. For many years, it was thought that transmission by beetles results from a simple mechanical process involving contamination of the beetle's mouth parts (Smith, 1965).

However, more recently, a more complex biologic phenomenon has been suggested (Fulton *et al.*, 1975, 1980; Fulton and Scott, 1977). The transmission is more than a mechanical event, since the virus persists in the insects and can be detected in the haemolymph of chrysomelid beetles. In many instances it is thought that the insect is inoculated after regurgitating sap from the foregut. Retention of virus for up to 8–10 days suggests that transmission is not merely by mechanical means (Walters, 1969; Selman, 1973; Fulton *et al.*, 1980; Gamez and Moreno, 1983).

Beetle-transmitted viruses have many similar properties, such as being relatively stable, readily mechanically transmitted, and usually present at a high concentration in infected plants. Furthermore, beetle-transmitted viruses are highly antigenic. All are isometric, contain RNA, and are approximately 25–30 nm in diameter.

MITES

Mites are small, about 0.2 mm long, and belong to the family Eriophyidae (order: Acarina; class: Arachnida) and possess mouth parts that are specifically adapted for piercing and sucking. Although 14 or more mite-transmitted viruses have been reported (Slykhuis, 1973; 1980), pigeon pea sterility mosaic disease is the only one reported among the tropical legumes and is transmitted by *Aceria cajani*. The agent that causes pigeon pea sterility mosaic disease has not yet been identified. Damage caused by mite feeding (phytotoxemia) could easily be confused with signs of virus infection.

Possibilities for Virus Disease Control

Considerable effort has been made to find chemicals that will directly eliminate or restrict virus multiplication in crop plants (Semal, 1967; Lockhart and Semancik, 1968, 1969; Dawson, 1976, 1978; Dawson and Schlegel, 1976; Gupta, 1977; Hansen, 1979; Schuster, 1979; Maekawa *et al.*, 1980; Cassels and Long, 1980, 1982; Tomlinson, 1982; Klein and Livingston, 1982; Dawson and Grantham, 1983; Dawson and Lozoya-Saldana, 1984; Turner and Dawson, 1984; Wambugu *et al.*, 1985). However, because of ineffectiveness, phytotoxicity, economic or other considerations, no viricides have been marketed. Furthermore, although tetracycline can be used to control, at least temporarily, mycoplasma-like organisms (Maramorosch, 1982), the cost of continuous antibiotic treatments is prohibitive for large-scale use in the field. So the majority of control measures for viruses and mycoplasmas are indirect, designed to reduce sources of inoculum within and outside the crop; to limit spread by vectors; and to minimize the effects of infection on yield. Before control of virus spread can be attempted, it is necessary to identify the vector(s), the mode of transmission and sources of inoculum. A detailed knowledge of the ecology of the vectors is often needed before effective control measures can be implemented. No single method will work in all cases and, therefore, it is best to use a combination of measures (integrated control) to combat virus diseases (Broadbent, 1969).

Often, insects are responsible for secondary spread of virus in the field. In the case of non-persistent viruses, secondary spread can be rapid and does not require colonization of the crop by the vector. On the contrary, it is transient vectors moving through a field that usually acquire and transmit non-persistent virus(es) in a matter of seconds (Halbert *et al.*, 1981; Atiri *et al.*, 1986). To control the spread of non-persistent viruses, therefore, one must effectively control initial inoculum or primary spread (Simons, 1959; Simons and Zitter, 1980; Falk and Duffus, 1988).

CHEMICAL CONTROL

The use of insecticides to prevent virus transmission by vectors has been only partially successful because some insects transmit viruses, particularly non-persistent types, before they die from the effects of insecticides (Broadbent, 1969; Wyman et al., 1979; Loebenstein and Raccah, 1980; Asjes, 1981; Jayasena and Randles, 1985). Also, the costs and hazards of using insecticides make them increasingly unattractive.

Synthetic organophosphates have reportedly reduced the spread of some persistent and semi-persistent viruses (Burt et al., 1960; Swenson, 1968; Plumb, 1981). However, recently, Rice et al. (1983a) demonstrated that the organophosphate demeton-S-methyl has the potential to increase the spread of potato virus Y. Still, the search for effective chemicals continues, and a newer class of insecticides, the synthetic pyrethroids, has been reported to be effective in reducing the transmission of non-persistent viruses (Gibson et al., 1982; Rice et al., 1983b; Gibson and Cayley, 1984; Atiri et al., 1987). The efficacy has been attributed to their rapid knockdown action (Briggs et al., 1974), which incapacitates aphids even before they feed and consequently prevents transmission.

Commercially, oil sprays have been used and appear to affect transmission of non-persistent and semi-persistent viruses (Bradley et al., 1962; Bradley, 1963; Loebenstein et al., 1970; Peters and Lebbink, 1973; Vanderveken, 1977; Loebenstein and Raccah, 1980; Simons and Zitter, 1980; Dewijs, 1980; Asjes, 1981; Simons, 1982). These have been tested on several crops. Costs, availability, and the special precautions associated with the use of mineral oils are constraints to their adoption in the tropics.

NON-CHEMICAL CONTROL

Barriers

Barrier crops have been reported to be useful in controlling aphid-transmitted viruses. For example, Lima and Gonçalves (1985) and Shoyinka (1975) demonstrated that maize planted as a barrier around cowpea reduced the incidence of cowpea aphid-borne mosaic virus, a non-persistent aphid-transmitted virus. The in-coming aphids landed first on maize where they probed briefly and lost the non-persistently transmitted virus they were carrying. In some cases, however, barriers may actually attract vectors — for example, maize attracts chrysomelid vectors of legume viruses — so the barrier crop must be carefully selected.

Reflective Mulches

Reflective surfaces laid on the soil around plants have also been found to be highly effective in controlling aphid vectors in certain crops (Simons, 1982). Aluminium strips or plastic sheets (grey or white) may be used as a mulch and have been shown to be successful in protecting peppers against cucumber mosaic virus and potato virus Y in Israel (Loebenstein *et al.*, 1975) and summer squash against watermelon mosaic virus in the Imperial valley of California, USA (Wyman *et al.*, 1979). Wyman *et al.* (1979) showed that the prevalence of virus in plots with the mulch was reduced 77–94 per cent compared with untreated plots.

The mulches are thought to act as a repellent by reflecting UV light as the aphids come to land (Smith *et al.*, 1964; Smith and Webb, 1969). Disadvantages of mulches are their cost and their decreased efficiency as the plant canopy develops and covers them. They are, therefore, only economical for high-value crops but have been successful against non-persistent viruses in several crops (Loebenstein and Raccah, 1980).

Mulches have also been used to control the spread of whitefly-transmitted viruses, but the mechanism of action is different from that described for aphid-transmitted viruses. The colour of the mulch attracts *B. tabaci*, and heat reflected from the mulch kills the whiteflies, thereby reducing virus incidence in treated plots (Cohen and Melamed-Madjar, 1978; Cohen, 1982). Using this method alone, therefore, is effective only if daytime temperatures can generate the heat necessary to kill the whiteflies. In cooler climates, insecticides can be incorporated into an attractive mulch (Cohen, 1982).

Genetic Resistance

The host plant can be resistant to the vector or to the virus. For years genetic resistance to the vector was advocated (Painter, 1951), with little progress in selection for at least 20 years. The availability of cheap and effective insecticides in the 1950s and 1960s discouraged the allocation of enough resources to investigate vector resistance in plants.

However, the development of resistance to pesticides in insects, the high research and development costs of new chemicals, coupled with the extensive and expensive testing as dictated by the high safety standards and finally the public awareness of the hazards of heavy pesticide use all contributed to creating new interest in breeding for vector resistance in plants (Gibson and Plumb, 1977; Dunn, 1978; Jones, 1987).

A few reports demonstrate that vector resistance in legumes is at times associated with a decrease in virus spread. Amin (1985) identified resistance in groundnut to the thrip *F. schultzei*, which is the vector of tomato spotted wilt virus, the causal agent of bud necrosis disease in groundnut. Resistance to the eriophyid mite *A. cajani*, which vectors the sterility mosaic disease of pigeon pea has been reported by Muniyappa and Nangia (1982). Soybean genotypes resistant to the aphid species *A. citricola*, *M. persicae* and *Rhopalosiphum maidis*, vectors of soybean mosaic virus, have recently been identified (Gunasinghe *et al.*, 1988). In none of the cases has the mechanism of control been clearly defined. It is often not easy to differentiate between resistance to the vector and resistance to virus multiplication in the plant, and sometimes both mechanisms may be at work in reducing virus incidence in the field.

As early as 1951, Painter identified three types of resistance in plants to insects:

- non-preference, more recently called antixenosis, which describes plant genotypes having an adverse effect on insect behaviour,
- antibiosis, which describes cases where plant genotypes have an adverse effect on insects' growth, reproduction, survival, and
- tolerance, which describes the ability of a plant to support insect colonization without harmful effects on its growth and development.

Cultivation of resistant varieties is an effective way of controlling plant virus diseases. Resistant sources have been identified, and resistant varieties have been developed to several legume viruses (Drijfhout, 1978; Walkey and Innes, 1979; Rios *et al.*, 1980; Hartwig and Keeling 1982; Patel *et al.*, 1982; Walkey *et al.*, 1983; Lim, 1985; Lima *et al.*, 1986; Singh *et al.*, 1987; Culver and Sherwood, 1987; Rossel and Thottappilly, 1988; Thottappilly *et al.*, 1988). However, for many important viruses, no resistance genes are yet known.

The genetic control of whitefly-transmitted geminiviruses of beans (*Phaseolus vulgaris* L.) has met serious difficulties due to the lack of immune genotypes. Therefore, a different approach has been followed to incorporate 'tolerance' into susceptible cultivars by combining different defence mechanisms, such as hypersensitivity, mature plant resistance and limited expression of disease signs, in genotypes selected as parental materials (Morales and Niessen, 1988a).

Crop genotypes with resistance to vectors or viruses promise savings to farmers by reducing expenditures on pesticides, and such benefits should not be underestimated, particularly in subsistence farming in the tropics and sub-tropics. Savings could be substantial even where host-plant resistance to insects or virus invasion is incomplete and insecticides are needed to complement resistance. When moderate vector resistance is combined with slight virus resistance, significant improvement in virus control can be achieved (Romanow *et al.*, 1986; Gunasinghe *et al.*, 1988). However, not all forms of vector resistance are equally effective in reducing virus spread, and some forms may in fact increase virus prevalence, as reported by Atiri *et al.* (1984). Ultimately, an integrated approach, minimizing chemicals through reliance on host-plant resistance, cultural practices and natural enemies, is the most promising method to control virus spread.

We wish to thank Drs K. F. Harris and S. R. Singh for critically reviewing this chapter.

References

A'Brook, J. 1964. The effect of planting date and spacing on the incidence of groundnut rosette disease and of the vector, Aphis craccivora Koch, at Mokwa, northern Nigeria. *Annals of Applied Biology*, 54, 199-208.

Abate, T. 1983a. Screening of haricot bean varieties against bean fly and African bollworm (nursery 1), Nazret, 1982-1983. Nazret Research Station. Addis Ababa, Institute of Agricultural Research, 7p.

Abate, T. 1983b. Screening of haricot bean varieties against bean fly and African bollworm (nursery 2), Nazret, Jima, Kkobo, Makele, Nazret Research Station. Addis Ababa, Institute of Agricultural Research, 3p.

Abbassy, M.A., and Abdel-Rahim, W.A. 1981. Toxicological studies on male and female cowpea weevil, *Callosobruchus maculatus* (F.). *Bulletin de la Société entomologique d'Egypte, Ser. econ.* 10, 165-170.

Abdel-Salam, A.M., Assem, M.A., Abdel-Shaheed, G.A., and Ragab, F.Y. 1972. Field studies on controlling cowpea, Vigna sinensis, pest in U.A.R. *Zeitschrift fuer Angewandte Entomologie*, 70, 332-336.

Abdel-Wahab, A.M., Abdel-Rahim, W.A., and Rizk, M. 1975. Comparative susceptibility of male and female southern cowpea weevil *Callosobruchus maculatus* (F.) to thirteen insecticides (Coleoptera: Bruchidae). *Bulletin de la Société entomologique de l'Egypte, Ser. econ.*, 8, 63-68.

Abul-Nasr, S. 1956. Polyhedrosis-virus disease on the cotton leaf-worm, *Prodenia litura* F. *Bulletin de la Société entomologique de l'Egypte*, 41, 591-620.

Abul-Nasr, S. 1977. Ophiomyia phaseoli (Tryon). In Kranz, J., Schmutterer, H., and Koch, W., eds., *Diseases, Pests and Weeds in Tropical Crops*, Berlin, Verlag Pard Parey.

Abul-Nasr, S., and Assem, M. 1966a. The external morphology of the bean fly, *Melanagromyza phaseoli* (Tryon). *Bulletin de la Société entomologique de l'Egypte*, 50, 61-69.

Abul-Nasr, S., and Assem, M. 1966b. Some ecological aspects concerning the bean fly, *Melanagromyza phaseoli* (Tryon). *Bulletin de la Société entomologique de l'Egypte*, 50, 163-172.

Abul-Nasr, S., and Assem, M. 1968a. Studies on the biological processes of the beanfly, *Melanagromyza phaseoli* (Tryon.) (Diptera: Agromyzidae). *Bulletin de la Société entomologique de l'Egypte*, 52, 283-295.

Abul Nasr, S., and Assem, M. 1968b. Chemical control of the bean fly, *Melanagromyza phaseoli* (Tryon). *Bulletin de la Société entomologique de l'Egypte, Ser. econ.*, 11, 151-159.

Abul-Nasr, S., and Awadalla, A.M. 1957. External morphology and biology of the bean pod-borer, *Etiella zinckenella* Treit. *Bulletin de la Société entomologique de l'Egypte*, 41, 591-620.

Achan, P.D., Mathur, K.C., Dhamadhikari, P.R., and Manunath, T.M. 1968. Parasites of *Heliothis* spp. in India. Ascot, U.K., Commonwealth Institute of Biological Control, Technical Bulletin 10, 129-149.

Aciole, A. 1971. Nova praga do feijoeiro no estado do Ceara, *Chalcodermus* sp. (Col: Curculionidae). *Biológico*, 37, 17.

Adams, M.W. 1980. Energy inputs in dry bean production. In Pimantel, D., ed., *Handbook of Energy Utilization in Agriculture*, Boca Raton, FL, CRC Press, 123–126.

Adjadi, O., Singh, B.B., and Singh, S.R. 1985. Inheritance of bruchid resistance in cowpea. *Crop Science*, 25, 740–742.

Agpad-Verzola, E., and Cortado, R.V. 1969. Preliminary experiment in the control of *Heliothis armigera* Hübner attacking bean pods. *Philippine Journal Plant Industry*, 34, 187–191.

Agrawal, N.S., and Pandey, N.D. 1961. Bionomics of *Melanagromyza phaseoli* Coq. *Indian Journal of Entomology*, 23, 293–298.

Agyen-Sampong, M. 1976. Co-ordinated minimum insecticide trial; yield performance of insect resistant cowpea cultivars from IITA compared with Ghanaian cultivars. *Tropical Grain Legume Bulletin*, 5, 6.

Agyen-Sampong, M. 1978. Pests of cowpea and their control in Ghana. In Singh, S.R., van Emden, H.F., and Taylor, T.A., eds., *Pests of Grain Legumes: Ecology and Control*, London/New York, Academic Press, 85–92.

Ahmad, T.Y. 1938. The tur-pod fly, Agromyza obtusa Malloch. A pest of Cajanus cajan. *Indian Journal of Agricultural Sciences*, 8, 63–67.

Ahmed, M. 1971. Studies on the genera and species of tribe *Erythroneurini* (Cicadellidae, Typlocybinae) in east Pakistan. *Pakistan Journal of Zoology*, 3 (2), 175–192.

Ahmed, M. 1978. Whitefly (*Bemisia tabaci*) transmission of a yellow mosaic disease of cowpea (*Vigna unguiculata*). *Plant Disease Reporter*, 62, 224–226.

Ahmed, M., and Harwood, R.F. 1973. Studies on a whitefly-transmitted yellow mosaic of urd bean (*Phaseolus mungo*). *Plant Disease Reporter*, 57, 800–802.

Aina, J.O. 1975a. The distribution of coreids infesting cowpea pod in southwestern Nigeria. *Nigerian Journal of Entomology*, 1, 119–123.

Aina, J.O. 1975b. The life history of *Riptortus dentipes* F. (Alydidae, Heteroptera): a pest of growing cowpea pods. *Journal of Natural History*, 9, 589–596.

Aina, J.O. 1975c. The life history of *Anoplocnemis curvipes* F. (Coreidae, Heteroptera): a pest of cowpea pods. *Journal of Natural History*, 9, 685–692.

Akinfenwa, S. 1975. Bioecological study of *Maruca testulalis* (Geyer) in the Zaria area of northern Nigeria. Zaria, Nigeria, Ahmadu Bello University (MSc thesis).

Akingbohungbe, A.E. 1976. A note on the relative susceptibility of unshelled cowpeas to the cowpea weevil (*Callosobruchus maculatus* Fabricius) (Coleoptera: Bruchidae). *Tropical Grain Legume Bulletin*, 5, 11–13.

Akingbohungbe, A.E. 1977. Notes on the identity and biology of the *Riptortus* spp. (Heteroptera: Alydidae) associated with cowpeas in Nigeria. *Journal of Natural History*, 11, 477–483.

Akingbohungbe, A.E. 1982. Seasonal variation in cowpea crop performance at Ile-Ife, Nigeria, and the relationship to insect damage. *Insect Science Application*, 3, 287–296.

Akingbohungbe, A.E., Agbede, T., and Olaifa, J.I. 1980. Oviposition preference by the black cowpea moth, *Cydia ptychora* (Meyrick) (Lepidoptera: Tortricidae), for different varieties of cowpea. *Bulletin of Entomological Research*, 70, 439–443.

Aldana, F., Masaya, P., and Yoshii, K. 1981. La tolerancia al mosaico dorado del frijol comun y el combate químico del vector (*Bemisia tabaci* Genn) como medio de control. Paper prepared for the 27th annual meeting of the Programa Cooperative Centroaméricano para el Mejoramiento de Cultivos Alimenticios, Santo Domingo, Dominican Republic, 3, 9–29.

Ali, S.I., Singh, O.P., and Misra, U.S. 1983. Effectiveness of plant oils against pulse beetle, *Callosobruchus chinensis* Linn. *Indian Journal of Entomology*, 45(1): 6–9.

Allen, D.J. 1983. *The Pathology of Tropical Food Legumes. Disease Resistance in Crop Improvement.* Chichester, John Wiley and Sons. 413 p.

Allen, D.J., Anno-Nyako, F.O., Ochieng, R.S., and Ratinam, M. 1981. Beetle transmission of cowpea mottle and southern bean mosaic viruses in West Africa. *Tropical Agriculture* (Trinidad), 58(2), 171-175.

Allen, D.J., Anno-Nyako, F.O., Ochieng, R.S., and Ratinam, M. 1981. Beetle transmission of cowpea mottle and southern bean mosaic viruses in West Africa. *Tropical Agriculture* (Trinidad), 58, 171-175.

Alonzo, F. 1975. Estudios en *Phaseolus vulgaris* sobre el control de la mosca blanca *Bemisia tabaci* (Genn.) en la zona sur oriente de Guatemala. Paper prepared for a workshop on bean plant protection, CIAT, Cali, 18p.

Altieri, M.A., van Schoonhoven, A., and Doll, J. 1977. The ecological role of weeds in insect pest management systems: a review illustrated by bean (*Phaseolus vulgaris*) cropping systems. PANS, 23, 195-205.

Amin, P.W. 1983. Major field insect pests of groundnut in India and associated crop losses. *Indian Journal of Entomology*, Special Issue 2, 337-344.

Amin, P.W. 1985a. Resistance of wild species of groundnut to insect and mite pests. In ICRISAT, *Proceedings of an International Workshop on Cytogenetics of Arachis*, 31 Oct-2 Nov 1983, Patancheru, AP, ICRISAT.

Amin, P.W. 1985b. Apparent resistance of groundnut cultivar Robut 33-1 to bud necrosis disease. *Plant Disease*, 69, 718-719.

Amin, P.W. 1988. Insect and mite pests and their control. In Reddy, P.S., ed., *Groundnut*, New Delhi, Indian Council of Agricultural Research, 393-452.

Amin P.W., and Mohammad, A.B. 1980. Groundnut pest research at ICRISAT. Paper prepared for an international workshop on groundnuts, ICRISAT, 13-17 October.

Amin, P.W., and Palmer, J. 1985. Identification of groundnut Thysanoptera. *Tropical Pest Management*, 31, 286-291.

Amin, P.W., Singh, K.N., Dwivedi, S.L., and Rao, V.R. 1985. Sources of resistance to the jassid (*Empoasca kerri* Pruthi), thrips (*Frankliniella schultzei* (Trybom)) and termites (*Odontotermes* sp.) in groundnut (*Arachis hypogaea* L.). *Peanut Science*, 12, 58-60.

Amoako-Atta. B., Omolo, E.O., and Kidega, E.K. 1983. Influence of maize, cowpea and sorghum intercropping systems on stem/pod-borer infestations. *Insect Science and Its Application*, 4, 47-57.

Ananthakrishnan, T.N. 1969. Indian Thysanoptera. New Delhi, Council for Scientific and Industrial Research, Publications and Information Directorate, CSIR Zoological Monograph 1.

Ananthakrishnan, T.N. 1980. Thrips. In Harris, K.F., and Maramorosch, K. eds., *Vectors of Plant Pathogens*, New York, Academic Press, 149-164.

Anazonwu, D.L., and Johnson, S.J. 1986. Effects of host and density on larval colour, size and development of the velvet bean caterpillar, *Anticarsia gemmatalis* (Lepidoptera: Noctuidae). *Environmental Entomology*, 15, 779-783.

Andow, D.A. 1983. Plant diversity and insect populations: interaction among beans, weeds, and insects. Ithaca, NY, Cornell University, 211p. (PhD thesis)

Andrews, K.L. 1983. Slugs of the genus *Vaginulus* as pests of common bean, *Phaseolus vulgaris* in Central America. *Proceedings of the 10th International Congress on Plant Protection*, Brighton, 3, 951.

Andrews, K.L. 1984. El manejo integrado de plagas invertebradas en cultivos agronómicos, hortícolas y frutales. Zamorano, Proyecto Manejo Integrado de Plagas Invertegradas en Honduras, Escuela Agrícola Panamericana and Agency for International Development, Publication 7, 85p.

Andrews, K.L., and Barletta, H. 1985. Los secretos de la babosa, parte 2: control en primera. Zamorano, Escuela Agrícola Panamericana, Publication MIPH EAP 49, 16p.

Andrews, K.L., and Dundee, D.S. 1986. *Sarasinula plebeia* (Fischer) (alias *Vaginulus plebeius*) and other Veronicellid slugs of agricultural importance in Central America. Paper prepared for a regional slug seminar, Zamorano.

Andrews, K.L., and Lema, F. 1986. Dínamica poblacional de la babosa, *Vaginulus plebeius* (Stylomenatophora: Veronicellidae) en lotes de maíz-frijol en relevo. *Turrialba*, 36, 77–80.

Andrews, K.L., and Poe, S.L. 1980. Spider mites of El Salvador, Central America (Acari: Tetranychidae). *Florida Entomologist*, 63, 502–505.

Andrews, K.L., Valverde, V., and Avedilla, M. 1985. Rentabilidad del uso de cubiertas de plastico en habichuela para control de saltahojas, *Empoasca* sp. probablemente *kraemeri* (Ross and Moore) Honduras, *CEIBA*, 26, 140–148.

Annecke, D.P., and Moran, C.V. 1982. Insects and mites of cultivated plants in South Africa. Durban, Butterworths.

Anno-Nyako, F.O. 1984. Identification, partial characterization and some properties of a virus causing a mild mottle disease in soybean, *Glycine max* (L.) Merril in Nigeria, and the evaluation of local and exotic cowpeas (*Vigna unguiculata* (L.) Walp.) for grain legume viruses under natural conditions in Kumasi, Ghana. Kumasi, Ghana, University of Science and Technology, 115 p. (PhD thesis).

Anno-Nyako, F.O. 1986. Semipersistent transmission of an 'extra mild' isolate of cowpea mild mottle virus on soyabean by whitefly *Bemisia tabaci* Genn. in Nigeria. *Tropical Agriculture* (Trinidad), 63(3), 193–194.

Anno-Nyako, F.O., Vetten, H.J., Allen, D.J., and Thottappilly, G. 1983. The relation between cowpea golden mosaic and its vector, *Bemisia tabaci*. *Annals of Applied Biology*, 102, 319–323.

Anonymous. 1964. Pests of arhar (*Cajanus indicus*). In *A Review of Research Division of Entomology (1947–1964)*, Dacca, East Pakistan Agricultural Research Institute, Department of Agriculture.

Anonymous. 1980. *Annual Research Report 1974 and 1975*. Fiji, Department of Agriculture. 141 p.

Anonymous. 1981. Soybean pests: description, damage and biology. In COPA (Commercial Oilseed Producers' Association), *Soybeans in Zimbabwe. Oilseeds Handbook*, Harare, COPA, 31–42.

Anonymous. 1985. Groundnut growing in Kenya. *Kenya Farmer*, September, 50, 30–31.

Ansa, O.A., Misari, S.M., and Shoyinka, S.A. 1988. Aetiology and economic importance of groundnut rosette virus in Africa. In Williams, A.O., Mbiele, A.L., and Nkouka, N., eds., *Virus Diseases of Plants in Africa*, Lagos, Nigeria, OAU/STRC Scientific Publication, 137–146.

Ansari, A.K. 1984. Biology of *Aphis craccivora* Koch and varietal resistance of cowpeas. University of Reading, UK. 273p. (PhD thesis).

Ansari, M.A., Pawar, A.D., and Ahmed, S.N. 1987. A note on pathogenicity of naturally occurring bacterium *Serratia marcescens* Bizio on some lepidopterous pests. *Plant Protection Bulletin*, 39, 27–28.

Appelbaum, S.W., Southgate, B.J., and Podler, H. 1968. The comparative morphology, specific status and host compatibility of two geographic strains of *Callosobruchus chinensis* (L.). *Journal of Stored Products Research*, 4, 135–146.

Appert, J. 1954. La bruche des arachides. *Annales du Centre de Recherches Agronomiques de Bambey*, 1954, 181–190.

Appert, J. 1964. Faune parasitaire du Niebe (*Vigna unguiculata* (L.) Walp.) = *V. catjang* (Burm.) Walp. en République du Sénégal. *Agronomie Tropical, Nogent*, 19, 788–799.

Appert, J. 1966. Les insectes d'arachide de Sénégal. In Centre de recherches agronomiques de Bambey, Rapport annuel, *Bulletin*, 7, 67–74.

Arant, F.S. 1938. Life history and control of the cowpea curculio. *Alabama Agricultural Experiment Station Bulletin*, 246, 34p.

Araújo, J.P.P., Rios, G.P., Watt, E.E., Neves, B.P., Fageria, N.K., Oliveira, I.P., Guimaraes, C.M., and Silveirafilho, A. 1984. Cultura do caupi, *Vigna unguiculata* (L.) Walp.: Descriço e recommendaçes técnicas de cultivo. Technical Bulletin 18, Goiñia, EMBRAPA-CNPAF, 82p.

Arbogast, R.T. 1984. Natural enemies as control agents for stored-product insects. Paper prepared for the third international working conference on stored-product entomology, Kansas State University, Manhattan, 23–28 October 1983, 360–375.

Arevalo, O.P. 1977. Azucares reductores y no reductores como posibles factores de resistencia del frijol hacia Epilachna varivestis (Muls.) (Coleoptera: Coccinellidae). Chapingo, Escuela Nacional de Agricultura, Colegio de Postgraduados, 70p. (MSc thesis)

Argikar, C.P., and Thobbi, V.V. 1957. An estimate of the damage caused by tur pod caterpillar, Exelastis atomosa W. to the pigeonpea grain. *Poona Agricultural College Magazine* 48, 25–26.

Arunin, A. 1978. Pests of soybean and their control in Thailand. In Singh, S.R., van Emden, H.F., and Taylor, T.A., eds., *Pests of Grain Legumes: Ecology and Control*, London/New York, Academic Press, 43–46.

Aryeetey, A.N., and Laing, E. 1973. Inheritance of yield components and their correlation with yield in cowpea (*Vigna unguiculata* (L.) Walp. *Euphytica*, 22, 386–392.

Asahina, S., and Turuoka, Y. 1970. Records of the insects visiting a weather ship located at the Ocean weather station 'Tango' on the Pacific, 5. Insects captured during 1968. *Kontyu*, 38, 318–330.

Asayama, T., and Osaki, N.A. 1970. Cytoplasmic polyhedrosis of the cotton leaf worm, *Prodenia litura* (F.). *Journal of Invertebrate Pathology*, 16, 2, 292–294.

Asayama, T., and Ohoishi, K. 1980. Field infection of *Spodoptera litura* larvae by the entomogenous fungus, *Nomuraea rileyi* and morphology of the fungus grown on the larvae. *Japanese Journal of Applied Entomology and Zoology*, 24, 105–107.

Ashby, J.W. 1984. Bean leaf roll virus. Kew, Surrey, *CMI/AAB Descriptions of Plant Viruses*, 286.

Asjes, C.J. 1981. Control of stylet-borne spread by aphids of tulip breaking virus in lilies and tulips, and hyacinth mosaic virus in hyacinth by permethrin sprays versus mineral oil sprays. Med. Fac. Landbourn, Rijksunin, *Gene*, 46, 1073.

Assa, A.D. 1976. Co-ordinated minimum insecticide trial: yield performance of insect resistant cowpea cultivars from IITA. *Tropical Grain Legume Bulletin*, 5, 9.

Atiri, G.I. 1984. Insect transmission characteristics of a Nigerian strain of cowpea aphid-borne mosaic virus. *Fitopatologia Brasileira*, 9(3), 495–503.

Atiri, G.I., and Thottappilly, G. 1985. *Aphis craccivora* settling behaviour and acquisition of cowpea aphid-borne mosaic virus in aphid-resistant cowpea lines. *Entomología Experimentalis et Applicata*, 39, 241–245.

Atiri, G.I., Ekpo, E.J.A., and Thottappilly, G. 1984. The effect of aphid resistance in cowpea on infestation and development of *Aphis craccivora* and on transmission of cowpea aphid-borne mosaic virus. *Annals of Applied Biology*, 104, 339–346.

Atiri, G.I., Enobakhare, D.A., and Thottappilly, G. 1986. The importance of colonizing and non-colonizing aphid vectors in the spread of cowpea aphid-borne mosaic virus. *Plant Protection*, 5(6), 406–410.

Atiri, G.I., Thottappilly, G., and Ligan, D. 1987. Effects of cypermethrin and deltamethrin on the feeding behaviour of Aphis craccivora and transmission of cowpea aphid-borne mosaic virus. *Annals of Applied Biology*, 110(No. 3), 445–461.

Attri, B.S., and Lal, R. 1976. Residue and residual toxicity of ethyl and methyl parathion on cowpea. *Indian Journal of Agricultural Sciences*, 44, 481–486.

Atwal, A.S. 1976. *Agricultural Pests of India and South-east Asia. Pests of Pulse Crops.* Ludhiana, Kalyani Publishers. 175p.

Augustine, M.G., Fisk, F.W., Davidson, R.W., Lapidus, J.B., and Cleary, R.W. 1964. Host plant selection by the Mexican bean beetle Epilachna varivestis. *Annals of the Entomological Society of America*, 57, 127–134.

Autrique, A. 1987. Recherches sur le controle de la mouche du haricot (*Ophiomyia* spp.) au Burundi. Bujumbura, Division Defense des Vegetaux, Institut des sciences agronomiques du Burundi, 13p.

Autrique, A., and Ntahimpera, L. 1986. Biological control of the black bean aphid in Burundi. *Phaseolus Beans Newsletter for Eastern Africa*, 5, 9–10.

Autrique, A., Remaudière, G., and Stary, P. 1985. Observations ecologiques sur les pucerons du haricot et du pois au Burundi. Paper prepared for an international conference on food legumes in Africa, Niamey, Association des universités partiellement ou entièrement de langue française.

Avalos, F. 1977. Control químico del barrenador de brotes Epinotia aporema Wlsm. en frijol. *Avances en Investigación* (Peru), 8, 1–5.

Avalos, F. 1982. Evaluación de resistencia a plagas de insectos en variedades de frijol. Taller nacional sobre manejo de plagas de frijol, Chiclayo, Peru, Instituto Nacional de Investigaciones y Promoción Agraria, Centro Internacional de Agricultura Tropical, and Centro Investigación y Promoción Agropecuaría, 8p.

Avalos, F., and Lozano, C. 1976. Comportamiento de 93 cultivares de frijoles amarillos al ataque del gusano pícador: avances en investigación. *Rev. Prog. CRIA I* (Peru), 6, 9–13.

Avidov, Z., Appelbaum, S.W., and Berlinger, M.J. 1965. Physiological aspects of host specificity in the Bruchidae. 2: Ovipositional preference and behaviour in *Callosobruchus chinensis* (L.). *Entomología Experimentalis et Applicata*, 8, 96–106.

AVRDC (Asian Vegetable Research and Development Center). 1976. Soybean report '75. Shanhua, AVRDC, 68p.

AVRDC. 1981. Progress report for 1979. Shanhua, Taiwan, AVRDC, 109p.

AVRDC. 1982. Vegetable pest control: insecticide evaluation tests. Shanhua, Taiwan, AVRDC, Table SB-15.

AVRDC. 1984. Progress report for 1982. Shanhua, Taiwan, AVRDC, 337p.

AVRDC. 1985. Progress report for 1984. Shanhua, Taiwan, AVRDC, 444p.

Ayoade, K.A. 1969. Insecticide control of the pod borer, *Maruca testulalis* Gey. on Westbred cowpea (*Vigna* sp.) *Bulletin of the Entomological Society of Nigeria*, 2, 23–33.

Ayyana, T., Arjuna Rao, P., Subbaratam, G.V., Krishna Murthy, B.M., and Narayana, K.L. 1982. Chemical control of *Spodoptera litura* Fabricius on the groundnut crop. *Pesticides* (Bombay), 16, 19–20.

Ayyar, P.N. 1934. A very destructive pest of stored products in India. *Bulletin of Entomological Research*, 25, 155–169.

Ayyar, T.V.R. 1963. *Handbook of Economic Entomology for South India.* Madras, Government Press. 516p.

Babu, C.S.J. 1978. Bionomics and control of bean fly Ophiomyia phaseoli (Tryon) (Diptera: Agromyzidae). *Mysore Journal of Agricultural Sciences*, 12, 522–523.

Babu, P.C.S., and Rajasekaran, B. 1981. A note on the control of the stemfly (*Ophiomyia phaseoli* Coq.) on cowpea (*Vigna unguiculata* L.). *Madras Agricultural Journal*, 68, 205–206.

Bainbridge-Fletcher, T. 1914. Some south Indian insects and other animals of importance—considered especially from an economic point of view. Madras, Government Press, 565p.

Bakhetia, D.R.C. 1976. *Anarsia ephippias* (Meyrick) (Lepidoptera: Gelechiidae) damaging the groundnut crop in the Punjab. *Journal of Research*, 14, 232–233.

Bakhetia, D.R.C. 1982a. Studies on the white grub, *Holotrichia consanguinea* Blanchard in the Punjab: control and yield losses due to white grub and collar rot of groundnut. *Journal of Soil Biology and Ecology*, 2, 40–46.

Bakhetia, D.R.C. 1982b. Studies on the white grub, *Holotrichia consanguinea* (Blanchard) in the Punjab. 4: control in groundnut through seed treatment with insecticides. *Indian Journal of Entomology*, 44, 310–317.

Bakhetia, D.R.C. 1983. Studies on the white grub, *Holotrichia consanguinea* (Blanchard) and collar rot (*Aspergillus niger* van Tiegh) of groundnut sown on different dates in Punjab. *Indian Journal of Agricultural Sciences*, 53, 846–850.

Bakhetia, D.R.C., and Brar, K.C. 1983. Seed treatment—a new and economical method to control white grub pest of groundnut. *Journal of Soil Biology and Ecology*, 3, 65–67.

Bakhetia, D.R.C., and Sidhu, A.S. 1976a. Biology and seasonal activity of the groundnut aphid *Aphis craccivora* Koh. *Journal of Research*, 14, 299–303.

Bakhetia, D.R.C., and Sidhu, A.S. 1976b. Studies on the chemical control of the groundnut aphid *Aphis craccivora* Koch. *Pesticides* (Bombay), 10, 22–24.

Banerjee, S.N., and Pramanik, L.M. 1964. An outbreak of *Euchreysops cnejus* (Fabr.) on golden gram (*Phaseolus aureus*) in West Bengal. *Science and Culture*, 30, 507.

Balder, B., Ramanujam, S., and Jain, H.K., eds. 1988. *Pulse Crops (Grain Legumes)*. New Delhi, Oxford & IBH Publishing, 626p.

Banks, H.J. 1977. Distribution and establishment of *Trogoderma granarium* Everts (Coleoptera: Dermestidae): climatic and other influences. *Journal of Stored Products Research*, 13, 183–202.

Baquero, M. Licha-. 1980. The witches' broom disease of pigeon-pea [*Cajanus cajan (L) Millsp.*] in Puerto Rico. *Journal of Agriculture of the University of Puerto Rico*, 64 (4), 424–441.

Barak, A.V., and Burkholder, W.E. 1985. A versatile and effective trap for detecting and monitoring stored product Coleoptera. *Agriculture, Ecosystems and Environment*, 12, 207–218.

Barfoot, P.D., and Connett, R.J.A. 1989. AGC's cowpea enzyme inhibitor gene potential market opportunity. *Biotechnology News and Information*, 1, 177–182.

Barroga, S.F. 1969. Control of lepidopterous pests attacking bush bean, *Phaseolus vulgaris* L. blossoms and pods. *Philippine Journal of Plant Industry*, 34, 159–162.

Barrow, R.M. 1968. Bionomics of a leaf-eating beetle (Diphaulaca n. sp.) on pigeonpea (*Cajanus cajan*) in Trinidad. Proceedings of the Caribbean Food Crops Society 6th Annual Meeting, Trinidad, 6, 38–41.

Bastos, J.A.M. 1965a. Ação de alguns inseticidas orgânicos sintéticos sobre Callosobruchus analis Fabr., 1775 (Col., Bruchidae): 1. Ação preventiva do malation e das misturas lindano e DDT. *Turrialba*, 15(2), 145–147.

Bastos, J.A.M. 1965b. Ação de alguns inseticidas orgânicos sintéticos sobre Callosobruchus analis Fabr., 1775 (Col., Bruchidae): 2. Ação curativa do malation. *Turrialba*, 15(2), 147–149.

Bastos, J.A.M. 1967. Proteção de alguns tipos de embalagens contra o ataque do gorgulho do feijão-de-corda, Callosobruchus analis Fabr., 1775 (Col., Bruchidae) e o gorgulho do milho, Sitophilus zea mais Mots., 1877 (Col., Curculionidae). In 1 Reunião da Sociedade Brasileira de Defensivos da Lavoura e Pecuária, São Paulo, 66–69.

Bastos, J.A.M. 1968. Influência das embalagens no controle do gorgulho Callosobruchus analis em feijão-de-corda, *Vigna sinensis*. *Turrialba*, 18(1), 76–79.

Bastos, J.A.M. 1969a. Substâncias orgânicas como atraentes para a postura do gorgulho, Callosobruchus analis Fabr. no feijão de corda, *Vigna sinensis* Endl. *Pesquisa Agropecuaria Brasileira*, 4, 127–128.

Bastos, J.A.M. 1969b. Influência da cor do feijão-de-corda, *Vigna sinensis* Endl. no ataque do gorgulho, *Callosobruchus analis*. *Turrialba*, 19(2), 296–297.

Bastos, J.A.M. 1970. Efeito da areia, em camadas de pequena espessura de feijão-de-corda (*Vigna sinensis* Endl.) no controle do gorgulho (*Callosobruchus analis* Fabr., 1775). *Pesquisas Agropecuarias do Nordeste*, Recife 2(2), 73–78.

Bastos, J.A.M. 1973a. Influência do tamanho das larvas do manhoso, *Chalcodermus bimaculatus* Fiedler, 1936 na emergência de adultos. *Pesquisas Agropecuarias do Nordeste*, Recife 5(1), 45–47.

Bastos, J.A.M. 1973b. Avaliação dos prejuizos causados pelo gorgulho, *Callosobruchus maculatus*, em amostras de feijão-de-corda, *Vigna sinensis*, colhidas em Fortaleza, Ceará. *Pesquisa Agropecuaria Brasileira*, 8, 131–132.

Bastos, J.A.M. 1974a. Profundidade de penetração de larvas do manhoso, *Chalcodermus bimaculatus* Fiedler, em solos arenosos. *Fitossanidade*, 1(1), 1–2.

Bastos, J.A.M. 1974b. Influência das diferentes fases de desenvolvimento do feijão-de-corda, *Vigna sinensis* Endl., na preferência do manhoso adulto, *Chalcodermus bimaculatus* Fiedler. *Fitossanidade*, 1(1), 2–3.

Bastos, J.A.M. 1974c. Controle do gorgulho do fejão-de-corda, *Callosobruchus maculatus* (Fabr., 1775) (Col., Bruchidae), com brometo de metila. *Turrialba*, 4(2), 230–232.

Bastos, J.A.M. 1974d. Periodo pupal do manhoso, *Chalcodermus bimaculatus* Fiedler, 1936 a diversas temperaturas. *Fitossanidade*, 1(1), 3–5.

Bastos, J.A.M. 1974e. Controle do manhoso, *Chalcodermus bimaculatus* Fiedler, no campo, com inseticida orgânicos sintéticos. *Fitossanidade*, 1(1), 7–9.

Bastos, J.A.M. 1974f. Desenvolvimento da fase pupal do *Chalcodemus bimaculatus* Fiedler, em alguns tipos de solos com diferentes teores de umidade. *Turrialba*, 24(2), 227–230.

Bastos, J.A.M., and Aguiar, P.A.A. 1971. Controle do gorgulho do feijão-de-corda, *Chalcodermus bimaculatus* (Fabr.) (Col., Bruchidae), com phostoxim. *Ciencia Agronómico*, 1(2), 59–62.

Bastos, J.A.M., and Assunção, M.V. 1975. Influência de diferentes tipos de embalagens na aço do phostoxim contra o gorgulho do feijão-de-corda, *Chalcodermus bimaculatus* Fabr. *Ciencia Agron.*, 5(1/2), 7–11.

Bath, J.E. and Chapman, R.K. 1968. Influence of aphid stage on acquisition and inoculation phases of pea enation mosaic virus transmission. *Annals of Entomological Society of America*, 61, 906–909.

Bath, J.E., and Tsai, J.H. 1969. The use of aphids to separate two strains of pea enation mosaic virus. *Phytopathology*, 59, 1377–1380.

Bato, S.M., and Sanchez, F.F. 1972. The biology and chemical control of *Callosobruchus chinensis* (Linn.) (Coleoptera: Bruchidae). *Philippine Entomologist*, 2, 167–182.

Battu, G.S. 1977. Occurrence of *Parasracophaga misera* (Walker) and *Campoletis* sp. as parasites of *Spodoptera litura* (F.) from India. *Current Science*, 46-568-569.

Becquer, A., and Fernandez, R. 1981. Dinamica de las poblaciones de afidos en plantaciones de frijol (*Phaseolus vulgaris* L.). *Ciencias de la Agricultura*, (Cuba), 8, 23–28.

Beebe, S. 1983. Mejoramiento para resistencia al *Apion godmani*. In IICA, *Taller Internacional sobre Apion y mustia hilachoza en Guatemala y Costa Rica*, Guatemala, Instituto Interamericano de Cooperación para la Agricultura, 50p.

Bell, C.H. 1984. Effects of oxygen on the toxicity of carbon dioxide to storage insects. In Ripp, B.E., ed., *Controlled Atmospheres and Fumigation in Grain Storage*, Amsterdam, Elsevier, 67–74.

Bell, J.V., and Hamalle, R.J. 1971. A bacterium and dipterous parasite in wild populations of cowpea curculio larvae: effects of treatment with spores of *Metarrhizium anisopliae*. *Journal of Invertebrate Pathology*, 17, 256–259.

Bennet, F.D. 1960. Parasites of *Ancylostomia stercoria* (Pyralidae: Lepidoptera) a pod borer attacking pigeonpea in Trinidad. *Bulletin of Entomological Research*, 59(4), 737–757.

Bergman, B.H.H. 1956. Mosaic and witches' broom disease of the groundnut (*Arachis hypogaea*) in West-Java and their vector *Orosius argentatus*. *Tijdschrift voor Plantenziekten*, 62, 291–304.

Berlinger, M.J. 1986. Host plant resistance to *Bemisia tabaci*. *Agriculture, Ecosystems and Environment*, 17, 69–82.

Bernabe, C.M. 1972. Effect of aphid infestation *Aphis craccivora* Koch on the yield of Los Baños bush sitao. *Philippine Entomologist*, 2, 209–212.

Bernardo, E.N. 1969. Effects of six host plants on the biology of black bean aphid, *Aphis craccivora* Koch. *Philippine Entomologist*, 1, 287–292.

Best, R.J. 1968. Tomato spotted wilt virus. In Smith, K.M., and Lauffer, M.A. eds., *Advances in Virus Research*, New York, Academic Press, 65–146.

Bhatnagar, V.S., and Davies, J.C. 1979. Arthropod endoparasitoids of insect pests (excluding *Heliothis* spp.) recorded at ICRISAT Center, Andhra Pradesh, India, 1974–79. Patancheru, India, ICRISAT, Progress Reports 3, Cropping Entomology. 17p.

Bhatnagar, V.S., Lateef, S.S., Sithanantham, S., Pawar, C.S., and Reed, W. 1982. Research on Heliothis at ICRISAT. In Reed, W., and Kumble, Vrinda, eds., Proceedings of the International Workshop on Heliothis Management, 15–20 November 1981, Patancheru, AP, ICRISAT, 385–397.

Bhatnagar, V.S., Lateef, S.S., Sithanantham, S., Pawar, C.S., and Reed, W. 1982. Research on *Heliothis* at ICRISAT. In ICRISAT, *Proceedings of the International Workshop on Heliothis Management, 15–20 Nov. 1981*, Patancheru, India, ICRISAT, 385–396.

Bhatnagar, V.S., Pawar, C.S., Jadhav, D.R., and Davis, J.C. 1985. Mermithid nematodes as parasites of *Heliothis* sp., and other crop pests in Andhra Pradesh, India. Proceedings of Indian Academy of Sciences. *Animal Science*, 94(5), 509–515.

Bhattacharya, A.K. 1984. Screening of soybean germplasm with special reference to losses caused by major pests (1983–84). Annual Research Report, Pantnagar, G.B. Pant University of Agriculture and Technology, Department of Entomology, 8p.

Bhattacharya, A.K. 1988. Insect pests of stored soybean and their management. National symposium on insect pests and diseases of soybean. Jawahar Lal Nehru Krishi Vishwa Vidyalaya University, R.A.K. College of Agriculture, Sehore, 25–26, (Abstract).

Bhattacharya, A.K., and Pant, N.C. 1969. Nature of growth inhibitors for *Trogoderma granarium* Everts (Coleoptera: Dermestidae) in lentil (*Lens esculenta* Moench) and french bean (*Phaseolus vulgaris* L.). *Journal of Stored Products Research*, 5, 379–388.

Bhattacharya, A.K., and Rathore, Y.S. 1977. Survey and study of the bionomics of major soybean insects and their chemical control. G.B. Pant University of Agriculture and Technology, *Research Bulletin*, 107, 324p.

Bhattacharya, A.K., and Rathore, Y.S. 1980. Soybean insect pests in India. In Corbin, F.T., ed., *World Soybean Research Conference II*, Boulder, CO, Westview Press, 291–301.

Bhattacharya, A.K., Chaudhary, R.R.P., and Ram, S. 1976. Survey of insect pests of soybean during various stages of crop growth at Govind Ballabh Pant University of Agriculture and Technology. Annual Report of Research, 1974–75, Pantnagar, G.B. Pant University of Agriculture and Technology, 76–77.

Bhattacherjee, N.S. 1976. Record of the parasites and predators of soybean leaf rollers in India. *Indian Journal of Entomology*, 38(4), 381–384.

Bhattacherjee, N.S. 1977. Preliminary studies on the effect of some soil insecticides on soybean nodulation. *Pesticides* (Bombay), 11, 38.

Bhattacherjee, N.S. 1980. Incidence of the stem fly, *Ophiomyia phaseoli* (Tryon) on soybean. *Indian Journal of Entomology*, 42, 280–282.

Bhattacherjee, N.S., and Gupta, S.I. 1972. A new species of *Heliothis* Ochsenheimer (Noct. Lepid.) infesting cotton and tur (*Cajanus indicus*) in India with observations on the three other common species of the genus. *Journal of Natural History, Bombay*, 6, 147–151.

Biezanko, C.M., Ruffinelli, A., and Link, D. 1974. Plantas y otras sustancias alimenticias de las onigas de los lepidopterous uriguoyos. *Revista de Centro Ciências Rurais*, 4, 107–148.

Bigot, L., and Vuattoux, R. 1981. Some biological and ecological data on Lepidoptera: Pterophoridae of the Lamto region (Ivory Coast). *Bulletin de l'Institut Fondamental d'Afrique Noire*, 41 (4), 837–843.

Bindra, O.S. 1965. Biology and bionomics of *Clavigralla gibbosa* spinola, the pod bug of pigeon pea. *Indian Journal of Agricultural Sciences*, 35 (4), 322–324.

Bindra, O.S., and Jakhmola, S.S. 1967. Incidence of and losses caused by some pod-infesting insects in different varieties of pigeonpea [*Cajanus cajan* (L.) Millsp.]. *Indian Journal of Agricultural Sciences*, 37, 177–186.

Bindra, O.S., and Sagar, P. 1976. Co-ordinated minimum insecticide trial: yield performance of insect resistant cowpea cultivars from IITA compared with Indian cultivars. *Tropical Grain Legume Bulletin*, 5, 8.

Bindra, O.S., and Singh, H. 1971a. Tur pod bug, *Clavigralla gibbosa* Spinola (Coreidae: Hemiptera). *Pesticides*, 5(2), 3–4, 32.

Bindra, O.S., and Singh, J. 1971b. Biological observations on the whitegrub, *Lachnosterna (Holotrichia) consanguinea* Blanchard (Coleoptera: Scarabeidae) and the relative efficacy of different insecticides against the adults. *Indian Journal of Entomology*, 33 (2), 225–227.

Birch, N., Southgate, B.J., and Fellows, L.E. 1985. Wild and semi-cultivated legumes as potential sources of resistance to bruchid beetles for crop breeders: a study of *Vigna/Phaseolus*. In Wickens, G.E., Goodin, J.R., and Field, D.V., eds., *Plants for Arid Lands*, London, George Allen and Unwin, 303–320.

Birch, N.E., Fellows, L.E., Evans, S.V., and Doherty, K. 1986. Paraaminophenylalanine in *Vigna*: possible taxonomic and ecological significance as a seed defence against bruchids. *Phytochemistry*, 25(12), 2745–2749.

Bird, J., and Maramorosch, K. 1975. *Tropical Diseases of Legumes*. New York, Academic Press, 171 pp.

Bird, J., and Maramorosch, K. 1978. Viruses and virus diseases associated with whiteflies. *Advances in Virus Research*, 22, 55–109.

Bird, J., and Sánchez, J. 1971. Whiteflies transmitted viruses in Puerto Rico. *Journal of Agriculture of the University of Puerto Rico*, 55, 461–466.

Bird, J., Perez, J.E., Alconero, R., Vakili, N.C., and Melendez, P.L. 1972. A whitefly-transmitted golden yellow mosaic virus of *Phaseolus lunatus* in Puerto Rico. *Journal of Agriculture of the University of Puerto Rico*, 56, 64–74.

Bird, J., Sánchez, J., and Vakili, N.G. 1973. Golden yellow mosaic of beans (*Phaseolus vulgaris*) in Puerto Rico. *Phytopathology*, 63, 1435.

Black, L.M. 1959. Biological cycles of plant viruses in insect vectors. In Burnet, F.M., and Stanley, W.M., eds., *The Viruses*, New York, Academic Press, 2, 157–185.

Blanco, S., and Bencoo, P. 1981. Presencia del virus del mosaico dorado del frijol (BGMV) en Cuba. *Ciencias de la Agricultura* (Cuba), 9, 118–119.

Blatchford, S.M., and Hall, D.W. 1963. Methods of drying groundnuts. 1, natural methods. *Tropical Science*, 5, 6–33.

Boardman, N.K. 1980. Energy from the biological conversion of solar energy. *Philosophical Transactions of Royal Society of London*, A, 295, 477–489.

Bock, K.R. 1971. Notes on East African plant virus diseases. 1: cowpea mosaic virus. *East African Agricultural and Forestry Journal*, 37, 60–62.

Bock, K.R. 1973. East African strains of cowpea aphid-borne mosaic virus. *Annals of Applied Biology*, 74, 75–83.

Bock, K.R., and Conti, M. 1974. Cowpea aphid-borne mosaic virus. Kew, Surrey, CMI (Commonwealth Mycological Institute), *CMI/AAB Descriptions of Plant Viruses*, 134p.

Bogdan, A.V. 1977. *Tropical Pasture and Fodder Plants*. London, Longman, 475p.

Bohlen, E. 1978. *Crop Pests in Tanzania and Their Control*. Berlin/Hamburg, Verlag Paul Parey, 142p.

Boica Junior, A.L., and Vendramin, J.D. 1986. Desenvolvimento de *Bemisia tabaci* (Gennadius, 1889) (Homoptera, Aleyrodidae) em genotipos de feijao (*Phaseolus vulgaris* L.). *Anais da Sociedade Entomológica do Brasil*, 15, 231–238.

Bonato, E.R. 1981. Programa nacional de pesquisa de soja. In *Seminário Nacional de Pesquisa de Soja*, volume 1, Londrina, EMBRAPA-CNPS, 765–793.

Bonnefil, L. 1965. Las plagas del frijol en Centroamerica y su combate. Paper prepared for the 11th annual meeting of the Programa Cooperativo Centroamericano para el Mejoramiento de Cultivos Alilmenticios, Panama.

Booker, R.H. 1963. The effect of sowing date and spacing on rosette disease of groundnut in northern Nigeria, with observations on the vector, *Aphis craccivora*. *Annals of Applied Biology*, 52, 125–131.

Booker, R.H. 1965. Pests of cowpeas and their control in northern Nigeria. *Bulletin of Entomological Research*, 55, 663–672.

Booker, R.H. 1967. Observation on three bruchids associated with cowpea in northern Nigeria. *Journal of Stored Products Research*, 3, 1–15.

Borges, M., Lourdes, V. de, and Louro, D. 1974. A. Biting insect as vector of broad bean mottle virus. *Agronomia Lusitana*, 36, 215–216.

Bos, L. 1981. Wild plants in the ecology of virus diseases. In Maramorosch, K., and Harris, K.F., eds., *Plant Diseases and Vectors, Ecology and Epidemiology*, Academic Press, New York, 1–33.

Bosq, J.M. 1937. Lista preliminar de los hemipterous (Heteropteros) especialmente relacionados con la agricultura nacional. *Revista de la Sociedad Entomológica Argentina*, 9, 111–134.

Boswell, K.F., and Gibbs, A.J. 1983. *Viruses of Legumes: Descriptions and Keys from Virus Identification and Data Exchange*. Canberra, Australian National University. 139 p.

Bowling, C.C. 1980. The stylet sheath as an indicator of feeding activity by the southern green stink bug on soybeans. *Journal of Economic Entomology*, 73, 1–3.

Bowyer, J.W., and Atherton, J.C. 1971. Summer death of frenchbean: new hosts of the pathogen vector relationship and evidence against mycoplasmal etiology. *Phytopathology*, 61, 1451–1455.

Bradley, R.H.E. 1963. Some ways in which a paraffin oil impedes aphid transmission of potato virus Y. *Canadian Journal of Microbiology*, 9, 369–380.

Bradley, R.H.E., Wade, C.V., and Wood, F.A. 1962. Aphid transmission of potato virus Y inhibited by oils. *Virology*, 18, 327–328.

Brady, U.E., Jay, E.G., Redlinger, L.M., and Pearman, G. 1975. Mating activity of *Plodia interpunctella* and *Cadra cautella* during exposure to synthetic pheromones in the field. *Environmental Entomology*, 4, 441–444.

Brar, K.S. 1981. Note on the comparative susceptibility of groundnut varieties to *Aphis craccivora* Koch. *Madras Agricultural Journal*, 3, 207–208.

Brar, K.S., and Sandhu, G.S. 1975. A note on the evaluation of resistance among different cultivars of groundnut against aphid and grey weevil. *Science and Culture*, 41, 445–448.

Brar, K.S., and Sandhu, G.S. 1980a. Biology of Holotrichia consanguinea Blanchard infesting groundnut in the Punjab. Indian Journal of Entomology, 42, 426–433.

Brar, K.S., and Sandhu, G.S. 1980b. Bionomics and control of white grubs in India. Oilseeds Journal, 10, 44–55.

Braune, H.J. 1982. Effect of structure of host egg mass on the effectiveness of egg parasite of Spodoptera litura (F.) (Lepidoptera : Noctuidae). Drosera, 1, 7–16.

Briggs, G.G., Elliott, M., and Farnham, A.W. 1974. Structural aspects of the knockdown of pyrethroids. Pesticide Science, 5, 643–649.

Broad, G.H. 1966. Groundnut pests. Rhodesia Agricultural Journal, September–October, Bulletin 2427, 4p.

Broadbent, J.A., Kuku, F.O., and Oyeniran, J.S. 1968. The internal mycoflora of market groundnuts in Ibadan. Ibadan, Nigerian Stored Products Research Institute, 6th annual report, 27–37.

Broadbent, L. 1969. Disease control through vector control. In Maramorosch, K., ed., Viruses, Vectors and Vegetation, New York, Interscience Publishers, 593–630.

Broersma, D.B., Bernard, R.L., and Luckman, W.H. 1972. Some effects of soybean pubescence on populations of the potato leaf hopper. Journal of Economic Entomology, 65, 78–82.

Brower, J.H. 1984. Trichogramma: potential new biological control method for stored product Lepidoptera. Paper prepared for the third international working conference on stored-product entomology, Kansas State University, Manhattan, 23–28 October 1983, 454–471.

Bruce, W.A., and LeCato, G.L. 1979. Pyemotes tritici: potential biological control agent of stored-product insects. In Rodriguez, J.G., ed., Recent Advances in Acarology, volume 1, New York, Academic Press, 213–220.

Brucher, E.G. 1941. Contribución preliminar al estudio de la polilla del frijol. Bol. Sanit. Veg. (Chile), 1, 63–69.

Buckmire, K.U. 1978. Pests of grain legumes and their control in the Commonwealth Caribbean. In Singh, S.R., van Emden, H.F., and Taylor, T.A., eds., Pests of Grain Legumes: Ecology and Control, London/New York, Academic Press, 179–191.

Buddenhagen, I.W., Gibbs, A.J., Persley, G.J., Reddy, D.V.R., and Wongkaew, S. 1986. Improvement and change of food legume agriculture in Asia in relation to disease. In Wallis, E.S., and Byth, D.E., eds., Proceedings 18, Inkata Press Pty. Ltd, Australia, 138–155.

Burges, H.D. 1962. Studies on the dermestid beetle Trogoderma granarium Everts. 5: reactions of diapause larvae to temperature. Bulletin of Entomological Research, 53, 193–213.

Burges, H.D. 1963. Studies on the dermestid beetle Trogoderma granarium Everts. 6: factors inducing diapause. Bulletin of Entomological Research, 54, 571–587.

Burges, H.D., Canning, E.V., and Hurst, J.A. 1971. Morphology, development and pathogenicity of Nosema oryzaephili in Oryzaephilus surinamensis. Journal of Stored Products Research, 8, 127–137.

Burrell, N.J., Grunday, J.K., and Harkness, L. 1965. Growth of Aspergillus flavus and production of aflatoxin in groundnuts, part 5. Tropical Science, 6, 2, 74–90.

Burt, P.E., Heathcote, G.D., and Broadbent, L. 1960. The use of soil insecticides to control potato aphids and virus diseases. Annals of Applied Biology, 48, 580–590.

Busoli, A.C., Lara, F.M., Nunes Jr., D., and Guidi, M. 1977. Preferência de Elasmopalpus lignosellus (Zeller, 1848) (Lepidoptera: Phycitidae) para diferentes culturas. Anais da Sociedade Entomológica do Brasil, 6, 73–79.

Butler, G.D., Henneberry, T.J., and Clayton, T.E. 1983. Bemisia tabaci (Homoptera: Aleyrodidae): development, oviposition, and longevity in relation to temperature. Annals of the Entomological Society of America, 76, 310–313.

Caballero, R., and Andrews, K.L. 1985. *Anagrus* sp. y otros enemigos naturales del lorito verde (*Empoasca* spp) en el cultivo del frijol en Honduras. *CEIBA*, 26, 149–152.

Cadena, L.D., and Sifuentes, J.A. 1969. Prueba comparativa de la efectividad de 4 insecticidas para combatir la conchinchuela del frijol (*Epilachna varivestis*) bajo condiciones de campo. *Agricultura Técnica en México*, 2, 440–444.

Caldwell, B.E., Howell, R.W., Judd, R.W., and Johnson, H.W., eds. 1973. Soybeans: improvement, production and uses. Madison, WI, American Society of Agronomy, Agron. Ser. 16, 681p.

Caltagirone, L.E. 1981. Land mark examples in classical biological control. Annual Review of Entomology, 26, 213–32.

Cameron, E. 1938. A study of the natural control of the pea moth, *Cydia nigricana* Steph. *Bulletin of Entomological Research*, 29, 277–313.

Cameron, P.J., Allan, D.J., Walker, G.P., and Wightman, J.A. 1983. Management experiments on aphids (*Acyrthosiphon* spp.) and beneficial insects in lucerne. *NZ Journal of Experimental Agriculture*, 11, 343–349.

Campbell, W.V. 1980. Resistance of groundnuts to insects and mites. In ICRISAT, *Proceedings of an International Workshop on Groundnuts*, 13–17 October, Patancheru, AP, ICRISAT, 149–157.

Campbell, W.V. 1983. Management of arthropods on peanut in Southeast Asia. In University of Georgia, *Annual Report, Peanut Collaborative Research Support Program*, 115–133.

Campbell, W.V. 1986. Management of arthropods on peanuts. Paper prepared for a CRSP peanut workshop, Khon Kaen, 19–21 August.

Campbell, W.V., and Brett, C.H. 1966. Varietal resistance of beans to the Mexican bean beetle. *Journal of Economic Entomology*, 59, 899–902.

Campbell, W.V., Emery, D.A., and Gregory, W.C. 1971. Registration of GP-NC343 peanut germplasm. *Crop Science*, 11, 605.

Campbell, W.V., and Wynne, J.C. 1980. Resistance of groundnuts to insects and mites. Paper prepared for an International Workshop on Groundnuts, Patancheru, ICRISAT, 13–17 October.

Campbell, W.V., Wynne, J.C., Emergy, D.A., and Mozingo, R.W. 1977. Registration of NC 6 peanuts. *Crop Science*, 17, 346.

Campos, J. 1972. Insecticidas impregnados a la semilla del maíz para el control de *Elasmopalpus lignosellus* Zeller (Lepidoptera: Pyralidae). *Revista Peruana de Entomología*, 15, 348–351.

Cantwell, G.E., and Cantelo, W.W. 1982. Potential of *Bacillus thuringiensis* as a microbial agent against the Mexican bean beetle. *Journal of Economic Entomology*, 75, 348–350.

Cantwell, G.E., Cantelo, W.W., and Cantwell, M. A. 1985a. Effect of a parasitic mite *Coccipolipus epilachne* on fecundity, food consumption and longevity of the Mexican bean beetle. *Journal of Entomological Science*, 20, 199–203.

Cantwell, G.E., Canatelo, W.W., and Schroder, R.F.W. 1985b. The integration of a bacterium and parasites to control the Colorado potato beetle and the Mexican bean beetle. *Journal of Entomological Science*, 20, 98–103.

Cardenas, A.M. 1982. Enfermedades virales del frijol transmitidas por la mosca blanca *Bemisia tabaci* Genn., con enfasis en Latinoamérica. *Revista Chapingo* (Mexico), 7, 13–18.

Cardona, C., and Posso, C.E. 1987. Bean varietal resistance to stored grain weevils: sources, mechanisms, and factors of resistance. *Bean Newsletter*, 9, 1–4.

Cardona, C., van Schoonhoven, A., Gomez, L., Garcia, J., and Garzon, F. 1981. Effect of artificial mulches on *Empoasca kraemeri* Ross and Moore populations and dry bean yields. *Environmental Entomology*, 10, 705–707.

Cardona, C., Flor, C.A., Morales, F.J., and Pastor-Corrales, M. 1982a. Field problems of beans in Latin America. 2nd ed. Cali, CIAT, 184p.

Cardona, C., Gonzalez, R., and van Schoonhoven, A. 1982b. Evaluation of damage to common beans by larvae and adults of *Diabrotica balteata* and *Cerotooma facialis*. *Journal of Economic Entomology*, 75, 324-327.

Cardona, C., Posso, C.E., Kornegay, J., Valor, J., and Serrano, M. 1989. Antibiosis effects of wild dry bean accessions on the Mexican bean weevil and the bean weevil (Coleoptera: Bruchidae). *Journal of Economic Entomology*, 82, 310-315.

Carlos, Cruz. 1975. Observations on pod borer oviposition and infestation of pigeonpea varieties. *Journal of Agriculture of the University of Puerto Rico*, 59 (1), 63-68.

Carner, G.R. 1980. Sampling pathogens of soybean insect pests. In Kogan, M., and Herzog, D.C., eds., *Sampling Methods in Soybean Entomology*, New York, Springer-Verlag, 559-572.

Carper, J. 1988. *The Food Pharmacy*. New York, Bantam Books, 367p.

Carrillo, S.J. 1977. Control biológico de la conchuela del frijol *Epilachna varivestis* Mulsant en Mexico. Agricultura Técnica en México, 4, 63-71.

Carter, D.J., and Deeming, J.C. 1980. *Azygophleps albovittata* Bethune-Baker (Lepidoptera: Cossidae) attacking groundnuts in northern Nigeria, with descriptions of the immature and imaginal stages. *Bulletin of Entomological Research*, 70, 399-405.

Carter, W. 1973. *Insects in relation to plant disease*. New York, John Wiley and Sons, 2nd ed. 759 pp.

Carvalho, R.P.L., and Machado, M.U.M. 1967. A entomofauna dos produtos armazenados: contribuição para o estudo do Callosobruchus maculatus (Fabricius) Col., Bruchidae. *B. Port. Ci. Nat.*, 11, 133-240.

Cassels, A.C., and Long, R.D. 1980. The regeneration of virus-free plants from cucumber mosaic virus- and potato virus Y-infected tobacco explants cultured in the presence of virazole. *Zeitschrift fuer Naturforsch*, 35C, 350-351.

Cassels, A.C., and Long, R.D. 1982. The elimination of potato viruses X, Y, S and M in meristem and explant cultures of potato in the presence of virazole. *Potato Research*, 25, 165-173.

Castro, Z.B., Cavalcante, R.D., Santos, D.M.L.L., and Cavalcante, M.L.S. 1975. Ocorrência de *Diabrotica speciosa* (Germar, 1824) em diversas culturas no Estado do Ceará. *Fitossanidade*, 1(2), 51-52.

Caswell, G.H. 1973. The impact of infestation on commodities. *Tropical Stored Products Information*, Nigeria, 25, 19.

Caswell, G.H. 1981. Damage to stored cowpea in the northern part of Nigeria. *Samaru Journal of Agricultural Research*, 1, 11-19.

Caswell, G.H., and Akibu, S. 1980. The use of pirimiphos methyl to control bruchids attacking selected varieties of stored cowpea. *Tropical Grain Legume Bulletin*, 17/18, 9-11.

Cavalcante, R.D., Melo, Q.M.S., Cavalcante, M.L.S. and Chagas, F.A. 1979. *Promecops* sp. (Coleoptera, Curculionidae), praga do feijoeiro macassar no Ceará. *Fitossanidade*, 3, 60.

Chalfant, R.B. 1972. Cowpea curculio: control in southern Georgia. *Journal of Economic Entomology*, 66, 727-729.

Chalfant, R.B. 1976. Chemical control of insect pests of the southern pea in Georgia. *Georgia Agricultural Experiment Station Research Bulletin*, 197, 31p.

Chalfant, R.B. 1985. Entomological research on cowpea pests in the USA. In Singh, S.R., and Rachie, K.O., eds., *Cowpea Research, Production and Utilization*. Chichester, John Wiley and Sons, 267-274.

Chalfant, R.B., and Canerday, T.D. 1972. Feeding and oviposition of the cowpea curculio and laboratory screening of southern pea varieties for insect resistance. *Journal of the Georgia Entomological Society*, 7, 272-277.

Chalfant, R.B., and Gaines, T.P. 1973. Cowpea curculio: correlations between chemical composition of southern pea and varietal resistance. *Journal of Economic Entomology*, 66, 1011-1013.

Chalfant, R.B., Suber, T.D., and Canerday, T.D. 1972. Resistance of southern peas to the cowpea curculio in the field. *Journal of Economic Entomology*, 65, 679-682.

Chambers, J. 1987. Recent developments in techniques for detection of insect pests. In Lawson, T.J., ed., *Stored Product Pest Control*, Thornton Heath, BCPC Publications, BCPC Monograph 37, 151-161.

Chambliss, O.L., and Rymal, K.S. 1982. Response of cowpea curculio to volatile extracts from southern pea pods. *Horticultural Science*, 17, 152.

Chandola, R.P., Trehan, K.B., and Bagrecha, L.R. 1970. Varietal resistance to *Bruchus* sp. in cowpea (*Vigna sinensis*) under storage conditions. *Current Science*, 38, 370-371.

Chang, V.C.S. 1977. Transovarial transmission of the Fiji disease virus in *Perkinsiella saccharicida* Kirk. *Sugarcane Pathol. News*, 18, 22-23.

Chant, S.R. 1959. Viruses of cowpea, *Vigna unguiculata* L. (Walp.), in Nigeria. *Annals of Applied Biology*, 47(3), 565-573.

Chari, M.S., and Patel, H.K. 1967. The bionomics of tur plume moth (*Marasmarcha liophanes* Mey.) on pigeonpea (*Cajanus cajan* Millsp.). *Andhra Agricultural Journal*, 14 (5), 158-164.

Chari, M.S., Patel, G.J., Patel, P.N., and Raj, S. 1976. Evaluation of cowpea lines for resistance to aphid, *Aphis craccivora* Koch. *Gujarat Agricultural University Research Journal*, 1, 130-132.

Chaturvedi, G.S., Aggarwal, P.K., and Sinha, S.K. 1980. Growth and yield of determinate and indeterminate cowpea in dryland agriculture. *Journal of Agricultural Science*, Cambridge, 94, 137-144.

Chaudhary, R.R.P., and Bhattacharya, A.K. 1976. Larval developmental behaviour of *Ephestia cautella* (Walker) on several food commodities. *Bulletin of Grain Technology*, 16, 3-8.

Chaudhary, R.R.P., Bhattacharya, A.K., and Rathore, R.R.S. 1976. Field tests for the control of seed maggot, *Delia platura* Mg. attacking soybean. *Science and Culture*, 42(8), 422-425.

Chaudhary, R.R.P., Krishnana, Y.S., and Bhattacharya, A.K. 1972. Soybean at Pantnagar. *Research Bulletin* 2, 72.

Cherian, M.C., and Basheer, M. 1940. *Euborella stali* Dohrn (Forficulidae) as a pest of groundnut in south India. *Indian Journal of Entomology*, 2, 155-158.

Cherian, M.C., and Basheer, M. 1942. Studies on *Stomopteryx nerteria* Meyr. A pest of groundnut in the Madras Presidency. *Madras Agricultural Journal*, 30(11), 379-381.

Chiang, H.S., and Jackai, L.E.N. 1988. Tough pod wall: a factor involved in cowpea resistance in pod sucking bugs. *Insect Science and Its Application*, 9, 389-393.

Chiang, H.S., and Singh, S.R. 1988. Pod hairs as a factor in *Vigna vexillata* resistance to the pod sucking bug, *Clavigralla tomentosicollis*. *Entomología Experimentalis et Applicata*, 47, 195-199.

Chiu, S.C., and Chou, L.Y. 1976. Hymenopterous parasitoids of *Spodoptera litura* Fab. *Journal of Agricultural Research of China*, 25(3), 227-241.

Chiykowski, L.N. 1981. Epidemiology of diseases caused by leafhopper-borne pathogens. In Marmorosch, K., and Harris, K.F., *Plant Diseases and Vectors, Ecology and Epidemiology*, New York, Academic Press, 106-159.

Chou, T.M., Kuo, C.H., and Cheng, E.Y. 1984. The occurrence of insecticide resistance in three lepidopteran pests on vegetables. *Journal of Agricultural Research of China*, 33, 331-336.

Choudhary, M.J. 1969. Bionomics of *Clavigralla gibbosa* Spin. (Coreidae: Hemiptera) a pest of *Cajanus cajan* Sprengl. *Labdev Journal of Science and Technology*, B (Life Science), Poona, India, 7 (3), 200-201.

Chu, Y.I. 1979. Some notes on the lepidopterous rice insect pests at Jawa Timur, Indonesia. National Taiwan University, *Phytopathologist and Entomologist*, 6, 38–43.

Chyan, J.C., Chow, L.Y., and Chiu, R.J. 1984. Hedylepta indicata: its biology and natural enemies. *Journal of Agricultural Research of China*, 33, 181–189 (in Chinese).

CIAT (Centro Internacional de Agricultura Tropical). 1974. *Annual report 1973*. Cali, CIAT, 1770–175.

CIAT. 1975. *Annual report 1974*. Cali, CIAT, 25–129.

CIAT. 1976. *Annual report 1975*. Cali, CIAT, 129–136.

CIAT. 1977. *Annual report 1976*. Cali, CIAT, 15–22.

CIAT. 1980. *Annual report 1979*. Cali, CIAT, 87p.

CIAT. 1981. *Annual report 1980*. Cali, CIAT, 132p.

CIAT. 1982. *Annual report 1981*. Cali, CIAT, 157–159.

CIAT. 1984. *Annual report 1983*. Cali, CIAT, 54–62.

CIAT. 1988. *Annual report 1987*. Cali, CIAT.

Clarke, J.F.G. 1954. The correct name for a pest of legumes. *Proceedings of the Entomological Society of Washington*, 56, 309–310.

Clausen, C.B. 1978. Introduced parasites and predators of arthropod pests: a world review. US Department of Agriculture, Handbook 480, 545p.

Cockbain, A.J. 1971. Epidemiology and control of weevil-transmitted viruses in field beans. *Proceedings of the 6th British Insecticide and Fungicide Conference I*, 302–306.

Cockbain, A.J. 1983. Viruses and virus-like disease of Vicia faba L. In Hebblethwaite, P.D. ed., *The Faba Bean (Vicia faba L.), A Basis for Improvement*, London, Butterworths, 421–462.

Cohen, S. 1982. Control of whitefly vectors of viruses by color mulches. In Harris, K.F., and Maramorosch, K. eds., *Pathogens, Vectors, and Plant Diseases: Approaches to Control*, New York, Academic Press.

Cohen, S., and Melamed-Madjar, V. 1978. Prevention by soil mulching of the spread of tomato yellow leaf and virus transmitted by Bemisia tabaci (Gennadius) (Homoptera: Aleyrodidae) in Israel. *Bulletin of Entomological Research*, 68, 465–470.

Constantino, A.F.T. 1956. O carneiro do feijão Acanthoscelides obtectus (Say). Estudos, Ensaios, Documentos Jts. Invest Ultramar 15. Lisboa, Ultramar, 174p.

Conway, J.A. 1975. Investigations into the origin, development and control of Caryedon serratus (Col. Bruchidae) attacking stored groundnuts in the Gambia. Paper prepared for the first international working conference on stored-product entomology, Savannah, GA, 7–11 October 1974.

Conway, J.A. 1976. The significance of Elasmolomus sordidus (F.) (Hemiptera: Lygaeidae) attacking harvested groundnuts in the Gambia. *Tropical Science*, 18, 187–190.

Conway, J.A. 1983. Notes on the biology and ecology of the groundnut seed beetle Caryedon serratus (Ol.) under field conditions in Senegambia. *Tropical Stored Products Information*, 45, 11–13.

Corpuz, L.R. 1969. The biology, host range and natural enemies of Nezara viridula L. *Philippine Entomologist*, 1, 227–239.

Corrêa-Ferreira, B.S. 1985. Criação massal do percevejo verde, Nezara viridula (L.) EMBRAPA-CNPSo Londrina, Parána, Brazil, documentos 11, 16p.

Corrêa-Ferreira, B.S. 1986. Ocorrência natural do complexo de parasitoides de ovos de percevejos da soja no Pará. *Anais da Sociedade Entomológica do Brasil*, 15, 189–199.

Corrêa-Ferreira, B.S., and Moscardi, F. 1985. Potencial de consumo dos principais insetos predadores ocorrantes na cultura da soja. Resultados Pesq. Soja 1984/85, Documento 15, 79.

Corrêa-Ferreira, B.S., Panizzi, A.R., Newman, G.G., and Turnipseed, S.G. 1977.

Distribuição geográfica abundância estacional dos principais insetos-pragas de soja e seus predadores. *Anais da Sociedade Entomológica do Brasil*, 6, 40–50.

Corseuil, E., and Redaelli, D.C. 1966. Pragas da soja. *Granja*, 22, 31A–31D.

Corseuil, E., and Terhorst, A. 1965. A broca do colo da soja. *Divulgaçã. Agronômica*, 17, 6–11.

Corseuil, E., Cruz, F.Z., and Meyer, L.M.C. 1974. Insetos nocivos à soja norio Grande do Sul. Universitade Fed. Rio Grande do Sul, Fac. Agronomia, Porto Alegre, 36p.

Costa, A.S. 1965. Three whitefly-transmitted virus diseases of beans in São Paulo, Brazil. *FAO Plant Protection Bulletin*, 13, 1–2.

Costa, A.S. 1969. Whiteflies as virus vectors. In Maramorosh, K., and Koprowski, H., eds., *Viruses, Vectors and Vegetation*, New York, Interscience, 95–119.

Costa, A.S. 1975. Increase in the population density of *Bemisia tabaci*, a threat of widespread virus infection of legume crops in Brazil. In Bird, J., and Maramorosch, K., eds., *Tropical Diseases of Legumes*, New York, Academic Press, 27–47.

Costa, A.S., 1976. Whitefly-transmitted plant diseases. *Annual Review of Phytopathology*, 14, 429–449.

Costa, A.S., Gasper, J.O., and Vega, J. 1983. Angular mosaic of Jalo bean induced by a carlavirus transmitted by *Bemisia tabaci*. *Fitopatologia Brasileira*, 8(2), 325–337.

Costa, C.L., and Batista, M.F. de 1979. Viroses transmitidas por Coleopteros no Brasil. *Fitopatologia Brasileira*, 4, 177–179.

Costa, C.L., Lin, M.T., and Sperandeo, C.A. 1981. Besoures crisomelideos vectores do serotipo IV do "cowpea severe mosaic virus" isolado do feijoeiro. *Fitopatologia Brasileira*, 6, 523.

Costa, C.L., Lin, M.T., Kitajima, E.W., Santos, A.S., Mesquita, R.C.M., and Freire-Filho, F.R. 1978. *Cerotoma arenata* (Oliv.). Un crisomelideo vector do mosaico da vigna do Brasil. *Fitopatologia Brasileira*, 3, 81–82.

Costa, C.L., and Rossetto, C.J. 1972. Investigações sobre pragas do feijoeiro no Brasil. In Universidade de Vicosa, Anais do I Siposio Brasileiro de Feijão, 2, 283–302.

Costa, E.C., and Link, D. 1982. Dispersão de adultos *Piezodorus guildinii* e *Nezara viridula* (Hemiptera: Pentatomidae) en soja. *Revista Centro Ciências Rurais*, 12, 51–57.

Costa, E.C., Link, D., and Mario, J.L. 1980. Danos causados por *Nezara viridula* (L.) em feijoeiro (*Phaseolus vulgaris* L). *Revista Centro Ciências Rurais*, 11, 251–256.

Crowe, T.J. 1985. Field crop pests in Burma: an annotated list. Rangoon, Office of the FAO representative, 35p.

Crowell, H.H. 1976. Seed-corn maggot control on sweet corn and snap beans. *Oreg. Veg. Dig.*, 25, 1–3.

Culver, J.N., and Sherwood, J.L. 1987. Resistance to peanut stripe virus in *Arachis* germ plasm. *Plant Disease*, 71, 1080–1082.

Cupertino, F.P., Costa, C.L., Lin, M.T., and Kitajima, E.W. 1981. Infecçao natural do feijoeiro pelo virus do mosaico seveno do caupi no centro-oeste do Brasil. *Fitopatologia Brasileira* 6, 529.

Cuthbert, F.P. Jr. and Davis, B.W. 1972. Factors contributing to cowpea curculio resistance in southern peas. *Journal of Economic Entomology*, 65, 778–781.

Cuthbert, F.P. Jr. and Fery, R.L. 1975a. CR 17-1-13, CR 18-13-1, CR 22-2-21, cowpea curculio resistant southern pea germplasm. *Horticultural Science*, 10(6), 628.

Cuthbert, F.P. Jr. and Fery, R.L. 1975b. Relationship between cowpea curculio injury and *Choanephora* pod rot of southern peas. *Journal of Economic Entomology*, 68, 105–106.

Cuthbert, F.P. Jr. and Fery, R.L. 1979. Value of plant resistance for reducing cowpea curculio damage to southern pea (*Vigna unguiculata* (L.) Walp). *Journal of the American Society for Horticultural Science*, 104, 2, 199–201.

Cuthbert, F.P. Jr., Fery, R.L., and Chambliss, O.L. 1974. Breeding for resistance to the cowpea curculio in southern peas. *Horticultural Science*, 9, 69–70.

Dabrowski, Z.T., Bungu, D.O.M., and Ochieng, R.S. 1983. Studies on the legume pod borer, *Maruca testulalis* (Geyer). 3, Methods used in cowpea screening for resistance. *Insect Science and Its Application*, 4, 1/2, 141–145.

Damsteegt, V.D., and Hewings, A.D. 1987. Relationships between *Aulacorthum solani* and soybean dwarf virus: Effect of temperature on transmission. *Phytopathology*, 77, (3), 515–518.

Daoust, R.A., Fernandes, P.M., Magalhaes, B.P., and Yokoyama, M. 1984. Pathogenicity of *Beauveria bassiana* applied to cowpea foliage and cucurbitaceous tubers to adult *Diabrotica speciosa* and *Cerotoma* sp. (Coleoptera: Chrysomelidae) in Brazil. Paper presented at the Annual Meeting of the Society of Invertebrate Pathology, 17th, University of California, Davis.

Daoust, R.A., Roberts, D.W., and Neves, B.P. das. 1985. Distribution, biology and control of cowpea pests in Latin America. In Singh, S.R., and Rachie, K.O., eds., *Cowpea Research, Production and Utilization*, Chichester, John Wiley and Sons, 251–266.

Daoust, R.A., Roberts, D.W., and Soper, R.S. 1982. Surveys for insect pathogens on pest and nonpest species of cowpea in Brazil, with particular emphasis on fungal disease agents. Proc. 1st Natl. Meet. Cowpea Research Brazil, Reun. Nac. Pesqui. Caupi, RENAC, Goiânia, GO, Brazil, 56–59.

Daoust, R.A., Roberts, D.W., and Soper, R.S. 1983. The enzootic and epizootic occurrence of disease in insect species associated with cowpeas in central, north and northeast Brazil. *Ann. Rep. Bean Improv. Coop.* 26, 86–87.

Das, B.B., and Misra, D.P. 1984. New records of alternate hosts of groundnut leafminer, *Aproaerema modicella* Deventer (Gelechiidae: Lepidoptera). *Indian Journal of Agricultural Science*, 54(9), 776.

Daugherty, D.M., Neustadt, M.H., Gehrke, C.W., Cavanagh, L.E., Williams, L.F., and Green, D.E. 1964. An evaluation of damage to soybeans by brown and green stink bugs. *Journal of Economic Entomology*, 57, 719–722.

Davey, P.M. 1958. The groundnut bruchid, *Caryedon gonagra* (F.). *Bulletin of Entomological Research*, 49, 385–404.

Davey, P.M., Hall, D.W., Conveney, P.L., and Raymond, W.D. 1959. The effect of insect infestation on the quality of decorticated groundnuts with special reference to storage at low and high humidities. *Tropical Science*, 1, 296–307.

David, B.V., and Santhanaraman, T. 1964. First record of the green nettle slug caterpillar, *Thosea aperiens* Wlk., in India. *Madras Agricultural Journal*, 51 (12), 499–502.

David, B.V., Vijayaraghavan, S., and Ramaswamy, K.A. 1965. Field trials for the control of groundnut aphid. *Oilseeds Journal*, 9, 188–191.

Davies, J.C. 1975. Use of menazon insecticide for control of rosette disease of groundnuts in Uganda. *Tropical Agriculture* (Trinidad), 52, 359–367.

Davies, J.C. 1976. The incidence of rosette disease in groundnut in relation to plant density and its effect on yield. *Annals of Applied Biology*, 82, 489–501.

Davies, J.C., and Lateef, S.S. 1975. Insect pests of pigeonpea and chickpea in India and prospects for control. In ICRISAT, *Proceedings, International Workshop on Grain Legumes, ICRISAT, 13–16 January 1975, Hyderabad, India*, Patancheru, India, ICRISAT, 319–331.

Davies, J.C., and Lateef, S.S. 1978. Recent trends in grain legume pest research in India. In Singh, S.R., van Emden, H.F., and Taylor, T.A., eds., *Pests of Grain Legumes: Ecology and Control*, London, U.K., Academic Press, 25–31.

Davis, C.J. 1961. Introduction, liberation and establishment of parasites to control *Nezara viridula var. smaragdula* (Fabr.) in Hawaii (Heteroptera: Pentatomidae). *Proceedings of the Hawaiian Entomological Society*, 18, 369–375.

Davis, C.J. 1967. Progress in the biological control of the Southern green stink bug, *Nezara viridula var. smaragdula* (Fabr.) in Hawaii (Heteroptera: Pentatomidae). *Mushi* (suppl.), 39, 9–16.

Davis, C.J. 1970. Recent introductions for biological control in Hawaii. *Proceedings of the Hawaiian Entomological Society*, 20, 521–525.

Davis, C.J., and Krauss, N.L.H. 1963. Recent introduction for biological control in Hawaii. *Proceedings of the Hawaiian Entomological Society*, 18, 245–249.

Davis, J.C. 1972. Studies on the ecology of *Aphis craccivora* Koch (Hem., Aphididae), the vector of rosette disease of groundnuts, in Uganda. *Bulletin of Entomological Research*, 62, 169–181.

Davis, J.J. 1969. Bean fly and its control. *Queensland Agricultural Journal*, 95, 101–106.

Davis, R.E., and Whitcomb, R.F. 1971. Mycoplasma, rickettsiae, and chlamydiae: Possible relation to yellows diseases and other disorders of plants and insects. *Annual Review of Phytopathology*, 9, 119–154.

Davis, R.E., and Worley, J.F. 1973. Spiroplasma: motile, helical microorganism associated with corn stunt disease. *Phytopathology*, 63, 403–408.

Dawson, W.O., and Grantham, G.L. 1983. Effect of 2-thiouracil on RNA and protein synthesis in synchronous and asynchronous infections of tobacco mosaic virus. *Intervirology*, 19, 155–161.

Dawson, W.O. 1976. Guanidine inhibits tobacco mosaic virus RNA synthesis at two stages. *Intervirology*, 6, 83–89.

Dawson, W.O. 1978. Time-course of actinomycin-D inhibition of tobacco mosaic virus multiplication relative to the rate of spread of the infection. *Intervirology*, 9, 304–309.

Dawson, W.O., and Lozoya-Saldana, H. 1984. Examination of the mode of action of Ribavirin against tobacco mosaic virus. *Intervirology*, 22, 77–84.

Dawson, W.O., and Schlegel, D.E. 1976. The sequence of inhibition of tobacco mosaic virus by actinomycin D, 2-thiouracil, and cycloheximide in a synchronous infection. *Phytopathology*, 66, 177–181.

de Bortoli, S.A. 1980. Danos de *Hedylepta indicata* (Fabricius, 1975) (Lepidoptera: Pyralidae) no feijoeiro (*Phaseolus vulgaris* L.) e efeitos de desfolha e dobra de foliolos sobre a produtividade de cultura. Ph.D. Dissertation. Escola Superior de Agricultura Luis de Queiroz de Universidade de Sao Paulo, Sao Paulo, Brazil. 129p.

de Bortoli, S.A., and Giacomini, P.L. 1981. Acao de alguns inseticidas granulados sistemicos sobre *Bemisia tabaci* (Gennadius, 1889) (Homoptera-Aleyrodidae) e *Empoasca kraemeri* (Ross and Moore, 1957) (Homoptera: Cicadellidae) e seus efeitos na produtividade de feijoeiro (*Phaseolus vulgaris* L.). *Anais da Sociedade Entomológica do Brasil*, 10, 97–104.

de Lima, C.P.F. 1979. *Liriomyza trifolii* (Diptera: Agromyzidae), an important new leafminer pest in Kenya. *Kenya Entomology Newsletter*, 10, 8.

De Long, D.M. 1971. The bionomics of leafhoppers. *Annual Review of Entomology*, 16, 179–210.

De Wijs, J.J. 1980. The characteristics of mineral oils in relation to their inhibitory activity on the aphid transmission of potato virus Y. *Netherlands Journal of Plant Pathology*, 8, 291–300.

DeBach, P. 1962. An analysis of success in biological control of insects in the Pacific area. *Proceedings of the Hawaiian Entomological Society*, 18, 69–79.

Deitz, L.L., van Duyn, J.W., Bradley, J.R. Jr., Rabb, R.L., Brooks, W.M., and Stinner, R.E. 1976. A guide to the identification and biology of soybean arthropods in North Carolina. *North Carolina Agricultural Experiment Station Bulletin*, 238, 1–264.

Demange, J.M. 1975. Les Myriapodes Diplopodes nuisibles a l'arachide au Senegal. *Oléagineux*, 30, 19–24.

Demski, J.W., Reddy, D.V.R., and Sowell, G. 1984a. Peanut stripe, a new virus disease of peanuts. *Phytopathology*, 74, 627 (abstract).

Demski, J.W., Reddy, D.V.R., Sowell, G., and Bays, D. 1984b. Peanut stripe virus—a new seed-borne potyvirus from China infecting groundnut (*Arachis hypogaea*). *Annals of Applied Biology*, 105, 495–501.

Derrick, K.S., and Newsom, L.D. 1984. Occurrence of a leafhopper-transmitted disease of soybeans in Louisiana. *Plant Disease*, 68, 343–344.

Deshmukh, P.D., Rathore, Y.S., and Bhattacharya, A.K. 1977. Studies on growth and development of *Diacrisia obliqua* (Walker) (Lepid: Arctiidae) on sixteen plant species. *Zeitschrift für Angewandte Entomologie*, 84, 431–435.

Desmarchelier, J., and Wohlgemuth, R. 1984. Response of several species of insects to mixtures of phosphine and carbon dioxide. In Ripp, B.E., ed., *Controlled Atmosphere and Fumigation in Grain Storages*, Amsterdam, Elsevier, 75–82.

Deuse, J.P.L., and Pointel, J.G. 1975. Assessment of research at farm level storage in francophone Africa. In *Proceedings of the First International Working Conference on Stored-Product Entomology, Savannah, Georgia, USA, Oct. 7–11, 1974*, 85–92.

Dhanorkar, B.K., and Daware, D.G. 1980. Differences in number of aphids found on lines of cowpea in a replicated trial. *Tropical Grain Legume Bulletin*, 19, 3–4.

Dhingra, K.L., and Chenulu, V.V. 1983. Symptomatology and transmission of witches' broom disease of soybean in India. *Current Science*, 52, (12), 603–604.

Diaz, G. 1976. *Urbanus proteus* (L.) en Azapa (Lep., Hesperidae). *Idesia*, 4, 159–161.

Dick, K.M. 1987. Losses caused by insects to groundnuts stored in a warehouse in India. *Tropical Science*, 27, 65–75.

Dick, K.M., and Credland, P.F. 1986. Changes in the response of *Callosobruchus maculatus* (Coleoptera: Bruchidae) to a resistant variety of cowpea. *Journal of Stored Products Research*, 22, 227–233.

Dina, S.O. 1977. Effects of monocrotophos on insect damage and yield of cowpea (*Vigna unguiculata*) in southern Nigeria. *Experimental Agriculture*, 13, 155–159.

Dina, S.O. 1979. Synthetic pyrethroids for the control of cowpea insect pests. *Journal of Agricultural Science*, 93, 735–747.

Dina, S.O. 1981. Response of three cowpea varieties to organophosphorus insecticides. *Tropical Grain Legume Bulletin* 23, 6–10.

Distant, W.I. 1980. Insecta Rhynchota Hemiptera—Heteroptera. Biologia Centralia-Americana, London 1(4), 78–79.

Djamin, A. 1961. The biology of *Maruca testulalis* (Geyer), with a consideration of its control. University of the Philippines, Quezon City (BSc thesis).

Doi, Y., Teranaka, M., Yora, K., and Asuyama, H. 1967. Mycoplasma or group-like microorganisms found in the phloem elements of plants infected with mulberry dwarf, potato witches broom, aster yellows, or paulocunia witches broom. *Nippon Shokubutsu Byori Gakkaishi*, 22, 259–266.

Don-Pedro, K.N. 1980. A population explosion of *Aphis craccivora* Koch. following DDT application in a cowpea plot (*Vigna unguiculata*) cultivar (Prima) in Nigeria. *Journal of Natural History*, 14, 617–619.

Don-Pedro, K.N. 1983. Level of parasitization of *Maruca testulalis* (Geyer) (Lepidoptera: Pyralidae) larvae in early and late cowpea (*Vigna unguiculata*) in Nigeria. *Révue de Zoologie Africaine*, 97, 678–683.

Dorge, S.K., Dalaya, V.P., and Kaul, O.B. 1966. Studies on bionomics and control of groundnut aphid, *Aphis craccivora* Koch. Labdev. *Journal of Science and Technology*, 4, 165–167.

Drake, C.J. 1920. The southern green stink bug in Florida. *State Plant Board Quarantine Bulletin*, 4, 41–94.

Drifjhout, E. 1978. Genetic interaction between *Phaseolus vulgaris* and bean common mosaic virus with implications for strain identification and breeding for resistance. *Agricultural Research Report*, Wageningen, Centre for Agricultural Publishing and Documentation, 1-90.

Dudley, N.J., Mueller, R.A.E., and Wightman, J.A. 1989. Application of dynamic programming for guiding IPM on groundnut leafminer in India. *Crop Protection*, 8, 5, 349-357.

Duerden, J.C., and Cutler, J.R. 1957. The storage of groundnuts under tropical conditions. I. The effects of prolonged storage on undecorticated and decorticated groundnuts. *Journal of the Science of Food and Agriculture*, 8, 600-604.

Duffus, J.E. 1963. Possible multiplication in the aphid vector of sowthistle yellow vein virus with an extremely long latent period. *Virology*, 21, 194-202.

Duffus, J.E. 1965. Beet pseudo-yellow virus, transmitted by the greenhouse whitefly (*Trialeurodes vaporariorum*). *Phytopathology*, 55, 450-453.

Duffus, J.E. 1971. Role of weeds in the incidence of virus diseases. *Annual Review of Phytopathology*, 9, 319-340.

Duffus, J.E. 1975. A new type of whitefly-transmitted disease—a link to the aphid-transmitted viruses. In Bird, J., and Maramorosch, K., eds., *Tropical Diseases of Legumes*, New York, Academic Press, 79-88.

Duffus, J.E. 1979. Legume yellows virus, a new persistent aphid-transmitted virus of legumes in California. *Phytopathology*, 69, 217-221.

Duffus, J.E. 1987. White-fly transmitted viruses. In Harris, K.E., ed., *Advances in Disease Vector Research*, 4, New York, Springer-Verlag.

Duke, J.A. *Biomass Information Packages for 66 Developing Countries* (under review for possible publication by CRC Press). Beltsville, Maryland, USDA.

Duke, J.A. 1978. The quest for tolerant germplasm. In ASA Special Publication No. 32, *Crop Tolerance to Suboptimal Land Conditions*, Madison, WI, USA, American Society of Agronomy. 343p.

Duke, J.A. 1981. *Handbook of Legumes of World Economic Importance*. New York, NY, USA, Plenum Press. 345p.

Duke, J.A. 1981a. The gene revolution. In Office of Technology Assessment, *Background Papers for Innovative Biological Technologies for Lesser Developed Countries*, Washington, DC, USA, USGPO. 511p. Paper No. 1, 89-150.

Duke, J.A. 1982. Plant germplasm resources for breeding of crops adapted to marginal environments. In Christiansen, M.N., and Lewis, C.F., eds., *Breeding Plants for Less Favorable Environments*. New York, NY, USA, Wiley-Interscience, John Wiley and Sons. 459p. Chap. 12.

Duke, J.A. 1983. Nitrogen fixing trees. In *The International Permaculture Seed Yearbook*, Orange, MA, USA, 48-51.

Duke, J.A. 1985. A green world instead of the greenhouse. In *The International Permaculture Seed Yearbook*, Orange, MA, USA, 15-21.

Duke, J.A. 1989. New crops survey. In *Proceedings of the First National New Crops Symposium*, Oct. 23-26, 1988, Indianapolis.

Duke, J.A., and Ayensu, E.S. 1983. *Medicinal Plants of China*. Algonac, MI, USA, Reference Publications Inc.

Duke, J.A., and Bagby, M.O. 1982. Comparison of oilseed yields: a preliminary review. Typescript of paper presented in North Dakota.

Duke, J.A., and Wain, K.K. 1981. *Medicinal Plants of the World. Computer Index with More than 85,000 Entries*. 3 vols. 1654p.

Duke, J.A., Atchley, A.A., Ackerson, K.T., and Duke, P.K. 1987. *Handbook of Agricultural Energy Potential of Developing Countries*. 2 vols. Boca Raton, FL, USA, CRC Press.

Dunn, J.A. 1978. Resistance to some insect pests in crop plants. *Applied Biology*, 3, 34–85.

Dupree, M. 1970. Ultra-low-volume insecticide sprays for control of the cowpea curculio. *Journal of the Georgia Entomological Society*, 5, 39–41.

Dupree, M., and Beckham, C.M. 1955. The cowpea curculio—a pest of southern field peas. *Georgia Agricultural Experiment Station Bulletin N.S.*, 6, 32.

Durbern, J., and Dollet, M. 1980. Groundnut eyespot virus, a new member of the potyvirus group. *Annals of Applied Biology*, 96, 193–200.

Dutta, D.N., and Lal, R. 1980. Residues and residual toxicity of monocrotophos on cowpea. *Journal of Research Assam Agricultural University*, 1, 177–181.

Dwivedi, S.L., Amin, P.W., Rasheedunisa, Nigam, S.N., Nagabhushanam, G.V.S., Rao, V.R., and Gibbon, R.W. 1986. Genetic analysis of trichome characters associated with resistance to jassid (*Empoasca kerry* Pruthi) in peanut. *Peanut Science*, 13, 15–18.

Dyadechko, N.P. 1964. Thrips on fringe-winged insects (*Thysanoptera*) of the European part of the USSR. Kiev, Urozai Publishers, 344p.

Eastman, C.E. 1980. Sampling phytophagous underground soybean arthropods. In Kogan, M., and Herzog, D.C., eds., *Sampling Methods in Soybean Entomology*, New York, Springer-Verlag, 327–354.

Eastman, C.E., and Wuensche, A.L. 1977. A new insect damaging nodules of soybean: *Rivellia quadrifasciata* (Macquart). *Journal of the Georgia Entomological Society*, 12, 190–199.

Eastop, V.F. 1973. Biotypes of aphids. *Bulletin of the Entomological Society of New Zealand*, 2, 40–51.

Eastop, V.F. 1977. Worldwide importance of aphids as virus vectors. In Harris, K.F., and Maramorosch, K., eds., *Aphids as Virus Vectors*, New York, Academic Press, 3–47.

Eastop, V.F., and Hille Ris Lambers, D. 1976. *Survey of the World's Aphids*. The Hague, Dr. W. Junk, 573 pp.

Eaton, A. 1978. Studies on distribution patterns, ovipositional preference, and egg and larval survival of *Colaspis brunnea* (Fab.) in North Carolina Coastal Plain soybean fields. Chapel Hill, University of North Carolina, 86p. (PhD thesis).

Eckenrode, C.J., Gauthier, N.L., Danielson, D., and Webb, R. 1973. Seedcord maggot: seed treatments and granule furrow applications for protecting beans and sweet corn. *Journal of Economic Entomology*, 66, 1191–1194.

Egwuatu, R.I., and Taylor, T.A. 1977. Studies on the biology of *Acanthomia tomentosicollis* (Stal.) (Hemiptera: Coreidae) in the field and insectary. *Bulletin of Entomological Research*, 67, 249–257.

Egwuatu, R.I., and Taylor, T.A. 1977a. Insect species associated with *Cajanus cajan* (L.) Durce (Pigeonpea) in Nigeria and their monthly abundance. *East African Agricultural and Forestry Journal*, 42, (3), 271–275.

Egwuatu, R.I., and Taylor, T.A. 1977b. Studies on the biology of Acanthomia tomentosicollis (Stal.) (Hemiptera: Coreidae) in the field and insectary. *Bulletin of Entomological Research*, 67, (2), 249–257.

Egwuatu, R.I., and Taylor, T.A. 1979. Studies on the effects of nymphal density on the development of *Acanthomia tomentosicollis* Stal. *East African Agricultural and Forestry Journal*, 42, (30), 276–286.

El Baradi, T.A. 1975. Pulses 1. Cowpeas. *Abstracts on Trop. Agr.*, 1(12), 9–19.

El Sadiq, E.O., and Ahmed, A.H. 1986. Comparative studies on aphid transmission of the Sudanese strain of peanut stunt virus. *Journal of Phytopathology*, 115, 160–164.

El-Sawaf, S.K. 1954. A contribution to the host selection principle as applied to *Bruchus (Callosobruchus) maculatus* F. (Coleoptera: Bruchidae). *B. Soc. Fonad. ler Entomol.*, 38, 297–303.

El-Sebae, A.H., and Saleh, M.R. 1970. Aphicidal properties of safer insecticides against *Aphis craccivora* on cowpea crop. *Alexandria Journal of Agricultural Research* 18, 131-134.

Ellis, C.R. 1984. Injury by *Empoasca fabae* (*Homoptera: Cicadellidae*) to peanuts in southwestern Ontario. *The Canadian Entomologist*, 116, 1671-1673.

Elmore, J.C. 1949. Hibernation and host-plant studies of the Mexican bean beetle in California. *Journal of Economic Entomology*, 42, 464-466.

Ennis, T.H., and Chambliss, O.L. 1976. Pods resist insect penetration in curculio resistant southern peas. *Highlights of Agricultural Research*, Auburn, AL, USA, Auburn University, 23, 8.

Enyi, B.A.C. 1975. Effects of defoliation on growth and yield in groundnut (*Arachis hypogaea*), cowpeas (*Vigna unguiculata*), soyabean (*Glycine max*), and green gram (*Vigna aurens*). *Annals of Applied Biology*, 79, 55-66.

Ernst, E., and Araujo, R.L. 1986. *A Bibliography of Termite Literature 1966-1978*. In Broughton, P., and Fullarton, K.M., Chichester, New York, Brisbane, Toronto, and Singapore, John Wiley, 903p.

Espinosa, G.O., and Sanchez, V.J. 1982. El minador del frijol *Liriomyza* sp. (Agromyzidae, Diptera), una plaga de interés econóomico en el Valle del Catamayo. *Anales de Facultad de Ciencias Agropecuarias Universidad National, Laja Ecuador*, 10, 81-92.

Ezedinma, F.O.C. 1973. Effects of defoliation and topping on semi-upright cowpeas, *Vigna unguiculata* (L.) Walp. in a humid tropical environment. *Experimental Agriculture*, 9, 203-207.

Ezueh, M.A. 1982. Effects of planting dates on pest infestation, yield and harvest quality of cowpea (*Vigna unguiculata*). *Experimental Agriculture*, 18, 311-318.

Ezueh, M.I. 1976a. An evaluation of ULV sprays for the control of cowpea insect pests in southern Nigeria. *Tropical Grain Legume Bulletin*, 4, 15-18.

Ezueh, M.I. 1976b. Soil systemic insecticides for cowpea pest control. *African Journal of Plant Protection*, 2, 99-105.

Ezueh, M.I. 1981a. Nature and significance of preflowering damage by thrips to cowpea. *Entomología Experimentalis et Applicata*, 29, 305-312.

Ezueh, M.I. 1981b. The biological basis of resistance in cowpea to the cowpea moth, *Cydia ptychora* (Lepidoptera: Olethreutidae). *Annals of Applied Biology*, 99, 313-321.

Ezueh, M.I., and Dina, S.O. 1979. Pest problems of soybeans and control in Nigeria. In Corbin, F.T., ed., *World Soybean Research Conference II*, Boulder, CO, Westview Press, 275-283.

Ezueh, M.I., and Taylor, T.A. 1981. Yield resistance in cowpea, *Vigna unguiculata* to the cowpea moth, *Cydia ptychora*. *Annals of Applied Biology*, 99, 307-312.

Ezueh, M.I., and Taylor, T.A. 1984. Effects of time of intercropping with maize on cowpea susceptibility of three major pests. *Tropical Agriculture* (Trinidad), 61, 82-86.

Fagoone, I., and Toory, V. 1983. Preliminary investigations of host selection mechanisms by the leafminer, *Liriomyza trifolii*. *Insect Science and Its Application*, 4, 337-341.

Faleiro, J.R., and Singh, K.M. 1985. Yield infestation studies associated with insects infesting cowpea, *Vigna unguiculata* (L.) Walp in Delhi. *Indian Journal of Entomology*, 47, 287-291.

Faleiro, J.R., Singh, K.M., and Singh, R.N. 1985. Dissipation of carbofuran and carbaryl in cowpea. *Indian Journal of Entomology*, 47, 393-400.

Faleiro, J.R., Singh, K.M., and Singh, R.N., 1986. Pest complex and succession of insect pests in cowpea, *Vigna unguiculata* (L.) Walp. *Indian Journal of Entomology*, 48, 54-56.

Falk, B.W., and Duffus, J.E. 1988. Ecology and control. In Milne, R.S., ed., *The Plant Viruses, The Filamentous Plant Viruses*, volume 4, New York, Plenum Press, 275-296.

Falk, B.W., and Tsai, J.H. 1985. Serological detection and evidence for multiplication of maize mosaic virus in the planthopper, *Peregrinus maidis*. *Phytopathology*, 75, 852–855.

FAO (Food and Agriculture Organization of the United Nations). 1976. *FAO Yearbook*. Rome, FAO.

FAO (Food and Agriculture Organization of the United Nations). 1985a. *FAO Production Yearbook*, vol. 39. Rome, FAO. 330p.

FAO (Food and Agriculture Organization of the United Nations). 1985b. *Manual of pest control for food security reserve grain stocks*. FAO Plant Production and Protection Paper 63. Rome, FAO.

Farrell, J.A.K. 1976a. Effects of groundnut sowing date and plant spacing on rosette virus disease in Malawi. *Bulletin of Entomological Research*, 66, 159–171.

Farrell, J.A.K. 1976b. Effects of groundnut crop density on the population dynamics of *Aphis craccivora* Koch (Hemiptera, Aphididae) in Malawi. *Bulletin of Entomological Research*, 66, 317–329.

Farrell, J.A.K. 1976c. Effects of intersowing with beans on the spread of groundnut rosette virus by *Aphis craccivora* Koch (Hemiptera, Aphididae) in Malawi. *Bulletin of Entomological Research*, 66, 331–333.

Farrell, J.A.K., and Adams, A.N. 1966. Cowpea and bean yield responses to insecticides. Annual Report, Agricultural Research Council Central Africa, 57p.

Farrell, J.A.K., and Adams, A.N. 1967. Cowpea yield response to insecticide. Annual Report, Agricultural Research Council Central Africa, 95–96.

Feakin, S.F. 1973. *Pest Control in Groundnuts*. PANS Manual No. 2. London, Centre for Overseas Pest Research, Foreign and Commonwealth Office, Overseas Development Administration. 197p.

Fenili, G.A., Dallai, R., and Abukar, M.M. 1983. Groundnut pests in Somalia. *Rivista di Agricoltura Subtropicale e Tropicale*, 7, 343–350.

Ferreira, B.S.C. 1979. Incidência de parasitas em lagartas da soja. *Anais I Seminário Nacional de Pesquisa de Soja*, 2, 79–91.

Ferreira, B.S.C. 1980. Sampling *Epinotia aporema* on soybean. In Kogan, M., and Herzog, D.C., eds., *Sampling Methods in Soybean Entomology*, New York, Springer-Verlag, 234–281.

Ferreira, B.S.C., and Panizzi, A.R. 1978. Distribuição de ovos e lagartas de *Anticarsia gemmatalis* Hübner em plantas de soja. *Anais da Sociedade Entomológica do Brasil*, 7, 54–59.

Fery, R.L., and Cuthbert, F.P. Jr. 1978. Inheritance and selection of nonpreference resistance to the cowpea curculio in the southern pea (*Vigna unguiculata* (L.) Walp). *Journal of American Horticultural Science*, 103(3), 370–372.

Fery, R.L., and Cuthbert, F.P. Jr. 1979. Measurement of pod-wall resistance to the cowpea curculio in the southern pea (*Vigna unguiculata* (L.) Walp.). *HortScience*, 14, 29–30.

Fery, R.L., and Dukes, P.D. 1984. "Carolina Cream" southern pea. *Horticultural Science*, 17, 152.

Fescemyer, H.W., and Hammond, A.M. 1986. Effect of density and plant age on colour phase variation and development of larval velvet bean caterpillar, *Anticarsia gemmatalis* Hübner (Lepidoptera: Noctuidae). *Environmental Entomology*, 15, 784–787.

Fletcher, J., Irwin, M.E., Bradfute, O.E., and Granada, G.A. 1984. Discovery of a mycoplasma-like organism associated with diseased soybeans in Mexico. *Plant Disease*, 68(11), 994–996.

Fletcher, T.B. 1914. *Some South Indian Insects and Other Animals of Importance*. Dehra Dun, India, Bishen Singh Mahendra Pal Singh. 565p.

Fletchman, C.H.W. 1972. *Acaros de Importancia Agricola Novel*. Sao Paulo, Brazil. 150p.

Flint, M.L., and van den Bosch, R. 1981. *Introduction to Integrated Pest Management*. New York, Plenum Press.

Fluiter, H.J. de, and Ankersmit, G.W. 1948. Gegevens betreffende de aantasting van bonen (*Phaseolus vulgaris* L.) door de zwarte bonenluis (*Aphis (Doralis) fabae* Scop.). *Tijdschrift over Pflantenziekten*, 54, 1–13.

Foerster, L.A. 1978. Chemical control of soybean pests in Brazil. In Singh, S.R., van Emden, H.F., and Taylor, T.A., eds., *Pests of Grain Legumes: Ecology and Control*, London/New York, Academic Press, 253–258.

Fontanilla, S.D. 1959. Biological notes and control of lepidopterous pests of bush sitao (*Vigna sinensis* (L.) Savi x *Vigna sesquipedalis* Fruw.) blossoms and pods. Quezon City, University of the Philippines (BSc thesis).

Forbes, A.R., and MacCarthy, H.R. 1969. Morphology of the Homoptera, with emphasis on virus vectors. In Maramorosch, K., ed., *Viruses, Vectors and Vegetation*, New York, John Wiley, 211–234.

Ford, B.J., Strayer, J.R., Reid, J., and Godfrey, G.L. 1975. The literature of arthropods associated with soybeans. 4: a bibliography of the velvet bean caterpillar, Anticarsia gemmatalis Hübner. Illinois Natural History Survey Biological Notes 92, 15p.

Forsyth, J. 1966. *Agricultural Insects of Ghana*. Accra, Ghana University Press, 163p.

Fraga, C.P., and Ochoa, L.H. 1972. Aspectos morfológicos y bioecológicos de *Piezodorus guildinii* (West.) (Hemiptera, Pent.). *IDIA*, 28, 103–117.

Frazier, N.W. 1966. Nonretention of two semipersistent strawberry viruses through ecdysis by their aphid vector. *Phytopathology*, 56, 1318–1319.

Freitas, A.O. 1960. "Cabeca de fosforo", nova praga do feijoeiro en Pernambuco. *Arquivos do Instituto de Pesquisas Agronómicas*, 55, 345–363.

Fukushi, T. 1969. Relationships between propagative rice viruses and their vectors. In Maramorosch, K., ed., *Viruses, Vectors and Vegetation*, New York, John Wiley, 279–301.

Fulton, J.P., and Scott, H.A. 1977. Bean rugose mosaic and related viruses and their transmission by beetles. *Fitopatologia Brasileira*, 2, 6–9.

Fulton, J.P., Scott, H.A., and Gamez, R. 1975. Beetle transmission of legume viruses. In Bird, G., and Maramorosch, K., eds., *Diseases of Tropical Legumes*, New York, Academic Press, 123–131.

Fulton, J.P., Scott, H.A., and Gamez, R. 1980. Beetles. In Harris, K.F., and Maramorosch, K., eds., *Vectors of Plant Pathogens*, New York, Academic Press, 115–132.

Galileo, M.H.M., Gastal, H.A.O., and Grazia, J. 1977. Levantamento populacional de pentatómideos (Hemiptera) em cultura de soja [*Glycine max* (L.) Merrill] no município de Guaiba, Rio Grande do Sul. *Revista Brasileira Biología*, 37, 111–120.

Galvez, G.E. 1980. Aphid-transmitted viruses. In Schwartz, H.F., and Galvez, G.E., eds., *Bean Production Problems*, Cali, Colombia, CIAT, 218–228.

Galvez, G.E., and Cardenas, M.R. 1980. Whitefly-transmitted viruses. In Schwartz, H.F., and Galvez, G.E., eds., *Bean Production Problems*, Cali, Colombia, CIAT, 261–289.

Galwey, N.W. 1983. Characteristics of the common bean, *Phaseolus vulgaris*, associated with resistance to the leafhopper *Empoasca kraemeri*. *Annals of Applied Biology*, 102, 161–175.

Galwey, N.W., and Evans, A.M. 1982a. Alternative methods of interpreting measurements of resistance to the leafhopper *Empoasca kraemeri* (Ross and Moore) in the common bean, *Phaseolus vulgaris* L. *Euphytica*, 31, 225–236.

Galwey, N.W., and Evans, A.M. 1982b. The inheritance of resistance to *Empoasca kraemer* (Ross and Moore) in the common bean, *Phaseolus vulgaris* L. *Euphytica*, 31, 933–952.

Galwey, N.W., Temple, S.R., and Schoonhoven, A.V. 1985. The resistance of genotypes of two species of *Phaseolus* beans to the leafhopper *Empoasca kraemeri*. *Annals of Applied Biology*, 107, 147–150.

Gamez, R. 1971. Los virus del frijol en centroamerica. I: Transmisión por moscas blancas (*Bemisia tabaci* Genn.) y plantas hospedantes del virus del mosaico dorado. *Turrialba*, 21, 22–27.

Gamez, R. 1972a. Some properties and beetle transmission of bean yellow stipple virus. *Phytopathology*, 62, 759.

Gamez, R. 1972b. Los virus del frijol en Centro América. 2, Algunas propiedades y transmisión por crisomelidos del virus del mosaico rugoso del frijol. *Turrialba*, 22, 249–257.

Gamez, R. 1980. Beetle-transmitted viruses. In *Bean Production Problems*, Schwartz, H.F., and Galvez, G.E., eds., Cali, Colombia, CIAT, 239–255.

Gamez, R., and Moreno, R.A. 1983. Epidemiology of beetle-borne viruses of grain legumes in Central America. In Plumb, R.T., and Thresh, J.M., eds., *Plant Virus Epidemiology: The Spread and Control of Insect-borne Viruses*, Blackwell, 267–275.

Gangrade, G.A. 1961. Tur pod bug, *Clavigralla gibbosa* Spin. in Madhya Pradesh. *Science and Culture*, 27 (2), 101–102.

Gangrade, G.A. 1963. Assessment of damage to tur (*Cajanus cajan*) in Madhya Pradesh by the tur-podfly, *Agromyza obtusa* Malloch. *Indian Journal of Agricultural Sciences*, 33, 1, 17–20.

Gangrade, G.A. 1964. Losses of tur (*Cajanus cajan*) by *Melanagromyza obtusa* Malloch. *Indian Journal of Entomology*, 26, 364–365.

Gangrade, G.A. 1974. Insects of soybean. Jabalpur, Madhya Pradesh, India, Directorate of Research Services, 88p.

Gangrade, G.A., Kapoor, K.N., and Gujarati, J.P. 1971. Biology, behaviour, diapause and control of *Oberea brevis* Swed (Coleoptera: Cerambycidiae: Lamiidae) on soybean in Madhya Pradesh. *Entomologist*, 104, 260–264.

Gangrade, G.A., Singh, D.P., and Matkar, S.M. 1975. Soybean yield losses in response to damage by varying levels of three lepidopterous larvae. *Indian Journal of Entomology*, 37(3), 225–229.

Gangwar, S.K., and Thakur, A.N.S. 1988. Population levels of leaf folders (*Nacoleia diemenalis* Guen and *N. vulgaris* Guen) on soybean in East Khasi Hills (Meghalaya). National symposium on insect pests and diseases of soybean, 1–3 Nov., Jawahar Lal Nehru Krishi Vishwa Vidyalaya University, R.A.K. College of Agric. Sehore, 15 (Abstract).

Garcia, C.M., and Sosa, M.C. 1973. Evaluación de la resistencia de frijol hacia la conchuela *Epilachna varivestis* Muls. *Agrociencia*, 13, 3–13.

Garcia, J., Cardona, C., and Raigosa, J. 1979. Evaluación de poblaciones de insectos plagas en la asociación cana de azucar-frijol y su relacion con loos rendimientos. *Revista Colombiana Entomología*, 5, 17–24.

Garrett, R.G. 1973. Non-persistent aphid-borne viruses. In Gibbs, A.J., ed., *Viruses and Invertebrates*, New York, Elsevier, 476–492.

Gatehouse, A.M.R., and Boulter, D. 1983. Assessment of the anti-metabolic effects of trypsin inhibitors from cowpea (*Vigna unguiculata*) and other legumes on development of the bruchid beetle (*Callosobruchus maculatus*) 34, 345–350.

Gatehouse, A.M.R., Gatehouse, J.A., Dobie, P., Kilminster, A.M., and Boulter, D. 1979. Biochemical basis of insect resistance in *Vigna unguiculata*. *Journal of Science of Food and Agriculture*, 30, 948–958.

Gatehouse, A.M.R., Dobie, P., Hodges, R.J., Meik, J., Putszai, A., and Boulter, D. 1987. Role of carbohydrates in insect resistance in *Phaseolus vulgaris*. *Journal of Insect Physiology*, 33, 843–850.

Gaud, S. Medina, and Tuduri, J. Garcia. 1977. New arthropod records for Puerto Rico. *Journal of Agriculture of University of Puerto Rico*, 61 (3), 409–412.

Gautam, R.D., and Saxena, H.P. 1986. New record of white tailed mealy bug, *Ferrisia virgata* (Cockerell) (Hemiptera: Pseudococcidae) on pigeonpea. *International Pigeonpea Newsletter*, 5, 39–40.

Gazzoni, D.L. 1978. Report of the activities at the National Soybean Research Center of EMBRAPA (Londrina, Paraná, Brasil) on soybean entomology and insect pest management. Paper presented at the annual meeting of Southern Regional Research Project 5-74, Control Tactics and Management Systems for Arthropod Pests of Soybeans, Atlanta, Georgia.

Gazzoni, D.L., and Oliveira, E.B. 1979. Distribuição estacional de *Epinotia aporema* (Walsingham, 1914) e seu efeito sobre o rendimiento e seus componentes, e características agronómicas de soja c.v. UFV-1 semeada em diversas épocas. Anais I Seminário Nacional de Pesquisa de Soja II, 94–105.

Gerard, B.M. 1976. Measuring plant density effects on insect pests in intercropped maize cowpeas. In Monyo, J.H., Ker, A.D.R., and Campbell, M., eds., *Intercropping in Semi-arid Areas*, Report of a symposium held at the Faculty of Agriculture, Forestry and Veterinary Science, University of Dar es Salaam, Morogoro, Tanzania, 10–12 May, Ottawa, International Development Research Centre, IDRC-076e, 72p.

Gerling, D. 1986. Natural enemies of *Bemisia tabaci*, biological characteristics and potential as biological control agents: a review. *Agriculture, Ecosystems and Environment*, 17, 99–110.

Ghaderi, A. 1984. Fungal diseases in leafhopper control: research highlights. Michigan State University Bean/Cowpea Res. Support Project, 1, 1–3.

Ghosh, C.C. 1937. The pulse beetles (Bruchidae) of Burma. *Indian Journal of Agricultural Sciences*, 7, 395–412.

Ghosh, M.R. 1981. Incidence of some important insect pests on redgram (*Cajanus cajan*) in West Bengal. *Entomon*, 6 (3), 215–218.

Ghosh, S.K., and Raychaudhuri, S.P. 1972. Mycoplasma. The new chapter in plant pathology. *Current Science*, 41(7), 235–241.

Ghule, B.D., Dhumal, V.S., and Deokar, A.B. 1987. Chemical control of groundnut leaf miner. *Journal of Maharashtra Agricultural Universities*, 12(2), 257–259.

Gibbs, A.J., ed. 1973. *Viruses and Invertebrates*. Amsterdam, North Holland, 673 pp.

Gibson, R.W., and Cayley, G.R. 1984. Improved control of potato virus by mineral oil plus pyrethroid cypermethrin applied electrostatically. *Crop Protection*, 3, 469–478.

Gibson, R.W., and Plumb, R.T. 1977. Breeding plants for resistance to aphid infestation. In Harris, K.F., and Maramorosch, K., eds., *Aphids as Virus Vectors*, New York, Academic Press, 473–500.

Gibson, R.W., Rice, A.D., and Sawicki, R.M. 1982. Effects of the pyrethroid deltamethrin on the acquisition and inoculation of viruses by *Myzus persicae*. *Annals of Applied Biology*, 100, 49–54.

Giga, D.P., and Smith, R.H. 1981. Varietal resistance and intraspecific competition in cowpea weevil *Callosobruchus maculatus* and *C. chinensis* (Coleoptera: Bruchidae). *Journal of Applied Ecology*, 18, 755–766.

Giga, D.P., and Smith, R.H. 1983. Comparative life history studies of four *Callosobruchus* species infesting cowpeas with special reference to *Callosobruchus rhodesianus* (Pic) (Coleoptera: Bruchidae). *Journal of Stored Products Research*, 19, 189–198.

Gill, C.C. 1970. Aphid nymphs transmit an isolate of barley yellow dwarf virus more efficiently than do adults. *Phytopathology*, 60, 1747–1752.

Gillier, P. 1970. Influence des attaques d'*Aphanus sordidus* sur la qualité des graines d'arachide. *Oléagineux*, 25, 465–466.

Gillier, P., and Bockelee-Morvan, A. 1979. La protection des stocks d'arachide contre les insectes. *Oléagineux*, 34, 131–137.

Gillon, D., and Gillon, Y. 1979a. Distribution spatiale des principales éspèces d'iules (Myriapodes Diplopodes) dans une zone cultivée au Sénégal. *Bulletin d'ecologie*, 10, 83–93.

Gillon, D., and Gillon, Y. 1979b. Estimation du nombre et de la biomasse des iules (Myriapodes Diplopodes) dans une zone cultivée au Sénégal. *Bulletin d'ecologie*, 10, 95–106.

Gilman, D.F., McPherson, R.M., Newsom, L.D., Herzog, D.C., and Williams, C. 1982. Resistance in soybeans to the southern green stink bug. *Crop Science*, 22, 573–576.

Glass, E.H. 1975. Integrated pest management: rationale, potential, means and implementation. *Entomological Society of America Special Publication*, 75–2, 141p.

Goering, C.E. 1981. Vegetable oil as diesel fuel. Progress report. Appendix 10. In USDA, *Vegetable Oil as Diesel Fuel, Seminar II, Oct. 21–22, 1981*. Peoria, IL, USA.

Gold, C.S., Wightman, J.A., and Pimbert, M. 1989. The use of mulches for reducing termite damage to drying groundnut pods. *International Arachis Newsletter*, in press.

Gomez, L.A., and Schoonhoven, A.V. 1977. Oviposición del *Empoasca kraemeri* en frijol y evaluacion del parasitismo por Anagrus sp. *Revista Colombia de Entomología*, 3, 29–38.

Gonzales, B.J.E. 1960. Control químico de *Empoasca kraemeri* Ross y Moore en el frijol. *Revista Peruana de Entomología Agrícola*, 3, 59–62.

Gonzalez, R., Cardona, C., and Schoonhoven, A.V. 1982. Morfología y biología de los crisomélidos *Diabrotica balteata* (Le Conte) y *Cerotoma facialis* (Erichson) como plagas del frijol comun. *Turrialba*, 32, 257–264.

Goodman, R.M., and Bird, J. 1978. Bean golden mosaic virus. Kew, Surrey, CMI (Commonwealth Mycological Institute), *CMI/AAB Descriptions of Plant Viruses*, 12, 192, 4 pp.

Goodman, R.M., and Nene, Y.L. 1976. Virus diseases of soybeans. In Goodman, R.M., ed., *Expanding the Use of Soybeans*, Urbana, University of Illinois, INTSOY Series 10, 91–96.

Gough, N., and Brown, J.D. 1988. Insecticidal control of white grubs (Coleoptera: Scarabaeidae) on the Atherton Tableland, with observations on crop losses. *Journal of Agricultural and Animal Sciences*, 45, 9–17.

Gould, H.J., and Mayor, J.G. 1975. Alternative seed treatments to dieldrin for the control of bean seed fly (*Delia* spp.). *Plant Pathology (London)*, 24, 245–246.

Govindan, R., Rangswamy, H.R., Devraj, K.C., Devaiah, M.C., and Viswanath, B.N. 1977. Biology of the redgram bud weevil (*Ceuthorrhynchus asperulus* Fabricius) (Coleoptera: Curculionidae). *Mysore Journal of Agriculture Sciences*, 11 (2), 191–194.

Graham, P.H. 1978. Some problems and potentials of *Phaseolus vulgaris* L. in Latin America. *Field Crops Research*, 1(4), 295–318.

Graham, W.M. 1970. Warehouse ecology studies of bagged maize in Kenya. II. Ecological observations on an infestation by *Ephestia (Cadra) cautella* (Walker) (Lepidoptera, Phycitidae). *Journal of Stored Products Research*, 6, 157–167.

Granada, G.A. 1979. Machismo disease of soybeans. 1. Symptomatology and transmission. *Plant Disease Reporter*, 63, 47–50.

Grazia, J., del Vechio, M.C., Balestieri, F.M.P., and Ramiro, Z.A. 1980. Estudo das ninfas do pentatomideos (Heteroptera) que vivem sobre soja [*Glycine max* (L.P.) Merrill]: I—*Euschistus heros* (Fabricius) e *Piezodorus guildinii* (Westwood). *Anais da Sociedade Entomológica do Brasil*, 9, 39–51.

Greathead, D.J. 1968. A study in East Africa of beanflies (Diptera: Agromyzidae) affecting *Phaseolus vulgaris* and their natural enemies, with the description of a new species of *Melanagromyza* Hend. *Bulletin of Entomological Research*, 59, 541–561.

Greathead, D.J. 1975. Biological control of the beanfly *Ophiomyia phaseoli* (Tryon). (Dip: Agromyzidae) by *Opius* spp. (Hym: Braconidae) in the Hawaiian Islands. *Entomophaga*, 20, 313–316.

Green, A.A. 1959. The control of insects infesting groundnuts after harvest in The Gambia. I. A study of the groundnut borer *Caryedon gonagra* (F.) under field conditions. *Tropical Science*, 1, 200–205.

Greene, G.L. 1971a. Economic damage levels of bean leaf roller populations on snap beans. *Journal of Economic Entomology*, 64, 673–674.

Greene, G.L. 1971b. Instar distributions, natural populations, and biology of the bean leaf roller. *Florida Entomologist*, 54, 213–219.

Grundlach, C.M., and Chambliss, O.L. 1977. Resistance in the southern pea, *Vigna unguiculata* (L.) Walpers to the cowpea curculio, *Chalcodermus aeneus* Boheman: the role of tannin. *Horticultural Science*, 12, 234.

Grunewaldt-Stocker, G., and Nienhans, F. 1977. Mycoplasma-ahnliche Organismen als krankheitserreger in Pflanzen. *Acta Phytomedica* (Heft 5), Berlin, Verlag Paul Parey, 1–115.

Guagliumi, P. 1966. Insetti e aracnidi delle Planti comunidel Venezuela segnalati nel periodo 1938–1963. Rela 2: Monograf. Agraicia subtropicali Tropicali, Inst. Agron. Per 17-Oltremare, Firenze, 86, 391p.

Guevara, J. 1962. El combate del picudo del ajote mediante la combinación de variedades resistentes e insecticidas. *Agricultura Tecnica (Mexico)*, 2, 17–29.

Guevara, J. 1969. Resistencia a insectos. In Brauer, O., ed., *Fitogenetica Aplicada*. Editorial Limusa and Wiley, Mexico, D.F., Mexico. 518p.

Guevara, J., Patino, G., and Casas, E. 1962. Seleccion de variedades de frijol resistentes al picudo del ejote. *Agricultura Tecnica (Mexico)*, 12, 10–12.

Gujarati, J.P., Kapoor, K.N., and Gangrade, G.A. 1971. Incidence and control of seed corn maggot, *Hylemyia cilicrura* (Rond.) on soybean. *Indian Journal of Entomology*, 33(3), 366–368.

Gujarati, J.P., Kapoor, K.N., and Gangrade, G.A. 1973a. Biology of *Scopula remotata* Guen. (Lepidoptera: Geometridae) on soybean. *Jawahar Lal Nehru Krishi Vishwa Vidyalaya Research Journal*, 7, 162–165.

Gujarati, J.P., Kapoor, K.N., and Gangrade, G.A. 1973b. Biology of soybean leafminer, *Stomopteryx subsecivella* (Lepidoptera: Gelechiidae). *Entomol.*, 106(1323), 187–191.

Guled, A.A. 1988. Mechanism of resistance of selected cowpea (*Vigna unguiculata* L.) accessions to the beanfly (*Ophiomyia phaseoli* Tryon). College, Laguna, Philippines, University of the Philippines at Los Baños.

Gunasinghe, U.B., Irwin, M.E., and Kampmeier, G.E. 1988. Soybean leaf pubescence affects aphid vector transmission and field spread of soybean mosaic virus. *Annals of Applied Biology*, 112, 259–272.

Gupta, B.M. 1977. Inhibition of plant virus infections by antiviral agents. In Harris, K.F., and Maramorosch, K., eds., *Aphids as Virus Vectors*, New York, Academic Press, 455–471.

Gupta, P.K., and Singh, J. 1981. Important insect pests of cowpeas (*Vigna unguiculata* L.) in agroecosystem of eastern Uttar Pradesh. *Indian Journal of Zootomy*, 22, 91–95.

Habib, R. 1973. Memorandum on possibilities of biological control of *Heliothis armigera*. Commonwealth Institute of Biological Control, Rawalpindi, Pakistan, 18p.

Hagel, G.T., Burke, D.W., and Sibernagel, M.J. 1981. Response of dry bean selections to field infestations of seed-corn maggot in Central Washington. *Journal of Economic Entomology*, 74, 441–443.

Hagen, A.F. 1974. Mexican bean beetle control with systemic insecticides on dry beans in Western Nebraska. *Journal of Economic Entomology*, 67, 137.

Hagstrum, D.W. 1984. The population dynamics of stored products insect pests. In *Proceedings of the Third International Working Conference on Stored Product Entomology*. Kansas State University, Manhattan, Kansas, USA, Oct. 23–28, 1983,, pp. 10–19.

Hagstrum, D.W., and Sharp, J.E. 1975. Population studies on *Cadra cautella* in a citrus pulp warehouse with particular reference to diapause. *Journal of Economic Entomology*, 68, 11–14.

Hagstrum, D.W., and Stanley, J.M. 1979. Release-recapture estimates of the population density of *Ephestia cautella* (Walker) in a commercial peanut warehouse. *Journal of Stored Products Research*, 15, 117–122.

Haidvogl, M., Fritsch, G., and Grubauer, H.M. 1979. Poisoning by raw garden beans (*Phaseolus vulgaris* and *Phaseolus coccineus*) in children. *Paediatrie and Paedologie*, 14, 293.

Haines, C.P. 1981. Laboratory studies on the role of an egg predator, *Blattisocius tarsalis* (Berlese) (Acarina: Ascidae), in relation to the natural control of *Ephestia cautella* (Walker) (Lepidoptera: Pyralidae) in warehouses. *Bulletin of Entomological Research*, 48, 27–32.

Haji, F.N.P. 1981. Biología, danos e controle do adulto de Diabrotica speciosa (Germar, 1824) (Coleoptera, Chrysomelidae), em cultura de batatinha (*Solanum tuberosum* L.). Piracicaba, ESALQ (PhD thesis).

Halbert, S.E., Irwin, M.E., and Goodman, R.M. 1981. Alate aphid (Homoptera Aphididae) species and their relative importance as field vectors of soybean mosaic virus. *Annals of Applied Biology*, 97, 1–9.

Hall, M.J.R. 1985. The blister beetle: a pest of man, his animals and crops. *Zimbabwe Scientific Newsletter*, 19, 11–15.

Halliday, D. 1967. Build-up of free fatty acid in Northern Nigerian groundnuts. *Tropical Science*, 9, 211–237.

Hallman, G. 1979. Importancia de algunas relaciones naturales plantas-artropodos en la agricultura de la zona Calida del Tolima Central. *Revista Colombia de Entomología*, 5, 19–26.

Halteren, P. van. 1971. Insect pests of cowpea, *Vigna unguiculata* (L.) Walp. in the Accra plains. *Ghana Journal of Agricultural Science*, 4, 121–123.

Hambleton, E.J. 1935. Alguns dados sobre lepidopteros brasileiros do Estado de Minas Gerais. *Revista de Entomología*, 5, 1–7.

Hamid, S., Shah, M.A., and Anwar, A.M. 1977. Some ecological and behavioural studies on *Aphis craccivora* Koch (Hem.: Aphidae). Commonwealth Institute of Biological Control, Tropical Bulletin 19, 99–111.

Hammad, S. M. 1955. On some dipterous leaf-miners from Egypt. *Bulletin de la Société Entomologie d'Egypte*, 39, 391–394.

Hammad, S.M. 1978. Pests of grain legumes and their control in Egypt. In Singh, S.R., van Emden, H.F., and Taylor, T.A., eds., *Pests of Grain Legumes: Ecology and Control*, London/New York, Academic Press, 135–137.

Hammond, R.B. 1983. Parasites of the green cloverworm (Lepidoptera: Noctuidae) on soybeans in Ohio. *Environmental Entomology*, 12, 171–173.

Hammond, R.B. 1984. Development and survival of the Mexican bean beetle, *Epilachna varivestis* (Mulsant) on two host plants. *Journal of Kansas Entomological Society*, 57, 695–699.

Hansen, A.J. 1979. Inhibition of apple chlorotic leaf spot virus in *Chenopodium quinoa* by ribavirin. *Plant Disease Reporter*, 63, 17–29.

Harmsen, R., Bliss, F.A., Cardona, C., Posso, C.E., and Osborn, T.C. 1987. Transferring genes for arcelin protein from wild to cultivated beans: implication for bruchid resistance. NDBC/BIC Meetings, October 27–29, 1987, Denver, CO, USA. 3p.

Harris, C.R., Svec, H.J., and Begg, J.A. 1966. Mass rearing of root maggots under controlled environmental conditions: seed-corn maggot, *Hylemya cilicrura*; bean seed fly, *H. liturata; Euxesta notata*; and *Chaetopsis* sp. Journal of Economic Entomology, 59, 407–410.

Harris, K.F. 1977. An ingestion–egestion hypothesis of noncirculative virus transmission. In Harris, K.F. and Maramorosch, K., eds., *Aphids as Virus Vectors*, New York, Academic Press, 165–220.

Harris, K.F. 1978. Aphid-borne viruses: ecological and environmental aspects. In Kurstak, K., and Maramorosch, K., eds., *Viruses and Environment*, New York, Academic Press, 311–337.

Harris, K.F. 1979. Leafhoppers and aphids as biological vectors: vector–virus relationships. In Maramorosch, K., and Harris, K.F., eds., *Leafhopper Vectors and Plant Disease Agents*, New York, Academic Press, 217–308.

Harris, K.F. 1980. Aphids, leafhoppers and planthoppers. In Harris, K.F., and Maramorosch, K., eds., *Vectors of Plant Pathogens*, New York, Academic Press, 1–13.

Harris, K.F. 1981a. Arthropod and nematode vectors of plant viruses. *Annual Review of Phytopathology*, 19, 391–426.

Harris, K.F. 1981b. Horizontal transmission of plant viruses. In McKelvey, J.J. Jr., Eldridge, B., Maramorosch, K., eds., *Vectors of Disease Agents, Interactions with Plants, Animals, and Man*, New York, Praeger, 92–108.

Harris, K.F. 1983. Stenorrhynchous vectors of plant viruses: virus–vector interactions and transmission mechanisms. *Advances in Virus Research*, 28, 113–140.

Harris, K.F., and Bath, J.E. 1973. Regurgitation of *Myzus persicae* during membrane feeding—its likely function in non-persistent plant viruses. *Annals of Entomological Society of America*, 66, 793–796.

Harris, K.F., and Maramorosch, K., eds. 1977. *Aphids as Virus Vectors*. New York, Academic Press, 559pp.

Harris, K.F., and Maramorosch, K., eds. 1980. *Vectors of Plant Pathogens*. New York, Academic Press, 467pp.

Harris, K.F., and Maramorosch, K., eds. 1982. *Pathogens, Vectors and Plant Diseases: Approaches to Control*. New York, Academic Press.

Harris, R.M. 1969. Population increase of *Steneotarsonemus pallidus* (Banks) following spray applications of dimethoate. *Plant Pathology*, 18, 113–115.

Harris, V.E., and Todd, J.W. 1980. Duration of immature stages of the southern green stink bug, *Nezara viridula* (L.) with a comparative review of previous studies. *Journal of the Georgia Entomological Society*, 15(2), 114–124.

Harris, W.V. 1961. *Termites: Their Recognition and Control*. London, Longmans Green and Co. 187p.

Harris, W.V. 1969. *Termites as Pests of Crops and Trees*. London, Commonwealth Institute of Entomology. 41p.

Hartwig, E.E., and Keeling, B.L. 1982. Soybean mosaic virus investigations with susceptible and resistant soybeans. *Crop Science*, 22, 955–957.

Hartwig, E.E., and Kilen, T.C. 1989. Breeding soybeans resistant to foliar feeding insects. In Pascale, A.J., ed., *World Soybean Research Conference IV*, Buenos Aires, Argentina, Impresiones Amawald S.A., 2039–45.

Harwood, H.J. 1981. Vegetable oils as an on-the-farm diesel fuel substitute: the North Carolina situation. *RTI Final Report FR-41U-1671-4*. Research Triangle Park, North Carolina. 65p.

Hassan, A.S. 1947. The bean fly *Agromyza phaseoli* Coq. in Egypt. *Bulletin Soc. Fouad I Ent.*, 31, 217–224.

Hassan, S.M., and Moawed, S.M. 1973. Combination of (virus + insecticides) for control of cotton leafworm, *Spodoptera littoralis* (Boisd.). Paper prepared for the first pest control conference, Assuit, Cairo, 129–132.

Hassan, S.M., and Moawed, S.M. 1974a. Toxicological studies on the effect of nuclear polyhedrosis for control of the cotton leafworm *Spodoptera littoralis* (Boisd.). Paper prepared for a symposium on the use of isotopes in pesticides and pests control, Beirut, Lebanon, 175–180.

Hassan, S.M., and Moawed, S.M. 1974b. Effect of polyhedrosis virus on some biological features of cotton leafworm, *Spodoptera littoralis* (Boisd.). Paper prepared for the second pest control conference, Alexandria University, Egypt.

Haytowitz, D.B., and Matthews, R.H. 1986. Composition of foods: legumes and legume products. *Ag. Handbook*, 8–16. USDA, Washington, DC, USA. 156p.

Hazarika, S.H., and Abdus, S. 1961. Insects associated with arhar (*Cajanus indicus* Spreng.), in East Pakistan. *Scientist (Pakistan)*, 4, 18–20.

Hebblethwaite, M.J., and Logan, J.W.M. 1985. Report on a visit to Western Sudan to assess termite damage to groundnuts *Arachis hypogaea* (Hedysarae). Overseas assignment report of project no. A1402/1403. Tropical Development and Research Institute, London. 71p.

Heinerman, J. 1988. *Heinerman's Encyclopedia of Fruits, Vegetables and Herbs*. Wesr Nyzck, NJ, USA, Pante Publishing Co. 400p.

Heinrich, W.O. 1966. "Verruga", a scale pest of coffee in Brazil. *World Crops*, 18 (1), 38–42.

Heinrichs, E.A., Gastal, H.A.O., and Galileo, M.H.M. 1979. Incidence of natural control agents of the velvet bean caterpillar and response of its predators to insecticide treatments in Brazilian soybean fields. *Pesquisa Agropecuária Brasileira*, 14, 79–87.

Helm, C.G., Kogan, M., and Hill, B.G. 1980. Sampling leafhoppers on soybean. In Kogan, M., and Herzog, D.C., eds., *Sampling Methods in Soybean Entomology*, New York, Springer-Verlag, 206–282.

Hely, P.C. 1948. Beanfly control. *Agricultural Gazette of New South Wales*, 419–420.

Heong, K.L. 1981. Searching reference of the parasitoid, *Anisopteromalus calandrae* (Howard) for different stages of the host, *Callosobruchus maculatus* (F.) in the laboratory. *Researches on Population Ecology*, 23, 177–191.

Hernandez, J.C., Vera, J.G., Schoonhoven, A.V., and Cardona, C. 1984. Efecto de la asociación maíz-frijol sobre poblaciones de insectos plagas con énfasis en *Empoasca kraemeri* (Ross and Moore). *Agrociencia (Mexico)*, 57, 25–35.

Herzog, D.C. 1980. Sampling soybean looper on soybean. In Kogan, M., and Herzog, D.C., eds., *Sampling Methods in Soybean Entomology*, New York, Springer-Verlag, 141–168.

Herzog, D.C., and Todd, J.W. 1980. Sampling velvet bean caterpillar on soybean. In Kogan, M., and Herzog, D.C., eds., *Sampling Methods in Soybean Entomology*, New York, Springer-Verlag, 107–140.

Hetrick, L.A. 1947. The cowpea curculio, its life history and control. *Virginia Agricultural Experiment Station Bulletin*, 409, 23p.

Highland, H.B., and Roberts, J.E. 1984. Feeding preferences and colonization abilities of three aphid vectors (Homoptera: Aphididae) of peanut mottle virus on selected host plants. *Environmental Entomology*, 13, 970–974.

Hilder, V.A., Gatehouse, A.M.R., Sheerman, S.E., Barker, R.F., and Boulter, D. 1987. A novel mechanism of insect resistance engineered into tobacco. *Nature*, 330, 160–163.

Hill, D.S. 1975. *Agricultural Insect Pests of the Tropics and Their Control*. Cambridge, England, Cambridge University Press. 516p.

Hill, J., and Schoonhoven, A.V. 1981. Effectiveness of vegetable oil fractions in controlling the Mexican bean weevil on stored beans. *Journal of Economic Entomology*, 74, 478–479.

Hill, L.D., ed. 1976. *World Soybean Research*. Danville, IL, USA, The Interstate Printers and Publishers Inc. 1073p.

Hille Ris Lambers, D. 1972. Aphids: their life cycles and their role as virus vectors. In de Box, J.A., ed., *Viruses of Potatoes and Seed-potato Production*, Wageningen, Centre for Agricultural Publishing and Documentation, 36–56.

Ho, T.H. 1967. The bean-fly (*Melanagromyza phaseoli* Coq.) and experiments on its control. *Malaysian Agricultural Journal*, 46, 149–157.

Hobbs, H.A. 1981. Transmission of bean curly dwarf mosaic virus and bean wild mosaic virus by beetles in Costa Rica. *Plant Disease*, 65, 491–492.

Hobbs, H.A., and Fulton, J.P. 1979. Beetle transmission of cowpea chlorotic mottle virus. *Phytopathology*, 69(3), 255–256.

Hochman, C.L. 1980. Ocorrencia de larvas da semente *Delia platura* (Meigen, 1826) (Diptera: Anthomyiidae) em feijoeiro, no estado do Parana. *Anais de Sociedade Entomológica do Brasil*, 9, 293–294.

Hochmuth, R.C., Hallman, J.L., Dively, G., and Schroder, R.F.W. 1987. Effect of the ectoparasitic mite, *Coccipolipus epilachnae* (Acari: Podapolipidae) on feeding, fecundity, and longevity of soybean-fed adult Mexican bean beetles (Coleoptera: Coccinellidae) at different temperatures. *Journal of Economic Entomology*, 80, 612–616.

Hodges, R.J. 1979. A review of the biology and control of the rice moth *Corcyra cephalonica* Stainton (Lepidoptera: Galleriinae). *Tropical Products Institute Report* G125. London, UK, Overseas Development Natural Resources Institute.

Hodges, R.J. 1984. Biological methods for integrated control of insects and mites in tropical stored products. IV. The use of insect diseases. *Tropical Stored Products Information*, 48, 27–33.

Hoffman, W.E. 1935. The food plants of *Nezara viridula* (L.) (Hemiptera: Pentatomidae). *Proc. Int. Congr. Entomol.* (Madrid), 6, 811–816.

Holley, R.H., Wynne, J.C., Campbell, W.V., and Isleib, T.G. 1985. Combining ability for insect resistance in peanuts. *Oléagineux*, 40, 203–207.

Honda, Y., Iwaki, M., Saito, Y., Thongmeearkom, P., Kittisak, K., and Deema, N. 1983. Mechanical transmission, purification and some properties of whitefly-borne mungbean yellow mosaic virus in Thailand. *Plant Disease*, 67, 801–804.

Honda, Y., Iwaki, M., Thongmeearkom, P., Deema, N., and Srithongehai, W. 1982. Blackgram mottle virus occurring on mungbean and soybean in Thailand. *JARQ* (Japan) 16(1), 72–77.

Horn, N.L., Newsom, L.D., Varmer, R.G., and Jenson, R.L. 1970. Effects of virus diseases on soybeans in Louisiana. *Louisiana Agriculture*, 13, 12.

Howe, R.W., and Currie, J.E. 1964. Some laboratory observations on the rates of development, mortality and ovipositions of several species of Bruchidae breeding in stored pulses. *Bulletin of Entomological Research*, 55, 437–477.

Howe, R.W., and Freeman, J.A. 1955. Insect infestation of West African produce imported into Britain. *Bulletin of Entomological Research*, 46, 643–666.

Huignard, J., Rojas-Rousse, D., and Alzouma, I. 1984. L'activité réproductrice et le développement de *Bruchidius atrolineatus* (Pic) sur les gousses seches de *Vigna unguiculata* (Walp) en zone sahelienne, mise en évidence d'une diapause imaginale. *Insect Science and Its Application*, 5, 41–49.

Hull, R. 1971. Mycoplasma-like organisms in plants. *Review of Plant Pathology*, 50, 121–130.

Hull, R. 1972. Mycoplasma and planta diseases. *PANS*, 18, 154–164.

Hull, R., and Adams, A.N. 1968. Groundnut rosette and its assistor virus. *Annals of Applied Biology*, 62, 139–145.

Hulse, J.H. 1979. Foreword. In Hawtin, G.C., and Chancellor, G.J., eds., *Food Legume Improvement and Development*. Ottawa, Ontario, International Development Research Centre, IDRC-126e. 216p.

Hunter, D.K., Collier, S.J., and Hoffman, D.F. 1973a. Effectiveness of a granulosis virus of the Indian meal moth as a protectant for stored inshell nuts: preliminary observations. *Journal of Invertebrate Pathology*, 22, 481–482.

Hunter, D.K., Collier, S.J., and Hoffman, D.F. 1975. Compatibility of malathion and the granulosis virus of the Indian meal moth. *Journal of Invertebrate Pathology*, 25, 389–390.

Hunter, D.K., Hoffman, D.F., and Collier, S.J. 1973b. Cross infestation of a nuclear polyhedrosis virus of the almond moth to the Indian meal moth. *Journal of Invertebrate Pathology*, 22, 186–192.

Hussain, M.H., and Abdel-Aal, Y.A.I. 1982. Toxicity of some compounds against the cowpea seed beetle *Callosobruchus maculatus* (Fab.) (Coleoptera: Bruchidae). *International Pest Control*, 24, 12.

Hussein, M.Y.B. 1978. Soil application of granular carbofuran to control bean fly, *Ophiomyia phaseoli* (Tryon.). *Pertanika*, 1, 36–39.

Ibrahim, A.E. 1980. Biotic factors affecting different species in the genera *Heliothis* and *Spodoptera* in Egypt. Cairo, Institute of Plant Protection, 2, 56p.

ICRISAT (International Crops Research Institute for the Semi-Arid Tropics). 1976a. Pulse entomology annual report 1975–76, part a: pigeonpea entomology. Patancheru, India, ICRISAT. 49p.

ICRISAT. 1976b. Pigeonpea pests. In ICRISAT, *Annual Report 1975–76*, Patancheru, India, ICRISAT. 102.

ICRISAT. 1977. Pulse entomology annual report 1976–77, part a: pigeonpea entomology. Patancheru, India, ICRISAT. 52p.

ICRISAT. 1982a. Pigeonpea insect pests—surveys. In ICRISAT, *Annual Report 1981*, Patancheru, India, ICRISAT, 125–128.

ICRISAT. 1982b. Pulse entomology (pigeonpea) report of work, June 1981 to May 1982. Patancheru, India, ICRISAT, Departmental Progress Report—9, Pulse Entomology. 103p.

ICRISAT. 1982c. *Annual Report for 1981*. Patancheru, India, ICRISAT.

ICRISAT. 1983. *Annual Report for 1982*. Patancheru, India, ICRISAT.

ICRISAT. 1984. *Annual Report for 1983*. Patancheru, India, ICRISAT.

ICRISAT. 1985. *Annual Report for 1984*. Patancheru, India, ICRISAT.

ICRISAT. 1986. *Annual Report for 1985*. Patancheru, India, ICRISAT.

ICRISAT. 1987. *Annual Report for 1986*. Patancheru, India, ICRISAT.

IITA (International Institute of Tropical Agriculture). 1981. *Annual Report*. Ibadan, Nigeria, IITA, 185p.

IITA. 1982. *Annual Report*. Ibadan, Nigeria, IITA, 217p.

IITA. 1983. *Annual Report*. Ibadan, Nigeria, IITA, 218p.

IITA. 1984. *Annual Report*. Ibadan, Nigeria, IITA.

IITA. 1988. *Annual Report for 1987 (GLIP)*. Ibadan, Nigeria, IITA.

Ingram, W.R. 1969a. A note on the failure to control aphid infestation on beans with insecticides in Uganda. *East Afr. Agric. For. J.*, 34, 276–281.

Ingram, W.R. 1969b. Observations on the pest status of bean flower thrips in Uganda. *East African Agriculture and Forestry Journal*, 34, 482–484.

Irwin, M.E., and Goodman, R.M. 1981. Ecology and control of soybean mosaic virus. In Harris, K.F., and Maramorosch, K., eds., *Plant Diseases and Vectors: Ecology and Epidemiology*, New York, Academic Press, 181–220.

Irwin, M.E., Avalos, F., Chicoma, F., Chiroque, J., Alcalá, P., and Cárdenas, E. 1981. The soybean pest management program in the Selva alta of Peru. East Lansing, Michigan State University, INTSOY country reports, 33p.

Isaravurak, S., and Potan, N. 1988. Agroclimatology of Thailand grain legume growing areas. Paper prepared for the Workshop on Agroclimatology of Asian Grain Legume Growing Areas, 4–17 December, Patancheru, India, ICRISAT.

Ishiie, T., Doi, Y., Yora, K., and Asuyama, H. 1967. Suppressive effects of antibiotics of tetracycline group on symptom development of mulberry dwarf disease. *Nippon Shokubutsu Byori Gakkaiho*, 33, 267–275.

Islam, W., Ahmed, K.N., Nargis, A., and Islam, U. 1983. Occurrence, abundance and extent of damage caused by insect pests of groundnuts (*Arachis hypogaea*). *Malaysian Agricultural Journal*, 54 (1), 18–24.

Ivbijaro, M.F. 1983. Preservation of cowpea, *Vigna unguiculata* (L.) Walp. with the neem seed, *Azadirachta indica*. *A. Juss. Prot. Ecol.*, 5, 177–182.

Iwaki, M. 1979. Virus and Mycoplasma diseases of leguminous crops in Indonesia. *Review of Plant Protection Research*, 12, 88–97.

Iwaki, M., Roechan, M., Hibino, H., Tochihara, H., and Tantera, D.M. 1980. A persistent aphidborne virus of soybean, Indonesian soybean dwarf virus (transmitted by *Aphis glycines*). *Plant Disease*, 64 (11), 1027–1030.

Iwaki, M., Roechan, M., Saleh, N., Sugiura, M., and Hibino, H. 1978. Identity of mycoplasma-like agents of legume witches' broom in Indonesia. Bogor, Indonesia, *Contributions*, Central Research Institute for Agriculture, 41, 1–11.

Iwaki, M., Thongmeearkom, P., Honda, Y., and Deema, N. 1983. Soybean leaf crinkle: a new whitefly-borne disease of soybean. *Plant Disease*, 67 (5), 546–548.

Iwaki, M., Thongmeearkom, P., Prommin, M., and Honda, Y. 1982. Whitefly transmission and some properties of cowpea mild mottle virus on soybean in Thailand. *Plant Disease*, 66 (5), 365–368.

Jackai, L.E.N. 1978. Induction and host-selection behavior in the soybean looper, *Pseudoplusia includens* Walker (Lepidoptera: Plusiinae). Urbana, University of Illinois (PhD thesis).

Jackai, L.E.N. 1981a. Relationship between cowpea crop phenology and field infestation by the legume pod borer, *Maruca testulalis*. *Annals of the Entomological Society of America*, 74, 402–408.

Jackai, L.E.N. 1981b. Use of an oil soluble dye to determine the oviposition sites of the legume pod-borer *Maruca testulalis* (Geyer) (Lepidoptera: Pyralidae). *Insect Science and Its Application*, 2, 205–207.

Jackai, L.E.N. 1982. A field screening technique for resistance of cowpea (*Vigna unguiculata*) to the pod-borer *Maruca testulalis* (Geyer) (Lepidoptera: Pyralidae). *Bulletin of Entomological Research*, 72, 145–156.

Jackai, L.E.N. 1983a. Efficacy of insecticide application at different times of day against the legume pod-borer, *Maruca testulalis* (Geyer) (Lepidoptera: Pyralidae), on cowpea in Nigeria. *Protection Ecology*, 5, 245–251.

Jackai, L.E.N. 1983b. Using trap plants in the control of insect pests of tropical legumes. Paper prepared for an international workshop on integrated pest control for grain legumes, Goiâna, GO, 3–9 April.

Jackai, L.E.N. 1984a. Studies on the feeding behavior of *Clavigralla tomentosicollis* (Stal) (Hemiptera: Coreidae) and their potential use in bioassays for host plant resistance. *Zeitschrift für Angewandte Entomologie*, 98, 344–350.

Jackai, L.E.N. 1984b. Using trap plants in the control of insect pests of tropical legumes. In Matteson, P.C., ed., *Proceedings of an International Workshop on Integrated Pest Control in Grain Legumes*, Brasilia, EMBRAPA, 101–112.

Jackai, L.E.N. 1987. Large plot entomological evaluation of four elite soybean varieties in Mokwa, Nigeria. Paper prepared for the seventh annual national soybean conference, Ahmadu Bello University, Zaria.

Jackai, L.E.N. 1989. A laboratory procedure for rearing the cowpea coreid, *Clavigralla tomentosicollis* Stal. (Hemiptera), using dry cowpea seeds. *Bulletin of Entomological Research*, 79, 275–281.

Jackai, L.E.N., and Daoust, R.A. 1986. Insect pests of cowpeas. *Annual Review of Entomology*, 31, 95–119.

Jackai, L.E.N., and Raulston, J.R. 1982. Rearing two maize stem borers and a legume pod borer on artificial diet. Ibadan, IITA, *Research Briefs*, 3, 1–6.

Jackai, L.E.N., and Raulston, J.R. 1988. Rearing the legume pod borer, *Maruca testulalis*, Geyer (Lepidoptera: Pyralidae) on artificial diet. *Tropical Pest Management*, 34, 166–172.

Jackai, L.E.N., and Singh, S.R. 1981. Studies on some behavioral aspects of Maruca testulalis on selected species of *Crotalaria* and *Vigna unguiculata*. *Tropical Grain Legume Bulletin*, 22, 3–6.

Jackai, L.E.N., and Singh, S.R. 1983a. Suitability of selected leguminous plants for development of *Maruca testulalis* larvae. *Entomología Experimentalis et Applicata*, 34, 174–178.

Jackai, L.E.N., and Singh, S.R. 1983b. Varietal resistance on integrated pest management of cowpea (*Vigna unguiculata*) pests. *Insect Science and Its Application*, 4, 199–204.

Jackai, L.E.N., and Singh, S.R. 1987. Entomological research on soybeans in Africa. In Singh, S.R., Rachie, K.O., and Dashiell, K.E., eds., *Soybeans for the Tropics: Research, Production and Utilization*, Chichester, John Wiley and Sons, 17–24.

Jackai, L.E.N., and Singh, S.R. 1988. Screening techniques for host plant resistance to cowpea insect pests. *Tropical Grain Legume Bulletin*, 35, 2–18.

Jackai, L.E.N., Dashiell, K.E., and Bello, L.L. 1988. Evaluation of soybean genotypes for field resistance to stink bugs in Nigeria. *Crop Protection*, 7, 48–54.

Jackai, L.E.N., Dashiell, K.E., Shannon, D.A., and Root, W.R. 1985. Soybean production and utilization in subsaharan Africa. In Shibles, R., ed., *World Soybean Research Conference III*, Boulder, CO, Westview Press, 1193–1202.

Jackai, L.E.N., Singh, S.R., Raheja, A.K., and Wiedijk, F. 1985. Recent trends in the control of cowpea pests in Africa. In Singh, S.R., and Rachie, K.O., eds., *Cowpea Research, Production and Utilization*, Chichester, John Wiley and Sons, 233–245.

Jagtap, A.B., Ghule, B.D., and Deokar, A.B. 1984. Assessment of losses in yield of 'Phule Pragati' groundnut caused by insect pests. *Indian Journal of Agricultural Sciences*, 54(8), 697–698.

Jai Rao, K., and Thirumalachar, D.K. 1977. New record of alternate host plants of groundnut leaf miner *Stomopteryx subsecivella* Zeller (Syn.: *S. nerteria* Meyrick) (Lepidoptera: Gelechiidae). *Current Science*, 46(3), 91–92.

Jain, H.K. 1988. Introduction. In Balder, B., Ramanujam, S., and Jain, H.K., eds., *Pulse Crops (Grain Legumes)*, New Delhi, Oxford & IBH Publishing Co., pvt., Ltd., 626p., vii–ix.

Jalali, S.K., Singh, S.P., and Ballal, C.R. 1987. Role of host plants on *Spodoptera litura* (Fabricius) on the degree of parasitism by *Cotesia marginiventris* (cresson) (Hymenoptera: Braconidae). *Indian Journal of Agricultural Sciences*, 57(9), 676–678.

Janardan, Singh and Nath, Paras. 1985. Effects of some granular insecticides on white grub populations in groundnut and sugar cane. *Pesticides*, October 1985, 66–68.

Jang, Y.D., and Yun, Y.N. 1983. A study on the biology of primary parasites of the cowpea aphid *Aphis craccivora* (Aphididae, Homo.) and its hyperparasites. *Korea Journal of Plant Protection*, 22, 237–243.

Jansen, W.P., and Staples, R. 1971. Specificity of transmission of cowpea mosaic virus by species within the subfamily Galerucinae, family Chrysomelidae. *Journal of Economic Entomology*, 64, 365–367.

Jarry, M., and Bonet, A. 1982. La bruche de haricot. *Acanthoscelides obtectus* Say (Coleoptera, Bruchidae), est-elle un danger pour le cowpea, *Vigna unguiculata* (L.) Walp. *Agronomie*, 2, 963–968.

Jayant, K.P., and Nagarkatti, S. 1984. Record of true parasitism in *Peribaea orbata* (Wied) (Diptera: Tachnidae). *Entomon*, 9(1), 77–78.

Jayaraj, S. 1982. Biological and ecological studies on *Heliothis*. In Reed, W., and Kumble, Vrinda, eds., *Proceedings of the International Workshop on Heliothis Management*, 15–20 November 1981, Patancheru, India, ICRISAT, 7–37.

Jayasena, K.W., and Randles, J.W. 1985. The effect of insecticides and a plant barrier row on aphid populations and the spread of bean yellow mosaic potyvirus and subterranean clover red leaf virus in Vicia fabae in South Australia. Annals of Applied Biology, 107, 355–364.

Jenson, R.L., and Newsom, L.D. 1972. Effect of stink bug-damaged soybean seeds on germination, emergence and yield. Journal of Economic Entomology, 65, 261–264.

Jepson, W.F. 1948. An annotated list of insects associated with groundnuts in East Africa. Bulletin of Entomological Research, 39, 231–236.

Jerath, M.L. 1968. Insecticidal control of Maruca testulalis on cowpea in Nigeria. Journal of Economic Entomology, 61, 413–416.

Johnson, H.W., et al. 1967. Growing soybeans. Washington, DC, USA, USDA Farmers Bulletin, 2129, 1–10.

Johnson, R.A., and Gumel, M.H. 1981. Termite damage and crop loss studies in Nigeria—the incidence of termite-scarified groundnut pods and resulting kernel contamination in field and market studies. Tropical Pest Management, 27, 343–350.

Johnson, R.A., Lamb, R.W., and Wood, T.G. 1981. Termite and crop loss studies in Nigeria—a survey of damage to groundnuts. Tropical Pest Management, 27, 325–342.

Johnston, C.D. 1986. Caryedon serratus (Olivier) (Bruchidae) established in northern South America, with additional host and locality records from Mexico. Coleopterists Bulletin, 264–265.

Johnstone, G.R., Ashby, J.W., Gibbs, A.J., Duffus, J.E., Thottappilly, G., and Fletcher, J.D. 1984. The host range, classification and identification of eight persistent aphid-transmitted viruses causing diseases in legumes. Netherlands Journal of Plant Pathology, 90, 225–245.

Jones, A.T. 1987. Control of virus infection in crop plants through vector resistance: a review of achievements, prospects and problems. *Annals of Applied Biology*, 111, 745–772.

Jones, C.G., Hoggard, M.P., and Blum, M.S. 1981. Pattern and process in insect feeding behaviour: a quantitative analysis of the Mexican bean beetle, *Epilachna varivestis*. *Entomología Experimentalis et Applicata*, 30, 254–264.

Jones, W.A. 1988. World review of the parasitoids of the southern green stink bug. *Nezara viridula* (L.) (Heteroptera: Pentatomidae). *Annals of the Entomological Society of America*, 81, 262–273.

Jones, W.A., and Jones, M.G. 1980. *Pests of Field Crops*, 2nd ed. London, E. Arnold, 448p.

Jones, W.A., and Sullivan, M.J. 1978. Susceptibility of certain soybean cultivars to damage by stink bugs. *Journal of Economic Entomology*, 71, 534–536.

Jones, W.A., and Sullivan, M.J., 1979. Soybean resistance to the southern green stink bug, *Nezara viridula*. *Journal of Economic Entomology*, 72 (4), 628–632.

Jones, W.A., and Sullivan, M.J. 1982. Role of host plants in population dynamics of stink bug pests of soybean in South Carolina. *Environmental Entomology*, 11, 867–875.

Joplin, C. E. 1974. Pulse crops of the world and their important insect pests. Burnaby, BC, Simon Fraser University (Master's thesis). 134p.

Joshi, B.G., and Sitaramaiah, S. 1979. Neem kernel as an oviposition repellent for *Spodoptera litura* (F.) moths. *Phytoparasitica*, 7, 199–202.

Joshi, B.G., Ramprasad, G., and Sitaramaiah, S. 1982. Effect of neem seed kernel suspension on *Telenomus remus* an egg parasite of *Spodoptera litura*. *Phytoparasitica*, 10, 61–63.

Joshi, B.G., Sitaramaiah, S., Satyanarayana, S.V.V., and Ramprasad, G. 1979. Note on natural enemies of *Spodoptera litura* (F.) and Myzus persicae (Sulz) on flue cured tobacco in Andhra Pradesh. *Science and Culture*, 45(6), 251–252.

Joshi, G. 1976. Surface preference on the pulse-halves of Cajanus indicus Prengl by the larvae of the rice moth *Corcyra cephalonica (Stainton)*. *Zeitschrift für Angewandte Zoologie*, 63 (2), 167–169.

Jotwani, M.G., and Sircar, P. 1967. Neem seed as a protectant against bruchids, *Callosobruchus maculatus* Fab. infesting some leguminous seeds. *Indian Journal of Entomology*, 29(1), 21–24.

Junyi, Gai, Xia, J.K., Cui, Z.L., Ren, Z.J., Pu, F.H., and Ji, D.F.J. 1985. A study on resistance of soybeans from southern China to soybean agromyzid fly (*Melanagromyza soja* Zehntner). In Shibles, R., ed., *World Soybean Research Conference III*, Boulder, CO, Westview Press, 1240–1245.

Kabir, A.K.M.F. 1978. Pests of grain legumes and their control in Bangladesh. In Singh, S.R., van Emden, H.F., and Taylor, T.A., eds., *Pests of Grain Legumes: Ecology and Control*, London, U.K., Academic Press, 33–36.

Kadam, M.V., and Patel, G.A. 1972. Pests of pulses. In Government of Maharashtra, *Crop Pests and How to Fight Them*, Bombay, Government of Maharashtra, 61–68.

Kaiser, W.J. 1979. Natural infection of cowpea and mung bean by alfalfa mosaic virus in Iran. *Plant Disease Reporter*, 63, 414–418.

Kaiser, W.J., and Schalk, J.M. 1975. Transmission studies with pea leaf-roll virus on pulse crops in Iran. *FAO Plant Protection Bulletin*, 23, 169–173.

Kalshoven, L.G.E. 1981. Pests of crops in Indonesia. Jakarta, Indonesia, P.T. Ichtiar Bani-van Hoeve (revised and translated from Dutch), 701p.

Kamal, M. 1951. The biological control of the cotton leaf-worm, *Prodenia litura* F. in Egypt. *Bulletin Société Fouad I d'Entomologie*, 35, 221–270.

Kapadia, M.N. 1975. Some studies on bionomics and control of blue butterfly (*Euchrysops cnejus* Fab.) as a pest of tur (*Cajanus cajan* Millsp.). Junagadh, Gujarat, India, Gujarat Agricultural University (Master's thesis).

Kapadia, M.N., Bharodia, R.K., and Vora, V.J. 1982. Biology and estimation of incidence of groundnut leaf miner, *Stomopteryx subsecivella* Zell. (Gelechiidae: Lepidoptera). *Gujarat Agricultural University Research Journal*, 8(1), 37–39.

Kaplan, L. 1965. Archeology and domestication in American *Phaseolus* (beans). *Economic Botany*, 19, 358–368.

Kapoor, K.N. 1966. Bioecological studies on *Clavigralla gibbosa* Spin. (Coreidae: Hemiptera) the tur pod bug. Jabalpur, Madhya Pradesh, India, Jawaharlal Nehru Krishi Vishwa Vidyalaya (Master's thesis).

Kapoor, K.N., Gujarati, J.P., and Gangrade, G.A. 1972. Bionomics of *Lamprosema indicata* Fabricius (Lepidoptera: Pyralidae), on pests of soybean in Madhya Pradesh. *Indian Journal of Entomology*, 34, 102–105.

Kapoor, K.N., Gujarati, J.P., and Gangrade, G.A. 1973. Chemical control of soybean stemfly, *Melanagromyza phaseoli* (Tryon). *Pesticides*, 7 (7), 31–32.

Kapoor, K.N., Gujarati, J.P., and Gangrade, G.A. 1975. *Cantheconidia furcellata* Wolff as a predator of *Prodenia litura* Fabr. larvae. *Indian Journal of Entomology*, 37 (3), 275.

Kapoor, S. 1964. Nutritional studies on *Rhizopertha dominica* (Bostrychidae, Coleoptera). 1: effects of various natural foods on larval development. *Indian Journal of Entomology*, 26, 288–295.

Karel, A.K. 1981. *The Problems and Progress of Heliothis armigera* management in Tanzania. Morogoro, Tanzania, University of Dar es Salaam, 31p.

Karel, A.K. 1984a. A list of insects attacking beans in East Africa. Sokoine University of Agriculture, Morogoro, Tanzania. 4p.

Karel, A.K. 1984b. Effect of insecticide application on the insect pests and yield of common bean, *Phaseolus vulgaris* L., in Tanzania. *Bean Improvement Cooperative (USA) Annual Report*, 27, 193–195.

Karel, A.K. 1985a. A bibliography of bean flies, *Ophiomyia phaseoli* (Tryon), *O. centrosematis* (de Meij.) and *Melanagromyza spencerella* (Greathead) (Diptera: Agromyzidae). East Lansing, MI, Michigan State University, Bean/Cowpea CRSP Monograph 2, 21p.

Karel, A.K. 1985b. Host-plant resistance in common beans to foliar beetle (*Ootheca bennigseni*) (Weise). *Bean Improvement Cooperative (USA) Annual Report*, 28, 13–14.

Karel, A.K. 1985c. Resistance to bean fly, *Ophiomyia phaseoli* (Tryon), in common beans. In Minjas, A.N., and Salema, M.P., eds., *Proceedings of the Third Regional Bean Workshop*, Morogoro, Tanzania, Sokoine University of Agriculture, 45–47.

Karel, A.K. 1985d. Yield losses from and control of bean pod borers *Maruca testulalis* (Lepidoptera: Pyralidae) and *Heliothis armigera* (Lepidoptera: Noctuidae) in field beans. *Journal of Economic Entomology*, 78, 1323–1326.

Karel, A.K., and Maerere, A.P. 1985. Evaluation of common bean cultivars for resistance to bean fly (*Ophiomyia phaseoli*) (Tryon). *Bean Improvement Cooperative (USA) Annual Report*, 28, 15–16.

Karel, A.K., and Malinga, Y. 1980. Leafhopper and aphid resistance in cowpea varieties. *Tropical Grain Legume Bulletin*, 20, 10–11.

Karel, A.K., and Matee, J.J. 1986. Yield losses in common beans following damage by bean fly, *Ophiomyia phaseoli* (Tryon) (Diptera: Agromyzidae). *Bean Improvement Cooperative (USA) Annual Report*, 29, 115–116.

Karel, A.K., and Materu, R.D.R. 1983. The effect of insecticide application and plant populations on insect pests and yield of intercropped maize and beans. *Bean Improvement Cooperative (USA) Annual Report*, 26, 43–45.

Karel, A.K., and Mughogho, R.M.K. 1985. The effect of insecticide application and plant populations on the insect pests and yield of common bean (*Phaseolus vulgaris* L.). *Journal of Economic Entomology*, 78, 917–921.

Karel, A.K., and Ndunguru, B.J. 1980. *Review of Appropriate Agriculture Production Practices for Small Farmers in Tanzania*. Rome, Italy, Food and Agriculture Organization of the United Nations (FAO). 75p.

Karel, A.K., and Rweyemamu, C.L. 1984. Yield losses in field beans following foliar damage by *Ootheca bennigseni* (Weise). *Journal of Economic Entomology*, 77, 761–765.

Karel, A.K., and Rweyemamu, C.L. 1985. Resistance to foliar beetle, *Ootheca bennigseni* (Coleoptera: Chrysomelidae) in common beans. *Environmental Entomology*, 14, 662–664.

Karel, A.K., and Schoonhoven, A.V. 1986. Use of chemical and microbial insecticides against pests of common beans. *Journal of Economic Entomology*, 79, 1692–1696.

Karel, A.K., Ndunguru, B.J., Price, M., Semuguruka, S.H., and Singh, B.B. 1981. Bean production in Tanzania. In CIAT, *Potential for Field Beans in Eastern Africa*. Cali, Colombia, Centro Internacional de Agricultura Tropical (CIAT), 122–154.

Kashyap, N.P., and Adlakha, R.L. 1971. New records of insect pests of soybean crop. *Indian Journal of Entomology*, 33, 467–468.

Katundu, J.M. 1980. Agromyzid leafminer: a new pest to Tanzania. *Tropical Grain Legume Bulletin*, 20, 8–10.

Kayumbo, H.Y. 1975. Cowpea pests in Tanzania. Proceedings IITA Collaborators Meeting on Grain Legume Improvement. Ibadan, IITA, 9–13 June, 179p.

Kayumbo, H.Y. 1977. Insect pest populations in mixed crop ecosystems. *Tropical Grain Legume Bulletin*, 8, 24–27.

Keever, D.W., Arbogast, R.T., and Mullen, M.A. 1985. Population trends and distribution of *Bracon hebetor* Say (Hymenoptera: Braconidae) and lepidopterous pests in commercially stored peanuts. *Environmental Entomology*, 14, 722–725.

Keever, D.W., Mullen, M.A., Press, J.W., and Arbogast, R.T. 1986. Augmentation of natural enemies for suppressing two major insect pests in farmers' stored stock peanuts. *Environmental Entomology*, 15, 767–770.

Kellen, W.R., and Hoffman, D.F. 1987. Laboratory studies on the dissemination of a granulosis virus by healthy adults of the Indian meal moth *Plodia interpunctella* (Lepidoptera, Pyralidae). *Environmental Entomology*, 16, 1231–1234.

Kennedy, J.S., Day, M.F., and Eastop, V.F. 1962. A complex of aphids as vectors of plant viruses. London, Commonwealth Institute of Entomology, 1–114.

Kester, K.M., Smith, G.M., and Gilman, D.F. 1984. Mechanisms of resistance in soybean (*Glycine max* (L.) Merrill) genotype PI 171444 to the southern green stink bug *Nezara viridula* (L.) (Hemiptera: Pentatomidae). *Environmental Entomology*, 13, 1208–1215.

Khaemba, B.M., and Khamala, C.P.M. 1981. Relation of pod age to the expression of resistance in cowpea *Vigna unguiculata* (L.) to common pod sucking bugs *Riptortus dentipes* (F.) and *Anoplocnemis curvipes* (F.) (Hemiptera: Coreidae). *Kenya Journal of Science and Technology*, 2, 47–52.

Khaemba, B.M., and Latigo, M.W.O. 1982. Effects of infestation and transmission of common bean mosaic virus (CBMV) by the black bean aphid *A. fabae* on the common bean *P. vulgaris*. *East African Agricultural and Forestry Journal*, 47(1–4), 1–4.

Khaemba, B.M., and Ogenga-Latigo, M.W. 1985. Effects of the interaction of two levels of the black bean aphid, *Aphis fabae* Scopoli (Homoptera: Aphididae), and four stages of plant growth and development performance of the common bean, *Phaseolus vulgaris*, under greenhouse conditions in Kenya. *Insect Science and Application*, 6, 645–648.

Khamala, C.P.M. 1978. Pests of grain legumes and their control in Kenya. In Singh, S.R., van Emden, H.F., and Taylor, T.A., eds., *Pests of Grain Legumes: Ecology and Control*, London/New York, Academic Press, 127–134.

Khamala, C.P.M., Oketch, L.M., and Okeyo-Owuor, J.B. 1978. Insect species associated with *Cajanus cajan*. *Kenya Entomologists Newsletter*, 8, 3–5.

Khan, M.I., and Raodeo, A.K. 1978. Importance of larval parasite in the control of Stomopteryx subsecivella Zeller. Journal of the Maharashtra Agricultural University, 3(3), 261–263.

Khan, M.I., and Raodeo, A.K. 1979. Studies on the soil application of systemic insecticides for the control of groundnut leaf miner, *Stomopteryx subsecivella* Zeller (Lepidoptera: Gelichiidae). *Journal of the Maharashtra Agricultural University*, 4(1), 29–31.

Khan, T.N., and Rachie, K.O. 1972. Preliminary evaluation and utilization of pigeon pea germplasm in Uganda. *East African Agricultural and Forestry Journal*, 38(1), 78–82.

Khare, R.N., Krishnamurthy, K., and Pingole, S.V. 1966. Milling losses of food grains. Part 1: Studies on losses of redgram (*Cajanus cajan*) during milling. *Bulletin of Grain Technology*, 4, 125–132.

Killinger, G.B. 1968. Pigeonpea (*Cajanus cajan* L. Druce) a useful crop for Florida. *Proceedings of Soil Crop Science Society Florida*, 28, 162–167.

Kim, T.H., and Eckkenrode, C.J. 1987. Bionomics of the bean seed maggot, *Delia florilega* (Diptera: Anthomyiidae) under controlled conditions. *Environmental Entomology*, 16, 881–886.

King, A.B.S., and Saunders, J.L. 1984. Las plagas invertebradas de cultivos anuales alimenticios en América Central: una guía para su reconocimiento y control. London, England, Overseas Development Administration (ODA). 182p.

King, E.G. and Coleman, R.J. 1989. Potential for biological control of *Heliothis* species 1,2. *Annual Review of Entomology*, 34, 53-75.

King, E.G., Powell, J.E., and Smith, J.W. 1982. Prospects for utilization of parasites and predators for the management of *Heliothis* spp., *Annual Review of Entomology*, 27, 103-122.

Kiritani, K. 1964. Natural control of populations of the southern green stink bug, *Nezara viridula. Research on Population Ecology* (Kyoto) (Kotai Gun Sectai no Kenkyu), 6, 88-98.

Kiritani, K. 1965. The natural regulation of the population of the southern green stink bug *Nezara viridula* L. *Proceedings of the International Congress of Entomology* (London), 12, 375.

Kiritani, K. 1970. Studies on the adult polymorphism in the southern green stink bug, *Nezara viridula* L. *Proceedings of the International Congress on Entomology* (London), 12, 375.

Kiritani, K., and Kimura, K. 1965. The effect of population density during nymphal and adult stages on the fecundity and other reproductive performances. *Japanese Journal of Ecology*, 15, 233-236.

Kiritani, K., and Kimura, K. 1966. A study of the nymphal aggregation of the cabbage stink bug, *Eurydema rugosum* Motschulsky (Heteroptera: Pentatomidae). *Japanese Journal of Applied Entomology and Zoology*, 1, 21-28.

Kiritani, K., Hokyo, N., Kimura, K., and Nakasuji, F. 1965. Imaginal dispersal of the southern green stink bugs, *Nezara viridula* L., in relation to feeding and oviposition. *Japanese Journal of Applied Entomology and Zoology*, 9, 29-97.

Kisimoto, R. 1973. Leafhoppers and planthoppers. In Gibbs, A.J., ed., *Viruses and Invertebrates*, New York, Elsevier, 137-156.

Kiula, B.A., and Karel, A.K. 1985. Effectiveness of vegetable oils in protecting beans against Mexican bean weevil (*Zabrotes subfasciatus* Boheman). *Bean Improvement Cooperative (USA) Annual Report*, 28, 3-5.

Klein, R.E., and Livingston, C.H. 1982. Eradication of potato virus X from potato by ribavirin treatment of cultured potato shoot tips. *American Potato Journal*, 59, 359-365.

Kobayashi, T. 1959. The developmental stages of some species of the Japanese Pentatomidae (Hemiptera). 7. Developmental stages of *Nezara* and its allied genera (Pentatomidae S. str.) (In Japanese, English summary). *Japanese Journal of Applied Entomology and Zoology*, 3, 221-231.

Kobayashi, T. 1976a. Pod borers and the seed pest complex in Asian soybeans. In Goodman, B.M., ed., *Expanding the Use of Soybeans*, Proceedings of a Conference for Asia and Oceania, Urbana, IL, University of Illinois, College of Agriculture, 171-173.

Kobayashi, T. 1976b. Insect pests of soybean in Japan and their control. *PANS*, 22, 336-349.

Kobayashi, T., and Cosenza, G. 1987. Integrated control of soybean stink bugs in the Cerrados. *JARQ*, 20(4), 230-236.

Kogan, M., and Greden, R.D. 1970. The host-plant range of *Lema trilineata daturaphila* (Coleoptera: Chrysomelidae). *Annals of the Entomological Society of America*, 63, 1175-1180.

Kogan, M., and Turnipseed, S.G. 1987. Ecology and management of soybean arthropods. *Annual Review of Entomology*, 32, 507-538.

Kogan, M., Turnipseed, S.G., Shepard, M., de Oliveira, E.G., and Borgo, A. 1977. Pilot insect pest management program for soybean in southern Brazil. *Journal of Economic Entomology*, 70, 661-663.

Kogan, M., Waldbauer, G.P., Boileau, G., and Eastman, C.E. 1980. Sampling bean leaf beetles on soybean. In Kogan, M., and Herzog, D.C., eds., *Sampling Methods in Soybean Entomology*, New York, Springer-Verlag, 201-236.

Köhler, C.S., and Mehta, P.N. 1972. Relationships of insect control attempts by chemicals to components of yield of cowpeas in Uganda. *Journal of Economic Entomology*, 65, 1421–1427.

Köhler, C.S., and Rachie, K.O. 1971. Notes on the control and biology of Heliothis armigera (Hübner) on pigeonpea in Uganda. *East African Agricultural and Forestry Journal*, 36 (3), 296–297.

Kolavalli, S., Williams, S. and Kauffman, H. 1987. Potential for soybean production and processing in Africa. In Singh, S.R., Rachie, K.O., and Dashiell, K.E., eds., *Soybeans for the Tropics: Research, Production and Utilization*, Chichester, John Wiley and Sons, 137–148.

Kolte, S.J., and Nene, Y.L. 1972. Studies on symptoms and mode of transmission of the leaf crinkle virus of urd bean (*Phaseolus mungo*). *Indian Phytopathology*, 25, 401–404.

Kondo, E., and Ishibashi, N. 1984. Infectivity and multiplication of *Steinernema feltiae* (Str. Mexican) on common cutworm *Spodoptera litura* (F.) *Japanese Journal of Applied Entomology and Zoology*, 28(4) 229–236.

Konje, C.B. 1988. Host plant resistance in cowpea: *Nezara viridula* (L.) (Hemiptera: Pentatomidae) and *Riptortus dentipes* (Fabricius) (Hemiptera: Alydidae) cowpea pod-sucking bugs. University of Ibadan (MSc thesis).

Kornegay, J.L., and Temple, S.R. 1986. Inheritance and combining ability of leafhopper defence mechanisms in common bean. *Crop Science*, 1153–1158.

Kornegay, J.L., Cardona, C., and Schoonhoven, A.V. 1986. The mechanisms of resistance in common beans to the leafhopper *Empoasca kraemeri*. *Entomología Experimentalis et Applicata*, 40, 273–279.

Kornegay, J.L., Cardona, C., van Esch, J., and Alvarado, M. 1988. Identification of common bean lines with ovipositional resistance to *Empoasca kraemeri* (Homoptera: Cicadellidae). *Journal of Economic Entomology* (in press; accepted for publication June 3, 1988).

Korytkowski, C., and Torres, M. 1966. Insect damaging cultures of pigeonpea (*Cajanus cajan*) in Peru. *Revista Peruana de Entomología?*, 9, 3–9.

Koyama, N. 1950. Studies on the food eating habits of *Epilachna vigintioctomaculata* Motschulsky I. On food plants. *Oyo Kontyu*, Japan. 6, 25–33.

Krishnaiah, K., Ramakrishnan, N., and Reddy, P.C. 1985. Control of *Spodoptera litura* (Fabr) on black gram by nuclear polyhedrosis. *Indian Journal of Agricultural Sciences*, 55(12), 775–776.

Kuhn, C.W., and Bock, K.R. 1975. Peanut mottle virus. *CMI/AAB Descriptions of Plant Viruses*, 141.

Kumar, N.G., Thontadarya, T.S., and Kulkarni, K.A. 1980. Some natural enemies of the pod borer, *Cydia ptychora* Meyrick (Lepidoptera: Tortricidae). *Current Research*, 9, 146–147.

Kumar, N.G., Thontadarya, T.S., and Kulkarni, K.A. 1981. Seasonal incidence of the pod borer, *Cydia ptychora* Meyrick (Lepidoptera: Tortricidae) on soybean crop at Dharwad. *Mysore Journal of Agricultural Science*, 15(2), 227–279.

Kumar Rao, J.V.D.K., and Sithanantham, S. 1989. Impact of nodule infestation by *Rivellia angulata* on N_2-fixation, growth and yield of pigeon pea (*Cajanus cajan* L. Mill sp.) grown in a vertisol. *Biology and Fertility of Soils*, 7(2), 95–100.

Kundu, G.G. 1984b. Effect of infestation by various insect pests on soybean crop. In progress report of All India Co-ordinated Research Project on Soybean, CIARU, 45–46.

Kundu, G.G., and Goswani, K. 1985. Evaluation of soybean germplasms for resistance to the stemfly, *Ophiomyia phaseoli* (Tryon). *Journal of Entomological Research*, 9(1), 54–56.

Kunkel, L.O. 1922. Insect transmission of yellow stripe disease. *Hawaii Plant Record*, 26, 58–64.

Labeyrie, V. 1957. Influence des techniques de recoltes des haricots secs sur l'intensité des attaques de la bruche (*Acanthoscelides obtectus*). *Académie Agricole de France*, 43, 138–140.

Labeyrie, V., and Maison, P. 1954. Sur les relations entre la ponte d'*Acanthoscelides obtectus* (Say) dans la nature et les estades phenologiques de *Phaseolus vulgaris* (Linne). *Comptes rendus hebdomadaires des séances de l'Académie des sciences*, 238, 1920–1922.

Lal, O.P. 1974. Occurrence of *Chauliops fallax* Scott (Hemiptera: Lygaeidae) on French bean and horse gram in Himachal Pradesh. *Indian Journal of Entomology*, 36, 67–68.

Lal, S.S., Yadava, C.P., and Dias, C.A.R. 1981. Major pest problems of pigeonpea in Uttar Pradesh, India. *International Pigeonpea Newsletter*, 1, 30–31.

Lall, B.S. 1959. On the biology and control of bean fly, *Melanagromyza phaseoli*. *Science and Culture*, 24, 531–532.

Lamb, R.W. 1979. Report on a visit to Nigeria and the Republic of Niger to survey termite damage to groundnuts, September 15–October 28, 1979. Centre for Overseas Pest Research, London, Report CVR/80/2 (limited distribution). 17p.

Langlitz, H.O. 1966. The economic species of Empoasca in the coastal and sierra regions of Peru. *Revista Peruana de Entomología*, 7, 54–70.

Lapidus, J.B., Cleary, R.W., Davidson, R.H., Fisk, F.W., and Augustine, M.G. 1963. Chemical factors influencing host selection by the Mexican bean beetle *Epilachna varivestis* Muls. *Journal of Agriculture and Food Chemistry*, 1, 462–463.

Lateef, S.S. 1977. Pest control strategy in the semi-arid tropics with specific reference to pigeonpea (*Cajanus cajan* Millsp.) and chickpea (*Cicer arietinum* L.). In *Chemicalisation of Plant Production in the Tropics and Sub-tropics*, vol. 3, Leipzig, GDR, KMU, 106–116.

Lateef, S.S., and Reddy, Y.V.R. 1984. Parasitoids of some pigeon-pea pests at ICRISAT. *International Pigeonpea Newsletter*, 3, 46–47.

Lateef, S.S., and Reed, W. 1980. Development of a methodology for open field screening for insect pest resistance in pigeonpea. In ICRISAT, *Proceedings of International Workshop on Pigeonpea, 15–19 Dec*, Patancheru, India, ICRISAT, 315–322.

Lateef, S.S., and Reed, W. 1983. Review of crop losses caused by insect pests in pigeonpea internationally and in India. In Entomological Society of India, *Crop Losses due to Insect Pests. Special Issue, Indian Journal of Entomology*, Hyderabad, 2, 284–291.

Lateef, S.S., Bhagwat, V.R., and Reed, W. 1986. Progress in the search for insect pest resistance in pulses at ICRISAT. *Annual Plant Resistance to Insects Newsletter*, 12, 49–50.

Lateef, S.S., Reed, W., and Bhagwat, V.R. 1987. Antibiosis to *Heliothis armigera* in pigeonpea. *Annual Plant Resistance to Insects Newsletter*, 13, 54–55.

Lateef, S.S., Reed, W., and Lasalle, J. 1985. *Tanaostigmodes cajaninae* LaSalle (Hymenoptera: Tanaostigmatidae), a potential pest of pigeonpea in India. *Bulletin of Entomological Research*, 75, 305–312.

Latheef, M., and Irwin, R.D. 1980. Effects of companionate planting on snap bean insects, *Epilachna varivestis* and *Heliothis zea*. *Environmental Entomology*, 9, 195–198.

Lathroop, F.H., and Keirstead, L.G. 1946. Black pepper to control the bean weevil. *Journal of Economic Entomology*, 39, 534.

Laurence, G.A. 1971. Insect pests of pigeonpea and their control. *Journal of Agricultural Society, Trinidad and Tobago*, 71, 4, 501–504.

Lays, J.F., and Autrique, A. 1987. *La mouche du haricot*. Institut des Sciences agronomiques du Burundi. Fiche technique no 008. 18p.

Le Cato, G.L., Collins, J.M., and Arbogast, R.T. 1977. Reduction of residual populations of stored-product insects by *Xylocoris flavipes* (Hemiptera: Anthocoridae). *Journal of the Kansas Entomological Society*, 50, 84–88.

Le Pelley, R.H. 1959. *Agricultural Insects of East Africa*. Nairobi, Kenya, East Africa High Commission. 307p.

Lee, H.S. 1965. Field evaluation of several low toxicity insecticides for controlling the bean pod borer, *Maruca testulalis* Geyer. *Plant Protection Bulletin* Taiwan, 7, 67–70 (in Chinese).

Lee, K.E., and Wood, T.G. 1971. *Termites and Soils*. London and New York, Academic Press. 251p.

Lee, S.Y. 1976. Notes on some agromyzid flies destructive to soybeans in Taiwan. *Formosan Science* (Taiwanke Nsuehu), 30, 4–10 (in Chinese).

Lefroy, H.M. 1906. *Indian Insect Pests*. New Delhi, India, Today and Tomorrow Printers.

Leite F.A., and Ramalho, F.S. 1979. Biología da cigarrinha verde, *Empoasca kraemeri* (Ross and Moore, 1957) em feijão e feijão-de-corda. *Anais da Sociedade Entomológica do Brasil*, 8(1), 93–101.

Letourneau, D.K., and Altieri, M.A. 1983. Abundance patterns of a predator, *Orius tristicolor* (Hemiptera: Anthocoridae) and its prey *Frankliniella occidentalis* (Thysanoptera: Thripidae): habitat, attraction in polyculture versus monoculture. *Environmental Entomology*, 12, 1464–1469.

Leuck, D.B. 1966. Biology of the lesser cornstalk borer in South Georgia. *Journal of Economic Entomology*, 59, 797–801.

Leuck, D.B., and Dupree, M. 1965. Parasites of the lesser cornstalk borer. *Journal of Economic Entomology*, 58, 779–780.

Lewis, T. 1973. *Thrips: Their Biology, Ecology, and Economic Importance*. London and New York, Academic Press. 349p.

Licha-Baquero, M. 1980. The witches' broom disease of pigeon pea (*Cajanus cajan* (L.) Millsp.) in Puerto Rico (caused by mycoplasma-like organisms and a virus, *Empoasca* vectors). *Journal of Agriculture of the University of Puerto Rico*, Agricultural Experiment Station (USA), 64, 424–441.

Lim, S.M. 1985. Resistance to soybean mosaic virus in soybeans. *Phytopathology*, 75, 199–201.

Lima, A.M.C. 1940. Insetos do Brasil: Hemiptera. Rio de Janeiro, Escola Nacional de Agricultura, 2, 351p.

Lima, J.A.A., and Gonçalves, M.F.B. 1980. Transmisibilidade de "Cowpea mosaic virus" pelo manhoso *Chalcodermus bimaculatus*. *Fitopatologia Brasileira*, 5, 414–415.

Lima, J.A.A., and Gonçalves, M.F.B. 1985. O uso de barreira viva visando o controle do "Cowpea aphid-borne mosaic virus" em cultura de feijao-de-corda (*Vigna unguiculata*). *Fitopatologia Brasileira*, 10, 321.

Lima, J.A.A., and Santos, A.A. dos 1988. Viral diseases of cowpea in Brazil. In Watt, E.E., and Araupo, J.P.P. de, eds., *Cowpea Research in Brazil*, chapter 12, 213–232, IITA/EMBRAPA, 360 p.

Lima, M.G.A. de, Daoust, R.A., and Soper, R.A. 1984. Patogenicidade de fungos a *Elasmopalpus lignosellus* e outros lepidopteros pragas do caupi (*Vigna unguiculata* Walp) pulverizados diretamente numa torre calabrada. Congr. Bras. Entomol., 9th, Londrina, RP, Brazil.

Lima, J.A.A., Santos, C.D.G. and Silveira, L.F.S. 1986. Comportamento de genótipos de campi em relação aos dois principais virus que ocurrem no Ceará. *Fitopatol. Bras.* 11, 151–161.

Lin, C.S. 1981. Resistance of beans to insects. *Chinese Journal of Entomology*, 1, 1–6.

Lin, M.T., and Rios, G.P. 1988. Cowpea diseases and their prevalence in Latin America. In Singh, S.R., and Rachie, K.O., eds., *Cowpea Research, Production and Utilization*, Chichester, John Wiley and Sons, 199–204.

Lipinsky, E.S., and Kresovich, S. 1980. Sorghums as energy crops. In *Proceedings, Bio-Energy '80. World Congress and Exposition, April 21–24 1980, Atlanta, Georgia; Washington, DC*. The Bio-Energy Council, 91–93.

List, P.H., and Horhammer, L. 1969–1979. *Hager's Handbuch der Pharmazeutischen Praxis*. Vols. 2–6. Berlin, Springer-Verlag.

Litsinger, J.A., Price, E.C., and Hereirra, R.T. 1980. Small farmer pest control practices for rainfed rice, corn and grain legumes in three Philippine provinces. *Philippine Entomologist*, 4, 65–86.

Litsinger, J.A., Quirino, C.B., Lumaban, M.D., and Bandong, J.P. 1978. Grain legume pest complex of rice-based cropping systems at three locations in the Philippines. In Singh, S.R., Taylor, T.A., and van Emden, H.F., eds., *Pests of Grain Legumes: Ecology and Control*, New York/London, Academic Press, 309–320.

Lockey, R.F., and Bukantz, S.C. 1989. Allergy and Immunology. *JAMA*, 271(19), 2824–2825.

Lockhart, B.E.L., and Semancik, J.S. 1968. Inhibition of the replication of a plant virus by actinomycin D. *Virology*, 36, 504–506.

Lockhart, B.E.L., and Semancik, J.S. 1969. Differential effect of actinomycin D on plant virus replication. *Virology*, 39, 362–365.

Lockwood, J.A., and Story, R.N. 1985. The diurnal ethology of the southern green stink bug, *Nezara viridula* (L.), in cowpeas. *Journal of Entomological Science*, 21, 175–184.

Loebenstein, G., and Harpaz, I. 1960. Virus diseases of sweet potatoes in Israel. *Phytopathology*, 50, 100–104.

Loebenstein, G., and Raccah, B. 1980. Control of non-persistently transmitted aphid-borne viruses. *Phytoparasitica*, 8, 221.

Loebenstein, G., Alper, M., and Levy, S. 1970. Field tests with oil sprays for the prevention of aphid-spread viruses in peppers. *Phytopathology*, 60, 212–215.

Loebenstein, G., Alper, M., Levy, S., Palevitch, D., and Menagem, E. 1975. Protecting peppers from aphid-borne viruses with aluminium foil and plastic mulch. *Phytoparasitica*, 3, 43–53.

Logan, J.W.M. 1988. Overseas Development Natural Resources Institute and the International Crops Research Institute for the Semi-Arid Tropics Collaborative Project for the Control of Termites in Groundnuts, 1986–87. Final report project A1402 (Unpublished, limited distribution).

Lopez, J.D. Jr., Ridgway, R.L., and Pinnel, R.E. 1976. Comparative efficacy of four insect predators of the bollworm and tobacco budworm. *Environmental Entomology*, 5, 1160–1164.

Lorz, A.P., et al. 1955. Production of southern peas (cowpeas) in Florida. *Bulletin of the Florida Agricultural Experiment Station*, 557.

Lourençao, A.L., and Miranda, M.A.C. 1987. Resistência de soja a insetos. VIII. IAC 78–2318, Linhagem com resistência múltipla. *Bragantia*, 46, 65–72.

Lucas, B.S., and Hill, J.H. 1980. Characteristics of the transmission of three soybean mosaic virus isolates by *Myzus persicae* and *Rhopalosiphum maidis*. *Phytopathologische Zeitschrift*, 99(1), 47–53.

Lyman, J.M., and Cardona, C. 1982. Resistance in lima beans to a leafhopper, *Empoasca kraemeri*. *Journal of Economic Entomology*, 75, 281–286.

MacFoy, C.A., and Dabrowski, Z.T. 1984. Preliminary studies on cowpea resistance to *Aphis craccivora* Koch (Hom.:Aphididae). *Zeitschrift für Angewandte Entomologie*, 97, 202–209.

MacFoy, C.A., Dabrowski, Z.T., and Okech, S. 1983. Studies on the legume pod borer, *Maruca testulalis* (Geyer). 6. Cowpea resistance to oviposition and larval feeding. *Insect Science and Its Application*, 4, 147–152.

Maekawa, K., Furusawa, I., and Okuno, T. 1980. Effects of actinomycin D and ultraviolet irradiation on multiplication of brome mosaic virus in host and non-host cells. *J. Gen. Virology*, 53, 353–356.

Magalhães, B.P., and Silva, A.B. 1981. Controle de carunchos em feijão caupi (*Vigna unguiculata* (L.) Walp.) armazenado com óleos vegetais. Pesquisa em Andamento, 42, Belém, EMBRAPA-CPATU.

Makkouk, K.M., and Kumari, S. 1989. *Apion arrogans*, a weevil vector of broad bean mottle virus. *FABIS*, 25, 26–27.

Malaka, S.L.O. 1972. Some measures applied in the control of termites in parts of Nigeria. *Nigerian Entomologists Magazine*, 2, 137–141.

Mali, V.R. 1986. Virus diseases of French bean in the tropics. In Raychandhuri, S.P., and Verma, J.P., eds., *Review of Tropical Plant Pathology*, volume 3, New Delhi, Today and Tomorrow's Printers, 421–480.

Mali, V.R., and Thottappilly, G. 1986. Virus diseases of cowpea in the tropics. In Raychandhuri, S.P., and Verma, J.P., eds., *Review of Tropical Plant Pathology*, volume 3, New Delhi, Today and Tomorrow's Printers, 361–403.

Mancia, J.E. 1973a. Evaluación de insecticidas sistémicos granulados para el combate del picudo de la vaina del frijol *Apion godmani* (Wagn). In XIX *Reunión Anual Programa Cooperativo Centroamericano para el Mejoramiento de Cultivos Alimenticios (PCCMCA), San José,, Costa Rica. 13p.*

Mancia, J.E. 1973b. Evaluación de variedades de frijol tolerantes al picudo de la vaina Apion godmani (Wagn). *SIADES (El Salvador)*, 2, 15–20.

Mancia, J.E. 1973c. Biología y control de la babosa del frijol *Vaginulus plebeius* (Fisher) en El Salvador. Ministerio de Agric. y Ganaderia, El Salvador, Circular 96. 12p.

Mancia, J.E. 1973d. La biología del pucido de la vaina del frijol *Apion godmani* (Wagn) y su distribución en El Salvador. SIADES (*El Salvador*), 2, 22–29.

Mancia, J.E., and Roman, M.C. 1973. Biología de la conchela del frijol común *Epilachna varivestis* (Muls). In *XXV Reunion Anual Programa Cooperativo Centroamericano para el Mejoramiento de Cultivos Alimenticios (PCCMCA)*, San Jose, Costa Rica. 10p.

Mancia, J.E., Diaz, A., and Gracias, O. 1973a. Utilización de insecticidas sistémicos granulados en el control de mosca blanca *Bemisia tabaci* (Genn) e infección virosa en frijol. In *XIX Reunión Anual Programa Cooperativo Centroamericano para el Mejoramiento de Cultivos Alimenticios (PCCMCA)*, San José, Costa Rica. 9p.

Mancia, J.E., Roman, M.C., and Gracias, O. 1973b. Efectividad de varios insecticidas en el combate del picudo de la vaina del frijol común *Apion godmani* (Wagn). *SIADES (El Savador)*, 2, 2–14.

Mancia, J.E., Gracias, O., and Cortes, M. 1974. Determinación de la mejor época de control del picudo de la vaina del frijol común *Apion godmani* (Wagn). *SIADES (El Salvador)*, 3, 59–66.

Mandahar, C.L. 1987. *Introduction to plant viruses*, 2nd ed., New Delhi, S. Chand and Company. 568p.

Manjunath, T.M., Bhatnagar, V.S., Pawar, C.S., and Sithanantham, S. 1985. Economic importance of *Heliothis* spp. in India and assessment of their natural enemies and host plants. Paper prepared for the International Workshop on Biological Control of *Heliothis*, 11–15 November, New Delhi, India.

Manjunath, T.M., Phalak, V.R., and Subramanian, S. 1970. First record of egg parasites of Heliothis armigera (Hübner) (Lep: Noctuidae) in India. Ascot, U.K., Commonwealth Institute of Biological Control, Technical Bulletin 13, 111–115.

Manochai Keerati-Kasikorn and Preecha Singha. 1986. A study of the age at which pods were attacked by the subterranean ant. *Proceedings of the Fifth International Groundnut Conference, Chiang Mai, March 19–21, 1986*, 261–263.

Maramorosch, K. 1963. Arthropod transmission of plant viruses. *Annual Review of Entomology*, 8, 369–414.

Maramorosch, K. 1964. Virus–vector relationships: vectors of circulative and propagative viruses. In Corbett, M.K., and Sisler, H.D., eds., *Plant Virology*, Gainesville, University of Florida, 148–174.

Maramorosch, K., ed. 1969. *Viruses, Vectors and Vegetation*. New York, Interscience Publishers, 666p.

Maramorosch, K. 1974. Mycoplasmas and rickettsia in relation to plant diseases. *Annual Review of Microbiology*, 28, 301–324.

Maramorosch, K. 1982. Control of vector-borne mycoplasmas. In Harris, K.F., and Maramorosch, K., eds., *Pathogens, Vectors and Plant Diseases, Approaches to Control*, New York, Academic Press, 265–295.

Maramorosch, K., and Harris, K.F., eds. 1979. *Leafhopper Vectors and Plant Disease Agents*. New York, Academic Press, 654p.

Maramorosch, K., Granados, R.R., and Hirumi, H. 1970. Mycoplasma diseases of plants and insects. *Advances in Virus Research*, 16, 135–193.

Maramorosch, K., Hirumi, H., Kimura, M., and Bird, J. 1975. Mollicutes and rickettsia-like plant disease agents (Zoophytomicrobes) in insects. *Annals New York Academy of Science*, 266, 276–292.

Maramorosh, K., and Harris, K.F., eds. 1981. *Plant Diseases and Vectors, Ecology and Epidemiology*. New York, Academic Press, 368p.

Mariga, I.K., Giga, D.P., and Maramba, P. 1985. Cowpea production constraints and research in Zimbabwe. *Tropical Grain Legume Bulletin*, 30, 9–14.

Martin, F.W. 1984. *CRC Handbook of Tropical Food Crops*. Boca Raton, FL, USA, CRC Press. 296p.

Martin, F.W., and Ruberte, R.M. 1975. *Edible Leaves of the Tropics*. Mayaguez, Antillian College Press. 235p.

Martin, J.H., Leonard, W.H., and Stamp, D.L. 1976. *Principles of Field Crop Production*. 3rd ed. New York, Macmillan Publishing. 1118p.

Martinez, R.M. 1978. Efecto de dos plagas en la producción del frijol (*Phaseolus* spp.). Chapingo, Mexico, Colegio de Postgraduados. 112p. (MSc thesis).

Matakot, L., Mapangou-Divassa, S., and Delobel, A. 1987. Evolution des populations de *Caryedon serratus* (Ol.) (Coleoptera: Bruchidae) dans les stocks d'arachide au Congo. *L'Agronomie Tropicale*, 42, 69–74.

Matee, J.J., and Karel, A.K. 1984. Investigation on chemical control of bean fly, *Ophiomyia phaseoli* (Tryon) on common beans. *Bean Improvement Cooperative (USA) Annual Report*, 27, 187–189.

Materu, M.E.A. 1968. The biology and bionomics of *Acanthomia tomentosicollis* (Stal) and *A. horrida* Germ (Coreidae: Hemiptera) in Arusha area of Tanzania. Kampala, Makerere Univ. College (Univ. of East Africa). (PhD. dissertation).

Materu, M.E.A. 1970. Damage caused by *Acanthomia tomentosicollis* Stal. and *A. horrida* Germ. (Hemiptera: Coreidae). *East African Agriculture and Forestry Journal*, 35 (4), 429–435.

Materu, M.E.A. 1971. Population dynamics of *Acanthomia* sp. (Hemiptera: Coreidae) or beans and pigeonpeas in the Arusha area of Tanzania. *East African Agriculture and Forestry Journal*, 36 (4), 361–383.

Mathur, Y.K., and Kausal, P.K. 1984. Relative susceptibility of some high yielding varieties of groundnut to the rust red flour beetle, *Tribolium castaneum* Herbst. (Tenebrionidae, Coleoptera). *Bulletin of Grain Technology*, 22, 144–148.

Matteson, P.C. 1981. Egg parasitoids of hemipteran pests of cowpea in Nigeria and Tanzania, with special reference to *Ooencyrtus particiae* Subba Rao (Hymenoptera: Encyrtidae) attacking Clavigralla tomentosicollis Stal. (Hemiptera: Coreidae). *Bulletin of Entomological Research*, 71, 547–554.

Matteson, P.C. 1982. The effects of intercropping with cereal and minimal permethrin application on insect pests of cowpeas and their natural enemies in Nigeria. *Tropical Pest Management*, 28, 373–380.

Maxwell-Lefroy, H., and Howlett, F.M. 1909. *Indian Insect Life: A Manual of the Insects of the Plain (Tropical India)*. Reprinted in 1971 by Today and Tomorrow's Publishers, New Delhi. 786p.

May, A.W.S. 1958. Control of potato pests in southern Queensland. *Queensland Agricultural Journal*, 84, 161–165.

Mayeux, A. 1984. Le puceron de l'arachide: biologie et controle. *Oléagineux*, 39, 425–435.

Mayo, J.K. 1945. Soybeans in Nigeria. *Tropical Agriculture*, 22, 226–229.

Mbata, G.N. 1986. The susceptibility of varieties of groundnuts to infestation by *Tribolium castaneum* during storage. *Tropical Science*, 26, 187–196.

Mbata, G.N. 1987. Studies on the susceptibility of groundnut varieties to infestation by *Plodia interpunctella* (Hübner) (Lepidoptera: Pyralidae). *Journal of Stored Product Research*, 23, 57–64.

McClanahan, R.J. 1981. Effectiveness of insecticides against the Mexican bean beetle. *Journal of Economic Entomolology*, 74, 163–164.

McDonald, D. 1966. *Aflatoxins: Poisonous Substances that can be present in Nigerian Groundnuts*. Samaru Miscellaneous Paper 53. 11p.

McDonald, D., and Harkness, C. 1966. Growth of *Aspergillus flavus* and production of aflatoxin in groundnuts, part VI. *Tropical Science*, 6, 131–154.

McDonald, D., and Harkness, C. 1968. Aflatoxin in the groundnut crop at harvest in northern Nigeria. *Tropical Science*, 8, 148–161.

McFarlane, J.A. 1970. Control of the bean bruchid *Acanthoscelides obtectus* (Say) by synergized pyrethrins powder. *Pyrethrum Post*, 10, 34–40.

McGauhey, W.H. 1975. Compatibility of *Bacillus thuringiensis* and granulosis virus treatments of stored grain with four grain fumigants. *Journal of Invertebrate Pathology*, 26, 247–250.

McGuire, J.U., and Crandall, B.S. 1967. Survey of insect pests and plant diseases of selected food crops of Mexico, Central America and Panama. International Agricultural Development Service (IADS); Agricultural Research Service, U.S. Department of Agriculture; and Agency for International Development (AID). 157p.

Mchowa, J.W., and Mitumbili, E.G. 1987. Activities of the groundnut entomology research team in Malawi. Proceedings of the First Regional Groundnut Plant Protection Group Tour. SADCC/ICRISAT Regional Groundnut Program for Southern Africa, 68–72.

McKelvey, J.J., Guevara, J., and Cortes, A. 1947. *Apion* pod weevil: a pest of beans in Mexico. *Journal of Economic Entomology*, 40, 476–479.

McKelvey, J.J., Smith, A.C., Guevara, J., and Cortes, A. 1951. Biología y control de los picudos del genero *Apion* que atacan al frijol en Mexico. *Instituto Nacionale Investigación Agricola Mexico, Folleto Tecnico 8*, 7–42.

Medina, M.R., and Guerra, L. 1973. *Evaluación del comportamiento génético del frijol infestado en forma natural con chicharrita (*Empoasca fabae*) (Harris), picudo* Apion godmani *(Wagner) y conchuela del frijol* Epilachna varivestis *en Calera, Zacatecas*. CIANE, Mexico. 13p.

Mehta, P.N., and Nyiira, Z.M. 1973. An evaluation of five insecticides for use against pests of cowpeas (*Vigna unguiculata* (L.) Walp.) with special reference to green pod yield. *East African Agricultural and Forestry Journal*, 39, 99–104.

Meiners, J.P., Waterworth, H.E., Lawson, R.H., and Smith, F.F. 1977. Curly dwarf mosaic disease of beans from El Salvador. *Phytopathology*, 67, 163–168.

Melamed-Madjar, V., and Tam, S. 1970. Tests with alternative insecticides in the control of earwigs in peanuts. *International Pest Control*, September/October 1970, 29–30.

Mellors, W.K., and Bassow, F.E. 1983. Temperature-dependent development of Mexican bean beetle (Coleoptera: Coccinellidae) immatures on snap bean and soybean foliage. *Annals of the Entomological Society of America*, 76, 692–698.

Menten, L.A., and Menten, J.O.M. 1984. Epoca de ataque de Acanthoscelides obtectus (Say) ao feijoeiro (*Phaseolus vulgaris* L.) sob condicoes de campo. *Turrialba*, 34, 333–336.

Mercer, P.C. 1976. Effect of defoliation on yield of two groundnut cultivars in Malawi. *Oléagineux*, 31, 69–72.

Messina, F.J., and Renwick, J.A.A. 1983. Effectiveness of oils in protecting stored cowpeas from the cowpea weevil (Coleoptera: Bruchidae). *Journal of Economic Entomology*, 76, 634–636.

Messina, F.J., and Renwick, J.A.A. 1985. Dispersal polymorphism of *Callosobruchus maculatus* (Coleoptera: Bruchidae): variation among populations in response to crowding. *Annals of the Entomological Society of America*, 78, 201–206.

Metcalf, C.L., Flint, W.P., and Metcalf, R.L. 1962. *Destructive and Useful Insects: Their Habits and Control*. 4th ed. New York, McGraw-Hill. 1087p.

Michael, P.J., Woods, W., Lawrence, P.J., Fisher, W., Bailey, P., and Swincer, P. 1984. Introduced parasites for the control of Australian noctuid pests. *Proceedings of the Fourth Australian Applied Entomological Research Conference, Adelaide, 24–28 September 1984*. Pest Control Recent Advances and Future Prospects.

Michels, G.J., and Burkhardt, C.C. 1981. Economic threshold levels of the Mexican bean beetle on pinto beans in Wyoming. *Journal of Economic Entomology*, 74, 5–6.

Middlekauff, W.W., and Stevenson, E.E. 1952. Insect injury to blackeye bean seeds in central California. *Journal of Economic Entomology*, 45, 940–946.

Miles, P.W. 1959. Secretion of two types of saliva by an aphid. *Nature* (Lond.), 183, 756.

Miles, P.W. 1968. Insect secretions in plants. *Annual Review of Phytopathology*, 6, 137–164.

Miles, P.W. 1972. The saliva of Hemiptera. *Advances in Insect Physiology*, 9, 183–255.

Miller, L.A., and McClanahan, R.J. 1960. Life history of the seed-corn maggot, *Hylemia cilicrura* (Rond.) and *H. liturata* (Mg.) (Diptera: Anthomyiidae) in southwestern Ontario. *Canadian Entomologist*, 42, 211–221.

Miner, F.D. 1961. Stink bug damage to soybeans. *Arkansas Farm Research*, 10, 12.

Miner, F.D. 1966. Biology and control of stink bugs (Pentatomidae) on soybeans. *Arkansas Agricultural Experiment Station Bulletin*, 708, 3–40.

Miner, F.D., and Wilson, T.H. 1966. Quality of stored soybeans as affected by stink bug damage. *Arkansas Farm Research*, 15, 2.

Miranda, C. 1967. Fechas de siembra e incidencia de *Empoasca* spp. en frijol. In *XIII Reunion Anual Programa Coperativo Centroamericano para el Mejoramiento de Cultivos Alimenticios (PCCMCA)*, San José, Costa Rica. 52.

Misari, S.M., Harkness, C., and Fowler, A.M. 1980. Groundnut production, utilization, research problems and further research needs in Nigeria. ICRISAT (International Crop Research Institute for the Semi-Arid Tropics, *Proceedings of the International Workshop on Groundnuts, 13–17 October 1980, Patancheru, A.P., India.*

Misari, S.M., and Sylvester, E.S. 1983. Coriander feathery red vein virus, a propagative plant rhabdovirus, and its transmission by the aphid *Hyadaphis foeniculi* Passerini. *Hilgardia*, 51, 38p.

Mital, V.P. 1969. Studies on the relative resistance and susceptibility of some important groundnut *Arachis hypogaea* (L.) varieties to groundnut bruchid *Caryedon gonagra*, Fabricius (Bruchidae, Coleoptera). *Bulletin of Grain Technology*, 7, 75–79.

Mitchell, W.C. 1965. An example of integrated control of insects: status of southern green stink bug in Hawaii. *Agriculture Science Review*, 3, 32–35.

Miyazaki, S., and Sherman, M. 1966. Toxicity of several insecticides to the southern green stink bug, *Nezara viridula* L. *Proceedings of the Hawaiian Entomological Society*, 19, 281–287.

Mohamed, A.H., and Karel, A.K. 1986. Effect of plant populations on insect pests and seed yield of common bean intercropped with maize. In Minjas, A.N., and Salema, M.P., eds., *Proceedings of the 4th Regional Bean Workshop*. Sokoine University of Agriculture, Morogoro, Tanzania, 69–77.

Mohammad, A. 1981. The groundnut leafminer *Aproaerema modicella (Stomopteryx subsecivella* Zeller) (Lepidoptera: Gelechiidae): a review of world literature. Patancheru, AP, India, ICRISAT, Groundnut Improvement Program. Occasional Paper 3.

Montalvo, C.G., and Sosa, C. 1973. Evaluación de la resistencia de frijol hacia la conchela *Epilachna varivestis* Muls. (Coleoptera: Coccinellidae). *Agrociencia* (Mexico), Series D, 10, 3–13.

Monte, O. 1934. Borboletas que vivem em plantas cultivadas. Série Agricola 21, Secretaria de Agricultura do Estado de Minas Gerais, Belo Horizonte, 220p.

Montecinos, M. 1982. Control cultural y quimíco de *Hylemia platura* Meig. en el cultivo del frijol. University of Chile, Santiago. 61p. (B.Sc. thesis)

Montecinos, M., Arretz, P., and Araya, J.E. 1986. Chemical control of *Delia platura* in *Phaseolus vulgaris* with seed and soil treatments in Chile. *Crop Protection*, 5, 427–429.

Montero, M.P. 1967. Control químico de *Stegasta bosquella chamlo y Epinotia aporema* Heinr. en mani. *Revista Peruana Entomología*, 10, 56–61.

Moraes, G.J. 1981. Acaros e insetos associados a algumas culturas irrigadas do sub-médio São Francisco. Tec. Bull. 4, Petrolina, EMBRAPA-CPATSA, 32p.

Moraes, G.J. 1982. Insetos e ácaros associados a algumas culturas na região de Ouricuri PE: Práticas de controle em uso pelos agricultores. EMBRAPA-CPATSA, Res. Bull. 15, Petrolina, 36p.

Moraes, G.J., and Oliveira, C.A.V. 1981. Comportamento de variedades de *Vigna unguiculata* Walp em relação ao ataque de *Empoasca kraemeri* Ross & Moore, 1957. *Anais da Sociedade Entomológica Brasil*, 10, 255–259.

Moraes, G.J., and Ramalho, F.S. 1980. Alguns insetos associados a *Vigna unguiculata* Walp no Nordeste. EMBRAPA-CPATSA, Res. Bull. 1, Petrolina, 10p.

Moraes, G.J., Magalhães, A.A., and Oliveira, C.A.V. 1981. Resistência de variedades de *Vigna unguiculata* ao ataque de *Liriomyza sativae* (Diptera, Agromyzidae). *Pesq. Agropec. Bras.*, 16(2), 2 19–21.

Moraes, G.J., Oliveira, C.A.V., Albuquerque, M.M., Salviano, L.M.C., and Possidio, P.L. 1980. Efeito da época de infestação de *Empoasca kraemeri* Ross and Moore, 1957 (Cigarrinha verde do feijoeiro) (Hom., Typhlocibidae) na cultura de *Vigna unguiculata* Walp (Feijão macassar). *Anais da Sociedata Entomológica do Brasil*, 9(1), 67–74.

Moraes, G.J., Sardana, B., and Oliveira, C.A.V. 1982. Nivel de dano económico de *Empoasca kraemeri* em *Vigna unguiculata*. *Pesquisa Agropecuária Brasileira*, 17(12), 1701–1705.

Morales, F. 1986a. Transmisión de virus de plantas por insectos. Miscelanea. *Sociedad Colombiana de Entomología*, 2, 3–22.

Morales, F. 1986b. Virus diseases of beans in the tropics. In Raychandhuri, S.P., and Verma, J.P., eds., *Review of Tropical Plant Pathology*, volume 3, New Delhi, Today and Tomorrow's Printers, 405–419.

Morales, F.J., and Gamez, R. 1989. Beetle-transmitted viruses. In Schwartz, H.F., and Comales, M.P., eds., *Bean Production Problems in the Tropics*, Cali, Colombia, CIAT, 363–377 (654p.).

Morales, F.J., and Niessen, A.I. 1988a. Comparative responses of selected Phaseolus vulgaris germ plasm inoculated artificially and naturally with bean golden mosaic virus. *Plant Disease*, 72, 1020–1023.

Morales, F.J., and Niessen, A.I. 1988b. Isolation and partial characterization of bean dwarf mosaic. *Phytopathology*, 78(6), 858.

Morey, C.S. 1972. Biología y morfología larval de *Epinotia aporema* (Wals) (Lepidoptera—Olethreutidae). *Universidad República Facultad Agronomía Montevideo Boletin* Rep. Fac. Agron. Montevideo Bol. 123, 14p.

Morrison, D.E., Bradley, J.R., Jr., and Duyn, J.W. van. 1979. Populations of corn earworm and associated predators after application of certain soil applied pesticides to soybean. *Journal of Economic Entomology*, 72, 97–100.

Morton, J.F. 1976. The pigeon pea (*Cajanus cajan* Millsp.), a high protein tropical bush legume. *Hortscience*, 11(1), 11–19.

Moscardi, F. 1983. Utilizacâo de *Baculovirus anticarsia* para controle da lagarta da soja *Anticarsia gemmatalis*. EMBRAPA, Com. Tech. 23, 13p.

Moscardi, F. 1989. Production and use of entomopathogens in Brazil. Paper prepared for Biotech. Biology Pest Novel Plant—Pest Res. Insect Pest Management, Boyce Thompson Institute, Cornell University, Ithaca, NY (in press).

Moscardi, F., and Corso, I.C. 1981. Açâo do *Baculovirus anticarsia* sobre a lagarta da soja (*Anticarsia gemmatalis* Hübner 1818) e outros lepidopteros. Anais I Seminário Nacional de Pesquisa de Soja, II, 51–57.

Moscardi, F., and Ferreira, B.S.C. 1985. Biological control of soybean caterpillars. In Shibles, R., ed., *World Soybean Research Conference III*, Boulder, Westview Press.

Mound, L.A. 1963. Host-correlated variation in *Bemisia tabaci* (Gennadius) (Homoptera: Aleyrodidae). *Proceedings of the Royal Entomological Society of London*, Series A, 38, 171–180.

Mound, L.A. 1973. Thrips and whiteflies. In Gibbs, A.J., ed., *Viruses and Invertebrates*, volume 31, Amsterdam, North-Holland Publishing Co., 232–242.

Mound, L.A., and Halsey, S.H. 1978. *Whitefly of the world*, New York, John Wiley and Sons, 340p.

Moutia, A. 1945. *Annual Report*, 1944. Division of Entomology, Department of Agriculture, Mauritius, 14–19.

Msangi, R.B., and Karel, A.K. 1985. Host-plant resistance in common beans to bean fly *Ophiomyia phaseoli* Tryon. In Minjas, A.N., and Salema, M.P., eds., *Proceedings of the 3rd Regional Bean Workshop*, Morogoro, Sokoine University of Agriculture, 60–63.

Mukhopadhyay, S., and Choudhuray, A.K. 1986. Virus diseases of vegetable crops. In Raychandhuri, S.P., and Verma, J.P., eds., *Review of Tropical Plant Pathology*, volume 3, New Delhi, Today and Tomorrow's Printers, 481–520.

Mundhe, D.R. 1980. Studies on the susceptibility of twenty varieties of soybean to the leaf miner, *Stomopteryx subsecivella* Zeller. *Research Bulletin Marathwada Agricultural University*, 4(1), 10–11.

Muniyappa, V. 1980. Whiteflies. In Harris, K.F., and Maramorosch, K., eds., *Vectors of Plant Pathogens*, New York, Academic Press, 115–132.

Muniyappa, V., and Nangia, N. 1982. Pigeon pea cultivars and selections for resistance to sterility mosaic in relation to the prevalence of eryophyid mite *Acetia cajani* Channabasavanna. *Tropical Grain Legume Bulletin*, 25, 28–30.

Muniyappa, V., and Reddy, D.V.R. 1983. The transmission of cowpea wild mottle virus in a nonpersistent manner. *Plant Disease*, 67, 391-393.

Muniyappa, V., and Reddy, H.R. 1976. Studies on the yellow mosaic disease of horsegram (Dolichos biflorus Linn.) 1: Virus vector relationships. *Mysore Journal of Agricultural Science*, 10, 605-610.

Muniyappa, V., Rajeshwari, R., Bharathan, N., Reddy, D.V.R., and Nolt, B.L. 1987. Isolation and characterization of a geminivirus causing yellow mosaic disease of horsegram. *Journal of Phytopathology*, 119(1), 81–87.

Murguido, C. 1983. Efectos de varios insecticidas sobre el saltahojas de los frijoles (*Empoasca* sp., Homoptera: Cicadellidae). *Ciencia y Tecnología Agrícola (Cuba)*, 6, 67–77.

Murugesan, S., and Chelliah, S. 1977. Transmission of greengram yellow mosaic virus by the whitefly, *Bemisia tabaci* (Genn.). *Madras Agricultural Journal* (India), 64(7), 437–441.

Mushobozy, D.M., and Karel, A.K. 1986. Resistance to bean fly (*Ophiomyia phaseoli* Tryon) in common beans. In Minjas, A.N., and Salema, M.P., eds., *Proceedings of the 4th Regional Bean Workshop*, Morogoro, Sokoine University of Agriculture, Tanzania, 62–68.

Myers, J.G. 1929. Notes on some natural enemies of *Plodia interpunctella* and *Silvanus surinamensis* in Australia. *Bulletin of Entomological Research*, 20, 425–430.

Naik, L.K., Devaiah, M.C., and Govindan, R. 1979. Parasitization of red gram bud weevil, *Cuthorrhynchus asperulus* Faust by *Diaparsis* sp. (Hymenoptera: Ichneumonidae). *Current Research*, 8 (12), 214–215.

Nair, M.R.G.K. 1975. *Insects and mites of Crops in India*. New Delhi, Indian Council of Agricultural Research, 405p.

Nair, N.G., and Nene, Y.L. 1973a. Studies on the yellow mosaic of urd bean (*Phaseolus mungo* L) caused by mung bean yellow mosaic virus. 1, Virus–vector relationship. *Indian Journal of Farm Sciences*, 1, 62–70.

Nair, N.G., and Nene, Y.L. 1973b. Studies on the yellow mosaic of urd bean (*Phaseolus mungo* L.) caused by mung bean yellow mosaic virus. 2, Transmission studies. *Indian Journal of Farm Sciences*, 1, 109–110.

Naito, A., Harnoto, A., Igbal, A., and Hattori, I. 1983. Pod borer *Etiella hobsoni* (Butler) of soybean in Indonesia. Bogor, Indonesia, Central Research Institute for Food Crops, 15p.

Nakasuji, F., Yamanaka, H., and Kiritani, K. 1976. Predation of larvae of the tobacco cutworm *Spodoptera litura* (Lepidoptera, Noctuidae) by Polistes wasps. *Kontyu*, 44(2), 205–213.

Namba, R. 1956. A revision of the flies of the genus *Rivellia* (Otitidae, Diptera) of America north of Mexico. *Proceedings of the United States National Museum*, 106, 21–84.

Nangju, D., Flinn, J.C., and Singh, S.R. 1979a. Control of cowpea pests by utilization of insect-resistant cultivars and minimum insecticide application. *Field Crops Research*, 2, 373–385.

Nangju, D., Nwanze, K.F., and Singh, S.R. 1979b. Planting data, insect damage and yield of cowpea in western Nigeria. *Experimental Agriculture*, 15, 1–10.

Nanne Roe, H.W. 1968. Estudio sobre dos especies de Laspeyresia (Olethreutidae, Lepidoptera) en frijol. (thesis), University of Costa Rica, San José.

Narayanan, N., and Sheldrake, A.R. 1975. ICRISAT pulse physiology annual report 1974–75, part a: pigeonpea physiology. Chapter 4, flower drop, pod set and pod development, Patancheru, India, ICRISAT, 44–49.

NAS (National Academy of Sciences). 1973. *Toxicants Occurring Naturally in Foods*. Washington, DC, USA, National Academy of Sciences. 624p.

NAS (National Academy of Sciences). 1980. *Shrub and Tree Species for Energy Production*. Washington, DC, USA, National Academy of Sciences. 237p.

Nault, L.R., and Ammar, El Desouky 1989. Leafhopper and planthopper transmission of plant viruses. *Annual Review of Entomology*, 34, 503–529.

Nault, L.R., and Gordon, D.J. 1988. Multiplication of maize stripe virus in *Peregrinus maidis*. *Phytopathology*, 78, 991–995.

Nault, L.R., and Rodriguez, J.G. 1985. *The Leafhoppers and Planthoppers*. New York, John Wiley and Sons.

Nawale, R.N., and Jadhav, L.D. 1980. Bionomics of tur pod bug *Clavigralla gibbosa* Spinola (Coreidae: Hemiptera). *Journal of Maharashtra Agricultural University*, 3 (3), 275–276.

Nayar, K.K., Ananthakrishnan, T.N., and David, B.V. 1976. *General and Applied Entomology*. New Delhi, Tata McGraw-Hill Publishing. 589 p.

Ndlovu, T.M., and Giga, D.P. 1988. Studies on varietal resistance of cowpeas to the cowpea weevil, *Callosobruchus rhodesianus* (Pic). *Insect Science and Its Application*, 9, 123–128.

Ndoye, M. 1978. Pests of cowpea and their control in Senegal. In Singh, S.R., van Emden, H.F., and Taylor, T.A., eds., *Pests of Grain Legumes: Ecology and Control*, London/New York, Academic Press, 113–115.

Negron, J.F., and Riley, T.J. 1987. Southern green stink bug, *Nezara viridula* (Heteroptera: Pentatomidae), feeding in corn. *Journal of Economic Entomology*, 80(3), 666–669.

Nene, Y.L. 1973. Control of *Bemisia tabaci* Genn., a vector of several plant viruses. *Indian Journal of Agricultural Sciences*, 43, 433–436.

Nene, Y.L., Rathi, Y.S.P., Nair, N.G., and Naresh, J.S. 1972. Diseases of mung and urd beans. In Nene, Y.L., ed., *Survey of the Viral Diseases of Pulse Crops in Uttar Pradesh*, G.B. Pantnagar Pant University of Agriculture and Technology, Research Bulletin 4, 6–153.

Neves, B.P. das. 1982a. Avaliação de danos causados pelo "manhoso" (*Chalcodermus* sp.) em caupi (*Vigna unguiculata* (L.) Walp). In Resumos da 1 Reunião Nacional de Pesquisa de Caupi, Goiânia GO, 1982, Documento 4, Goiânia, EMBRAPA-CNPAF, 62.

Neves, B.P. das. 1982b. Determinaço de resistencia varietal ao "manhoso" (*Chalcodermus* sp.) em caupi (*Vigna unguiculata* (L.) Walp). In Resumos da 1 Reunião Nacional de Pesquisa de Caupi, Goiânia GO, 1982, Documento 4, Goiânia, EMBRAPA-CNPAF, 65.

Neves, B.P. das. 1982c. Método para avaliação da resistência varietal ao *Chalcodermus* sp. em *Vigna unguiculata* (L.) Walp., em larga escala. In Resumos da 1 Reunião Nacional de Pesquisa de Caupi, Goiânia GO, 1982, Documento 4, Goiânia, EMBRAPA-CNPAF, 68–70.

Neves, B.P. das., Araújo, J.P.P. de, and Watt, E.E. 1982a. Estudo da resistência varietal e dos danos causados pela *Maruca testulalis* em caupi. In Resumos da 1 Reunião Nacional de Pesquisa de Caupi, Goiânia GO, 1982, Documento 4, Goiânia, EMBRAPA-CNPAF, 66.

Neves, B.P. das, Rios, G.P., and Carvalho, J.R.P. de. 1982b. Flutuação populacional da *Empoasca kraemeri, Cerotoma arcuata* e *Diabrotica speciosa* e seus efeitos na produção de caupi (*Vigna unguiculata* (L.) Walp.). In Resumos da 1 Reunião Nacional de Pesquisa de Caupi, Goiânia GO, 1982. Documento 4, Goiânia, EMBRAPA-CNPAF, 67–68.

Newsom, L.D., Dunigan, E.P., Eastman, C.E., Hutchinson, R.L., and McPherson, R.M. 1978. Insect injury reduces nitrogen fixation in soybeans. *Louisiana Agriculture*, 21, 15–16.

Nickel, J.L. 1960. Temperature and humidity relationships of *Tetranychus desertorum* (Banks) with special reference to distribution. *Hilgardia*, 30, 41–100.

Nielson, M.W. 1968. The leafhopper vectors of phytopathogenic viruses (Homoptera, Cicadellidae): Taxonomy, biology and virus transmission. USDA Technical Bulletin 1382, 386p.

Nielson, M.W. 1979. Taxonomic relationships of leafhopper vectors of plant pathogens. In Maramorosch, K., and Harris, K.F., eds., *Leafhopper Vectors and Disease Agents*, New York, Academic Press, 2–37.

Nielson, M.W. 1985. Leafhopper systematics. In Nault, L.R., and Rodriguez, J.G., eds., *The Leafhoppers and Planthoppers*, New York, John Wiley and Sons, 11–39.

Nienhaus, F. 1981. Virus and similar diseases in tropical and sub-tropical areas. Eschborn, Deutsche Gesellschaft fuer Technische Zusammenarbeit, 216p.

Nienhaus, F., and Sikora, R.A. 1979. Mycoplasmas, spiroplasmas and rickettsia-like organisms as plant pathogens. *Annual Review of Phytopathology*, 17, 37–58.

Nilakhe, S.S., and Chalfant, R.B. 1982. Cowpea cultivars screened for resistance to insect pests. *Journal of Economic Entomology*, 75, 223–227.

Nilakhe, S.S., Chalfant, R.B., and Singh, S.V. 1981a. Damage to southern peas by different stages of the southern green stink bug. *Journal of the Georgia Entomological Society*, 16, 409–414.

Nilakhe, S.S., Chalfant, R.B., and Singh, S.V. 1981b. Evaluation of southern green stink bug damage to cowpeas. *Journal of Economic Entomology*, 74, 589–592.

Nogueira, O.L. 1981. Cultura do feijão caupi no Estado do Amazonas. Manaus, EMBRAPA-UEPAE, Boletin Técnico 4, 21p.

Norris, D.M., and Kogan, M. 1980. Biochemical and morphological bases of resistance. In Maxwell, F.G., and Jennings, P.R., eds., *Breeding Plants Resistant to Insects*, Chichester, John Wiley and Sons, 23–62.

NSCIC (National Soybean Crop Improvement Council). 1966. *Soybean Farming* (rev. ed.). Urbana, IL, USA. 34p.

Nwanze, K., and Horber, E. 1976. Seed coats of cowpeas affect oviposition and larval development of *Callosobruchus maculatus* (F.). *Environmental Entomology*, 5, 213–218.

Nyiira, Z.M. 1971. The status of insect pests of cowpea, *Vigna unguiculata* (L.) Walp. in Uganda and their control. *PANS*, 17, 194–197.

Nyiira, Z.M. 1973. Pest status of thrips and lepidopterous species on vegetables in Uganda. *East African Agricultural and Forestry Journal*, 39, 131–135.

Nyiira, Z.M. 1978. Pests of grain legumes and their control in Uganda. In Singh, S.R., van Emden, H.F., and Taylor, T.A., eds., *Pests of Grain Legumes: Ecology and Control*, London, Academic Press, 117–121.

Oblisami, G., Ramamoorthi, K., and Rangaswami, G. 1969. Studies on the pathology of some crop pests of South India. *Mysore Journal of Agricultural Science*, 3(1), 86–98.

Ochieng, R.S. 1977. Studies on the bionomics of two major pests of cowpea (*Vigna unguiculata* L.); *Ootheca mutabilis* Sahlb. (Coleoptera: Chrysomelidae) and *Anoplocnemis curvipes* F. (Hemiptera: Coreidae). Ibadan, Nigeria, University of Ibadan, 267p. (PhD thesis).

Ochieng, R.S., and Bungu, D.O.M. 1983. Studies on the legume pod borer, *Maruca testulalis* (Geyer). 4: A model for mass rearing: Rearing on artificial diet. *Insect Science and its Application*, 4, 83–88.

Ochse, J.J. 1931. *Vegetables of the Dutch East Indies*. B.V. Amsterdam, A. Asher & Co. 1005p. (Reprinted 1980)

Odak, S.C., Deshpande, B.V., and Dhamdhare, S.V. 1967. An estimate of the damage caused by plume moth, *Exelastis atomosa* and podfly (*Agromyza obtusa*) to tur. *Journal of Agriculture College*, Gwalior, 8, 1–3.

Odak, S.C., Dhamdhare, S.V., and Deshpande, B.V. 1968. New record of *Demarchus pubipennis* Jacoby, feeding in *Cajanus cajan* (L.). *Indian Journal of Entomology*, 30 (4), 323.

Odebiyi, J.B. 1981. Field populations of *Sitobion nigrinectaria* Theo. attacking pigeonpea in Kenya. *Nigerian Journal of Agricultural Sciences*, 1 (2), 135–139.

Oei-Dharma, H.P. 1969. *Use of Pesticides to Control Economic Pests and Diseases in Indonesia*. Leiden, E.J. Brill, 199p.

Ofuya, T.I. 1984. Studies on cowpea varietal resistance to the black cowpea moth, *Cydia ptychora* (Meyrick) (Lepidoptera: Tortricidae). University of Ife, Nigeria (PhD thesis).

Ofuya, T.I. 1986. Predation by *Cheilomenes vicina* (Coleoptera: Coccinellidae) on the cowpea aphid, *Aphis craccivora* (Homoptera: Aphididae): Effect of prey stage and density. *Entomophaga*, 31, 33–35.

Ofuya, T.I. 1988. Varietal resistance of cowpeas to the cowpea aphid, *Aphis craccivora* Koch (Homoptera: Aphididae) under field and screenhouse conditions in Nigeria. *Tropical Pest Management*, 34, 445–447.

Ofuya, T.I., and Akingbohungbe, A.E. 1988. Susceptibility of cowpea varieties to damage by the black cowpea moth, *Cydia ptychora* (Meyrick) (Lepidoptera: Tortricidae). *Insect Science and Its Application*, 9(1), 73–76.

Ogunlana, M.O., and Pedigo, L.P. 1974a. Economic injury level of the potato leafhopper on soybeans in Iowa. *Journal of Economic Entomology*, 67, 29–32.

Ogunlana, M.O., and Pedigo, L.P. 1974b. Pest status of the potato leafhopper on soybeans in Central Iowa. *Journal of Economic Entomology*, 67, 201–202.

Ohiagu, G.E. 1985. Arthropod invaders as a threat to food and raw material security. Paper presented at a symposium of the 18th annual conference of the Entomological Society of Nigeria, Ahmadu Bello University, Zaria, October 6–9.

Ojehomon, O.O. 1968. Flowering, fruit production and abscission in cowpea, *Vigna unguiculata* (L.) Walp. *Journal of the West Africa Science Association*, 13, 227–234.

Ojehomon, O.O. 1970. Effect of continuous removal of open flowers on the seed yield of two varieties of cowpea, *Vigna unguiculata* (L.) Walp. *Journal of Agricultural Science*, Cambridge, 74, 375–381.

Ojo, K.O. 1988. Inheritance of resistance to the soybean leaf defoliator (*Spodoptera littoralis*) (Boisd.). University of Ibadan (MSc thesis).

Okeyo-Owuor, J.B., Agwardo, P.O., and Simbi, C.O.J. 1983. Studies on the legume pod-borer, *Maruca testulalis* (Geyer). 5: Larval population. *Insect Science and Its Application*, 4, 75–81.

Okeyo-Owuor, J.B., and Ochieng, R.S. 1981. Studies on the legume pod borer, *Maruca testulalis (Geyer)*. 1: Life cycle and behavior. *Insect Science and Its Application*, 1, 263–268.

Okeyo-Owuor, J.B. 1978. Insect pod borers of pigeonpea, *Cajanus cajan* (L) Millsp. and their influence on developing pods and final seed yield in Kenya. Nairobi, Kenya, University of Nairobi (Master's thesis). 150p.

Okwakpam, B.A. 1967. Three species of thrips in cowpea flowers in the dry season at Badeggi, Nigeria. *Nigerian Entomologists' Magazine*, 45–46.

Oladiran, A.O., and Oso, B.A. 1985. Interactions between fungicides, insecticides and spraying regimes in the control of irrigated cowpeas in northern Nigeria. *Journal of Agricultural Science*, Cambridge, 105, 45–49.

Olagbaju, A.R. 1988. Studies on bionomics and population assessment of *Aspavia armigera* (F.) (Hemiptera: Pentatomidae) on cowpea and rice. University of Ibadan (MSc thesis).

Olaifa, J.I. 1977. Observations on a braconid parasite of *Cydia ptychora* a pest of mature cowpeas in southern Nigeria. *Proceedings of the Nigerian Society of Plant Protection*, 48p.

Olaifa, J.I., and Akingbohungbe, A.E. 1981. Aspects of the biology of the black cowpea moth, *Cydia ptychora* (Lepidoptera: Torticidae) related to host plant phenology. *Annals of Applied Biology*, 97, 129–134.

Olaifa, J.I., and Akingbohungbe, A.E. 1981b. Studies on the life history and life stages of the black cowpea moth, *Cydia ptychora*. *Insect Science and Its Application*, 1, 151–160.

Olaifa, J.I., and Akingbohungbe, A.E. 1982. Seasonal population fluctuation in the black cowpea moth, *Cydia ptychora* (Meyrick) (Lepidoptera: Tortricidae). *Insect Science and Its Application*, 3, 73–77.

Oliveira, A.M., Pacova, B.E., Sudo, S., Rocha, A.C.M., and Barcellos, D.F. 1979. Incidencia de *Zabrotes subfasciatus* (Boheman, 1833) e *Acanthoscelides obtectus* (Say, 1831) em diversos cultivares de feijao armazenado (Col. Bruchidae). *Anais da Sociedade Entomologíca do Brasil*, 8, 39–46.

Oliveria, F.J., and Santos, J.H.R. 1983. Prediçăo de periodos de estocagem para sementes de *Vigna sinensis* (L.) Savi injuriadas peol *Callosobruchus maculatus* (F., 1775). *Ciencia Agronomia*, 14(1/2), 1–14.

Oliveira, J.P., and Araújo, A.D. 1979. Utilizaçao de armadilhas adesivas coloridas na coleta de *Empoasca kraemeri* Ross and Moore, 1957, em feijão *Vigna unguiculata* (L.) Walp. *Fitossanidade*, 3, 10–11.

Oliveira, J.V. 1971. Ataque do *Callosobruchus analis* no feijão comercializado em Fortaleza-Cereá-Brasil. *B. Soc. Cult. Recr. Eng. Agron. Moss.* 1(2), 18–21.

Oliveira, J.V., Da Silva, I.P., and Fernandez, M.B. 1981. Dinamica populacional de "cigarrinha verde" *Empoasca kraemeri* (Ross and Moore, 1957), em cultivares de feijao. *Anais Sociedade Entomológica do Brasil*, 10, 21–26.

Oliveira, J.V., Da Silva, I.P., Pereira, J.L.L., Teixeira, L.L.C., and Netto, R.A.C. 1984. Influência de óleos vegetais na viabilidade de ovos e emergência de adultos de *Callosobruchus maculatus* (Fabr., 1775) (Col., Bruchidae) em feijão *Vigna unguiculata* Walp. In Resumos do Congresso Brasileiro de Entomologia, 9, Londrina, Sociedade Entomológica do Brasil, 145p.

Onayama, K., Moustafa, M., and El Attal, Z.M. 1985. Enhancement of the efficiency of some insecticides against thrips and cotton leafworm by mineral oils. *Journal of Agricultural Science*, Cambridge, 105, 63–66.

Opender, K. 1985. Azadirachtin interaction with development of *Spodoptera litura* Fab. *Indian Journal of Experimental Biology*, 23, 160–163.

Osborn, T.C., Blake, T., Gepts, P., and Bliss, F.A. 1986. Bean arcelin 2: genetic variation, inheritance and linkage relationships of a novel seed protein of *Phaseolus vulgaris* L. *Theoretical and Applied Genetics*, 71, 847–855.

Osborn, T.C., Burrow, M., and Bliss, F.A. 1988a. Purification and characterization of arcelin seed protein from common bean. *Plant Physiol.*, 86, 399–405.

Osborn, T.C., Alexander, D.C., Sun, S.S.M., Cardona, C., and Bliss, F.A. 1988b. Insecticidal activity and lectin homology of arcelin seed protein. *Science*, 240, 207–210.

Osuji, F.N.C. 1982. Radiographic studies of the development of *Callosobruchus maculatus* Fabricius (Coleoptera: Bruchidae) in cowpea seeds. *Journal Stored Products Research*, 18, 1–8.

Otanes, Y., and Quesales, F. 1918. The bean fly. *Philippine Agriculture*, 7, 2–31.

Otieno, D.A., Hassanali, A., and Njoroge, P.E.W. 1984. Chemical basis of TVu 946 cowpea stem resistance to *Maruca testulalis* (Geyer). Nairobi, International Centre of Insect Physiology and Ecology, Annual Report.

Otieno, D.A., Odindo, M.O., Okeyo-Owuor, J.B., and Sabwa, D.M. 1981. Studies on the legume pod-borer, *Maruca testulalis* (Geyer). 6, Field survey on pathogenic organisms. *Insect Science and Its Application*, 4, 211–215.

Owusu-Akyaw, M. 1987. Resistance of some varieties of cowpea (*Vigna unguiculata* (L.) Walp.) to attack by the cowpea storage weevil, *Callosobruchus maculatus* (F.) (Coleoptera: Bruchidae). Kumasi, University of Science and Technology, 259p. (PhD thesis).

Pacheco, F. 1970. Plagas del valle del Yaqui. Instituto Nacional de Investigación Agrícola, SAG, Circ. CIANO 53, 124p.

Padmanabhan, M.D., Lewin, H.D., and Saroja, R. 1973. Soil treatment to control groundnut pod borer (*Euborella stali* Dohn.). *Pesticides*, August 1973, 34–35 and 40.

Pagham, D.E., Timmins, F.M., and Ranga Rao, G.V. (In press). Mechanisms of resistance in groundnut (*Arachis hypogaea* L.) to Aphis craccivora (Koch). *Annals of Applied Biology*.

Paguio, O.R., and Kuhn, C.W. 1976. Aphid transmission of peanut mottle virus. *Phytopathology*, 66, 473–476.

Painter, R.H. 1941. The economic value and biological significance of plant resistance to insect attack. *Journal of Economic Entomology*, 34, 358–637.

Painter, R.H. 1951. *Insect Resistance in Crop Plants*. New York, Macmillan, 520p.

Pal, S.K. 1972. A note on leaf weevil *Cyrtozemia cognata* Marshall (Curculionidae: Coleoptera) infesting Kharif crops of dryland farming. *Annals of Arid Zone*, 11 (1–2), 132.

Palaniswamy, M.S. 1977. Effectiveness of different insecticides against the pod borer, *Euborella stali* Dohn. infesting groundnut in Tamil Nadu. *Pesticides*, March 1977, 53–54.

Panchabhavi, K.S., Thimmaiah, G., and Desai, M.K.S. 1972. Report on the incidence of *Alcides collaris* Pascoe (Curculionidae: Coleoptera) on redgram at Dharwar. *Science and Culture*, 38 (7), 325–326.

Pandey, N.D. 1962. Studies on the morphology, bionomics and control of some Indian Agromyzidae. *Agra University Journal of Research Science*, 11, 39–43.

Pandey, N.D., Mathur, K.K., Pandey, and Tripathi, R.A. 1986. Effect of some plant extracts against pulse beetle, *Callosobruchus chinensis* Linnaeus. *Indian Journal of Entomology*, 48(1), 85–90.

Pandey, N.D., Misra, R.L., and Tripathi, R.A. 1977. Relative susceptibility of some groundnut varieties to the almond moth, *Cadra cautella* Walker (Phycitinae, Lepidoptera). *Bulletin of Grain Technology*, 15, 105–110.

Pandey, N.D., Misra, S.C., and Pandey, U.K. 1978. Some observations on the biology of *Polymmatus boeticus* L. (Lepidoptera: Lycaenidae) a pest of Cajanus cajan (L.) Millsp. *Indian Journal of Entomology*, 40 (1), 81–82.

Pandey, N.D., Singh, S.R., and Tiwari, G.C. 1976. Use of some plant powders, oils and extracts as protectant against pulse beetle *Callosobruchus chinensis* Linn. *Indian Journal of Entomology*, 38(2), 110–114.

Pandit, P.V. 1965. Effect of time of sowing and varieties of tur on the incidence of its major insect pests, bioecological studies on *Exelastis atomosa* Wlm. (Pterophoridae: Lepidoptera), the tur plume moth. Jabalpur, Madhya Pradesh, India, Jawaharlal Nehru Krishi Vishwa Vidyalaya (PhD thesis). 83 p.

Panizzi, A.R. 1980a. Uso de cultivar armadilla no controle de percevejos em soja. Trigo e Soja, 47, 11–14.

Panizzi, A.R. 1980b. Manejo de pragas da soja: situação atual e perspectivas futuras. Anais VI Congress Brasileiro de Entomologíca, 303–322.

Panizzi, A.R. 1985. Dynamics of phytophagous pentatomids associated with soybean in Brazil. In Shibles, R., ed., *World Soybean Research Conference III*, Boulder, Westview Press, 674–680.

Panizzi, A.R. 1986. Assessoria em manejo integrado de pragas da soja no Paraguai et Bolivia. Technical Report 6p.

Panizzi, A.R. 1987. Nutritional ecology of seed-sucking insects of soybean and their management. *Memórias do Instituto Oswaldo Cruz*, 82, 161–175.

Panizzi, A.R. 1988a. Biology of *Megalotomus parvus* (Hemiptera: Alydidae) on selected leguminous food plants. *Insect Science and Its Application*, 9, 279–286.

Panizzi, A.R. 1988b. Desempenho de adultos de *Leptoglossus zonatus* (Hemiptera: Coreidae) en semente verde de milho e vagem verde de soja. *Resultados de Pesquisa de Soja* (in press).

Panizzi, A.R., and Ferreira, B.S.C. 1980. Geometrideos em soja flutuação estacional e ressurgência após o uso de insecticidas. *Pesquisa Agropecuiána Brasileira*, 15, 159–161.

Panizzi, A.R., and Rossini, M.C. 1987. Impacto de várias leguminosas na biología de ninfas de *Nezara viridula* (Hemiptera: Pentatomidae). *Revísta Brasileira de Biología*, 47, 507–512.

Panizzi, A.R., and Slansky, Jr., F. 1985a. Review of phytophagous pentatomids (Hemiptera: Pentatomidae) associated with soybean in the Americas. *Florida Entomologist*, 68, 184–214.

Panizzi, A.R., and Slansky, Jr., F. 1985b. Legume host impact on performance of adult *Piezodorus guildinii* (Westwood) (Hemiptera: Pentatomidae). *Environmental Entomology*, 14, 237–242.

Panizzi, A.R., Corrêa, B.S., Gazzoni, D.L., Oliveira, E.B., Newman, G.G., and Turnipseed, S.G. 1977a. Insetos da soja no Brasil. EMBRAPA, Bol. Tec. 1, 20p.

Panizzi, A.R., Corrêa, B.S., Newman, G.G., and Turnipseed, S.G. 1977b. Efeito de inseticidas na população das principais progas da soja. Anais la Sociedade Entomológica do Brasil, 6, 264–275.

Panizzi, A.R., Ferreira, B.S.C., Neuaier, N., and Queiroz, E.F. 1979. Efeitos da época de semeadura e do espaçadosà entre fileiras na população de artrópodos associados à soja. *Annais 1er Seminar Nacionale Pesquisa Soja*, 11, 113–125.

Panizzi, A.R., Galileo, M.H., Gastal, H.A.O., Toledo, J.F.F. and Wild, C.H. 1980. Dispersal of *Nezara viridula* and Piezodorus guildinii nymphs in soybeans. *Environmental Entomology*, 9, 293–297.

Panizzi, A.R., Panizzi, M.C.C., Bays, I.A., and Almeida, L.A. 1986. Danos por percevejos em genotipos de soja com sementes pequena. *Pesquisa Agropecuíana Brasileira*, 21, 571–577.

Panizzi, M.C.C., Bays, I.A., Kiihl, R.A.S., and Porto, M.P. 1981. Identificação de genótipos fontes resistência a percevejos—pragas da soja. *Pesquisa Agropecuíana Brasileira*, 16, 33–37.

Paramanik, L.M., and Basu, A.C. 1967. Record of two insect pests of pigeonpea (*Cajanus cajan*) in West Bengal. *Indian Agriculture*, 11 (2), 145–148.

Parh, I.A. 1976. A progress report on studies on the bionomics of *Empoasca* spp. associated with cowpea, *Vigna unguiculata* (L.) Walp. Ibadan, University of Ibadan, 194p.

Parh, I.A. 1983a. Species of *Empoasca* associated with cowpea, *Vigna unguiculata* (L.), Walp, in Ibadan, and three ecological zones in south-western Nigeria (Homoptera: Cicadellidae). *Revue de Zoologie Africaine*, 97, 202–210.

Parh, I.A. 1983b. The effects of *Empoasca dolichi* Paoli (Hemiptera: Cicadellidae) on the performance and yield of two cowpea cultivars. *Bulletin of Entomological Research*, 73, 25–32.

Parh, I.A., and Taylor, T.A. 1981. Studies on the life cycle of the cicadellid bug *Empoasca dolichi* Paoli, in southern Nigeria. *Journal of Natural History*, 15, 829–835.

Parpia, H.A.B. 1981. Utilization. In ICRISAT, *Proceedings of the International Workshop on Pigeonpea, 15–19 Dec*, Patancheru, India, ICRISAT, 484–486.

Passoa, S. 1983. Lista de los insectos asociados con los granos básicos y otros cultivos selectos en Honduras. *CIIBA*, 25, 1–97.

Patel, G.M., Shah, A.H., Patel, M.B., and Patel, C.B. 1985. First record of *Coccidohystrix insolita* (Green) as a pest of pigeonpea in south Gujarat. *Gujarat Agricultural University Research Journal*, 11 (1), 61.

Patel, P.N., Mligo, J.K., Leyna, H.K., Kuwite, C., and Mmbaga, E.T. 1982. Sources of resistance, inheritance, and breeding of cowpeas for resistance to a strain of cowpea aphid-borne mosaic virus from Tanzania. *Indian Journal of Genetics*, 42, 221–229.

Patel, R.C., Patel, R.M., Madhukar, B.V.R., and Patel, R.B. (1974). Oviposition behavior of *Heliothis armigera* in cotton Hybrid-4, *Current Science*, 43, 588–589.

Patel, R.K., and Singh, D. 1977. Serious incidence of pod borer Maruca testulalis Gey. on red gram at Varanasi. Science and Culture, 43 (7), 319.

Patel, V.C., and Pitre, H.N. 1971. Transmission of bean pod mottle virus to soybean by the striped blister beetle, Epicanta vittata. Plant Disease Reporter, 55, 628–629.

Patnaik, H.P., Samalo, A.P., and Samalo, B.N. 1986. Susceptibility of some early varieties of pigeonpea for pod borers under protected conditions. *Legumes Research*, 9 (1), 7-10.

Pattinson, I., and Thornton, I. 1965. The quality of unshelled groundnuts in the Gambia with special reference to insect and fungal attack. *Tropical Science*, 7, 67-74.

Pawar, C.S., and Srivastava, C.P. 1985. Bionomics of the pigeonpea thrip *Megalurothrips usitatus* Bagnall. *International Pigeonpea Newsletter*, 4, 56-58.

Pearson, E.O. and Darling, R.C.M. 1958. The insect pests of cotton in tropical Africa. London, U.K. Empire Cotton Growers and Commonwealth Institute of Entomology, 355p.

Pedigo, L.P., Hutchins, S.H. and Higley, L.G. 1986. Economic injury levels in theory and practice. *Annual Review of Entomology*, 31, 341-68.

Pereira, J. 1983. The effectiveness of six vegetable oils as protectants of cowpeas and Bambarra groundnuts against infestation by *Callosobruchus maculatus* (F) (Coleoptera: Bruchidae). *Journal of Stored Products Research*, 19(2), 57-62.

Perez, G. 1985. Himenopteros parasitoides de *Apion* spp. (Coleoptera: Curculionidae; Apionidae) en Tepoztlan, Morelos. *Folia Entomológica Mexicana*, 63, 39-46.

Perrin, R.M. 1977. Pest management in multiple cropping systems. *Agro-Ecosystems*, 3, 93-118.

Perrin, R.M. 1978. Varietal differences in the susceptibility of cowpea to larvae of the seed moth: *Cydia ptychora* (Meyrick) (Lepidoptera: Tortricidae). *Bulletin of Entomological Research*, 68, 47-56.

Perrin, R.M., and Ezueh, M.I. 1978. The biology and control of grain legume olethreutids (Tortricidae). In Singh, S.R., van Emden, H.F., and Taylor, T.A., eds., *Pests of Grain Legumes: Ecology and Control*, London/New York, Academic Press, 201-217.

Perrin, R.W. 1976. Host-plant relationships of the cowpea podborer *Cydia ptychora* (Meyr.). *Tropical Grain Legume Bulletin*, 5, 10.

Perry, D. 1967. Premature death of groundnut plants in northern Nigeria. *Experimental Agriculture*, 3, 211-214.

Perry, L.M. 1980. *Medicinal Plants of East and Southeast Asia*. Cambridge, UK, MIT Press. 620p.

Peters, D. 1973. Persistent aphid-borne viruses. In Gibbs, A.J., ed., *Viruses and Invertebrates*, Amsterdam, North-Holland Publishing Co., 464-475.

Peters, D., and Lebbink, G. 1973. The effect of oil on the transmission of pea enation mosaic virus during short inoculation probes. *Entomología Experimentalis et Applicata*, 16, 185-190.

Pflucker, O.S. 1981. Pests of pigeonpea on the northern coast of Peru. In ICRISAT, *Proceedings of International Workshop on Pigeonpea, 15-19 Dec*, Patancheru, India, ICRISAT, 355-358.

Phelps, R.J. 1956. Investigation on the biology of *Piezotrachelus varium* (Wagner) and *Apion (Conapion) chirindanum* Wagner. *Journal of the Entomological Society of Southern Africa*, 19, 86-99.

Phelps, R.J., and Oosthuizen, M.J. 1958. Insects injurious to cowpeas in the Natal Region. *Journal of the Entomological Society of Southern Africa*, 21, 286-295.

Philpotts, H. 1965. Effect of soil temperature on nodulation of cowpeas (*Vigna sinensis*). *Australia Journal of Experimental Agriculture and Animal Husbandry*, 7, 372-376.

Pierce, H.D., Pierce, A.M., Millar, J.G., Wong, J.W., Verigin, V.G., Oehlschlager, A.C., and Borden, J.C. 1984. Methodology for the isolation and analysis of aggregation pheromones in the genera *Cryptolestes* and *Oryzaephilus*. Paper prepared for the Third International Working Conference on Stored Product Entomology, Kansas State University, Manhattan, Kansas, USA, October 23-28, 1984, 121-137.

Pierre, R.E. 1975. Observations on the golden mosaic of bean (*Phaseolus vulgaris* L.) in Jamaica. In Bird, J., and Maramorosch, K., eds., *Tropical Diseases of Legumes*, New York, Academic Press, 55-59.

Pillemer, E.A., and Tingey, W.M. 1976. Hooked trichomes: a physical plant barrier to a major agricultural pest. *Science*, 193, 482–484.

Pio-Ribeiro, G., Wyatt, S.D., and Kuhu, C.W. 1978. Cowpea stunt: a disease caused by a synergistic interaction of two viruses. *Phytopathology*, 68, 1260–1265.

Pirone, T.P. 1969. Mechanism of transmission of stylet-borne viruses. In Maramorosch, K., eds., *Viruses, Vectors and Vegetation*, New York, Interscience Publishers, 199–210.

Pirone, T.P., and Harris, K.F. 1977. Non-persistent transmission of plant viruses by aphids. *Annual Review of Phytopathology*, 15, 55–73.

Pitre, J.H.N., and Kantack, J.E. 1962. Biology of the banded cucumber beetle, *Diabrotica balteata*, in Louisiana. *Journal of Economic Entomology*, 55, 904–906.

Pizzamiglio, M.A. 1979. Aspectos da biologia de *Empoasca kraemeri* (Ross and Moore, 1957) (Homoptera: Cicadellidae) em *Phaseolus vulgaris* (Linnaeus, 1753) e ocorrência de parasitismo em ovos. *Anais da Sociedade Entomológica do Brasil*, 8, 369–372.

Ploaie, P.G. 1981. Mycoplasmalike organisms and plant diseases in Europe. In Maramorosch, K., and Harris, K.F., eds., *Plant Diseases and Vectors: Ecology and Epidemiology*, New York, Academic Press, 61–104.

Plumb, R.T. 1981. Chemicals in the control of cereal virus diseases. In Jenkyn, J.F., and Plumb, R., eds., *Strategies for the Control of Cereal Diseases*, Oxford, Blackwell Scientific Publications, 135–145.

Pointel, J.G., Deuse, J.P.L., and Hernandez, S. 1979. Evaluation et evolution de l'infestation de stocks experimentaux d'arachides en coque au Sénégal par *Caryedon gonagra* F. (Coleoptera: Bruchidae). *Agronomie tropicale*, 34, 196–207.

Pohronezny, K., McSorley, R., and van Waddill, H. 1981. Integrated management of pests of snap bean in Florida. *Proceedings of the Florida State Horticultural Society*, 94, 137–140.

Polhill, R.M., and Ravin, P.H. 1981. *Advances in Legume Systematics*. 2 vols. Kew, Richmond, Surrey, UK, Royal Botanic Gardens. 1049p.

Pollard, G.V., and Elie, A. 1981. Studies on the economic importance of the blossom thrips, *Frankliniella insularis* (Thripidae, Thysanoptera) on pigeonpea, *Cajanus cajan*, in Trinidad. *Tropical Agriculture*, 58 (3), 281–286.

Posada, O.L., de Polania, I.Z., de Arevalo, E.S., Saldarriga, A., Garcia Rao, F.A., and Cardenas, Y.R. 1970. Lista de insectos daninos y otras plagas en Colombia. Programa Nacional de Entomología, Miscellaneous Publication, 17, 202p.

Prando, H.F., and da Cruz, F.Z. 1986. Aspectos da biologia de *Liriomyza huidobrensis* (Blanchard, 1926) (Diptera, Agromyzidae) em laboratorio. *Anais da Sociedade Entomológica do Brasil*, 15, 77–88.

Press, J.W., Flaherty, B.R., and Arbogast, R.T. 1974. Interactions among *Plodia interpunctella*, *Bracon hebetor* and *Xylocoris flavipes*. *Environmental Entomology*, 3, 183–184.

Press, J.W., Flaherty, B.R., and Arbogast, R.T. 1975. Control of the red flour beetle, *Tribolium castaneum*, in a warehouse by a predaceous bug, *Xylocoris flavipes*. *Journal of the Georgia Entomological Society*, 10, 76–78.

Press, J.W., Flaherty, B.R., and Arbogast, R.T. 1979. Vertical distribution of the predator *Xylocoris flavipes* (Reuter) (Hemiptera: Anthocoridae). *Journal of the Kansas Entomological Society*, 52, 561–564.

Press, J.W., Flaherty, B.R., and McDonald, L.L. 1981. Survival and reproduction of *Bracon hebetor* on insecticide-treated *Ephestia cautella* larvae. *Journal of the Georgia Entomological Society*, 16, 231–234.

Press, J.W., Cline, L.D., and Flaherty, B.R. 1982. A comparison of two parasitoids, *Bracon hebetor* (Hymenoptera: Braconidae) and *Venturia canescens* (Hymenoptera: Ichneumonidae) and a predator *Xylocoris flavipes* (Hemiptera: Anthocoridae) in suppressing residual populations of the almond moth, *Ephestia cautella* (Lepidoptera: Pyralidae). *Journal of the Kansas Entomological Society*, 55, 725–728.

Prevett, P.F. 1961. Field infestation of cowpea (*Vigna unguiculata*) pods by beetles of the families Bruchidae and Curculionidae in northern Nigeria. *Bulletin of Entomological Research*, 52, 635–646.

Price, M., and Dunstan, W.R. 1983. The effect of four insecticides on leaf miner damage of cowpeas in Tanzania. *Tropical Grain Legume Bulletin*, 27, 23–26.

Price, M., Chambuya, R.I., and Machange, F.Z. 1983. Insecticide evaluation and timing of spray application for insect control in cowpeas in Tanzania. *Tropical Grain Legume Bulletin*, 28, 4–8.

Proctor, D.L., and Ashman, F. 1972. The control of insects in exported Zambian groundnuts using phosphine and polyethylene lined sacks. *Journal of Stored Products Research*, 8, 127–137.

Pryde, E.H., and Doty, H.O., Jr. 1981. World fats and oils situation. In Pryde, E.H., Princen, L.H., and Mukherjee, K.D., eds., *New Sources of Fats and Oils*. Champaign, IL, USA, American Oil Chemists' Society. AOCS Monograph 9. 340p.

Purcell, A.H. 1979. Leafhopper vectors of xylem-borne plant pathogens. In Maramorosch, K., and Harris, K.F., eds., *Leafhopper Vectors and Plant Disease Agents*, New York, Academic Press, 603–625.

Puttarudraiah, M. 1947. Some observations on the biology and habits of redgram (*Cajanus cajan*) flower bud borer (*Euproctis scintillans*). *Mysore Agriculture Journal*, 24, 20–24.

Quaintance, A.L. 1898. Three injurious insects: bean leaf-roller, corn delphax, Canna leaf-roller. *Florida Agricultural Experiment Station Bulletin*, 45, 53–75.

Quinderé, M.A.W., and Barreto, P.D. 1982. Suscetibilidade do caupi ao *Callosobruchus maculatus* (F., 1775): Estudos preliminaris. In Resumos da 1 Reunãio Nacional de Pesquisa de Caupi, Goiânia, GO, 1982, Documento 4, Goiânia, EMBRAPA-CNPAF, 291.

Radke, S.G., Yendol, W.G., and Benton, A.W. 1972. Studies on parthenogenetic viviparous and sexual forms of the cowpea aphid, *Aphis craccivora* Koch. *Indian Journal of Entomology*, 34, 319–342.

Raghupathy, A., and Rathnaswamy, R. 1970. Studies on comparative susceptibility of seeds of certain redgram [*Cajanus cajan* (L.) Millsp.] varieties to pulse beetle, *Callosobruchus chinensis* L. (Bruchidae: Coleoptera). *Madras Agriculture Journal*, 57, 106–109.

Ragsdale, D.W., Larson, A.D., and Newson, L.D. 1979. Microorganisms associated with feeding and from various organs of *Nezara viridula*. *Journal of Economic Entomology*, 72, 725–727.

Raheja, A.K. 1973. A report on the insect pest complex of grain legumes in northern Nigeria. Paper prepared for 1st IITA Grain Legumes Improvement Workshop, Ibadan, Nigeria, 295–299.

Raheja, A.K. 1975. Millepedes on groundnuts, *Arachis hypogaea*. *Nigerian Journal of Plant Protection*, 1, 91–92.

Raheja, A.K. 1976a. Assessment of losses caused by insect pests of cowpeas in northern Nigeria. *PANS*, 22, 229–233.

Raheja, A.K. 1976b. U.L.V. spraying for cowpea in northern Nigeria. *PANS*, 22, 327–332.

Rahman, L. 1975. Bangladesh coordinated soybean research project in Bangladesh (Report from Bangladesh Agric. Univ.). Paper prepared for forum on soybean, R/5, Bangladesh Coordinated Soybean Research Project Rep. 1, 9–10 Dec. 1975.

Raina, A.K. 1970. *Callosobruchus* spp. infesting stored pulses (grain legumes) in India and a comparative study of their biology. *Indian Journal of Entomology*, 32, 303–310.

Raina, A.K. 1972. Observations on bruchids as field pests of pulses. *Indian Journal of Entomology*, 33(2), 194–197.

Raina, A.K., Benepal, P.S., and Sheikh, A.Q. 1980. Effects of excised and intact leaf methods, leaf size, and plant age on Mexican bean beetle feeding. *Entomología Experimentalis et Applicata*, 27, 303–306.

Rajagopal, D., Siddaramegowda, T.K., and Rajagopal, B.K. 1982. Incidence of pineapple mealybug, *Dismicoccus breviceps* (Cockerell) on *Rhizobium* nodules of redgram and groundnut. *Journal of Soil Biology and Ecology*, 2(2), 97–98.

Ram, C., and Yadava, C.P.S. 1982. Seed treatment of groundnut for control of white grub, *Holotrichia consanguinea* (Blanchard). *Indian Journal of Entomology*, 44, 121–124.

Ramakrishnan, N., Saxena, V.S., and Dhingra, S. 1984. Insecticide resistance in the population of *Spodoptera litura* (F.) in Andhra Pradesh. *Pesticides*, 18, 23–27.

Ramalho, F.S. 1978. Efeitos da época de infestação da cigarrinha verde, *Empoasca kraemeri* Ross and Moore, 1957. *Anais da Sociedade Entomológica do Brasil*, 7(1), 30–32.

Ramalho, F.S., and Ramos, J.R. 1979. Distribução de ovos de *Empoasca kraemeri* Ross and Moore, 1957 na planta de feijao. *Anais da Sociedade Entomológica do Brasil*, 8, 85–91.

Ramalho, M.A., Botelho, W., and Salgado, L.O. 1977. Comportamento de algumas variedades de feijao (*Phaseolus vulgaris* L.) quanto a susceptibilidade ao caruncho *Acanthoscelides obtectus* (Say, 1831). *Anais da Sociedade Entomológica do Brasil*, 6, 238–242.

Raman, K.V., Singh, S.R., and van Emden, H.F. 1978. Yield losses in cowpeas following leafhopper damage. *Journal of Economic Entomology*, 71, 836–838.

Raman, K.V., Singh, S.R., and van Emden, H.F. 1980. Mechanism of resistance to leafhopper damage in cowpea. *Journal of Economic Entomology*, 73, 484–488.

Ramasubbaiah, K., and Lal, R. 1975. Studies on residues of phosphamidon in cowpea crop. *Indian Journal of Entomology*, 37, 179–184.

Ramiro, Z.A. 1977. Observações sobre a biología de *Plusia oo* (Cramer, 1782) em condições de laboratório, alimentadas com Folhas de soja. *Biología*, 43, 47–54.

Ranga Rao, G.V., Wightman, J.A., and Ranga Rao, D.V. (In preparation). Pheromone trap data. Patancheru, ICRISAT.

Ranjnauth, G.L., Pegus, J.E., and Haque, S.Q. 1987. Laboratory rearing of *Cerotoma arcuata* (Oliv.) a beetle vector of cowpea severe mosaic virus. *Tropical Agriculture* (Trinidad), 64(3), 191–192.

Rao, B.N., and Rao, B.H.K. 1977. Occurrence of *Ophiomyia recticulipennis* on French bean in Hyderabad. *Indian Journal of Entomology*, 39, 281.

Rao, V.P. 1968. *Heliothis* spp. and their parasites in India. *PANS*, August 1968.

Rao, V.P. 1974. Biology and breeding techniques for parasites and predators of *Ostrinia* spp. and *Heliothis* spp. Bangalore, India, CIBC Final Technical Report, US PL-480 Project, 86p.

Rathi, Y.P.S., and Nene, Y.L. 1974. Some aspects of the relationship between mung bean yellow mosaic virus and its vector *Bemisia tabaci*. *Indian Phytopathology*, 27, 459–462.

Ratnam, N.N. 1979. Dry matter production and harvest index trends in groundnut (*Arachis hypogaea* L.). *Madras Agriculture Journal*, 66(4), 218–221.

Rawat, R.R., Kapoor, K.N., Misra, U.S., and Dhamdere, S.V. 1969a. A record of predatory mite *Bochartia* sp. (Erythraeidae: Acarina) on *Clavigralla gibbosa* Spinola. *Journal of the Bombay Natural History Society*, 66(2), 403–404..

Rawat, R.R., Singh, Z., and Jakhmola, S.S. 1969b. Effect of infestation of blossom thrips on pod setting in pigeonpea, *Cajanus cajan* (L.) Millsp. *Indian Journal of Agricultural Sciences*, 39(9), 623–625.

Rawnsley, J. 1959. The natural relationship between the hymenopterous parasite, *Bracon hebetor*, and its host, the cocoa moth, *Ephestia cautella*: the importance of this relationship in designing chemical control. Accra, Ghana Cocoa Marketing Board, Insect Control Unit, Publication, 7, 1–3.

Raychandhuri, S.P., and Nariani, T.K. 1977. *Virus and Mycoplasma Diseases of Plants in India*. New Delhi, Oxford and IBH, 102p.

Redden, R.J., Dobie, P., and Gatehouse, A.M.R. 1983. The inheritance of seed resistance to *Callosobruchus maculatus* F. in cowpea (*Vigna unguiculata* L. Walp.). I. Analysis of parental F_1, F_2, F_3 and backcross seed generations. *Australian Journal of Agricultural Research*, 34, 681–695.

Reddy, D.V.R. and Black, L.M. 1966. Production of wound tumor virus and wound tumor soluble antigen in the insect vector, *Virology*, 30, 551–561.

Reddy, D.V.R., and Wightman, J.A. 1988. Tomato spotted wilt virus: thrips transmission and control. Advances in Disease Vector Research, 5, 202–220.

Reddy, D.V.R., Nene, Y.L., and McDonald, D. 1986. Virus disease problems of groundnut, chickpea, and pigeonpea in Asia. In *Technical Bulletin*, 19, Tropical Agriculture Research Center, Japan, 67–75.

Reddy, D.V.R., Iizuka, N., Ghanekar, A.M., Murthy, V.K., Kuhn, C.W., Gibbons, R.W., and Chohan, J.S. 1978. The occurrence of peanut mottle virus in India. *Plant Disease Reporter*, 62(3), 224–226.

Reddy, K.V.S. 1973. Studies on the gram caterpillar, *Heliothis armigera* (Hübner) (Lepidoptera: Noctuidae) with special reference to its biology, host preference and estimation of loss in red gram. Bangalore, India, University of Agricultural Sciences. 132p. (PhD thesis).

Reddy, M.V., and Sammaiah, C. 1988. *Odontotermes brunneus* (Hagen) (Termitidae: Isoptera) as a new pest of maize and groundnut. *Entomon*, 13, 47–50.

Redlinger, L.M., and Davis, R. 1982. Insect control in postharvest peanuts. In Pattee, H.E., and Young, C.T., eds., *Peanut Science and Technology*. Yoakum, Texas, USA, American Peanut Research and Education Society Inc., 520–571.

Reed, C.F. 1976. *Glycine max* (L.) Merr. Typescript submitted to USDA.

Reed, W. 1965a. *Heliothis armigera* (Hübner) in Western Tanganyika. 1, Biology with special reference to the pupal stage. *Bulletin of Entomological Research*, 56, 117–125.

Reed, W. 1965b. *Heliothis armigera* Hb. (Noctuidae) in western Tanganyika. 2: Ecology, natural and chemical control. *Bulletin of Entomological Research*, 56, 127–140.

Reed, W. 1983. Estimation of crop loss to insect pests in pulses. In Entomological Society of India, *Crop Losses due to Insect Pests. Special issue, Indian Journal of Entomology*, Hyderabad, 2, 263–267.

Reed, W., and Pawar, C. 1982. *Heliothis*: a global problem. In Reed, W., and Kumble, Vrinda, eds., *Proceedings of the International Workshop on Heliothis Management*, 15–20 November 1981, Patancheru, AP, ICRISAT, 9–14.

Reed, W., Lateef, S.S., and Sithanantham, S. 1980. Pest management in low input pigeonpea. In ICRISAT, *Proceedings of International Workshop on Pigeonpea, 15–19 Dec. 1980*, Patancheru, India, ICRISAT, 99–105.

Reed, W., Lateef, S.S., Sithanantham, S., and Pawar, C.S. 1989. Pigeonpea and chickpea insect identification handbook. Patancheru, India, ICRISAT, *Information Bulletin 26*.

Reichmuth, Ch., Wohlgemuth, R., Levinson, A.R., and Levinson, H.Z. 1976. Studies on the use of pheromone-baited traps for control of Lepidoptera in stores. *Zeitschrift für Angewandte Entomologie*, 82, 95–102.

Rejesus, R.S. 1976. Insect pest diversity and succession in Asian soybeans. In Goodman, R.M., ed., *Expanding the Use of Soybean*, Proceedings of a conference for Asia and Oceania, Urbana, University of Illinois, College of Agriculture, 97–103 (INTSOY Ser. 10).

Remaudière, G., Aymonin, G., and Autrique, A. 1985a. Les plantes hôtes des pucerons africains. In Remaudière, G., and Autrique, A., eds., *Contributions a l'ecologie des aphides africains*, Rome, Italy, Food and Agriculture Organization of the United Nations (FAO), Plant Production and Protection Papers, 64, 103-139.

Remaudière, G., Eastop, V.F., and Autrique, A. 1985b. Distribution des aphides de la région ethiopienne. In Remaudière, G., and Autrique, A., eds., *Contributions a l'ecologie des aphides africains*, Rome, Italy, Food and Agriculture Organization of the United Nations (FAO), Plant Production and Protection Papers, 64, 77-93.

Rice, A.D., Gibson, R.W., and Stribley, M.F. 1983a. Alarm pheromone secretion by insecticide susceptible and resistant *Myzus persicae* treated with demeton-S-methyl; aphid dispersal and transfer of plant viruses. *Annals of Applied Biology*, 103, 375-381.

Rice, A.D., Gibson, R.W., and Stribley, M.F. 1983b. Effects of deltamethrin on walking, flight and potato virus y-transmission by pyrethoid-resistant *Myzus persicae*. *Annals of Applied Biology*, 102, 229-236.

Rios, G.P., Watt, E.E., Araujo, J.P.P. de, and Neves, B.P. das. 1980. Identification of sources of resistance to the principal disease of southern pea (*Vigna unguiculata* (L.) Walp.) in Brazil. *Bean Improvement Cooperative (USA) Annual Report*, 23, 106.

Ripa, S.R. 1981. La pollilla del frijol y alfalfa. *Investigación y Progreso Agropecuario (Chile)*, 4, 12-14.

Risbec, J. 1950. La faune entomologique des cultures au Sénégal et au Soudan français. Travaux du Laboratoire d'entomologie du secteur soudanais de recherches agronomiques. Gouvernement general de l'Afrique occidentale française.

Risch, S. 1976. Effect of variety of cowpea (*Vigna unguiculata* L.) on feeding preference of three chrysomelid beetles, *Cerotoma ruficornis, Diabrotica balteata* and *Diabrotica adelpha*. *Turrialba*, 26, 327-334.

Risch, S.J. 1980. Fewer beetle pests on beans and cowpea interplanted with banana in Costa Rica. *Turrialba*, 32, 210-212.

Rizzo, H.F. 1971. Aspectos morfológicos y biológicos de *Edessa meditabunda* (F.) (Hemptera: Pentatomidae). *Revista Peruana de Entomología Agricola*, 14, 272-281.

Rizzo, H.F.E. 1968. Aspectos morfológicos y biológicos de *Nezara viridula* (L.) (Hemiptera: Pentatomidae). *Agronomia Tropical*, 18, 249-274.

Rizzo, H.F.E. 1972. Insectos y otros animales enemigos de la soja (*Glycine max*) en la Argentina. *Fitotechia Latinoamérica*, 8, 44-49.

Robert, P. 1985. A comparative study of some aspects of the reproduction of three *Caryedon serratus* strains in presence of its potential host plants. *Oecologia*, 65, 425-430.

Roberts, M.J., and Chipeta, F.M. 1973. The effects of an insecticide spraying trial on the yield of cowpeas. *Research Bulletin Bunda College Agricultural University of Malawi*, 4, 24-31.

Robertson, L.A.D. 1973. Notes on the insect parasites of some lepidopterous pests in Tanzania. *East African Agricultural and Forestry Journal*, 39, 82-93.

Rodriguez, J.R. 1983. Resistencia varietal al mosaico dorado del frijol y control químico del vector (mosca blanca) en Papautla, Veracruz. Escuela de Agricultura, Universidad de Guadalajara, México. 12p. (BSc thesis).

Roesingh, C. 1980. Resistance to flower thrips, *Megalurothrips sjostedti* (Trybom) in cowpea. Stuttgart, West Germany, Universität Homenhein, 64p. (PhD thesis).

Rogers, D.J. 1974. Studies on host-plant resistance involving the French bean (*Phaseolus vulgaris* L.) and the bean fly (*Melanagromyza phaseoli* Tryon). Brisbane, University of Queensland. (MSc thesis).

Rogers, D.J. 1979. Host-plant resistance to *Ophiomyia phaseoli* Tryon (Diptera: Agromyzidae) in *Phaseolus vulgaris*. *Journal of the Australian Entomological Society*, 18, 245-250.

Rogers, D.J., Teakle, R.E., and Brier, H.B. 1983. Evaluation of *Heliothis* nuclear polyhedrosis virus for control of *Heliothis armigera* on navy beans in Queensland, Australia. *General and Applied Entomology*, 15, 31-34.

Rolston, L.H. 1974. Revision of the genus *Euschustus* in middle America (Hemiptera: Pentatomidae). *Entomologica Americana*, 48, 1–102.

Romanow, L.R., Moyer, J.W., and Kennedy, G.G. 1986. Alteration of efficiencies of acquisition and inoculation of watermelon mosaic virus 2 by plant resistance to the virus and to an aphid vector. *Phytopathology*, 76, 1276–1281.

Roongsook, D., Sitchawat, T., Knapp, F.W., and Tiemtaisong, A. 1973. The effect of phorate and malathion on beanfly control and yield of mungbean. *Journal of Agricultural Science*, 6, 283–286.

Roonwal, M.L. 1979. *Termite Life and Termite Control in Tropical South Asia*. Jodhpur, Scientific Publishers. 177p.

Rose, D.J.W. 1962. Pests of groundnuts. *Rhodesia Agricultural Journal*, 59, 197–198.

Rose, J.W., Iles, M.J., and Ward, A. 1988. Cereal losses caused by army-worm in southern Africa: current information and research proposals. *Insect Science and Its Application*, 9(6), 697–699.

Rose, R.I., Chiang, H.S., and Harnoto, I. 1978. Pests of grain legumes and their control in Taiwan. In Singh, S.R., van Emden, H.F., and Taylor, A.T., eds., *Pests of Grain Legumes: Ecology and Control*, London, Academic Press, 67–71.

Ross, H.H., and Moore, T.E. 1957. New species in the *Empoasca fabae* complex (Homoptera: Cicadellidae). *Annals of the Entomological Society of America*, 50, 118–121.

Ross, J.P. 1963. Transmission of bean pod mottle virus by beetles. *Plant Disease Reporter*, 47, 1049–1050.

Rossel, H.W. 1986. Rice yellow mottle and African soybean dwarf, newly discovered virus diseases of economic importance in West Africa. Paper prepared for an international symposium on virus diseases of rice and leguminous crops, Tsukuba, Japan, 1–4 October 1985. Tropical Agriculture Research Series, 19, 146–153.

Rossel, H.W., and Thottappilly, G. 1985. Virus diseases of important food crops in tropical Africa. Ibadan, IITA, IITA Publication Series, 67p.

Rossel, H.W., and Thottappilly, G. 1988. Control of virus diseases in Africa's major food crops through breeding for resistance. In Williams, A.O., Mbiele, A.L., and Nkouka, N., eds., *Virus Diseases of Plants in Africa*, Lagos, OAU/STRC Scientific Publication, 169–187.

Rossel, H.W., Thottappilly, G., and Anno-Nyako, F.O. 1982. Soybean 'dwarf' in Nigeria, a whitefly-transmitted disease of high risk potential. Paper prepared for the 3rd annual national soybean conference, Makurdi, Benue State, Nigeria, 7–9 February 1982.

Rossetto, C.J. 1989. Breeding for resistance to stink bugs. In Pascale, A.J., ed., *World Soybean Research Conference IV*, Buenos Aires, Impresiones Amawald S.A., 60p.

Rossetto, C.J., De Santis, L., Paradela, O., and Pompeu, A.S. 1974. Especies de tripses coletados em culturas de feijoeiro. *Bragantia*, 33, 9–14.

Rossetto, C.J., Igue, T., Miranda, M.A.C. de, and Lourençao, A.L. 1986. Resistência de soja a insetos: VI. Comportamento de genótipos em relaçáo a percevejos. *Bragantia*, 45 (2), 323–335.

Rossetto, C.J., Lourençao, A.L., Igue, T., and Miranda, M.A.C. de. 1981. Picadas de alimentacao de *Nezara viridula* em cultivares e linkagens de soja de diferentes grans de suscetibilidade. *Bragantia*, 40, 104–114.

Rouzière, A. 1986. Storage of shelled groundnut seed in controlled atmospheres. I. Preliminary trials 1979–1982. *Oléagineux*, 41, 339–344.

Rowe, A.G. 1980. Alternative crops 3: grain legumes. *Zimbabwe Agriculture Journal*, 77(5), 221–227.

Ruelle, J.E. 1985. Order *Isoptera* (termites). In Scholtz, C.H., and Holm, E., eds., *Insects of Southern Africa*, Durban, Butterworths, 502p.

Ruffinelli, A., and Piran, A.A. 1959. Hemipterous heterópteros del Uruguay. Facultad de Agronomía de Montevideo, Biol. 51, 17p.

Ruhendi, J.A., and Litsinger, J.A. 1979. Insect-suppressing effect of rice stubble height, tillage practices, and straw mulch in wetland rice-cowpea cropping pattern. *International Rice Research Newsletter*, 4, 26–27.

Ruppel, R.F. 1982. The seedcorn maggot in dry beans. *Michigan Dry Bean Digest*, 6, 5.

Ruppel, R.F., and De Long, D.M. 1956. *Empoasca* (Homoptera: Cicadellidae) from highland crops of Colombia. *Bulletin of Brooklyn Entomological Society*, 51, 85–92.

Ruppel, R.F., and Idrobo, E. 1962. Lista preliminar de insectos y otros animales que danan frijoles en América. *Agricultura Tropical*, 18, 651–679.

Ruppel, R.F., Russel, H.L., and Love, A.P. 1981. Residual efficacy of grain protectants against the bean weevil. *Michigan Dry Bean Digest*, 5, 21.

Russell, L.M. 1975. *Whiteflies on beans in the western hemisphere*. Paper prepared for workshop on bean plant protection, Centro Internacional de Agricultura Tropical, CIAT, Cali, Colombia. 21p.

Rwamugira, W.P., and Karel, A.K. 1984. Varietal evaluation of common beans to bean fly *Ophiomyia phaseoli* Tryon. *Bean Improvement Cooperative (USA) Annual Report*, 27, 186–187.

ymal, K.S., and Chambliss, O.L. 1976. Cowpea curculio feeding stimulant from southern pea pods. *Journal of the American Society of Horticultural Science*, 101, 722–724.

Saboo, K.C., and Puri, S.N. 1978. Effect of insecticides on incidence of sucking pests and yield of groundnut, *Arachis hypogaea* Linn. *Indian Journal of Entomology*, 40, 311–315.

Sachan, J.N., and Gangwar, S.K. 1980. Insect pests of soybean in Khasi Hills of Maghalaya and their control. *Bulletin of Entomology*, 21(1–2), 105–112.

Sagar, P., and Mehta, S.K. 1982. Field screening of exotic cowpea cultivars against jassid *Amrasca biguttula* (Tshida) (Cicadellidae: Homoptera) in Punjab. *Journal Research*, Punjab Agricultural University, 19, 222–223.

Saharia, D. 1980. Natural regulation of population of *Aphis craccivora* Koch. on cowpea. *Journal of Research*, Assam Agricultural University, 1, 171–76.

Saint-Smith, J.H., MacCarthy, G.J.P., Rawson, J.E., Langford, S., and Colbran, R.C. 1972. *Peanut Growing Advisory Leaflet 1178*, Division of Plant Industry, Department of Primary Industries, Australia. 18p.

Sakimura, K. 1962. The present status of thrips-borne viruses. In Maramorosch, K., ed., *Biological Transmission of Disease Agents*, New York, Academic Press, 33–40.

Sakimura, K. 1963. *Frankliniella fusca* an additional vector for the tomato spotted wilt virus with notes on *Thrips tabaci*, another vector. *Phytopathology*, 53, 412–415.

Salas, L., and Ruppel, R.F. 1959. Efectividad de insecticidas aplicados en polvo para controlar las principales plagas del frijol y del maiz almacenados en Colombia. *Agricultura Tropical*, 15, 93–108.

Salguera, V. 1983. Importancia de *Apion* sp. en Guatemala. In *Taller Internacional sobre Apion y Mustia hilachoza en Guatemala y Costa Rica*. Guatemala, Instituto Interamericano de Cooperación para la Agricultura (IICA). 50p.

Salifu, A.B. 1986. Studies on aspects of the biology of the flower thrips, *Megalurothrips sjostedti* (Trybom) with particular reference to resistance in its host cowpea, *Vigna unguiculata* (L.) Walp. Wye College, University of London, 267p. (PhD thesis)

Salifu, A.B., and Singh, S.R. 1987. Evaluation of sampling methods for *Megalurothrips sjostedti* (Trybom) (Thysanoptera: Thripidae) on cowpea. *Bulletin of Entomological Research*, 77, 451–456.

Salifu, A.B., Hodgson, C.J., and Singh, S.R. 1988a. Mechanism of resistance in cowpea, *Vigna unguiculata* (L.) Walp. genotype, TVx 3236 to the bean flower thrips, *Megalurothrips sjostedti* (Trybom) (Thysanoptera: Thripidae). 1: Ovipositional nonpreference. *Tropical Pest Management*, 34, 180–184.

Salifu, A.B., Singh, S.R., and Hodgson, C.J. 1988b. Mechanism of resistance in cowpea, *Vigna unguiculata* (L.) Walp. genotype, TVx 3236 to the bean flower thrips, *Megalurothrips sjostedti* (Trybom) (Thysanoptera: Thripidae). 2. Nonpreference and antibiosis. *Tropical Pest Management*, 34, 185–188.

Salinas, P.J. 1976. Presencia de *Elasmopalpus lignosellus* (Zeller) (Lepidoptera: Pyralidae) en los Andes venezolanos. *Agronomía Tropical*, 26, 71–76.

Sanap, M.M., and Deshmukh, R.B. 1988. Efficacy of nuclear polyhedrosis virus against *Heliothis armigera* (Hubner) infesting pigeonpea. *Indian Journal of Pulses Research*, 1(1), 80–82.

Sanchez, P. 1977. El frijol asociado con maíz y su respuesta a la conchuela (*Epilachna varivestis* Muls.) y al picudo del ejote (*Apion* spp.). Chapingo, Mexico Colegio de Postgraduados, Escuela Nacional de Agricultura, 117p. (MSc thesis)

Sandana, H.R., and Verma, S. 1986. Preliminary studies on the prevalence of insect pests and their natural enemies on cowpea crop in relation to weather factors at Delhi. *Indian Journal of Entomology*, 48(4), 448–458.

Sandhu, G.S. 1977. Some insects recorded as pests of fodder crops at Ludhiana (Punjab). *Journal of Research* (Punjab Agricultural University), 14(4), 449–459.

Sandhu, G.S. 1978. Note on the incidence of *Stomopteryx subsecivella* (Zell.) (Lepidoptera: Gelechiidae) on lucerne at Ludhiana. *Indian Journal of Agricultural Sciences*, 48(1), 53–54.

Sands, W.A. 1962. Observations on termites destructive to trees and crops. Lagos, Nigeria, Ministry of Agriculture Technical Report 17, *Samaru Research Bulletin*, 26, 1–14.

Sands, W.A. 1965. Termite distribution in man-modified habitats in West Africa with special reference to species segregation in the genus *Trinervitermes* (Isoptera, Termitidae, Nasutitermitinae). *Journal of Animal Ecology*, 34, 557–571.

Sandsted, R. 1980. Energy inputs in snapbean production. In Pimantel, D., ed., *Handbook of Energy Utilization in Agriculture*. Boca Raton, FL, USA, CRC Press, 127–128.

Sandsted, R.F., How, R.B., Muka, A.A., and Sherf, A.F. 1971. Growing dry beans in New York State. Ithaca, New York State College of Agriculture, New York University (at Cornell University). *Information Bulletin 2*, 22p.

Sangappa, H.K. 1977. Effectiveness of oils as surface protectants against the bruchid, *Callosobruchus chinensis* L. infestation on redgram. *Mysore Journal of Agricultural Sciences*, 11(3), 391–397.

Sangappa, H.K., and Balaraju, E.S. 1977. A note on *Callosobruchus chinensis* L. as field pest of redgram (*Cajanus cajan* sp.). *Current Research*, 6, 105–106.

Santos, A.A. dos, Silva, P.H.S. da, and Mesquita, R.C.M. 1982. Insetos associados ê cultura do caupi (*Vigna unguiculata*) no Estado do Piaui. In Resumos da 1 Reunião Nacional de Pesquisa de Caupi, Goiânia, GO, Documento 4, Goiânia, EMBRAPA-CNPAF, 60–61.

Santos, J.H.R. 1971. Aspectos da biología do *Callosobruchus maculatus* (Fabr., 1775) (Col., Bruchidae) sobre sementes de *Vigna sinensis* Endl. Piracicaba, ESALQ, 87p. (MSc thesis)

Santos, J.H.R. 1976. Aspectos da resistência de cultivares da *Vigna sinensis* (L.) Savi ao ataque do *Callosobruchus maculatus* (F., 1775) (Col., Bruchidae), mantidas no estado do Ceará-Brasil. Piracicaba, ESALQ, 194p. (PhD thesis)

Santos, J.H.R., and Bastos, J.A.M. 1977. Nivel de controle económico do manhoso, *Chalcodermus bimaculatus* Fiedler: 1. Primeira aproximação. In Relatório Téchnico 1976, Fortaleza, Universidade Federal do Ceará, Centro de Ciências Agrárias, Departamento de Fitotecnia, 59–69.

Santos, J.H.R., and Bastos, J.A.M. 1979. Porcentagem de sementes de cultivares de feijão-de-corda, *Vigna sinensis* (L.) Savi, atacadas pelo *Chalcodermus bimaculatus* Fiedler, 1936 (Col., Curc.): Terceira lista. In Relatório da programa de pesquisa corn a cultura do feijoeiro, Fortaleza, Universidade Federal do Ceará, 49–56.

Santos, J.H.R., and Lopes, L.O. 1979. Suscetibilidade de cultivares de feijão-de-corda, *Vigna sinensis* (L.) Savi, ao ataque da lagarta das vagens, *Etiella zinckenella* (Treitschke, 1832) (Lep., Phycitinae): Segunda lista. In Relatório da programa de pesquisa com a cultura do feijoeiro, Fortaleza, Universidade Federal do Ceará, 66–73.

Santos, J.H.R., and Oliveira, F.J. 1978a. Influência do ataque das lagartas das vagens, *Etiella zinckenella* (Treitschke, 1832) (Lep., Phycitinae), sobre a produção do feijão-de-corda, *Vigna sinensis* (L.) Savi. In Relatório da programa de pesquisa com a cultura do feijoeiro, Fortaleza, Universidade Federal do Ceará, 68–75.

Santos, J.H.R., and Oliveira, F.J. 1978b. Nivel de controle económico do manhoso, *Chalcodermus bimaculatus* Fiedler, 1936 (Col., Curc.): Segunda aproximação. In Relatório da programa de pesquisa com a cultura do feijoeiro, Fortaleza, Universidade Federal do Ceará, 83–87.

Santos, J.H.R., and Quinderé, M.A.W. 1988. Biology, importance and management of Brazilian cowpea pests. In Watt, E.E., and Araújo, J.P.P., eds., *Cowpea Research in Brazil*, Brasilia, IITA/EMBRAPA, 267–300.

Santos, J.H.R., and Vieira, F.V. 1971. Ataque do *Callosobruchus maculatus* (F.) a *Vigna sinensis* Endl. 1. Influência sobre o poder germinativo de sementes do c.v. 'Seridó.' *Ciencia Agronómica*, 1(2), 71–74.

Santos, J.H.R., Alves, J.F., and Benevides, E.C. 1973. Fitossanidade feijoeiro *Vigna sinensis* (L.) Savi: 1. Efeito do etoato etilico e do parathion etilico sobre a produtividade da variedade 'Pitiuba'. In Relatório de Pesquisa, Fortaleza, Universidade Federal do Ceará, Centro de Ciências Agrárias, Departamento de Fitotecnia, 47–53.

Santos, J.H.R., Alves, J.F., and Oliveira, F.J. 1978a. Perdas de peso em sementes de *Vigna sinensis* (L.) Savi decorrente do ataque de *Callosobruchus maculatus* (F., 1775) Col., Bruchidae): Primeira aproximação. *Ciencia Agronómica*, 8(1/2), 55–56.

Santos, J.H.R., Teófilo, E.M., and Oliveira, F.J. 1978b. Porcentagens de sementes de cultivares de feijão-de-corda, *Vigna sinensis* (L.) Savi, atacadas pelo *Chalcodermus bimaculatus* Fiedler, 1936 (Col, Curc.): Segunda lista. In Relatório de Pesquisa 1977, Fortaleza, Universidade Federale Ceará, Centro de Ciências Agrárias, Departamento de Fitotecnia, 58–7.

Santos, J.H.R., Andrade, J.M., Nogueira, R.S.A., Mesquita, A.L.M., Araújo, F.E., Oliveira, F.M.E.S., Fontes, J.M., Silva, F.M.S.E., Lima-Verde, L.W., Vasconcelos, M.F.R., Gonçalves, M.F.B., Alves, M.T., and Barros, P. 1979. Efeitos de materiais de origem vegetal e do malation na preservação de sementes de *Vigna sinensis* (L.) Savi, contra o ataque do *Callosobruchus maculatus* (F., 1775) (Col., Bruchidae). Fortaleza, Tec. Bull. DNOCS 37(1), 5–14.

Santos, J.H.R., Beleza, M.G.S., and Silva, N.L. 1981. A mortalidade do *Callosobruchus maculatus* em gãos, de *Vigna sinensis*, tratados com óleo de algodão. *Ciencia Agronómica*, 12(1/2), 45–48.

Santos, J.H.R., Teófilo, E.M., Almeida, J.M., and Oliveira, F.J. 1977a. Percentagens de sementes de cultivares de *Vigna sinensis* (L.) Savi, atacadas pelo *Chalcodermus bimaculatus* Fiedler, 1936 (Col., Curc.). In Relatório de Pesquisa 1976, Fortaleza, Universidade Federal do Ceará, Centro de Ciências Agrárias, Departamento de Fitotecnia, 70–74.

Santos, J.H.R. dos, Vieira, F.V., and Pereira, L. 1977b. Importância relativa dos insetos e ácaros hospedados nas plantas do feijão-de-corda, nos perímetros irrigados do DNOCS, especialmente no Ceará. 1. Primeira lista. Convênio do Fitossanidade DNOCS/UFC, Univ. Federal do Ceará, Centro de Ciências Agrárias, Fortaleza, 29p.

411

Santos, R.B., and Sutton, B.G. 1983. Effect of defoliation on reproductive development of the peanut. *Australian Journal of Agricultural Research*, 34, 527–535.

Sarup, P., Jotwani, M.G., and Pradhan, S. 1961. Relative toxicity of some important insecticides to the bean aphid, *Aphis craccivora* Koch. *Indian Journal of Entomology*, 22, 105–108.

Sathe, T.V. 1987. New records of natural enemies of *Spodoptera litura* (Fab) in Kolhapur, India. *Current Science India*, 56(20), 1083–1084.

Sathorn, Sirisingh, and Manochai, Keerati-Kasikorn. 1986. Management of arthropods on peanuts in Thailand. Paper prepared for the Peanut CRSP Workshop, Khon Kaen, Thailand, 19–21 August, 1986, 35–39.

Sathorn, Sirisingh, and Manochai, Keerati-Kasikorn. 1987. Effect of monocrotophos on thrips population, yellow spot virus and peanut yield. *Proceedings of American Peanut Research and Education Society*, 19, 18.

Satpathy, J.M., Das, M.S., and Naik, K. 1979. Effect of multiple and mixed cropping on the incidence of some important pests. *Journal of Entomological Research*, 1(1), 78–85.

Sauer, H.F. 1939. Notas sobre *Elasmopalpus lignosellus* Zeller (Lep. Pyr.) séria praga dos cereais no Estado de São Paulo. *Archivos del Instituto de Biología*, 10, 199–206.

Sauer, H.F. 1946. Constatação de Himenópteros e Dípteros entomóçagos no Estado de So Paulo. Boletin Fitossanitario, 3, 7–23.

Saunders, O.J.L., King, A.B.S., and Vargas, S.C.L. 1983. Plagas de cultivos en America Central—Una lista de referencia. Departamento de Producción Végetal, Centro Agronómico Tropical de Investigación y Enseñanza. Turrialba, Costa Rica.

Savalia, B.M. 1971. Some studies on bionomics and control of tur plume moth (*Trichoptilus congrualis* Walker) under Junagadh conditions. Gujarat, India, Gujarat Agricultural University. (MSc thesis).

Saxena, H.P. 1971. Insect pests of pulse crops. In *New Vistas in Pulse Production*, Delhi, Indian Agricultural Research Institute, 87–101.

Saxena, H.P. 1974. Severe and widespread occurrence of *Maruca testulalis* Geyer in red gram, *Cajanus cajan*. *Entomology News*, 4, 21.

Saxena, H.P. 1978. Pests of grain legumes and their control in India. In Singh, S.R., van Emden, H.F., and Taylor, T.A., eds., *Pests of Grain Legumes: Ecology and Control*, London/New York, Academic Press, 15–31.

Saxena, H.P., Kumar, S., and Prasad, S.K. 1971. Efficacy of some systemic granular insecticides against galerucid beetle, *Madurasia obscurella* Jacoby infesting kharif pulses. *Indian Journal of Entomology*, 33, 470–471.

Saxena, H.P., Sircar, P., and Phokela, A. 1969. Studies on the chemical control of pea leaf miner, *Phytomyza atricornis* (Meigen) and pod borer, *Etiella zinckenella* (Treitschke). *Labdev. Journal of Science and Technology*, 7, 318–322.

Saxena, M.C. 1976. Soybeans in India. In Goodman, R.M. ed., Expanding the use of soybean. Urbana, University of Illinois, INTSOY Series 10, 226–231.

Schalk, J.M., and Fery, R.L. 1982. Southern green stink bug and leaffooted bug: effect on cowpea production. *Journal of Economic Entomology*, 75, 72–75.

Schalk, J.M., and Rassoulian, G. 1973. *Callosobruchus maculatus*: observations of attack on cowpea in Iran. *Journal of Economic Entomology*, 66, 579–580.

Schiller, J.M., Sampoapol, R., and Thirathon, A. 1982. Interdependence of disease and insect pest control in rainfed peanut production. *Thai Journal of Agricultural Science*, 15, 33–50.

Schmutterer, H. 1969. *Pests of Crops in Northeast and Central Africa*. Stuttgart, Federal Republic of Germany, Gustav Fischer-Verlag. 296p.

Scholtz, C.H., and Holm, E. (eds.) 1985. *Insects of Southern Africa*. Durban, Butterworths. 502p.

Schoof, H.F. 1941. The effects of various relative humidities on life processes of the southern cowpea weevil, *Callosobruchus maculatus* (F.) at $30 \pm 8°C$. Ecology, 22, 297–305.

Schoonhoven, A. van. 1976. Pests of stored beans and their economic importance in Latin America. In Proc. Symposium on Trop. Stored Products Entomology held at the 15th Int. Congress of Entomol., Entomol. Soc. Am., College Park, MD, USA, 691–698.

Schoonhoven, A. van. 1978. Use of vegetable oils to protect stored beans from bruchid attack. *Journal of Economic Entomology*, 71, 254–256.

Schoonhoven, A. van, and Cardona, C. 1982. Low levels of resistance to the Mexican bean weevil in dry beans. *Journal of Economic Entomology*, 75, 567–569.

Schoonhoven, A. van, and Cardona, C. 1980. Insects and other bean pests in Latin America. In Schwartz, H.F., and Galvez, G.E., eds., *Bean Production Problems: Disease, Insect, Soil and Climatic Constraints of Phaseolus vulgaris*, Cali, Colombia, Centro Internacional de Agricultura Tropical (CIAT), 363–412.

Schoonhoven, A. van, Cardona, C., Garcia, J., and Garzon, F. 1981. Effect of weed covers on *Empoasca kraemeri* (Ross and Moore) populations and dry bean yields. *Environmental Entomology*, 10, 901–907.

Schoonhoven, A. van, Cardona, C., and Valor, J. 1983. Resistance to the bean weevil and the Mexican bean weevil (Coleoptera: Bruchidae) in noncultivated common bean accessions. *Journal of Economic Entomology*, 76, 1255–1259.

Schoonhoven, A. van, Gomez, L.A., and Avalos, F. 1978a. The influence of leafhopper (*Empoasca kraemeri*) attack during various bean (*Phaseolus vulgaris*) plant growth stages on seed yield. *Entomología Experimentalis et Applicata*, 23, 115–120.

Schoonhoven, A. van, Hallman, G.J., and Temple, S.R. 1985. Breeding for resistance to *Empoasca kraemeri* (Ross and Moore) in *Phaseolus vulgaris* L. In Nault, L.R., and Rodriguez, J.G., eds., *Leafhoppers and Planthoppers*. New York, Wiley, 405–422.

Schoonhoven, A. van, Piedrahita, J., Valderrama, R., and Galvez, G. 1978b. Biología, dano y control del acaro tropical *Polyphagotarsonemus latus* (Banks) (Acarina: Tarsonemidae) en frijol. *Turrialba*, 28, 77–80.

Schotman, C. 1986. Report on the pigeonpea pod borer workshop, 21–23 Nov. 1985, St. John's, Antigua. *Pigeonpea Development Culture*, 24, FAO-Santiago, 44p.

Schreiner, I., Nafus, D., and Bjork, C. 1986. Control of *Liriomyza trifolii* (Burgess) (Dip.: Agromyzidae) on yard-long (*Vigna unguiculata*) and pole beans (*Phaseolus vulgaris*) on Guam: effect on yield loss and parasite numbers. *Tropical Pest Management*, 32, 333–337.

Schroder, R.F.W. 1979. Host specificity tests of *Coccipolipus epilachnae*, a mite parasitic on the Mexican bean beetle. *Environmental Entomology*, 8, 46–47.

Schumann, F.W., and Todd, J.W. 1982. Population dynamics of the southern green stink bug (Heteroptera: Pentatomidae) in relation to soybean phenology. *Journal of Economic Entomology*, 75, 748–753.

Schuster, G. 1979. One source of interactions of virazole and plant hormones in virus infected plants. *Phytopathologische Zeitschrift*, 94, 72–79.

Schultz, G.A., Irwin, M.E., and Goodman, R.M. 1983. Factors affecting aphid acquisition and transmission of soybean mosaic virus. *Annals of Applied Biology*, 103, 87–96.

Schwalbe, C.P., Burkholder, W.E., and Boush, G.M. 1974. *Mattesia trogodermae* infection rates as influenced by mode of transmission, dosage, and host species. *Journal of Stored Products Research*, 10, 161–167.

Scott, H.A., and Phatak, H.C. 1979. Properties of blackgram mottle virus. *Phytopathology*, 69, 346–348.

Scott, L.B. 1940. The bean pod borers in Puerto Rico. *Journal of Agriculture of University of Puerto Rico*, 24, 35–47.

Seelig, R.A., and Roberts, E. 1960. *Green and Wax Snap Beans, Fruit and Vegetable Facts and Pointers*. Washington, DC, USA, United Fruit and Vegetable Association.

Selman, B.J. 1973. Beetles—polyphagous Coleoptera. In Gibbs, A.J., ed., *Viruses and Invertebrates*, Amsterdam, North-Holland Publishing Co., 157–177.

Semal, J. 1967. Effects of actinomycin D in plant virology. *Phytopathologische Zeitschrift*, 259, 55–71.

Sepswasdi, P. 1976. Control of soybean insect pests in Thailand. In Goodman, R.M., ed., *Expanding the Use of Soybeans*, Urbana, Il, University of Illinois, INTSOY Ser. 10, 104–107.

Shaheen, A.H. 1977. Survey of pests attacking soybean plants in Egypt, with some ecological notes. *Agricultural Research Review*, Egypt, 55, 59–65.

Shapas, T.J., Burkholder, W.E., and Boush, G.M. 1977. Population suppression of *Trogoderma glabrum* using pheromone luring for protozoan dissemination. *Journal of Economic Entomology*, 70, 469–474.

Sharma, S.K., and Kaul, C.K. 1970. Relative efficiency of insecticides against gram pod borer *Heliothis armigera*. *Annals of Arid Zone*, 8, 43–80.

Sharma, S.R., and Varma, A. 1982. Applied transmission of two cucumo-viruses from plants also infected with tobamovirus. *Zentralblatt fuer Mikrobiologie*, 137, 415–419.

Sheldrake, A.R., and Narayanan, A. 1977. Experimental investigations on source–sink relationship. II-3, Effect of flower removal, and II-4, Effect of defoliation. In ICRISAT, *Pulse Physiology Annual Report 1976–77*, Part I, Pigeonpea, Patancheru, ICRISAT, 39–59.

Sheldrake, A.R., Narayanan, A., and Venkataratnam, N. 1979. The effect of flower removal on the seed yield of pigeonpeas (*Cajanus cajan*). *Annals of Applied Biology*, 19, 383–390.

Shetgar, S.S., and Thombre, U.T. 1984. Occurrence of natural enemies on soybean leaf miner and relative susceptibility of some soybean varieties to its attack. *Journal of Maharashtra Agricultural University*, 9(2), 218–219.

Shoyinka, S.A. 1975. Attempted control of virus incidence in cowpeas by the use of barrier crops. Nigerian Society of Plant Protection, NSPP Abstracts, Occasional publication 1, 27.

Shoyinka, S.A., Bozarth, R.F., Rees, J., and Rossel, H.W. 1978. Cowpea mottle virus: a seed borne virus with distinctive properties infecting cowpea in Nigeria. *Phytopathology*, 68(5), 693–699.

Siddappaji, C., and Gowda, T.K.S. 1980. Rhizobial nodules eating insect—*Rivellia* sp., a new pest of pulse crops in India. *Current Research*, 9(7), 122–123.

Siddappaji, C., Reddy, M.P., and Pattanshetti, H.V. 1974. Crab caterpillar—*Stauropus alternus* Wlk. (Notodontidae: Lepidoptera). A new pest of sapota (*Achras sapota* L.). *Current Research*, 3(19), 631.

Sifuentes, A. 1978. Control de plagas del frijol en Mexico. Instituto Nacional Investigaciones Agrícolas (INIA), *Folleto Divulgativo* No. 69. 22p.

Silva, A.B., and Magalhães, B.P. 1980. Insetos nocivos ê cultura do feijão caupi (*Vigna unguiculata*) no Estado do Pará. Res. Bull. 3, Belém, EMBRAPA-CPATU, 22p.

Silva, A.G. d'A., Gonçalves, C.R., Galvão, D.M., Gonçalves, A.J.L., Gomes, J., Silva, M.N., and Simoni, L. 1968. Quarto catalogo dos insetos que vivem nas plantas do Brasil—Seus parasitas e predadores. Rio de Janeiro, Ministry of Agriculture, parte 11, 1, 622p.

Silveira Neto, S., Berti Fo., E., and Carvallo, R.P.L. 1973. Flutuação populacional de algumas pragas da soja em *Assis* sp. *Solo* 64, 21–25.

Simon, J.P., Parent, M.P., and Auclair, J.L. 1982. Isozyme analysis of biotypes and field populations of the pea aphid, *Acyrthosiphon pisum*. *Entomologia Experimentalis et Applicata*, 32, 186–192.

Simons, J.N. 1959. Factors affecting secondary spread of nonpersistent aphid-borne virus. *Proceedings of the Florida State Horticultural Society*, 72, 136.

Simons, J.N. 1982. Use of oil sprays and reflective surfaces for control of insect-transmitted plant viruses. In Harris, K.F., and Maramorosch, K., eds., *Pathogens, Vectors, and Plant Diseases. Approaches to Control*, New York, Academic Press, 71-73.

Simons, J.N., and Zitter, T.A. 1980. Use of oils to control aphid-borne viruses. *Plant Disease*, 64, 542.

Singh, B.B., and Merrett, P.J. 1980. Leaf miner. A new pest of cowpeas. *Tropical Grain Legume Bulletin*, 21, 15-17.

Singh, B.B., and Ntare, B.R. 1985. Development of improved cowpea varieties in Africa. In Singh, S.R., and Rachie, K.O., eds., *Cowpea Research, Production and Utilization*, Chichester, John Wiley and Sons, 105-116.

Singh, B.B., Hadley, H.H., and Bernard, R.L. 1971. Morphology of pubescence in soybeans and its relationship to plant vigour. *Crop Science*, 11, 3-16.

Singh, B.B., Thottappilly, G., and Rossel, H.W. 1987. Breeding for multiple virus resistance in cowpea. *Agronomy Abstracts*, 79.

Singh, D., and Sidhu, H.S. 1976. Demonstration, extraction and trapping efficacy of female sex pheromone of the rice moth, *Corcyra cephalonica* (Stainton). *Journal of Research, Punjab Agricultural University*, 13, 85-90.

Singh, D.P., and Singh, K.M. 1966. Certain aspects of bionomics and control of *Oberea brevis* a new pest of bean and cowpea. *Labdev Journal of Science and Technology*, 4(3), 174-177.

Singh, G., Misra, P.N., and Tiwari, S.C. 1979. Efficacy of some insecticides in controlling the stemfly of pea. *Indian Journal of Agricultural Sciences*, 49, 50-52.

Singh, H., and Dhooria, M.S. 1971. Bionomics of the pea pod borer, *Etiella zinckenella* (Treitschke). *Indian Journal of Entomology*, 33(2), 123-130.

Singh, O.P. 1987. Insect pests of soybean in Madhya Pradesh (from 1967 to 1986). A paper prepared for a soybean workshop held at Dharwed, Karnataka, 1-3 May, 1-34.

Singh, O.P., and Gangrade, G.A. 1977. Note on girdle beetle infestation in relation to dates of planting of soybean. *Indian Journal of Agricultural Sciences*, 53(7), 615-616.

Singh, O.P., and Jakhmola, S.S. 1983. New record of *Cydia ptychora* Meyrick as a pod-borer pest of soybean in Madhya Pradesh. *Indian Journal of Agricultural Sciences*, 53, 615-616.

Singh, O.P., Jakhmola, S.S., and Gangrade, G.A. 1978. New foodplants of the girdle beetle, *Oberea brevis* Swed. (Col.: Cerambycidae, Lamunae) in India. Pflanzenschutz Umweltschutz, *Anzeiger für Schädlingskunde*, 51(6), 88-89.

Singh, R., and Patel, H.K. 1968. Bionomics of tur pod bug (*Clavigralla gibbosa* Spinola) on pigeonpea (*Cajanus cajan* Millsp.). *Andhra Agriculture Journal*, 15(3), 80-87.

Singh, R., and Patel, H.K. 1972. Record of some new host plants of, and biological notes on, *Gampsocoris pulchellus* (Dallas) (Hemiptera: Neididae—Berytidae). *Indian Journal of Agricultural Sciences*, 42(11), 977-979.

Singh, S.R. 1977a. Cowpea cultivars resistant to insect pests in world germplasm collection. *Tropical Grain Legume Bulletin*, 9, 3-7.

Singh, S.R. 1977b. Grain legume entomology: training booklet. Ibadan, IITA, 48p.

Singh, S.R. 1978. Resistance to pests of cowpea in Nigeria. In Singh, S.R., van Emden, H.F., and Taylor, T.A., eds., *Pests of Grain Legumes: Ecology and Control*, London/New York, Academic Press, 267-279.

Singh, S.R. 1980. Biology of cowpea pests and potential for host plant resistance. In Haris, M.K., ed., *Biology and Breeding for Resistance to Arthropods and Pathogens in Agricultural Plants*, College Station, Texas A&M University, Bulletin MP-1451, 398-421.

Singh, S.R. 1983. Host plant resistance in cowpeas, beans and soybeans. In Matteson, P.C., ed., Proc. of Int. Workshop in Integrated Pest Control for Grain Legumes, Goiânia, GO, 117–129.

Singh, S.R. 1985. Insects damaging cowpeas in Asia. In Singh, S.R., and Rachie, K.O., eds., *Cowpea Research, Production and Utilization*, Chichester, John Wiley and Sons, 247–250.

Singh, S.R. 1987. Host plant resistance for cowpea insect pest management. *Insect Science and its Application*, 8, 765–769.

Singh, S.R., and Allen, D.J. 1979. Cowpea pests and diseases. Ibadan, International Institute of Tropical Agriculture (IITA), IITA Manual Series No. 2, 113p.

Singh, S.R., and Allen, D.J. 1980. Pests, diseases, resistance and protection of *Vigna unguiculata* (L.) Walp. In Summerfield, R.J., and Bunting, A.H., eds., *Advances in Legume Science*, London, Royal Botanical Gardens, and Ministry of Agriculture, Fish and Food, 419–443.

Singh, S.R., and Jackai, L.E.N. 1985. Insect pests of cowpeas in Africa: their life cycle, economic importance, and potential for control. In Singh, S.R., and Rachie, K.O., eds., *Cowpea Research*, Production and Utilization, Chichester, John Wiley and Sons, 217–231.

Singh, S.R., and Jackai, L.E.N. 1988. The legume pod-borer, *Maruca testulalis* (Geyer): past, present and future research. *Insect Science and its Application*, 9, 1–5.

Singh, S.R., and Rachie, K.O. 1987. Introduction to soybeans. In Singh, S.R., Rachie, K.O., and Dashiell, K.E., eds., *Soybeans for the Tropics: Research, Production and Utilization*, Chichester, John Wiley and Sons, xv–xx.

Singh, S.R., and Taylor, T.A. 1978. Pests of grain legumes and their control in Nigeria. In Singh, S.R., van Emden, H.F., and Taylor, T.A., eds., *Pests of Grain Legumes: Ecology and Control*, London/New York, Academic Press, 99–111.

Singh, S.R., and van Emden, H.F. 1979. Insect pests of grain legumes. *Annual Review of Entomology*, 24, 255–278.

Singh, S.R., Luse, R.A., Leuschner, K. and Nangju, D. 1978. Groundnut oil treatment for the control of *Callosobruchus maculatus* (F.) during cowpea storage. *Journal of Stored Products Research*, 14, 77–80.

Singh, S.R., Rachie, K.O., and Dashiell, K.E. 1987. *Soybeans for the Tropics: Research, Production and Utilization*. Chichester, UK, John Wiley and Sons, 230p.

Singh, S.R., Singh, B.B., Jackai, L.E.N., and Ntare, B.R. 1983. Cowpea research at IITA. Ibadan, IITA Information Series, 14, 20p.

Singh, S.R., van Emden, H.F., and Taylor, T.A., eds. 1978a. *Pests of Grain Legumes: Ecology and Control*. London/New York, Academic Press, 454p.

Singh, S.R., van Emden, H.F., and Taylor, T.A. 1978b. The potential for the development of integrated pest management systems in cowpeas. In Singh, S.R., van Emden, H.F., and Taylor, T.A., eds., *Pests of Grain Legumes: Ecology and Control*, London/New York, Academic Press, 328–336.

Singh, S.R., Williams, R.J., Rachie, K.O., Rawal, K., Nangju, D., Wien, H.C., and Luse, R.A. 1975b. VITA-5 cowpea. *Tropical Grain Legume Bulletin*, 5, 41–42.

Singh, S.R., Williams, R.J., Rachie, K.O., Rawal, K., Nangju, D., Wien, H.C., and Luse, R.A. 1975a. VITA-3 cowpea. *Tropical Grain Legume Bulletin*, 1, 18–9.

Singh, Y., Saxena, H.P., and Singh, K.M. 1980. Exploration of resistance of pulse beetles 3. Growth and development of *Callosobruchus maculatus* Fabricius. *Indian Journal of Entomology*, 42, 622–626.

Singh, Z. 1973. *Southern Green Stink Bug and Its Relationship to Soybean*. Delhi, Metropolitan Book Co. Ltd., 105p.

Sinha, M.M., and Yadav, R.P. 1983. *Apion clavipes*, a new pest of pigeonpea in Bihar, India. *International Pigeonpea Newsletter*, 2, 69–70.

Sinha, R.C. 1968. Recent work on leafhopper transmitted viruses. *Advances in Virus Research*, 13, 181–223.

Sinha, R.C. 1973. Viruses and leafhoppers. In Gibbs, A.J., ed., *Viruses and Invertebrates*, Amsterdam, North-Holland, 493–511.

Sinha, R.C. 1981. Vertical transmission of plant pathogens. In McKelvey, J.J. Jr., Eldridge, B.E., and Maramorosch, K., eds., *Vectors of Disease Agents—Interactions with Plants, Animals and Man*, New York, Praeger, 109–121.

Sinha, R.C. 1984. Transmission mechanisms of mycoplasma-like organisms by leafhopper vectors. In Harris, K.F., ed., *Current Topics in Vector Research*, volume 2, New York, Praeger, 93–109.

Sinha, R.C., and Chiykowski, L.N. 1969. Synthesis, distribution and some multiplication sites of wheat striate mosaic virus in a leafhopper vector. *Virology*, 38, 679–684.

Sinha, S.K., and Savithri, K.S. 1978. Biology of yield in food legumes. In Singh, S.R., van Emden, H.F., and Taylor, T.A., eds., *Pests of Grain Legumes: Ecology and Control*, London/New York, Academic Press, 233–240.

Sitaramaiah, S., Joshi, B.G., Prasad, G.R., and Satyanarayana, S.V.V. 1975. *Harpactor costallis* Stal (Reduviidae: Heteroptera)—a new predator on tobacco caterpillar (*Spodoptera litura* F.). *Science and Culture*, 41(11), 545–546.

Sithanantham, S. 1987. Insect pests of pigeonpea and chickpea and their management. In Rao, M.V., and Sithanantham, S., eds., *Plant Protection in Field Crops*. Hyderabad, India, Plant Protection Association of India, 159–173.

Sithanantham, S., and Reed, W. 1980. Studies on the exotic parasite, *Eucelatoria* sp. (Tachinidae: Diptera) on *Heliothis armigera* at ICRISAT Center during 1978–80. Paper prepared for third workshop, *All India Coordinated Research Project Biology Control* (Crop Tests and Weeds, Ludhiana, Punjab, 27–30 October 1980), 113–117.

Sithanantham, S., Kumar Rao, J.V.D.K., Reed, W., and Dart, P.J. 1981a. Studies on nodule damage in pigeonpea. In ICRISAT, *Proceedings of the International Workshop on Pigeonpeas*, ICRISAT, 15–19 Dec. 1980, Patancheru, India, Vol. 2, 409–415.

Sithanantham, S., Lateef, S.S., and Reed, W. 1981b. Podfly susceptibility in pigeonpea: some aspects of oviposition preferences. In ICRISAT, *Proceedings of the International Workshop on Pigeonpeas*, ICRISAT, 15–19 Dec. 1980, Patancheru, India, Vol. 2, 329–335.

Siva Rao, D.V., Thippeswamy, M., and Murty, P.S.S. 1984. Studies on field evaluation of insecticides on rainfed groundnut. *Pesticides*, December 1984, 35–38.

Sivasubramaniam, P., and Palaniswamy, G.A. 1983. Studies on the chemical control of groundnut leaf miner *Aproaerema modicella* Dev. *Madras Agricultural Journal*, 70(7) 485–486.

Sivasubramaniam, P., and Palaniswamy, G.A. 1986. Loss due to leaf hopper and thrips in groundnut. *Madras Agricultural Journal*, 73, 530–531.

Slansky, Jr., F., and Panizzi, A.R. 1987. Nutritional ecology of seed sucking insects. In Slansky, Jr., F., and Rodriguez, J.G., eds., *Nutritional Ecology of Insects, Mites, Spiders and Related Invertebrates*, Chichester, John Wiley and Sons, 283–320.

Slater, J.A. 1972. The occurrence of *Elasmolomus sordidus* (F.), a potential pest of peanuts, in Brazil (Hemiptera: Lygaeidae). *Biológico*, 38, 394–397.

Slykhuis, J.T. 1973. Viruses and mites. In Gibbs, A.J. (ed.), *Viruses and Invertebrates*, Amsterdam, North Holland Publishing Co., 391–405.

Slykhuis, J.T. 1980. Mites. In Harris, K.F., and Maramorosch, K., eds., *Vectors of Plant Pathogens*, New York, Academic Press, 325–356.

Smiley, R.L. 1974. A new species of *Coccipolipus* parasitic on the Mexican bean beetle (Acarina: Podapolipidae). *Wash. Acad. Sci.*, 64, 298–302.

Smith, C.E. 1924. Transmission of cowpea mosaic by bean-leaf beetle. *Science*, 60, 268.

Smith, F.F., and Poos, F.W. 1931. The feeding habit of some leafhoppers of the genus *Empoasca*. *Journal of Agricultural Research*, 43, 267–285.

Smith, F.F., and Webb, R.E. 1969. Repelling aphids by reflective surfaces, a new approach to the control of insect-transmitted virus. In Maramorosch, K., ed., *Viruses, Vectors and Vegetation*, New York, Interscience, 631–639.

Smith, F.F., Johnson, G.V., Hahn, R.P., and Bing, A. 1964. Repellency of reflective aluminum to transient aphid virus vectors. *Phytopathology*, 54(7), 748 (Abstr.).

Smith, J.G. 1978. Pests of soybean in Brazil. In Singh, S.R., van Emden, H.F., and Taylor, T.A., eds., *Pests of Grain Legumes: Ecology and Control*, London/New York, Academic Press, 167–177.

Smith, J.W., and Barfield, C.S. 1982. Management of preharvest insects. In Pattee, H.E., and Young, C.T., eds., *Peanut Science and Technology*, Yoakum, Texas, American Peanut Research and Education Society, 825p.

Smith, J.W., Sams, R.L., Agnew, C.W., and Simpson, C.E. 1985. Methods for estimating damage and evaluating the reaction of selected peanut cultivars to the potato leafhopper, *Empoasca fabae* (Homoptera: Cicadellidae). *Journal of Economic Entomology*, 78, 1059–1062.

Smith, K.G. 1963. The study of an insect population living on bagged groundnuts stored in southern Nigeria with particular reference to the behaviour of *Trogoderma granarium* Everts (Col., Dermestidae). *Journal of the West African Scientific Association*, 8, 44–45.

Smith, K.M. 1965. Plant virus–vector relationships. *Advances in Virus Research*, 11, 61–95.

Snow, J.W., Cantelo, W.W., Baumhover, A.H. Goodenough, J.L., Graham, H.M., and Raulston, J.R. 1974. The tobacco budworm on St. Croix, US Virgin Islands. Host-plants, population survey and estimates. *Florida Entomologist*, 57(3), 297–301.

Southgate, B.J. 1958. Systematic notes of species of *Callosobruchus* of economic importance. *Bulletin of Entomological Research*, 49, 591–599.

Southgate, B.J. 1964. Distribution and hosts of certain Bruchidae in Africa. *Tropical Stored Products*, 7, 277–279.

Southgate, B.J. 1978. The importance of the Bruchidae as pests of grain legumes, their distribution and control. In Singh, S.R., van Emden, H.F., and Taylor, T.A., eds., *Pests of Grain Legumes: Ecology and Control*, London/New York, Academic Press, 219–229.

Southgate, B.J., and McFarlane, J.A. 1979. Host records of *Specularius* species (Coleoptera: Bruchidae) with notes on the infestation of pigeonpeas (*Cajanus cajan* L.) by these beetles. *East African Agricultural and Forestry Journal*, 42(2), 219–223.

Sower, L.L., and Whitmer, G.P. 1977. Population growth and mating success of Indian meal moths *Plodia interpunctella* and almond moths *Cadra cautella* in the presence of synthetic sex pheromone. *Environmental Entomology*, 6, 17–20.

Spangler, H.G. 1987. Ultrasonic communication in *Corcyra cephalonica* (Stainton) (Lepidoptera: Pyralidae). *Journal of Stored Products Research*, 23, 203–211.

Spencer, K.A. 1959. A synopsis of Ethiopian Agromyzidae (Diptera). *Transactions of the Royal Entomological Society*, London, 11, 237–329.

Spencer, K.A. 1961. Notes on the African Agromyzidae (Diptera). Stuttgart, Beitr. Naturk, 46, 5p.

Spencer, K.A. 1973. *Agromyzidae (Diptera) of Economic Importance*. Hague, W. Junk B.V. 418p.

Sreenivasulu, P., Iizuka, N., Rajeshwari, R., Reddy, D.V.R., and Nayudu, M.V. 1981. Peanut green mosaic virus—a member of the potato virus Y group infecting groundnut (*Arachis hypogaea*) in India. *Annals of Applied Biology*, 98, 255–260.

Srikanth, J., and Lakkundi, N.H. 1988. Host preference studies of cowpea aphid *Aphis craccivora* Koch. *Indian Journal of Plant Protection*, 16, 103–107.

Srinivasan, S., and Siva Rao, D.V. 1984. New off-season summer hosts of the groundnut leaf miner, *Aproaerema modicella* Deventer (*Stomopteryx subsecivella* Zell.) (Lepidoptera: Gelechiidae) in Andhra Pradesh. *Entomon*, 9(1), 11–12.

Srinivasan, S., and Siva Rao, D.V. 1986. New report of parasites of groundnut leafwebber, *Aproaerema modicella* Deventer (Lepidoptera: Gelechiidae). *Entomon*, 12(2), 117–119.

Srivastava, A.S., and Katiyar, S.S.L. 1972. *Epilachna vigintioctopunctata* F. and *E. dodecastigma* Muls. as pests on cowpea. *Zeitschrift für Angewandte Entomologie*, 71, 169–172.

Srivastava, A.S., Katiyar, S.S.L., and Srivastava, K.M. 1971. Damage of *Agromyza obtusa* M. (Dipt. Agromyzidae) to *Cajanus cajan* Lin. *Labdev Journal of Science and Technology*, 9-B(1), 71–73.

Srivastava, B.K. 1964. Pests of pulse crops. In Pant, N.C., ed., *Entomology in India*. New Delhi, Entomological Society of India, 83–91.

Srivastava, B.K., and Bhatia, S.K. 1959. The effect of host species on the oviposition of *Callosobruchus chinensis* Linn. (Coleoptera: Bruchidae). *Annals of Zoology (Agra)*, 3, 37–42.

Srivastava, K.K., and Srivastava, B.K. 1988. Varietal resistance and toxicity of insecticides against leaf folder, *Lamprosema indicata* Fab. on soybean. *Pesticides*, 22(12), 45–47.

Srivastava, K.M., Singh, L.N., and Sinha, S.C. 1977. Note on the incidence of *Anarsia ephippias* Meyrick in red gram (*Cajanus cajan* L.) *Indian Journal of Agricultural Research*, 11(1), 55–56.

Srivastava, O.S. 1973. Varietal susceptibility/resistance of different varieties of soybean to *Ephestia cautella* Walk. (Phycitidae: Lepidoptera). A storage pest of stored soybean. *Bulletin of Grain Technology*, 11, 203–205.

Stam, P.A. 1978. Relation of predators to population dynamics of *Nezara viridula* (L.) in a soybean ecosystem. Baton Rouge, Louisiana State University, 220p. (PhD thesis)

Stam, P.A., Newsom, L.D., Lambremont, E.N. 1987. Predation and food as factors affecting survival of *Nezara virudula* (L.) (Hemiptera: Pentatomidae) in a soybean ecosystem. *Environmental Entomology*, 16(6), 1211–1216.

Standaert, D.Y, Autrique, A., Bianquis, A., Bizimana, A., and Iyamugerna, P. 1985. Protection du haricot conservé en greniers traditionnels contre la bruche *Acanthoscelides obtectus* (Say) par de la laterite en poudre en tant que matière de charge comme telle au support au pirimiphos-methyl. Institut des sciences agronomiques du Bujumbura, Burundi. 5p. (Mimeograph).

Steele, W.M. 1972. Doctoral thesis. University of Reading, UK. 242p.

Stern, V.M., Smith, R.F., van der Bosch, R., and Hagen, K.S. 1959. The integrated control concept. *Hilgardia*, 29, 81–101.

Stevens, L.M., Strinhauer, A.L., and Elden, T.C. 1975. Laboratory rearing of the Mexican bean beetle and the parasite, *Pediobius foveolatus*, with special emphasis on parasite longevity and host parasite ratios. *Environmental Entomology*, 4, 953–957.

Stevenson, W.A., Kaufman, W., and Sheets, L.W. 1957. The salt-marsh caterpillar and its control in Arizona. *Journal of Economic Entomology*, 50, 179–280.

Stone, K.J. 1968. Reproductive biology of the lesser cornstalk borer. 1. Rearing technique. *Journal of Economic Entomology*, 61, 1712–1714.

Stone, M.W. 1965. Biology and control of the lima bean pod borer in southern California. Washington DC, *USDA Technical Bulletin* 1321, 146p.

Storey, H.H., and Bottomley, A.M. 1928. The rosette disease of peanuts (*Arachis hypogaea* L.). *Annals of Applied Biology*, 15, 26–45.

Strand, E.G. 1948. Soybeans in American farming. Washington, DC, *USDA Technical Bulletin*, 966, 1–66.

Su, H.C.F. 1976. Toxicity of a chemical component of lemon oil to cowpea weevils. *Journal of the Georgia Entomological Society*, 11, 297–301.

Su, H.C.F. 1977. Insecticidal properties of black pepper to rice weevils and cowpea weevils. *Journal of Economic Entomology*, 70, 18–21.

Su, H.C.F., Speirs, R.D., and Mahany, P.G. 1972. Citrus oils as protectants of black-eyed peas against cowpea weevils: laboratory evaluation. *Journal of Economic Entomology*, 65, 1433–1436.

Subasinghe, S.M.C., and Fellowes, R.W. 1978. Recent trends in grain legume pest research in Sri Lanka. In Singh, S.R., van Emden, H.F., and Taylor, T.A., eds., *Pests of Grain Legumes: Ecology and Control*, London/New York, Academic Press, 37–41.

Sudhakar, K., and Vereesh, G.K. 1985. Crop loss estimates due to termites (*Odontotermes obesus* and *Microtermes obesi*) on dryland crops. *Journal of Soil Biology and Ecology*, 5, 58–64.

Sugawara, M., Kojima, M., and Murayama, D. 1970. Retention of inoculativity in the transmission of potato leaf roll virus in the green peach aphid, *Myzus persicae* Sulz. *Memoirs of Faculty of Agriculture* Hokkaido University, 7, 462–467.

Summerfield, R.J., Huxley, P.A., and Steele, W.M. 1974. Cowpea (*Vigna unguiculata* (L.) Walp.). *Field Crop Abstracts*, 27(7), 301–312.

Summerfield, R.J., Pate, J.S., Roberts, E.H., and Wien, H.C. 1985. The physiology of cowpeas. In Singh, S.R., and Rachie, K.O., eds., *Cowpea Research, Production and Utilization*, Chichester, John Wiley and Sons, 65–102.

Sun Huan, Ling Yi-Lu and Gai Jun-yi. 1987. Cropping systems and research with soybean in China. In Singh, S.R., Rachie, K.O., and Dashiell, K.E., eds., *Soybeans for the Tropics: Research, Production and Utilization*, Chichester, John Wiley and Sons, 119–124.

Sundara Babu, P.C. 1969. Trials against the aphid, *Aphis craccivora* Koch on groundnut with some modern synthetic insecticides. *Madras Agricultural Journal*, 56, 452–454.

Suteri, B.D., Kothyari, B.P., and Purohit, S.K. 1985. Relationship of soyabean mosaic virus with its vector *Aphis craccivora*. *Indian Phytopathology*, 38(2), 234–237.

Swaine, G. 1969. Studies on the biology and control of pests of seed beans (*Phaseolus vulgaris* L.) in northern Tanzania. *Bulletin of Entomological Research*, 59, 323–329.

Swamiappan, M., Jajaraj, S., Chandy, K.C., and Sundarmurathy, V.T. 1976. Effect of activated kaolinitic clay on some storage insects. *Zeitschrift für Angewandte Entomologie*, 80, 385–389.

Swenson, K.G. 1968. Role of aphids in the ecology of viruses. *Annual Review of Phytopathology*, 6, 351–374.

Sylvester, E.S. 1956. Beet yellows virus transmission by the green peach aphid. *Journal of Economic Entomology*, 49, 789–800.

Sylvester, E.S. 1962. Mechanisms of plant virus transmission by aphids. In Maramorosch, K., eds., *Biological Transmission of Disease Agents*, New York, Academic Press, 11–31.

Sylvester, E.S. 1969a. Virus transmission by aphids—a view point. In Maramorosch, K., eds., *Viruses, Vectors and Vegetation*, New York, Interscience Publishers, 159–173.

Sylvester, E.S. 1969b. Evidence of transovarial passage of sowthistle yellow vein virus in the aphid *Hyperomyzus lactucae*. *Virology*, 38, 440–448.

Sylvester, E.S. 1980. Circulative and propagative virus transmission by aphids. *Annual Review of Entomology*, 25, 257–286.

Sylvester, E.S. 1985. Multiple acquisition of viruses and vector-dependent prokaryotes: Consequences on transmission. *Annual Review of Entomology*, 30, 71–88.

Sylvester, E.S., and Osler, R. 1977. Further studies on the transmission of the filagree red-leaf virus by the aphid *Acyrthosiphon pelargonni zerozalphum*. *Environmental Entomology*, 6, 39–42.

Sylvester, E.S., and Richardson, J. 1970. Infection of *Hyperomyzus lactucae* by sowthistle yellow vein virus. *Virology*, 42, 1023–1042.

Ta'Ama, M. 1983. Yield performance of thrips resistant cultivars on insecticide application. *Tropical Grain Legume Bulletin*, 27, 26–28.

Talekar, N.S. 1987. Insects damaging soybean in Asia. In Singh, S.R., Rachie, K.O., and Dashiell, K.E., eds., *Soybeans for the Tropics: Research, Production and Utilization*, Chichester, John Wiley and Sons, 25–45.

Talekar, N.S., and Chen, B.S. 1983. Identification of sources of resistance to lima bean pod borer (*Etiella zinckenella*) (Lepidoptera: Pyralidae) in soybean (*Glycine max*). *Journal of Economic Entomology*, 76, 38–39.

Talekar, N.S., and Chen, B.S. 1986. The beanfly pest complex of tropical soybean. In Sulzberger, E.W., ed., *Soybean Tropical and Subtropical Cropping Systems*, Shanhua, Tainan, Taiwan, Asian Vegetable Research and Development Center (AVRDC), 257–274.

Talekar, N.S., Lee, E.M., and Sun, L.T. 1977. Absorption and translocation of soil and foliar applied ^{14}C-carbofuran and ^{14}C-phorate in soybean and mungbean seeds. *Journal of Economic Entomology*, 70, 685–688.

Tamada, T. 1970. Aphid transmission and host range of soybean dwarf virus. *Annals of Phytopathology Society Japan*, 36, 266–274.

Tamada, T. 1975. Studies on the soybean dwarf diseases. Report of Hokkaido Prefectural Agricultural Experiment Station, 25, 1–144.

Taylor, C.E. 1958. The bean stem maggot. *Rhodesia Agricultural Journal*, 55, 634–636.

Taylor, C.E. 1959. Control of bean stem maggots by insecticidal dressing. *Rhodesia Agricultural Journal*, 56, 195–196.

Taylor, D.E. 1980. Soybean semi-loopers. *Zimbabwe Agricultural Journal*, 77, 111–112.

Taylor, D.E. 1981. *Hilda patruelis*, the groundnut hopper. *Zimbabwe Agricultural Journal*, 78, 177–178.

Taylor, D.E., and Kunjeku, E. 1983. Development of an economic threshold for semi-loopers (Lepidoptera: Noctuidae) on soybeans in Zimbabwe. *Zimbabwe Journal of Agricultural Research*, 21, 89–100.

Taylor, T.A. 1964. The field pest problems on cowpeas, *Vigna sinensis* L. in southern Nigeria. *Nigerian Grower Producer*, 3, 1–4.

Taylor, T.A. 1965. Observations on the bionomics of *Laspeyresia ptychora* Meyr. (Lepidoptera: Eucosmidae) infesting cowpea in Nigeria. *Bulletin of Entomological Research*, 55, 761–773.

Taylor, T.A. 1967. The bionomics of *Maruca testulalis* (Geyer) (Lepidoptera: Pyralidae), a major pest of cowpeas in Nigeria. *Journal of West Africa Science Association*, 12, 111–129.

Taylor, T.A. 1968. The effects of insecticide application on insect damage and the performance of cowpea in southern Nigeria. *Nigerian Agricultural Journal*, 5, 29–37.

Taylor, T.A. 1969a. On the population dynamics and flight activity of *Taeniothrips sjostedti* (Trybom) (Thysanoptera: Thripidae) on cowpea. *Bulletin of Entomological Society of Nigeria*, 2, 60–71.

Taylor, T.A. 1969b. Preliminary studies on the integrated control of the pest complex on cowpea, *Vigna unguiculata* Walp, in Nigeria. *Journal of Economic Entomology*, 62, 900–902.

Taylor, T.A. 1975. Effects of orange and grapefruit peels on *Callosobruchus maculatus* infestation of cowpea. *Ghana Journal of Agricultural Science*, 8, 169–172.

Taylor, T.A. 1977. Mixed cropping as an input in the management of crop pests in tropical Africa. *Afr. Environ.*, 2/3, 111–126.

Taylor, T.A. 1978. *Maruca testulalis*: an important pest of tropical grain legumes. In Singh, S.R., van Emden, H.F., and Taylor, T.A., eds., *Pests of Grain Legumes: Ecology and Control*, London/New York, Academic Press, 193–200.

Taylor, T.A., and Ezedinma, F.O.C. 1964. Preliminary investigations on field pests of cowpeas and methods of control. *Nigerian Agricultural Journal*, 1, 8–11.

Taylor, W.E. 1978. Recent trends in grain legume pest research in Sierra Leone. In Singh, S.R., van Emden, H.F., and Taylor, T.A., eds., *Pests of Grain Legumes: Ecology and Control*. London/New York, Academic Press, 93–98.

TDRI. 1984. *Insects and Arachnids of Tropical Stored Products: Their Biology and Identification (A Training Manual)*. Slough, UK, Overseas Development Natural Resources Institute.

Tej Kumar, S., and Devaraj Urs, K.C. 1983. Estimation of crop loss in groundnut due to the leaf miner *Aproaerema modicella* (Lepidoptera: Gelechiidae). *Indian Journal of Entomology*, Special Issue, 2, 345–351.

Telek, L., and Martin, F.W. 1981. Okra seed: a potential source for oil and protein in the humid lowland tropics. In Pryde, E.H., Princen, L.H., and Mukherjee, K.D., eds., *New Sources of Fats and Oils*. Urbana, IL, USA, American Oil Chemists' Society, AOCS Monograph 9. 37–53.

Tengkano, W., and Soehardjan, M. 1985. Insect pests in relation to growth stages of soybean. In Somaatmadja, S., Ismunadji, M., Sumarno, Syam, M., Manurung, S.O., and Yuswadi, eds., *Kedelai*, Bogor, Indonesia, Agency for Agricultural Research and Development, Central Research Institute for Agriculture, 295–318 (in Indonesian).

Thakkar, V.K., Talati, G.M., and Vyas, H.N. 1981. Comparative efficiency of some insecticides against aphid (*Aphis craccivora* Koch) infesting groundnut in relation to their toxicity to coccinellid predator. *Indian Journal of Plant Protection*, 9, 132–136.

Thevasagayam, E.S., and Canagasingham, I.S.C. 1961. Some observations on the insect pests of dhal (*Cajanus cajan*) and their control. *Tropical Agriculture*, 116(4), 287–298.

Thontadarya, T.S., Jai Rao, K., and Kumar, N.G. 1979. Occurrence of the groundnut leaf miner *Biloba* (*Stomopteryx*) *subsecivella* (Zeller) on berseem (*Trifolium alexandrinum* L.) in Karnataka. *Current Research*, 8(4), 65.

Thontadarya, T.S., Reddy, K.V.S., and Govindan, R. 1982. A new pod borer. *Adisura marginalis* (Walker) (Lepidoptera: Noctuidae) on red gram *Cajanus cajan* L. *Journal of the Bombay Natural History Society*, 79, 222.

Thottappilly, G. 1969. Untersuchungen über das Blattrollvirus der Erbse und seine Vektoren. 1: Übertragungsversuche mit verschiedenen Blattlaiesarten, die sich an viruskranken *Pisum sativum*—pflanzen entwickelt hatten. *Phytopathologische Zeitschrift*, 64, 327–337.

Thottappilly, G. 1970. Untersuchungen über das Blattrollvirus der Erbse und seine Viktoren. 2: Bestandigkeit des virus in vektor *Acyrthosiphon pisum*. *Zeitschrift für Pflanzenkrankheiten Pflanzenpathologie und Pflanzenschutz*, 77, 555–561.

Thottappilly, G., and Rossel, H.W. 1985. Worldwide occurrence and distribution of virus diseases. In Singh, S.R., and Rachie, K.O., eds., *Cowpea Research, Production and Utilization*, Chichester, John Wiley and Sons, 155–171.

Thottappilly, G., and Rossel, H.W. 1987. Viruses affecting soybean. In Singh, S.R., Rachie, K.O., and Dashiell, K., eds., *Soybeans in the Tropics: Research, Production and Utilization*, Chichester, John Wiley and Sons, 53–68.

Thottappilly, G., Eastop, V.F., and Bath, J.E. 1977a. Morphological variation within *Acyrthosiphon pisum* and in ability to transmit broad bean severe chlorosis virus. *Entomología Experimentalis et Applicata*, 22, 29–34.

Thottappilly, G., Kao, Ya-chu, Hooper, G.R., and Bath, J.E. 1977b. Host range, symptomatology, and electron microscopy of a persistent, aphid-transmitted virus from alfalfa in Michigan. *Phytopathology*, 67, 1451–1459.

Thottappilly, G., Rossel, H.W., and Singh, B.B. 1988. Virus diseases of cowpea in Nigeria and development of multiple virus resistant cowpea lines. Paper prepared for the 5th International Congress of Plant Pathology, Kyoto, Japan, 20–27 Aug.

Thottappilly, G., Tsai, J.H., and Bath, J.E. 1972. Differential transmission of two bean yellow mosaic virus strains and comparative transmission of biotypes and stages of the pea aphid. *Annals of Entomological Society of America*, 65, 912–915.

Todd, J.W. 1989. Ecology and behaviour of *Nezara viridula*. *Annual Review of Entomology*, 34, 273–292.

Todd, J.W., and Herzog, D.C. 1980. Sampling phytophagous Pentatomidae on soybean. In Kogan, M., and Herzog, D.C., eds., *Sampling Methods in Soybean Entomology*, New York, Springer-Verlag, 438–478.

Todd, J.W., Jellum, M.D., and Leuck, D.B. 1973. Effects of Southern green stink bug damage on fatty acid composition of soybean oil. *Environmental Entomology*, 2, 685–689.

Tomlinson, J.A. 1982. Chemotherapy of plant viruses and virus diseases. In Harris, K.F., and Maramorosch, K., eds., *Pathogens, Vectors and Plant Diseases. Approaches to Control*, New York, Academic Press, 23–44.

Torres, M. 1968. Un control químico de *Epinotia* en frijol. *Revista de Peruana Entomología*, 25, 617–620.

Tsai, J.H. 1979. Vector transmission of mycoplasmal agents of plant diseases. In Witcomb, R.F., and Tully, T.G., eds., *The Mycoplasmas*, volume 3: *Plant and Insect Mycoplasmas*, New York, Academic Press, 266–307.

Tsai, J.H., Bath, J.E., and Igbokwe, E.C. 1972. Biological and transmission characteristics of *Acyrthosiphon pisum* biotypes efficient and nonefficient as vectors of pea enation mosaic virus. *Annals of the Entomological Society America*, 65, 1114–1119.

Tsedeke, A., and Adhanom, N. 1980. Chemical control of African bollworm (*Heliothis armigera* Hübner) with ultra-low volume spray. *Ethiopia Journal of Agricultural Science*, 3, 49–55.

Tsedeke, A., Tasesse, G., and Kemal, A. 1982. *Arthropod Pests of Grain Legumes in Ethiopia: Their Importance and Distribution*. Addis Ababa, Artistic Printers, 56p.

Turner, J.W. 1980. Insect pests in southern Queensland. *Queensland Agricultural Journal*, March–April 1980, 172–176.

Turner, J.W., and Brier, H. 1979. Effects of leaf hopper (jassid) control on the yield of peanuts and navybeans. *Tropical Grain Legume Bulletin*, 16, 23–25.

Turner, M.S., and Dawson, W.O. 1984. Specificity of the actinomycin-D-sensitive function of some RNA plant viruses. *Intervirology*, 21, 224–228.

Turner, N. 1932. The Mexican bean beetle in Connecticut. *Journal of Economic Entomology*, 25, 617–620.

Turner, N. 1935. Effect of Mexican bean beetle injury on crop yield. *Journal of Economic Entomology*, 28, 147–149.

Turnipseed, S.G. 1973. Insects. In Caldwell, B.E., ed., *Soybeans: Improvement, Production and Uses*, Madison, WI, American Society of Agronomy, 545–572.

Turnipseed, S.G. 1975. Manejo das pragas da soja no sul do Brasil. *Trigo e Soja*, 1, 4–7.

Turnipseed, S.G. 1977. Influence of trichome variations on populations of small phytophagous insects in soybean. *Environmental Entomology*, 6, 815–817.

Turnipseed, S.G. 1980. Soybean insects and their natural enemies in Brazil—a comparison with the southern United States. In Corbin, F.T., ed., *World Soybean Research Conference II*, Boulder, CO, Westview Press, 785–790

Turnipseed, S.G. 1983. Insecticide use and selectivity in soybean. In Matteson, P.C., ed., Proceedings of the International Workshop in Integrated Pest Control for Grain Legumes, April 3–9, Goiâna, Brazil, 227–237.

Turnipseed, S.G., and Kogan, M. 1976. Soybean entomology. *Annual Review of Entomology*, 21, 247–282.

Turnipseed, S.G., and Kogan, M. 1987. Integrated control of insect pests. In Madison, W.I., *Soybeans: Improvement, Production and Uses*, 2nd ed., American Society of Agronomy Monograph 16, 779–817.

Turnipseed, S.G., and Newsom, L.D. 1989. Chemical control of soybean insect pests. In Pascale, A.J., ed., World Soybean Research Conference IV., Buenos Aires, March 1989, 1509–1518.

Turnipseed, S.G. and Shepard, M. 1980. Sampling Mexican bean beetle on soybean. In Kogan, M. and Herzog, D.C., eds., *Sampling Methods in Soybean Entomology*, New York, Springer-Verlag, 186–200.

Turnipseed, S.G. and Sullivan, M.J. 1976. Plant resistance in soybean insect management. In Hill, L.D., ed., World Soybean Research, Danville, Illinois, Interstate Printers and Publishers, 549–550.

Turnipseed, S.G., Heinrichs, E.A., da Silva, R.F.P., and Todd, J.W. 1974. Response of soybean insects to foliar applications of a chitin synthesis inhibitor TH 6040. *Journal of Economic Entomology*, 67, 760–702.

Unseld, E., and Klotz, U. 1989. Benzodiazepines: are they of natural origin? *Pharmaceutical Research (New York)*, 6(1), 1–3.

USDA (United States Department of Agriculture). 1976. Groundnut bruchid (*Caryedon serratus*) (Olivier) in Puerto Rico. *Cooperative Plant Pest Report*, 1, 261–262.

Usua, E.J. 1976. Description of the larva and pupa of *Maruca testulalis* (Geyer). *Nigerian Science Journal*, 10, 179–189.

Usua, E.J., and Singh, S.R. 1978. Parasites and predators of the cowpea pod-borer, *Maruca testulalis* (Lepidoptera: Pyralidae). *Nigerian Journal of Entomology*, 2, 100–102.

Usua, E.J., and Singh, S.R. 1979. Behavior of the cowpea pod borer *Maruca testulalis* Geyer. *Nigerian Journal of Entomology*, 3, 231–239.

Utida, S. 1954. "Phase" dimorphism observed in the laboratory population of the cowpea weevil, *Callosobruchus quadrimaculatus*. *Oyo Dobutsugaku Zasshi*, 18, 161–168.

Utida, S. 1972. Density dependent polymorphism in the adult of *Callosobruchus maculatus* (Coleoptera, Bruchidae). *Journal of Stored Products Research*, 8, 111–126.

Vakilli, N.G., and Maramorosch, K. 1974. "Witches broom" disease caused by mycoplasma like organisms on pigeonpeas (*Cajanus cajan*) in Puerto Rico. *Plant Disease Reporter*, 58, 96.

Val, V.M.C. 1985. History and development of soybean production in South America. In Shibles, R., ed., *World Soybean Research Conference III*, Boulder, CO, Westview Press, 1215–1220.

Valdez, L.C. 1989. Host plant resistance in cowpea, *Vigna unguiculata* (L.) Walp. var. *unguiculata*, to the pod borer, *Maruca testulalis* (Geyer) (Pyralidae: Lepidoptera). College, Laguna, University of the Philippines at Los Baños (MSc thesis)

Valverde, R., Moreno, R., and Gamez, R. 1978. Beetle vectors of cowpea mosaic virus in Costa Rica. *Turrialba*, 28(1), 90–92.

van Dam, W., and Wilde, G. 1977. Biology of the bean leafroller *Urbanus proteus* (Lepidoptera: Hesperiidae). *Journal of Kansas Entomological Society*, 50, 157–160.

van der Goot, P. 1930. Agromyzid flies of some native legume crops in Java. Shanhua, Taiwan, Tropical Vegetable Information Service, AVRDC, 98p. (translated from Dutch)

van der Laan, P.A. 1949. Over de bestrijding van het katjangvhegje op kedelee met insecticiden. Mededelingen van het Instituut voor plantenziekten Buitenzorg, 109, 29p. (in Dutch with English summary)

van Velson, R.J. 1961. Witches broom on pigeonpea induced by mealy bug (*Planococcus*), i.e., *Pseudococcus critici* infestation. Papua, New Guinea, *Journal of Agriculture*, 14(2–3), 129.

Vanderveken, J.J. 1977. Oils and other inhibitors of nonpersistent virus transmission. In Harris, K.F., and Maramorosch, K., eds., *Aphids as Virus Vectors*, New York, Academic Press, 435–454.

Varma, A.N., and Kashyap, R.K. 1980. Termites—their damage and control in field crops. *Memoirs of the Entomological Society of India*, New Delhi, 8. 53p.

Varma, B.K., and Mangalasain, 1977. *Dasychira mendosa* Hb. (Lepidoptera: Lymantridae), a pest of *Cajanus cajan* L. Millsp. in Hyderabad. *Indian Journal of Plant Protection*, 5(1), 95–98.

Varma, G.C., and Singh, P.P. 1987. Effect of insecticides on emergence of *Trichogramma brasiliensis* (Hymenoptera, Trichogrammatidae) from parasitized host eggs. *Entomophaga*, 32, 443–448.

Varma, P.M. 1963. Transmission of plant viruses by whiteflies. *National Institute of Science Bulletin* (India), 24, 11–33.

Vea, E.V., and Eckenrode, C.J. 1976a. Resistance to seedcorn maggot in snap beans. *Environmental Entomology*, 5, 735–737.

Vea, E.V., and Eckenrode, C.J. 1976b. Seedcorn maggot injury on surviving bean seedlings influences yield. *Journal of Economic Entomology*, 69, 545–547.

Vea, E.V., Webb, D.R., and Eckenrode, C.J. 1975. Seedcorn maggot injury. *New York's Food and Life Sciences Bulletin*, 55, 3p.

Verdcourt, B. 1970. Studies in the Leguminosae—Papilionoideae: IV. *Kew Bulletin*, 24, 542–546.

Verma, S., and Lal, R. 1976. Evaluation of phorate, monocrotophos and carbaryl against the pests of cowpea crop. *Entomologists' Newsletter*, 6 (8/9), 52–53.

Verma, S., and Lal, R. 1978. Evaluation of pesticides against the pests of cowpea crop (*Vigna sinensis* Savi.). *Indian Journal of Entomology*, 40, 54–58.

Verma, S., and Pant, N.C. 1975. Resistance of phorate on mung and arhar crops. *Entomologists' Newsletter*, 5(3), 21.

Vetten, H.J., and Allen, D.J. 1983. Effects of environment and host on vector biology and incidence of two whitefly-spread diseases of legumes in Nigeria. *Annals of Applied Biology*, 102, 219–227.

Vick, K.W., Coffelt, J.A., Silhacek, D.L., and Oberlander, H. 1985. Methoprene and sex pheromone as control agents for the almond moth (Lepidoptera: Phycitidae) on peanuts stored in the shell. *Journal of Economic Entomology*, 78, 258–262.

Vidano, C., and Conti, M. 1965. Transmission con afidi d'un 'cowpea mosaic virus' isolato da *Vigna sinensis* Endl. in Italia. *Annali Accademia Italiana de Scienze*, Torino 99, 1041–1050.

Vieira, F.V., and Santos, J.H.R. 1974. Dados biométricos do manhoso, *Chalcodermus bimaculatus* Fiedler, 1936 (Col., Curc.). *Ciencia Agronómica*, 4(1/2), 47–50.

Vieira, F.V., Bastos, J.A.M., and Pereira, L. 1975. Influência do *Chalcodermus bimaculatus* Fiedler, 1936 (Col., Curc.) sobre o poder germinativo do feijão-de-corda, *Vigna sinensis* (L.) Savi. *Fitossanidade* 1, 47–48.

Vietmeyer, N.D. 1986. Lesser-known plants of possible use in agriculture and forestry. *Science*, 232.

Villas Bôas, G.L., and Panizzi, A.R. 1980. Biología de *Euschistus heros* (Fabricius, 1798) em soja (*Glycine max* (L.) Merrill). *Anais da Sociedade Entomológica do Brasil*, 9, 105–113.

Vir, S. 1982. Relative resistance of some cowpea varieties to the pulse beetle, *Callosobruchus maculatus* F. *Pestology*, 6(7), 9–11.

Vishakantaiah, M., Jayaramaiah, M., and Visweswara Gowda, B.L. 1973. Observations on tur podfly *Melanagromyza obtusa* Malloch. (Diptera: Agromyzidae) in Mysore. *Current Research*, 2(8), 62.

Vishwa, N., and Srivistava, A.S. 1981. Comparative efficiency of insecticides for the control of white grub, *Holotrichia consanguinea* Blanch. in groundnut. *Indian Journal of Entomology*, 43, 413–415.

Waddill, V., and Shepard, M. 1975. A comparison of predation by the pentatomids *Podisus maculiventris* (Say) and *Stiretrus anchorago* F. on the Mexican bean beetle, *Epilachna varivestis* Mulsant. *Annals of the Entomological Society of America*, 68, 1023–1027.

Waghray, R.N., and Singh, S.R. 1965. Effect of N, P and K on the fecundity of the groundnut aphid, *Aphis craccivora* Koch. *Indian Journal of Entomology*, 27, 331–334.

Waldbauer, G.P. 1977. Damage to soybean seeds by South American stink bugs. *Anais da Sociedade Entomológica do Brasil*, 6, 224–229.

Walker, P.T. 1960. Insecticide studies on East African agricultural pests III. Seed dressing for the control of bean fly, *Melanagromyza phaseoli* Coq. in Tanganyika. *Bulletin of Entomological Research*, 50, 781–793.

Walkey, D.G.A., and Innes, N.L. 1979. Resistance to bean common mosaic virus in dwarf beans (*Phaseolus vulgaris* L.). *Journal of Agricultural Science*, 92, 101–118.

Walkey, D.G.A., Innes, N.L., and Miller, A. 1983. Resistance to bean yellow mosaic virus in *Phaseolus vulgaris*. *Journal of Agricultural Science*, 100, 643–650.

Wallace, G.B. 1939. French bean diseases and bean fly in East Africa. *East African Agricultural and Forestry Journal*, 5, 170–175.

Wallis, E.S., Whiteman, P.C., and Byth, D.E. 1979. Pigeonpea: a new crop for Queensland. *Queensland Agricultural Journal*, 105(6), 487–492.

Walters, H.J. 1969. Beetle transmission of plant viruses. *Advances in Virus Research*, 15, 339–363.

Walters, H.J., and Henry, D.G. 1970. Bean leaf beetle as a vector of the cowpea strain of southern bean mosaic virus. *Phytopathology*, 60, 177–178.

Walters, H.J., and Surin, P. 1973. Transmission and host range studies of broad bean mottle virus. *Plant Disease Reporter*, 57, 833–836.

Wambugu, F.M., Secor, G.A., and Gudmestad, N.C. 1985. Eradication of potato virus y and s from potato by chemotherapy of cultivated axillary bud tips. *American Potato Journal*, 62, 667–672.

Watson, M.A. 1972. Transmission of plant viruses by aphids. In Kado, C.I., and Agrawal, H.O., eds., *Principles and Techniques in Plant Virology*, chapter 5, New York, Van Nostrand Reinhold, 131–167.

Watson, M.A., and Okusanya, B.A.M. 1967. Studies on the transmission of groundnut rosette virus by *Aphis craccivora* Koch. *Annals of Applied Biology*, 60, 199–208.

Watson, M.A., and Plumb, R.T. 1972. Transmission of plant pathogenic viruses by aphids. *Annual Review of Entomology*, 17, 425–452.

Watson, M.A., and Roberts, F.M. 1939. A comparative study of the transmission of *Hyoscynmus* virus 3, potato virus Y and cucumber virus 1 by the vectors *Myzus persicae* (Sulz)., *M. circumflexus* (Buckton) and *Macrosiphum gei* (Koch). *Proceedings of the Royal Society of London* B, 127, 543–576.

Watson, M.A., and Roberts, F.M. 1940. Evidence against the hypothesis that certain plant viruses are transmitted mechanically by aphids. *Annals of Applied Biology*, 27, 227–233.

Weaving, A.J.S. 1980. Observations on *Hilda patruelis* Stal. (Homoptera: Tettigometridae) and its infestation of the groundnut crop in Rhodesia. *Journal of the Entomological Society of Southern Africa*, 43, 151–167.

Weder, J.K.P. 1981. Protease inhibitors in the Leguminosae. In Polhill, R.M., and Raven, P.H., eds., *Advances in Legume Systematics*, Kew, UK, Royal Botanic Gardens, 533–560.

Weingartner, K.E. 1987. Processing, nutrition and utilization of soybeans. In Singh, S.R., Rachie, K.O., and Dashiell, K.E., eds., *Soybeans for the Tropics: Research, Production and Utilization*, Chichester, John Wiley and Sons, 149–178.

Wells, P.W., Dively, G.P., and Schalk, J.M. 1984. Resistance and reflective foil mulch as control measures for the potato leafhopper (Homoptera: Cicadellidae) on *Phaseolus* species. *Journal of Economic Entomology*, 77, 1046–1051.

Wessels, C.L. 1978. Residues in soybean plants (*Glycine max* (L.) Merr.) of aldrin and dieldrin following soil application and of endosulfan and DDT following foliar application. *Rhodesian Journal of Agricultural Research*, 16, 205–210.

Wheatley, A.R.D., Wightman, J.A., Williams, J.H., and Wheatley, S.J. 1989. The influence of drought stress on the distribution of insects on four groundnut genotypes grown near Hyderabad, India. *Bulletin of Entomological Research* (submitted).

Whigham, D.K. 1981. Soybeans. *Glycine max*. In McClure, T.A., and Lipinsky, E.S., eds., *CRC Handbook of Biosolar Resources*, vol. II, Resource Materials. Boca Raton, FL, USA, CRC Press, 95–104.

Whitcomb, R.F. 1972. Transmission of viruses and mycoplasmas by anchenorrhynchous Homoptera. In Kado, C.I., and Agrawal, H.O., eds., *Principles and Techniques in Plant Virology*, New York, Van Nostrand Reinhold, 168–203.

Whitcomb, R.F. 1981. The biology of spiroplasmas. *Annual Review of Entomology*, 26, 397–425.

Whitcomb, R.F., and Davis, R.E. 1970. Mycoplasma and phytarboviruses as plant pathogens persistently transmitted by insects. *Annual Review of Entomology*, 15, 405–464.

Whitney, W.K., and Gilmer, R.M. 1974. Insect vectors of cowpea mosaic virus in Nigeria. *Annals of Applied Biology*, 77, 17–21.

Wickramasinghe, N., and Fernando, H.E. 1962. Investigations on insecticidal seed dressings, soil treatments and foliar sprays for the control of *Melanagromyza phaseoli* (Tryon) in Ceylon. Bulletin of Entomological Research, 53, 223–240.

Wien, H.C., and Tayo, T.O. 1978. The effect of defoliation and removal of reproductive structures on growth and yield of tropical grain legumes. In Singh, S.R., van Emden, H.F., and Taylor, T.A., eds., *Pests of Grain Legumes: Ecology and Control*, London/New York, Academic Press, 241–252.

Wightman, J.A. 1972. Grass grubs and soil water. *Proceedings of Soil and Plant Water Symposium*, DSIR Information Series 96, 227–280.

Wightman, J.A. 1987. Sitona discoideus in New Zealand, 1975-1973: distribution, population studies and bionomic strategy (Coleoptera: Curculionidae). *New Zealand Journal of Zoology*, 13, 221–240.

Wightman, J.A. 1989. The contribution of insects to low groundnut yields in Southern Africa. In ICRISAT, *Proceedings of the Third Regional Groundnut Workshop in Southern Africa, Lilongwe, Malawi, March 1988*. Patancheru, ICRISAT (International Crop Research Institute for the Semi-Arid Tropics), (in press).

Wightman, J.A., and Amin, P.W. 1988. Groundnut pests and their control in the semi-arid tropics. *Tropical Pest Management*, 34, 218–226.

Wightman, J.A., and Southgate, B.J. 1982. Egg morphology, host and probable regions of origin of the bruchids (Coleoptera: Bruchidae) that infest stored pulses—an identification aid. *New Zealand Journal of Experimental Agriculture*, 10, 95–99.

Wightman, J.A., and Wightman, A.S. 1988. An evaluation of five insecticides for the control of foliage and soil insects in a groundnut crop in Malawi. Unpublished internal report.

Wilde, G., and van Schoonhoven, A. 1976. Mechanisms of resistance to *Empoasca kraemeri* in *Phaseolus vulgaris*. *Environmental Entomology*, 5, 251–255.

Wilde, G., van Schoonhoven, A., and Gomez-Laverde, L. 1976. The biology of *Empoasca kraemeri* on *Phaseolus vulgaris*. *Annals of Entomological Society of America*, 69, 442–444.

Wille, J.E. 1943. *Entomología Agrícola del Peru*. Lima, Peru, Ministry of Agriculture. 466p.

Wille, J.E. 1946. Experimentos con los nuevos insecticidas DDT y gammexane ejecutados en la Estación Experimental Agrícola de la Molina hastas fines de mayo de 1946. La Molina, Peru, Est. Exp. Agric. Bol. 29, 23p.

Williams, J.O. 1986. Preliminary observation on the susceptibility of selected varieties of soybean (*Glycine max*) to *Tribolium castaneum* (Herb). (Coleoptera: Tenebrionidae) in Nigeria. *Tropical Grain Legume Bulletin*, 33, 42–44.

Williams, R.J. 1975. A whitefly transmitted mosaic of lima bean in Nigeria. *Tropical Grain Legume Bulletin*, 1(1), 11.

Williams, R.J. 1976. A whitefly-transmitted golden mosaic of lima beans in Nigeria. *Plant Disease Reporter*, 60(10), 853–857.

Wilson, C.T. 1973. *Peanuts—Culture and Use*. Stillwater, OK, USA, American Peanut Research and Education Association, 684p.

Wilson, J.W., and Genung, W.G. 1957. Insect problems in the production of southern peas (cowpeas). *Proceedings of the Florida State Horticultural Society*, 69, 217–223.

Wilson, K.G. 1981. Aspects of the physiological ecology of the Mexican bean beetle, *Epilachna varivestis* Mulsant. Raleigh, NC, USA, North Carolina State University 81p. (PhD dissertation).

Windsor, I.M., and Black, L.M. 1973. Evidence that clover club leaf is caused by a rickettsia-like organism, *Phytopathology*, 63, 1139–1148.

Wishart, G. 1943. Note on the establishment in Canada of imported parasites of pea moth, *Laspeyresia nigricana* Steph. *Canadian Entomologist*, 75, 237–238.

Witethom, B. 1980. Natural control of the rice moth *Corcyra cephalonica* Stainton (Lepidoptera, Galleriinae) by a parasitic wasp *Bracon hebetor* Say (Hymenoptera, Braconidae) and the effect of some common insecticide treatments on the host-parasite relationship. *Research Report*, BIOTROP, Bogor, Indonesia.

Wolcott, G.N. 1933. The lima bean pod-borer caterpillar of Puerto Rico. *Journal Dep. Agric. Puerto Rico*. 17, 241–255.

Wolfenbarger, D., and Sleesman, J.P. 1961. Resistance to the Mexican bean beetle in several bean genera and species. *Journal of Economic Entomology*, 54, 1018–1022.

Wolfenbarger, D., and Sleesman, J.P. 1963. Variation in susceptibility of soybean pubescent types, broad bean and runner bean varieties and introduction to the potato leafhopper. *Journal of Economic Entomology*, 56, 893–897.

Woodruff, J.G. 1973. *Peanuts: Production, Processing, Products*. Westport, CO, Avi Pub. Co. Inc. 330p.

Woodruff, J.G. 1981. Peanuts *Arachis hypogaea*. In McClure, T.A., and Lipinsky, E.S., eds., *Handbook of Biosolar Resources Vol. II, Resource Materials*, Boca Raton, FL, CRC Press. 575p.

Wraight, S.P., and Roberts, D.W. 1987. Insect control efforts with fungi. *Journal of Industrial Microbiology*, 28(2), 77–87.

Wu Leung, Woot-Tsuen, Butrum, R.R., and Chang, F.H. 1972. Part I. Proximate composition mineral and vitamin contents of East Asian food. In FAO, *Food Composition Table for Use in East Asia*, Rome, Italy, FAO, 334p.

Wyman, J.A., Toscano, N.C., Kido, K., Johnson, H., and Mayberry, K.S. 1979. Effects of mulching on the spread of aphid-transmitted watermelon mosaic virus to summer squash. *Journal of Economic Entomology*, 72, 139–143.

Xu, Z., Yu, Z., Lui, J., and Barnett, O.W. 1983. A virus causing peanut mild mottle in Hubei Province, China. *Plant Disease*, 67, 1029–1032.

Yadav, D.N., Patel, R.R., and Patel, R.C. 1987. Natural enemies of the groundnut leafminer, *Aproaerema modicella* Deventer (Lepidoptera: Gelechiidae) and their impact on its infestation in Anand (Gujarat). *Gujarat Agricultural University Research Journal*, 13(1), 13–16.

Yadav, H.S., Gangrade, G.A., and Jakhmola, S.S. 1974. Note on the relationship between thrips and pod setting in the flowers of pigeonpea. *Indian Journal of Agricultural Sciences*, 44(8), 555–556.

Yang, C., and Liu, H. 1966. Biological observations on *Stomopteryx subsecivella* Zell. in Den Bei District, Kwantung. [In Chinese] *Acta Entomologica Sinensis*, 15(1), 39–46. [English summary in *Review of Applied Entomology Ser. A*, 54, 483.]

Yen, D.F. 1973. A natural enemy list of insects of Taiwan. Taipei, National Taiwan University, 106p.

Yoshida, T., and Hasegawa, M. 1977. Distribution of stizolamine in some leguminous plants. *Phytochemistry*, 16(1), 131–132.

Young, W.R., and Candia, D. 1962. Biología y control de la "doradilla" en el campo Cotaxtla, Veracruz. *Agrícultura Tecnica (Mexico)*, 2, 33–38.

Young, W.R., and Sifuentes, J.A. 1959. Biological and control studies on *Estigmene acrea* (Drury), a pest of corn in the Yaqui Valley, Sonora, Mexico. *Journal of Economic Entomology*, 52, 1109–1111.

Yukawa, J., and Kiritani, K. 1965. Polymorphism in the southern green stink bug. *Pacific Insects*, 7, 639–642.

Zaumeyer, W.J., and Thomas, H.R. 1957. A monographic study of bean diseases and methods for their control. *Washington, DC, USDA, Technical Bulletin Agricultural Research Series Handbook*, 868, 255p.

Zaumeyer, W.J., and Thomas, H.R. 1962. Bean diseases and how to control them. *Washington, DC, USDA, Technical Bulletin Agricultural Research Series Handbook*, 225.

Zaz, G.M., and Kushwaha, K.S. 1983. Quantitative incidence of tobacco caterpillar, *S. litura* (F.) and related natural enemies in sole crops. *Indian Journal of Entomology*, 45(2), 201–202.

Zettler, F.W., and Wilkinson, R.E. 1966. Effect of probing behaviour and starvation of *Myzus persicae* on transmission of bean common mosaic virus. *Phytopathology*, 56, 1079–1082.

Zettler, J.L. 1982. Insecticide resistance in selected stored product insects infesting peanuts in the southeastern United States. *Journal of Economic Entomology*, 75, 359–362.

Zimmerman, A. 1907. Die Krauselkrankheit der Erdnuesse (*Arachis hypogaea*). Der Pflanzer, 3, 129–133.

Zungoli, P.A., Steinhauer, A.L., and Linduska, J.J. 1983. Evaluation of diflubenzuron for Mexican bean beetle (Coleoptera: Coccinellidae) control and impact on *Pediobius foveolatus* (Hymenoptera: Eulophidae). *Journal of Economic Entomology*, 76, 188–191.

Index